applied
management science
a quick & dirty approach

applied
management science

a quick & dirty approach

Rick Hesse
Department of Management
San Diego State University

Gene Woolsey
Department of Engineering
Colorado School of Mines

assisted by

H.S. Swanson
Department of Engineering
Colorado School of Mines

SCIENCE RESEARCH ASSOCIATES, INC.
Chicago, Palo Alto, Toronto, Henley-on-Thames, Sydney, Paris
A Subsidiary of IBM

Compositor   Western Printing Services Ltd.
Acquisition Editor   David Bruce Caldwell
Project Editor   Ronald Q. Lewton
Text and Cover Design   Parallelogram
Editing and Production   Phoenix Publishing Services

Acknowledgments

The epigraph is reprinted with permission from *Psychology Today* Magazine. Copyright © 1974 Ziff-Davis Publishing Company.

The quotation on pages 62–63 is reprinted by permission from TIME, The Weekly Newsmagazine; Copyright Time Inc. 1975.

The chapter-opening photographs were provided by:

Stock, Boston/Elizabeth Hamlin   Chapter 10
Stock, Boston/Ellis Herwig   Chapters 3, 5, 7
Photophile/Geahard Julius   Chapters 1, 4
Stock, Boston/Peter Menzel   Chapter 11
Photophile/Gordon Menzie   Chapter 2
Photophile/Leonard Rhodes   Chapter 8
Photophile/L. D. Smithey   Chapter 6
Stock, Boston/Harry Wilks   Chapter 9

Library of Congress Cataloging in Publication Data

Hesse, Rick
    Applied management science.

    Bibliography: p.
    Includes index.
    1. Operations research.   I.   Woolsey, Robert, E. D.
joint author.   II.   Title.
T57.6.H47   001.4'24   79-9420
ISBN 0-574-19345-6

10   9   8   7   6   5   4   3   2   1

I believe that all academics should be prepared to popularize what they are doing. Popularization is especially important for scientists who are engaged in work that may have social implications. Unless the public and politicians are reasonably informed, you see, they have no possible basis on which to make judgments. . . . Making complicated ideas simple and not misleading is a difficult, time-consuming business. Too many scientists feel that they can't be bothered with the stupid public and must get on with their research. But the best scientists are generally good popularizers.

Edmund Leach
Psychology Today, July 1974

contents

preface

For over thirty years the field known as management science (and also as operations research, decision sciences, quantitative analysis) has been growing in complexity and usefulness. The gap between actual business practice and theory has steadily widened, to the point that some operations research courses can be characterized as nothing more than Math Appreciation 101. It is our intention to provide a practical guide to management science that bridges the gap between theory and practice and yet at the same time provides concepts that are mathematically correct. The authors are academic applied mathematicians with much real-world experience in solving operations research problems. This book is an amalgam of our two backgrounds, ideas, and experiences, and has been almost a decade in coming to fruition. Although our tone may at times seem flippant, no disrespect of persons, institutions, or businesses is intended. The sometimes casual style of writing should not mislead readers into thinking that the subject matter is neither important nor without factual base.

TO THE PROFESSOR

Every OR book is arranged in a different order, and the way we have ordered the material may be different from the way you have been teaching your course. Many chapters are interchangeable and can be taught in a different order. Our arrangement of the subject matter simply seems the most logical to us. The field of operations research has no underlying thread that would order topics in a standard way because many problems and techniques can be seen from different viewpoints. Thus some authors would put linear programming first and have every chapter as a variation of linear programming; others would see all problems as network problems and use that as a foundation; while the most elite realize that everything is *really* a calculus of variation problem and deals with information theory and automatic controls!

This book has been used for a standard semester course for junior undergraduates in a business school. There is more than enough for a semester's course, and four or five sections would need to be deleted if one section were covered every hour (assuming 42–45

hours per semester). It has also been used as the primary textbook for an undergraduate introductory class, but could be an excellent supplement for an advanced undergraduate class in business or engineering. It would also fit well into a beginning graduate class where students are more mature and quicker to learn.

One of the pleasures of teaching this book that the professor will quickly appreciate is the absence of the complaining question from future-shocked students, "Where is this technique used?" This should free a great deal of energy to be put to better use than defending appreciation of mathematics!

Finally, the cases and problems are included so that the professor may choose among many ways to teach the course: as a case course, using groups and having presentations; as a lecture course with cases assigned as homework problems; or as a lecture course with students simply doing the problems and an occasional selected case (say one for every section). The modularity of the book also lends itself well to a self-paced or personalized system of instruction, if the professor is so inclined.

TO THE STUDENT

This book is primarily designed for the student who will never take another management science course. After using this text, he or she should be able (1) to understand the processes and techniques involved in operations research and (2) recognize types of problems that occur in the business world and find logical ways to solve them.

For the student who finds this field interesting and wants to pursue it, we expect that the foundation laid in this course will be of great value as a practical reminder when the mathematics gets too thick in the advanced courses. Such tools as matrix algebra, differential and integral calculus, and statistics will be necessary as the student progresses deeper into the complexities underlying the theory, but it is not our intention here to provide theorems and proofs for techniques shown valid years ago. Rather, we provide a common-sense approach (with good mathematical references) as a basis for further study.

TO THE INTERESTED READER

It is the authors' hope that many people will read un-aided through this book to acquaint themselves with the problems and techniques of operations research. To this end, there is an example and a solved case for every section so that the reader can become acquainted with the types of problems and techniques without having to solve a multitude of cases and problems.

ACKNOWLEDGMENTS

The authors wish to acknowledge their debt to several groups of people who have made this book possible. First, we thank the practitioners who have provided the grist for the mill—the actual settings and problems they have encountered and resolved, successfully and unsuc-cessfully, in their own businesses. Secondly, we are grateful to the students at the Colorado School of Mines, University of Southern California, and San Diego State University who have labored through var-ious editions of this book and provided many of the problems and cases for it. They have helped to elimi-nate many errors in both the manuscript and answer book. Thirdly, we are indebted to the teaching assistants who, through time and effort spent during the last seven years, provided inestimable help in proofing as well as their own perspectives.

We would like especially to acknowledge the assis-tance of our colleague Hunter Swanson at the Colorado School of Mines, who worked on several sections of this book to help us over some rough spots. His labor as well

as his solid contribution to this book are appreciated. We would also like to thank the numerous other col-leagues who read this book in early editions and pro-vided many helpful suggestions for improvement:

John J. Bernardo, University of Kentucky
Chuanyu E. Chen, Montclair State College
Norman L. Chervany, University of Minnesota
Robert L. Childress, University of Southern California
T. G. Eschenbach, University of Alaska
Guisseppi A. Forgionne, California State Polytechnic University
Dave Goodman, Southern Methodist University
Manfred W. Hopfe, California State University, Sac-ramento
James B. Lee, Montana State University
Herbert Lyon, University of Houston
Mildred G. Massey, California State University, Los Angeles
Jill Mellick, Golden Gate University
Bill Peters, University of New Mexico
W. E. Pinney, University of Texas at Arlington
Barry Render, University of New Orleans
Mark G. Simkin, University of Hawaii
Philip R. Swenson, Utah State University
Willard I. Zangwill, University of Chicago

Finally, to our wives and children who have had to endure the sound of typing late into the night, long hours away from home, and disgruntled spirits during the pressures of writing and rewriting, we can only humbly say "Thanks" for putting up with us and supporting us.

San Diego, California   Rick Hesse

Golden, Colorado   Gene Woolsey

1
introduction

1.1 QUICK & DIRTY MANAGEMENT SCIENCE

The whole philosophy behind "Quick & Dirty" management science is to present a simple way to attack complex problems. We define *management science* (or operations research) as "the use of logic and mathematics in such a way as not to interfere with common sense." When used, it should look, feel, and taste like good old common sense. (This should do away with the circular definition that "management science is what scientific managers do.") Most management science (abbreviated MS) or operations research (OR) techniques are so esoteric that hardly anyone understands what is being done and, as a consequence, either the technique is not used or the answer is ignored. Most MS/OR books require the use of calculus, matrix algebra, simple algebra, and other higher mathematics for the student to be able to understand and use the techniques. This book will require the student to know—

1. how to add and subtract,
2. how to multiply and divide,
3. know the left from the right,
4. that one number is bigger than another.

It will also require a lot of patience and repetition, which still seem to be the prime ingredients of learning. Doing the simple things well should be the goal, not just a stopover on the way to sophistication. The work required for understanding the concepts is simple, although time-consuming, and will lead to a practical understanding.

Most books present a lot of material on the derivation of techniques, but only a few exercises using them. Furthermore they hardly ever include any "real-world" problems. The problems are artificial, data appears mysteriously, and implementation is ignored. Finally, it is unfortunate that disastrous consequences that may result from an improper application of operations research are never mentioned. It is the authors' intention to correct these faults with this textbook, a radical (and, we hope, a pioneer) departure from the many texts now available.

In this book we are interested in approaching problems that are *real*. By real we mean that these problems are actually encountered in business and industry, sometimes on a daily basis. We assert that in order for the reader to use this book properly, he or she must recognize that learning is a process where first the baby must crawl, then walk, before it can run. The reader who expects to use this book as a tool to become an instant operations researcher must seek

elsewhere. It is hoped that this foundation will be a firm footing for thoughtful problem solvers in business and industry. It will be suggested later that the simple techniques should be used first. There are a number of reasons for this approach: (1) As they are simpler, there is a higher probability that they will be used; (2) there is a good chance that the user will understand what he or she is doing; and (3) simpler techniques are usually cheaper, a fact that gains instant credibility outside of grant-supported institutions. Again, it is learning to do a few common things uncommonly well that provides the firmest foundation.

It would be hoped that some readers might want to go on to more complex techniques to enable them to solve more complex problems. Thus they may wish to progress from this simple "paper and pencil" approach to more difficult problems requiring minicomputers, and finally to full-scale models necessitating large computer systems. A few of these techniques will be presented in the chapters on linear programming and integer programming. The reader should beware, however, of such statements as, "Complex problems require sophisticated solutions." The example set by Alexander the Great when confronted with the Gordian knot should keep us honest. (The Gordian knot was one that could not be untied, so Alexander, in a bold stroke, cut it with his sword, thus simplifying the solution greatly.)

This book is an attempt to popularize, without prostituting, operations research—a first step in understanding an exciting approach to problem solving. With our collective tongues firmly in our respective cheeks, we offer this book as a giant step *backward*.

1.2 MANAGEMENT SCIENCE: INTRODUCTION

Russ Ackoff, a management science professor at the University of Pennsylvania, says that we don't really have problems, we have *messes*. Problems appear in textbooks and also in a vacuum (never tied to the real world). Therefore Ackoff suggests that we deal in "mess management," or how to make problems out of messes. In real-world problems there are no answer books; there are just chaotic conglomerations of conflicting opinions, figures, wants, and desires. The first thing that must be done in management science is to determine what the manager wants done. The best way to begin doing this is to—

1. ask basic, simple questions,
2. observe relevant operations,
3. start paraphrasing the problem,
4. listen to feedback from the manager.

Then the chances of actually discovering the real problem are greatly increased. Once you know the problem to be solved, you have a much better chance of solving it. As an example of trying to discover the problem in the mess, consider the following.

INCIDENT: PATROLLING PARKING

A telephone company manager hired a consultant to work on a scheduling problem that involved trying to minimize the number of female operators at night. The consultant asked the simple question, "Why?" The response was that it was costly to keep several night guards in the parking lot so that the women could be safely escorted to their cars. (Men didn't need to be escorted, and none of them had been raped yet.) Operating on the principle of "doing the dumb things first," the consultant suggested replacing the women operators with men. Unfortunately that wasn't the answer (because it wasn't the problem), and it became obvious to the manager that the problem was more complex than that. Certainly there were costs in patrolling the parking lot, but they were very small compared to the total number of operators being hired and the potential savings of minimizing the number of operators to meet union requirements. After the consultant pointed out these facts, the problem could be restated, but was still very difficult to solve. (The authors have four different colleagues working independently on this problem, with minimal results so far.)

Thus asking *basic, simple questions* and suggesting *simple solutions* led to a definition of the problem through *feedback* from the manager. Another example illustrates the importance of asking simple questions.

INCIDENT: SIMPLE QUESTIONS, SIMPLE ANSWERS

This classic story from the same consultant involves a long tunnel bored through a mountain for a highway. As the highway tunnel began to be used, it was quickly recognized that the multimillion dollar ventilation system was not operating up to expectations. Exhaust gases were building up in the tunnel faster than they could be removed. It had been determined that the buildup was worse in the center of the tunnel and that redesign of the ventilation system would cost several thousand dollars. The consultant sent one of her slowest students to the site for free consulting, knowing that sometimes the slowest students ask the dumbest, simplest questions. The first question the student asked was, "What's the problem?" The answer was that people were complaining of being nauseous after driving through the tunnel. The student then asked, "Why?" The answer was that in the hot climate, people left their windows open, and as they drove through the long tunnel with its carbon monoxide buildup, the fumes would enter the cars. The student then suggested the solution: spend $200 on two signs, one at each end of the tunnel, saying, *"For safety's sake, roll up your windows."* Of course, the suggested solution solved the problem, except that since it did not use up the amount budgeted for the new ventilation system, it was not an acceptable solution. The actual problem was how to use all the money allocated.

INCIDENT: SNOW JOB

Another problem developed in an area replete with snow during six months of the year. A consultant had extolled the virtues of his students before an audience of skeptical county and city officials at a professional seminar. A city manager asked the consultant if any of his students were present. Two students were quickly produced. To test the students' abilities, the city manager presented them with the following problem: It seems that the city manager was always catching hell from the city council, which met at 6:00 A.M. every Tuesday morning. The usual complaint was that the streets of the town had not been sufficiently plowed. The city manager said, "If I tell you how many plows and sand trucks I have and their rate of work, what is the first question you would ask me to help solve my problem?" The two students flipped a coin to decide who would answer. The winner turned to the city manager and said, "Please produce a map of the town showing where the council members live and the routes they drive to the council chambers. Plow those streets *first.*"

Thus a lot of problems that may seem complex at first can be found to be quite simple; while others that, at first, seem simple after interaction with the manager are found to be complex.

INCIDENT: NO TIME LOST

One of the earliest examples in management science of determining the problem concerns complaints about the slowness of the elevators in a high-rise office building. The management had tried everything: staggering the two elevators, one going to

even floors, the other to odd; hiring operators to speed up the service; staggering one elevator to service the first 25 floors, the second to service the next 25, and so on. Finally one consultant had a brilliant idea and promised that for $500 and a couple of workers over the weekend, the complaints would be reduced to almost nothing. The company in desperation yielded to the request, and on Monday morning was surprised to see no changes in the elevators, nor in the speed of the service. The only change was that each elevator door was now a full-length mirror. The number of complaints showed a dramatic decline.

The solution used the difference between perceived time and real time in the following way: As people were waiting at the elevators, the women would look at themselves in the mirrors and make adjustments, while the men would look at the women, and before they knew it, the elevator was there. What was actually done was to create the illusion of not waiting. The problem was not to make the elevators operate more efficiently, but simply to reduce the time a user thought he or she was having to wait. (Did you ever notice that some companies play music over the telephone while you are on hold?)

INCIDENT: THE RIGHT ANSWER TO THE WRONG QUESTION

When one works in Canada, one rapidly discovers that operations research is called operation*al* research and is a profession that originated in England during World War II. Giving the English their due, there is also the story that the original operational research group was the first to discover the principle of giving the right answer to the wrong question. The first known example took place in the celebrated study of optimum utilization of Spitfires and Hurricanes during the battle of Britain. Whenever a Spitfire or Hurricane returned to the aerodrome, careful note was made upon pads made up for the purpose, as to where each bullet hole appeared on the aircraft. This information was then meticulously diagrammed and correlated. Additional armor to protect the plane and pilot was then suggested on the basis of these data. This study experienced the principle of giving the right answer to the wrong question when an unnamed group captain noted that they were counting holes and making recommendations on the basis of the planes that *returned.*

Peter Drucker, author of many books on management, has said that the wrong answer to the right question is not fatal, for further answers may be sought. But the right answer to the wrong question can be disastrous.

Asking the right questions is not so much an art as it is using common sense and not jumping to conclusions. One of the reasons we don't like to ask questions is that we are afraid of appearing stupid. However, to ask probing questions without ruffling feathers is a difficult task indeed. Until you understand people's problems, you can't help them.

INCIDENT: UNDERMINING ASSUMPTIONS

The last story concerns a mining company that was running into the problem of success (a common problem that has been the downfall of those who can't cope with success). In this case the company was making good progress in digging for ore, but as they got farther and farther back into the tunnels, it took longer and longer to get the ore out, since they had only one track per tunnel. An empty cart would come from the dumping station down to the end of the tunnel, be loaded, and then sent back to be dumped. As the tunnels got longer, so did the wait for another cart to be filled. The problem presented was one of trying to determine where double tracks should be placed to speed up the system of getting the ore out and returning empty cars. The cost involved enlarging tunnels and adding track at appropriate bottlenecks. The main part of the cost was enlarging and shoring up the tunnels. The first questions the consultant asked were, "How wide are the tracks, how much clearance is there between tracks and how much between the walls and the tunnels, and how wide is the tunnel now?" The information was quickly provided, and it didn't take long for the consultant to determine that sufficient tunnel width existed to lay two tracks at each and every bottleneck. The company had just *assumed* that the tunnels needed to be widened, but no one had bothered to measure to be sure. The moral is that when you *assume* you make an *ass* out of *u* and *me*.

Not all messes are as easy to solve as the preceding examples, but a great many are this way, simply because someone didn't ask some basic questions and listen to the feedback. Thus the first thing you should do with the knowledge of operations research is to be sure the solution fits the problem that the manager actually wants to solve. The formulation of a mess into a problem lies much more in the realm of *quantitative analysis* than *quantitative methods*. It is at this point that even the most skilled students realize that they may not be well equipped to analyze, since most math-oriented courses present problems to be solved rather than messes to be analyzed. This book is designed to help you learn how to analyze as well as to solve, to think as well as to do.

Analysis requires the ability to think in "circular" fashion, to look at the mess again and again, turn it over, and view it from many angles, not just one side. It also requires the ability to think in "parallel," holding many possibilities in mind simultaneously. This can be a very uncomfortable feeling for those who have not practiced it, but it is absolutely necessary for good problem formulation—hence the "team approach" in operations research where several people can brainstorm a mess until it becomes a well-defined problem. This is in contrast to problem-solving or quantitative methods which most often are very direct, linear, sequential, and lock-step.

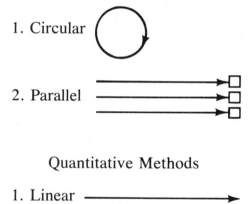

Quantitative Analysis

1. Circular

2. Parallel

Quantitative Methods

1. Linear

2. Sequential

1.3 SOLUTION

Once the mess has been changed into a problem, we will see that there are many different ways that the problem can be formulated. It might be formulated as a table of numbers or a map of distances that looks like a network. Once you have decided upon the problem formulation, there may be many different solution techniques available. In this book you will learn several ways to formulate problems and then several ways to solve them. The genius in problem solving is the person who so formulates the problem and chooses the solution technique that the solution is obvious or simple. There are essentially three different ways to solve operations research problems:

1. Change the problem to fit the solution technique.
2. Change the solution technique to fit the problem.
3. Invent a whole new way to solve the problem.

Usually we choose alternative 1 or 2, although there will be several occasions in this book when we will point out the need for a new technique, which might allow you to become rich and famous.

The important thing to remember is that there are several ways that a problem can be approached and solved. The solution technique should be something that makes sense (that is, the method may not be understood in the sense that all the math is understandable, but that the results make sense and the steps of solution are not impossible). Thus we come to *Woolsey's first law:* "Managers would rather live with a problem they can't solve than use a technique they don't trust." In simple behavioral terms, I would rather not jump out of the frying pan into the fire! This does not mean that managers understand all the mathematics behind it, but it does mean that they believe it can solve their problem. In management science, solution techniques are called *algorithms*, which simply means a clearly defined procedure.

Furthermore, operations research people are hung up on finding the optimum, because that's what we did in our classroom work as students. We found the optimum to nonexistent problems and were hung or ostracized if we didn't. But in the real world, where the data are suspect to begin with and the environment is so turbulent and dynamic that today's optimal answer is tomorrow's near-optimal, managers don't really care if you find the *optimum*. This leads us to *Woolsey's second law:* "Managers don't want the best solution; they simply want a better one." Better than what? Better than what they have right now, for a reasonable price in a reasonable amount of time. The problem with finding the optimum is that sometimes to get from 98 percent to 100 percent of the optimal value may take as long as reaching the 98 percent solution, and managers have neither the money nor the time to waste. This leads to *Woolsey's third law:* "If the solution technique will cost you more than you will save, don't use it!"

The solution techniques fall into the classification of quantitative methods and as such require the ability to think in a linear fashion (not jump ahead or think of several possibilities simultaneously). If one has ever observed brilliant math professors solve problems at the blackboard in a single bound, the impression is given that instead of executing many steps methodically, the answer simply "appears" much like a vision to a clairvoyant. But what actually happens is that the professor is able to do many simple steps very quickly in his mind because he is very good at the simple basics. Where most math students fall down is in the ability to add, subtract, multiply, and divide *symbols,* and hence they get lost in the *methods* (not just the analysis) because they try to do several steps at a time or simultaneously. Another thing that good math professors do is recheck their work mentally once or twice looking for flaws in their mechanics. Again, most math students are afraid to go back and check for fear of finding something wrong or not getting the same answer twice. Many good math people make plenty of mistakes, maybe even more than poor math people, but the difference is that they recognize them and correct them. Thus a word of advice from the authors: Take everything one step at a time. Learn to do the basics, the simple things, well. Don't try to do analysis when doing the solution techniques, but after the technique has been completed, check the answer to see if it "makes sense" (analysis).

The solution techniques (algorithms) will first be labeled either *quick* or *long*. Quick means that the method is very simple and instructions are easy to follow. Long means that it will be a little more involved (either intricate or very lengthy). Second, the algorithm will be labeled either *dirty* or *clean*. Dirty is a mathematical term to indicate that the solution technique cannot be promised to yield an optimal answer, although it may even do so 99 percent of the time. Clean means that the algorithm can be shown to yield a mathematically optimal solution. (However, even the use of a clean algorithm with data that is incorrect or suspicious may yield a dirty answer.) Many of the algorithms that are "Quick & Dirty" are *heuristic,* meaning a procedure based upon common sense and practical considerations but not necessarily optimal.

1.4 DATA

An OR/MS model without data is like a person without a soul. There are too many journal articles that use only fictitious data and do not face the problems of real data gathering. The data can be unavailable, tremendously expensive to get, jealously guarded by a department or an individual, or simply incomplete.

INCIDENT: DIRTY DATA

Each semester our classes are given the assignment of going to a local business and obtaining the costs for inventory problems—usually just the costs of carrying inventory (a combination of cost of capital, insurance, handling, storage, and so on)—and the students are amazed at the reaction of business people. Some business people have no idea what they are talking about; others try valiantly to help the students with some answers; and the smart ones know the figures but won't say so. It is always a valuable experience for any student to find out how hard it is to obtain actual figures and how threatening it can be to the person being asked. If the person doesn't know what the student is talking about, he or she is afraid to admit it, so usually he or she turns the student away or fakes it. This leads to *Woolsey's first law of data*: "The data is wrong." If you ask a machinist how long it takes to machine a piece, will he know how long it will take to the closest minute? Always! Will he give you an answer? Never!

After the direct approach fails, the next move is usually to the accounting office. There the wispy young OR analyst stands trembling at the desk of one of the accountants, buried deep in facts and figures, asking for time estimates. Finally the accountant at the next desk yells, "Toni, just give him a number!" With numbers clutched tightly in hand, the analyst runs back to the office to plug them into the latest algorithm. This leads to *Woolsey's second law of data*: "If you ask the accounting department to give it to you, they'll give it to you every time!"

A wise person once said of computing that the object was insight, not numbers.

INCIDENT: PITFALLS OF COLLECTING DATA

An energetic young man was heading out to an open-pit copper mine to time the arrivals, loading, and departures of dump trucks between the mine and the mill. As he was on his way, his instructor happened to meet him. The instructor was immediately alarmed at the prospect of what the young man was about to do and asked where his binoculars were. Not understanding, the young man asked why he would need them, whereupon the wise instructor informed him of the average life span of those who stand by the roadside with clipboard and stopwatch attempting to time teamster-driven trucks. The instructor pointed out that the young man had a high probability of appearing as an impurity in a copper ingot, coming out of the other end of the mill. The student quickly procured a topographic map of the area and soon located an appropriate spot to take the data (through binoculars).

Thus when trying to obtain data, one should be very aware of the environment and the fact that it may pose a threat to those who are being counted, measured, and observed. It is always a good rule of thumb to wear a hard hat in a plant, for tools have been known to fall upon unsuspecting data gatherers.

INCIDENT: A MORE PERFECT UNION

An enterprising young junior college student landed a job in a machine shop, having had some experience with lathes and metal working. Applying all she knew about operations research, she quickly cut down the time to produce parts so that she was making 40 parts a day within three days. Upon arrival at work the fourth day, she was greeted by the shop steward who wanted to comment upon her performance. The student was quick to explain that she was still getting the hang of it but should be able to up her production to 50 parts per day. The shop steward interrupted her and said that the student didn't quite understand. He then showed her a book which said that according to union standards only 15 of these pieces could be made per day. She was working far over the rate of the other employees and was advised that if she wanted to maintain her health, she ought to make 15 a day, and only 15. Being quick to learn, the student turned out 14 pieces in the first 3 hours, then set up her lathe for the 15th, and read books by the lathe the rest of the day, and was never bothered by the shop steward again!

In this case we see that sometimes data can be constant and that union rules and regulations can certainly have an effect upon OR models. Unless cooperation is secured with the union, the best models in the world may simply yield a theoretically optimal production rate.

INCIDENT: DEAD-END FOR DATA

A young student worked part-time as a switchboard operator for a large department store. Her class assignment was to get some information for a discounting problem from the department store. Being shy of interviewing people, she decided to get the information by telephone. What she experienced was a maze of transferred calls as one manager after another shuttled her around, until after five minutes of dead silence on the other end of the phone she realized that she had been transferred to a dead-end connection for people considered troublemakers!

Remember that gathering and validating data is threatening to many people, expensive, and time consuming. Often the data provided to the questioner is subject to ignorance, error, and evasion and must therefore be treated very carefully.

A final story illustrates the need to be alert to what the real data is and thus the actual problem that needs to be solved.

INCIDENT: A PROBLEM OF DEFINITION

A town in the western United States desired to build a new fire station to better serve its citizens. The old station dated back to territorial days and was a beautiful old relic, but not large enough for the new fire equipment. The town hired a consultant to help in determining the location of the new station, and was interested in knowing what data to collect. Many questions were asked about what the real objective was, such as whether to (1) locate near the buildings with the highest insurance rates or (2) minimize the maximum time to get to any house or building. Finally the consultant asked if he had all the information. The fire chief assured him that he did, whereupon the consultant stated that he had heard differently. The problem as he saw it was not where to locate the new firehouse but what to do with the old one. It seemed that the old station house was in an old part of town that was now mostly a Chicano neighborhood, and the council representative from that district had drummed up considerable support to keep the old station house. He argued that the proposed closing of the old station was another example of exploitation. All the *proposed* locations would be out of his neighborhood and thus reduce fire protection for his people. The problem rapidly became a classic example of the political hot potato. Further, the town could not afford to keep two station houses, so the result was a stalemate. The fire chief was rather surprised that the consultant had done his homework, and asked, "What can you do?"

The consultant suggested that the local chapter of the state Historical Society, which had been trying to save historical landmarks for 15 years and had never been successful, might be persuaded that the old station house was something that could be saved. The present fire equipment could be housed there and the station restored to its former glory and preserved for a small cost which the Society could support. The result would be that the community would have the protection it needed and would not be insulted by the removal of the station house. This proposal was unanimously passed by the City Council, to the delight of the Historical Society, the D.A.R., and the Chicano community.

1.5 CASES

Our primary instruments for teaching the use of management science are the cases in each section. These cases have been rigorously class-tested and are ranked in each section in the order of difficulty, the easier ones coming first. They are *real* cases in that they have come directly from actual situations in business, with perhaps some names and data changed to protect the guilty or the innocent. Some of them have been simplified to a great extent and, as always, they can never duplicate the real situation, that is, you never get to see the original *mess* from which they came.

However, it still should be a challenge for you to formulate and solve some of these, even though the Quick & Dirty algorithms are easy. This is because the data is sometimes cleverly hidden in the words and, as in all cases, there is a need for interpretation and feedback. In most textbook problems there is no need for any feedback since all the variables and constants are clearly given and all you have to do is to plug in the formula. In these present cases it may be necessary for you to formulate and set up the solution and then check with the instructor (who has the answer book and thus is all-wise and all-knowing) and find out if you have decoded the words properly. A lot of problem solving involves communication and feedback, and it is hoped that this will be something that will be learned from these cases.

Another point in favor of the case method is that some of these cases are large enough for teams to work on (or a team could divide up the work on several small ones), thus reinforcing a concept vital to operations research: the team approach to problem solving. You may notice as you begin to work in teams that the human dynamics become quite interesting. There is the disturbing property in mathematics of answers being right or wrong, and invariably where two or more are gathered together, several answers appear. The problem becomes (1) which solution you will hand in, (2) how is that decided, and (3) who gets blame and credit for the work? These are very real difficulties in problem solving and should not be discounted.

Each section of the book has an example with each Quick & Dirty algorithm, and then a case and solution following it. Then there are three or more cases for each section to give you some realistic ideas of situations where the algorithms have been used. Following these cases will be additional short problems which will allow you to sharpen your skills.

Your homework in this book will be done in a very different manner from math courses that you may have had previously. In most math courses the *answer* is important, and perhaps some work showing how you arrived at that answer. In these case studies the *recommendation* is the first important thing to show, then the *numerical answer,* and finally the *math work* or supporting calculations. It is suggested that the format be as follows:

1. *Recommendation.* This should be what you recommend to the manager (or professor) as far as action to take, given the problem stated in the case. This should be in English, not numbers or Greek symbols.

2. *Numerical Answer(s).* This should be the answer to the math problem and may contain all the numbers and Greek symbols usually found in math textbooks. This answer may differ from the recommendation, as it is the answer to the math part of the case, the outcome of applying the Quick & Dirty algorithm, which may yield several answers, one of which must be recommended, or the recommendation may round the math answer.

3. *Math Work.* This should be included for reference for the manager if it is desired to see how you arrived at the answer and recommendation. Of course the work should be neat and orderly, logically presented, so that the manager can follow the solution easily.

Examples of this format may be found throughout this book.

In this book you will find an interdependence between problem (analysis) and solution techniques (methods), and this makes it difficult to classify and organize the book according to problem types or solution techniques. Therefore there will be a brief introduction of each problem type and several solution techniques that could be used. Each problem type will have a solved case to show you how it might be approached, and then the cases will follow.

1.6 MODELS

One of the fundamental concepts of the practice of operations research or management science is the whole idea of a *model* of something. In the authors' generation a model had a very definite meaning which differs from that of today. Usually it meant a model plane, made of balsa wood, paper, glue, decals, wire, a one-piston engine, and hours of patient toil to put it all together so that it might fly. The result was something that looked like the real thing, and even acted like the real thing to the extent that it flew.

Nowadays we still have model planes like the above; however, the ones most often seen are those that are made of plastic and snap together. The primary difference seems to be that the new models require little or no skill to construct. Admittedly, they *do* fly, but somehow lack the resiliency, when crash landed, of the more carefully constructed models.

From the above discussion we can, at once, create some general truths about models of all kinds, includ-ing those in this book. We note that usually models that require no skill in construction, or brains on the part of the assembler, do not hold together as well as those that do. We further note that the more realistic the model is, the more time and money must go into it. We also pay a premium price for convenience. The less we have to do or understand, the more we pay (in one way or another). It can be easily verified that the component parts for a really professional model, which requires many hours of construction, cost less than the plane made of plastic that one can take out of the box and launch. We begin to get the sneaky feeling that it's not what the model appears to be that is important, but rather what goes into it. A model is the better, the more nearly it approximates the real thing; in short, if it acts just like the real article. However, some funny things can go wrong with this concept. We tend to assume that just because something *looks* like something else, it will also *act* like that something else. Little experience with other people is needed to convince us that there is precious little correlation between looking sexy, smart, or brave and *being* any of these.

Whenever a simple model is tried, there is always some other OR graduate heard saying that the model will never fly because it is (gasp, choke!) *unsophisticated.* The implication is clear:

$$\text{sophisticated model} = good$$
$$\text{unsophisticated model} = bad$$

As we have stated earlier, these words have lost their meaning. As Humpty Dumpty says in *Through the Looking Glass,* "a word . . . means just what I choose it to mean—neither more nor less. The question is, . . . which is to be master—that's all."[1] Turning to the Oxford Universal Dictionary for an even more complete definition of "sophisticate" we find that the definitions are: "1. To mix with some foreign or inferior substance; to adulterate . . . 2. . . . to render less genuine or honest. 3. To corrupt, pervert, mislead. 4. To falsify by misstatement or by unauthorized alteration."

We quickly conclude from this that the next time someone says he or she wants a sophisticated model, we should ask whether the model is wanted adulterated, ungenuine, dishonest, corrupted, perverted, misleading, or simply falsified. The execution of this bear trap will gleefully be left as an exercise for the student (after all the grades have been posted).

In the early years of operations research, B.C. (before computers), a model of a system was literally that; that is, a copy of the real situation was constructed to scale. A shining example of this would be the actual scale model of the Mississippi–Missouri river drainage basin constructed by the Corps of Engineers in the 1930s. Another excellent example would be the David Taylor model basin of the U.S. Navy where scale-model ships are floated in simulated seas to see how they survive. If the Corps of Engineers wanted to see how much of Missouri would be flooded if the Mississippi river went two feet over the levees, they just played a hose on that part of the model long enough to *see* what would happen. If the U.S. Navy had a sneaky suspicion that the new Sink-jack nuclear sub might rather run upside down, they just built a model of it, put it in a tank where some GS-7s were wading (to simulate waves) and noted that, yes indeed, the periscope was always upside down.

There was something really neat about these models. In the case of the flood model, if congressional representatives stood with their feet planted in the area that might be flooded and got their feet wet, they were quickly convinced that their constituents deserved (nay, *needed*) another dam. Three guesses whose budget gets increased to *build* the dam. In the case of the upside-down sub, *anyone* knew that a retrofit was needed before Admiral Rickover would approve the sub. We conclude at once that the best thing about the physical model is that anyone can plainly see the result, and even better, *why* the result happens.

Unfortunately, what works well for one thing, by being similar to it, may be very inefficient in another case. For example, Neanderthal man, if he had followed this kind of reasoning, might have been long delayed in inventing the wheel. He would have noticed that locomotion of a burden from one point to another by people or beasts required legs. Therefore the first cart might have looked like Figure 1.1(a) instead of Figure 1.1 (b).

Figure 1.1

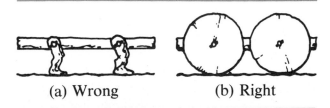

(a) Wrong (b) Right

Upon giving the legged cart (with the burden of one saber-toothed tiger) in Figure 1.2(a) a push, he would quickly notice the undesirable result shown in Figure 1.2(b). Nothing daunted, our sturdy caveman would then add another leg as seen in Figure 1.3(a); unfortunately this would lead to the result shown in Figure 1.3(b). Noting that, at least, the cart was not flat on the ground as before, he would reiterate until he got to the situation shown in Figure 1.4. Finally, after a few more tries, he would get to the state shown in Figure 1.5, which leads to a desired wheel-like optimum.

Figure 1.2

(a) Action (b) Reaction

Figure 1.3

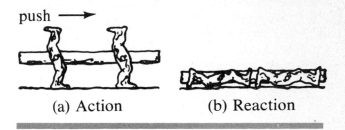

(a) Action (b) Reaction

Upon the final move from Figure 1.5 to optimality [Figure 1.1(b)], he would be promoted from Neanderthal (nondegree) to Cro-Magnon (junior executive) status. The final result (homo atomicus-transistorus) is still with us today.

We are therefore to conclude that a physical model is best *if* we can construct one that is more efficient (or just as efficient) as the real thing. Physical models are good because they are so clearly similar to the real system that the customer needs little convincing when we conclude that if a model does *X*, so will the real system. Physical models are persuasive because common sense supports the obvious conclusions. If a person can *see* something happen (in a model) and the model is a scale version of the real situation, common sense assures acceptance. (Exceptions to this rule are rare and have only appeared in federal, state, and local government and all sectors of private industry.)

Figure 1.4

Figure 1.5

The budding analyst knows that a victory has been won when the customer slaps her forehead and says something appropriate like "Of course, it *must* be true. It's just like *common sense!*" An edifying example follows.

Sometime ago, in a nameless southern state, a TV station wished to connect four antennas with coaxial cable on top of a mountain. A diagram of the situation may be found in Figure 1.6. Now as coaxial cable for this application ran something on the order of $3.50 a running *inch* and the distances between the antennas were in *miles,* the station executive became fascinated with the problem. Various methods were tried to find the way to lay the cable that would minimize length (and thus cost) to the station. We note these in Figure 1.7.

In desperation, two different consultants were hired. The first one, wearing a black hat and cape, used his sword to suggest Figure 1.8. Unfortunately, as he could not explain *why* this was any better than the others, Zorro was fired and a local academic was hired. She listened to the problem, consulted a physics book, and stated that the minimum length/minimum cost diagram (as generated by her FORTRAN IV program, run on the school 370/168 with JCL) was as shown in Figure 1.9.

The station manager was overjoyed to hear that this was indeed the optimum solution and said, "I'll write you a check right now, but first would you take

Figure 1.8

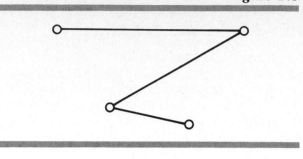

Figure 1.9

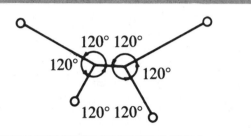

just a minute and explain *why* this is the right answer?" The professor began well, explaining the necessary Cartesian distance idea in her best QM452 style. As she went on getting into the necessary trigonometry, she noticed a slightly glazed look on the face of the station manager. As she gave it her big finish, the proof that the interior angles must all be exactly 120°, she noted with alarm that the pen had slipped from the fingers of the station manager. (She still doesn't know why she was not paid.)

As the problem *had* to be solved, a council of war was called. One of the reporters at the station said, "I have a friend who does things like this all the time, using junk around the house to explain solutions to complicated problems." "Get him," said the station manager. The friend listened to the problem, looked at the diagram, and said, "I can do it." Upon being asked how, he replied, "With a map to scale, two pieces of sheet plastic, four Popsicle sticks, a hot tub, a cup of detergent, a teaspoon of glycerine, and a crayon. Leaving the room, the station manager was heard to mutter something like; "I've got to *see* this." Overhearing this remark, the new consultant asked him to stay and watch.

The consultant punched four holes in each one of the pieces of sheet plastic exactly where the antennas should be on the map. He then ran the four Popsicle sticks through the four holes in the pieces of plastic when they were held about an inch apart. The final rigid construction is shown in Figure 1.10.

At this point a hot tub was run, and the cup of detergent (low phosphate, biodegradable for Sierra Club readers) and the glycerine were dumped in and stirred well. Now the construction was dipped into the

Figure 1.6

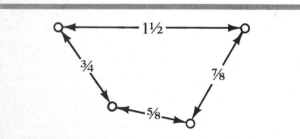

Figure 1.7

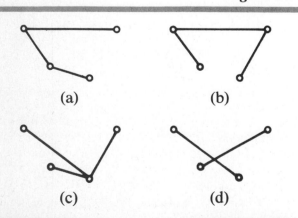

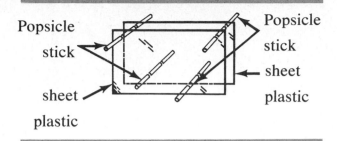

Figure 1.10

Popsicle stick

Popsicle stick

sheet plastic

sheet plastic

water and removed. As it was taken from the tub, a soap bubble was noted between the sticks. Holding it up to the light, the consultant traced out where the bubble was on the outside of one of the plastic sheets. He then handed the construction to the station manager, still dripping, and said: *"That's* the way you should lay the cable." The side view of the construction may be seen in Figure 1.11, the lines representing the connecting bubble.

The station manager, without a moment's hesitation, wrote a check for the consulting fee. While doing so, he was overheard to mutter, "Well, it's clear to me why it works, because of the fact that the bubble has surface tension and thus takes up the least distance between all the points. On the other hand I sure wish that you had done something on a *computer.*"

Let's pause a moment and realize that the soap bubble is an analog computer of sorts and will come up with the *same* solution found by the professor in Figure 1.9. The difference is that almost anyone who has understood a little of natural phenomena knows that soap bubbles will take the least space and surface possible. (That's why blowing bubbles produces spheres instead of cubes.) So the proof to most people is obvious and just common sense. The professor had the right answer; she just couldn't sell it. She could show the model mathematically, prove that it was right, but this also assumed that the customer was educated enough in physics, trigonometry, and algebra to comprehend the proof (which he wasn't). However, we should also recall that being educated and being smart are two different things. Having a Ph.D. no more makes you smart than being in a garage makes you a car. Of course on the other hand, the reason our hero used a crayon was probably because his school didn't allow him to handle anything sharp.

Figure 1.11

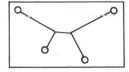

After reading this far, hopefully, you are beginning to get the message: "Verily, we say unto you that inside of every fat complicated (even sophisticated) mathematical model is a thin elegant model trying to get out." Again, let's turn to our trusty dictionary to look up the definition for *elegant.* We find it has the definition of *"ingenious simplicity."* You must realize that having the right answer isn't enough, but having a model that makes sense is extremely important. For this reason we will try in this book not to just tell you things that work, but hopefully, as often as we can, tell you the kernel of common sense that you will need to understand and eventually use the method. Remember that the right answer not used is the *wrong* answer.

Given sufficient education and a native acceptance of logic and mathematics, it is usually cheaper to build a mathematical model of something than to construct a physical model. For example, if we added another three or four antennas, building a physical model of the above example tends to become rather messy. Usually when dealing with the complex, many-faceted problems that confront the typical industrial concern, physical models are just not possible. This is indeed a painful truth.

However, in this book we will try to stay away from the complicated, mathematical models and present pictorial models, or simple tables of numbers, or, at worst, simple mathematical formulas. The thin elegant model will be presented in very simple, common-sense terms, and then at the end of each chapter we will make comments on the fat complicated mathematical model.

Now the purpose of all this discussion has been to let you know that in this book we will present several models, derived from problems that came from messes. These models are simplifications (sometimes gross) of real-world messes. Like the plastic or balsa-wood airplane models, they can provide a great learning experience about several techniques in operations research. However, you should be warned that—

1. models are *simplifications* of reality,
2. optimal answers to models may not be optimal (or even feasible) in reality,
3. all answers need to be checked *with* and *against* reality.

As this is an introduction to management science, the models presented are basic and simple, and you are encouraged to continue on to higher courses and more complicated modeling. While this book is not explicitly teaching how to *build* (formulate) models, it intends to teach by example how to *recognize* models and thus, implicitly, eventually how to build them.

1.7 REVIEWS

Most chapters of this book contain two review exams to help you prepare for midterms and finals. It is assumed that you have read all the material and have worked on all the cases, either in teams or individually. Obviously it would not be possible to have a test consist of several cases, so some problems of a more "artificial" nature are included, along with questions about the cases already solved. The problems are included to test the ability to do certain algorithms, to perform the methods, the mechanics. The other questions are included to attempt to check if you understand the case and what has happened and "what would happen if . . . ." These questions are often directed more at analysis rather than just mechanics. There are also included several "give-away" questions which are very simple to answer *if* you either have done the homeworks or understand the solutions to the cases.

You should try to work the problems for one of the exams at your leisure, but alone, to see what areas of learning are strongest and weakest. At that point, team members might gather and help each other with their weak points and/or receive additional assistance from your instructor. Then you should take the other exam, alone, under time-limit pressure to see what other weaknesses you might have. (Remember that "the optimal answer after you need it is worthless!")

We have always given these exams as "open book and open notes" because it is the authors' belief that in the real world one has access to certain materials and formulas. However, beware, for "open-book" tests are usually much more difficult than "closed-book" tests, and they require the ability to know what to look for, where to look for it, and to solve problems with real-time constraints.

1.8 OTHER FEATURES

At the end of each chapter there is a section titled "Bridging the Gap: The Interface" which is meant to help you if you are interested further in the topic of the chapter. The section is designed to put some of the algorithms into more mathematical terms for those who are interested, to comment on further extensions of some of the algorithms, and finally to bridge the gap between the practice of management science and the mathematical and theoretical framework without getting into too much detail.

As an antidote to our Quick & Dirty approach, the following fable by an early critic of academic popularization is presented. It is hoped that we have struck the balance in our approach.

The Wizard Who Oversimplified: A Fable*
HAROLD PETERSON

In a certain kingdom, there was a school for the education of princes approaching manhood. Since the king and his court spent much of their time playing chess—indeed, chess was called the sport of kings—it was decided that the subject called "games" should be added to the curriculum of this school. A wizard was engaged to develop the course.

Never having played chess himself, the wizard was a little uncertain about what to teach in this course. (Only a little uncertain because his ignorance of chess was outweighed by his strong confidence in his general ability.) He sought the advice of a colleague in another kingdom and from him received the following communication:

"Above all else, a course in games should be rigorous and intellectually challenging. We wizards long ago concluded that chess, as actually played, is so complicated that it is impossible to formulate a body of principles and decision rules; these are essential to the rigorous analysis of any subject. We have therefore introduced a few simplifying assumptions. For example, in chess, the pieces move in a bewildering fashion—some forward, some on the diagonal, and some even at a right angle; we have tidied up this confusion by assuming that all pieces move according to the same rule. With such assumptions, we have been able, albeit with great difficulty, to develop a model, a set of principles, and decision rules which are teachable and intellectually challenging. A 700-page treatise describing these is enclosed."

The wizard was much impressed by the 700-page treatise and used it in his course. He found that it was teachable, and that the task of learning this model and solving problems with the decision rules was indeed rigorous and intellectually challenging, as proved by the fact that good students did well on their examinations, while poor students failed them.

The wizard maintained an active correspondence with wizards in other kingdoms about the model and its decision rules. In this correspondence, the game was referred to as "chess" although this was solely for convenience of expression; it was taken for granted that everyone knew that their game was not quite like chess as played in the real world. Eventually, some of this correspondence came to the king's attention. Although he didn't understand the formulas and the jargon, he did notice that the word "chess" was mentioned, so he commanded the wizard to appear before him.

At this audience, the wizard asked, "How can I serve you, O King?"

* *Reprinted by permission from the* Quarterly Journal of Economics, *vol. 79, no. 2 (May 1965).*

And the king replied: "I understand that you are teaching the princes how to play chess. I wish to improve my own game. Can you help me?"

"What we call chess may not be exactly like your game, your majesty. So before answering your question, I must analyze the problem. Please describe chess as you play it."

So the king explained the game of chess. As he did so, the wizard noted that it had the same physical layout, the same number of pieces, and apparently the same objective as the game he taught in school. It seemed clear therefore that the solution was simply to apply the decision rules for this game, although he of course did not immediately reveal this fact to the king for he wanted to preserve his reputation for wizardry. Instead, he said thoughtfully: "I will study the problem and return in ninety days."

At the appointed time, the wizard appeared again, carrying a crimson pillow on which lay a spiral-bound report with a Plexiglas cover. It was a paraphrase of the 700-page manuscript. "Follow the rules in this report, your majesty, and you will become the best chess player in the world," he said.

The king avidly studied the report, but soon ran into difficulty. He summoned the wizard again. "I see reference to kings, and men, and squares, which are familiar terms to me; but what is all this about 'jumping,' and 'double jumping,' and 'countervailing force,' 'suboptimization'; and where do you mention queens, rooks, bishops, and knights?"

"But your majesty, as I have clearly explained in the introduction, it was necessary to simplify the environment a trifle. I doubt that these simplifications lessen the practical usefulness of what I have written, however."

"Have you by chance watched some chess players to find out?" asked the king.

"Oh, no, your gracious majesty, but I do carry on an extensive correspondence with other wizards. This is better than observing actual practice because it is generally agreed that wizards are smarter than chess players."

"And your princes. Are they equipped to play chess in the real world because of what they have learned in your course?"

"No offense intended, sir, but we wizards do not believe this to be a proper question. The purpose of our course is to teach princes to think, not to prepare them for a mere vocation."

At this point, the king lost his patience, but since he was a kindly king, he sent the wizard back to his schoolroom rather than to a dungeon.

Moral for economics professors: an education in checkers does not prepare one for a life of chess.

Moral for operations researchers: half a loaf is not necessarily better than no bread; it may be only chaff.

Moral for businessmen: A consultant who wants to play his own game rather than yours is worthless.

Supplementary Problems

1. Explain in *your own words* the difference between quantitative analysis and quantitative methods.
2. Give Woolsey's two laws of data and briefly explain them in *your own words*.
3. According to Chapter 1,
   a. give two definitions for "sophisticated":
   b. give the definition of "elegant":

1.9 REFERENCE

1. L. Carroll, *Through the Looking Glass* (New York: Grosset & Dunlap, 1946, pp. 229–230).

2
machine scheduling

INTRODUCTION

In machine shops where there is a lot of production on several machines there are many ways that these jobs could be scheduled, and some ways will take less time than others. The trick is to determine quickly how to schedule a batch of jobs so that everyone is busy (slack or idle time is minimized). Assume that there are ten jobs to be scheduled on two machines, a drilling machine and a reamer. Each piece must be drilled before it is reamed, so order is important. To determine the number of ways that these ten jobs could be ordered, realize that you are free to pick any of the ten jobs to go first, then there are only nine to pick from for the second, eight for the third, and so on. This comes out to $(10)(9)(8)(7)(6)(5)(4)(3)(2)(1) = 3,628,800$ possible ways these jobs could be done. We immediately come to grips with the problem of combinatorials: there are an increasingly huge number of possibilities, and we must choose between them in some rational manner. If there were only two jobs to be done, there would be no problem. The idea is to find some rational way to make the decision without becoming hopeless or irrational. The same situation confronts us when we go to the grocery store and are overwhelmed by an array of laundry soaps: flakes, granules, liquids, tablets, presoak, enzymes, biodegradable, phosphates, regular size, deluxe, economy, jumbo, with bleach, without, with colored sprinkles, . . . ad nauseum! What sets in then is what Alvin Toffler describes as *future shock*. Our eyes glaze over, we become catatonic, and in a trancelike state we reach for the soap that has the most obnoxious advertising (that jingle keeps going through our head) and make an irrational (or arational) decision.

There was a soap manufacturer whose advertising showed a woman taking her laundry out of the machine. The laundry was so bright that she had to wear sunglasses. Another beautiful commentary showed a man and a wife in bed. They had to wear sunglasses because the laundry detergent had gotten their sheets so bright. A few weeks after the first appearance of the ads on TV, a trailer was added where the wife took off her sunglasses and added that you really didn't need sunglasses after all. Why? Because the company had received so many complaints from users of the laundry detergent that their clothes weren't coming out that bright. The point is, after seeing something this obnoxious and vowing that you will never buy that soap, here you stand in front of a line of laundry soaps trying to make a decision, and in this aisle there are powders, granules, tablets, liquids; presoaks with bleach, enzymes, or

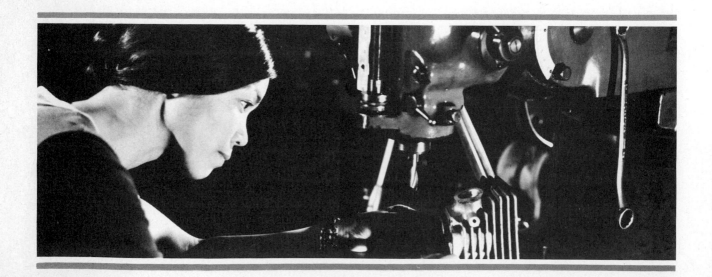

phosphates; regular size, economy, deluxe, giant, and so on. Finally you pick the soap you vowed you would never buy. You can't forget the name of it!

Alvin Toffler, author of *Future Shock,* points out that in chaotic, overload situations, we tend to revert to familiar behavior and old habit patterns. In operations research this can be very dangerous. What works in simple situations that we can comprehend may be one of the worst things we can do in complex situations. What is needed is some Quick & Dirty method that doesn't violate common sense. This section is devoted to some of these methods, attempts to find at least a good order of jobs in complex situations. To begin with, we will take a simple situation, solve that problem, and then make it more complex.

One of the risks in working with simplified problems is that one tends to oversimplify reality, with the result that the solution doesn't fit reality at all. The consultant should not ignore the problems of data collection, data estimation, conflicting schedules, machine breakdowns, or outside customer pressure and pretend that they do not exist. If these problems are ignored and a simplified solution is forced on the manager, catastrophe may result. It is a similar situation to the one in which Sir Isaac Newton explained to the Royal Artillery major that, neglecting air resistance, the cannonball should land right *there.*

As a final word of caution, the authors cheerfully point out that *none* of the methods presented here should be used straightaway. In an actual machine-shop situation there are many factors to be considered in an actual, *usable* schedule. Some of these are extremely subtle, for example, the knowledge by the shop supervisor that a given lathe has a higher than average need for preventive maintenance; thus he or she will not load it as much as another. The use of these algorithms should in no way abrogate the use of common sense.

2.1 TWO-MACHINE PROBLEM

Given five jobs on two machines, they are to be processed first on machine A and then on machine B. The processing times in hours are given in Table 2.1.

Quick & Clean Johnson Algorithm[1]

1. Find the smallest number in the chart and circle it.
2. If it appears in column A, schedule the job as soon as possible (on the left).
3. If it appears in column B, schedule it on the right, as late as possible.
4. Cross off that job and go back to step 1.

Example. The smallest number (processing time) is 2 hours for job 2 on machine B. It is in the machine B column (the right-hand column), thus job 2 is scheduled last (on the right). The job is then crossed off. (– – – –2). The smallest number is now a tie of 3 between job 1, machine A, and job 4, machine B. *In case of a tie, pick either job.* It won't make any difference in the final answer and simply indicates alternate solutions. Therefore let us arbitrarily pick the first smallest number, and since 3 appears for job 1 on the left, schedule job 1 first (1 – – – –2). The smallest number is now 3 for job 4, machine B, which means it should be scheduled as late as possible (on the right) (1 – – –4–2). Now the smallest number remaining is a 4 for job 3, machine A, and job 5, machine B. Thus the final schedule will look as follows: 1 – 3 – 5 – 4 – 2. This is the ordering that will give the least total processing time and the least idle time out of the 120 possible orderings. (There are some alternate orderings that would give the same time.)

Total Time

To determine the total time for these five jobs, multiply the total time for the latest job by the number of machines doing the processing. One way to determine the total time is to make up a schedule as shown in Table 2.2. Thus the total time is (2)(28) = 56 hours. The idle time would be total time − (time on machine A + time on machine B) = 56 − (26 + 22) = 8 hours. This could also be graphed on a time line, which is called a Gantt chart (Figure 2.1, page 16).

Let us compare this schedule (1–3–5–4–2) to our original ordering (1–2–3–4–5) shown in Table 2.3. The total time here is (2)(30) = 60 hours and idle time is 60 − (26 + 22) = 12 hours. There are four

Table 2.1

Job	Machine A	Machine B
1	3	6
2	7	2
3	4	7
4	5	3
5	7	4
Total	26	22

Table 2.2

Job	Machine A		Machine B	
	In	*Out*	*In*	*Out*
1	0	3	3	9
3	3	7	9	16
5	7	14	16	20
4	14	19	20	23
2	19	26	26	28

Table 2.3

Job	Machine A		Machine B	
	In	*Out*	*In*	*Out*
1	0	3	3	9
2	3	10	10	12
3	10	14	14	21
4	14	19	21	24
5	19	26	26	30

more hours of idle time, which means an operator is spending four more hours doing nothing. Management does not tend to like operators standing around doing nothing for four hours. Of course they could be asked to clean up the shop or do some other janitorial chore. (The least measurable instant of time is the time it takes from the instant the shop supervisor asks a machinist to pick up a broom to the time the whole shop is on strike.) This also brings up the problem of computing total time and why the total time is taken as the time it takes the last job to be finished times the number of machines. It is simply a standard measure to compare two different orderings. *If we are lucky* we can find some odd jobs for machinist B to do and keep him or her from looking like there is nothing to do. This is the scheduler's main problem, for difficulties arise quickly between machinists when one is doing all the work.

The rationale behind Johnson's machine-scheduling algorithm is to schedule short jobs first on machine A from left to right so that machinist B has something to do as soon as possible. It should be clear that to minimize *total* idle time, starting idle time must be as small as possible. Scheduling short jobs on machine B from right to left will ensure that machine A is kept busy as much as possible relative to machine B. The really satisfying thing about this last argument is the symmetry it makes with the first argument above.

tool and die

A small tool and die shop is set up by a business person in his garage in Fallbrook, California, and he works on orders from other small businesses in the area. There are six large machines now in use and two employees working the machines. Essentially there are only two things that can be done since there are only two persons to run the six machines. The company has no inventory and must wait for the material to arrive for each specific job. Thus scheduling has tended to be impulsive and rather haphazard. What is needed is a simple ordering algorithm that can be applied by hand when the need arises. For a typical week the jobs and hours of labor required for tooling and production are given below. Time is in hours. Find the ordering and schedule of the tooling and production sections that will minimize the idle and total time, with the requirement that the tooling be done first. Compare the optimal schedule with the way the jobs are ordered in the table. What is the difference in the idle time?

Job	Tooling	Production
16	6	9
17	8	6
23	8	7
38	—	3
39	5	4
41	16	9
42	11	16

Solution

Recommendation. Change the original order of jobs from 16–17–23–38–39–41–42 to an optimal schedule of 38–16–42–41–23–17–39. This saves 22 idle hours.

Numerical Answer

Optimal Schedule

idle time = total time − machine time
total time = 59 hours per machine (2 machines)
= 118.

Note that we use the longest time for the production process for *both* processes.

Figure 2.1

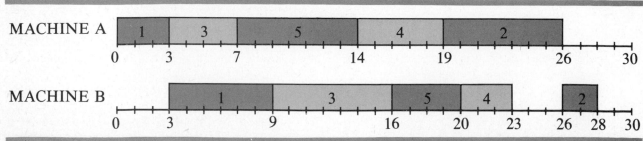

machine time = 108 hours.

This is the total time from the preceding table, the actual time that pieces are in process.

idle time = 118 − 108 = 10 idle hours.

Original Schedule

idle time = 70 hours per machine (2 machines) − 108
= 140 − 108 = 32 idle hours.

Thus there is a savings of 22 hours of idle time.

Math Work

Job	Tooling	Production
~~16~~	⑥⁸	~~9~~
~~17~~	8	⑥⁸
~~23~~	8	⑦⁴
~~38~~	⓪¹	~~3~~
~~39~~	5	④²
~~41~~	16	⑨⁵
~~42~~	⑪⁶	~~16~~

Total 54 + 54 = 108 machine hours

The following steps 1–6 are not required under "Math Work," but are included as an explanation to the student.

1. The smallest number in the above table is 0 for job 38 and appears on the left; thus job 38 is scheduled first (38– – – – – –). Job 38 is then crossed off.
2. The smallest remaining number is 4, the production time for job 39, which appears on the right, so that job 39 is scheduled on the right (38– – – – – –39). Job 39 is then crossed off from the table.
3. The smallest remaining number is 6, and there are two of them: jobs 16 and 17. Since job 16 appears on the left, and 17 on the right, it makes no difference which one we pick first; the job ordering will remain the same. Thus we have 38–16– – – –17–39, and cross off both jobs 16 and 17.
4. The next smallest number is 7 and appears on the right for job 23. Thus it is put as far right as possible, and then job 23 is crossed off the table (38–16– – –23–17–39).
5. The next smallest number is 9 appearing for job 41 on the right and is scheduled as far right as possible, and then job 41 is crossed off (38–16–41–23–17–39).
6. Only job 42 remains and must be scheduled third (38–16–42–41–23–17–39).

Optimal Schedule

Job	Tooling In	Tooling Out	Production In	Production Out
38	0	0	0	3
16	0	6	6	15
42	6	17	17	33
41	17	33	33	42
23	33	41	42	49
17	41	49	49	55
39	49	54	55	59

total time = 59(2) = 118 hours.
idle time = 118 − 108 = 10 hours.

Original Schedule

Job	Tooling In	Tooling Out	Production In	Production Out
16	0	6	6	15
17	6	14	15	21
23	14	22	22	29
38	22	22	29	32
39	22	27	32	36
41	27	43	43	52
42	43	54	54	70

total time = 70(2) = 140 hours.
idle time = 140 − 108 = 32 hours.

cable division

In January the Cable Division of a global company received contracts for over 3000 miles of transatlantic cable to run from the Virgin Islands to Brazil, Venezuela, and Florida. This required the immediate start-up of its production facilities which had been idle since August. It also required the modification of the assembly lines, especially the rolling mills and core extruders. Other modifications were also necessary so that within 60 days production of the SF cable could begin. These modifications must be designed by the production engineering department and then produced by an outside job shop within 6 weeks (42 calendar days or 30 working days). Each designer is responsible for several designs and has given estimates of how long each design will take and then how long the job shop will require to produce the modifications according to specifications.

The contract will take an estimated two years to complete, with 45 miles of SF cable being produced per week. An additional 200 people must be hired within the next 2 months, but care must be taken that all personnel will be trained and ready for production work at the same time, rather than having some waiting around for other parts of production to be qualified and ready to run.

Given the data below for two of the designers, determine the optimal ordering for each designer so as to minimize the time necessary to design and build the equipment, and state whether there will be any delay caused by the original ordering. Time estimates are in days.

Charlie's Jobs	Design Stage	Job Shop
Creel modification	5	7
Core extruder 1	3	6
Rolling mill 2	7	3
Jointing SF modification	6	8
Shaver 3	4	2

Max's Jobs	Design Stage	Job Shop
Core extruder 2	8	5
Rolling mill 1	4	6
Welding 1	5	4
Shaver 2	7	2
Welding 2	2	3
Jacket 3	1	2

INCIDENT: RIGID REQUIREMENTS

To illustrate the "least measurable instant of time" and the reality of difficulties that can arise from scheduling some machinists more than others, consider the following case. A consultant was hired by a foundry to do a complex simulation of the shop. She was instructed that if there were a variance of more than 15 minutes in the work of any machinist, the whole shop threatened to go on strike. This much more complex situation required a considerably more complex simulation program to try and find a sequence that would satisfy the rigid requirements.

silk screen shirts corporation

In 1969 Morgan Dean Oliver began silk screening shirts in his garage for friends who wanted their favorite logo or saying emblazoned across a shirt. Now, over 10 years later, he is working from a two-story factory building on Clairemont Boulevard.

The printing and packaging of shirts consists of basically three processes. Pulling consists of taking the shirts out of inventory and laying them out so that they can be put through the machine. For t-shirts this means getting a roll of t-shirts out and laying the chest or back area flat, so there wouldn't be any wrinkles. Girls' shirts and golf shirts come in plastic bags, so they have to be unwrapped and all pins and tags removed before being laid out. Rugby shirts come on hangers and are easily taken out of inventory, but they have long sleeves which are cumbersome when laying out the shirts. Debbie, the woman doing the pulling, said she could prepare 240 t's, 60 golf or 60 girls' shirts, or 80 rugby shirts per hour.

Printing is done on a hand machine, and Debbie can do both the pulling and the printing. The hand machine takes five minutes to set up and then can do shirts at a rate of 80 per hour, regardless of the kind of shirt.

Folding is preparing the shirts for delivery. T-shirts are put into rolls of 12, and 5 rolls can be done in one hour. Girls', golf, and rugby shirts are folded individually and can be done at the rate of 30 per hour. This is done by Arnold and obviously must be done after Debbie has both pulled and printed each job.

Mr. Oliver has eight jobs as of right now and would like to know how to arrange these to minimize the total idle time. Given the size and type of each job below, first of all construct a timetable for Debbie and Arnold and a schedule for the jobs as ordered. Then determine the optimal ordering and schedule and find out how much time has been saved. (Round all times to minutes; remember these are estimates anyway.)

Job	Quantity and Type
Born Again Christians	50 t-shirts
Dirty Dan's	40 t-shirts
Boat House	10 rugbys
Chart House	24 golfs
Old Ox	20 girls', 4 golfs, 24 t-shirts
Red Onion	24 girls', 12 golfs
The Black	20 t-shirts, 10 girls'
Magnolia's Peach	48 t-shirts, 24 girls'

INCIDENT: INTUITION VERSUS RATIONALITY

Frederick Taylor, the father of scientific management and time and motion study, determined from his studies that the simple use of intuition on the part of the machinists was not nearly as good as using some rational, heuristic approach that could be *taught* to and *used* by the machinists. It is interesting that this result has been known for over 50 years, and yet is seldom used.

gordon and smith surfboards

Gordon and Smith have been producing surfboards for years and currently employ 12 people to help with

Table 2.4

| | Production Team I | | | | Production Team II | | | |
Job	Foamer	Shaper	Glasser	Sander	Hot Coater	Pin Striper	Finish Sanding	Box and Crate
O.B. 1	5	115	20	37	15	80	15	10
P.B. 1	5	230	20	28	17	82	15	10
P.B. 2	5	145	18	33	10	78	15	10
M.B. 1	5	150	19	30	18	45	15	10
O.B. 3	5	110	20	40	15	70	15	10
M.B. 2	5	110	18	40	14	70	15	10
L.J. 1	5	130	15	35	12	73	15	10
L.J. 2	5	165	10	30	12	65	15	10
C.V. 1	5	225	17	25	18	80	15	10

the design, production, and distribution of their surfboards. For a long time they have been known for their quality work and their unique design, which is instantly recognized by surfers everywhere.

Their basic production process consists of an initial process of a foamer, and then shaping when the board is given its basic shape. After that the board is glassed and sanded. A hot coating follows, and then pin striping (a distinct design of Gordon and Smith) and the finishing sanding and buffing are done. Finally the board is boxed and crated and is ready for shipment.

Production teams have been formed, and the many processes have been merged into two processes or production teams, with each team being treated as if it were one huge process. The idea behind this was for each team to take about as much time for a board as the other team, and hopefully reduce idle time. Nine orders have been received for this week, and the time in minutes for each basic part of the production is given in Table 2.4. Add these various times to give the production times of the two teams and then determine the optimal ordering and schedule of these nine jobs. Then compare the idle time and total time with the original ordering (the way they came into the shop).

INCIDENT: ANOTHER COMMON SENSE SOLUTION

A foundry used a large numerically controlled machine which required five human operators. After the operations on this machine, each piece had to be worked on by a second machine, but not until certain measurements had been taken. Certain that the process could be more efficient, the company hired a consultant to give advice. The consultant knew that the first rule is to *look at what is happening now* and

so proceeded to spend a day looking over the operations. One of the things he noticed was that when a large piece was finished on the first machine, it took 5 men 20 minutes to haul it across the shop to be measured at the calibration center. It then took another 20 minutes to haul it back to the second machine (which was no more than a minute away from the first one). Since this happened at least once a day, and each worker was being paid $6.50 per hour, it was costing $21.66 per day or $5632 per year (approximately) to do this. The consultant simply suggested that the calibration device (highly portable and easily carried by one person) be moved to the area where it was needed. Since the consultant's contract called for payment of 10 percent of yearly savings, the consultant made $563 for a few hours of simple observation and years of collected wisdom. This again illustrates the need to use common sense with even the best of algorithms.

Supplementary Problems

1. Pat and Debby are grading MS tests which are each two pages long. Pat is grading the first sheet and Debby the second, which must be done after the first one. The following are the times in minutes for several tests that must be graded. Determine the optimal order.

Test	Page 1	Page 2
1	9	10
2	30	27
3	20	11
4	5	16
5	23	7
6	11	13

Order ___ ___ ___ ___ ___ ___

2. Given the following schedule:

Job	A In	Out	B In	Out
1	0	4	4	8
2	4	6	8	12
3	6	15	15	17

a. Why can't job 2 start until "8" on machine B?

_____

_____

b. Why can't machine B start on job 3 at "12"?

_____

3. Darlene has five loads of clothes to wash and dry and would like to know the optimal ordering so as to mimimize time, given the following times in minutes:

Load	Washing	Drying
Pants	30	20
Blouses	20	10
Towels	35	25
Lingerie	15	5
Sheets	30	15

a. Optimal Order: _____

b. If the last load is done at 135 minutes, give

Total time: _____

Idle time: _____

c. Why does this problem have a "precedence" relationship?

4. Given the Gordon & Smith Surfboards case, what differences are there in the job ordering compared to the optimal one if the Sander is included in Production Team I instead of Production Team II? Show your new time totals for each team and work, as well as the old and new orders.

Old order: _____

New order: _____

Job	Team I	Team II
O.B. 3		
P.B. 1		
P.B. 2		
M.B. 1		
O.B. 1		
M.B. 2		
L.J. 1		
L.J. 2		
C.V. 1		

5. Given the following schedule for five jobs on two machines, draw a Gantt chart.

Job	Machine A In	Out	Machine B In	Out
1	0	2	2	8
2	2	9	9	13
3	9	12	13	15
4	12	14	15	16
5	14	17	17	19

Idle time: _____

A: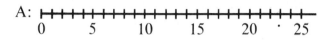

B: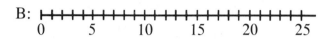

2.2 M-MACHINE PROBLEM

When there are more than two machines (M>2), everything is up for grabs. Under some very special conditions there is a Quick & Clean (optimal) algorithm for three machines but mostly we must depend upon a heuristic to help us get a "good" answer. If you desire to become rich and famous, you would do well to develop an algorithm that would be quick and efficient and optimal for three or more machines. Two approaches will be shown, one a modification of Johnson and the other a technique by Gupta.

Quick & Dirty Johnson Algorithm[1]

1. Set up the table of jobs and machine times with the proper ordering of machines (that is, in the order that each piece must be machined).
2. Set up a Johnson two-machine problem by using the first machine as machine A and the last machine as machine B and determine an ordering and the total and idle times.
3. Set up a Johnson two-machine problem with the total time for the first two machines versus the last two machines. Determine the order and total and idle times.
4. Do the same thing with three machines, four machines, and so on, up to and including $M - 1$ (where M is the number of machines). Always pair off the same number of machines.
5. Pick the ordering that gives you the least total and idle times. This is not guaranteed to be optimal.

Table 2.5

Job	Machine A	B	C	D	E
1	4	3	7	2	8
2	3	7	2	8	5
3	1	2	4	3	7
4	3	4	3	7	2
5	2	5	1	4	3
Total	13	21	17	24	25

Table 2.7

Numerator	Job	Machine A	B	C	D	E	Denominator	Job Value
-1	1	4	3	7	2	8	7	-1/7
-1	2	3	7	2	8	5	9	-1/9
-1	3	1	2	4	3	7	3	-1/3
1	4	3	4	3	7	2	7	1/7
-1	5	2	5	1	4	3	5	-1/5

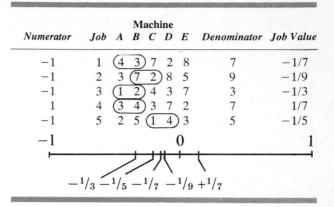

-1 0 1

$-\frac{1}{3}$ $-\frac{1}{5}$ $-\frac{1}{7}$ $-\frac{1}{9}$ $+\frac{1}{7}$

The rationale behind this scheme is to order jobs first that get through the first machines the quickest and order jobs last that finish up quickly. Only $M - 1$ problems need be solved for N jobs on M machines versus $N!$, which is a very small fragment. To ensure optimality, all $N!$ orders would have to be investigated.

Example. Given the data shown in Table 2.5, two-machine problems can be developed as shown in Table 2.6. The best ordering of these four two-machine combinations yields a total time of 185 hours and 85 idle hours (3–5–1–2–4), but is not guaranteed to be the best or optimal.

Another approach, which is by Gupta[2], orders by job values computed as follows.

Quick & Dirty Gupta Algorithm

For each job:
1. If the machine time on the first machine is greater than or equal to the machine time on the last machine, set the numerator equal 1 for that job. Otherwise set the numerator equal -1.
2. Find the smallest sum of the two connecting machine times (A+B, B+C, C+D, and so on) and use that as the denominator.
3. Rank order the job values from most negative to most positive. That is the ordering to use.

Example. Using the same data as in Table 2.5, we can obtain the job shown in Table 2.7. The order is 3–5–1–2–4 which gives an idle time of 85 hours and a total time of 185 hours. The rationale behind this heuristic is that the numerator separates those jobs that start early and those that finish fast while the denominator orders jobs first or last, depending on how small successive machine times are. It should be noted that the intuitive justification for Gupta's method is really a restatement of Johnson's two-machine method. The negative sign forces short-starting jobs on the first process *to the left.* The positive sign pushes the jobs with long starting times *to the right.* The relative value of the denominators determines *how much* the jobs are pushed to the left or right.

mercury division

The Mercury Division of an East Coast manufacturer has four machines that it uses in its production process. One of the machines can do many different jobs,

Table 2.6

Job	Machine A	E	Job	Machine A+B	D+E	Job	Machine A+B+C	C+D+E	Job	Machine A+B+C+D	B+C+D+E
1	4	8	1	7	10	1	14	17	1	16	20
2	3	5	2	10	13	2	12	15	2	20	22
3	1	7	3	3	10	3	7	14	3	10	16
4	3	2	4	7	9	4	10	12	4	17	16
5	2	3	5	7	7	5	8	8	5	12	13
Order	3–5–2–1–4		3–1–4–2–5			3–5–4–2–1			3–5–1–2–4		
Total Time	200 hours		205 hours			215 hours			185 hours		
Idle Time	100 hours		105 hours			115 hours			85 hours		

which permits a reduction of the idle time. This press machine can be set up to either punch holes or break (bend corners). Given this versatility, the machine can virtually always be running. For example, the machine can start out punching shelves and then breaking hats. Some jobs do not have to go through all the processes. This type of scheduling set up by the supervisor allows the press machine to run all day except for the time required to change the dies. This time is also kept to a minimum because only three persons know how to change the machine and they have done it for many years. The problem is that the other areas of the shop are experiencing an uneven load. As far as total time is concerned, it might be possible that the scheduling now used is not the least total time. The jobs must first be processed on the press, then welded, tagged, and finally painted, in that order. Given the jobs and machine times below (time in minutes), determine the job order and the schedule you would use, remembering that punching or breaking can be done on the press machine. Also determine the total time and the idle time.

Jobs	Process I Punch	Process I Break	Process II Form	Process III Weld	Process III Tag	Process III Paint
Shelves	1000	1000	3000	—	1000	3000
Hats	500	1000	—	1000	—	—
Standards	1000	800	1800	2000	—	1000
Brackets	—	1000	1000	2000	—	—
Base	—	500	4000	2000	—	—
Kick base	2000	500	3000	—	100	500
Panel rail	1000	500	2500	300	500	500
Top panel rail	—	—	1000	200	—	500

Solution

Recommendation. Order jobs: Top panel rail – brackets – standards – base – shelves – panel rail – kick base – hats. This will reduce idle time to 14,400 minutes (230 hours).

Numerical Answer

$$
\begin{aligned}
\text{total time} &= 18,700 \text{ minutes (3 processes)} \\
&= 56,100 \text{ minutes} \\
\text{machine time} &= 41,700 \text{ minutes} \\
\text{idle time} &= 56,100 - 41,700 \\
&= 14,400 \text{ minutes.}
\end{aligned}
$$

Math Work

1. Using Johnson's method, use the first and last processes for a two-machine algorithm.

Job	Punch/Break	Weld/Tag/Paint
Shelves	(2000)[8]	4000
Hats	1500	(1000)[4]
Standards	(1800)[7]	3000
Brackets	(1000)[4]	2000
Base	(500)[2]	2000
Kick base	2500	(600)[3]
Panel rail	1500	(1300)[6]
Top panel rail	(0)[1]	700

Order

Top panel – base – brackets – standards – shelves – panel – hats – kick base.

Schedule

Job	Punch/Break In	Punch/Break Out	Form In	Form Out	Weld/Tag/Paint In	Weld/Tag/Paint Out
Top panel	0	0	0	1,000	1,000	1,700
Base	0	500	1,000	5,000	5,000	7,000
Brackets	500	1,500	5,000	6,000	7,000	9,000
Standards	1,500	3,300	6,000	7,800	9,000	12,000
Shelves	3,300	5,300	7,800	10,800	12,000	16,000
Panel	5,300	6,800	10,800	13,300	16,000	17,300
Hats	6,800	8,300	13,300	13,300	17,300	18,300
Kick base	8,300	10,800	13,300	16,300	18,300	18,900

total time = 18,900(3) = 56,700 minutes
idle time = 56,700 − 41,700 = 15,000 minutes.

2. Now we take the first two processes versus the last two processes and solve the two-machine problem that results.

Job	Punch/Break and Form	Form and Weld/Tag/Paint
Shelves	(5000)[8]	7000
Hats	1500	(1000)[2]
Standards	(3600)[4]	4800
Brackets	(2000)[3]	3000
Base	(4500)[7]	6000
Kick base	5500	(3600)[5]
Panel	(4000)[6]	3800
Top panel	(1000)[1]	1700

Order

Top panel – brackets – standards – panel – base – shelves – kick base – hats.

Schedule

Job	Punch/Break In	Out	Form In	Out	Weld/Tag/Paint In	Out
Top panel	0	0	0	1,000	1,000	1,700
Brackets	0	1,000	1,000	2,000	2,000	4,000
Standards	1,000	2,400	2,400	4,600	4,600	7,600
Panel	2,800	4,300	4,600	7,100	7,600	8,900
Base	4,300	4,800	7,100	11,100	11,100	13,100
Shelves	4,800	6,800	11,100	14,100	14,100	18,100
Kick base	6,800	9,300	14,100	17,100	18,100	18,700
Hats	9,300	10,800	17,100	17,100	18,700	19,700

total time = 19,700 (3) = 59,100 minutes
machine time = 41,700 minutes
idle time = 59,100 − 41,700 = 17,400 minutes.

This schedule is not better than the first one.

3. Let us now use Gupta's algorithm (see Table 2.8). To determine the numerator for the Shelves, compare the time of the first process (Punch/Break) with the last (Weld/Tag/Paint). Since 200 is less than 4000, the numerator is −1. Otherwise it would be +1. The same process is done for all the other jobs.

To determine the denominator, take the smallest sum of two adjacent processes. Thus for Shelves we take the smallest amount of (2000 + 3000) and (3000 + 4000) which is 5000. The same is done for all processes.

The ratio is simply the numerator divided by the denominator, and is put on a number line as shown in Figure 2.2.

Schedule

Job	Punch/Break In	Out	Form In	Out	Weld/Tag/Paint In	Out
Top panel	0	0	0	1,000	1,000	1,700
Brackets	0	1,000	1,000	2,000	2,000	4,000
Standards	1,000	2,800	2,800	4,600	4,600	7,600
Base	2,800	3,300	4,600	8,600	8,600	10,600
Shelves	3,300	5,300	8,600	11,600	11,600	15,600
Panel	5,300	6,800	11,600	14,100	15,600	16,900
Kick base	6,800	9,300	14,100	17,100	17,100	17,700
Hats	9,300	10,800	17,100	17,100	17,700	18,700

total time = 18,700 (3) = 56,100 minutes.
idle time = 56,100 − 41,700 = 14,400 minutes.

This is the best of the three schedules.

fibre containers

Fibre Containers has five main machines through which the cardboard goes to become a box. Not all boxes need to be run through each machine, and some need processing by only one. However, there is a certain order that must be maintained: slitter, rotary press, taper, D/C, and box maker. The problem Fibre Containers has is to fit the various jobs on the different machines, minimizing the total time and idle time for the machinists. On any given day they have from six to nine jobs to be done.

The times for seven jobs are given (in hours) for a particular day. Ignoring such things as customer priority, determine the job order and a time schedule

Table 2.8

Numerator	Job	Punch/Break	Form	Weld/Tag/Paint	Denominator	Ratio
−1	Shelves	2000	3000	4000	5000	−1/5000
1	Hats	1500	0	1000	1000	1/1000
−1	Standards	1800	1800	3000	3600	−1/3600
−1	Brackets	1000	1000	2000	2000	−1/2000
−1	Base	500	4000	2000	4500	−1/4500
1	Kick base	2500	3000	600	3600	1/3600
1	Panel	1500	2500	1300	3800	1/3800
−1	Top panel	0	1000	700	1000	−1/1000

Figure 2.2

JOB	TOP PANEL	BRACKETS	STANDARDS	BASE	SHELVES		PANEL	KICK BASE	HATS
RATIO	−1/1000	−1/2000	−1/3600	−1/4500	−1/5000	0	1/3800	1/3600	1/1000

for these seven jobs. When the jobs are started by Fibre Containers at the beginning of each day, they consider the possibility of not being able to finish all the jobs by the end of the day. Another bottleneck sometimes occurs due to a large shortage of cardboard in the United States.

Using the Johnson and Gupta algorithms, determine a good job order and the resulting schedule. What is the total time difference between the original schedule and your recommendation?

Job	Slitter	Rotary Press	Taper, D/C and Box Maker
Planet Plastics	1.6	—	2.0
Essick Manufacturing	2.1	5.6	3.6
Alliance Rubber	—	3.8	12.8
Modern Aire	4.8	—	—
Bernham Groves I	—	4.4	5.4
Bernham Groves II	1.9	2.4	2.1
Bernham Groves III	1.4	2.0	2.3

INCIDENT: AUDITING APPLICATION

The Veterans' Administration conducts a yearly audit of all its hospitals and facilities and uses its own team of accountants and CPAs. The team basically performed three functions and tried to look as busy as possible. Finally the manager, suspecting that something was inefficient, decided to optimize her own department and thus set up and solved the problem as a three-machine problem with several jobs. Formerly it took 15 days to perform each audit, and using the results of the simple three-machine heuristic it was cut down to five days. This caused considerable consternation in surrounding departments. The result was that the managers of the adjoining departments arranged it so that this manager was offered a higher position in another agency, which she accepted.

This illustrates that the M-machine algorithm is certainly not limited to solving problems that only involve machines, but that any process that requires time is a candidate for efficient job scheduling.

indiana metal enameling company

The Indiana Metal Enameling Company builds and installs metal signs. It is a well-established company with a gross income of several million dollars per year. It is most concerned with pleasing customers and will go to almost any length to do so. This includes working overtime to get a job out on time, moving workers from one job station to another (they

have quite a bit of flexibility in this as many of their people can do many different jobs), or even hiring on a temporary basis. For a very large job (such as 600 Shell Oil price marker signs which took 45 days), they may simply clear the decks of all other jobs and devote all the time to one main job.

The following machine scheduling problem is made up of figures from the fabrication schedule of architectural jobs. Times are in hours, and the jobs must be processed on each machine in the order specified from left to right. Determine the job order that best reduces idle time and total minimum time, using any method you wish. As a solution give the time schedule for each job and machine and determine idle and total times. Once the schedule is determined, draw a Gantt chart and see if there is any way that the idle time might be further reduced by using less than four workers to run the machines.

Job	Shear and Set Up	Strip Form and Set Up	Weed and Buff	Steel Pickle
Woolo Store	3	27	13	6
Police Building	4	11	4	1
North Shore Hospital	2	1	0	1
Good Samaritan Hospital	4	30	8	7
Eric Substation	3	23	8	3

INCIDENT: INCENTIVE FOR COMMUNICATION

As an exercise in the communication of important truths, we require our students each semester to write up a Quick & Dirty algorithm for the *M*-machine scheduling problem so that a machinist could understand and use it. It has to be one $8\frac{1}{2}$ by 11 inch page long, neat, and legible, with an example and simple instructions. We then take these to a shop supervisor and ask him to divide them into three piles: one pile for those he can neither read nor understand, the second pile for those he can understand, and the third pile for the ones that would be good enough for him to keep and actually use. Needless to say, the largest pile is the first, with three or four in the second and one in the third. Grades are then assigned as F, C, and A, respectively.

One student, in pile one, objected to the grading and wanted to see the dumb SOB who couldn't read his Quick & Dirty. A plant tour was arranged with the class, the high point being when the student was introduced to the shop supervisor. The supervisor towered over the student, standing 6' 6" with a neck size only exceeded by his bicep measurement. The student comprehended at once that he had a rather severe communication problem. He further was considerably impressed with the thought that, "If this guy knew what I *called* him, he might react in a negative and rather physical way." The student became highly motivated to communicate in some useful way, now that the proper incentive had been supplied.

archer machine products

Archer Machine Products is a machine shop. Approximately 80 percent of all their jobs are through closed bids to large aircraft manufacturing companies. The remaining 20 percent are of a special nature that do not require submitting bids and are not competitive.

Because such a large share of Archer's contracts are of a competitive nature, it is extremely important that they be able to estimate the costs of a particular job accurately. If the estimates for a job are too conservative, the company stands to lose a great deal of money if it should be awarded the contract. If the costs estimated for a job are much higher than those that would be incurred, Archer, in all likelihood, will lose that bid to another company.

On November 10, Archer was invited to bid on a contract for a large aircraft plant in the Midwest. This contract would entail the manufacture of 1000 vertical stabilizer bars, 1000 horizontal stabilizer bars, 1000 third-member skin braces, 1000 dovetailed stabilizer brackets, 1000 fuel-hatch hinges, and 1000 fourth-member cross braces. Mr. Archer, President, needed to know how much the bid for this job should run. Bids usually run 10 percent over the cost estimate.

There are five different machines on which these various pieces of equipment have to be produced. The sequence of machining for completing the task is as follows: drilling, first milling, honing, second milling, and polishing. The time required to machine 1000 of each on the various items is given in hours. All 1000 of each product must be processed before proceeding to the next station.

	Drill	Mill 1	Honing	Mill 2	Polisher
Vertical stabilizer bar	15	92	3	25	10
Horizontal stabilizer bar	30	105	6	10	7
Third-member skin brace	8	76	6	45	15
Fourth-member cross brace	8	76	6	48	13
Dovetailed stabilizer bracket	24	105	30	15	9
Fuel-hatch hinge	3	45	0	2	0

The operator of the honing machine receives $5.00 per hour, while the remaining operators are paid $3.50 per hour each. The costs of maintaining equipment have been broken down into per-hour costs. For the drill press this cost is $0.15 per hour, milling machines are each $0.35 per hour, the honing machine is $0.11 per hour, and the polisher is $0.05 per hour.

Use the Gupta algorithm to determine a good ordering of these jobs and give a breakdown of the respective costs involved. Assume that all operators and machines must be charged whether idle or not. Once the ordering of jobs has been determined, give the time schedule for each job and machine, idle tiem, and total time. Finally, give your estimate of the bid.

Supplementary Problems

1. Ted, a starving young business student, would like to make some extra money to buy groceries as soon as possible. He is working on five stained-glass windows and would like to know a good ordering for completing them as quickly as possible. Using the Gupta algorithm determine the ordering and schedule.

Window	Cut Glass	Cut Lead	Assemble	Solder	Putty	Clean
Daffodil	5	7	12	3	3	4
Parrot	10	20	30	9	9	11
Roses	7	9	15	5	5	6
Sunset	3	6	10	7	7	8
Geometric	10	18	13	8	8	6

Ordering ——— —— —— —— —— ——

Machine time ——————————————————

Total time ———————————————————

Idle time ————————————————————

2. Give the answer for the ordering for the Archer Machine case:

—— —— —— —— —— ——

If you were to compare the first and last processes using Johnson's algorithm, would there be a different ordering? Explain briefly.

3. Consider the Archer Machine case.
   a. What would happen to total time and costs if

honing, mill 2, and polishing were all done by one machinist instead of three, and why?

___

b.   If drill 1 and mill 1 were done by one operator, what would happen to time and costs? Why?

___

c.   If there were only two operators (combining parts a and b), what algorithm would you use and why?

___

d.   What is the percent idle time for the original solution?

___

4.   Use the Gupta algorithm to determine a good ordering for a body shop, given the following data.

Car	Putty	Sand	Prime	Paint
'57 Chevy	6	5	8	9
'72 Malibu	6	9	2	2
'40 Ford	5	12	17	4
'77 Pacer	10	3	3	5
'66 Mustang	8	4	1	30
'71 Pickup	2	8	10	13
'69 Gremlin	1	7	6	$\frac{1}{2}$

Order: ___ ___ ___ ___ ___ ___ ___

5.   Give the schedule for the original order in problem 4 for the first three cars:

Car	Putty	Sand	Prime	Paint
'57 Chevy				
'72 Malibu				
'40 Ford				

2.3 DUE DATES

Now let us complicate matters by allowing due dates for each job. This means that the situation is more dynamic than the preceding ones and that all jobs are not due at the same time. To simplify matters for the present, let us assume that these jobs are all done on one process (or that if they are done on several machines we will simply take the total time). We will present two heuristic algorithms for scheduling jobs; one will minimize the number of jobs that will be late and the other will minimize the latest any one job will be. Unfortunately this will usually not yield the same ordering, so that the manager will have to use his or

her judgment as to which jobs are scheduled first and which will be late.

Again, this problem is not limited strictly to job shops, but can take place in many business situations. The dilemma in a grocery store is whether to have a quick-service line (usually ten items or less). In other words, do they want to have one, which will mean that not as many people will have to wait in the checkout lines, but those who do wait will have to wait longer if they have more than ten items; or if they do not have the quick-service line, then more people will be waiting, with those with full baskets waiting less and those with ten items or less waiting more.

This problem arises in the time-sharing service offered by computer service companies. The dilemma here is whether you keep a few customers happy or a lot of customers late. Lag time is the amount of waiting time from entering commands on the terminal to the response. The idea of time-sharing is that several persons use the computer simultaneously and have the illusion of being the only user on the machine. If the lag time is too great, then customers will complain or stop using the service. The Harvard Business School purposely does not own a computer, but rather rents time-sharing from three or four companies. Then if the response time for a certain company is too long, they simply dial another one and use their service—a good example of free enterprise.

Quick & Clean Algorithm: N-job, one-process sequencing to minimize the number of late jobs.[3]

Given that we have the due dates and processing times for all the jobs,

1.   Order all jobs by increasing due dates (earliest first) from left to right.
2.   Starting with the first job, determine the total time it takes to do all the jobs until one of the jobs will be late. Then go to step 3. If there are no late jobs, the sequence is optimal. *Stop*.
3.   Find the job in the sequence up to and *including* the first late job that has the largest processing time and put that job at the end. Then go back to step 2.

Example.   Given the eight jobs with processing time and due dates (in days), find the optimal sequence.

Job	1	2	3	4	5	6	7	8
Due date	5	8	10	11	14	17	20	21
Time	4	3	2	3	4	2	5	3
Finish date	4	7	9	12*	16*	18*	23*	26*

Here the first late job would be job 4, due on the 11th and done by the 12th. (It would not be late if done on the 11th.) Thus we look at the first four jobs and find the job with the largest processing time. This is job 1 with a processing time of four days. We put this job at the end and now have the sequence 2–3–4–5–6–7–8–1. Finally, we position job 7 at the end.

Job	2	3	4	5	6	8	1	7
Due date	8	10	11	14	17	21	5	20
Time	3	2	3	4	2	3	4	5
Finish date	3	5	8	12	14	17	21*	26*

Thus we have a sequence of 2–3–4–5–6–8–1–7 which will have two jobs late (1 and 7). Job 7 will be 6 days late, job 1 will be 16 days late, a total of 22 late days. The original sequence had 5 late jobs and 12 late days.

Quick and Clean Algorithm: N-job, one process sequencing to minimize the latest any job will be

1. Order all jobs by increasing due date (earliest first) from left to right.
2. *Stop.* Sequence is optimal.

The original ordering will minimize the latest any job will be. Thus although there are 5 jobs late, the latest is only 5 days late, versus the second ordering which will have only 2 jobs late, but one will be late by 21 days. Now you can appreciate the dilemma that the manager is faced with: The choice is five people mad (but not very) or just two people mad (and one fuming). In the real world of getting jobs done, there is a simple heuristic which usually aids in decision making: *Put the screamers first.* Those who scream loudest often get serviced quickest (or if too loud and obnoxious, not at all). Notice that no priority or importance of the customer has been attached to these jobs. We will deal with that later.

An important point to notice in the first scheduling algorithm for due dates is that the first job that was late (job 4) is not necessarily the one that should be put at the end. The real culprit for making jobs late is the one that took the longest. To make a homey analogy, in a family where several people are using the same bathroom and you are late for work and can't get in to brush your teeth, the person to get mad at is not necessarily the guy ahead of you, but the one who took the longest. Thus the first job is put last instead of job 4.

the amforge corporation—1600-ton press

The Amforge Corporation makes steel forgings. The process of forging is to stamp the raw steel into the basic shape the final part will take so that the machining time will be cut to a minimum. Production planning, job scheduling, and machine scheduling are done on a job-shop basis according to shop capacity and customer requirements. In production planning there are two schedules: long range and short range. The long-range schedule has orders that cover from one to six months. The short-range schedule, also called the revolving schedule, consists of all orders lasting from 1 to 30 days. There are five schedules used by this company in making decisions on when to run the various jobs. These schedules are (1) schedule of forging equipment by type and capacity, (2) schedule of auxiliary and material preparation equipment, (3) schedule of tools and dies needed for the jobs and engineer design time, (4) schedule of raw-stock arrival, (5) schedule of workforce at time of production. The general manager stresses that job scheduling is no cut and dried thing due to factors such as equipment breakdowns, die failures, absenteeism, late arrival of raw materials, oversold condition of some production units, and extreme customer pressure. The revolving job schedule or short-range schedule allows new orders to come in at any time. This requires schedule reshuffling. All the other factors mentioned above complicate making a stable scheduling plan.

Assuming that production for December has been completed, and all steel has been cut to run the jobs, schedule the jobs for the month of January. Assume 22 working days, 10 hours per day for each machine involved. Only one job may be done at a time and once a job is started, it must be completed. Jobs are due at the end of a day. Determine two schedules: one that will minimize the number of late customers, and another that will minimize the maximum lateness of any customer who is late. As a manager, which one would you choose and why?

Customer	Order Size	Due Date	Job Hours for Month
John Deere (K39644)	1,100	3	10
Barton Instruments–2F	2,500	21	40
Barton Instruments–1F	2,500	5	22
Norris Industries	30,000	10	45
Jetco (J9570)	250	1	5
Major Safe–T2	1,200	2	15
Major Safe–J2	1,200	4	12
Chiksan (A856B)	600	13	40
Talley–463	500	19	20

Solution

Recommendation. It is recommended that the following ordering be used: Jetco (J9570) – John Deere (K39644) – Major Safe-J2 – Barton Instruments-1F – Major Safe-T2 – Chiksan (A856B) – Norris Industries – Talley-463 – Barton Instruments-2F. This reduces the number of late jobs and also keeps each job late by less than five days. It is assumed that this is better than having four jobs late and a lot of customers upset over scheduling problems. Major Safe-T2 and Norris Industries will be late.

Numerical Answer. Ordering by minimizing the number of late jobs yields a schedule of Jetco – John Deere – Major Safe-J2 – Barton-1F – Chiksan – Talley – Barton-2F – Major Safe-T2 – Norris, where Major Safe-T2 is late by 14.4 days and Norris is late by 10.9 days. By placing the two late jobs in the order given in the recommendation section, the lateness is reduced to 4.4. and 4.9 days without making any other jobs late.

Ordering by minimizing the maximum lateness results in the schedule of Jetco – Major Safe-T2 – John Deere – Major Safe-J2 – Barton-1F – Norris – Chiksan – Talley – Barton-2F and will have four jobs late. Major Safe-J2 late 0.2 day, Barton-1F late 1.4 days, Norris late 0.9 day, and Chiksan late 1.9 days.

Math Work. The jobs are ordered by due date, and if any ties, by least processing time (see Table 2.9). The initial ordering will give the minimum maximum lateness. The first late job is Major Safe-J2, but the T2 job is the one with the most processing time, and so it is put at the end. Then the next late job is Chiksan, but the job with the most processing time up to that point is Norris so it is put at the end.

---

the amforge corporation—700- and 750-ton presses

Referring to the previous Amforge case, there are two presses that are very similar to each other: the 700-ton and the 750-ton presses. For scheduling purposes it has proven convenient to treat these as

one machine which essentially doubles the hours available. The jobs that are run on these presses are smaller in size and require less pressure and temperature than the 1600-ton press, but more pieces are required to be processed. Given the number of hours required for each job, and the due date in terms of working days, schedule the two presses as one press with 20 hours per day available. Jobs are due at the end of the day. Determine the optimal schedule that will minimize the number of late jobs and the optimal schedule that will minimize the latest any one job will be and decide which of the schedules you will use. Also see if you can reduce the amount of total late time by rearranging jobs without changing the ones that are late.

Customer	Order	Due Date	Job Hours for Month
Caterpillar–SH	4,800	10	20
Chiksan (S104F)	1,600	21	10
Caterpillar–9S	8,600	21	50
Ross (10865985)	5,700	9	35
Caterpillar–8L	10,000	12	80
Talley–301	1,000	16	40
Sparton–484	1,700	1	10
Sparton–487	1,800	1	10
Talley–11	300	14	5
Fab Products (2630)	8,600	11	50
Murdock (9219167)	40,000	8	110

INCIDENT: DUE FOR A JOB

The problem of due dates can be quite vexing, especially when your shop is behind in orders and customers are threatening to take their orders elsewhere. An interesting case involves a firm with a tremendous scheduling problem. They had a two-month backlog and it was getting worse. In desperation they finally turned to outside help and enlisted the aid of a student trained in Quick & Dirty methods for the summer. While being interviewed for the job he was shown about the plant and then finally shown a nice office where he awaited further interviewing. After sitting alone in the office for a while, he poked

Table 2.9

	Jetco	T2	Deere	J2	1F	Norris	Chiksan	Talley	2F	T2	Norris
Process time	5	15	10	12	22	45	40	20	40	15	45
Due date (hours)	10	20	30	40	50	100	130	190	210	20	100
Total	5	20	30	42*	64*	109*	149*	169	209		
Revised total	5		15	27	49		89	109	149	164*	209*

his head out the door to ask the secretary what was happening. She informed him that she understood that he was now the new head of production scheduling, and that was his office. Panic-stricken at the thought of actually having to implement what he had learned in the classroom, he nevertheless buckled down and by the end of the summer, working 18-hour days, seven days a week, he had eliminated the backlog and dropped the in-process inventory by $800,000.

term papers

The usual strategy for term papers is to wait until the last moment to do them. If there are several due around the same time, things can become complicated. Let us assume that you have three classes which require several term papers: English, philosophy, and biology. We will also assume that the professor for each class will not be fooled by such excuses as "the dog ate my term paper," or "I left my 3×5 cards on the plane back from Hawaii" (this one requires a good tan and can only be used during the spring semester after Easter vacation). Thus it will actually be necessary to do the term papers.

We will also further assume that you are a smart student who wants to get organized at the beginning of the semester. The due dates for all of your term papers (in weeks) are determined, having been given out the first day of class. Each paper is due at the end of that week. You have estimated the time (in weeks) to do each one as if it were the only paper you were working on. This also counts "all nighters," staying up the night before to put it all together and type it.

Schedule the papers so that you minimize the latest any paper will be, and minimize the number of late papers. Comment on which of the two schedules you would use and why. What if you started to work on the first term paper the week before it was due (in the fourth week)? How would this change the number of late papers in each case? A theorem called "complementary slackness" is at work here (and will be discussed later).

Course	Due Date	Time Estimate
Biology	6	1
	12	1
	15	1
Philosophy	8	3
	15	1
English	4	1
	8	4
	15	4

INCIDENT: COMMUNICATING THE SOLUTION

A consultant was called in to demonstrate his Quick & Dirty to a supervisor in Houston, Texas, who was quite impressed with what could be done. A little mini-computer by DEC was used, and the instructions for the data and the results were in simple English. The only objection the supervisor had was that most of the workers, being Mexican-American, were more familiar with Spanish than with English. Undismayed, and knowing that a consultant has to fill the needs of his customers, the consultant reprogrammed the computer on the spot. Instead of typing out "Two-machine job shop, how many jobs are to be done?," the reprogrammed version typed: "Dos processos maquina, entre el numero de trabajos para hacer." It then continued in Spanish to direct the user to type in the data and reported the result (also in Spanish). This case simply points out the necessity of *communicating* the right answer to someone, rather than just being right. A mathematician would have stopped at being right, while businesspeople want to see the right answer understood and used.

bathroom madness

Consider the dilemma of five guys living in a house with only one bathroom (this is a real case, the names have not been changed to protect anyone, innocent or guilty). Sandy is a flower grower and usually gets up at 6:45 A.M. and spends five minutes in the bathroom. He must be at work, which is 25 minutes away, at 7:00 A.M. Needless to say he doesn't make it.

George is in the Navy and must report to the base by 7:00 A.M. Allowing 20 minutes driving time to make it to the base, he must leave the house by 6:40 A.M. George spends 25 minutes using the bathroom in the mornings.

Rick is a professor (and author) and must be at school by 7:30 A.M. (five minutes driving time) and spends 30 minutes in the bathroom (most of that time is spent drying his hair so that his natural will cover up his little bald spot).

Brent is a grocery checker leaving the house by 8:30 A.M. and spends 45 minutes in the bathroom (he takes several showers, turning it on and off every five minutes).

Pete is currently unemployed and must be at the unemployment office by 8:00 A.M. to pick up his check. The way Pete drives it only takes him ten minutes to drive about the same distance George does in 20. Pete spends 40 minutes in the bathroom.

The ideal for each person is to sleep as long as possible before getting up, using the bathroom, and leaving the house, thus getting as much sleep as possible. If everyone were to sleep as late as possible, how many would be late to work (or the unemployment office)? If everyone had to be on time for work, how many would not get to sleep as late as they wanted?

Assume that the time to get dressed is negligible (although Pete is never quite sure what to wear and Sandy has only one outfit to wear). Also breakfast is so rare around the house that there is no time wasted eating.

Use common sense to help restore order to this mad household! You will have to adapt the algorithm or develop your own for this problem.

1. Minimize the number of people getting up early and still making it to work on time.
2. Minimize the total lateness without changing the rising times.
3. Minimize the amount of "earliness" (getting up earlier than they want to) with no one being late.

Supplementary Problems

1. Given the following jobs, order them to minimize the number of late jobs.

Job	1	2	3	4	5	6	7	8	9
Due date	5	6	7	2	6	8	3	5	4
Time	1	2	1	$1\frac{1}{2}$	$\frac{1}{2}$	3	2	1	1

Late jobs: _____

Total lateness: _____

2. Given the following jobs with due dates:

Job	1	2	3	4	5	6	7	8	9	10
Due date	3	10	5	9	6	8	3	5	2	4
Time	1	1	1	3	2	2	1	3	1	2

a. Minimize the number of late jobs.

Late jobs: _____

Total lateness: _____

b. What is the most any job will be late if you minimize maximum lateness? _____

3. Given the Bathroom Madness problem, state two ways this differs from the standard due-date problem. _____

_____

_____

2.4 WAITING TIME

Consider the problem when all jobs are due *now*. This situation occurs frequently when the boss gives the secretary five jobs to type up and wants them all immediately (and there is only one secretary to do them); or at a computer center which receives several batch jobs to do and, not having multipartioning, has to decide which jobs get done first. Here we will allow priorities and give a Quick & Clean algorithm for the case without and with priorities to minimize the total time to complete the jobs and the total time the jobs have to wait until processed.

Quick & Clean Algorithms: Minimize the Total Waiting Times for One Process

1. Order all jobs by increasing processing times (smallest first) from left to right.
2. *Stop.* Sequence is optimal.

Example. Let us assume that the previous example (page 26) now has just one due date for all jobs.

Job	3	6	2	4	8	1	5	7
Time	2	2	3	3	3	4	4	5
Total	2	4	7	10	13	17	21	26
Wait	0 +	2 +	4 +	7 +	10 +	13 +	17 +	21 = 74

The total waiting time is 74 days.

If we had simply ordered the jobs as originally done we would have the following:

Job	1	2	3	4	5	6	7	8
Time	4	3	2	3	4	2	5	3
Total	4	7	9	12	16	18	23	26
Wait	0 +	4 +	7 +	9 +	12 +	16 +	18 +	23 = 89

The total waiting time is 89 days.

What this algorithm shows is that it pays to get the small jobs done first and leave the longer ones for last. This is precisely what is usually done in computing centers, which will run long jobs (45 minutes or more) during the evening hours and promise only 24-hour turnaround.

Quick & Clean Algorithm: Minimize the Total Waiting Times for One Process with Weighting

Now let us assign priorities or weights to each job. This frequently happens in computer centers, especially with multiprocessing computers. In most cases an original priority is assigned, and then the priority rises as the job waits in the queue; the longer the wait, the higher the priority becomes.

1. Order all jobs by increasing ratio of processing time to priority (smallest first) from left to right. Priority 1 would be the lowest. (If your priority ranking is the opposite, simply multiply priority by processing time.)
2. *Stop.* Sequence is optimal.

Example. Let us take the same example again and assign priorities to the jobs. Priority will be from 1 to 10, with 10 as the highest.

Job	1	2	3	4	5	6	7	8
Time	4	3	2	3	4	2	5	3
Priority	6	5	10	9	8	2	4	6
Ratio	2/3	3/5	1/5	1/3	1/2	1	5/4	1/2

The jobs should be done in the order 3–4–8–5–2–1–6–7. Notice that this is slightly different than the order without priorities. If the manager is still not satisfied with the order, ask what priority his or her favorite jobs should have and recompute.

Now let us assume that the priority numbers were ranked in the opposite order, priority 10 being lowest and 1 highest. (This works well when the jobs have been ranked in order of importance, 1 being the most important.)

Job	1	2	3	4	5	6	7	8
Time	4	3	2	3	4	2	5	3
Priority	6	5	10	9	8	2	4	6
Product	24	15	20	27	32	4	20	18

The job ordering is 6–2–8–3–7–1–4–5. The jobs are ranked from the smallest product to the largest and this will minimize the waiting times for the jobs in the order of decreasing importance.

computer center 10 a.m. batch

At a northeastern university the University Computer Center makes batch runs at 10 A.M., 2 P.M., and 4 P.M. every day. There have been complaints that the jobs always seem to take too long and that everybody is always waiting for his or her job. The center has several remote batch terminals on the campus, one of which is located in the basement of the School of Business. These remote job entry terminals (RJE) are convenient for running jobs that have a low volume of output, high volume of computation, and a small number of cards due to the slow I/O devices.

The jobs are processed through the RJE at 10 A.M., 2 P.M., and 4 P.M., and then the output is delivered through the remote printer, is bundled with the cards, and delivered to the user room.

It has been argued that jobs should be processed on a shortest job first basis, while others would like to see a priority system put into effect. For this computer center, a priority of 10 is the highest priority and is assigned to only a few users. Priority 1 is for undergraduates who are juniors, 2 is for seniors, 3 is for master's candidates; these are all unfunded accounts. The morning batch is usually small due to the fact that jobs are run at night and the queue is fairly empty. Given the 10 A.M. batch shown, determine the schedule with and without priority. Is there a difference at all in the two schedules?

Job	Minutes	Priority
1255	3	10
1260	6	2
1248	9	4
1268	12	10
1277	7	8
1256	3	4
1283	5	2
1294	8	5
1297	5	1
1301	2	3

Solution

Recommendation. Order by priority, 1255 – 1301 – 1256 – 1277 – 1268 – 1294 – 1248 – 1283 – 1260 – 1297. The use of priorities is recommended, with the assumption that priority numbers are handled properly and that funded accounts are given higher priorities since the center needs those funds to keep in operation.

Numerical Answer. The total waiting time without priority is 188 minutes for the 10 jobs, or an average of 18.8 minutes each (see Table 2.9). There is no sense in giving the total weighted waiting time, as this has no real meaning. However, the unweighted waiting time will be more (it must be) with priority, but the least important jobs will be waiting the longest.

Math Work. If the ratios are ordered from smallest to largest, they give the order with priority. If the table is set up by processing time from smallest to largest, it gives the optimal ordering without priority. The total waiting time is larger with priority (Table 2.9). It is those with priority 2 or 1, however, that will have to wait longer.

Table 2.9

Total Waiting Time without Priority

Job	1301	1255	1256	1283	1297	1260	1277	1294	1248	1268	
Time	2	3	3	5	5	6	7	8	9	12	
Priority	3	10	4	2	1	2	8	5	4	10	
Ratio	0.67	0.30	0.75	2.50	5.00	3.00	0.88	1.60	2.25	1.20	
Total	2	5	8	13	18	24	31	39	48	60	
Wait		2 +	5 +	8 +	13 +	18 +	24 +	31 +	39 +	48	= 188 minutes

Total Waiting Time with Priority

Job	1255	1301	1256	1277	1268	1294	1248	1283	1260	1297	
Time	3	2	3	7	12	8	9	5	6	5	
Total	3	5	8	15	27	35	44	49	55	60	
Wait	0 +	3 +	5 +	8 +	15 +	27 +	35 +	44 +	49 +	55	= 241 minutes

computer center 2 P.M. batch

At 2 P.M. the number of jobs being processed by the University Computer Center has picked up considerably, and this also holds true for the remote batch terminal at the School of Business. The University has an IBM 370 model 50 and three remote job entry terminals (RJE), one of which is at the School of Business. In this case there are 20 jobs waiting to be processed, with the time estimates on the job cards and the priority numbers. Determine the optimal ordering for these jobs with and without priority and also determine the total waiting times. Which order would you recommend and why?

Job	Minutes	Priority
1306	3	10
1481	5	8
1344	2	10
1356	10	2
1328	1	4
1382	6	10
1383	3	10
1345	5	8
1355	2	10
1386	15	4
1346	5	6
1376	20	1
1401	8	2
1390	3	10
1379	7	10
1366	12	1
1351	10	2
1342	6	5
1321	3	1
1407	5	8

INCIDENT: SIMPLY SCHEDULING

A large computer manufacturing company has developed a sophisticated (remember the definition of sophisticated?) production and control system that it sells to customers at considerable cost. It has a plant in a southwestern state which produces parts for its computers, and thus has an ideal opportunity to use its own system. However, it doesn't use it; managers complain that it is too complicated, they can't read the output and can't explain it to the shop supervisors. Reportedly they use some simple Quick & Dirty heuristics that are programmed on a competitor's minicomputer. The competitor was required in the contract not to reveal what its minicomputer is being used for or the site. This unnamed company is *still* selling the system at the time of this printing. This again simply illustrates the first law of problem solving: *Do the simple things first.* If in applying the Quick & Dirtys in this or any other section it becomes necessary to do something more complicated, make sure that you have at least tried scheduling with the simple methods first.

telephone installation

Due to a new contract, a large business firm in the South has experienced a rapid expansion in personnel. Since the multimillion-dollar contract will ensure business for the next three years, management feels safe in making some major changes, among which is the addition of several phone lines for each department in the company. Each department feels that it has first priority for installation, and claims that it cannot do work without the phones. Obviously, some departments will have to wait longer than others, and the problem is to schedule installation in some equitable and rational manner. Given the number of working days for each installation, schedule the departments according to the two different ways of determining ordering: by shortest time and by priorities. Management has assigned priorities to each department and would like to know if there is any difference between the two different schedules. A priority of 1 is the highest. Also find the waiting times. Are they significantly different?

Department	Time	Priority
Accounting	8	4
Marketing	5	3
Production	6	1
Engineering	7	2
Sales	9	5
Personnel	4	6

INCIDENT: SIMPLE QUESTIONS PRODUCE SIMPLE SOLUTIONS

As a final lesson that the most important thing in job-shop problems is observing what is happening, consider the following story. It seems that during the Korean War there was a small bomb factory somewhere on the East Coast. The bombs that they made were routinely nondestructively tested before leaving the factory (the destructive testing is very spectacular). Unfortunately the Air Force started double-checking them and retested (nondestructively) all the bombs sent to them. The result of the Air Force's test was that the bombs tested by the factory were consistently found to be 90 percent defective. Further, it was found that bombs *not* tested at the factory, when tested by the Air Force, were 100 percent effective. So, the Air Force came to them and said, "Please don't send us any more tested bombs. We want only the untested bombs, as we have found them to be more reliable." The factory's OR group immediately formed a group to study the problem and designed a fantastic probabilistic scheduling model that was supposed to make the whole problem go away. After two months, 90 percent of the bombs were still defective after they had been tested. At this point a representative from the Air Force showed up and said, "You people must understand this is a very grave problem, because when our people load these bombs and fly over the bad guy's area to drop them, they would rather they go 'boom' instead of 'thud.' Some of our pilots might get the feeling that perhaps the trip wasn't worth it. So we'd like you people to get with it." Well, one engineer snuck into the meeting and said, "Look, why don't we go and see how they're testing bombs before we do any more work on the model." The OR group threw him out because he obviously didn't have a Ph.D.

Shortly after that, the engineer submitted his resignation to the corporation. On his way out he decided to be a bad guy. So he wrote the Air Force office concerned and asked them to let him go and see how they were testing the bombs. He found that the bombs were being tested in the following way: A little old lady sits on a chair and a bomb comes along on a conveyor belt. She takes the test panel off and reaches inside for a piece that looks kind of like a 75-mm shell. She puts it in a vertical tester that's got little electrodes on the end which connect with the electrodes from the bomb. She then presses a button. If the light goes green, it means that the connections are right and the bomb is working. She then puts it back into the bomb, puts the panel back on, and goes to the next bomb.

It only took a minute for the engineer to see what was happening. Remember, the bombs are lying horizontally when she takes the panel off. She has to reach inside and pick up a thing about a foot long and four inches around and put it in a vertical tester. She then presses a button on the tester; if the test light glows green, she puts the thing back in the bomb. Now look at Figure 2.3.

Any good industrial engineer will tell you that when people have to move a piece of work from horizontal to vertical, the dominant hand will support the work from *below*. But when a piece of work must be taken from vertical to horizontal, the dominant hand will support and guide the work from *above*. So what was happening was that every time the little old ladies tested the thing in the bomb, they put it in *backwards*.

Now some of Ph.D.'s from the OR group were less

Figure 2.3

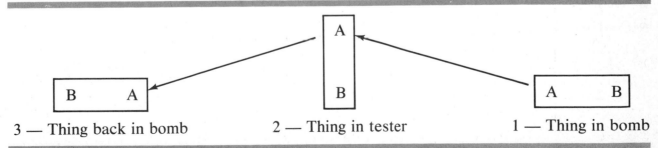

3 — Thing back in bomb   2 — Thing in tester   1 — Thing in bomb

than impressed by this discovery and pointed out that if the engineer was right that *all* of the tested bombs would have been defective, rather than the 90 percent found by the Air Force. The engineer then coolly asked the boss of the testing group how many women were testing the bombs. The boss replied that he had 20 employees doing the testing. The engineer then asked how many of the women were *left-handed*. It was found that there were two south-paws in the group.

automobile repair

One of the big problems with scheduling automobile repair is determining when the car will be ready. Most schedulers figure that if they are within a day, that is close enough. The scheduler has already made out the sheet for the day and has realized that all of the cars cannot get done by 5 P.M. as promised. He has estimated how many minutes each job will take (divided by the number of mechanics) and has assigned priorities of 1, 2, and 3 for each job (1 being the most important). 1 means get it done at all costs; 2 means get it done if you can; and 3 means don't worry about it. 1s are usually given to friends of the boss, big tippers, or jobs that have been waiting for three days already.

3s are given to people who are too pushy, those who made the mistake of saying "get to it when you can" (not pushy enough), friends of the scheduler's ex-wife, or those who look too straight. 2s are assigned as a default category; everyone else goes into this one (including the family from Potosi, Missouri, on their vacation and stranded for the last three hours).

Let us assume that the shop opens at 8:00 A.M. and closes at 5:00 P.M. with an hour for lunch. Determine the schedule without priority and with priority. How many jobs and which ones must wait until the next day? Will all the priority 1s get done the first day? Note the differences in schedules.

Job	Repair (minutes)	Priority
'71 Datsun	5	3
'72 Chevy Nova	50	1
'70 Toyota	65	2
'73 Torino	80	3
'72 Mustang	140	1
'70 Mustang	20	3
'72 Impala	95	1
'73 Fiat Spider	35	3
'70 240 Z	125	2
'71 Duster	110	2

Supplementary Problems

1. The IRS is auditing a local CPA, and the CPA needs to get certain accounts in order depending upon the client's income. If the accounts with priority 1 are the highest, give the two different orders that minimize total waiting time and use priorities.

Account	1	2	3	4	5	6	7	8
Time (hours)	10	25	15	5	30	6	9	20
Priority	3	10	7	1	4	3	2	6

a. Order for minimum waiting time:

___ ___ ___ ___ ___ ___ ___ ___

Total waiting time: _____

b. Order for priorities:

___ ___ ___ ___ ___ ___ ___ ___

Total waiting time: _____

2. In the Telephone Installation case, the priorities have changed so that 10 is the highest and 1 is the lowest. Determine the appropriate ordering with priorities. What is the difference in total waiting time?

New order: ___ ___ ___ ___ ___ ___

Old total time: _____

New total time: _____

3. A procrastinating student has five homework assignments due tomorrow. With 1 being the highest priority, determine the optimal ordering of these assignments.

Class	Time (hours)	Priority
Accounting	3	2
Finance	2	5
Bus. Law	2	2
The Block	5	1
Marketing	2	4

a. Optimal ordering: ___ ___ ___ ___ ___

b. If you reverse priority numbers (1 is lowest), will this always reverse the ordering? Explain.

_____

4. Give the four valid principles of job scheduling:

a. _____

b. _____

c. _____

d. _____

2.5 BRIDGING THE GAP: THE INTERFACE

Bridging the gap between actual practice today in the real business world and the mathematical theory taught in the classrooms for the last 20 years is no simple task. For the interested student, some references are included for further investigation. Some mathematical notes to tie in the algorithms to previous texts are presented in this section that may help you recognize some of the algorithms from previous works or to assure the mathematically minded that a Quick & Clean is indeed optimal in terms of classical calculus.

1. All jobs in Sections 2.1 and 2.2 have been assumed to be required to be done in order on machines A, B, C, D, E, . . . , X, Y, Z. There are other algorithms that are Quick & Clean for two machines that will allow different combinations of machine orderings for the jobs. Thus if there are two machines (A, B), there exists a modification for the Johnson algorithm that will allow jobs to have orderings on the machines as (A, B), (B, A), (A), (B), and give an optimal ordering that will minimize the total time.[4]

2. Since the machine times are fixed and constant, any algorithm that minimizes the total time will also minimize the idle time, and vice versa. This follows since

$$T_I = T_T - T_M$$

where T_I is idle time, T_T is total time, and T_M is machine time. Since the time on the machines is fixed and constant (simply the sum of all the machine times in the table), when the total time T_T gets smaller, so must T_I.

3. For the three-machine problem (a special case of Section 2.2), if

$$\min (A_i) \geq \max (B_i)$$

or

$$\min (C_i) \geq \max (B_i)$$

then the Johnson Quick & Dirty algorithm performed on the two-machine problem made up by adding machine time $A_i + B_i$ versus $B_i + C_i$ will be an optimal algorithm (Quick & Clean).

4. For Section 2.3, once the order to reduce the total late jobs has been achieved, it is possible to reduce total lateness without making more jobs late. The algorithm for this is published by Heck and Roberts.[5]

As a final note to this section, job shop, machine shop, production scheduling, and related problems constitute a very difficult art, and one that is learned primarily by being on the location where the jobs are being done and getting a feeling for the work and the attendant problems. These few Quick & Cleans and Quick & Dirtys are simply a beginning attempt to hack away at the complexities of real scheduling problems. These algorithms point out some of the valid principles of real scheduling:

1. *Make the jobs wait versus machinists.* You are not going to get more work done by having machinists stand around idle. Also, for many large numerically controlled machines it may take several machinists to operate one machine, and thus there is a very large cost for an "operator" or machine to be idle.

2. *Keep everyone busy as much as possible.* In the area of human relations, much resentment can build up when others see people standing around doing nothing and getting paid for it. Another interesting facet is that being idle is really not much fun and leads to a sense of uselessness.

3. *There is a trade-off between keeping a few people (or jobs) waiting a long time versus having a lot of people (or jobs) waiting a short time.* Here the scheduler has to make a decision between a few people being very mad and lots of people being slightly mad. The worst thing to do is to try for both and end up with everyone being mad. It is a sad fact of life that someone will be mad at you, so you simply might as well choose who will be mad rather than trying to avoid any being mad at you.

4. *Priorities can make a difference in scheduling.* Some jobs or people may be more important than others, and it may make a difference in how you schedule these jobs whether you take that into account or not. Again, your calculations produce two optimal algorithms and you must decide how to schedule the jobs.

2.6 REVIEWS

Review 1: Open book and notes; show all work; and write legibly.

1. (9 points) In "The Wizard Who Oversimplified" briefly explain what each of the following means in terms of education and school:

   a. the wizard: _____

   b. the 700-page treatise: _____

   c. the extensive correspondence: _____

2. (6 points) Give definitions of:

   a. heuristic: _____

   b. algorithm _____

3. (8 points) For the Indiana Metal Enameling Company case, give the schedule for the first two jobs in the best ordering for all the machines.

4. (10 points) In the Department of Public Administration there is one secretary who must type and another who must ditto and collate exams. The following are the times (in minutes) for several exams that must be done. Determine the optimal ordering.

Test	Typing	Ditto and Collate
1	10	30
2	20	10
3	15	27
4	5	7
5	30	13
6	23	11
7	9	16

Order: ___ ___ ___ ___ ___ ___ ___

5. (10 points) Give a schedule for the original order (1–7) of the jobs in problem 4 for the first four tests (1–4).

Test	Typing		Ditto and Collate	
	In	*Out*	*In*	*Out*
1				
2				
3				
4				

6. (12 points) Give the four valid principles of job scheduling:

    a. _____

    b. _____

    c. _____

    d. _____

7. (10 points) Use the Gupta algorithm to determine a good ordering for these accounting jobs; rank the job values on the number line.

Customer	Consultation	Balance Assets	Prepare Financial Statement	Prepare Income Tax
Jackson	4	4	2	1
Johnson	2	6	6	3
Michaels	6	2	5	8
Smith	7	5	7	2
Baldwin Co.	9	27	10	16
Moore	1	12	9	7
Kitcher	$\frac{1}{2}$	1	–	$\frac{1}{2}$

Order: ___ ___ ___ ___ ___ ___ ___

−1	0	+1

8. (12 points) Given the following jobs, order them (a) to minimize the number of late jobs and (b) to minimize maximum lateness for any one job.

Job	1	2	3	4	5	6	7	8
Due date	5	2	6	3	4	8	3	7
Production time	1	$\frac{1}{2}$	2	1	2	$\frac{1}{2}$	$1\frac{1}{2}$	1

a. — — — — — — — —

b. — — — — — — — —

9. (7 points) Given the Telephone Installation case, what difference does it make if the personnel department now receives a priority of 2 instead of 6? Give the two resulting orderings, the original and the new one (you don't have to show your work on the original ordering).

Old: — — — — — —

New: — — — — — —

10. (16 points) Give the two different orders for these seven jobs with and without priority. Assume that a 1 is the highest priority and give the total waiting times.

Job	1	2	3	4	5	6	7
Time	3	7	6	4	8	10	2
Priority	1	4	5	8	6	3	2

Without priority: — — — — — — —

Waiting time: _____

With priority: — — — — — — —

Waiting time: _____

Review 2: Open book and notes; show all work; and write legibly.

1. (12 points) Jack and Fred are gardeners, and they divide their work into cutting and trash-bagging the cuttings. The cutting must be done first (by Jack) and then the trash-bagging (by Fred). Time is in minutes.

Job	Cutting	Bagging
Lawn	30	10
Hedge	15	20
Trees	20	45
Shrubbery	25	25

a. Determine the optimal ordering of these jobs.   Order: ———— ———— ———— ————

b. Determine the schedule from the original ordering (not optimal) and also the total time and the idle time.

Job	Cutting		Bagging	
	In	*Out*	*In*	*Out*
Lawn				
Hedge				
Trees				
Shrubbery				

Total time: ————

Idle time: ————

2. (10 points) Given the Cable Division case, consider Charlie's jobs. Let us assume that we have found that the jointing SF modification takes three days and ten days for design and job shop rather than six and eight.
   a. Does this change the optimal ordering from your homework answer? How?

   _____

   _____

   b. Given the optimal schedule in your homework, if you kept the same ordering, will this make the project earlier or later? Which and why? Explain your answer or show math.

3. (6 points) Give the definition of "sophisticated." What does this mean in relation to "optimal" solutions and Quick & Dirty algorithms? _____

   _____

   _____

4. (10 points) John makes furniture of several types. He wants to cut down the idle time of his machine operators. Each job must be done in order on the machines from left to right. Give a good ordering using the Gupta algorithm.

Job	Jigsaw	Router	Driller	Sander
1	4	6	2	3
2	5	8	3	6
3	3	1	4	5
4	3	5	2	8
5	7	4	3	5
6	8	5	4	4

Order: _____ _____ _____ _____ _____ _____

5. (10 points) Give the schedule for the original order in problem 4 for the first three jobs.

Job	Jigsaw		Router		Driller		Sander	
	In	*Out*	*In*	*Out*	*In*	*Out*	*In*	*Out*
1								
2								
3								

6. (12 points) A commercial artist has several jobs due at specific times. She has listed the due dates and time to complete each job.

Job	1	2	3	4	5	6	7
Due date	8	5	11	15	10	21	19
Time	3	2	1	6	4	3	7

a. Determine the order that minimizes maximum lateness, the number of jobs late, and total lateness.

Order minimizing maximum lateness: ── ── ── ── ── ── ──

Number of late jobs:── Total lateness:──

b. Determine the order that minimizes the number of late jobs, number of jobs late, and total lateness.

Order minimizing number of late jobs: ── ── ── ── ── ── ──

Number of late jobs: ── Total lateness: ──

c. Which of the two orders would you pick and why? _____

_____

7. (6 points) Explain the difference between a *mess* and a *problem*. _____

_____

_____

8. (12 points) A certain carpenter has an inspector due at 8:00 A.M. and he needs to get some necessary jobs done before the inspector comes so that they will not hold up other portions of the project. Given the jobs, with the priority 1 being the highest, give the two different orders that minimize total waiting time and use priorities.

Job	1	2	3	4	5	6	7	8
Time	10	5	20	25	15	30	20	10
Priority	2	5	1	3	7	10	4	6

a. Order minimizing total waiting time: ___ ___ ___ ___ ___ ___ ___ ___
   Total waiting time: _____
b. Priority ordering: ___ ___ ___ ___ ___ ___ ___ ___
   Total waiting time: _____

9. (10 points) For the Term Papers case, assume that the biology paper due in week 12 takes two weeks (not one). What changes will that make in the schedule and ordering that you came up with for your correct homework answer which minimized the number of late jobs?

a. What changes are there in late jobs? _____

_____

b. Amount of lateness? _____

_____

10. (6 points) For the Computer Center 2 P.M. Batch case, give the total waiting time for the following jobs in the ordering with and without priority.

Job	With Priority	Without Priority
1342		
1356		
1345		

11. (6 points) Illustrate the three ways to solve problems in operations research (see the section in Chapter 1 on Solutions) with the three algorithms of Johnson and Gupta (Sections 2.1 and 2.2) and explain.

a. _____

_____

b. _____

_____

c. _____

_____

2.7 REFERENCES

1. S. M. Johnson, "Optimal Two and Three Stage Production Schedules with Set-Up Times Included," *Naval Research Logistics Quarterly,* vol. 1, 1954, pp. 61–68.
2. J. N. D. Gupta, "A Functional Heuristic Algorithm for the Flowshop Scheduling Problem," *Operational Reserach,* vol. 22, 1971, pp. 39–48.
3. J. M. Moore, "An N-Job, One-Machine Sequencing Algorithm for Minimizing the Number of Late Jobs," *Management Science,* vol. 15. Sept 1968, pp. 102–109.
4. J. R. Jackson, "An Extension of Johnson's Result on Job-Lot Scheduling," *Naval Research Logistics Quarterly,* vol. 3, Sept. 1956, pp. 201–204.
5. H. Heck and S. Roberts, "A Note on the Extension of a Result on Scheduling with Secondary Criteria," *Naval Research Logistics Quarterly,* vol. 19, June 1972, pp. 403–405.
6. R. W. Conway, W. L. Maxwell, and L. W. Miller, *Theory of Scheduling* (Don Mills, Ont.: Addison-Wesley, 1967), pp. 31–32.
7. E. L. Lawler, "Optimal Sequencing of a Single Machine Subject to Precedence Constraints," *Management Science,* vol. 19, Jan. 1973, p. 544.
8. L. G. Mitten, "A Scheduling Problem," *Journal of Industrial Engineering,* vol. 10, Mar.-Apr. 1959, pp. 131–135.
9. W. E. Smith, "Various Optimizers For Single-Stage Production," *Naval Research Logistics Quarterly,* vol. 3, 1956, pp. 59–66.

3
inventory

INTRODUCTION

Inventory problems are common to almost all business situations. Each business has some raw materials, stock items, supplies, or production items waiting to be used or shipped. Whenever material is being held, there are costs involved: warehouses, handling, insurance, breakage, theft, spoilage, obsolescence, cost of tied-up capital, and numerous other costs involved with the very fact that some goods are on hand. Even an ordinary office must have supplies of paper, felt-tip pens, and so on, and not only is there a cost for keeping these somewhere, but there is also a cost associated with being out of supplies. A production shop must have a certain amount of raw material on hand, and subassemblies may have to be stored somewhere also. Retail stores must have a supply of goods on hand and anticipate when they will run out of stock so as to order far enough in advance to meet customer demand.

The two basic questions that need to be asked in inventory situations are, *how much* should be ordered at a particular time, and *how often*? These are very simple questions to answer when there are only a few items to be considered. The problem arises, as in most OR cases, when the number of possibilities or items gets to be huge. Running a small mom and pop store can be done without the aid of computers and fancy warehouses, but when the store becomes a chain of 50 with 3 warehouses, the problem becomes overwhelming. A lot of decisions need to be made, each one fairly simple. It is estimated that 20 percent of the items in most stores account for 80 percent of the volume. Thus the other 80 percent of the items are low in demand, and since they do not move through the store quickly, they must be kept elsewhere. This can result in high expenses when a lot of items must be stored and moved up front on demand.

Thus inventory can be classified as "A," "B," or "C." "A" inventory constitutes the 20 percent that account for most of the inventory cost. In a department store this would be color TVs, freezers, and such. "B" inventory would range from toasters down to expensive tools. "C" inventory are small tools down to nuts, bolts, and nails. To sum up:

"A" inventory is counted (constantly)
"B" inventory is counted (regularly)
"C" inventory is (usually) weighed (occasionally).

Most of the mathematics for inventory problems

were developed a long time ago, and this book will not spend time proving formulas; the object is to use them, not to prove them. References will be given for the interested student.

The basic tension in these types of problems is between fixed costs and variable costs. Fixed costs are represented by the rent for a warehouse or building, or its purchase price, employees' wages, taxes, and so forth. Variable costs, however, are proportional to the amount of inventory that is kept. They may comprise handling charges, insurance, breakage, and so forth. There is a basic struggle to maintain a balance between fixed costs and variable costs. When fixed costs are too high, there is an attempt to lower them by spreading them over more time, volume, and so on.

Finally a word on *material requirements planning* (MRP) is in order. This is a relatively new approach to inventory and production control, which makes a careful distinction between dependent and independent demand. There are materials that must be ordered simultaneously to make certain products. Thus a product may need some plastic, wire, and sheet metal, which must all be ordered together. There may be a lead time of several weeks needed for the different parts (called parts explosion). Planning for the materials required has become very complicated yet necessary for any large plant. The reason behind the development of material requirements planning is the recent availability of an inexpensive high-speed core for computers. Previously, most companies simply could not afford to store, for quick reference, the bills of materials and ordering policies for thousands and thousands of parts and pieces of equipment. The interested reader is directed to books by Orlicky,[1] Wight,[2] and Plossl.[3] As the construction of a material requirements plan is an extremely involved process, we abdicate responsibility and will not discuss it further here, except to present a sample of different lot-sizing methods that could be used with such a plan.

INCIDENT: ADDED BREAKFAST, ADDED PROFIT

During the last few years McDonald's has advertised that they are open for breakfast. First it was Egg McMuffin, then pancakes and sausages, then scrambled eggs and sausage, sweet rolls and coffee, and so on. McDonald's is open from 7 to 11 A.M. to serve breakfast (or Big Macs) and thus is trying to combat the high fixed costs of owning the property and taxes. In this way fixed costs are spread over more hours of operation, and the variable profit will increase.

INCIDENT: PUTTING SCHOOL BUILDINGS TO WORK

Many communities offer public education in shifts around the year and/or several times a day. Rather than build another public school (high fixed cost) they have simply utilized the current buildings and added more teachers (higher variable costs) which they would have had to hire for new buildings anyhow. This way the building doesn't sit empty for most of the day or for three months during the summer (not to mention vacations, weekends, and holidays). The taxpayers are beginning to realize that a tremendous amount of money as well as their own tax dollars are invested in these buildings and need to be spread out over more time.

In each of these cases the fixed cost of the overhead was too high. There are also occasions when the variable costs are too high.

INCIDENT: LOW DEMAND, HIGH INVENTORY

A large midwestern auto parts manufacturer (mostly piston rings) was experiencing unusually high costs of carrying some auto parts. Investigation revealed that too many low-demand items were being held (for instance, five sets of distributors and parts for 1950 Packards, while the demand was only one every four years). The cost for setting up new production for one distributor was less than storing it for four years.

INCIDENT: TOO MUCH TOO SOON

A firm was processing titanium ingots and felt that it had an unusually high amount in inventory. At $10 per ingot, the value of the inventory was $6,000,000. By the time the OR group had developed a fancy model to determine how many to produce and how many to store, the inventory clerks had simply reduced the excess inventory by cutting it in half each month until they had only two weeks' production left.

3.1 ECONOMIC ORDER QUANTITY

The simplest and most standard model of inventory problems was developed by Wilson.[4] The basic assumptions for this model are as follows:

1. *Constant demand.* We know how much is needed each week, month, or year, and that this amount remains constant. This assumption, of course, simplifies the problem, but we will change this assumption as we work with more complicated models.
2. *No price breaks or quantity discounts.* We will assume that the price for each item remains the same, regardless of how many are ordered or produced.
3. *No shortages or backorders allowed.* It will be assumed that we will never run out of inventory. Thus we will order in time to allow for delivery or production (called lead time) and will assume that we do not run out of needed items.
4. *Instantaneous delivery or production of all items.* This simply means that all items are delivered almost simultaneously or produced so quickly that the complete lot size is on hand in a very short amount of time.
5. *Constant lead time.* The time between ordering items and receiving them is constant.

A pictoral representation of this situation is shown in Figure 3.1. Thus we start with a certain quantity Q, and over time T it reduces to zero. We then order more (or produce more), and the situation is repeated again. The quantity and time are related to each other by the demand D. If the demand is 100 units per month and we produce a quantity of 200 units, we can see that it will take 2 months to use up 200 units (assuming our demand is constant). Thus $T = Q/D$. (In this case $T = 200/100$, which is two months.)

The costs associated with this model are twofold:

1. *Fixed costs.* These are expenses that do not vary according to the size of the order or production. They are usually called ordering costs if we are ordering material and may be the cost of doing the paperwork involved with the ordering. If we are producing items, then the fixed costs are called set-up costs and are the costs of setting up a machine or production line. In both cases it makes no difference how many items will be ordered or produced.
2. *Variable costs.* These are costs per item over time. Thus it makes a difference how many items we have and/or how long we have them. Such costs might be insurance (if on a per-item basis), theft, spoilage or breakage, warehouse rental (again, if prorated per item), handling, and cost of capital (the money now tied up in goods that have not yet been sold).

Determining what these costs actually are is the province of a branch of metaphysics known as accounting, and probably only the accounting office knows for sure which costs are being treated as variable and which as fixed. When a warehouse is rented, some of the cost is allocated to fixed overhead, and some may be allocated to variable overhead. Sorting this out can be very difficult, not only for the student, but for the actual business. Many times there is not even an agreement within the accounting office itself. It must also be noted that *the point in time when the accountants check the inventory can have a profound influence on the method used.* Only the most stupid inventory controller will not try to reduce inventories in the face of an imminent visit from the accounting department.

For any period of time the cost of carrying inventory will be the sum of the fixed costs and the variable costs. The fixed cost will be denoted by C_o, the cost of ordering, and will be incurred each time there is an order or production. The variable cost is C_c, the cost of carrying one item for one period of time, times the

Figure 3.1

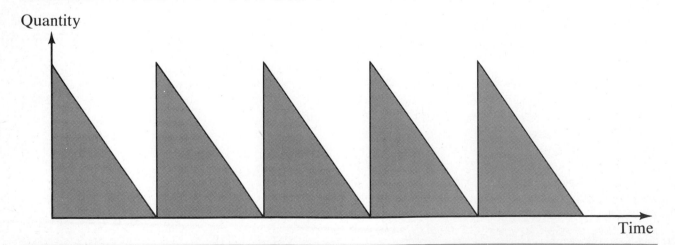

average inventory times the amount of time. The demand over time will be denoted by D, and the quantity to order or produce will be denoted by Q.

Let us assume that we have the following problem:

$$D = 50 \text{ units per month}$$
$$C_o = \$100$$
$$C_c = \$0.25 \text{ per unit per month.}$$

If we were to order enough to last for a whole year, we would order 600 units. This would ensure enough units for the whole year and certainly reduce our fixed costs for the year. Ordering only once would cost just $100. This is shown graphically in Figure 3.2. The variable costs would be $0.25 per unit per month times the average inventory times the amount of time (12 months). The average amount of inventory is simply the average of having all units on hand (600) and none (0). During the whole year the inventory averages out to having 300 units on hand. Thus,

$$\text{total cost for year} = \$100 + \$0.25\ (300)\ (12)$$
$$= \$100 + \$900 = \$1000.$$

Notice that although the fixed cost ($100) is low in comparison to the variable cost, the variable cost is considerably higher. This is because we are carrying so much inventory. To consider what our costs would be if we were to reduce our average inventory by ordering every month (remember, we need 50 per month), consult Figure 3.3. Note that here we have gone to the other extreme. Although our variable

Figure 3.2

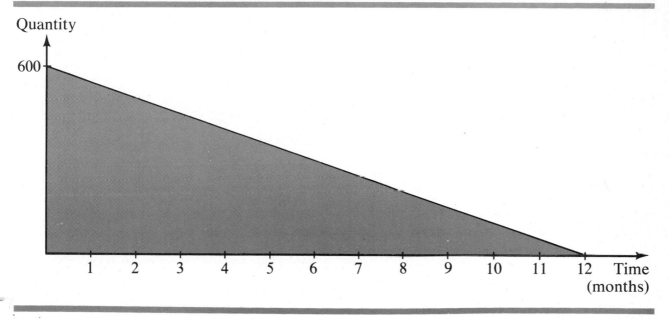

Figure 3.3

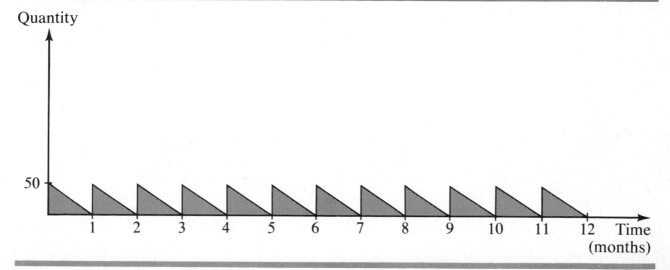

costs will be low (not much inventory), we are ordering many times (12 times in a year), and our fixed cost for the year will be \$1200:

total cost for year = \$100(12) + \$0.25(25) (12)
= \$1200 + \$75 = \$1275.

The fixed cost is \$100 times the 12 times necessary to order. The variable cost is \$0.25 per unit per month times the average inventory of 25 (start at 50, end at 0) times 12 months. Here we see that the variable costs are much lower than the fixed costs. In both cases we are either carrying too much inventory or ordering too often.

Consider now the costs involved if 200 are ordered each time (see Figure 3.4). By ordering 200 items each time, we will have to order only 3 times during the year, so the fixed costs will be \$300. The average amount of inventory will be 100 units, so the variable costs will be \$0.25(100(12) = \$300. This means that both the variable and the fixed costs are equal:

total cost for year = \$100(3) + \$0.25(100)(12)
= \$300 + \$300 = \$600.

This is our lowest total cost for the year, and it is no accident that the variable costs equal the fixed costs.

To investigate this further, let us look at the fixed costs as the size of the order Q increases (see Figure 3.5). By just looking at the fixed costs, it would make sense to order in as large a quantity as possible. But let us also look at the variable costs as the size of the order increases (see Figure 3.6). Now we see that

variable costs increase as the amount of inventory increases. The total costs are the sum of the two, and can be expressed as shown in Figure 3.7 (page 50).

Notice that where the total cost for the year is the lowest, fixed costs equal variable costs. A benefit of this knowledge is that if you know your fixed and variable costs, you can determine whether your present ordering policy is correct by comparing the two costs. If variable costs are too high, you are carrying too much inventory (ordering too much and not often enough). If fixed costs are too high, you are ordering too often and in small quantities.

One final word about the total cost curve (Figure 3.7). The curve is fairly flat near the optimal amount Q to order or produce. Because of this, if the value of Q is off by 10 or 20 percent, the cost will only be affected by a small amount. This helps ensure against data that is slightly off, erroneous guesses, and so on. It explains why so many businesses can order materials without having an idea of what they are doing and still remain afloat. But if there are gross errors in the ordering quantity, there is no protection against going out of business.

Quick & Clean Algorithm: Economic Order Quantity[4]

Given the following information:

D = demand per unit time
C_o = cost of ordering (or set-up cost)
C_c = cost of carrying per item per unit of time

follow these steps:

Figure 3.4

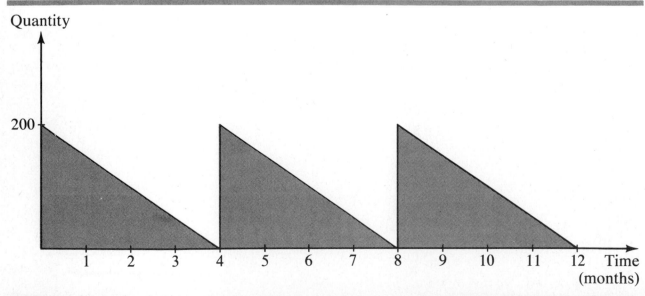

Figure 3.5

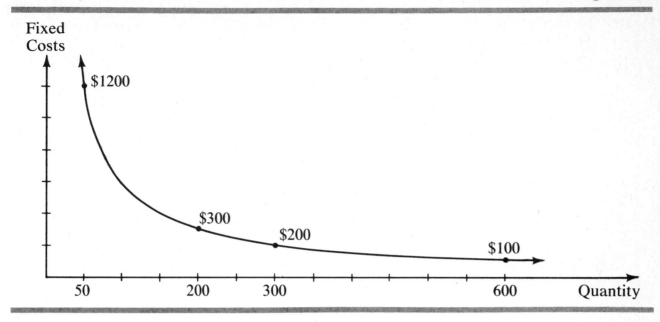

Figure 3.6

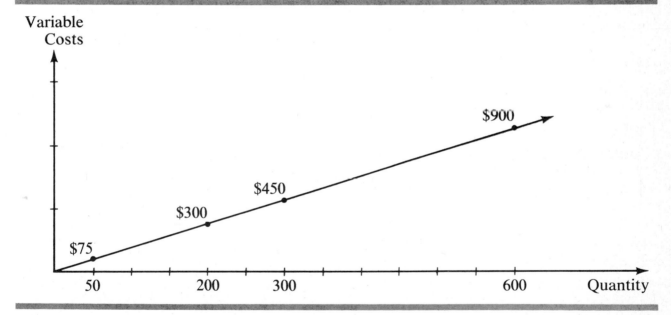

1. Find the economic order quantity (EOQ):

$$\text{quantity } Q = \sqrt{\frac{2DC_o}{C_c}}.$$

2. Find the amount of time T it will take Q units to be used:

$$T = \frac{Q}{D}.$$

This is the time between orders.

3. Then you obtain the average total costs (ATC):

$$\text{ATC} = \frac{C_o D}{Q} + \left(\frac{Q}{2}\right) C_c$$

or

$$\text{ATC} = \sqrt{2DC_o C_c}$$

(a shortcut formula for the optimal value of Q only).

Example. For our example, where $D = 50$ units per month, $C_o = \$100$, and $C_c = \$0.25$ per unit per month,

1. $Q = \sqrt{2(50)(100)/0.25} = \sqrt{40{,}000} = 200$ units.

Figure 3.7

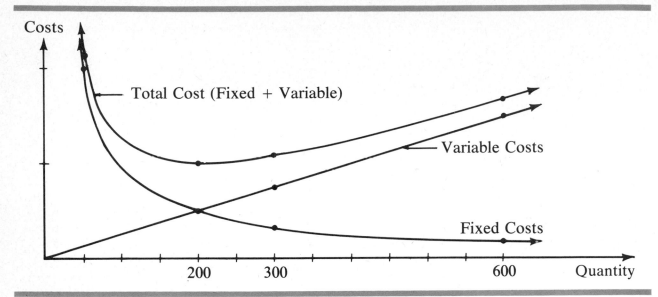

2. $T = 200/50 = 4$ months. Order or produce 200 units every 4 months.
3. ATC $= \$100(50)/200 + (200/2)\$0.25 = \$25 + \$25 = \$50$ per month.

Thus the total cost for the year equals 12($50) = $600. These are the exact same figures we arrive at on the preceding pages.

A Word of Caution

Make sure that demand and carrying cost are always in the same time units (for example, months, years, or weeks). If demand is in months and carrying cost in years, wrong answers may develop.

spark plugs

Marv's Enco Service Station of Charleston buys Champion spark plugs from outside suppliers at $4.00 per set of four. The total annual need is 500 sets at a rate of 2 sets per working day (250 working days per year). Marv has been buying in lots of 500 each year and using a storage room in the back. Since the items are not perishable, he figures that this is the easiest way of ordering. He has determined his carrying cost to be $0.50 per set per year and the cost of ordering to be $10.00.

During this last year, storage space has come to be very critical, and Marv is now beginning to wonder whether his ordering policy is optimal. He was very sure that his policy was correct, because he had been doing it that way for years. Besides, he figured that

storing things in inventory was free, until he realized that all the money he had in parts, the cost of constantly moving things around in the storeroom, and counting how many of each part he had from time to time amounted to quite a bit.

Determine what his economic order quantity should be and what his average total costs are under the two policies.

Solution

Recommendation. It is recommended that Marv change his ordering policy to order a gross (12 dozen, or 144) of spark plugs every 72 working days (14 weeks, 2 days).

Numerical Answer

$$EOQ = 141.4$$
$$T = 70.70 \text{ days (working)}$$
$$ATC = \$70.70/yr$$

Recommended Policy	Old Policy
$Q = 144$	$Q = 500$
$T = 72$ working days	$T = 250$ working days
ATC $= \$70.72/yr$	ATC $= \$135.00/yr$

Math Work. $D = 500$ sets per year, $C_c = \$0.50$ per set per year, and $C_o = \$10.00$ per order,

$$Q = \sqrt{2(500)(10)/0.50} = \sqrt{20,000} = 141.4$$
$$T = 141.4/2 \text{ sets/day} = 70.70 \text{ working days}$$
$$ATC = 500(10)/141.4 + (141.4/2)(0.50)$$
$$\$35.35 + \$35.35 = \$70.70.$$

Since 141.4 is so close to 144 (1 gross), it is suggested that Marv simply order a gross of sets of spark plugs each time:

$$T = 144/2 = 72 \text{ working days}$$
$$\text{ATC} = 500(\$10)/144 + (144/2)(\$0.50)$$
$$= \$34.72 + \$36.00 = 70.72.$$

Under Marv's old policy, the costs were

$$\text{ATC} = 500(\$10)/500 + (500/2)(\$0.50)$$
$$= \$10 + \$125 = 135.00/\text{yr}.$$

Looking at the costs for the old policy it becomes apparent that Marv had been holding too much inventory and not ordering often enough.

INCIDENT: KEEP IT SIMPLE

A large midwestern brewery decided to forecast inventory requirements for its distributors, and after using several sophisticated and complicated forecasting models, came up with a simple formula using last year's sales, this year's trend, and a fudge factor to determine how much beer should be ordered by each distributor. The distributors then promptly ordered what they wanted anyway. *Moral:* You must sell your model to the right user.

r & b wire manufacturing company, inc.

The R & B Wire Manufacturing Company, Inc., produces wire baskets and carts for self-service laundries. To produce these units it is necessary for the company to stock raw wire and tubing. The wire comes on large spools called Alabama stands, and the tubing comes on wooden pallets. These raw materials can be delivered to the company immediately by any one of four sources. The real question is to find out how much wire and tubing should be ordered and when to be the most economically feasible.

The following information was gathered by the production manager:

Warehouse area	8835 ft²
Cost	$0.0886/ft²/mo
Office expense for ordering	$38.50
Alabama stands: Size = 16 ft²	Demand = 9/mo
Pallets of tubing: Size = 9 ft²	Demand = 6/mo

Assume that the Alabama stands and the pallets of tubing must be ordered separately. Will the optimal quantities exceed the available warehouse area?

INCIDENT: WAREHOUSING ON A LARGE SCALE

To give you an idea of the size of warehouses and some of the costs involved, it is interesting to look at the new warehouse that Sears opened in Los Angeles. It is computerized and has 1,700,000 square feet of floor space or storage; 90 carloads of merchandise can be handled at one time. Fifteen hundred electric carts, programmed by computer, move through the aisles. Sears also has completely automated cash registers that will update the inventory for each store and department as a sale is made. They know down to the penny the cost of carrying inventory.

durham signs

Durham Signs is a small commercial sign shop that uses Duraply (a trademark for a type of plywood) in the construction of many of its signs. This material is purchased in 4 × 8-ft and 4 × 10-ft sheets. The price of Duraply fluctuates, but averages $11.57 per sheet for 4 × 8's and $15.17 per sheet for 4 × 10's. Demand for the smaller sheets of plywood is 186 per year and for the larger sheets 62 per year. Mr. McConnell, the owner, figures his carrying costs to be 5 percent annually of the cost of capital invested.

Both size sheets are obtained from the same supplier and delivered regardless of quantity for $10.00 per order of each size. Mr. McConnell usually does not have them delivered though, because his own truck can pick them up for a cost of only $6.00 per order. However, the Durham Signs truck is only capable of carrying 20 sheets at a time, so orders have been limited to this quantity. Mr. McConnell has begun to question his practice lately, wondering how much he has been saving, if anything. Therefore he would like to know if his total costs could be reduced by ordering larger quantities, even if it means paying the larger delivery fee.

Determine the cost of having the supplier deliver an economic lot size of 4 × 8's and the cost of Mr. McConnell making his own pick-ups (remember his truck can only hold 20 sheets). Then determine the cost of delivering the 4 × 10's in the two different manners. What would you recommend as the policy for Durham Signs?

INCIDENT: McDONALD'S KEEPS IT FRESH

At McDonald's Hamburgers the turnover is so rapid that the cost of the tied-up capital is minimal, but one of the largest costs was found to be handling the materials that were used. As hamburgers and fries are used, the freezer has to maintain a first in–first out order. Thus oldest hamburgers are put on the top shelves, the newest on the bottom, and these are continually reordered during the day. The largest cost is therefore the use of an employee to stock the freezer.

health data management systems

The problem is to determine when to purchase the three types of paper used in the office of Health Data Management Systems, and how much. Presently there is a reorder time of 90 days for all three types of paper, with 13 boxes of one-ply line printer paper, 3 boxes of two-ply line printer paper, and 8 boxes of teletype paper being purchased. The demand is assumed fixed with no shortages being allowed. The present policy meets demand, but there is a suspicion that a cheaper solution exists. Since each type of paper must be ordered separately (at a cost of $10.00 per order, regardless of size) it is possible that there are better reordering times. The annual demand is as follows:

one-ply line printer paper	52 boxes/yr
two-ply line printer paper	12 boxes/yr
teletype paper	32 boxes/yr

Three possible vendors and their prices, including penalties, for the items under consideration are listed in the following table:

Vendor	Cost per Box	Penalties
Moore Business Forms	$12.80/$18.62/$12.80	$9 on orders of less than 6
Woehrmyer	$11.84/15.82/$11.04	None
Standard Register	$12.55/$17.18/$11.84	None

The cost per box is for one-ply, two-ply, and teletype paper. The table shows that Woehrmyer is the most favorably priced, and thus is used by Health Data Management Systems. Before this comparison was made, Moore was used, and now $135.68 per year is being saved. Health Data now wants to determine if further savings can be made by changing the ordering policy. The amounts ordered will be determined by storage costs and the cost of the money tied up in inventory. Using a figure of 8 percent per year as the cost of money and 1 dollar per box per year as the commercial storage and handling costs, determine the optimal policy for each type of paper (one-ply, two-ply, and teletype) and compare the average total costs of the old and new policies. Were any of the old policies good guesses? What recommendations would you make?

INCIDENT: NO INVENTORY, NO COST!

A brewery, which will remain nameless, has the ideal inventory problem. The demand for its product has been so high (even presidents of the United States have been known to fly by to get a few cases) that even by expanding its single-plant capacity to 20,000,000 barrels per year it could not supply all the demand for just Texas and California. As a result, it has a limited market, and *no inventory of beer.* Distributors must have their trucks at the brewery ready to receive shipment. If they are not there, the beer is shipped by common carrier (C.O.D.). The distributors are thus highly motivated to cooperate with the production plan of the brewery.

pacific telephone

Axminster central office is where the dial tone comes from for the subscribers with prefixes 291 through 299 in Los Angeles. For telephone service to be installed, a service order must be sent to the central office from the business office. Depending upon the type of service wanted, different length jumpers (wire) are run in on the intermediate distributing frame (IDF), the main distributing frame (MDF), and/or the number group (NG). The average jumper length for the IDF is 110 feet, for the MDF 170 feet, and for the NG 2.5 feet (30 inches).

Step-by-step orders have jumpers run in on the IDF and MDF only. Number 5 cross bar (#5X-bar) orders are run in on the MDG and NG only, one apiece. These service orders average 75 per day, 20 percent being #5X-bar. X-bar number changes average 12 per day, with work being done in the NG only. Special circuits, which are separate from service orders, consist of burglar alarms, computer lines, and WATS lines (numbers beginning with 800) and are run in on the MDF only. Each special circuit averages 3 jumpers, and there are an average of 12 special circuits per day. Trunk facility orders (TFO) average 24 jumpers each, with 5 TFOs falling due each day. TFOs run in on the MDF only. This is summarized below:

	IDF	MDF	NG	Demands per Day
Step-by-step	1	1		60
#5X-Bar		1	1	15
X-Bar number			1	12
Special circuits		3		12
TFO		24		5
Average length (feet)	110	170	2.5	
Storage limit (rolls)	500	1000	100	

The cost of carrying inventory is mainly the cost of the capital that is tied up. Thus a cost of $\frac{1}{2}$ percent per month is put on the use of money. The cost to make an order for any particular type of wire is put at $110 per order (each order must be separate, the different wires may not be ordered together). The following costs are given for the different types of wire:

IDF jumpers cost $0.98/100 ft, with 2000 ft/roll
MDF jumpers cost $0.80/100 ft, with 2000 ft/roll
NG jumpers cost $0.18/100 ft, with 5000 ft/roll

Assume that there are 30 days in each month, and use months for time units. Determine how many rolls should be ordered and how often for each type of wire. (Do all calculations in terms of rolls.) Is there enough storage space for each type of wire? If not, how much wire can be ordered? Determine the average total costs for each situation, and then determine what you would recommend to be done.

Supplementary Problems

1. Consider the Dean's office with the normal problem of office supplies and inventory. Classify each item according to the A, B, C classification:

____Typewriters   ____Bond Paper
____Paper Clips   ____Typewriter Ribbons
____Pencils   ____Desks
____Grade Change Forms ____Desk Calendars
____File Folders   ____File Cabinets

2. Given the Health Data Management case, assume that Woehrmyer just went into bankruptcy due to the low prices they charged. Decide the following:
   a. How much one-ply line-printer paper they should order, how often, and from whom.

_____
_____

   b. How much will they save over the *original* policy stated in the case? _____
_____
_____

3. The dairy case in a supermarket can hold 60 gallons of milk while the refrigerator in back can hold 300 more. Consider that the average daily demand is 120 gallons per day and the cost of ordering is $10.00. The carrying cost is determined at 10¢ per gallon per month.

   a. Determine the EOQ. _____
_____

   b. What is the A.T.C. per year? _____

   c. How many gallons of milk *can* be ordered given the restriction that the milk must be refrigerated? _____
_____

   d. If milk should not be stocked longer than two days, how does this affect the ordering policy?
_____

3.2 PRICE BREAKS

One of the simple problems that arise in inventory calculations is the opportunity to take advantage of price breaks. A manufacturer or distributor may want to offer a discount to consumers if they buy in larger quantities. The advantage for the manufacturer is that of knowing with more certainty that demand will be high. For the consumer the advantage is some monetary savings. Balanced against these savings, though, will be a higher level of inventory. The common mistake is to assume that larger quantities should always be ordered if storage room is available. Also, if the items are perishable, larger quantities may take so long to be used that they spoil. Obsolescence is another problem; although the per-unit cost for large volumes of items may be very attractive, by the time the normal rate of demand will have used these items, no one may want them anymore and you will have a warehouse full of hula hoops.

What most merchants fail to take into account is

the fact that there is extra money tied up, and depending upon their cash-flow situation, money may be very precious indeed. Quite a number of merchants neglect the fact that it takes money to have inventory, and then when they are cash-bound and need to order some other items, they realize that their cash is tied up in inventory that will take two years to get rid of. (But we got such a good price on it!)

In this Quick & Dirty algorithm we will balance the savings from volume buying and lower average fixed costs with the increase in variable (carrying) costs. We will ignore the fact that there may be an optimum amount to order at some point other than the earliest point at which we get each discount. Thus we will simply compute the average total cost for each discount quantity and choose the smallest cost. Before, the price of the goods was not included in the average total cost formula because the price per item never changed. But now, since that price decreases as the quantity increases, we will include it in the ATC formula.

Quick & Dirty Algorithm: Price Break[5]

Given the following information:

P = price per item at each price break
Q = smallest quantity that must be ordered for each price break
D = demand per unit of time (weeks, months, or years, for example)
C_o = cost per order (or set-up)
C_c = carrying cost per item per unit of time

determine the average total cost (ATC) for each quantity for which there is a price break and choose the quantity that yields the lowest ATC:

$$\text{ATC} = \frac{DC_o}{Q} + \left(\frac{Q}{2}\right)C_c + PD.$$

Example. The Society for the Advancement of Management (SAM) is a student organization at the School of Business at Pennsylvania State University.

SAM operates a coffee and donuts concession where they offer daily fresh donuts and fresh perked coffee. The operation is certainly a success, netting thousands of dollars a year and financing a very active social budget. The coffee is bought by the case (a dozen 1-pound cans), and SAM is given a discount of $0.60 per case, or $0.05 per can. Thus if two cases are bought, a savings of $1.20 per case is realized. Mike, the social chairperson and the person most interested in cost savings, has figured that it costs $3.00 per order to go and pick up the coffee and $0.15 per can per week to store it. The SAM office uses two cans each day (10 cans per week) and wants to know the optimal quantity to order.

If D = 10 cans per week, C_o = $3.00 per order, and C_c = $0.15 per can per week, we can develop the data shown in Table 3.1.

Notice that the increased cost of carrying inventory overcomes the savings from the discount and the average fixed costs after a while. In fact, the first and last terms, the average fixed cost and the total price, both decrease as Q gets larger. The middle term is the average variable cost and *may* have C_c go down (because it may be a percentage of the cost of capital, and as Q increases the price goes down), but it is soon overridden by the $(Q/2)$ term increasing. So we see that there is a trade-off here between savings occurring from the average fixed cost and the cheaper price of larger lot sizes and the increased cost of storing larger amounts.

In this example, even if the coffee were bought at $2.00 per can, the carrying cost would be prohibitive. For 10 cases the coffee would take 12 weeks to be used, and the average total cost would be $29.95. The lowest cost is for 3 cases (36 cans), but it is certainly very close to the cost of 2 dozen cans.

kopy king

Toni's Kopy King is a sole proprietorship which was established in 1971 in Houston, Texas. It began in the rear of a moderately profitable insurance business by Mr. Borelli. Originally started as an aside to the insurance business, Kopy King proved more prosperous than Toni had initially anticipated. In its rela-

Table 3.1

Q	P	Fixed Costs C_oD/Q	+	Variable Costs $(Q/2)C_c$	+	Price PD	=	Average Total Costs ATC
12	$2.45/can	$2.50	+	$0.90	+	$24.50	=	$27.90
24	$2.40/can	$1.25	+	$1.80	+	$24.00	=	$27.05
36	$2.35/can	$0.83	+	$2.70	+	$23.50	=	$27.03
48	$2.30/can	$0.63	+	$3.60	+	$23.00	=	$27.23

tively short life span of three years it built its annual sales to $150,000. Kopy King is a print shop which produces a variety of products (letterheads, embossed envelopes, invoices, contracts, multi-part forms, post cards, tickets, business cards, fliers, and business proposals) and services (collating, stapling, binding, Xeroxing, and personalized Christmas cards).

Kopy King had been taking advantage of the largest discount offered by the Kirk Paper Company, and as a result had a 400,000-sheet inventory. It had not considered the cost of capital that was tied up. Given the price breaks below, determine how much it should order and how often. Kopy King's estimate of its cost of capital is 50 percent (extremely high), and it estimates its fixed costs at $10.00 per order. It needs 7 cartons (35,000 sheets) of high-grade and 7 cartons of low-grade paper each month.

| Quantity | White Paper Cost per Carton | |
	High Grade	Low Grade
3 cartons	$25.15	$22.25
10 cartons	$22.10	$19.40
40 cartons	$20.30	$17.95

Solution

Recommendation. Order quantities of 40 cartons of both high-grade and low-grade paper every $5\frac{1}{2}$ months (approximately). This will yield the lowest ATC in both cases, assuming that there is enough storage room and that the high estimate of the cost of capital is reasonable.

Numerical Answer

High Grade
$Q = 3$ cartons, ATC = $2411.46/yr, $T = 0.428$ mo
$Q = 10$ cartons, ATC = $1995.65/yr, $T = 1.428$ mo
$Q = 40$ cartons, ATC = $1929.20/yr, $T = 5.714$ mo

Low Grade
$Q = 3$ cartons, ATC = $2165.69/yr, $T = 0.428$ mo
$Q = 10$ cartons, ATC = $1762.10/yr, $T = 1.428$ mo
$Q = 40$ cartons, ATC = $1708.30/yr, $T = 5.714$ mo

Math Work. The following data is given:
$C_o = \$10.00$ per order, regardless of the size of the order (high grade and low grade are ordered separately).
$D = 7$ cartons per month for both high-grade and low-grade paper, and $C_c = 50$ percent of the cost per carton per year. To make sure that D and C_c are in the same units, change D to 7 cartons per month times 12 months per year, that is, 84 cartons per year.

High Grade
For $Q = 3$ cartons, $C_o = \$10.00$, $D = 84$ cartons per

year, $C_c = (0.5)(\$25.15) = \$12.57$ per carton per year, and $P = \$25.15$ per carton,

$$\text{ATC} = \frac{DC_o}{Q} + \frac{QC_c}{2} + PD$$

$$= \frac{\$10(84)}{3} + \frac{3(\$12.57)}{2} + 84(\$25.15)$$

$$= 280.00 + \$18.86 + \$1856.40$$

$$= \$2411.46/\text{yr}.$$

For $Q = 10$, $C_c = (0.5)(\$22.10) = \$11.05$ per carton per year, and $P = \$22.10$ per carton,

$$\text{ATC} = \$84.00 + \$55.25 + 1856.40 = \$1995.65/\text{yr}.$$

For $Q = 40$, $C_c = (0.5)(\$20.30) = \$10.15$ per carton per year, and $P = \$20.30$ per carton,

$$\text{ATC} = \$21.00 + \$203.00 + 1705.20 = \$1929.20/\text{yr}.$$

Low Grade
For $Q = 3$ cartons, $C_o = \$10.00$, $D = 84$ cartons per year, $C_c = (0.5)(\$22.25) = \$11.13$ per carton per year, and $P = \$22.25$ per carton,

$$\text{ATC} = \frac{DC_o}{Q} + \frac{QC_c}{2} + PD$$

$$- \frac{\$10(84)}{3} + \frac{3(\$11.13)}{2} + \$84(\$22.25)$$

$$= \$280.00 + \$16.69 + \$1869.00$$

$$= \$2165.69/\text{yr}.$$

For $Q = 10$ cartons, $C_c = (0.5)(\$19.40) = \$9.70$ per carton per year, and $P = \$19.40$ per carton,

$$\text{ATC} = \$84.00 + \$48.50 + \$1629.60 = \$1762.10/\text{yr}.$$

For $Q = 40$ cartons, $C_c = (0.5)(\$17.95) = \$8.98$ per carton per year, and $P = \$17.95$ per carton,

$$\text{ATC} = \$21.00 + \$179.50 + \$1507.80$$
$$= \$1708.30/\text{yr}.$$

Time

For $Q = 3$,

$$T = 3 \text{ cartons}/7 \text{ cartons/mo} = \frac{3}{7} \text{ mo} = 0.428 \text{ mo}.$$

For $Q = 10$,

$$T = 10 \text{ cartons}/7 \text{ cartons/mo} = \frac{10}{7} \text{ mo} = 1.428 \text{ mo}.$$

For $Q = 40$,

$$T = 40 \text{ cartons}/7 \text{ cartons/mo} = \frac{40}{7} \text{ mo} = 5.714 \text{ mo}.$$

INCIDENT: RECORD PROFIT

Boogie-Down Records in downtown Miami, open until midnight every night of the year, is a large discount record store that deals with large volumes of records. Maria Hernandez, the manager, was asked about quantity discounts and related an interesting story. Some record companies are so anxious to have a large number of records ordered that they will offer a discount for orders above a certain quantity. If not all those records are sold, they can be returned to the manufacturer at full cost (as if the discount had *not* been given). In this way B. D. Records can sometimes make money without ever selling a record (and that's not a bad way to make a living).

middlearth

Middlearth is a candle-making firm established in 1970 when two individuals began making candles for swap meets. This small venture has now grown into a corporation with annual sales of a quarter of a million dollars, shipping to 300 cities across the nation. Middlearth produces 23 different types of candles and 19 types of planters. The production of candles and planters are completely different entities within the corporation as they involve different processes and personnel. Attention is concentrated on the production of candles which are wood or ceramic filled with wax. They fall into five basic groups: cirio wood, manzanita, gourd, ceramic, and turned wood. The ceramic candles have been the poorest sellers, and at present Middlearth has an excess inventory.

The rapid growth rate accompanied by increased demand (which far exceeds production) has caused many production and cost problems for the corporation. As a result, there is an opportunity loss associated with capital at 40 percent per year. Middlearth also has a problem of determining the amount and time to order its supplies. An example of this is the policy concerning shipping boxes. The average demand for shipping boxes is 1436 per month, and the policy has been to order the largest lot size available on the grounds that it is the cheapest and reordering would not take place as quickly as for the smaller lots. The cost of ordering has been determined at $6.66 every time an order is placed, regardless of size. This includes the cost of labor and determining what needs to be ordered. The price break is as follows:

500 boxes at $0.55/box
1000 boxes at $0.50/box
2500 boxes at $0.38/box

Determine which lot size gives the cheapest average total cost of ordering and storing inventory, how often the lot should be ordered, and the ATC.

INCIDENT: OLD BEER FLATTENS SALES

Stamm Brewery, like most breweries, sells beer through distributors, and it is those distributors that actually buy the beer from the brewery, and not the private consumer. Yet Stamm does advertising to the private consumer through TV, newspapers, radio, magazines, and so on. Stamm is dependent upon the distributor to buy beer and then sell it to taverns, grocery stores, and liquor stores. In an effort to promote more beer sales through the distributors, Stamm would hold yearly contests among the distributors to see which one would sell the most beer. But the smaller distributors would complain that the larger ones had an unfair advantage, so the contest was changed to the biggest percentage increase in sales. Then the larger ones would complain that this was unfair. Regardless of the contest rules, it was certain that not everyone would be satisfied. However, the biggest problem was "stockpiling"; that is, a distributor would buy two months' supply of beer during the one-month contest, and then just sell "old" beer to his outlets. The problem with that is that "old" beer tastes flat and the consumer blames the brewery for this. Thus in the marketing contests Stamm had to face up to the dilemma that the "discount" offered to the distributors might result in "old" beer being sold to their outlets. The "discount" in this case would be a free trip to Hawaii or a Cadillac to the winning distributor, and would be an incentive to buy and sell more beer.

vanier graphics

Vanier Graphics is a printing business that has been in operation over 25 years. It staffs about 35 to 40 printers, operators, and stockcrew on an average 8-hour shift, with three shifts daily. Administrative staff is about 45 to 55 employees, not including salespersons. Vanier Graphics has a plant in Los Angeles, the main distributing center, and three subsidiary companies, located in San Diego, Hawaii, and Oklahoma. Customer service throughout this area is about 30 regular major customers and about 7000 other regular customers throughout the year.

Vanier Graphics prints paper and forms in different sizes, colors, multisheets, qualities, and quantities. The warehouse space is approximately 25,000 square feet, and it has about a 6- to 8-week inventory supply of bulk-quantity rolled paper. This paper is stored in bins segregated by the quality of the paper, then by size, and then by color. The company carries approximately 142 stock items.

Most of the ordering is done by a computer program based on statistical data that Vanier Graphics has gathered. As an example, the company has received an order for 850 pounds of No. 15 white 9-inch paper to be printed. This is a monthly order that must be filled and represents the total of this type of paper to be used monthly. The cost of ordering this paper is put at $10.00, and it can be selected from one of two different sources. One choice is the mill, and because of its long delivery time of 4 to 8 weeks and a minimum of 2500-pound orders, Vanier Graphics retains a 3- or 4-week supply in inventory. The other choice is the Los Angeles distributor who can promise delivery in 1 week or less and there is no minimum order. Carrying costs have been figured at 12 percent of the cost of capital per year. Determine the amount to order and which supplier to order it from, how often to order, and the ATC.

Supplier	Quantity	Price
Los Angeles	Any	$33.00/100 lb
Mill	2,500	$32.50/100 lb
Mill	5,000	$32.00/100 lb
Mill	10,000	$31.50/100 lb

INCIDENT: VOLUME COMPARISONS CAN YIELD SURPRISES

A personal illustration of the danger inherent in buying larger quantities that eventually do not result in a savings can be found by careful grocery shopping. Every once in a while, if the price per pound or ounce is computed, it comes out that the larger size in fact costs more per unit than do smaller sizes. Although this does not seem to make sense, it has in fact been verified more than once by one of the authors. The fun begins, however, when you try to convince other shoppers that they will save money by buying the smaller sizes. This gets the same reaction as trying to give money away – most people simply will not believe it. We seem to have been taught that "bigger is better" and so it can't be true.

house plant helper

Mr. R. Richard Kimbrough decided to start his own small company, TLC (Tender Loving Care) Products. He designed a house plant helper, a chart made up of three pieces of circular cardboard explaining the care of house plants. These three pieces are then assembled in his garage with part-time labor. The three pieces must be grommeted to form a single unit, then covered with plastic (which is shrunk around the unit with an old hair dryer), and boxed (24 to a box). The cost of grommeting is $0.02 per unit, and bagging costs $0.04 per unit. The unit will retail for $1.79, and the retailer will make 100 percent on each unit. The house plant helper is designed to sell as an impulse item, put near checkout counters at supermarkets, department stores, and plant nurseries.

Mr. Kimbrough has a bid from the printer for the three circular cardboard pieces as follows:

10,000 units at $0.30/unit
75,000 units at $0.118/unit
250,000 units at $0.101/unit

He estimates sales of 10,000 per month and will store them in his garage so that inventory carrying costs will only be the cost of capital that is tied up. He estimates the value of money at 12 percent per year times the total cost of each assembled house plant helper. This is the cost of taking out a loan for production. Every time Mr. Kimbrough makes a new order, he must decide what type of paper he will use, if it will be varnished and/or polycoated, and what colors the house plant helper should be. He spends approximately 16 hours of his time (at $25 per hour) on the work involved with bids from printers and other decisions. Determine what lot size he should order to minimize the average monthly cost. However, in the first 6 months sales were only 2000 per month. Would that have affected his decision based on the estimate of 10,000 per month? Also find the reorder time and the ATC.

Supplementary Problems

1. Given the Vanier Graphics case,
   a. What is the EOQ for Los Angeles? ———
   b. What is the optimal ATC for the problem in terms of cost per year? ———————
   ———————————————

2. Given the Middlearth case,
   a. If you ordered 500 boxes per order, what is the ATC? ———————————
   b. If the opportunity loss associated with capital increased to 50 percent per year, for the 1000-box lot-size, what is the value of C_c? ———

c. If the price break for 2500 boxes were only $0.45 per box, what is the new ATC? ——

_____

3.3 SHORTAGES

Now let us look at another complication, shortages. There are times when firms can well afford to be out of items. These firms usually deal with items that are unique, expensive, and of high quality, like jewelry. Or there may be such a high demand for the item that no other store can provide it either (see the Datsun case, page 61). Another condition could be a monopoly where the competitor makes a decidedly inferior product. Skiing, tennis, and other sports equipment can be classified here, where some people will wait one or two months to get the right equipment. In any case, we are faced with a situation where we will allow shortages, that is, the store is out of the item but will backorder it for you. There may be some extra expense involved in doing the backordering, or the store may lose one out of every three customers, and determine that the cost to be short is one third the cost of the item. The situation is shown graphically in Figure 3.8: where S is the amount of shortage (the greatest number of items on backorder).

What is being stated is that even though it may cost more per unit per time period to be short or out of something than to carry it in inventory, there is a trade-off in costs because of the amount of time involved. A comparison of the original model without shortages and the one with shortages may help explain the cost savings. (See Figure 3.9, where C_s is the cost of the shortage).

Let us assume that we have an item with a demand of 10 units per month, a set-up cost (or ordering cost) of $8.00, and a carrying cost of $0.10 per item per month. The model without shortages (Figure 3.9a) shows the solution: the EOQ is 40 items, which would

take 4 months to be used. The graph in Figure 3.9b shows 40 items again, but this time 10 are allowed to be late, so that when the next 40 arrive, 10 will be given out right away, leaving 30 in inventory. If we assume a cost of $0.40 per item per month of being short, then our total cost for this second model would be

$8.00 + (30/2) (3 mos) $0.10
+ (10/2) (1 mo) ($0.40) = $14.50.

This compares favorably with the first model, which would have costs of

$8.00 + (40/2) (4 mos) $0.10 = $16.00

The difference can be seen in the graph in Figure 3.9c, which shows that the essential decision we are making is whether to carry 10 units in inventory for $3\frac{1}{2}$ months or be an average of 5 units short for just 1 month. The cost difference is $1.50 in favor of being short, even though it costs 4 times as much to be out of stock.

Quick & Clean Algorithm: Inventory with Shortage[4]

Given the following information:

D = demand per unit time
C_o = cost of ordering (or set-up)
C_c = cost of carrying per item per unit of time
C_s = cost of being short per item per unit of time,

follow these steps:

1. Find the total amount to order:

$$Q = \sqrt{\frac{(2DC_o)(C_s + C_c)}{C_c}} = \text{(old } Q)\sqrt{\frac{C_s + C_c}{C_s}}.$$

2. Find the maximum number of items to be short:

$$S = \sqrt{\frac{(2DC_o/C_s)C_c}{(C_c + C_s)}} = \text{(old } Q)\sqrt{\frac{C_o^2}{C_s(C_c + C_s)}}.$$

3. $Q - S$ will be the actual amount entering inventory. When Q items arrive, S will be given to waiting customers.
4. The amount of time it will take Q units to be used is

$$T = \frac{Q}{D}.$$

Figure 3.8

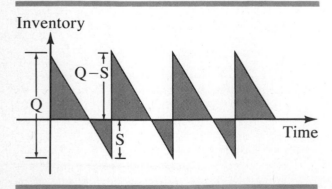

Inventory
Q–S
Q
S
Time

Figure 3.9

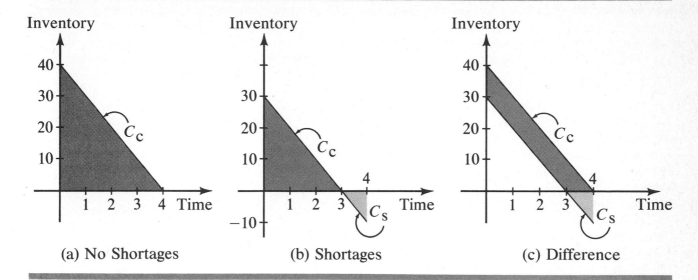

(a) No Shortages (b) Shortages (c) Difference

5. Then you obtain the average total cost:

$$\text{ATC} = \frac{DC_o}{Q} + \frac{(Q-S)^2 C_c}{2Q} + \frac{S^2 C_s}{2Q}.$$

If the amount of shortage S is zero, then the ATC formula is the same as the original ATC in Section 3.1.

Note that if, in the formula for Q, C_s were exorbitantly high, the ratio $\sqrt{(C_c + C_s)/C_s}$ would equal 1.00, and thus the formula simply reduces to the original EOQ formula. In other words, it is a more general formula. The first one simply assumed that the cost of being out was so high that it wasn't worth considering. Note also that the formula for S would reduce to zero if C_s were very high. This means that it would not be worth being short. One last point to note is that this formula for Q (shortage) will give a lower value than the first formula for Q. Because the cost of being short is tolerable, it is worth *not* carrying those S units in inventory for a long while and just incurring a higher cost for a shorter period of time. Of course, if the cost of being short were less than carrying inventory, you would *still* have inventory. This would be true for items that are custom-made or simply made to order.

Example. Let us take the previously mentioned problem with the following data: $D = 10$ items per month, $C_o = \$8.00$, $C_c = \$0.10$ per item per month, and $C_s = \$0.40$ per item per month.

$$Q = \sqrt{[(2)(10)(8)/0.10][(0.40 + 0.10)/0.40]}$$
$$= \sqrt{1600(5/4)} = 44.72.$$

Remember that without shortages the EOQ was 40,

and now with shortages Q is multiplied by $\sqrt{5/4}$, which increases the size of the order.

$$S = \sqrt{[(2)(10)(8)/0.40][0.10/(0.10 + 0.40)]}$$
$$= \sqrt{400(1/5)} = 8.94.$$

Again note that there is a multiplier effect ($\sqrt{1/5}$). If C_s were large, this multiplier would be extremely small, and thus S would be close to zero.

For convenience, let us round off Q to 45 and S to 9. Then the average total cost would be

$$\begin{aligned}
\text{ATC} &= 10(8)/45 + (45-9)^2(\$0.10)/(2\times45) + \\
&\qquad 9^2(\$0.40)/(2\times45) \\
&= \$1.78 + \$1.44 + \$0.36 \\
&= \$3.58/\text{mo.}
\end{aligned}$$

Comparing this with the 4-month period when we were ordering 40 and being short 10, over 4 months it would cost \$14.32 using the Quick & Clean algorithm, while the 40/10 plan would cost \$14.50 (a close guess).

The time to reorder is $T = 45/10 = 4.5$ months. So every $4\frac{1}{2}$ months we will order 45 items, but there will be 10 customers waiting for theirs when the order arrives, so that the initial inventory level will be only 35 items.

pappaseed

Pappaseed is a small plant shop located in Southampton, New York, which carries a wide variety of beautiful houseplants, a nice selection of pots and hangers, and a small assortment of plant-care items such as plant food, bug sprays, and so on. The shop was first opened two years ago and is still run solely by its owner. The first year that Pappaseed was open, there were almost three times the number of customers during the summer months (beach-browsing season) than during the rest of the year. Now that Pappaseed has established itself, the number of customers has become constant throughout the whole year.

All the plant-care items for the store are purchased exclusively at McBride's distributors, which is located several miles away. The orders are picked up by the owner herself as a chance to get away from the store and give her new assistant a chance to be on his own. The owner figures her time to be worth $10 an hour, and by the time she drives to McBride's, fills out the invoices, puts the plant food in the car, chats with McBride, and drives back, three hours elapse plus $1.50 worth of gas.

Pappaseed buys special plant food that sells for $3.50 a bottle. The food is used for rare beautiful plants. The demand for this plant food is two dozen bottles a week. The cost of carrying these bottles is figured to be 5 percent of the selling price per year. One problem that Pappaseed has is that the store runs short of bottles from time to time and loses sales. Last year the store lost sales of 48 bottles due to being short. The profit on each bottle is approximately 40 percent of the selling price, and the cost of being short is simply figured as 40 percent of the retail price.

Determine how many bottles of this special plant food should be ordered, how many Pappaseed can afford to be short if it promises to deliver the bottles eventually, and how often the owner should make her trip to McBride's to waste half a day. Also find the cost for such a policy.

Solution

Recommendation. The owner should order 60 dozen (720) bottles of plant food every 30 weeks. This is assuming that the fixed costs for ordering are as high as stated and that there is room for this many bottles. When she is short 79 bottles, she should reorder. The yearly cost will be $110.60.

Numerical Answer. The optimal quantity to order is

$$Q = 711 \text{ bottles.}$$

The most amount short is

$$S = 79 \text{ bottles.}$$

The highest level of inventory is

$$Q - S = 632 \text{ bottles}$$
$$ATC = \$110.58/\text{yr.}$$

Math Work. If the demand is 2 dozen bottles per week times 12 bottles per dozen times 52 weeks per year, then $D = 1248$ bottles per year.

$C_o = \$31.50$ for each order, $C_c = 5$ percent ($3.50 per bottle) per year = $0.175 per bottle per year, and $C_s = 40$ percent ($3.50 per bottle) per year = $1.40 per bottle per year. Then,

$$Q = \sqrt{\frac{2(1248)(31.50)(0.175+1.40)}{(0.175)(1.40)}}$$

$$= 710.943 \qquad 711 \text{ bottles}$$

$$S = \sqrt{\frac{2(1248)(31.50)(0.175)}{1.40(0.175+1.40)}}$$

$$= 78.99 \quad \approx 79 \text{ bottles}$$

$$ATC = \frac{\$31.50(1248)}{711} + \frac{(711-79)^2(\$0.175)}{2(711)}$$

$$+ \frac{(79)^2(\$1.40)}{2(711)}$$

$$= \$55.29 + \$49.15 + \$6.14 = \$110.58/\text{yr.}$$

Since 711 bottles is close to 720 (60 dozen), it is easier to order the "even" number of bottles. Then

$$ATC = \$54.60 + \$49.93 + \$6.07 = \$110.60.$$

Thus it would cost $0.02 more per year to order 60 dozen bottles (an even number) and be short a maximum of 79 bottles.

INCIDENT: FELLED SHORT BY FELT SHORTAGES

The Middlearth Candle Company had a situation where the demand far exceeded the supply of its candles. It was making a 50 percent profit on the cost of its candles, but would stop production for lack of felt for the bottom of the candles. The felt inventory situation was investigated, and it was observed that employees neglected to tell management when they were running out of felt. An examination of the highest daily usage of felt showed that no more than 10 feet would be used in any 1 day. Since it took 2 days from ordering to receiving the felt, a pink tag, which said *order more felt*, was put 20 feet from the end of the felt roll, and the workers were instructed to give it to the manager when it fell out. The cost of being short (stopping production) was so high that the company could not afford to stop making candles.

datsun

During 1971–1972 the Datsun 240Z was a very popular car, and demand far exceeded supply, so that dealers had to fight for as many cars as they could get each month. When the deliveries arrived at the port, they had to be sure to be right there to get the number they were promised, and then there was no guarantee as to color and accessories. Because of this demand, the company would not give the cars on consignment, but would rather charge C.O.D. Thus dealers would have to take out short-term loans, and the cost to keep a car on the lot averaged $0.93 per day per car.

This problem also affected the customer, who would usually have to be put on a waiting list and put down $50 hoping that he could get the Datsun 240Z in his choice of color and accessories. The dealer made a profit of around $600 per car. As an average of 1 in 20 customers would renege on the deal, the dealer would then lose $550 profit. An average Datsun dealer would sell 40 240Zs per month, and thus could fix the cost of a lost sale (or backorder) at $1100 dollars every 30 days (for 40 cars).

Ordering costs average $40 per order, regardless of the size of the order. Determine the optimal quantity the dealer should order, how often, and how many cars to have on the waiting list per order period.

INCIDENT: STEEL MILL SOLIDIFIES ASSETS

A steel mill had a large overhead crane that weighed 130 tons on which hung ladles of molten steel taken from the furnaces. A crucial part, the central planetary gear, cracked one day, and when it broke it was discovered that there was not an extra one in stock. The company immediately called up Ohio Steel for an extra one, but they didn't have one either; so the part had to be made to order. It was made within 24 hours, flown in, and installed the next day. By that time, though, two blast furnaces had cooled, with the result that the furnaces had to be rebuilt. Thus there was a loss incurred from nonproduction, the cost of rebuilding the furnaces, and the special order. The company reaction was to order 50 spares to make sure it would *never* happen again.

surfboard blanks

A small firm in Florida produces surfboard blanks. One type is very popular among surfers the world over for its maneuverability, light weight, and handling in the water. The other is a shorter board, a belly-board, capable of supporting a person's weight, and used for "hot dogging" while the rider is on his knees.

Both boards are made by a process that uses a new flexible but extremely sturdy type of polyfoam. Each board takes a different size piece of polyfoam, which is punched out on a cutter and then placed in a mold that heats it, shapes it, and laminates a plastic waterproof skin to it.

Polyfoam production costs $14.50 for each large-size board and $9.50 for each belly board. Production of the blanks is fairly simple and costs only $25.00 to set up. There is a demand for 350 of the large blanks every month, and the firm has a warehouse to store the blanks after production, which costs about 1 percent of the cost of the tied-up capital per month. Due to the board's popularity and its unique shape and style, the cost of being short is put at only $\frac{1}{2}$ percent of the cost of each board per month.

Recent production plans have been to produce 1000 large boards each production period and then make sure that the firm is never short. But the last six months have shown that the cost of being late is not too high, and it is necessary to determine if any shortage should be allowed at all, and if so, how much. Another concern is that the present warehouse capacity is for 600 large boards, and the warehouse would have to be expanded.

Determine the optimal policy and cost for such an action in light of the recent plans for large board production.

INCIDENT: A SPARE KEEPS THINGS COOL

Trucking lines that have refrigerated trucks carrying perishables must be careful that either an extra air compressor is carried or the trucks are no more than four hours away from a place where they can get a new one (or repairs). Otherwise they will incur the cost of damaged goods.

short-wired

Referring back to the Pacific Telephone case, the worst thing that could happen to a central office next to a power failure or major equipment failure is to run out of wire. The cost of running out of wire is estimated at $65 per hour (the cost for 13 frameworkers to sit around). This is $250 per day, and when calculated in terms of wire and daily demand the cost is as follows:

	Demand			Cost of Being Short
IDF	3.3 rolls/day	$520/ 3.3	=	$157.57/roll/per day
MDF	19.6 rolls/day	$520/19.6	=	$26.53/roll/per day
NG	0.0135 roll/day	$520/0.0135	=	$38518.52/roll/per day

Assuming a 30-day month and that the company will be short only once during each month, but the shortage will last 3 days, we can determine the cost of being short each month to be $(3/30) = 0.1$ of the costs above. Thus for the NG the cost of being short would be $3851.85 per month.

For the IDF, determine from the case on pages 52–53 what the new policy and ATC would be compared to the old policy and what you would recommend.

For the MDF, compare the old policy from the case on pages 52–53 with two alternatives:

1. $Q = 1200$, $S = 200$
2. $Q = 1300$, $S = 300$

and make your recommendation. (Our alternatives are limited because there is room for only 1000 rolls, and we cannot make larger orders which might realize some savings.)

INCIDENT: WATER OVER THE DAM

In Venezuela the government keeps extra bearings in stock for the penstock gates for its dams, realizing that if one gate breaks and cannot be replaced within a few hours, everything will go over the top, which in turn will result in floods, destruction of homes and towns, and public ill will.

c. n. & e. d. forms

The Communications Network and Engineering Division of Eastern Telephone Company in Boston must have a certain form to complete orders for special services. These forms are of teletype paper and can only be obtained from a printer in Worcester. The forms come in rolls and are ordered by the carton; there are 12 rolls per carton, and the company orders 20 cartons per month.

The purchase price (plus transportation cost) is $1110.96 for 20 cartons. The carrying cost per month is 2 percent of the price. The forms have no resale value, being an expense item only. However, if the company should run short of the forms, production would stop in the communications center as copies of the orders could not be sent to the various departments. This would result in a delay in completing orders. Lawsuits would ensue due to the failure of the company to complete orders when promised. In the communications center 28 people would be unable to work at capacity until the forms were delivered. All factors considered, Eastern Telephone has determined that it costs them $5000 per day if they run out of forms. Thus the cost of being short is $150,000 per carton per month. All orders are placed by phone, and when it is determined that there are no more forms, a call is placed to Worcester and within 2 days the new forms are delivered. Phone and time expense are figured to be $5.00 per order, regardless of size.

The present policy is to order when there are no more forms. Is this the optimal policy, or is there a better one? How much should be ordered, how many days' shortage should be allowed, and how often should they be ordered?

INCIDENT: BITING OFF MORE THAN YOU CAN CHEW

From *Time* magazine, October 27, 1975: "Like the greedy little boy whose eyes were bigger than his stomach, oil-rich Nigeria, thanks to a colossal spending binge, is in one dreadful financial mess. The most visible sign of it was outside Apapa, port for the capital city of Lagos. Last week no fewer than 406 ships of all shapes and sizes were backed up waiting their turn for dock space. At least one vessel has been stuck outside Apapa since last February. Maritime experts call it the worst shipping jam in modern history.

"Nigeria last year earned $8 billion from oil revenues, prompting the government of former Head of State Yakubu Gowon to embark on a gargantuan program to develop and modernize Black Africa's most populous country. Unfortunately, no one stopped to figure what would happen when all the goodies arrived. One item in desperate need of modernization was the port of Apapa itself; the ordered machinery and parts are stuck in ships unable to dock.

"More than half the waiting ships are loaded down with cement, 2.4 million tons of it. And that's only a part of the order. In all, Nigeria somehow managed to contract for 21 million tons of cement, about ten times the total amount that the lagoon port could handle in a year even without other cargo to unload. Because of the chemical makeup of the cement, much of it may not be usable for building after six months. Last week Brigadier Murtala Mohammed, who ousted Gowon in a coup last July, ordered an official inquiry to see whether the cement purchase was made to 'sabotage the economy through a deliberate embarrassment of riches.'

"Nigeria's economy, as one official puts it, is 'suddenly encased in a wave of cement.' The country is paying a demurrage charge of $4000 a day to many of the backed-up ships; total cost in the past six months: $18 million. Unscrupulous shipowners, the government believes, have added to the shambles by putting old tubs into line to collect for demurrage, since it is more than they can make on the high seas. Paperwork is so fouled up that one shipper collected for demurrage and for cargo, even though he docked with nothing in his hold. In a desperate effort to find relief, Nigeria has tried to revoke the supposedly irrevocable letters of credit from the Nigerian Central Bank that backed the purchases in the first place. That move is wreaking havoc among international traders, and may cause some producers and shippers to be bankrupted.

"Last week the Nigerian government belatedly requested a halt to the shipping of any cargo to its ports until further notice. If the request is honored, it should help matters some, but at least 50 more ships are already en route to Apapa and will join the line within the next month. If nothing is done, a large London shipping group estimates, the latest arrivals will have to wait ten years before unloading. At best, the port is not expected to be unscrambled for a year."

Supplementary Problems

1. Sears is having a sale on Craftsman toolboxes and is selling an average of 15 boxes each week at one store. It is estimated that the cost to order is $10.00 and cost of carrying a toolbox for a year is $2.00.
   a. Determine how many should be ordered, how often, and the ATC. _____
   _____
   b. If they are short, they figure that the cost is $2.00 per box per month. Using this added data, determine what the new quantity should be that they order. _____
   _____

2. Referring back to the R & B Manufacturing case (page 51), if the cost of being short is $0.75 per ft² per month, how would this change the ordering policy for the Alabama stands?

   Previous quantity _____

   Previous ATC _____

   New quantity _____

   New ATC _____

3. Give five examples of critical shortages given in this section.

   a. _____
   b. _____
   c. _____
   d. _____
   e. _____

3.4 UNEQUAL DEMAND

There are many times when companies know or can reasonably estimate their demand, but it is not constant throughout the year. The problem then becomes one of trying to determine how much to order and when to order when the demand is fluctuating. Seasonality can play a big part in demand fluctuation; beer and soft drinks are examples of industries where sales are much higher in the summer than in the winter months.

Many approaches to solving this problem have been attempted. One approach is to average the sales for the year and use this monthly average in the EOQ formula. This means that the same amount is ordered each time, but since the demand increases and decreases, the time between orders would differ. Another approach is to use the same monthly average for demand, determine $Q/D = T$, and use the time period as a constant between orders, thus varying the amount of each order. Neither case proves to be generally effective, and the method of Silver and Meal on the following pages has proven to be far superior.[6]

The rationale behind the method is to balance the average fixed costs with the average variable costs. But since the demand fluctuates, different quantities may be ordered at different times, instead of always ordering the same amount or always ordering every month.

Let us assume that we have the following demand for the next six weeks:

Week	1	2	3	4	5	6
Demand	100	50	50	30	20	100

If it costs $30.00 to order (or set up production) and $0.20 per item per week to carry it, we need to determine how much to order for the next few weeks. Then we will have another such problem to solve in the coming weeks. Unlike the problems with constant demand, we will always need to resolve these problems as new demand comes up. We will also assume that all inventory goes out at the beginning of the period (rather than all during the period) to simplify the math somewhat, but the answer should not be affected much.

Let us determine the cost for ordering for one week, two weeks, three weeks, and so on. From these different possibilities, we will choose the ordering policy that will minimize the average total cost.

One week

Ordering 100, the cost is $30 ordering + $0 for inventory = $30.

$$ATC = \frac{\$30}{1} = \$30.$$

Two weeks

Ordering 150, the cost is $30 ordering + (50 units) (0.20 per unit per week)(1 week storage) = $40.

$$ATC = \frac{\$40}{2} = \$20/wk.$$

Three weeks

Ordering 200, the cost is $40 for the first two weeks + (50 units)(0.20 per unit per week)(2 weeks) = $40 + $20 = $60.

$$ATC = \frac{\$60}{3} = \$20/wk.$$

Four weeks

Ordering 230, the cost is $60 + (30 units)(0.20 per unit per week)(3 weeks) = $78.

$$ATC = \frac{\$78}{4} = \$19.50/wk.$$

Five weeks

Ordering 250, the cost is $78 + (20 units) (0.20 per unit per week)(4 weeks) = $94.

$$ATC = \frac{\$94}{5} = \$18.80/wk.$$

Six weeks

Ordering 350, the cost is $94 + (100 units)(0.20 per unit per week)(5 weeks) = $194.

$$ATC = \frac{\$194}{6} = \$32.33/wk.$$

Figure 3.10

A	0	1	2	3	4	5	6	ORDER
B								
C								
D	Ratio							
E	1	2	3	4	5	6	7	
F								
G								

At this point the average total cost goes up, and there is no longer an advantage to ordering larger quantities, for the variable costs are too high. A simple Quick & Dirty will accomplish the same results as above.

Given known unequal demands, set-up (ordering) costs, and holding costs, the method of Silver and Meal computes the total average costs and finds the minimum. A simple *nomograph* is given which should help the inventory control clerk to quickly determine the order for the upcoming weeks (see Figure 3.10).

The demand is as follows:

Week	1	2	3	4	5	6
Demand	100	50	50	30	20	100

The Ratio is set-up cost/holding cost. Given set-up costs of $30.0 and holding costs of $0.20 per unit per week, Ratio = $30.0/$0.20 = 150. This amount is entered in column 0, row D.

Quick & Dirty Algorithm: Unequal Demand[6]

Follow these steps in completing the nomograph of Figure 3.11.

1. Enter the demand for each week in row B.
2. Multiply A times B and obtain row C. (This is the number of unit-weeks the items are stored.)
3. Add row C to the total of the last period and enter result in row D. The first entry in row D is the Ratio of set-up to holding costs.
4. Divide row D by row E and enter in row F. (This is the total average divided by the holding cost. To get the total average cost, multiply by the holding cost.)
5. When the value in row F increases, sum the demand (row B) up to the point *before* the value increases and order that amount. In this example we would order 100 + 50 + 50 + 30 + 20 = 250 units.

6. Multiply the lowest ratio in row F by C_c to get the ATC, which in this case is $18.80 (row G).

Here we can see that the little nomograph accomplishes what was done step by step before, but the nomograph becomes a simpler way to do this. Now after this order of 250 units is placed, which will satisfy the next five weeks' demand, we would have to start with another nomograph and the demand for the next few weeks, starting with 100 units for week 1 (our old week 6), then the next week's demand, and so on.

Another point to notice is that it is not always true that when the ratio in row F goes up, this will be the lowest average total cost. It could be that, after going up for a period or two, the ratio may go back down and be smaller than the first minimum. Just checking past a few periods from the minimum will sometimes benefit in savings. This will usually occur when there is a larger demand followed by some very small demands.

fibre containers company

The Fibre Containers Company must keep at least one month's supply of cardboard on hand for its production needs, and it has been considering changing its ordering policy. Currently it has been ordering monthly, after estimating its next month's sales, but it now feels confident enough to make estimates several months in advance. Another factor is that cardboard is becoming more difficult to obtain in the United States, and a backlog might help in case cardboard becomes a scarce commodity for a few months. A third factor in this decision is that there is now room at the factory for at least three months' supply of cardboard, with a possible five months' inventory if some small modifications can be made.

The monthly demand for the next six months has been estimated (in 1000 square feet) and is seasonal. The ordering cost is $15.00 (about 3 hours involved in

sales estimation and verification, order forms, phone calls, and so on), and the cost is currently holding at $15.50 per 1000 square feet with a delivery cost of $0.50 per 1000 square feet of cardboard. The inventory carrying costs have been estimated at 5 percent per year of the cost of goods. Determine what policy should be used for the next six months, given the following sales estimates:

Month	1	2	3	4	5	6
Sales	182	164	142	160	193	198

Solution

Recommendation. Order 346,000 square feet for month 1, 302,000 square feet in time for month 3, and at least 391,000 square feet for month 5. (You will need to know the demand for month 7, and so on, to decide if you want to order more.) This assumes that there are no large fluctuations in price or scarcity of cardboard.

Numerical Answer

$$Q_1 = 346, \quad \text{ATC} = \$13.03/\text{mo}$$
$$Q_2 = 302, \quad \text{ATC} = \$12.90/\text{mo}$$
$$Q_3 = 391, \quad \text{ATC} = \$14.17/\text{mo}.$$

Math Work. The ratio of fixed costs to variable costs is 225, $C_o = \$15.00$, and $C_c = (\$15.50$ per 1000 square feet + $0.50 per 1000 square feet) times 5 percent per year = $0.80 per 1000 square feet per year or $0.067 per 1000 square feet per month.

Since demand is in terms of months, the carrying costs must also be in months.

For the first and second orders the average in row F of Table 3.2 (page 66) keeps going up, so that the minimum is in the second month in both cases. For the third order we have no more information to tell if the second month is the minimum or not.

Each minimum ratio is multiplied by C_c (0.067) to get the average total cost.

Figure 3.11

A	0	1	2	3	4	5	6	ORDER
B	100	50	50	30	20	100		250
C	0	50	100	90	80	500		
D	150	200	300	390	470	970		
E	1	2	3	4	5	6	7	
F	150	100	100	97.5	94	161.6		
G					$18.80			

inglewood golf course

Inglewood Golf Course has a system of ordering range balls that entails, by mutual agreement, a regular monthly order of 400 dozen golf balls at $1.50 per dozen from Northern Golf Balls Company in Chicago.

Naturally, because the driving range is located outdoors, the demand to use the range varies with the seasons (that is, less people will hit range balls in the winter than in the summer). Consequently, the

Table 3.2

First Order				Second Order				Third Order	
A	0	1	2	3	A	0	1	2	3
B	182	164	142	160	B	142	160	193	198
C	0	164	284	480	C	0	160	386	594
D	225	389	673	1153	D	225	385	771	1365
E	1	2	3	4	E	1	2	3	4
F	225	194.5	224.3	288.25	F	225	192.5	257	341.25
G		$13.03			G		$12.90		

Third Order		
A	0	1
B	193	198
C	0	198
D	225	423
E	1	2
F	225	211.5
G		$14.17

manager has estimated the demand for balls (in dozens) on the range as follows:

Month	Jan.	Feb.	Mar.	Apr.	May	Jun.
Demand	100	100	200	400	450	500

Month	Jul.	Aug.	Sept.	Oct.	Nov.	Dec.
Demand	550	550	500	400	300	100

The fixed ordering costs have been determined from freighting costs, time to do the paper work, and other factors to be $12.00 per order, regardless of the size of the order. Actually the cost is quite complicated, involving cash discounts and varying freighting rates, with fixed and variable costs, but a detailed analysis has shown that the fixed cost for the ordering works out to $12.00 per order. The variable costs are 1 percent of the cost of tied-up capital, so that carrying costs are $0.015 per dozen per month.

Determine how much and how often Inglewood Golf Course should order.

INCIDENT: APPLE PIE ORDER

A grocery store which carries frozen dessert pies has noticed that demand for three different types of pies is not constant at all. The demand for apple, cherry, and blueberry pies seems to fluctuate from a total of 20 pies per week to 60 pies per week. With this knowledge and considering the cost of ordering pies each week from the distributor, the manager of the store has cut down costs by changing his ordering policy from 40 pies per week to using the method of unequal demand.

realistic toy company

The Realistic Toy Company of Toronto, Canada, produces various toys and, as would be expected, runs into trouble trying to satisfy demand around Christmas time. It is not unusual for demand to exceed the possible production rate (including overtime), and it is necessary to schedule production to minimize the costs involved. The president of the company has had increasing union difficulties concerning overtime and is considering a policy of not allowing any overtime.

Without overtime, 5000 of these toys can be produced per week. An average set-up cost of $200.00 is used per production period, and the average cost per toy is $10.00. The storage cost for each toy per week has been figured at $0.041, and there is also a cost of capital involved at 10 percent. This works out to be 1.9 cents per toy per week, so that the total carrying costs are $0.059 per toy per week.

Determine what the production policy should be, given the forecasted demands that follow and also determine the total costs. Does the new policy of no overtime affect your decision?

Week No.	39	40	41	42	43	44
Demand	200	200	200	400	600	900

Week No.	45	46	47	48	49	50
Demand	1100	1700	2100	2100	1800	1000

INCIDENT: STAMP OUT INVENTORY COSTS

An interesting personal application of the unequal demand model is buying postage stamps. Each month the number of letters written and mailed varies, especially during holiday seasons (Christmas, Valentine's day, Easter, birthdays, and so on). There is a cost associated with going to the post office and waiting in line (fixed cost) and then there is the variable cost of having your money tied up in stamps. The unequal demand model is useful in showing what common sense would say, namely, that you would not keep large numbers of stamps on hand for a long period of time.

cpa firm

After successful years with a large accounting firm and then three years with a Houston-based construction firm, Roberto Lopez decided to go into business for himself. At present he enjoys a growing practice that services approximately 100 small businesses and many individual tax clients. Like any successful business, Roberto's practice incurs considerable expenses. Following employee salaries and office rent, the highest expense item is document duplication. A major portion of this duplication expense is the cost of paper and film.

At present, Roberto's bookkeeper orders copy paper and film for their 3M model 209 when supplies are down to 1 box each of paper and film, which is enough for 2800 copies. A box of paper contains 4 packages of 700 sheets and a box of film contains 4 rolls. She has been buying three boxes each order, and delivery usually takes three or four days. The supplies are guaranteed fresh on the shelf for one year, and they now have in stock enough to last until the end of the year. Roberto suspects that his ordering policy is not optimal.

An interpretation of the meter readings contained in the copy machine maintenance log reveals the following expected monthly demand schedule:

Month	Jan.	Feb.	Mar.	Apr.	May	Jun.
Demand (copies)	1500	5000	5000	4000	600	900

Month	Jul.	Aug.	Sept.	Oct.	Nov.	Dec.
Demand (copies)	1400	500	700	1400	500	500

Roberto figures his only carrying expense related to paper and film is a cost of capital of 12 percent annually. At present film costs $19.23 per roll and paper $3.40 per 100 sheets. Ordering costs are $13.00 per order, and Roberto would like to determine how much paper and film to order at the beginning of next year. (Consider the two together with only one ordering cost.) Compare this order with the old policy and also compare the costs of the different policies. Would it make sense to order for the whole year? (Explain why the Quick & Dirty is "dirty.")

Supplementary Problems

1. With cold days coming a local clothing store is getting ready to order their winter coats. They figure the cost of ordering is $75.00 and the cost of carrying the coats at their central warehouse is $0.20 per coat per month. At the beginning of each month they ship from the warehouse to the local store. Demand is as follows:

Month	Aug.	Sept.	Oct.	Nov.	Dec.	Jan.
Demand	20	30	65	60	70	50

a. How many coats should they order for their first order? _____

b. What happens if only 100 coats can be stored in the central warehouse? Does this change the answer to (a) at all? Why or why not? _____

_____

2. Consider the dairy case at the supermarket, which has a cost of ordering of $10.00 and the carrying cost of $0.10 per gallon per month, and a daily demand as follows:

Day	S.	M.	T.	W.	Th.	F.	S.
Demand	90	120	110	100	100	200	200

How much should be ordered for the first order? _____

3.5 DISCOUNTING

There comes that horrible moment when, even though you have faithfully used your Quick & Dirty manual for ordering inventory, you have ordered some "dogs." They won't sell, they sit on the shelf for months, gathering dust, and you hate to discount them and lose money on them, and besides, you don't know how much to discount them. You are not the only one in this dilemma, and, if you are like most people, the one thing you would never dream of doing is to sell them below cost.

Quick & Clean Algorithm: Discounting[7]

Given the following information:

D = discount price
P = profit margin on cost (the percent markup)
Y = average number of years it would take all the "dogs" to be sold at the original price (the time to sell all of them divided by 2)
N = number of times good stock (same lot size as the "dogs") turns over during the year
S = current selling price
$L = S - D$ = loss per item by discounting the "dogs"

the discount price is

$$D = \frac{S}{(1 + PNY)}.$$

If X = the percentage of profit (instead of markup on cost), then

$$D = \frac{S(1 - X)}{1 + X(NY - 1)}$$

Example. The Lido ski sweater is a slow-moving item mainly because of its design. It is a well-made sweater, but, according to management, its main drawback is its frontal appearance. It retails at $29.95 with a 40 percent markup on cost. There were 10 of these sweaters in stock, and they were selling at the rate of one a year. Normally 10 sweaters would turn-over 2.5 times in a year.

Here we find that the profit margin $P = 40$ percent (or 0.40). It would take 10 years to sell all the slow-moving sweaters, thus the average number of years $Y = 5$. If these were any other sweater, they would sell 2.5 lots in a year, thus $N = 2.5$. The selling price $S = \$29.95$. Then,

$$D = \frac{29.95}{[1 + (0.40)(2.5)(5)]} = \frac{29.95}{6} = \$4.99.$$

Thus each sweater should be immediately discounted to sell at $4.99 each. The rationale behind this is as follows. Let us take one of the "dogs" and see what happens. It sells immediately for $4.99 which we will now put into our fast-moving stock. Since we will mark up the goods 40 percent, the $4.99 will return $2.00 each time a good sweater is sold, (0.40)($4.99). The good stock turns over 2.5 times a year, so that you will make 2.5(2) = $5.00 a year. Since it will take 5 years on the average for the "dogs" to clear out, 5(5) = $25. Now add your original $4.99, we have the original selling price of $29.95.

In other words, we can either hold on to the dogs and eventually sell all of them at $29.95, some this year, some 10 years from now (but it averages out to 5 years), or we can sell all of them now at $4.99, put that money into good stock, and in 5 years regain our losses. The discount price D is simply a break-even point. We don't have to discount them that low, but it gives us an idea of how low we can go. The wholesale price was $21.40, and we might simply want to discount the sweaters to $20.00. In that case, if all of them go relatively soon, we will *make money,* even though they have been sold below cost. The point is that money is tied up in inventory and is not moving.

logos bookstore

LOGOS is a nonprofit Christian bookstore located in Westwood, California. Although it is nonprofit, it still has problems similar to profit-oriented stores. It sells Christian and other religious books, and also a wide variety of posters and cards not found in many other stores. The manager has some books that are slow sellers. Some of these do not sell well because they are hardbacks and the publisher has just released the book in paperback. Few people want the hardback because of the higher price. Some are not sold because the book has been displayed in an area where people would not give it much attention. These books take up space and, more importantly, tie up badly needed capital.

The solution is to discount the books, which will result in the books' being sold quickly. Then that money can be put into faster moving inventory. The immediate cash will earn back the initial cost within the time that it would have taken to move the slow sellers at their present price.

The manager has three books to discount. The first is *The Future of Belief Debate,* edited by Gregory Baum. There are three copies and he estimated it might take two years to sell them. *The Bhagavad Gita,* edited by Ann Stanford, was one of those books that is now available in paperback. He has three of these and predicts that it will take him three years to get rid of them (at one book a year). The third book is *Contemplative Prayer,* by Thomas Merton. He has six of these and probably only two will be sold per year. His average markup is 40 percent on cost, and the average turnover is nine books of this type a year. The initial selling prices of these books are $4.95, $3.50, and $3.00, respectively. Determine the lowest price that could be set for each book.

Solution

Recommendation. Hold a 50%-off sale for the three books as follows:

The Future of Belief Debate – $2.50
The Bhagavad Gita – $1.75
Contemplative Prayer – $1.50

Numerical Answer. The discount price that represents the break-even point for each book is as follows:

The Future of Belief Debate – $2.25
The Bhagavad Gita – $1.25
Contemplative Prayer – $1.57

Math Work. *The Future of Belief Debate.* $S = \$4.95$, $N = 3$ sets of 3 per year, $P = 40$ percent, $Y = 1$ year average:

$$D = \frac{\$4.95}{[1 + 0.40(3)1]} = \$2.25.$$

The Bhagavad Gita. $S = \$3.50$, $N = 3$ sets of 3 per year, $P = 40$ percent, and $Y = 1.5$ years:

$$D = \frac{\$3.50}{[1 + 0.40(3)1.5]} = \$1.25.$$

Contemplative Prayer. $S = \$3.00, N = 1.5$ sets of 6 per year, $P = 0.40$ percent, and $Y = 1.5$ years:

$$D = \frac{\$3.00}{[1 + 0.40(1.5)1.5]} = \$1.57.$$

By having the 50%-off sale, we will "lose" 7¢ per book on *Contemplative Prayer* but be "making" much more on the other two types of books. This sale will not reduce the price so low that customers might resist buying them because they are "too cheap." It is assumed that at these prices all the books would sell within a reasonable amount of time.

INCIDENT: GREETINGS!

A book store in Atlanta can't get rid of a certain line of greeting cards and is sorry it ever bought them. They sold for 35¢ and were discounted down to 10¢ (well above the break-even point of 2¢ which the manager just could not believe). She cleared out the rack in two weeks.

precision tile company

Precision Tile Company is involved in many aspects of building swimming pools. They buy tile in very large quantities and sell primarily to other companies that install the tile on pools. They are the only company in the area that specializes in swimming-pool tiles, and they try to keep a supply of any tile someone might want to put on a pool. A few of the tiles they stock are made in the United States and can usually be ordered and picked up in a few weeks, but the majority of the tiles are imported from Japan. These tiles are usually ordered a year before delivery, and a factory has to be set up for each tile. Therefore the orders must be large to decrease the set-up cost per square foot of tile. Because of having to order so far in advance, the company cannot just buy more of a certain tile as soon as they find that it is a good seller, but rather they must guess what the public will like and order according to these estimates. The many different patterns of tile that they carry are changed frequently to keep on top of the competition. Most of the people who have a pool put in their backyard want the pool to be personalized. The most striking part of a pool is the tile, so that customers do not want the same tile that their friends and neighbors have.

With all these changes taking place, Precision Tile occasionally orders a tile that does not sell very well.

The management feels that there are outlets to sell these poor movers fairly quickly at a reduced price. The problem is to determine the price that a slow mover can be sold for without reducing overall profit once the tile has been determined a slow mover.

The markup is 30 percent of cost on all tiles. The accounting department figures the inventory turnover to be about three times per year. The selling price, as well as the number of years to sell, vary for each tile. There are two tiles that the company is currently concerned about. The management estimates that it will take two years to sell each of them. One of the tiles is now selling for $0.70 per square foot and the other for $1.05 per square foot. Determine the lowest price that these tiles could be sold for.

INCIDENT: FAIR TRADE LIMITATION

A liquor store in the northwest was interested in discounting some wines, but was up against the regulation of the fair trade price. The answer was obvious; namely, the price should be discounted immediately to the lowest allowable under the law. The next step was to show that since D was already determined, Y could be computed. When the owner saw that a wine or liquor was not moving faster than Y years, he lowered the price down to the fair trade price.

ski racquet shop

In recent years there has been a rapid growth in the ski industry. This may be due largely to the increased free time available to the everyday worker. Most of the free time is spent in recreational activities, skiing being just one of these activities. Tennis, golf, and camping are a few more. Whatever the cause, the American people now search out new and exciting recreational activities in which to participate, and an outgrowth of this search for more fun and sun has been the sporting goods store.

One of these outgrowth stores, which has recently expanded to a chain of five, is the Ski Racquet Shop, located in Torrance, California. It caters strictly to the ski bum, tennis buff, and hiking and camping enthusiast. Since its opening in 1966, sales have tripled with $2,000,000 being reached in 1973. The fiscal year, which had previously ended on June 30, was recently changed to March 31 to more closely correspond to the very seasonal sales pattern. The majority of the sales are held during February and

March. The sales percentages for the categories of skiing, tennis, and camping are 85, 10, and 5 percent, respectively. The markup on cost for all items was a standard 40 percent.

The Alpine Design goose down parka retails at $55.00, and there are currently three of these in inventory. It is estimated that one would be sold each year, while three parkas of the other brands would turn over twice a year.

There were two types of Olin skis that were slow moving. The main reason for this was the unfamiliarity of the new brand. The first type was the Mark 1 D model, which retailed at $155.00. There were 16 Mark 1 D model Olins in stock, and it was estimated that it would take 2 years to sell all of them, while the same number of the other types of skis would turn over 1.5 times in a year. The second type (Mark II VCE—Variable Cracked Edges) sells for $189.00, and the turnover and time to sell 10 of them was the same as the Mark 1 D. Thus it would take 2 years to clear out the stock, while 10 pairs of other skis would turn over 2.4 times a year. Determine the lowest discount prices that could be charged for these three items.

INCIDENT: GETTING BETTER WITH AGE

Another liquor store was interested in moving some of its slower stock, especially a red French wine which previously sold for $6.99 a bottle and took about a year to sell a dozen bottles. Having another dozen of these bottles left, the owner was anxious to get rid of them. When she marked them down to $2.50 a bottle, a customer came in and bought two bottles, proclaiming that they now sold for $10.00 per bottle and were increasing in value. The owner immediately canceled her sale for the other ten bottles and increased the price. Every three months she increased the price by $0.50 per bottle and thus more than paid for her carrying costs.

kinney's shoes

Kinney's Shoe Store on University Avenue is managed by Oscar Bravo and for the most part does a prosperous business. Yet every once in a while Oscar's store gets hold of a shoe that just won't sell, no matter how hard he tries to push it (via displays, suggestions from clerks, and so on). Oscar is currently stuck with a dog; it is a leather wallaby. This shoe looks like the suede wallaby, the only difference

being that it is made of leather, and for some reason is not as popular. It retails, like the suede shoe, for $16.99, with a 50 percent markup on cost. Oscar received 100 of both styles at the beginning of the year. In 6 months Oscar has sold 230 suede shoes as compared with 23 leather wallabys. Normally it would take two to three years to sell all of these at this rate, but Kinney's has a policy of scrapping "dogs" after one year, with no salvage value to the store.

Rather than taking a loss on these, Oscar is willing to discount the shoes, but he is also afraid of "losing" money. Determine the lowest discount price that he could charge for each leather wallaby if he were to simply keep the 77 shoes until they all sold at the current rate (use the Quick & Clean discounting formula). Then consider what price he might charge if the company policy were enforced and at the end of one year all the remaining 54 shoes were thrown out, with no salvage value. Make up your own formula and reasoning. The company is very concerned about their image of being with the trend in shoe fashion, and would not want a shoe that is out of style to be displayed so that the stock could be cleared out. On the other hand, Oscar doesn't want to take a loss because the main office made a mistake in ordering them in the first place. Determine what discount price Oscar should charge by comparing the results of the Quick & Clean and your own algorithm. Write up your algorithm on a single piece of paper with an example so that a store manager such as Oscar could read it and use it.

INCIDENT: BEATING INFLATION

The University Mechanical and Engineering Contractors were bidding on seven condominiums in Myrtle Beach. Five others had been completed previously, and the low bidder for the plumbing contract has since gone out of business. University was interested in bidding for the job and wanted to submit a low bid which would guarantee them the job and yet not be so low as to force them out of business. Since the task would take 18 months to complete, University determined the cost of buying all materials when they got the bid (getting a loan if necessary) and storing them on site with a chain-link fence and a watch dog. They determined that they would save money, since inflation was increasing much more rapidly than their other costs. By doing this, they were successful in getting the bid, saved the customer approximately $6500, and bid $4000 lower than their nearest competitor.

Supplementary Problems

1. A department store has some men's shirts from India that sell for $25.00 with a profit margin on cost of 40 percent. They are not selling as well as a similar American style that usually turns over at a rate of 24 per month. At the rate the Indian shirts are selling, it will take three years to sell the 144 shirts remaining. At what price should the store discount these shirts, or what is the break-even price?

2. Many stores figure their markup on retail rather than wholesale cost. Given that X = the markup percentage on retail:
   a. Express P in terms of X. _____
   b. Rework the Ski Racquet case for Mark I D model Olins if the markup were 40 percent of the retail price.

3. The local headshop is trying to sell some old psychedelic posters at the current price of $2.95. They aren't moving any more (only 10 per month) and newer posters are selling much better (100 per month). The shop marks their goods up 25 percent on cost.
   a. What is the lowest discount price possible for the old posters? _____
   b. What would the lowest discount price be if their markup were on the retail price, not wholesale? _____

3.6 REPLACEMENT

Replacement theory is concerned with two questions: when to buy a machine and when to replace it. In other words, how old should the machine or item be when we buy it, and how old should it be when we sell

it? Usually we settle the first question in the simplest manner and buy the item new. This somehow guarantees us that the variable costs of keeping the item up will be very low (even though the fixed costs are extremely high). Thus we are also hoping to keep the machine for a long period of time so that the fixed costs will be averaged out to a reasonable cost.

For instance, when we buy a new car, there is a tremendous initial cost (over $3000). It is hoped that the cost of keeping up the car will be negligible for the next three or four years, and thus the investment will work out to only $800 per year for a four-year period. On the other hand, buying a used car may result in an initial investment of only $1000, but repair expenses over a four-year period of several thousand dollars. Even so, it may turn out that to buy a machine that is older but requires more in repairs will give a lower average yearly cost.

Replacement theory is interested in balancing the average fixed costs (purchase price, initial investment) with the average variable costs (operating and repair). The two extremes would be to keep the machine indefinitely so that the initial investment would be averaged out over a long period of time (but with rising costs of keeping it repaired) or to buy a new one each year and have no repair expense, but a high cost of purchase (minus trade-in).

Consider the Illinois Slag & Ballast company which has an International Harvester Hough 70 loader, purchased two years ago at $35,000. The initial plan called for keeping the machine for five years (a life span of 10,000 operating hours) but the company is considering changing its policy. By the end of the second year its trade-in had dropped to $12,000. There are those in the company who would like to buy a newer machine and are convinced that the repair and operating expenses make the machine uneconomical to keep, and that it should be replaced right now. The figures for operating expenses and trade-in are given in Table 3.3.

Table 3.3

Year (A)	Purchase Price (B)	Trade-in Value (C)	Replacement Cost (D)	Yearly Operating Expense (E)	Total Operating Expense (F)	Total Expense (G)	Average Cost (H)
1	$35,000	$15,000		$ 5,000			
2	35,000	12,000		10,000			
3	35,000	10,000		15,000			
4	35,000	8,500		20,000			
5	35,000	7,700		25,000			
6	35,000	6,800		30,000			
7	35,000	6,000		35,000			

Quick & Clean Algorithm: Replacement[4]

The data in columns A, B, C, and E of Table 3.3 are supplied by the person with the problem. The information for yearly operating expenses may be actual expenses (historical data) or projected expenses. The yearly operating expenses are the expenses for that year only, and in this case are spiraling up each year. The purchase price in this case remains constant, although one may project increased (or even decreased) costs there.

To complete the blank columns, follow these steps:

1. Column $D = B - C$. This is the fixed cost of buying the new machine.
2. Column $F =$ the sum of column E up to and including the year you are working on. This is the total repair bill so far.
3. Column $G = D + F$. This is how much you have spent on the machine.
4. Column $H = G/A$. This is the average yearly expense (after trade-in).
5. Choose as the year to replace the machine the one that corresponds to the smallest average cost in column H.

Following the above steps for the data given in Table 3.3 for the Illinois Slag and Ballast Company, we obtain the results shown in Table 3.4.

Notice that if you were to replace the machine yearly, the cost would be high due to the expense of replacing the machine. On the other hand, if you waited until the end of the fifth year, the high cost would be high due to the increasing repair costs, even though the cost of buying a new machine (minus the trade-in) averages out to a little more than $5000 per year (versus $20,000 if a new one is bought each year).

A further note is in order. Depending upon the repair costs, the cost does not always go down and then rise, never to fall again. Some repair costs, like cars, are higher some years when everything falls apart, and then for the next few years they are lower

again. In other words, they tend to be cyclical. Even though the cost goes up, it may fall lower again in a few years, so it may pay to determine the averages for the next few years after the cost goes up.

rider lawn mowers

A-1 Rentals has several rider lawn mowers available for rental. These are the large mowers usually used for large open spaces, and they are quite a bit more expensive than the smaller gasoline-engine lawn mowers. Each of these rider mowers costs $500 but has a 10-year life span, depreciating by an even $50 each year, until the 10th year when there is no trade-in value at all. The rental office is concerned that the mowers are kept too long, and has projected the operating costs (beyond normal maintenance and the repainting they undergo every year) in the following table:

Year	1	2	3	4	5
Operating Expense	$100	$50	$50	$25	$25

Year	6	7	8	9	10
Operating Expense	$40	$55	$70	$95	$110

Notice that the operating expenses drop during the first five years, but are very high the first year while the machine is being broken in. Then for the last five years the projected expenses go up each year.

The normal procedure for A-1 Rentals has been to replace all mowers at the end of three years, but they have never had equipment of this type before, and figure that the extra expense of the initial investment should warrant a review of this standard policy. It is assumed that to buy a new mower in the next few years, the cost will not go up appreciably, so the cost of $500 will be used. Others at A-1 think that costs for mowers will go up by 5 percent each year and that this should not only be taken into account, but that it will make a difference in when to replace the current

Table 3.4

Year (A)	Purchase Price (B)	Trade-in Value (C)	Replacement Cost (D)	Yearly Operating Expense (E)	Total Operating Expense (F)	Total Expense (G)	Average Cost (H)
1	$35,000	$15,000	$20,000	$ 5,000	$ 5,000	$ 25,000	$25,000
2	35,000	12,000	23,000	10,000	15,000	38,000	19,000
3	35,000	10,000	25,000	15,000	30,000	55,000	18,333*
4	35,000	8,500	26,500	20,000	50,000	76,500	19,125
5	35,000	7,700	27,300	25,000	75,000	102,300	20,460

machines. Therefore determine with and without the inflationary costs of buying the new rider lawn mowers when they should be replaced.

Solution

Recommendation. Keep the rider lawn mowers for six years without inflation, indefinitely with inflation. It is assumed that the repair costs that have been estimated are close to correct. This will minimize the yearly average costs.

Numerical Answer. Average costs per year without inflation are $98.33 for the sixth year.

Average costs per year with inflation are $89.96 for the tenth year and going down.

Math Work. Using the Quick & Clean algorithm, we may compute the data shown in Table 3.5. Notice that within one or two years the average yearly costs are fairly close, which indicates that the minimum-cost curve is fairly shallow. This means that we could be one or even two years off the optimum point and still keep the costs close to the minimum.

sanitation department

The Dallas Sanitation Department is presently using D8 Caterpillar bulldozers in its land-fill dumps to bury and shovel garbage. This work is very strenuous on the clutch and undercarriage of these machines, such that every three or four years major repairs must be done. Cost data was found by taking the average costs of three identical machines working under the same strenuous conditions. In 1966 their purchase prices averaged $47,385.00 and in 1972 their average retail value was $76,241.00. Trade-in values were paralleled with costs from a similar machine, taking into account the excessively hard work that these machines have been doing.

Listed at the top of page 74 are the relevant costs. Determine the optimal time to trade in the D8 Caterpillar bulldozers to minimize the average yearly costs.

Table 3.5

Without Inflation

Year	Purchase Price	Trade-in Value	Replacement Cost	Yearly Operating Expense	Total Operating Expense	Total Expense	Average Cost
1	$500	$450	$ 50	$100	$100	$ 150	$150.00
2	500	400	100	50	150	250	125.00
3	500	350	150	50	200	350	116.67
4	500	300	200	25	225	425	106.25
5	500	250	250	25	250	500	100.00
6	500	200	300	40	290	590	98.33*
7	500	150	350	55	345	695	99.28
8	500	100	400	70	415	815	101.87
9	500	50	450	95	510	960	106.66
10	500	0	500	110	620	1120	112.20

With Inflation

Year	Purchase Price	Trade-in Value	Replacement Cost	Yearly Operating Expense	Total Operating Expense	Total Expense	Average Cost	Discount $(1.05)^{1-n}$
1	$500.00	$450	$ 50.00	$100	$100	$ 150.00	$150.00	$150.00
2	525.00	400	125.00	50	150	275.00	137.50	130.95
3	551.25	350	201.25	50	200	401.25	133.75	121.32
4	578.81	300	278.81	25	225	503.81	125.95	108.80
5	607.75	250	357.75	25	250	607.75	121.55	100.00
6	638.14	200	438.14	40	290	728.14	121.36	95.09
7	670.05	150	520.05	55	345	865.05	123.58	92.22
8	703.55	100	603.55	70	415	1018.55	127.32	90.48
9	738.73	50	688.73	95	510	1198.73	133.19	90.15
10	775.66	0	775.66	110	620	1395.66	139.56	89.96*

Year	Purchase Price	Trade-in Value	Repair Cost
1966	$ 47,385	$36,285	$ 1,785
1967	51,293	33,643	2,907
1968	55,524	27,957	7,976
1969	60,105	23,219	3,610
1970	65,063	18,480	3,518
1971	71,974	14,191	3,319
1972	76,241	12,794	8,961
1973	82,531	11,372	4,122
1974	89,340	10,424	3,998
1975	96,711	9,378	3,798
1976	104,690	8,542	10,406
1977	113,327	6,973	4,787
1978	122,676	5,243	4,643
1979	132,797	4,527	4,411
1980	143,753	3,942	12,086

INCIDENT: BEATING CAR PRICES

About 15 years ago a thorough study was done on when was the best time to buy a car and when to replace it. Extensive surveys were taken for a mid-sized car and the costs involved with repairs. Time intervals were three months. The study indicated that the best time to buy a car is when it is three years old, which is right after everything has fallen apart for the first time. Then it is worth keeping the car until it is seven and a half years old, when it should be driven to the nearest junkyard.

new cars

A study was made of three small compact cars: British, German, and American. They each average over 20 miles per gallon and are easy to handle. All three were purchased in 1968 and costs were determined over seven or eight years. Purchase prices and trade-in values were taken from *Kelly's Blue Book*; operating costs (liability insurance, gasoline, tune-ups, light maintenance, parts replacement, tires, and so on) were figured on 15,000 miles per year from personal experience, *Consumer Reports,* mechanics, and dealers. These are, of course, only estimates and should be taken as such. Another variable is that even within the same model, costs may vary considerably, and what held true for 1968 may not be true for the next year, and so on. Finally, the actual models of the cars are not disclosed in this case, but you are encouraged to perhaps gather your own data and do a study of two or three cars, determining the average operating costs per year and deciding which you would buy to minimize your investment per year. Also, there is no way of including subjective data such as handling, driving enjoyment, prestige, and so on. The cost of replacement is purchase minus trade-in. It is assumed that each car will survive the seven-year period.

From the data given in Table 3.6, determine the minimum yearly cost for each automobile and which of the three you would purchase under these conditions and assumptions.

INCIDENT: CHANGING TECHNOLOGIES

The Daily Breeze is interested in purchasing a new printing press but because of the change in technology, it becomes difficult to determine the new purchase price and trade-in. The worth of the old press drops because of the change in the last ten years in presses, and it is difficult to estimate what a new press of the old type would cost. Thus the Quick & Clean becomes more difficult to implement.

Table 3.6

| Year | German | | British | | American | |
	Replace	Operate	Replace	Operate	Replace	Operate
1	$1260.00	$ 737.55	$ 375.00	$ 851.75	$ 915.00	$ 880.00
2	1450.00	950.28	593.00	918.75	1565.00	905.00
3	1800.00	1013.92	1037.50	945.75	2310.00	1130.00
4	2105.00	825.55	1481.25	1023.75	2780.00	1155.00
5	2130.00	1056.29	1925.00	1015.75	3000.00	1518.00
6	2200.00	1001.42	2147.00	1275.45	3100.00	1650.00
7	2280.00	1041.38	2250.00	1416.81	3200.00	1780.00
8	2350.00	1102.45	—	—	—	—

theodore e. anvick—structural engineers

Theodore E. Anvick—Structural Engineers, Inc., located in Omaha, Nebraska, is a diversified firm that provides structural engineering services that include preliminary design, design, preparation of working drawings, and field inspections of schools, churches, commercial and industrial buildings, test facilities, and special structures.

In order for the firm to provide detailed structural design in the fastest and most economical way possible, several types of equipment are used. One of the most often used pieces of equipment is the Blu-Ray model 800 blueprint machine.

The machine has been in use for the past seven years. It was acquired at a cost of $800.00. Costs incurred by the operation of the machine include blueprint paper, labor, ammonia, and repairs. Paper costs 15¢ per sheet. Labor is charged at the rate of $8.00 per hour, and one person can run 20 sheets per hour. In the first year, labor amounted to $400 for the operation of this machine and increased $40 for each of the second and third years. The labor increase was $80 a year for each of the remaining years of operation. Ammonia has averaged out to be about $12.00 per month. As for repairs, at the beginning of the sixth year a new motor had to be installed along with new developing lights. The motor was $54.00. The belts and the developing tubes were $100.00 and $40.00, respectively. The new lights burned with twice the intensity of the original ones; thus labor costs were cut in half for the sixth year on because exposure time for each print was cut in half.

As time went on and the business grew, more jobs were acquired, and operation costs increased accordingly. Paper costs increased with 1000, 1100, 1200, 1400, 1600, 1800, and 2000 sheets used from years 1 through 7, respectively. In year 8 the number of prints is projected to be 2250. Labor costs went up along with the number of prints produced, although it was still charged at the rate of $8.00 per hour. Ammonia remained the same because a certain amount has to be kept in the machine regardless of whether it is running or not so that the seals won't dry out.

Each year the trade-in value declined, and the values for years 1 through 7 were, respectively, $750.00, $650.00, $550.00, $425.00, $325.00, $250.00, and $200.00. The figure of $200.00 is regarded as salvage value.

The executives of the firm have recently split into two factions. The first group feels that a new machine should have been purchased when the model 800 broke down last year and that they wasted that much money by repairing it. The second group, obviously, feels that the repair was warranted and that further savings would accrue by continued operation of the present machine. Those who favor discarding the machine contend that it would be less costly to purchase the blueprints from an outside service at $1.00 per sheet.

Determine what decision should have been made based on costs per sheet rather than just yearly costs (that is, the first column, instead of being years, should be total sheets: 1000, 2100, 3300, and so on).

Supplementary Problems

1. Zura Hall has a large color console TV set with the following costs for repair and trade-in. When is the *best* time to trade it in, given the figures below?

Year	Purchase Price	Trade-in Value	Repair Cost
1	$695	$400	$ 0
2	695	380	20
3	695	360	15
4	695	340	200
5	695	320	20
6	695	300	10
7	695	280	20

2. A college student has decided to buy a moped to get to and from school. It will cost $600 to get the deluxe Vespa and she estimates the following prices for resale, and operating. Given the data below determine when she should trade the moped in and the ATC:

Year	Purchase Price	Trade-in Value	Yearly Operating Expense
1	$600	$550	$20
2	580	525	35
3	560	510	45
4	550	500	50
5	540	475	55
6	520	470	60

3. Consider the New Cars case:
   a. What if there is a $100 rebate offered for each car? What does this do to your ATC for the British car? Show new total costs and ATC.

b. Explain why it doesn't make much difference if a $100 rebate is given on the German car.

3.7 MISCELLANEOUS: IMPUTING DATA AND DATA GATHERING

The most appropriate use of the previous formulas for economic order quantities, shortages, average total cost, and so on, is not necessarily to solve them. Most businesses are already ordering supplies, or being short of them. And if a business is keeping a good accounting of expenses, it is possible to determine the average fixed costs and variable costs associated with inventory. If the average fixed costs are extremely high in relation to the variable costs, this means that one is ordering too often and not carrying enough inventory. If the carrying costs (variable costs) are very high compared to the fixed costs, this means that the business is carrying too much inventory and not ordering often enough. In the Spark Plugs case, the average fixed costs were $10 per year and the variable costs were $125 per year when Marv was ordering 500 sets of spark plugs each year. This simply indicates (if his figures were correct) that he was carrying too much inventory. If his ordering policy is correct, then his cost of carrying inventory per item per year is much too high. In other words, his actions are imputing a different cost on variable and/or fixed costs.

Quick & Dirty Algorithm: Imputed Costs (Without Shortages)

Given the ordering policy and associated costs as follows:

1. $D = Q^2C_c/(2C_o)$ the demand is imputed to be this amount, or
2. $C_o = Q^2C_c/(2D)$ the ordering (set-up) cost is imputed to be this amount, or
3. $C_c = 2DC_o/Q^2$ the carrying cost is imputed to be this.

Looking at the example in Section 3.1, we had a demand of 50 units per month, an ordering cost of $100, and a carrying cost of $0.25 per unit per month. Let us assume that for this situation, the ordering policy had been to order 50 units each month. This would imply that

$$D = \frac{(50)^2(0.25)}{2(100)} = 3.125 \text{ units/mo.}$$

Thus for the lot size of 50 units to be an optimal lot

size (economic order quantity), the demand would have to be 3 units per month.

Or this ordering policy would impute the ordering cost to be

$$C_o = \frac{(50)^2(0.25)}{2(50)} = \$6.25/\text{order.}$$

This is smaller than the $100 which was estimated to be the cost of ordering. Again, we could impute the carrying cost as $C_o = 2(50)(100)/(50)^2 = \$4$ per unit per month instead of the $0.25 per unit per month.

As can be seen, this means that either the ordering policy of 50 units per month is wrong or the costs associated with inventory have been estimated poorly.

marv's enco service station

In the Spark Plugs case, Marv was ordering 500 sets of spark plugs each year and simply storing them in his service station. After much discussion it became evident to Marv that perhaps this did represent a lot of money tied up, and since it would take an entire year to get rid of 500 spark plug sets, perhaps he was wrong in some of his estimates of cost and demand. He also admitted that he didn't like to be out of anything, especially spark plugs.

Using his present ordering policy and his estimate of cost, determine the imputed value of carrying cost, ordering cost, and what he expects his demand to be by ordering so many spark plug sets. Remember that the demand was estimated to be 500 sets per year, the cost of ordering was $10.00 regardless of the size of the order, and the carrying cost was estimated at $0.50 per set per year.

If you were to go back to Marv, what figures would you use to impress on him that his ordering policy could use revision?

Solution

Recommendation. It is recommended that Marv be shown that he is imputing his cost of ordering the sets of spark plugs as $125.00. That should convince him that his costs are out of line, and that ordering more often will not make his costs go up (he estimated his costs of ordering at only $10.00).

Numerical Answer

Imputed demand = 6250 sets per year
or imputed ordering cost = $125.00
or imputed carrying cost = $0.04 per set per year.

Math Work

$$D = \frac{(500)^2(0.50)}{2(10)} = 6250/\text{yr}$$

$$C_o = \frac{(500)^2(0.50)}{2(500)} = \$125.00$$

$$C_c = \frac{2(500)(10)}{500^2} = \$0.04/\text{set/yr}$$

Thus the reader can see that given a current ordering policy, it is possible to impute what certain costs or demands might be. There will be no cases included for this section, but the application of this should be obvious.

The next part of this section will deal with the difficulty of obtaining the data.

Data Gathering

To gain experience in solving the Quick & Clean economic order quantity model, it is instructive to have to go out and gather the data. Stop by any of your local friendly merchants and ask them what their carrying costs are. Or ask them about fixed costs, how they divide overhead into fixed and variable, and so on. If you receive a blank stare, explain that carrying costs are the costs per item to carry the merchandise they sell or make. This might be the cost of insurance, tied-up capital (they could be making something on the money invested in the goods), handling, spoilage, theft, and so on.

You will find it instructive to explain to laypeople what costs are involved in handling merchandise, and to have to put it into terms they understand. If you are a business student, you will be amazed at how little businesspeople may know about their costs. On the other hand, you may experience the difficulty of getting information from businesses that very well know what their costs are. Finally, you may have an incident happen to you as the following true story illustrates.

INCIDENT: DEALING WITH CARRYING COSTS

A student visited with a service-station dealer that he had traded with for about five years (thus ensuring his being local and friendly). He told him that he was studying economic order quantity for inventory, and then asked him if he would mind answering some general questions concerning his inventory carrying cost. Now this student was not some 19-year-old wide-eyed sophomore, but an ex-Navy chief who had a lot of experience with life.

The initial response of the service-station manager was "that is confidential." The student told him that he did not intend to be nosy and he convinced him that he would not use his name nor the name of the service station, but just wanted to know his carrying costs. The manager reflected a little bit, but seemed to become uneasy. He said: "I am a businessman. I buy merchandise, pay cash, place it on the shelves in the stock room (which is quite large, approximately 400 square feet of floor space), and out front. I then sell it and I don't have time to be figuring inventory carrying costs, much less cost per item."

While the manager attended a car on the driveway, the student looked around and observed quite a volume of merchandise that included tires, batteries, oil, various filters, spark plugs, and other accessories. When the manager returned, he stated, "besides, that stuff you are learning is for the big outfits, the corporations, not for the small guy like me. That crap is Communism, bureaucracy, and government meddling!"

The student tried to explain that costs are tax deductible and loss of capital costs him money that could be applied to other uses. The manager then suggested that the student go home and inventory his child's toy box. He then pointed to a small storage cabinet where he kept gasoline filters and said, "You see this? I picked this up in a junkyard for free, painted it, and that's my inventory carrying cost. Ha, ha!"

The student then invited the manager over to a nearby bar for a beer to cool off. To this day, whenever the student drives in for gasoline, the manager comes running out to greet him with, "How's the inventory freak?"

INCIDENT: KNOWING YOUR COSTS

A few successful ventures by other students revealed the following data. Atlantis Bedding determined that it took 1 hour every 2 weeks at $10 an hour for placing orders, thus amounting to a monthly cost of $20. The cost of carrying was simply determined as 40 percent of the capital tied up each year, with no costs allocated for overhead or insurance.

Another service station determined that there was a loss of interest on the cash used to purchase gasoline (approximately $2000 per month) at 8 percent yearly interest. The time to prepare the orders was determined as 3 to 4 hours at $6.00 per hour. No costs were determined for the storage tanks, and since the station is owned, the manager figured that there were no costs there. It was also difficult to put a figure on the evaporation loss of gasoline, but it was acknowledged that the longer the gasoline is kept, the more loss there is.

INCIDENT: A DIARY OF FRUSTRATION

This student was very determined in her approach to several businesses as is reflected in her diary of events.

"September 24, 1979

6:30 P.M. Ventured into Great Goods Department Store. Asked sales clerk for data information about carrying costs, fixed costs, and so on. Was referred to three other sales clerks and finally was told that I must write to the buyers in New York for such data information. (Even purchased a belt I didn't need.)

7:00 P.M. Tried Jensen's Jewelers in the same shopping center. Was told that no one could answer *any* questions concerning carrying costs at *any* time.

7:30 P.M. After two turn-downs, I drove to Lea's Shoes in Fashion Valley. Asked salesman for needed data and again was told that I must write to buyers in New York. (I was so frustrated, I ended up buying a pair of shoes that hurt my feet!)

8:30 P.M. Shopped for a while . . . and thought maybe if I gave it one more try . . . . This time it was Buyers' Market in Fashion Valley. Went to the sports department and asked about the *desperately* needed data. This time I was told to come back another day, another time (the daytime preferably when someone was there)."

INCIDENT: PASSING THE BUCK

Another adventure is recounted by a student who would not be put off easily. "In an effort to obtain carrying costs, I called Discount Delight. I properly identified myself and then stated my question. And, to my dismay, the person on the other end of the line asked me if I was calling about a book. After rephrasing the question, I was transferred to the secretary. After introducing myself and stating my question, I was once again transferred to another party. This time I was given another number to dial and was reassured by the other party that 'those people can give you loads of numbers.' I thanked her and immediately after hanging up I dialed the number, only to get a busy signal. I waited a few minutes and then dialed again. The receptionist answered, whereupon I began my recitation for the third time. I was then transferred to three other people before I spoke to a supervisor in inventory control. The supervisor asked me to repeat where I was from and what I was doing. Eagerly, I repeated myself (this is the seventh time). Then the supervisor said that she couldn't give it to me because 'it was too involved,' and even if it were

available, she didn't think that she should give it to me anyway."

Supplementary Problems

1. Given the Health Data Management case (page 52), assume that the ordinal ordering policy for two-ply printer paper was correct.
    a. What are the values of:

    Q = —————————————————

    T = —————————————————

    ATC = ————————————————

    b. What is the implied value of C_c? —————

    c. What is the actual value of C_c in the case?

    —————————————————————

    d. Which one would you believe? Why? —————

    —————————————————————

2. If the average variable cost for an inventory situation (simplest model) is $100.00 per year for the optimal amount ($Q = 50$),

    a. What is the ATC? —————————————

    b. What is C_c? ————————————————

    c. If the demand is 1000 per year, what is C_o?

    —————————————————————

3.8 BRIDGING THE GAP: THE INTERFACE

By now many readers may be wondering, "How do I know that these formulas are really optimal?" The proper response is that most aren't, even though they may have mathematical respectability and be mathematically optimal. Again dirty data rears its ugly head, and, as we have seen in the previous section, the data may be exceptionally difficult to obtain or unreliable. Nevertheless, here are some mathematical considerations for the different algorithms.

1. For Section 3.1, the economic order quantity that minimizes the average total cost can be shown through calculus to be the same formula we found by setting the average fixed costs equal to the average variable costs:

$$\text{ATC} = \frac{C_o D}{Q} + \left(\frac{Q}{2}\right) C_c$$

Taking the derivative with respect to Q

(remember all those other letters and numbers are really constants):

$$\frac{d(\text{ATC})}{dQ} = \frac{-C_oD}{Q^2} + \frac{C_c}{2} = 0.$$

This is set equal to zero (where either a maximum, minimum, or an inflection point must be) and solved for Q:

$$\frac{C_c}{2} = \frac{C_oD}{Q^2}$$

$$Q^2C_c = 2C_oD$$

$$Q^2 = \frac{2C_oD}{C_c}$$

$$Q = \sqrt{\frac{2C_oD}{C_c}}.$$

Substituting this value of Q into the ATC formula,

$$\text{ATC} = \frac{C_oD}{\sqrt{\frac{2C_oD}{C_c}}} + \sqrt{\frac{2C_oD}{C_c}}\,\frac{C_c}{2} = \sqrt{2DC_oC_c}.$$

Notice that both the average fixed costs and the average variable costs are equal for the optimal value of Q. Finally it suffices to show that the second derivative is positive for that value of Q to prove that we have found a minimum extreme point, which will be positive for *any* value of Q (> 0 of course):

$$\frac{d^2(\text{ATC})}{d^2Q} = \frac{2C_oD}{Q^3}.$$

2. In Section 3.2 we concerned ourselves only with the specific price breaks and the quantities associated with them, and not the other possible quantities in between. Perhaps a hypothetical example might help, along with a graph of a couple of possible situations to explain the potential difficulties. Consider some product with price breaks at 10, 20, and 30 units. Two possible outcomes are shown in Figure 3.12.

    The Quick & Clean formula will correctly pick the optimal circled values, and in fact looks only at the values of $Q = 10$, 20, and 30. For the case on the left-hand graph it will find the optimal value of all the Q's, but for the graph on the right-hand side it has missed the optimal value ($\times$) which is between 10 and 20. Fortunately for ATC curves, they are usually very shallow, and since the data may be dirty anyway, the solution may be near-optimal.

3. The formulas for the economic order quantity Q and the optimal shortage amount S in Section 3.3 are derived in a similar fashion as for Section 3.1, except that now the ATC formula has two variables on which it depends, Q and S. Thus partial derivatives must be taken according to Q and S, which results in two nonlinear equations that must be solved simultaneously:

$$\text{ATC} = \frac{DC_o}{Q} + \frac{(Q-S)^2C_c}{2Q} + \frac{S^2C_s}{2Q}$$

$$= DC_0Q^{-1} + \frac{QC_c}{2} - SC_c + 2S^2C_cQ^{-1}$$

$$+ 2S^2C_sQ^{-1}$$

where all numbers and letters other than Q and S are constants.

$$\frac{\partial \text{ATC}}{\partial Q} = \frac{-DC_o}{Q^2} + \frac{C_c}{2} - \frac{S^2C_c}{2Q^2} - \frac{S^2C_s}{2Q^2} = 0$$

Figure 3.12

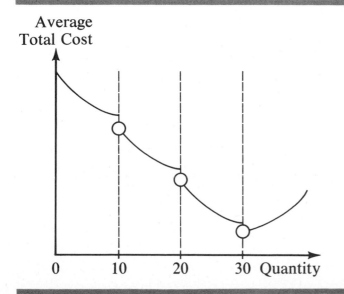

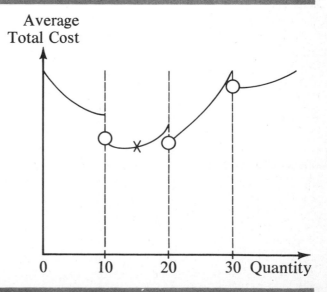

$$\frac{\partial(ATC)}{\partial S} = -C_c + \frac{SC_c}{Q} + \frac{SC_s}{Q} = 0.$$

Simplifying the two formulas, we get

$$2DC_o - C_cQ^2 + S^2C_c + S^2C_s = 0$$

or

$$Q^2 = 2DC_o + \frac{S^2(C_c+C_s)}{C_c}$$

$$QC_c - SC_c - SC_s = 0$$

or

$$Q = \frac{S}{C_c}(C_c+C_s).$$

Squaring the last formula and setting it equal to the first yields

$$\frac{2DC_o + S^2(C_c+C_s)}{C_c} = \frac{S^2(C_c+C_s)}{C_c^2}.$$

Simplifying,

$$2DC_oC_c + S^2(C_c + C_s)C_c = S^2(C_c + C_s)^2.$$

Solving for S^2,

$$S^2(C_c^2 + C_sC_c - C_c^2 - 2C_cC_s - C_s^2) = -2DC_oC_c$$

$$S^2 = \frac{2DC_oC_c}{C_s^2 + C_sC_c} = \frac{2DC_oC_c}{C_s(C_s + C_c)}.$$

Thus

$$S = \sqrt{\frac{2DC_oC_c}{C_s(C_s + C_c)}}$$

$$Q = \sqrt{\frac{2DC_oC_c}{C_s(C_s + C_c)}} \; \frac{(C_c + C_s)}{C_c}$$

$$= \sqrt{\frac{2DC_o}{C_c} \; \frac{(C_c + C_s)}{C_s}}.$$

Therefore we see that the two formulas given in Section 3.3 can be shown to give values for Q

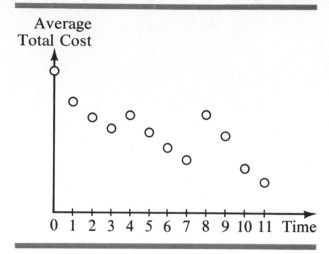

Figure 3.13

and S that represent the only extreme point for ATC, and can be shown by inspection to thus be a minimum (versus a maximum or a saddle point).

4. The section on replacement, Section 3.6, contains a very Quick & Dirty algorithm to decide when to replace a machine or some similar object. Depending upon the repair costs and trade-in values, the ATC for each time period may not be unimodal (having only one low point). The Quick & Dirty will stop after the ATC rises the first time and thus may miss a more optimal point. Again a graph (as shown in Figure 3.13) may help to show this.

Here we see that the ATC starts out high and by the third time period has reached a local minimum as the next time period yields a higher average cost. But we see that there is a lower local minimum for time period 7, and then it seems to be getting even lower for time period 11. The only way to ensure that these other local minima are not missed is to continue the computations indefinitely, which may be impractical due to a lack of time or data. Notice that we do not have a continuous curve that we could differentiate (and thus find all the local minima but not necessarily the global). Again considerations of the data (estimates for the most part) and the economy (very unstable) may allow us to use the Quick & Dirty with less compunction about not being "optimal."

3.9 REVIEWS

Review 1: Open book and notes; show all work; and write legibly

1. (10 points) Baskin Robbins' best selling ice cream is now chocolate mint chip (replacing vanilla and then rocky road). It is used up at an average of 10 barrels each week. It is estimated that the cost to order is $5.00 and the cost of carrying a barrel of ice cream is $13.00 per barrel per year. Determine how much should be ordered, how often, and what the average total cost (ATC) is.

$Q = $ _____

$ATC = $ _____

2. (15 points) A large business firm buys pencils for office supplies by the box. Approximately half a box is used every week, with the cost being $4.25 per box. If the ordering cost is $1.00 and the carrying cost is set at 10 percent per box per week of the cost tied up, determine how many boxes should be ordered and how often if the following price breaks are given.

Boxes	Price per Box
1	$4.25
2	$4.15
3	$4.05
4	$3.95
5	$3.85

$Q = $ _____

$ATC = $ _____

3. (10 points) For the Durham Signs case (page 51), what would be the economic order quantity for 4 × 8's if you allowed shortages, and the cost for a shortage is $C_s = \$1.7355$ per sheet per year? *Hint*: You could use the answer for no shortages rather than start from scratch. Assume that the 4 × 8's come from the suppliers; do *not* find the amount short S.

$Q = $ _____

4. (10 points) Determine the ATC for the Datsun case (page 61) if $Q = 20$ and $S = 10$. How does it compare with the current answer?

New ATC = _____

Old ATC = _____

5. (15 points) Assume the following demand for Boston ferns at Nurseryland for the first six months of the year. If it costs $10.00 to order the ferns, each fern costs $5.00, and the cost of carrying a fern is $0.02 per fern per month, determine how many ferns Nurseryland should order for their first order and the average total cost (ATC).

Month	1	2	3	4	5	6
Demand	25	50	30	45	100	75

$Q =$ _____

ATC = _____

6. (10 points)
    a. Explain why the algorithms for unequal demand and replacement are Quick & Dirty rather than Quick & Clean.

b. Why would it be better to order for 12 months in the CPA Firm case (pages 66–67) than for 8 months? What are the two ATCs (per month)?

7. (10 points) What would the discount price for the Kinney's Shoe case (page 70) be if the turnover of the good shoes (suede wallabys) were twice as much as the problem originally states?

8. (5 points) Give two examples of items that you would *not* discount even though they were selling slowly, and *why* you would not discount them (do not include fair trade items).

   a. _____

   b. _____

9. (15 points) A middle-aged professor has decided to buy a 1973 Honda 350 motorcycle. It cost him $500.00 by the time he bought a windshield, new tire, and helmet. He estimates the following costs for resale, operating, and so forth. Determine when he should sell the motorcycle (go for at least three quarters) and the lowest ATC. Is the answer any different if in the first year the mileage for each quarter is 1000, 800, 600, and 500, then it is 500 miles each quarter thereafter, and the average is computed as cost per mile?

Quarter	Purchase Price	Trade-in Value	Replacement Cost	Repair Cost	Total Repair Cost	Total Expense	Average Cost
1	$500	$450		$20			
2	500	400		30			
3	500	380		35			
4	500	370		40			
5	500	350		50			
6	500	325		60			
7	500	300		65			
8	500	275		70			

Review 2: Open book and notes; show all work, and write legibly

1. (10 points) Consider the Surfboard Blanks case (page 161).
   a. What is the yearly savings achieved by allowing shortages versus the original way of ordering 1000 boards without shortages?

   b. If you were still to order 1000 boards according to the old policy but allowed 400 to be short, would you save money compared to the old policy? Show your work.

2. (10 points) A contractor requires about 50 pounds of 8d finishing nails every three months. He doesn't like to tie up money in items not used for long periods of time since the cost of a loan is 11 percent per year, so he usually buys one-pound boxes when he goes to the store (which usually takes about half an hour). His salary is $10 per hour. Given the following prices, which quantity should he order? (Compute everything in terms of years.)

Quantity	Total Price
1-lb box	$1.62/lb
5-lb box	$7.50/5 lbs
50-lb barrel	$68.50/barrel

3. (10 points) A water-skiing fanatic bought a boat and motor for $5600 and obtained an estimate of the cost of upkeep. She would like to know when she should sell or trade in her boat at the lowest average total cost. Show your work.

Year	Purchase Price	Trade-in Value	Operating Expense
1	$5600	$4000	$1000
2	5700	3400	1200
3	5900	2800	1300
4	5900	1600	1500
5	6200	1300	1700
6	6300	1000	1800
7	6500	700	2000

4. (10 points) A music store has some guitars it ordered from Hong Kong that sell for $75.00 with a profit margin on cost of 65 percent. They are not selling as well as a similar Japanese model that usually turns over at a rate of two per month. At the rate the Hong Kong guitars are going, it will take five years to sell the dozen that are remaining. At what price should the store discount these guitars?

5. (10 points) At Jim's Widget Shop it costs Jim $16.00 to pick up a load of widgets in Denver. Jim pays $7.00 per widget and figures his cost of money invested at 15 percent per year. There is a constant demand of 125 widgets per month. The cost of insurance for widgets is $0.25 per widget per year and should be included in the carrying cost. Determine the number of widgets to order, how often they should be ordered, and the average total cost.

$Q =$ _____

$T =$ _____

$ATC =$ _____

6. (10 points)
   a. Explain the imputed cost of ordering of $125.00 in Marv's Enco Station case (page 76), in terms of average fixed and average variable costs in light of Marv's original policy.

   b. How would you explain the new ordering policy to Marv in light of $C_o = \$125.00$?

7. (10 points) Brenda's Bakery specializes in fruit cake during the holidays and has estimated orders for the six days prior to Christmas as 30, 45, 85, 100, 120, and 90. It costs $150 to fire up the ovens and make a batch of fruit cakes (regardless of the size of the order) and only about $0.15 per cake per day to store them in the refrigeration unit. Determine the batch size that should be made for the first batch and the ATC.

$Q = $ _____

$ATC = $ _____

8. (10 points) Given the Durham Signs case, how many of the 4 × 10's would Mr. McConnell order if he had unlimited capacity in his truck? How much would he save over the current recommendation?

9. (10 points) Monty's Den advertises a submarine sandwich special at prices as follows: 5 centimeters thick = 50¢, 7½ centimeters = 70¢, and 10 centimeters = 90¢.
   a. Determine the fixed and variable costs.

Fixed cost: _____

Variable cost: _____

   b. Give one reasonable explanation for what each of these costs might represent in the above case.

Fixed cost: _____

Variable cost: _____

10. (10 points) In the Sanitation Department case (page 73) the Department could have bought a repair policy which would have cost $6000 for the first year and $200(each year for the next three years (total of four years), with an option to renew the contract thereafter on the same terms. How does this change your recommendation? (Check years 1966, 1967, 1968, 1969, and 1973.)

Year	Yearly Operating Expense
1966	$6000
1967	$2000
1968	$2000
1969	$2000
1973	$2000

3.10 REFERENCES

1. J. A. Orlicky, *Material Requirements Planning* (New York: McGraw-Hill, 1975).
2. O. W. Wight, *Production and Inventory Management in the Computer Age* (Boston: Cahners Publishing, 1974).
3. G. W. Plossl, *Manufacturing Control* (Reston, Va.: Reston Publishing, 1973).
4. M. W. Sasieni, A. Yaspan, and L. Friedman, *Operations Research—Methods and Problems* (New York: Wiley, 1959). Economic order quantity algorithms, pp. 71–74; Inventory with shortage algorithms, pp. 75–80; Replacement algorithm, pp. 102–105.
5. G. Hadley and T. M. Whitin, *Analysis of Inventory Systems* (Englewood Cliffs, N.J.: Prentice-Hall, 1963), pp. 66–68.
6. E. A. Silver and H. C. Meal, "In Defense of 'A Simple Modification of the EOQ for the Case of Varying Demand Rate.'" Working paper 62, Dept. of Management Sciences, University of Waterloo, Waterloo, Ont., Canada, Jan. 1972.
7. G. Levary, "A Pocket-Sized Case Study in Operations Research Concerning Inventory Markdown," *Operations Research,* vol. 4, Dec. 1956, pp. 738–740.

4
networks

INTRODUCTION

A network consists of a series of nodes (circles) and branches or arcs (lines), as shown in Figure 4.1.[1]

The nodes may represent intersections of roads, work stations in a business, pumping stations for water, oil wells, logging centers, houses in a subdivision, sprinkler heads in a lawn, or junction boxes in electrical layout.

The branches may represent highways, runways, roads at a logging camp, electrical wires, water, gas, or oil lines, sewer lines, or work flow between work stations.

Thus to take one of the above examples, the network of Figure 4.1 may be a graphical representation of a forest with the nodes being logging centers where logs are cut and loaded on to trucks. The branches would represent the possible roads to those centers. In this chapter we will work with several problems resulting from this situation, where we might want to minimize the total amount of road to hook up all the logging centers (minimal spanning tree), or find the shortest route from the main center A to all the others. Again, we might be interested in visiting all the logging centers and returning back to A (traveling salesman). The numbers on the branches may represent distance, time, or expense between nodes. We will find in this chapter that many real-world problems arise as network representations.

Networks are very handy ways to visualize several problems in operations research, and with a minimal amount of work you should be able to find Quick & Dirty solutions to problems involving routing, flow, or scheduling. For several of the cases the original problem will be laid out, and then the resulting network diagram given. Thus you will be able to see how the problem was derived and, hopefully, you will then recognize the problem in its natural state in the real world.

Again, you should be cautioned that obtaining data for these problems is extremely difficult at times, or even if easily obtained, the data may not be exactly accurate. Remember that dirty data can turn a Quick & Clean algorithm into a Quick & Dirty one.

4.1 MINIMAL SPANNING TREE

The logging problem just mentioned can serve as a good example of the minimal spanning tree problem. We would like to connect all logging centers to each other by the minimum amount of roads (distance or expense). In network terms we want to find the set of

Figure 4.1

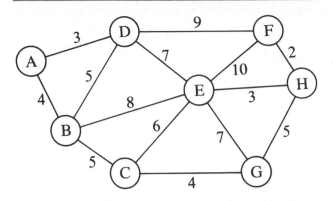

Figure 4.2

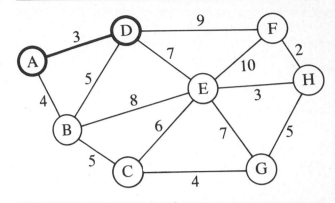

branches that will connect every node, and this is called a *span*, or *spanning the network*. When we have such a solution it looks like a *tree*, hence the name *minimal spanning tree*. In the logging case it may be that we are not so much interested in the shortest distance from each logging center to the highway (let's assume node H), because the cost of building the roads that will hold the heavy and long logging trucks is the major expense, and it won't hurt if the drivers have to drive a few extra miles as long as the total road network is a minimum (thus minimizing the major costs).

Another example might be laying sewer lines for a new housing division. What the city is concerned with (and the taxpayer) is the minimum amount of sewer lines to be installed, and not whether each individual house has the shortest sewer line to the main. The following algorithm is the simplest of the network algorithms that we will learn and will be the base for several others that follow.

Quick & Clean Algorithm: Minimal Spanning Tree[1]

1. To begin with, select *any* node in a network and circle it. Right now there are no connected nodes.
2. Find the nearest unconnected node to the circled node. Circle it and connect the branch between the two nodes.
3. Repeat step 2 until all nodes are circled and connected.

Example. Given the network of Figure 4.1, let us arbitrarily pick node D to begin with. We circle node D and then look for the nodes that are near node D. There are no connections yet, all the branches simply indicate possible connections. The unconnected nodes near D are A – 3 units, B – 5 units, E – 7 units, F – 9 units. The nearest node to D is node A. Circle it and connect it (Figure 4.2).

Now the unconnected nodes near A and D are B–A 4 units, B–D 5 units, E–D 7 units, and F–D 9 units. The nearest is the connection from B to A. Circle it and connect B to A (Figure 4.3).

Figure 4.3

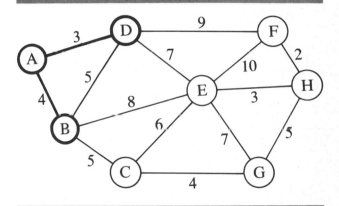

Now the unconnected nodes near A, B, and D are C–B 5 units, E–B 8 units, E–D 7 units, and F–D 9 units. (Notice that B to D does not count, since both nodes B and D have already been connected by other branches.) The nearest node is C. Circle it and connect it to B (Figure 4.4).

Figure 4.4

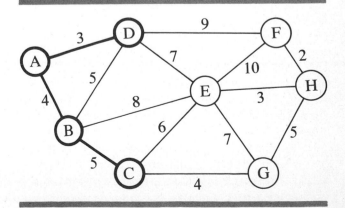

Completing the algorithm we get the minimal spanning tree shown in Figure 4.5. The total span is A–D 3 units, A–B 4 units, B–C 5 units, C–G 4 units, G–H 5 units, H–F 2 units, and E–H 3 units, which makes 26 units to span (connect) all the nodes. There is no other set of connecting branches that would connect all the nodes for less.

Figure 4.5

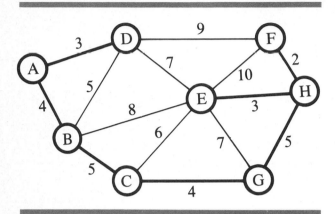

Notice the following points:

1. The spanning tree does *not* form a circuit (closed loop).
2. It does *not* necessarily form a single path (it splits at node H which has three branches from it, hence the name *tree*).
3. *Not* every possible connection or branch is used. Only those branches are used which will give the smallest total distance (or cost).

This is also known as the *greedy algorithm*, that is, you may be as greedy as you wish (we try to find the smallest connection each time), and the solution will be optimal. At every stage we are looking for the cheapest connection. Also we may have started at any node and come up with the same spanning tree.

southwestern bank

Southwestern Bank is considering the direct hook-up of computer terminals at its branch offices to the main office. The computer terminals can be "hard-wired" or use special phone lines with telecommunication devices. Hard-wired terminals cannot be moved, but the main computer does not have to be dialed up. With special phone lines there is the inconvenience of dialing the main center and more distortion on the lines, but the terminals can be used wherever there is a phone.

The computer company will charge for the necessary wiring to hook up all the branches to the main office. The bank has decided to use the special phone lines (which have a charge per mile) because of the

convenience of portability (cost did not actually enter into the decision). These phone lines may be connected either to the main office directly or to any branch. Determine where the branches are connected and how much actual mileage of special lines is used (Figure 4.6).

Figure 4.6

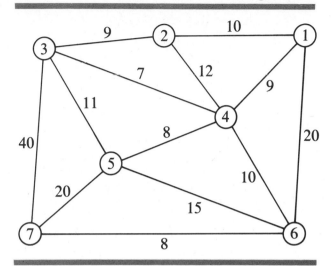

Solution

Recommendation

The following connections should be made to minimize the number of miles of connection (51 miles):

Main office to Wilshire	9
Main office to Westchester	7
Main office to Torrance	8
Main office to Santa Ana	10
Westchester to West Los Angeles	9
Anaheim to Santa Ana	8

Numerical Answer: total mileage = 9 + 7 + 8 + 10 + 9 + 8 = 51 miles.

Math Work. The results obtained by using the minimal spanning tree algorithm are given in Figure 4.7.

fort lauderdale country club

The Fort Lauderdale Country Club was faced with the problem of relocating three fairways on its golf course and thus of having to excavate ditches for the automatic sprinkling system. Since the cost of excavating ditches and laying pipe can get to be expensive, they were interested in determining where the pipe should be placed. They accepted the bid of an engineer to do the layout for $500.00.

In the meantime, an enterprising young OR student (who was working at the club) happened to see the blueprints and inquired about the problem. He

Figure 4.7

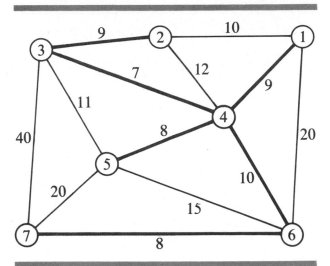

convinced the management that he could come back the next morning with the solution and it would cost them only $300.00. The next morning he produced the optimal solution (which also saved $350 in labor and materials per fairway) and more than paid for the price of his tuition for the course in OR.

The following restrictions had to be observed:

1. No more than six sprinklers per line from the main. (This is for best water pressure.)
2. No lines can pass under trees, sand traps, or greens.
3. Only one line per water-main connection.
4. Connectors from the water main to the sprinkler heads must be made directly to the sprinkler head. (The same holds true of connections between sprinklers.) Thus it is not allowed to connect water lines in the middle; there must always be a sprinkler head.

Given the possible water-line connections on the map in Figure 4.8, determine the minimum length of pipe that is needed while observing the above restrictions.

circuit-board analysis

In the early 1950s, transistors revolutionized the electronics industry. Miniaturized electronic components were now possible, and circuits that formerly measured cubic feet in volume were reduced to frac-

Figure 4.8

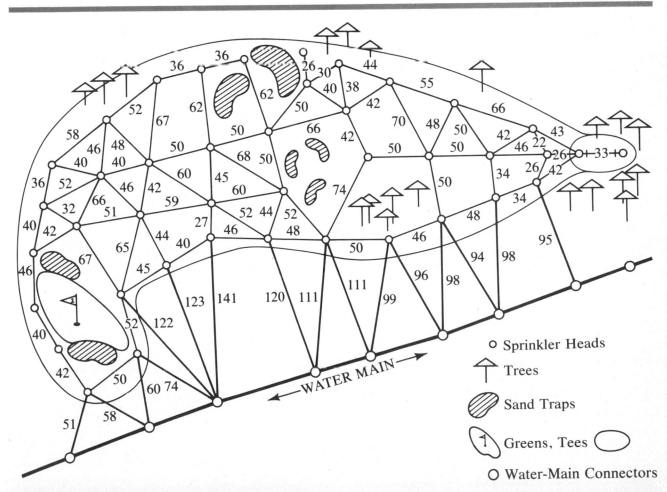

Figure 4.9

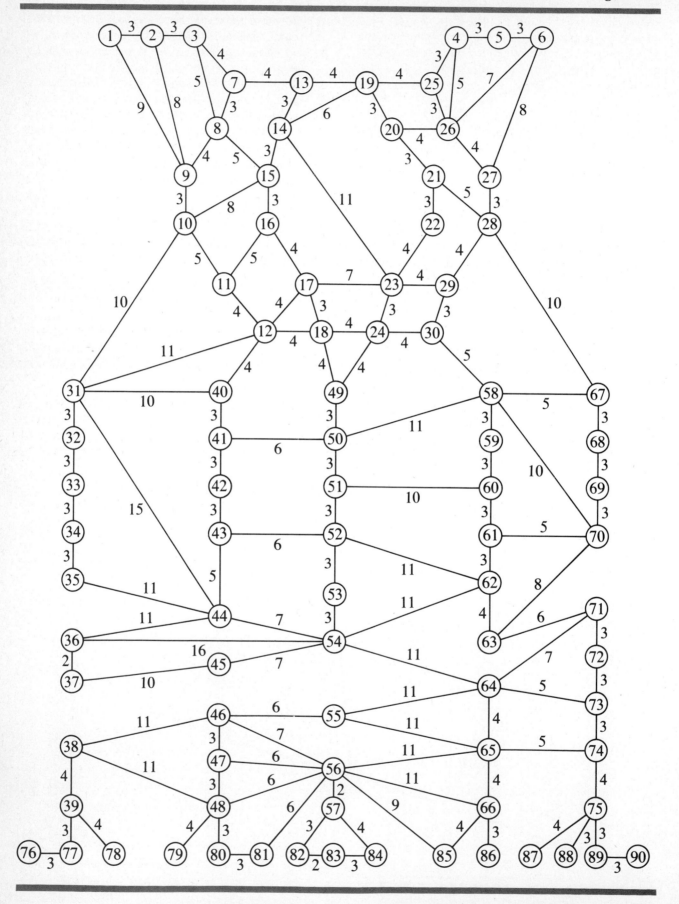

tions of cubic inches. This new solid logic technology provided some interesting problems from many standpoints. Numerically controlled machinery was now able to mass-produce circuits that before had to be hand-wired. Small computers were developed to test a large number of differing circuits in a matter of minutes that formerly took a technician days to check out.

The normal practice was to take standard boards (in this case 90 holes) and lay out different circuits on each one. In some cases all the holes might be used, in others only a subset might be used. Of course, for all these holes there must be circuit connections (usually a thin strip of copper or gold etched onto the board). It is important from a standpoint of electrical resistance to have as little length of connecting copper or gold as possible. Given the layout of a typical 90-hole board (Figure 4.9), determine which paths should be used to minimize the total distance (in units).

---

community college district

A local Community College offers many services to its student body, such as Adult Career Guidance,

Testing Centers, Financial Assistance, and so forth. In the past these services have been located in several different offices. Recently, however, the district leased a building to consolidate these services and reduce costs.

The existing air-conditioning system is adequate for the space it has to cool, but since several partitions have been constructed to create offices and testing rooms, there is poor ventilation. To solve the problem, the district intends to add ventilation pipes to the existing air-conditioning system, piping air to the offices and testing rooms.

Figure 4.10 shows the floorplan and locations of the vents. Additionally, the following information and stipulations are provided.

1. No more than three pipes may come from any one air source.

2. No more than ten air vents may be connected to any one air source.

3. The required pipe costs $1.50 per foot.

Find the minimum amount of pipe that will be needed to do the job and how much it will cost.

Figure 4.10

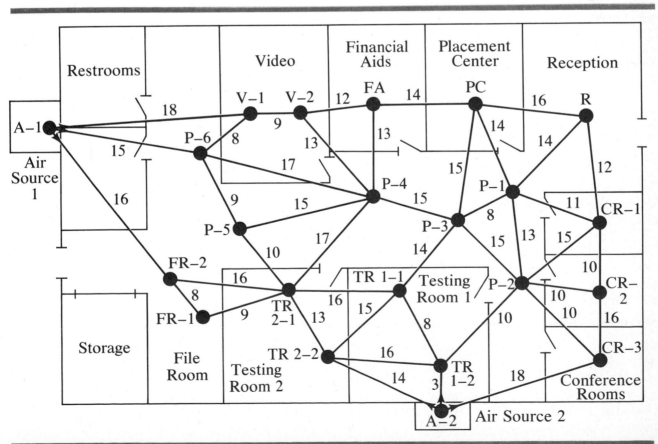

INCIDENT: LIGHTNING STRIKES ONCE

A large oil company in Texas was required to monitor the output of its wells. In order to do that, it was necessary to connect telemetry cables to meters at every well. The company considered the idea of stringing the cables on telephone-type poles to the control monitoring location. However, not even Lloyd's of London would insure them. (There seems to be some risk in connecting oil and gas wells with above-ground wires in an area of frequent lightning storms.) Therefore the lines had to be put underground (at $1 per yard), and it was important that the company determine the minimal spanning tree. The area covered 300 square miles. The company gave out bids for the job, and some were as high as $20,000, complete with a large computer rented for the occasion. An executive of the company was bemoaning his problems at an OR conference, and over a few drinks was shown by a well-known consultant in the field how easily the problem could be solved. The consultant earned $50 for his drink (the algorithm was executed on a cocktail napkin), and the company saved thousands of dollars.

the cortez mining and milling corporation

In the fall of 1971 an antipollution bill was passed by the Congress of the United States. The essence of the bill was simply the prohibition of any industry, large or small, foreign or domestic, located within the boundaries of the United States or its territories, from discharging any type of untreated waste materials into either the atmosphere or the waterways of the United States or its territories.

The industries that violated this new bill were given 12 months to comply, after which time, if antipollution devices were not installed, a court injunction would be filed against said industry and their operations halted until such devices were installed. Adequate funds would be allocated to each industry according to the size of the company and the amount of waste discharged into the environment. This made it impossible for each industry not to comply without penalty.

Out of the thousands of industries affected by this new law, one in particular, the Cortez Mining and Milling Corporation, sums up the actions taken by 90 percent of those industries involved. Upon receiving the notice to comply and the amount of allocation, sealed bids were solicited from construction firms for the construction of a treatment plant.

For years the mining and milling wastes, which consisted of sulfuric acid and other harmful liquids, had been disposed, untreated, into a nearby river. The operation consisted of seven independently operated mines and one milling plant. (Its function was to form concentrates of the valuable minerals, which reduced shipping costs.) Since a large profit was being shown from this operation, a treatment plant became necessary if operations were to be continued.

After all the bids were submitted, the company that came closest without going over the allocation was notified and given just one command: Build a treatment plant in 12 months! The construction company then called upon its chief OR analyst, giving him just one order: minimize costs. Three problems existed:

1. where to build the plant,
2. minimal paths from the mines and mill to the plant,
3. size of the pipe to be used from the mines and mill to the plant.

The following data was made available in order that a more accurate solution could be obtained:

Pipe	Cost	Capacity
20 in.	$0.50/ft	5 ton/hr
30 in.	$1.00/ft	10 ton/hr
50 in.	$1.50/ft	20 ton/hr

Each mine produces 3 tons of waste per hour, and the mill produces 11 tons of waste per hour. The total budget is $750,000.

In the problem of locating the plant, an infinite number of solutions are possible. However, since cost is a major factor, the problem is reduced down to two possibilities. Both occur along the river bed since any other location would produce an extra cost of obtaining access to the location (such as roads, bridges, tunnels, and so on). The two possible locations are given in Figures 4.11 and 4.12. Distances from the various mines are in miles. It is important to note that a 20-inch pipe cannot take the flow from two mines; thus a 30-inch pipe must be used, which increases costs. Therefore, although the minimal spanning tree algorithm may be used, one must be very careful.

INCIDENT: HOUSEHOLD HINT

A small building contractor decided to rewire his house. Showing the plans to his cousin, a bright young OR student, his cousin bragged that she could save him some money on the amount of wire to be used. Given the plans and an evening to work on

Figure 4.11

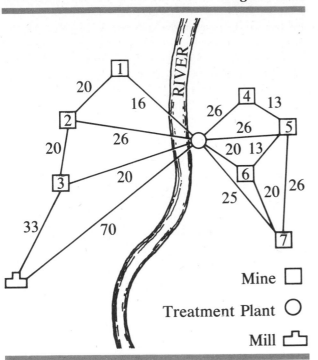

Figure 4.12

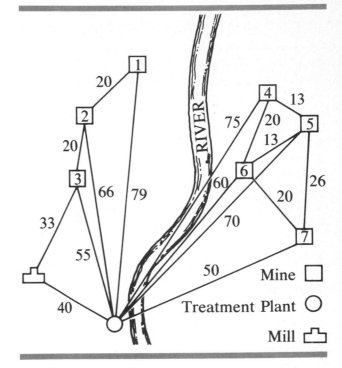

them, the student promptly used the minimal spanning tree algorithm and came up with 100 feet of wire less. Her cousin, not a big believer in anything mathematical, was amazed. Then to compound his amazement, the student showed the contractor how he could apply the technique himself. The contractor then used the technique for the plumbing and saved approximately $200 on both the plumbing and the wiring.

Supplementary Problems

1. Miss Westridge is having her 15-room mansion wired for an intercom system. Given the distance

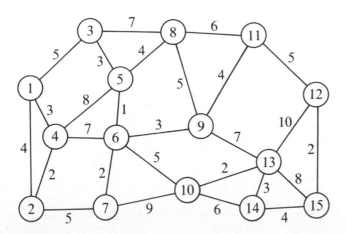

between rooms in the diagram at the bottom of column 1, determine the least amount of wire needed to connect every room.

2. Refer to the Cortez Mining and Milling case and the site shown in Figure 4.11.
   a. What is the cost of the solution at site A?
   b. If the cost for 50 inch pipe is only $1.25, what is the revised cost?
   c. How would the solution change (which connections) if all the pipe cost the same per foot regardless of the diameter of the pipe?

3. Explain why and how the minimal spanning tree algorithm must be changed to solve the Fort Lauderdale Country Club case.

4. Lawrence of Arabia would like to unite all the Arab villages and towns in the Northern African desert by building roads. Given the map below, determine the least number of miles of roads needed to connect all the towns and villages.

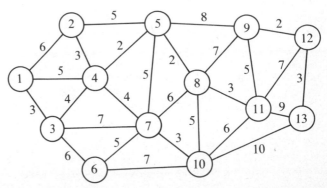

4.2 SHORTEST ROUTE

The problem of trying to get from point A to point B in the shortest amount of time, distance, or money is called the *shortest route* problem. There may be many ways to get from point A to point B, which would be advantageous for companies involved with deliveries to customers. (It is surprising how many truck drivers, uneducated in matrix algebra, can usually determine the shortest route to somewhere much quicker than an OR genius.) This problem especially occurs when only one delivery per run can be made. When other stops are included in the run, the problem becomes more difficult, and other techniques (shown later) must be used.

Returning to the logging problem in the previous section (Figure 4.1), we now might be interested in the shortest route from the main logging center A to all the others, or from A to H. In this case the branches would represent roads already constructed and thus would be possible routes. Thus we would now like to minimize the distance, time, or money it takes to travel from the starting node to any or all others. Certain simple changes in the minimal spanning tree algorithm will be required for our next algorithm.

Quick & Clean Algorithm: Shortest Route[2]

1. Start with the *first* node (the one from which you want to find the shortest route) and find the closest unconnected node to the origin. Circle the node, connect it, and write the distance to the origin above that node.
2. Find the next nearest node to the origin (either directly or next to circled nodes). Circle it, connect it, and write the distance to the origin above it.
3. Repeat until all nodes are circled and connected and you have the distance above each node.

Figure 4.13

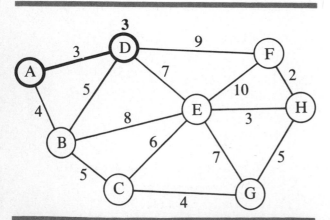

Example. Let us use the same network as in the minimal-spanning-tree example (Figure 4.1). The starting node is A and the nearest node to A (the origin) is node D (3 units away). The node is circled, connected to A, and the distance from D back to the origin (3) is written above the node (Figure 4.13).

The next nearest node to A is node B (4 units away). The node is circled, connected to A, and the distance from B back to the origin (4) is written above the node (Figure 4.14).

Figure 4.14

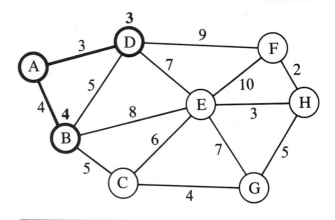

The next nearest node to the origin is node C, 9 units away (5 units from B which is 4 units from A). The node is circled, connected to B, and the distance of 9 is written above the node (Figure 4.15).

Figure 4.15

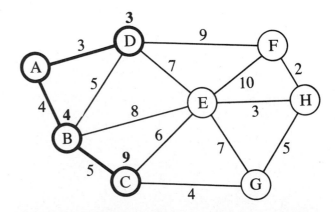

The final network looks as shown in Figure 4.16 and gives the paths and distances from A to every node. Thus the shortest route from A to E would be A–D–E and would be 10 units. The shortest route from A to F would be A–D–F and would be 12 units. This method gives all the shortest routes from A to every other node. Notice that at any time in the algorithm you always have the shortest route from the circled nodes back to the origin.

Figure 4.16

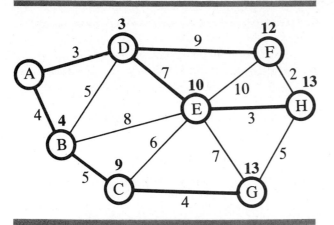

overland moving and storage company

The Overland Moving and Storage Company is located in Denver, Colorado. For years this company has been in the business of transporting or moving any equipment or items to any destination in the continental United States. Overland has just received a request from a customer who wants to move her household articles and furniture from Denver to Cleveland, Ohio.

Over the past couple of months Overland has been losing much of its profit to the increasing costs of excessive mileage traveled by its truck drivers and the extra time it takes to travel these longer routes. Because of these increasing costs, the company needs to determine the shortest route (in miles) from Denver to Cleveland. All possible routes are inter-

state highways with the exception of Chicago to Cleveland, which is a toll road. Speed limits are the same on all roads, and most factors are about equal. Thus what is needed is to determine the shortest route from Denver to Cleveland (Figure 4.17).

Solution

Recommendation
The shortest route from Denver to Cleveland is 1390 miles. It goes from Denver via Omaha to Des Moines, Chicago, and straight on to Cleveland. It is assumed that the toll is not a significant part of the cost involved in moving from Denver to Cleveland.

Route	Distance
Denver – Omaha	551
Omaha – Des Moines	137
Des Moines – Chicago	354
Chicago – Cleveland	348
	1390

Math Work. The network in Figure 4.18 (page 98) shows all the shortest distances from Denver.

INCIDENT: SIMPLE THINGS FIRST

A public utilities gas company in the south needed a map of all the shortest routes from the utility office to different sections of town. A computerized solution was going to be used (costing $2000) until an employee suggested the Quick & Dirty.

Figure 4.17

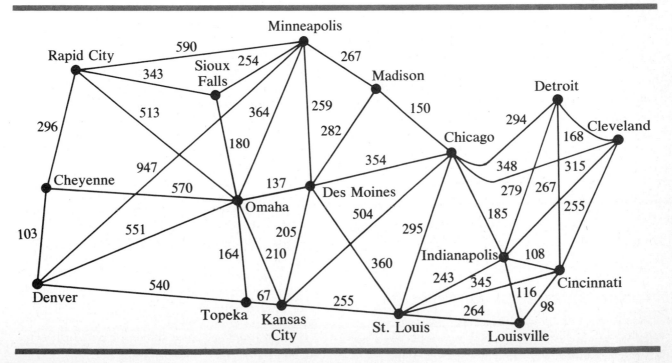

Figure 4.18

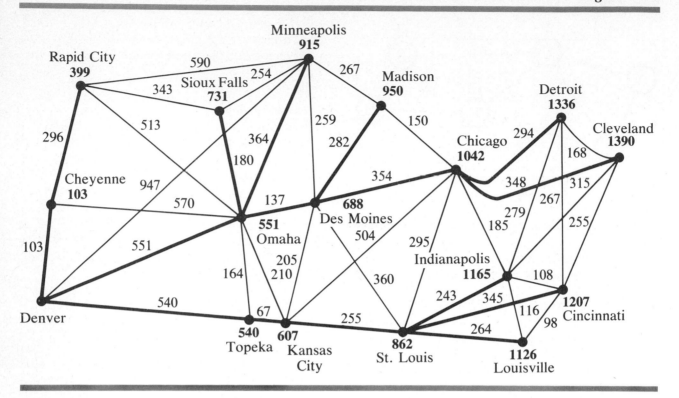

legal abstract firm

A Casper, Wyoming-based firm prepares legal abstracts. The preparation requires photostats of documents found in county government offices scattered throughout the county seats of the state.

The Wyoming highway system and population distribution being rough realities of the state's geography, automative expenses per mile, as well as food and lodging expenses per day for the driver/photographer and assistant remain within certain fixed limits throughout the state.

The owners of the legal abstracting firm wish to maximize the amount of information and minimize the cost per trip. Photographic work in any county seat can almost always be completed in one day or less, but no better estimate of work time can be given until the work has begun. Both maximization of information and minimization of cost can be achieved by minimizing the distance traveled.

Assuming that all county seats are visited frequently, the problem is one of finding the minimum distance from Casper to all the other county seats (Figure 4.19).

INCIDENT: TIME VERSUS DISTANCE

A professor in Colorado Springs wanted to know the shortest route from her house to the campus where she taught (approximately 45 minutes away). In laying out the map, times between points were used rather than distances. It also made a great difference at what time of the day she would leave the house for the campus. During rush hour, the time to go from point A to B could be significantly different from the time to go from point B to A. Thus the problem was not symmetrical as it was in the example.

brookside winery, southern area

The Brookside Winery is headquartered in Guasti, California, and has 16 tasting rooms located in Southern California. It is a family-owned and operated winery and sells directly from the tasting rooms. The company does not sell or distribute its wine to wholesalers, so that the tasting rooms are the only sales outlet. They are located at strategic spots along major highways to attract travelers and local residents to stop and participate in the free tasting programs, which usually consist of sampling 10 to 12 of Brookside's wines. Red wines, white wines, and fruit wines are its major items, but bread, cheese, glasses, and other sundry items are available also.

The Brookside Winery is interested in the shortest route from Bonita (near San Diego and its southernmost wine tasting room) to Ventura, just north of Los Angeles.

Figure 4.20 (page 100) shows a map of the 16 wine tasting rooms that Brookside has in Southern Cali-

Figure 4.19

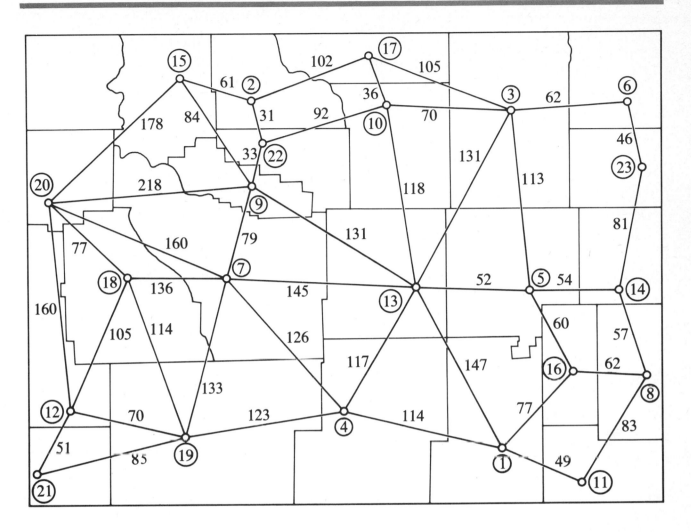

	County	County Seat		County	County Seat		County	County Seat
1.	Albany	Laramie	9.	Hot Springs	Thermopolis	17.	Sheridan	Sheridan
2.	Big Horn	Basin	10.	Johnson	Buffalo	18.	Sublette	Pinedale
3.	Campbell	Gillette	11.	Laramie	Cheyenne	19.	Sweetwater	Green River
4.	Carbon	Rawlins	12.	Lincoln	Kimmerer	20.	Teton	Jackson
5.	Converse	Douglas	13.	Natrona	Casper	21.	Uinta	Evanston
6.	Crook	Sundance	14.	Niodrara	Lusk	22.	Washakie	Worland
7.	Fremont	Lander	15.	Park	Cody	23.	Weston	Newcastle
8.	Goshen	Torrington	16.	Platte	Wheatland			

fornia and the distances between them. Assume that the problem is symmetrical, that is, that it is the same distance from point A to point B as from point B to point A.

INCIDENT: MAPPING IT OUT

A nursery chain in Minneapolis makes deliveries once a week from its main store to its other five branch stores. Each branch store requires at least half a truck load of plants, fertilizers, and so on, and therefore each delivery must be made from the main store to the branch store and back. Thus a shortest route algorithm was used to find the shortest route from the main store to all the others. This was done on a map with a felt-tip marker, plastered to the dashboard of the truck, and used by the driver.

circuit-board analysis

In the early 1950s, transistors revolutionized the electronics industry. Miniaturized electronic components were now possible, and circuits that formerly

Figure 4.20

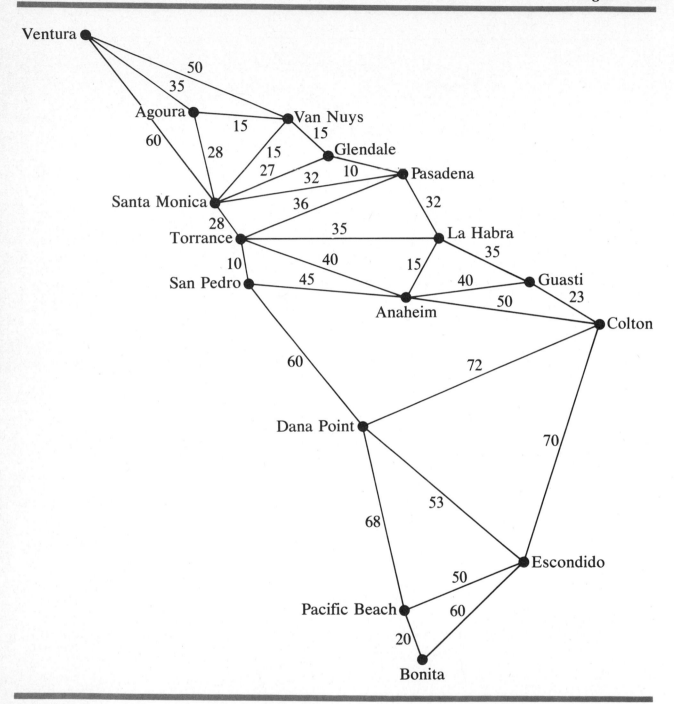

measured cubic feet in volume were reduced to fractions of cubic inches. This new solid logic technology provided some interesting problems from many standpoints. Numerically controlled machinery was now able to mass-produce circuits that before had to be hand-wired. Small computers were developed to test a large number of differing circuits in a matter of minutes that formerly took a technician days to check.

The normal practice was to take standard boards (in this case 90 holes) and lay out different circuits on each one. In some cases all the holes might be used; in others only a subset might be used. Of course, for all these holes there must be circuit connections (usually a thin strip of copper or gold etched onto the board). It is important from a standpoint of electrical resistance to have as little length of connecting copper or gold as possible. Given the layout of a typical 90-hole board (Figure 4.21), determine the shortest path from hole 1 to hole 90.

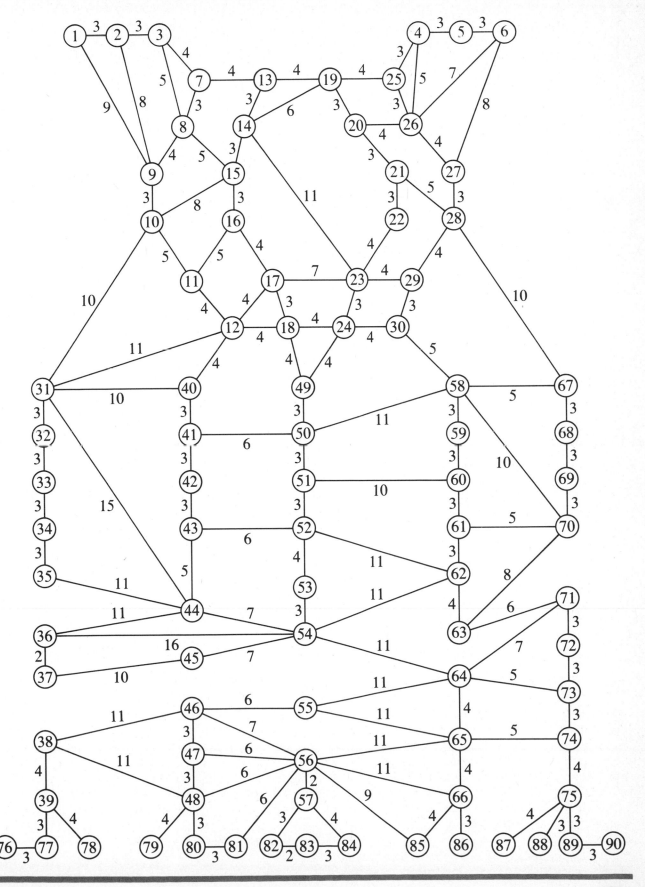

Figure 4.21

Supplementary Problems

1. A forest ranger has the task of finding the shortest route from the fire fighters' headquarters to major areas where fires could break out. Given the map at the bottom of the page, find the shortest route to all areas.

2. Domino's Pizza is drawing a lot of business from campus because they deliver. They need to know the shortest route to *each* of the locations below.

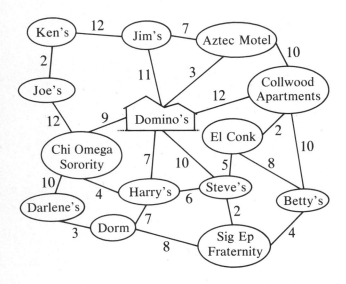

3. Refer to the Legal Abstracts Firm case and find the shortest route and distance between the following towns:
   a. from Rawlins to Kimmerer.
   b. from Torrington to Casper.
   c. from Casper to Basin.

4.3 TRAVELING SALESMAN

This problem has been one of the most interesting for operations researchers to work on because it is so simple to state and so very difficult to solve. For that reason there have been many Quick & Dirty algorithms, which have had varying degrees of effectiveness. Simply stated, the traveling salesman problem requires finding the minimum cost or length or time path that goes to each city once and only once and returns to the original city. To begin with, let us investigate some simple Quick & Dirty algorithms. The first makes use of the network layout and the important theorem that the optimal tour will never intersect itself on a map drawn to scale (Figure 4.22). Again we see that this network problem bears some similarity to the previous sections, except for the requirement that we want to stop at each possible location once and only once and end back where we started. This might be for delivery trucks, a salesman's tour (hence the name), or a guard making rounds. Referring to our logging example, it might be that the supervisor must visit each center and return to A at a minimum distance.

Quick & Dirty Algorithm: Traveling Salesman—Part I[3]

Given a network of distances that are geometrically proportional, construct a tour that makes a complete loop, taking the shortest paths possible. There can be no intersections. An example is shown in Figure 4.23.

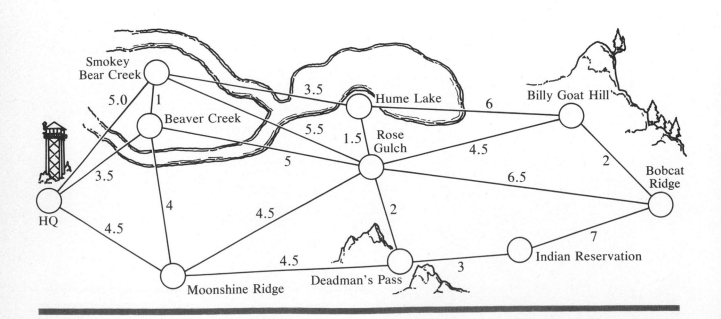

Figure 4.22

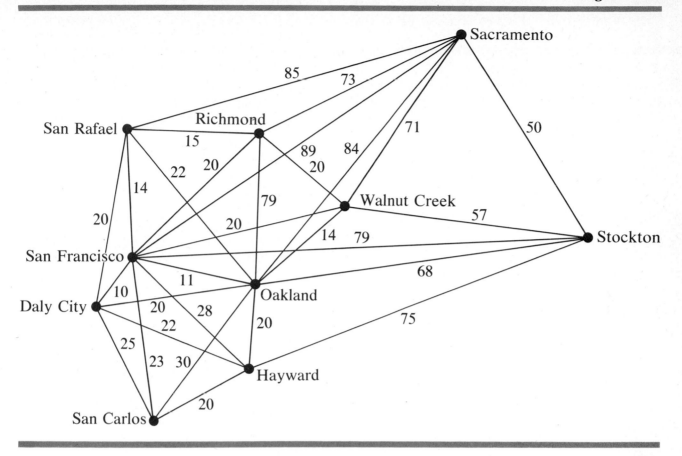

Figure 4.23

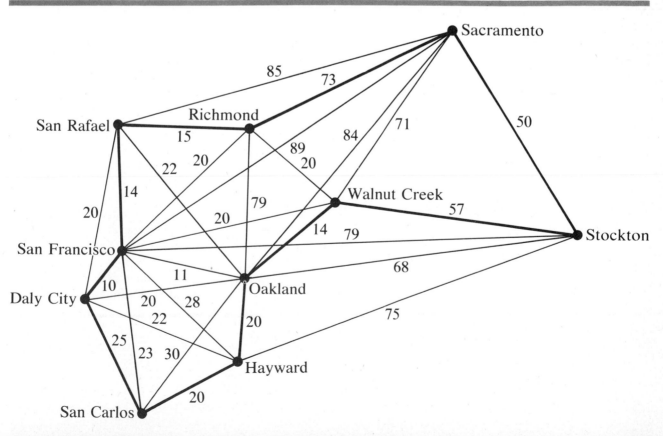

The second part of this algorithm involves larger problems and can be computerized. It was developed at Bell Laboratories while they were trying to solve very large traveling salesman problems (over 100 cities). The computer program makes many good approximations in a reasonable length of time and selects the best. To begin with, it will choose a random path (not necessarily free of intersecting branches), then it will remove three links (thus breaking it into three sections), and then it will connect the sections differently to see if a shorter tour develops. Our algorithm will be somewhat simpler. With networks having more alternate routes than the above problem it is possible to interchange some branches, which will yield a smaller tour by inspection.

Quick & Dirty Algorithm: Traveling Salesman—Part II[4]

1. Given a tour that does not intersect itself, remove any two links and reconnect differently if the new tour length is shorter.
2. Repeat until no further combinations are possible.

Example. Using a larger example than the tour from part I of the algorithm, in this tour the branches do not intersect with one another. The tour consists of connections A–B–C–D–E–F–G–H–I–J–K–L–M–N–O–A with a length of 111 (Figure 4.24).

Figure 4.24

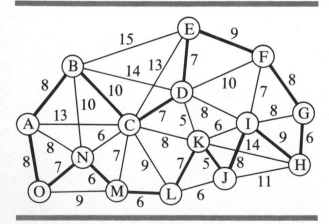

By inspection we see that branches I–J (8) and K–L (7) can be removed and replaced with branches I–K (6) and J–L (6), which gives an overall savings of 3 units for a tour of 108 (Figure 4.25).

Figure 4.25

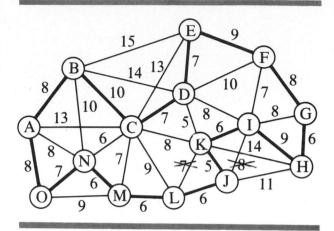

davis development company

The Davis Development Company operates the Onestop Gasoline Stations and Fastway Cleaners. By combining two dissimilar operations, Davis hopes to attract several types of customers for the same amount of fixed overhead. There are one manager and several part-time employees for each location, and both the gas station and the cleaner are in the same building. At the moment there are 9 outlets throughout the county. Davis purchases its gasoline supplies from a distributor located in University City, whose contract expires soon. Two other distributors have been invited to submit bids for next year's deliveries.

The current distributor wishes to minimize the transportation cost of delivering the gasoline to the 9 outlets in the county area. The distributor has stated that it costs them $3.35 per mile to make deliveries, and they estimate that there will be 26 routine and 3 nonroutine deliveries during the year (each delivery includes all 9 outlets). Thus they are interested in knowing the shortest distance from their office in University City to all 9 locations and return (Figure 4.26).

Determine the transportation costs to make one delivery so that a yearly estimate may be made. This will be used as a base for determining the cost of the bid.

Solution

Recommendation

At $3.35 per mile and 29 delivery trips, with each trip 142 miles, the total cost will be $13,795.30. The recommended route would be from the office in University City to Mountainside, Waycom, Belleview,

Figure 4.26

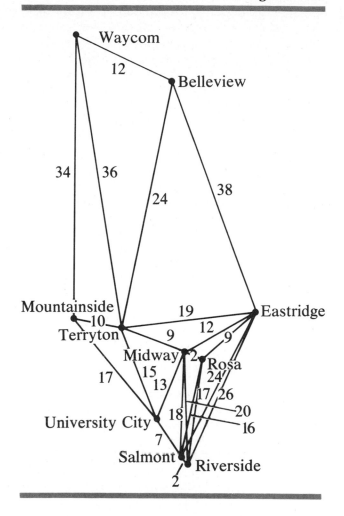

Figure 4.27

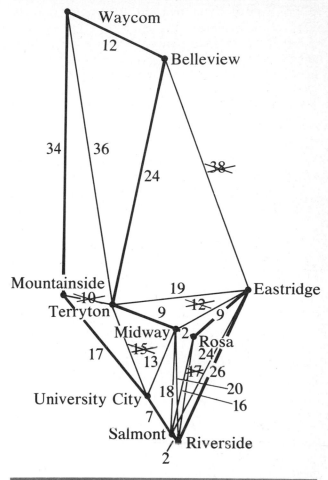

Terryton, Midway, Rosa, Eastridge, Riverside, and Salmont, then back to the University City office (Figure 4.27).

Numerical Answer. The route above covers a total distance of 142 miles, as follows:

distance = 17 + 34 + 17 + 24 + 9 + 2 + 9 + 26 + 2 + 7 = 142 mi

cost for one trip = 142 mi ($3.35/mi) = $475.70/trip

cost for year = 29 trips/yr ($475.70/trip) = $13,795.30/year.

Math Work. From part I of the algorithm the original route was University City to Terryton, Mountainside, Waycom, Belleview, Eastridge, Midway, Rosa, Riverside, and Salmont, back to the office in University City for a total distance of 149 miles.

From part II of the algorithm it can be seen that if we remove the leg University City to Terryton and go to Mountainside and then to Waycom on the one hand and, on the other hand, instead of going from

Belleview to Eastridge, we travel from Eastridge to Terryton and Midway and then add Rosa to Riverside, while not going from Eastridge to Riverside, we save 7 miles for the best route so far of 142 miles.

We thus removed links which equaled (15 + 10 + 38 + 12 + 17) = 92 miles and added links of (17 + 24 + 9 + 9 + 26) = 85 miles for savings of 7 miles.

southwestern bank

Southwestern Bank has its head office in the southwestern section of Los Angeles. It also maintains six branch banks that are located in the Wilshire district, West Los Angeles, Westchester, Torrance, Santa Ana, and Anaheim. There is a daily distribution of a computer printout that is delivered to each branch from the main office. This output shows a running daily balance for each customer of Southwestern

Bank. The bank has its own delivery service, but management has become unhappy with what it feels are excessive costs involved with the distribution system as it now works.

Given the mileage between cities (Figure 4.28), what recommendation would you make to the management of Southwestern Bank and why?

Figure 4.28

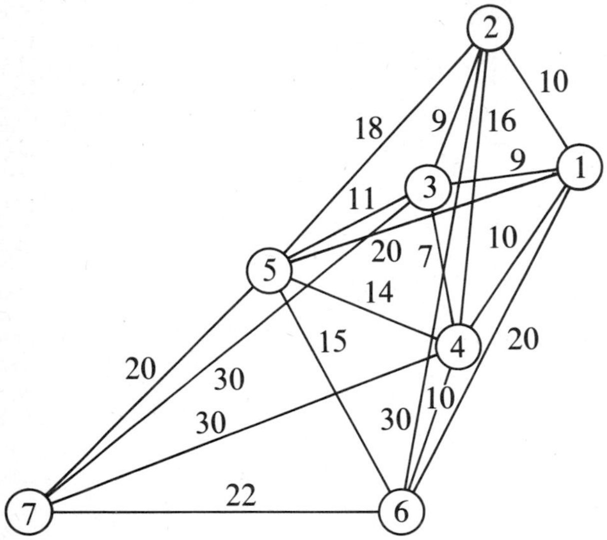

1. Wilshire
2. West Los Angeles
3. Westchester
4. Main Office
5. Torrance
6. Santa Ana
7. Anaheim

INCIDENT: CONTROLLING COSTS

A department chain store in the Minneapolis–St. Paul area has seven outlets, which must be visited once a week by the assistant controller for the purpose of delivering the paychecks. After leaving the main office, she must go to the bank, then visit all the outlets, and return to the main office. Thus the shortest circuit is desired, and rather than use fancy techniques that take forever to determine the answer, the assistant controller uses the Quick & Dirty method to find the shortest circuit.

porsche–audi dealers

A team of suppliers, engineers, and other specialists from the Porsche–Audi Corporation in Stuttgart, West Germany, and Englewood Cliffs, New Jersey,

will be visiting all Porsche–Audi dealers in the greater city area to provide parts and product briefings, technical assistance, counseling, and advice to sales and service personnel at each dealership. They will have several mobile vans of specialized equipment that must travel as a unit to each dealer. Therefore they are concerned with the most efficient method of visiting all Porsche–Audi dealers at the lowest expense, and the greatest expense seems to be in terms of gas mileage. Assume the speed between each dealer is the same.

The team must visit each dealer once, and the order of the visits is not critical, although they will return to the main dealer (11), from where they started, when the visits are over. Determine the shortest route to visit all dealers, assuming that the distances on the map in Figure 4.29 are accurate.

INCIDENT: BURGER ROUTE

Another case involves the vice president of a chain of family hamburger restaurants. In the Reno, Nevada, area there are 12 such outlets, and the minimum circuit must be determined for the weekly delivery of supplies. Since this method is Quick & Dirty, it is easy to show some savings that would result by rerouting the delivery system, thus saving money for the delivery of meat, buns, and so on. More importantly, it saves time for each of the outlets in that their deliveries can be made more quickly.

cable electronic company

Cable Electronic Company is an electronic parts manufacturer of cable television equipment. Cable maintains production facilities at Hoboken, New Jersey, and its distribution is spread throughout the United States, including a regional distributor in Torrance, California. The distributors are stocked with cable, cable fittings, power equipment, and amplifiers which are sold to cable systems within the distributors' regions.

The Torrance salesperson lives in Malibu, California, and is assigned to visit 25 cities once every week to see the clients. In the Los Angeles basin she is restricted to an average traveling speed of 25 miles per hour, which includes stopping times. The southeastern portion of her route includes several important customers who require more of her time. This causes her traveling speed to average out to only 20 miles per hour when in this area. The north and central areas of her route are relatively smaller

Figure 4.29

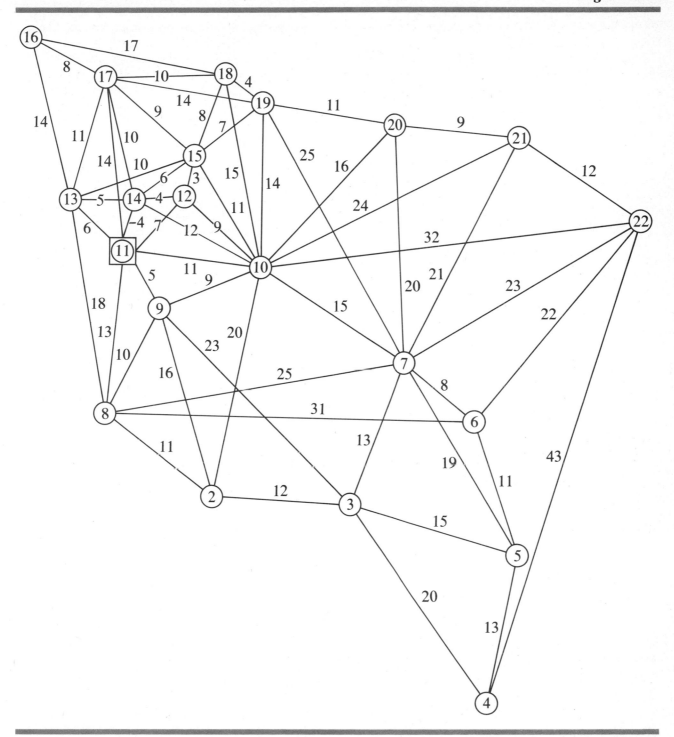

systems which in turn require less time, and she is able to average 28 miles per hour in these areas.

The Los Angeles region includes the following stops for the salesperson: Malibu, Santa Monica, Redondo Beach, Palos Verdes, Anaheim, Newport Beach, Oceanside, Escondido, San Diego, and El Cajon. While the last four are not in the basin geographically, they are considered as a part of this group of customers. The eastern area of the sales-

person's territory consists of Calexico, Yuma (Arizona), Blythe, Indio, Borrego Springs, Palm Springs, Twentynine Palms, and Riverside. The remaining cities are Hemet, Crestline, Big Bear, Hesperia, Apple Valley, Barstow, and Boron, which make up the north central area.

Determine from Figure 4.30 (page 108) the shortest distance tour that will allow the salesperson to visit every city once and only once.

Figure 4.30

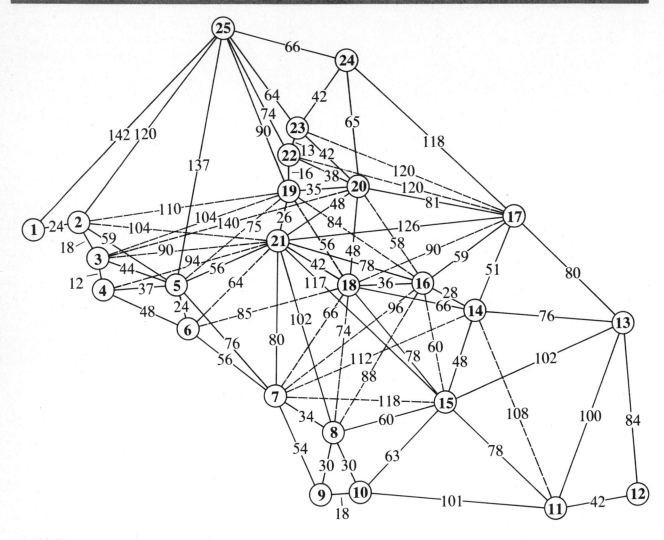

1. Malibu
2. Santa Monica
3. Redondo Beach
4. Palos Verdes
5. Anaheim
6. Newport Beach
7. Oceanside
8. Escondido
9. San Diego
10. El Cajon
11. Calexico
12. Yuma
13. Blythe
14. Indio
15. Borrego Springs
16. Palm Springs
17. Twentynine Palms
18. Hemet
19. Crestline
20. Big Bear
21. Riverside
22. Hesperia
23. Apple Valley
24. Barstow
25. Barton

Supplementary Problems

1. Find the minimum length traveling salesman tour for the network at the right.

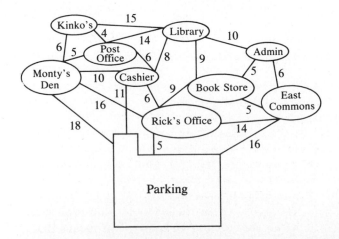

2. Given the following stops for a bakery delivery route, determine the minimum traveling salesman tour that will visit every stop once and only once.

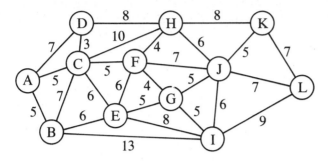

4.4 PERT

Necessity has been the mother of operations research more than once, and during the construction of the Polaris submarine there were so many parts being made and subsystems assembled and tested that it was necessary to coordinate all these activities. One of the things desired was to know ahead of time when bottlenecks would occur. Such occurrences as material shortages, production delays, workforce shortages, and so on, would make a difference in the final assembly and testing of the prototype submarine. It would make no sense at all for the whole project to be delayed because of the lateness of one small subsystem. Therefore a consulting company with cooperation from the Navy developed a system of forecasting possible bottlenecks which they labeled PERT (that is, program evaluation and review technique). The mathematics behind the system were so simple that it was necessary to create a terminology with PERT that would make it sound more exotic. The Polaris project was several months ahead of schedule because of this new technique, and the government was so impressed that it soon required PERT charts for every project that it financed. Managers could be seen with PERT charts all over the walls of their offices and essentially developing a PERT chart for going for coffee.

The network to be analyzed consists of a starting node and a finishing node, with arrows on the branches that indicate direction. The nodes are called *events* and are points in time, such as the moment an activity ends or starts. The branches are called *activities*, and these consume time. The activity between two nodes may take three days. The first node may be the event "start pouring the concrete foundation" and the second node the event "finish pouring the concrete foundation." The nodes (events) take no time, but the branch (activity) takes three days.

Notice that a network has some nodes with several activities coming into an event. This means that *all*

these activities must be finished before any others which leave that node (event) can be started. The analogy may be made of several campers or hikers meeting at a point. They cannot leave from that point until all of them have reached it; then they can split up again or proceed in unison.

The network depicted in Figure 4.31 has eight events, including a starting event A and an ending event H. There are activities between them with estimates, in days, of how long each activity will take. The problem is to determine how long it will take to finish

Figure 4.31

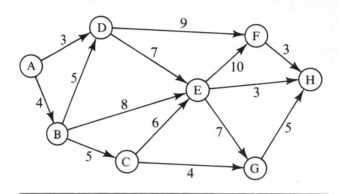

the entire project (get to node H) and what activities *must* be done on time to ensure that the project will be finished within the estimated amount of time. This path will be called the *critical path*. It will be the activities to be closely watched by management. This allows management to monitor only a few of the activities carefully and also to order them in priority of importance. For large projects this is absolutely necessary, as not every activity can be closely supervised. This permits *management by exception* where only the trouble spots or the potential trouble spots have to be closely examined.

Quick & Clean Algorithm: PERT[2]

1. Going from left to right, compute the earliest time T_E you could leave any node. (Remember that all activities have to be done before you can leave.)
2. Going from right to left, compute the latest time T_L you could leave any node without being late for the ones you are leaving for.
3. For each node, compute the slack time ($s = T_L - T_E$).
4. Circle each node with zero slack time and connect these nodes with the branches that have the longest paths. This is the *critical path*.

Example. Step 1 involves finding T_E for each node. Starting with node A, it is set to $T_E = 0$ to begin with. Node B can start its event at day 4 (0 + 4 = 4). Node D has two branches coming into it. The branch from A will take 3 days, while the one coming from B will take 4 + 5 = 9 days. Thus the earliest the event at node D can start is day 9. The rest of the values for T_E are computed and the network will look as shown in Figure 4.32. The whole project can thus be done on day 29 at the earliest. By then *all* the events and activities will have been finished.

Step 2 starts with the last node, H, and the latest time that we can start event H (finish the project) is day 29. Thus we set $T_E = T_L = 29$. Going to node G, the latest time we could start event G and still finish at node H by day 29 would be $T_L = 24$ (29 − 5 = 24). For node F the latest we could start event F is day 26. Node E has three branches coming out of it, and to determine the latest time we could start event E and not be late we must look at all three possibilities. If we are not to be late to node F, we must start by 26 − 10 = 16. For node H, 29 − 3 = 26 must be the latest we can start. Finally for node G, 24 − 7 = 17 is the latest we could start and not be late for the start of event G. Thus we must start by 16, 26, or 17. It is obvious that we must start by day 16, or we will be late for event F. Thus we pick the minimum time for T_L. The network will then look as shown in Figure 4.33.

Now to determine the slack (how much time an event can be delayed from its earliest start) we simply subtract T_E from T_L for each node. We then circle each node with zero slack and find the critical path by connecting these nodes with the path that will equal the value of T_E (and also T_L). You will notice that the path from node A to node D is not critical, for it has an activity of only 3 days and $T_E = 9$ for that node. The *critical path* is A–B–D–E–F–H (Figure 4.34), and any activity along that path that takes longer than the estimate will delay the project. These are the activities to watch closely; it may be that you will want to schedule overtime or extra personnel for those activities.

private contracting

Two brothers in the Las Vegas area want to try their hands at helping a friend do some private contracting. The friend has recently purchased a two-bedroom house on a probate real estate sale. Escrow closed March 3, and remodeling is to begin by tearing out everything but the living room, one bedroom, and the kitchen area. Additions consist of one bedroom, two baths, and a family and dining area. The approximate square footage at the start is 950; it will be increased to around 1650. Also included in the reconstruction of the house are complete replumbing and rewiring. This project is to be completed by June 15, with all

Figure 4.32

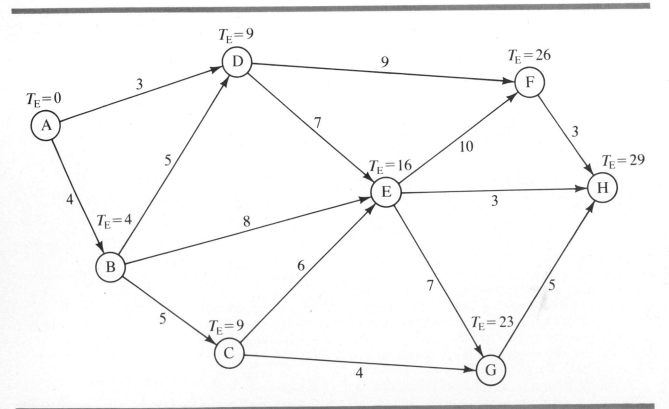

Figure 4.33

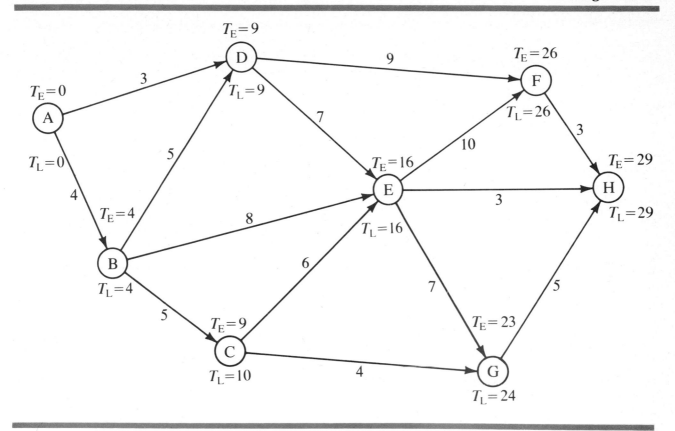

Figure 4.34

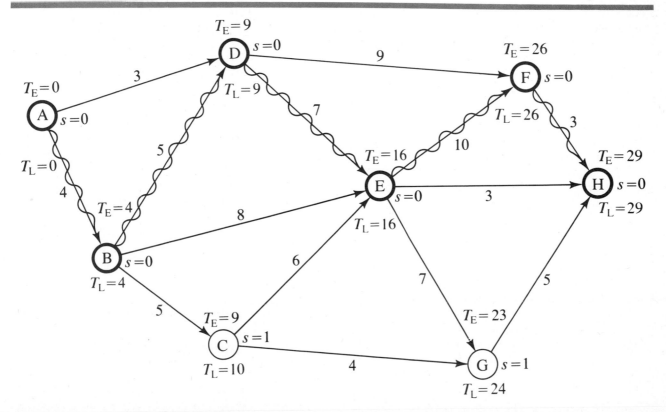

Figure 4.35

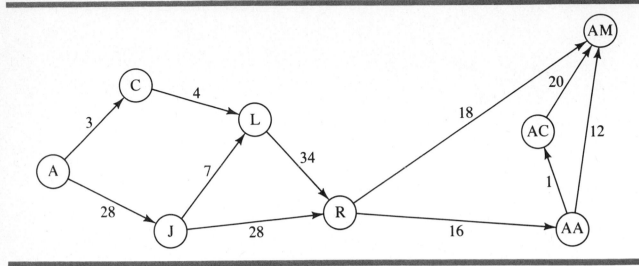

three working whenever time permits (mostly evenings and weekends).

The original diagram, which consisted of 39 nodes and 42 activities, has been reduced to the diagram shown in Figure 4.35. There are approximately 104 days available for work, and the estimates for each activity are in days and, of course, they are very rough. It has been taken into account that only a few hours will be available during the weekdays and that weekends would be full days (12–14 hours). Of course an advantage in Las Vegas is that the probability of lost days due to bad weather is fairly negligible.

Event J represents the finishing of the demolition of the old house (one bedroom, bathroom, and utility room), event L the pouring of the foundation for the new part of the house, event R the finishing of the walls, event AA the finishing of the roofing, and finally event AM is the finishing of the entire house. Determine the critical path and whether the project will be finished on time (assuming that the estimates are correct).

Solution

Recommendation

As the estimates go, the construction will be two days late. It is recommended that attention be paid to the critical path to see if any activity along that path can be shortened. If the demolition of the house, pouring of the foundation, finishing of the walls, or roofing can be done sooner, this will shorten the total time.

Numerical Answer. The critical path is A–J–L–R–AA–AC–AM with a time of 104 days.

Math Work. The earliest, latest, and slack times are given for each event (node) in Figure 4.36. The critical path is the path with slack of −2.

INCIDENT: THREATENING DATA

In the early days of PERT (early 1960s) managers did not know much about asking people to give time estimates for jobs. People would hem and haw and mostly lie or exaggerate about how long something would take. Therefore managers took to a form of indirect questioning. They first asked the employee how long the job would take if nothing went right (the most pessimistic time); then they asked how long it would take if everything went smoothly (the most optimistic time); finally they would ask how long the employee might expect it to take normally (the median time). These times were averaged together by weighting the normal time four times as much, adding the most pessimistic and the optimistic times, and dividing by 6. This became the estimate. All kinds of normal curves were drawn in an effort to show that this was a legitimate thing to do (besides it *looked* more mathematical). Nowadays a single estimate is used and determined by not asking questions in such a threatening manner.

INCIDENT: LARGE-SCALE APPLICATION

North American, for its Apollo project, needed to determine when the project should be completed. Several different methods of estimating this were

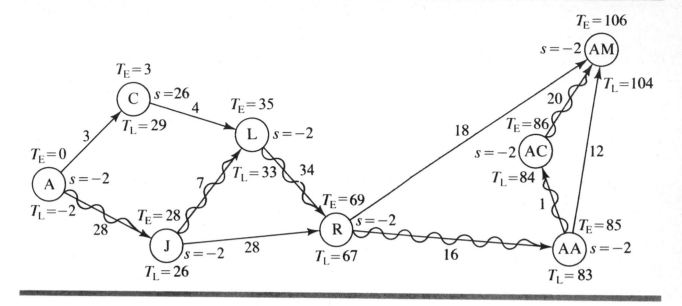

used, and one of them was PERT. The network consisted of 32,000 events and had to be computerized, but it gave the answer six weeks before any other method.

fibre containers

When an order for cardboard boxes is produced and delivered by Fibre Containers, it has a series of steps to go through. The saleswoman contacts the customer (1), and at the same time as she gets her order, she begins a credit check (2). The saleswoman must then make a sample to be approved by the customer (3). When the customer approves the box, a price quotation is made (4), and then the written order is made up (5). Then the cutting die (6), the cardboard (7), and the artwork to be printed on the box (8) are ordered. After the artwork is finished, the ink (10) and the printing plates (11) are ordered. When the cutting die and cardboard arrive, the boxes can be made (9), but the printing cannot be done until the artwork and boxes are finished. This is the second phase of the production (12). After this is all produced, the order is delivered (13).

Given the approximate time in days for each of these events, determine the critical path that the manager will have to watch closely (Figure 4.37, page 114).

INCIDENT: LOOK BEFORE YOU LEAP

The cost of *not* using PERT for periodic evaluation of where problems are occurring can be illustrated by an L.P. gas distributor with approximately 200 distributors and 175,000 customers. Up until July 1969 all accounting (accounts receivable, payroll, and so on) had been done on a decentralized basis with the corporate office handling payables and corporate payroll. In January 1968 a local newly established data-processing "consulting" firm was employed to study the effectiveness of the accounting systems and make recommendations. After a three-month study the consulting firm came back with a plan for centralization of all billings and inventory control and indicated a savings of $300,000 annually. It also made a recommendation that the consulting firm would contract to handle the entire development program.

Management did not believe the savings figure but gave approval for the program on the basis that if they just broke even, the centralized data base would give them access to much more information than they presently had. After 12 months, 6 months behind schedule (a *very* critical path!) and with thousands of dollars of overrun costs, the system was implemented and promptly collapsed. When the first centralized billing *was* accomplished, they were 6 months behind; on the second billing, they were 8 months behind. In September 1969 they decided to abandon the program and revert to decentralized billing. This resulted in the extraordinary expense of

Figure 4.37

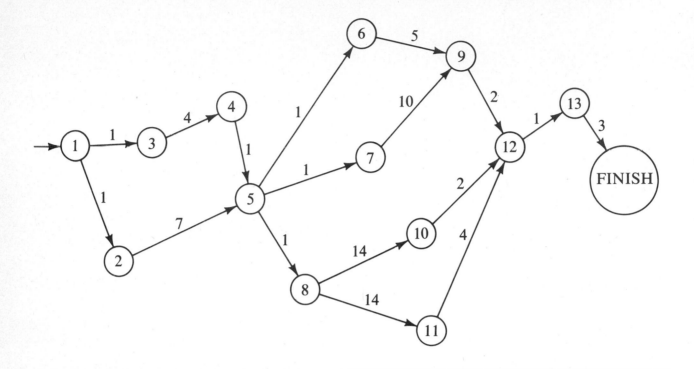

$600,000 after taxes incurred in the cancellation of the program. (Needless to say, it also caused incredible embarrassment to management when they tried to explain the losses to stockholders.) These costs resulted because of—

1. the high cost of the outside consultant,
2. a decision to buy a computer rather than rent one (and much larger than needed),
3. delays in projected schedules,
4. lost and late billings,
5. cost of initially collecting data for the central file (personnel).

The reasons for such a massive system failure were listed by the company as —

1. no company involvement and control over the local consultant,
2. complete lack of proper planning and scheduling of work by outside consultant, and very little reporting to company management on progress or costs (PERT),
3. consultant's recommendation was followed, allowing start-up of system *without* paralleling old manual system. (Thus billing could not get out on time.)

small building contractor

A small building contractor has laid out the following PERT chart and needs to determine the critical path. The time for each activity is given in days, and the start of each activity is designated by the numbers 5 through 24 (Figure 4.38).

INCIDENT: SIMPLICITY IS A KEY

Another case similar to the previous one (where there was *no* scheduling or PERT chart against which to match performance) had a happier ending. The State of California Teacher Preparation and Licensing Commission fired their computer and switched to human beings. The move cut teacher credential processing time by 900 percent. They took a giant step backward in a demodernization program which converted credential processing from a complex and costly automated system to a streamlined, fully manual operation. They got rid of $1,500,000 worth of computer and were able to reduce the staff from 240 persons to 106. At the same time, getting rid of the computer cut the credential processing time from an average of 95 days to the current average of

Figure 4.38

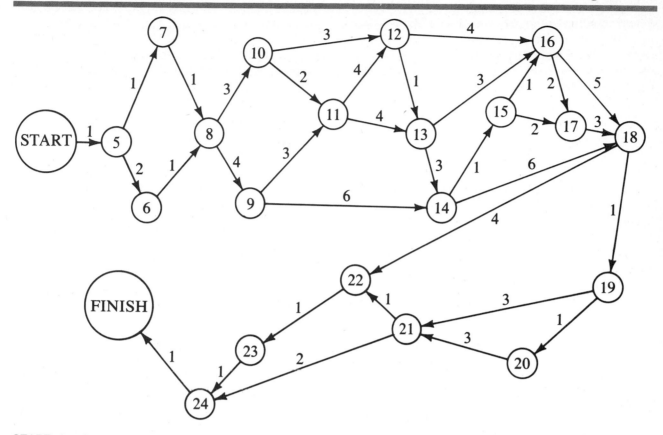

START	Land acquisition (1)		(13)	Top out plumbing
	Obtain house plans (2)		(14)	Install heating unit, wiring
	Take out loan (3)		(15)	Roofing
	Obtain building permit (4)		(16)	Wallboard
(5)	Temporary facilities: water, power, chemical toilets		(17)	Carpentry: hang doors, lay particle board, trim out closets and windows
(6)	Excavation: trenching for foundations, utilities; pour concrete		(18)	Clean up for painters
			(19)	Painting: walls and interior, trim
(7)	Order lumber		(20)	Floorlaying: lay linoleum, set cabinets, sinks
(8)	Rough plumbing		(21)	Electrician: hang fixtures, wall plugs
(9)	Floor joints		(22)	Final cleanup: touch up paint, lay carpet
(10)	Basic rough framing		(23)	Final excavation
(11)	Install overhead garage door		(24)	Final inspection
(12)	Siding			

10. Although the computer was unable to hold its job, the director said it was a good worker; it just couldn't compete with people.

production contract

A large international firm has a division that is located on the Gulf Coast. This division received a $50 million contract which would last for approximately 2 years and employ 300 people. Thus it was necessary, as soon as the award was announced, to schedule the hiring of personnel, the ordering of raw materials, the design and installation of the necessary engineering modifications to existing machinery, and the training of the new personnel. Time estimates were obtained by hiring a local consultant who spent two weeks interviewing each of the different managers involved. Given Figure 4.39 and the time estimates below, determine how long it will take to get production going and what activities seem to be critical.

INCIDENT: WHO USES PERT?

A consultant for a large aerospace firm in California reported that although the company had an entire room devoted to a huge PERT chart with thousands of events placed on the wall, the log-entry book showed that about the only time the manager visited the room was to show visitors around. Also it showed that the large majority of entries were for those who were keeping the chart current. When pressed about really using PERT, the manager produced a small cardboard chart with only about 10 events on it. The point the consultant was trying to make was that the ideas of events, activities, slack, and critical path are very valid, but that we tend to clutter up the valid concepts with a lot of trappings that become worshipped as ends in themselves (chart rooms, huge computer listings, and so on).

Figure 4.39

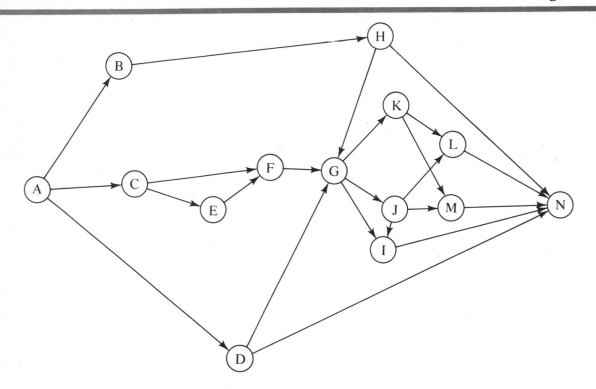

Activity	Description	Time Estimate (weeks)
A–B	Contract to materials department	1
A–C	Contract to engineering design department	2
A–D	Contract to personnel department	3
B–H	Order raw materials	2
H–G	Copper and plastics delivery	12
H–N	Steel-wire delivery	17
D–G	Hire set-up personnel	5
D–N	Hire production personnel	12
C–E	Engineering design for assembly-line modifications	7
C–F	Engineering design determining standard changes	10
E–F	Subcontracting work on assembly-line modifications	6
F–G	Installation of all modifications	3
G–K	Quality-control training	2
G–J	Inspection and qualifying of assembly line	2
G–I	Creel modifications	4
K–L,K–M	On-job training of operators	1,1
J–L	Core-extruder testing	2
J–M	Wire-wind testing	1
J–I	Jacket-line testing	3
L–N	Core-extruder final preparation	1
M–N	Wire-wind final preparation	1
I–N	Jacket and Creel final preparation	2

INCIDENT: BIGGER IS NOT BETTER

Here is another case where PERT was not used, so that actual results fell way below hoped-for expectations. An auto parts manufacturer in the Midwest used to have its board meetings on the second Tuesday of each month because it took that long for its manual accounting system to determine the state of the preceding month's sales, inventory, accounts receivable, and so on. Convinced by a computer salesperson that he could get more information quicker and with less personnel, the manufacturer decided to buy a machine. Now they meet on the third Tuesday of every month, have hired two new people (and fired no one), and have a computer utilization of 20 percent. (They have a machine that is much too large for their needs.)

As a final note on PERT, the initial T_E does not have to be 0, the last T_L does not have to be set equal to the last T_E, nor does the critical path have to have a slack of 0.

1. Instead of setting $T_E = 0$ for the initial node, it may be set to *any* number desired. Thus if event A will take place on the 30th day of the project, T_E may be set to 30 to begin with.
2. The T_L for the final node may also be set to any number desired (instead of being equal to the final T_E). If the project should be done on the 25th day, then set $T_L = 25$. In the example this would give the critical path a slack of −4 (4 days late) rather than 0. Or it may be that the project does not need to be done until day 32; thus $T_L = 32$ and the critical path will have a slack of +3 (3 days of slack).
3. For large projects there are computerized versions of PERT which require an activity time estimate, showing which nodes are successors and which are predecessors. The events are then ranked in the order of increasing amounts of slack.

Supplementary Problems

1. Darlene has planned the following activities that must be accomplished before she can leave for the Caribbean. Reservations have been made for March 30 and she will start activity '1' on March 10. Will she be on time? Show the

PERT values of T_E, T_L, and s and the critical path.

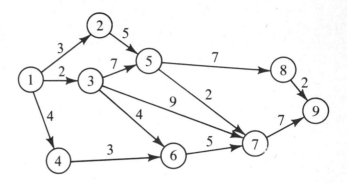

2. In order to pass the CPA examination, a student has laid out the following activities. Given that she has 82 hours to get ready for the examination, use the PERT algorithm to determine if she will be ready in time. Also show T_E, T_L, and s for each node and identify the critical path.

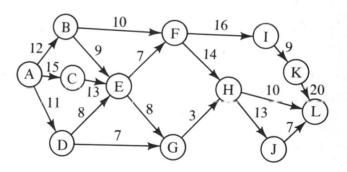

4.5 CPM

Another way of presenting scheduling information and the interactions between activities is a method known as critical-path method (CPM). Not to be outdone by the government, private industry rose to the challenge of making its own scheduling algorithms with different acronyms. This method bears a resemblance to a Gantt chart which uses a time line, usually in days or weeks, and thus "lays out" the progress of the events. For some people this algorithm is easier to read and understand, although it may not contain as much information as a PERT chart. This type of approach has proved very successful in the construction industry, where simple graphical solutions as well as computer printouts can be used. It gives the project supervisor a quick picture of where critical delays may occur. You must realize that this method is accomplishing the same goal as the PERT method, although it may seem different.

Quick & Clean Algorithm: CPM[2]

1. Draw a time line and mark it off in days (or weeks).
2. Moving from left to right, put each event on the time line (an event may appear several times) by adding to the number of days for the preceding activity.
3. Draw solid lines between events (nodes) when there is no slack or waiting.
4. Draw dashed lines between events that appear more than once. The event to the farthest right (of the similar ones) will have a solid line (or lines) from it. The other similar events will have only dashed lines. See Figure 4.41.
5. The critical path is the solid line from the beginning of the time line to the end.

Example. Given the same network as in the PERT example (Figure 4.40), let us construct a CPM chart. Taking the first three events (A, B, and D), we place them on the time line (Figure 4.41). Event A starts at time 0, while it takes 3 days to get to event D. Thus D is placed at time 3. Event B takes 4 days from A and is placed at time 4. But event D also has an activity coming from B which takes 5 more days. Thus a solid line is drawn to node D which is 5 days away from B. This leaves 2 node D's. The node that is farthest along the time line will be the one that all paths must eventually reach before anything else can be done from node D. Thus we connect the two (or more) node D's by dashed lines. The dashed lines stand for slack along that path and indicate that we may take up to 6 extra days coming from node A without delaying the schedule. Note that we don't have to go "forward" and find all the T_E's first, then come "backward" to determine the T_L's and finally the slack s. The final solution is shown in Figure 4.42.

You will notice that there are a few differences between the PERT approach and the CPM approach. The CPM chart may have several nodes with the same name (letter or number), which indicates that by using certain paths, this event will be reached sooner. The CPM method also uses dashed lines to indicate slack time, which is associated with activities rather than events as in PERT. While T_E, and T_L, and s are computed successively in PERT, CPM computes the slack at the same time as the chart is made. However, it is not as easy to determine the earliest or latest times that an event can start.

Figure 4.40

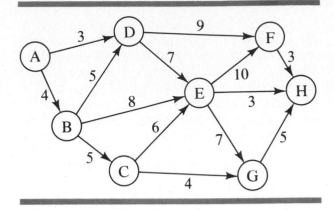

Figure 4.41

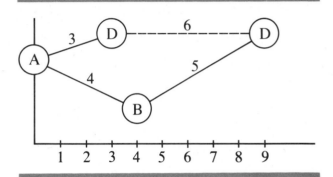

programmed console

The Biomedical Computing Laboratories in St. Louis, Missouri, developed the Programmed Console (originally called the four-week wonder because it was developed in four weeks by a graduate engineering class) to aid radiologists in the placing of radium implants in patients with cervical cancer. The problem for most radiologists was that when two or more radium needles had to be implanted it was difficult to determine how much radiation each part of the body would receive. It was important that the entire tumor received radiation and that the other parts of the body received none (or small dosages). Thus it was a matter of "feel" as to where the implants would go and how long the treatment should last (from 45 minutes to 4 hours). The Programmed Console was an analog/digital computer which would accept as input the placement of the needles (from the X-ray), the roentgen strength (entered by keyboard), and the program (entered via tape drive). It would give as output (on a cathode ray tube) the roentgen strength about the tumor in two dimensions, with the option of showing

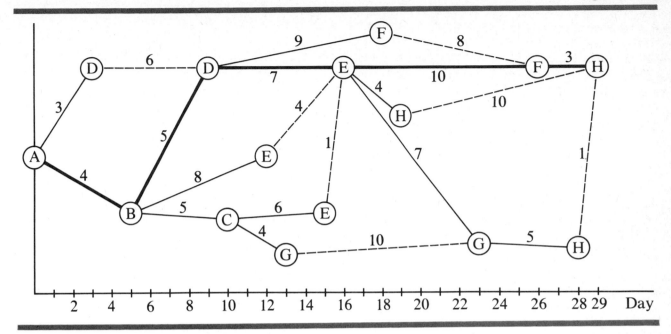

any one plane or a combination of five planes along the body.

What was needed to develop this system was a keyboard (to type in small commands and data), a rho–theta plotter (a telescoping pen, attached to a transducer, which would give the coordinates off an X-ray), a simple tape drive (a language machine that could read a strip of tape), the cathode ray tube, magnetic core, the logic circuitry, and the main frame to hold it all. The cathode ray tube, core, and reader were bought commercially, so that all that had to be considered there was the delivery time and the time to hook them up into the complete system. The rho–theta plotter was made from scratch, as was the keyboard. The toughest part was the logic circuitry, which needed extensive testing. The main frame was simple enough to design and build.

Given the network shown in Figure 4.43 (page 120), construct a CPM chart and determine the critical path. Time estimates are in weeks.

Solution

Recommendation

Special care and attention should be paid to the progress of all aspects of the logic circuitry: design, building, integration, and testing. This is the most crucial phase since it is a bottleneck to the whole project. If all estimates are correct, the Programmed Console will be finished in 16 weeks.

Numerical Answer. The critical path is E1–E2–E3–H1–H2–H3–H4 and will take 6 + 4 + 3 + 1 + 1 + 1 = 16 weeks.

Math Work. See the chart shown in Figure 4.44 (page 121).

INCIDENT: THEY REALLY DO USE IT!

To determine the validity of CPM, several students decided to go to a construction site and talk to the project manager. He said that not only had he heard of CPM, but he was in fact using it for this project. He showed them his chart, which was done by hand with a key to the different symbols on it. He showed them where his trouble spots were, which included two subcontractors, delays due to rains, and some shortage of personnel from one labor union. He knew that he was now four weeks behind and had two ideas of where he could make up most of that lost time. Since the contract had no penalty clauses (lost money for being late), he was not too worried about being late. This was because most of the delay was excusable and was not a reflection of his ability to get the work done.

united uranium

United Uranium supplies uranium fuel to nuclear-powered naval warships and submarines as well as civilian nuclear electrical generating plants across the nation. Presently United Uranium is planning to increase its reserves by purchasing uranium-rich

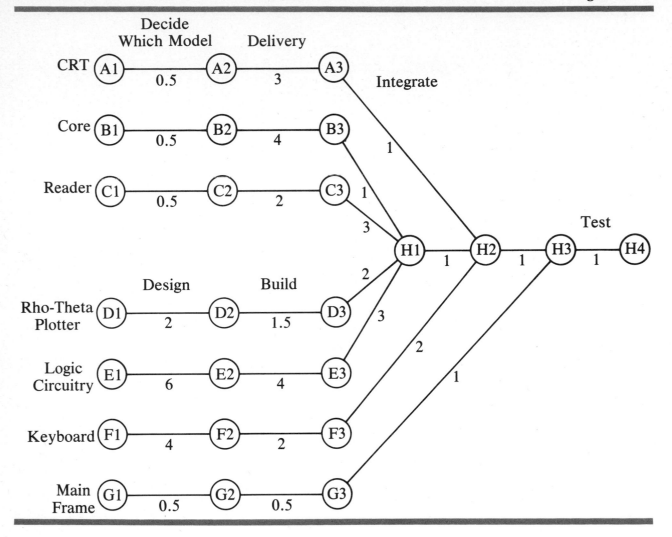

land in northern Colorado. Bids on the planned mountain subdivision, Glenshire #4A, must be submitted in 30 days to Western Properties, the corporation that owns the land. Before a proper bid can be submitted, several stages of planning must be completed.

Initially a sewer study A, taking two days, and an engineer's review for buildability B, taking three days, must be finished. Once A is completed, a water and drainage study C can be made requiring two days. The completion of both B and C allows a specification plan to be submitted to the county D, requiring two days and one day, respectively. Also, incidentals can be added to the engineer's review, and the assignments delegated E, once B is finished. The completion of E in three days will allow the preparation of necessary legal descriptions H, taking five days. The specification plan F will be returned from the county in four days. An A/D boundary map G can be started, once E and F are finished, requiring three days and one day, respectively. A field profile I can be made in five days, once F is completed. When the attorneys have completed H, a bond screening package K can

be started and will take three days. A subdivision bond and monumenting amount J can be set, once I and G are completed. This will require seven and three days, respectively, and will allow a subdivision agreement to be prepared L, requiring five days. Also the completion of J and K will allow the A/D proceedings to be started M, requiring three days and four days, respectively. The contract bid can be submitted N, once L and M are completed, and will require four and five days, respectively.

Complete the CPM chart on the Glenshire #4A mountain subdivision and find the critical path (Figure 4.45). Determine if the project will be completed within 30 days.

INCIDENT: CPM ACTS LIKE A MIRROR, NOT A MIRACLE

Building for the 1976 Olympics in Montreal had been going at a snail's pace, and all the CPM charts in the

Figure 4.44

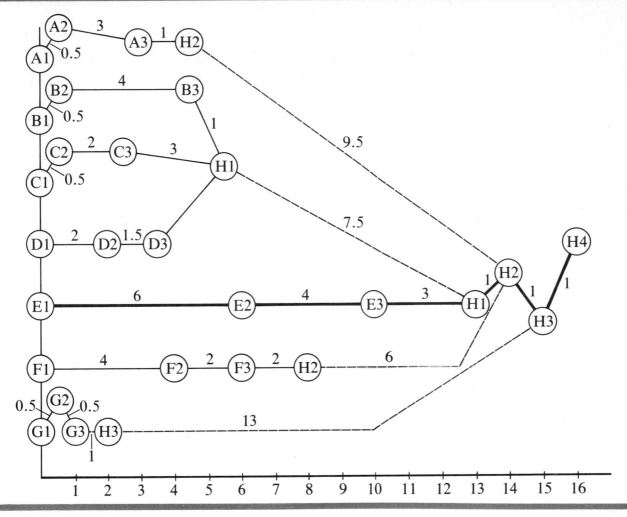

Figure 4.45

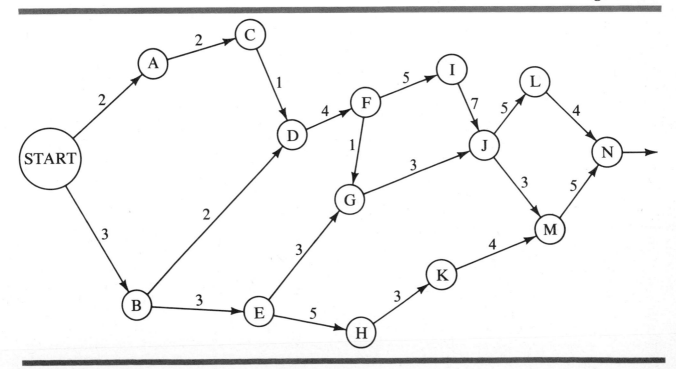

world couldn't help it. They simply showed how late these buildings would be, and the effect that a strike would have upon them. However, due to public pressure, most of the buildings were finished on time, and the Olympics were held. The other factor on finishing projects on time is known as Parkinson's law: *The available work fits the available space*. Thus many projects which could be done in two weeks will take ten if that is the deadline. Similarly, given a smaller amount of time, it is amazing how much work can get done.

The process of construction is complicated enough, without the added worries of the paperwork involved in getting started. There is the bureaucratic requirement of filing different permits, notifying the neighboring owners of the construction site, planning for materials requirements (ordering materials), letting out bids and contracts, and making up a budget for the whole project. Consider Figure 4.46, an example

Figure 4.46

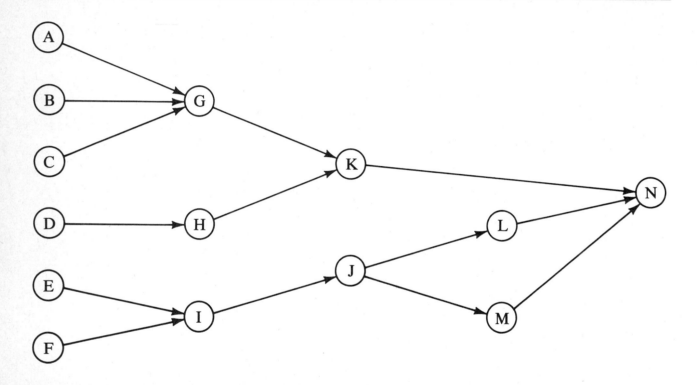

Activity	Explanation	Time Estimate (weeks)
A–G	Demolition: select, bid, let contract	6
B–G	File demolition permit	3
C–G	File encroachment letter	2
D–H	Shore and excavation: select, bid, let contract	5
E–I	Bid steel tonnage	2
F–I	Bid granite	1
G–K	Demolition work	12
H–K	Agreement with contiguous property owners	2
I–J	Set budget	2
J–L	Mill order steel	1
J–M	Order granite	1
K–N	Excavation and shore work	10
L–N	Steel delivery	15
M–N	Granite delivery	20

that is taken from an actual preconstruction phase of a 24-story office building on the East Coast. Determine the critical path by preparing a CPM chart.

INCIDENT: CPM DOES NOT REPLACE COMMON SENSE

In the early 1960s the mania of PERT/CPM had caught on, and almost every large project needed some sort of chart. Washington University of St. Louis was building a new dormitory for which they had a Ford Foundation matching grant. One of the stipulations of the grant was that a CPM chart should be run each week. The contractors, MacDonald Construction Company, were required to come to the University Computer Center each Friday afternoon for the running of the CPM program. Mr. MacDonald (known as Mr. Mac), who had been in the business for about 50 years, would lean with his back to the printer as the program would run, naming the critical activities off the top of his head as they would appear on the computer printout. He was never wrong. It only showed that operations research should not and does not replace common sense. For someone with 50 years' experience it was not hard to see that if the bricks were not delivered on time, he would be in trouble. But for those who have only a few years' experience in all the things that could possibly go wrong, it can be a very valuable aid.

parking structure

San Diego State University has approximately 32,000 students enrolled each semester, and most of these students are commuters from the surrounding area. As the school has expanded, so has the need for facilities, especially classrooms. As a result, new buildings have been erected, but usually at the expense of using an existing parking lot for the land. With the construction of the new Social Sciences and Humanities building, the need for parking became critical. At this time it was decided to build a high-rise (six-story) parking lot in a canyon across from the Business and Mathematics building. The construction took 18 months and was finished shortly after the 1975 fall semester.

The basic plan for construction was to do the gradings, put up a retaining wall and access road, and fence off the area. Then the main stairwells and elevator shafts were poured (the entire six stories). The parking lot was divided into three sections, with the west section being worked on first. When it was about three stories high, work began on the middle section, while work on the west section was continued. Finally work began on the east section when the west section was being completed. After completion of the middle section, a bridge was constructed from the sixth floor of the middle section to the first floor of the Business and Mathematics Building.

Thirty weeks before the beginning of the 1975 fall semester, the project manager of the Golden construction company was facing a set of activities and events as outlined in Figure 4.47. Unfortunately it is not possible to determine what each node stands for, but it is possible to determine how long the project will take as stated. Will the project be late, and if so, by how much? The time for each activity is in weeks. Draw a CPM chart.

Figure 4.47

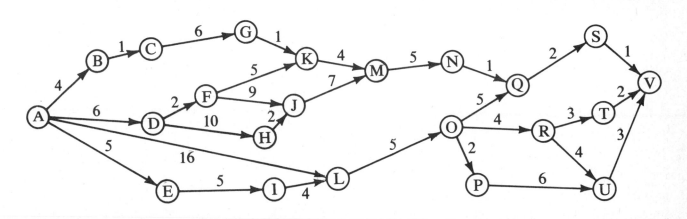

Supplementary Problems

1. Given the following network, determine the critical path by using the CPM method.

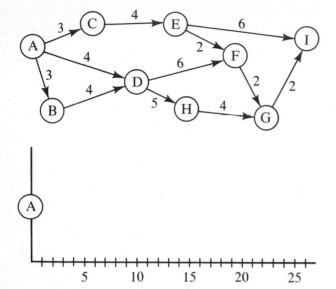

2. Given the CPM chart below, draw the original network diagram that it represents and fill in the other numbers on the CPM chart.

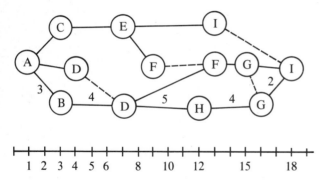

4.6 MAXIMAL FLOW/MINIMAL CUT

The final type of problem discussed in this chapter concerns finding the maximum flow that can occur from the "source" of a network to its "sink." An example of this type of problem may be a series of locks on a river (some in parallel). The source of the problem is the river traffic flow (mostly barges) coming into the lock system, and the sink is the end of the lock system. We are interested in seeing what is the maximum flow or the largest number of ships per hour that can flow through the system. Each branch on the network diagram is labeled with a capacity and an arrow, denoting the amount that can flow along that branch in the direction of the arrow during a fixed time period (minutes, hours, or days). These situations arise in any system that is pumping water, natural gas, sewage, or anything else through pipes.

The capacity for each branch is the amount of water, gas, or sewage that can flow through the pipe per minute or hour. What needs to be determined in this problem is how much water, gas, or sewage can flow through the system from the source to the sink per minute or hour, which gives this problem the name *maximal flow*.

Traffic systems can also be represented by networks, with the nodes being traffic centers, lights, or intersections and the branches being roads, airways, or canals. The system can also represent a river watershed system with the nodes being confluences or reservoirs and the branches being the rivers and tributaries.

The network shown in Figure 4.48 represents a simple system for which we want to determine the maximal flow. The first node (1) is labeled *source* and the last node (7) *sink*. The numbers along the branches indicate capacities, with the arrows pointing into the directions of flow. In this case flow is allowed in one direction only, but as in our example of a river with locks, it is possible for a branch to be represented as follows:

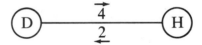

where the flow from D to H is four units per hour (four barges), but if the branch were used only from H to D, only two barges could pass per hour. We will assume that branches will be used in either one direction or the other, but that they can also have a dual capacity, which will be explained later.

Quick & Clean Algorithm: Maximal Cut[1]

1. Pick *any* path from source to sink and determine the maximum flow that can pass through all the branches on that path. There must be positive flow. This maximum flow is the minimum of all the current capacities.
2. Add that flow to the capacities leading back to the source along that path and subtract that flow from the capacities leading to the sink along that path.
3. When there are no more paths with positive flow, *stop: optimal.*

Example. To begin, let us pick arbitrarily the path 1–2–4–6–7, which goes from source to sink. The capacities for these branches are 3, 3, 3, and 7, and thus the minimum is 3, which is the maximum flow allowed through that path. The reason that we do not add these capacities is that we are restricted in flow by the smallest pipe or the most constrictive branch. Let us imagine that this is a water pipe system, and we

Figure 4.48

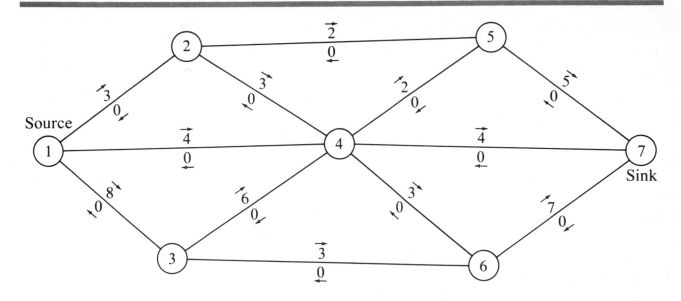

have connected 4 pipes together with capacities of 3, 3, 3, and 7 gallons per minute. It is obvious that we will not have 16 gallons per minute flowing through the system but only 3, since we are restricted by the smaller pipes.

We now add that flow of 3 to the capacities leading back on that path to the source (node 1). This simply means that we have the ability to decide to send some of that flow back along that path if we want to, and hence the reason in this algorithm is that we can pick *any* path and still come up with the optimal solution. We also subtract the maximum flow from the capacities on that path going to the sink, which means that we have less flow available going from source to sink.

To summarize this first flow, let us pick the path 1–2–4–6–7 from source to sink. The capacities along the branches are 3, 3, 3, and 7 units, and therefore the most that can flow along that path is 3 units. We then add that flow of 3 to the capacities leading back to node 1 (the source) along paths 1–2, 2–4, 4–6, and 6–7 and subtract it from the capacities going to the sink (Figure 4.49). (This is the possible flow we could take back.)

Figure 4.49

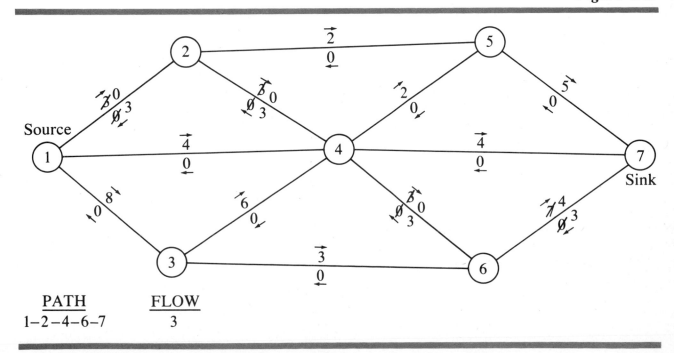

PATH	FLOW
1–2–4–6–7	3

Figure 4.50

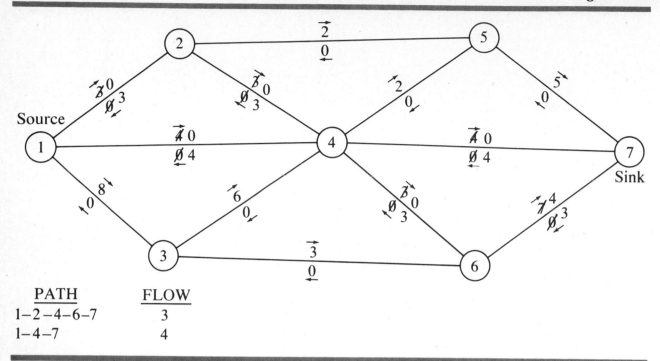

PATH	FLOW
1–2–4–6–7	3
1–4–7	4

Next let us pick the path 1–4–7, which will allow 4 units of flow (Figure 4.50).

Now since it is not possible for any flow to leave along path 1–2 or 1–4, we will pick the path 1–3–6–7 which has capacities of 8, 3, and 4 units, and the most flow that can go along this path is 3 units (Figure 4.51).

The next path to choose is 1–3–4–5–7 with capacities of 5, 6, 2, and 5 units, so that the most that can flow along that path is 2 units. The network will then look as shown in Figure 4.52.

The last path that can be chosen is 1–3–4–2–5–7, where we retrace some of the flow from node 4 to node 2, so that we have capacities of 3, 4, 3, 2, and 3 units, and the most that can flow from source to sink is 2 units (Figure 4.53).

Now there are no more paths from source to sink which can have a positive flow. It is impossible to get from 2 to 5, from 4 to 5, from 4 to 7, from 4 to 6, or from 3 to 6. In other words, the source is *cut off* from the sink (the wavy line in Figure 4.53). This is also called the *minimum cut;* that is, if the original

Figure 4.51

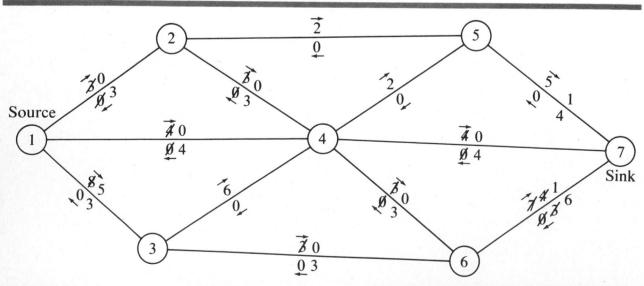

Figure 4.52

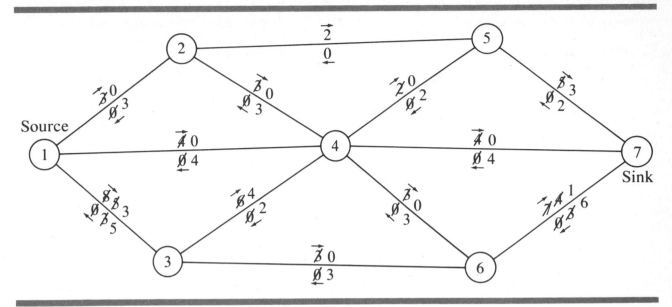

capacities from source to sink are taken as the cost of cutting off the flow along that branch, there is a minimum cost for cutting off the flow from source to sink. Thus if we were to cut off the flow from 1 to 2, from 1 to 4, and from 1 to 3, it would cost $3 + 4 + 8 = 15$ units. But the cut from 2 to 5, from 4 to 5, from 4 to 7, from 4 to 6, and from 3 to 6 costs $2 + 2 + 4 + 3 + 3 = 14$ units.

Path	Flow	Cut	Cost
1–2–4–6–7	3	2–5	2
1–4–7	4	4–5	2
1–3–6–7	3	4–7	4
1–3–4–5–7	2	4–6	3
1–3–4–2–5–7	2	3–6	3
	14		14

Notice that the maximal flow (14 units) is the minimum cut (cost of 14 units). We have inadvertently solved two problems simultaneously. By solving the maximum flow we find the minimum cut (the minimum cost to cut off the source(s) from the sink(s) completely).

Thus we could look at our original problem in a completely different manner. Rather than trying to find the maximum amount of flow, we could try to find the least expensive (minimum) cut. The interesting thing about this is that the maximum of one problem (the flow) is the minimum of the other problem (the cut). In operations research these two problems are known as primal and dual problems. It is an interesting property that for many problems (the primal) there exists another problem (the dual) so

Figure 4.53

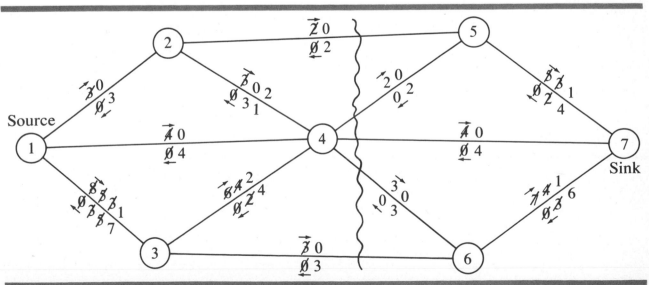

that the maximum of the primal equals the minimum of the dual. Many difficult problems have been solved by setting them in another form.

The only point the two problems have in common is the optimal solution to each. All other solutions to one problem are not feasible (or workable) solutions for the other. Thus the danger of setting a problem into the form of a dual and solving it is that if you do not find an optimal solution, you do not have a workable answer. In the case of flow/cut problems we will always use the flow algorithm, even to solve the cut problems, because it is easier (especially on larger problems), very methodical, and almost foolproof.

For our example we could establish cuts between nodes 1–2, 1–4, and 1–3 for a cost of 15 units. Another possible cut would be 5–7, 4–7, and 6–7 for a cost of 16 units. Still another cut would be 5–7, 4–7, 4–6, and 3–6 for a cost of 15 units. Although there are a finite number of cuts, it is not always obvious where they all are. However, of all the possible cuts, the minimum is a cost of 14 units.

shindana toy company

The Shindana Toy Company needs to determine the maximal flow of products through its toy factory for one year. The maximum capacity is figured for 1 shift, 40 hours a week, for 50 weeks. The company is interested in determining where bottlenecks will occur (minimal cut) so that it will be able to hire extra personnel if more output is desired.

Shindana produces seven dolls, and they must each go through several of the ten major operations at the plant. The first major operation is the oven, where molds form heads, arms, legs, and torsos and then bake these simultaneously. Six of the seven dolls are involved in this operation and then cooled. The other doll, Flip, is stuffed. After the body parts are formed, the heads go to be painted, and the other parts of the body are assembled. All doll faces except one are hand painted. Next the painted heads go to the sewing stalls to have hair sewn on. One doll requires a special machine because the hair must be parted on the side. (They must make 20,000 of these.) All the sewn-hair doll heads go through a grooming station next. Then they are attached to the body that has been assembled, or are sewn to a cloth body and sent to be stuffed. All the assembled bodies with their heads attached are then dressed and packaged. Given the flow diagram of Figure 4.54, determine the total number of units that can flow through the system, and where it might be advisable to use overtime, extra

Figure 4.54

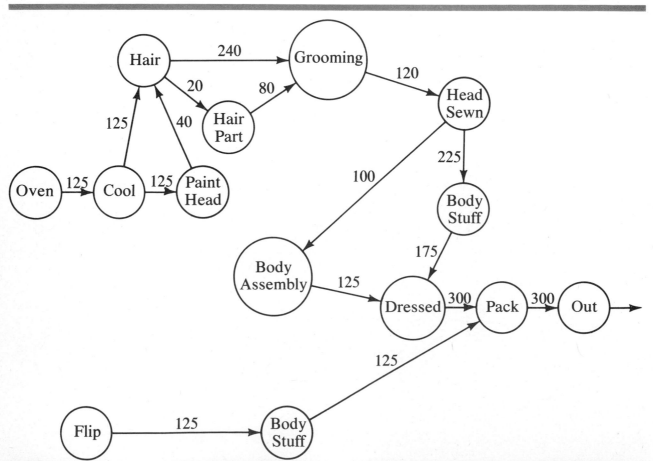

personnel, or machines if more output is desired. Note that there are two sources for this problem: Oven and Flip. The numbers on each branch represent capacity in 1000 units.

Solution

Recommendation

More capacity is needed in the grooming phase of making the six dolls, and more Flip dolls are needed to be stuffed. Otherwise there is plenty of capacity in the rest of the plant. 245,000 units can be made, of which 125,000 are the Flip dolls.

Numerical Answer

Cut	Cost
Flip–Body Stuff or	
Body Stuff–Pack	125,000
Grooming–Head Sewn	120,000
	——————
	245,000

Math Work. The paths used and the amount of resulting flow are given in Figure 4.55. 125,000

units have to flow from Flip to Body Stuff. The other paths are optional, and alternate paths may be taken to end up with a total flow of 245,000 units.

INCIDENT: BOTTLENECK IN PRODUCTION SQUEEZES PROFITS

A garment manufacturer is concerned that its production line function smoothly and effectively. To determine where the bottlenecks are, the flow of the entire operation is charted on a network, and the minimum cut produces the bottlenecks. This is where the company sees that they will have to hire more workers or increase the number of machines.

dam placement

On a river system a series of dams for flood control are to be built at a minimum cost. However, the cost of building the dams includes also the cost of relocating the people who are displaced by the rising waters of the reservoirs behind the dams. In many locations

Figure 4.55

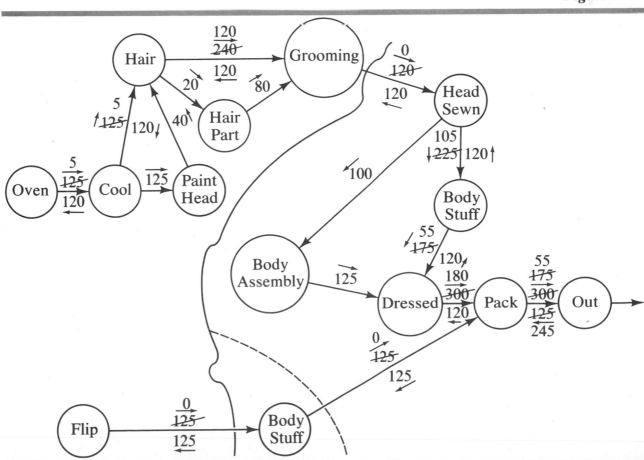

Figure 4.56

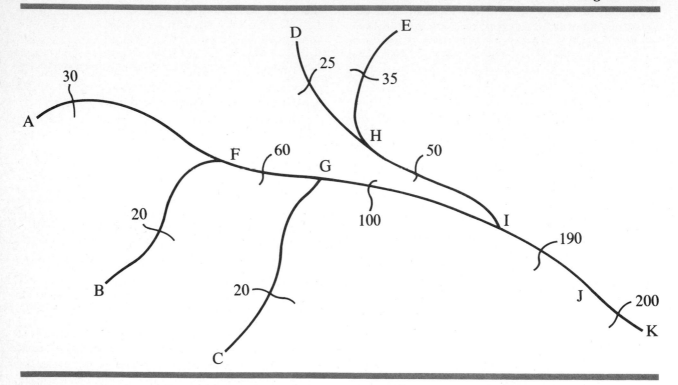

this can be quite a problem, not only costwise but also politically. Although there are many advantages from the dams (power, recreation, visitors, and new income), there are also many disadvantages (imbalancing the ecological system and displacing people and whole towns).

Figures 4.56 and 4.57 show two flow diagrams of the basin system. The first is taken from the map, with possible dam locations indicated by wavy lines. The approximate costs of building those dams are given in millions of dollars. Therefore the dam between A and F would cost $30,000,000 to build. The second flow diagram is the way it would be represented as a flow chart for solution by the Quick & Clean method.

Determine where the dams should be built to minimize the sum of the cost estimates for the flood-

Figure 4.57

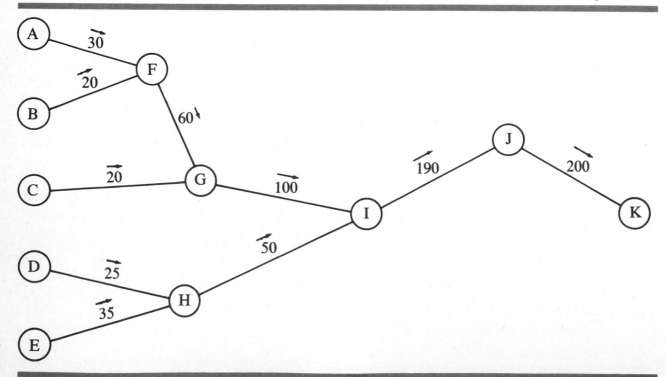

control system. By solving the maximal-flow problem, you will obtain the minimal cut for the system and thus find where the dams should be placed at the lowest cost. This, of course, does not include the inestimable cost of displacing people from their homes, nor does it include the savings due to prevented flood damage and possible deaths.

INCIDENT: TRAFFIC SLOWDOWNS

A traffic engineer wants to determine where the slowdowns might occur in the freeway system. She puts electric counters at strategic spots to determine the traffic flow along major arteries. Where the minimum cut occurs is where the traffic jams will take place and where the traffic system needs relief. Possible solutions are widening the freeway and/or opening up alternate routes around the congested area or controlling the flow on to the on-ramps in the minimum-cut areas.

traffic flow

The freeway system for San Diego county was well planned for the growth of the 1970s. San Diego county has experienced the largest growth rate of any county in California and has been well prepared for the last few years for the increase in traffic flow.

Assume that the source of the traffic flow will start at the downtown intersection of highways 5 and 94. The outlets for the traffic will be the smaller cities of Ocean Beach, Mission Beach, Pacific Beach, and La Jolla for the coastal beach towns; San Diego, East San Diego, and Chula Vista for the center of the city; Escondido, Clairemont, and Rancho Bernardo for North county; and El Cajon, La Mesa, and Lemon Grove for the eastern cities.

Highways 5, 805, 8, and 15 are interstate highways; 163 and 94 are county highways. Again, two flow diagrams are presented (Figure 4.58 and on page 132, Figure 4.59). The first is taken from the

Figure 4.58

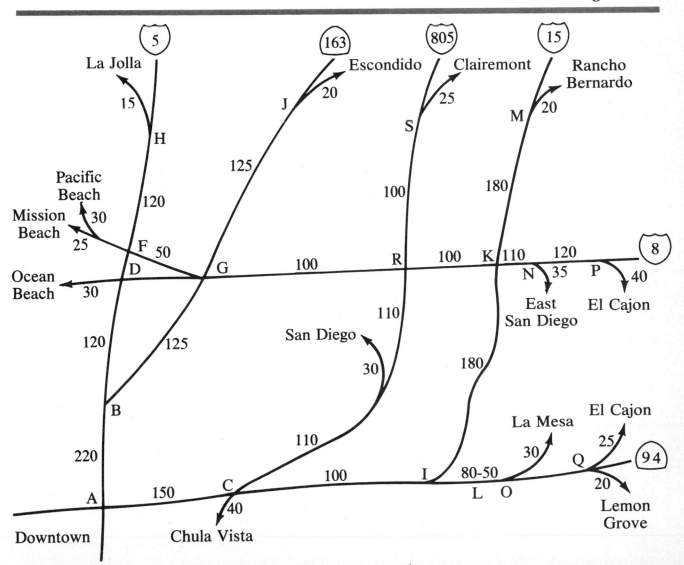

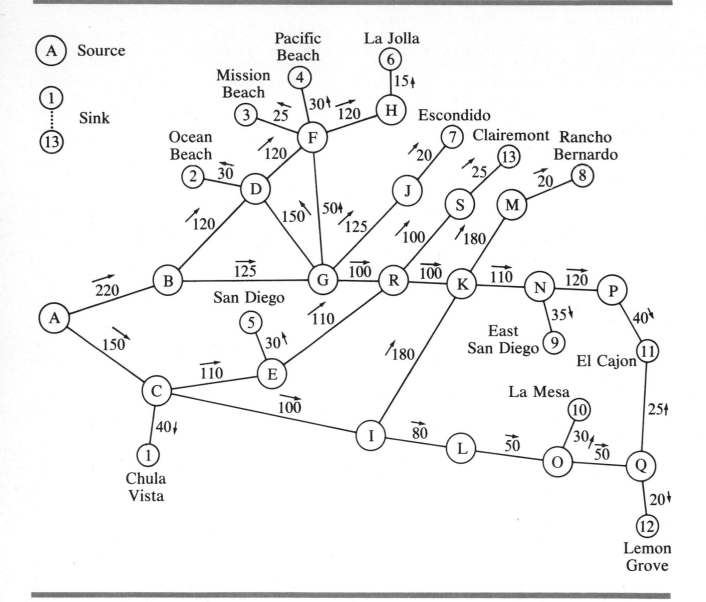

highway map with estimates of traffic flow. The second diagram is the flow diagram for the solution by the Quick & Clean algorithm.

In 1976 the traffic flow was 330 cars per minute, and it is figured that each year the traffic flow will increase by 10 cars per minute. The off ramps for each city are represented by the sinks, and the capacity is figured on the population for each city in 1980. Thus if the minimal cut for this freeway system is at all the sinks, the system is more than adequate. If the minimal cut is less than the projected traffic flow for 1980, then a bottleneck exists which may need to be widened soon. Using the maximal-flow algorithm, determine if such a bottleneck exists and if so, by how much the flow can be increased before another bottleneck occurs.

INCIDENT: MINIMAL CUT USED IN MILITARY BLOCKADE

During the Vietnam peace-keeping effort the U.S. Armed Forces had a vested interest in keeping tourists (and supplies) from coming down the Ho Chi Minh trail. The costs of bombing roads, destroying bridges, patrolling rivers, aerial electronic surveillance, and so on, were all computed and figures put on a network diagram of North Vietnam, Cambodia, Laos, and South Vietnam. The network was then solved as a maximal flow which produced the minimum cut. This cut was the place to bomb to interrupt the flow at the least ammunition cost.

Figure 4.60

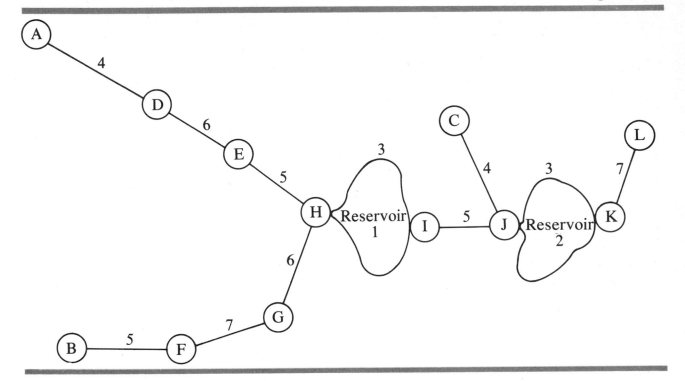

reservoir system

An important application of network flows is flood control, usually established by reservoir systems which also provide power and a more stable ecological system. The classic problems encountered are where to build reservoir systems, how much they should hold, at what level they should be maintained, and, given a series of flood or near flood inputs from the streams, whether they will check the flooding.

Given the river–reservoir system shown in Figure 4.60, determine whether the projected run-off of water will be checked by the present system. There are three sources A, B, and C and one sink L. It takes one day for the water to travel through the entire system. Reservoir 1 has a capacity of ten units and is currently holding six. Reservoir 2 has a capacity of nine units and is currently holding eight. Determine if the current holdings are too high for the reservoirs. Each reservoir can empty only three units of flow, regardless of how much is in it. A storm will produce the following amount of water during its duration:

Node A 2 units Node B 4 units Node C 3 units

To put this problem into a more proper network flow framework, it is possible to create a single source (super source) that will give the day's water flow. Also a fictitious branch from the source to the node at the downstream side of each reservoir is created. These branches should have a capacity equal to the volume of water stored in its corresponding reservoir for that day. Finally a fictitious branch is created from the upstream node of each reservoir going to the final node (sink). These branches should have a capacity equal to the remaining available storage for the corresponding reservoir for that day. Solve the maximal flow problem from Figure 4.61 (page 134) and then refer back to Figure 4.60 for a physical interpretation of the problem.

INCIDENT: DAM PROBLEMS WITH THE U.S. GOVERNMENT

The U.S. Army Corps of Engineers needed to determine where it was best to build dams in a river system for flood control. The cost of putting the dams along the tributaries was estimated, and the cost figures were put on a network diagram. The diagram was solved as a network algorithm and gave a starting solution for the optimum placement of dams for controlling the water flow within the river basin. In this case they were interested in the cheapest cost, but also in the flow of the river so that each dam will be able to generate power as well as serve as flood control.

Figure 4.61

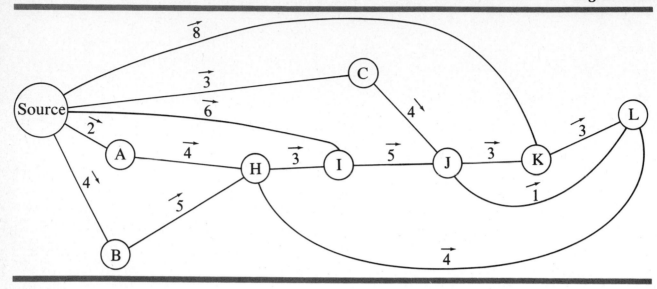

Supplementary Problems

1. Determine the maximum flow/minimal cut of the following network.

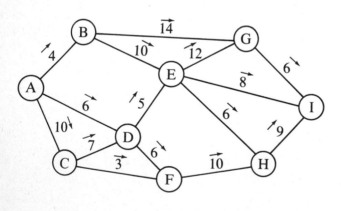

2. Refer to the Reservoir System case.
   a. In which reservoir do we have a problem? Why?
   b. What are two possible ways to solve this problem of flooding?
3. Consider the Dam Placement case.
   a. What would the minimum cost and cuts be if the cost from C–G were 40?
   b. What would the minimum cost and cuts be if the cost from H–I were 55?
4. As a combat engineer serving with the Marines, one of your jobs is to blow up bridges and roads behind enemy lines to cut off the retreat back to point M. The enemy is currently at positions A, B, and C and the escape routes are shown on the diagram, with the cost of either blowing up bridges or roads. Determine the minimum cost and which branches should be blown up by using the maximal flow algorithm.

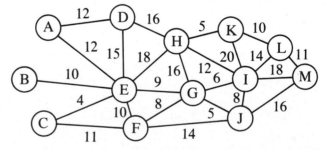

5. From what you have learned in this chapter, determine the algorithm that would be most appropriate to solve each of the problems described below:
   a. One person delivering paychecks to different branch offices. _____
   b. Rewiring an entire house. _____
   c. Scheduling completion of a new Navy missile. _____
   d. Placing of stoplights to control the flow of traffic through town. _____

4.7 BRIDGING THE GAP: THE INTERFACE

Figure 4.62

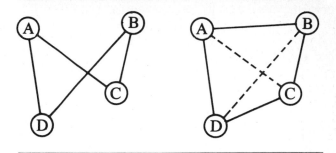

For the most part the network algorithms presented in this chapter have very simple mathematical bases, some of which have been adapted from tabular formats (such as the shortest route). Most textbooks in operations research did not even mention network problems in this network format until about 1975, even though these problems are easier to introduce and understand in this manner.

1. The mathematics behind the minimal spanning tree algorithm are quite simple and can be proved by contradiction. If there were a smaller branch that is not connected in the final solution, it could not have been connected to any node in the original diagram, which is an impossibility. A quick check for accuracy of the final solution is to see if there are any branches with small values that are not used in the answer. If there are some, then it is possible that a mistake was made in the implementation of the algorithm.

2. For the shortest route problem the network solution is actually a simple implementation of the dynamic programming algorithm, which can also be done in tabular format (see Hillier and Lieberman[5]). This analogy will be used in the dynamic programming section to give a visual representation of what dynamic programming is actually doing. The "principle of optimality" assures us that *all* the solutions generated by the Quick & Clean shortest route will in fact be shortest routes (optimal) back to the start.

3. In the traveling salesman section it was stated that the optimal tour will not intersect itself on a map drawn to scale. More correctly, we should say that the theorem is that the optimal tour will not intersect itself in the Euclidean plane. Digging back into our plane geometry we can show that given four or more nodes, the shortest paths connecting them will never intersect because if they do, another set can be found that has a smaller total.

    As shown in Figure 4.62, note that A–C and B–D are really the hypotenuses of two triangles, and that in fact there are only six possible branches, with A–C being longer than A–D or C–D and also B–D being longer than B–C or C–D. Thus we see that the nonintersecting loop on the right must be smaller than the intersecting loop on the left. It should also be apparent to the reader why these distances *must* be geometrically proportional for the theorem to always hold true.

4. Another algorithm can be developed to solve the maximal flow/minimal cut problem which is very Quick & Dirty. Simply take several cuts from source to sink, add up the capacities in the direction of cutting off flow from source to sink, and take the minimum of these. This should be an upper bound to the maximal flow and, of course, if you considered every single possible set of cuts, you would have a Long & Clean algorithm.

5. The maximal flow problem has the following mathematical representation, where X_{ij} is the amount of flow directly from node i to node j; there are N nodes; c_{ij} is the capacity in the arc from node i to node j; and node 1 is the source and node N is the sink:

$$\text{maximize flow} = \sum_{j=2}^{N} X_{1j} \text{ (flow from source)}$$

or

$$\sum_{i=1}^{N-1} X_{iN} \text{ (flow into sink)}$$

subject to

$$\sum_{i=1}^{N} X_{ij} = \sum_{k=1}^{N} X_{jk}$$

$i \neq j$, $k \neq j$ (conservation of flow at each node: what comes into node j must go out)

$$0 \leq X_{ij} \leq C_{ij} \qquad \text{for all } i, j, i \neq j$$

The Quick & Clean maximal flow algorithm was adapted from a tabular version so that the reader could more readily visualize the process. For further proof of optimality please refer to Liu[1] or Hillier and Lieberman.[5]

6. Last, it may be of some interest that the minimal spanning tree can be changed into a maximal spanning tree by choosing the largest distance rather than the smallest, *or* by keeping the algorithm the same and changing the problem by dividing the distance for each branch into 1 (using the reciprocals). This is a good example of either changing the algorithm to fit the problem or changing the problem to fit the algorithm. Now all we need is a reason to have a maximal spanning tree.

4.8 REVIEWS

Review 1: Open book and notes; show all work and write legibly.

1. (15 points) The following network represents several loudspeakers to be connected to a stereo receiver R.

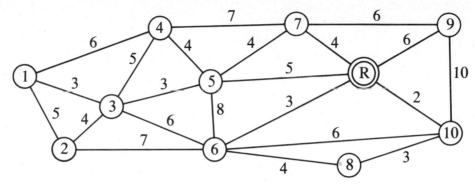

a. Determine the least number of feet of loudspeaker wire needed to connect all loudspeakers (nodes) to R in any fashion.

b. If the receiver R can only have up to three loudspeakers connected in series to each wire coming from the receiver (see diagram below), show the minimum amount of wire and how it will be hooked up.

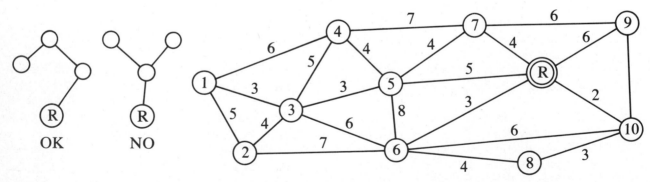

2. (10 points) Given the following network, find the critical path, T_E, T_L, and s given that T_E for node A is 0 and T_L for node J is 30.

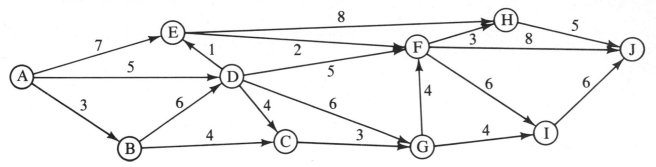

3. (9 points) For the Brookside Winery case, give the shortest route and distance:

a. From Bonita to Van Nuys: _____

b. From Bonita to La Habra: _____

c. From Bonita to Anaheim: _____

4. (8 points) Given the Traffic Flow case, if the capacity from L to O is increased from 50 to 60, where does the next bottleneck appear, and how much could that capacity be increased?

_____

_____

5. (15 points) Given the CPM chart below, answer the following questions:

a. What is the critical path and how long is it? _____

b. What paths have slack and how much? _____

c. Draw the original network and label the activity times and each node. Do *not* determine T_E, T_L, and so on.

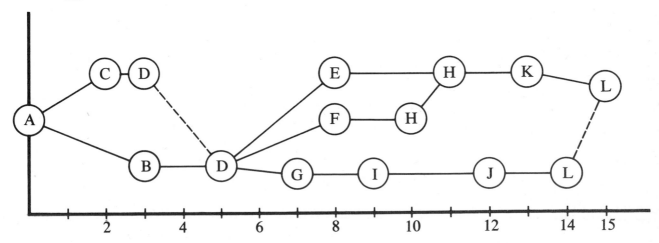

6. (10 points) Given the following cities whose distances are geometrically proportional, find the minimum traveling salesman tour that will visit every city once and only once.

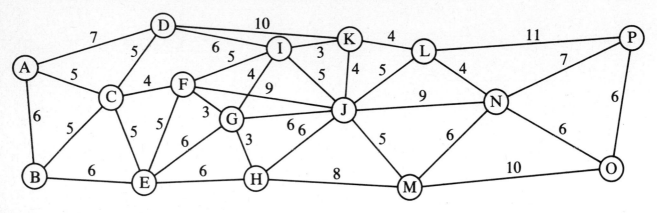

7. (8 points) For the Small Building Contractor case, what is the total time for the project if each of the following changes is made singly and independently from the original?

a. Activity 16–17 is reduced from 2 to 1: _____

b. Activity 16–17 is increased from 2 to 3: _____

c. Activity 11–13 is increased from 4 to 6: _____

d. Activity 14–18 is decreased from 6 to 4: _____

8. (10 points) Given below is a network of possible paths from A to I that represent infiltration of enemy troops from Northern Fungland to Southern Fungland. The numbers on each branch represent the costs of stopping enemy troop movement.

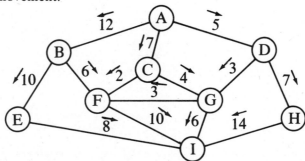

a. Give three possible cuts and their values (not necessarily optimal) that will stop the troop movement.

b. Solve for the minimal cut by using the maximal-flow algorithm and show the optimal cut. Assume that opposite flow is zero units.

Path	Flow	Cut	Cost

9. (10 points) Given the network below, find the shortest routes as follows:

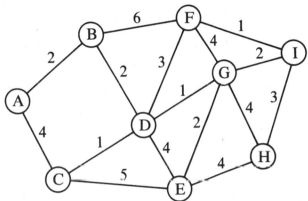

a. From A to E (show distances above nodes on network): _____

b. Then from E to F (just give path and distance; don't work it on the graph): _____

c. Finally from F back to A: _____

10. (5 points) Consider the Circuit Board case in the shortest route section. Give the following shortest routes:

Nodes	Route	Distance
9–24		
1–60		
1–36		
21–70		
63–10		

Review 2. Open book and notes; show all work and write legibly.

1. (10 points) A trapper wants to know the shortest distance to check on his traps and not check any of them twice. Given the map below, which is geometrically accurate, find the tour and the distance for the trapper to check all his traps and come back to where he started (Home).

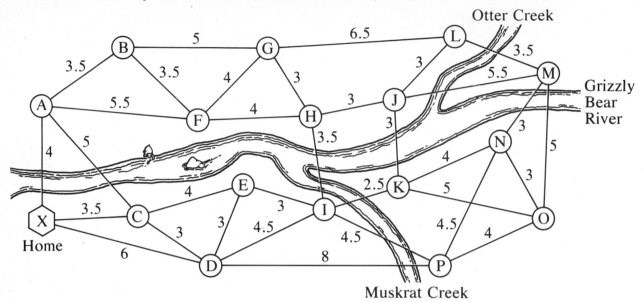

2. (10 points) Given the solution to the Porsche–Audi Dealers case, it is discovered that during one of California's frequent earthquakes the road from Pomona (22) to Monrovia (21) (and vice versa) is completely wiped out.

    a. What was the original total distance for the traveling salesman tour? _____

    _____

    _____

    b. What new changes would you make and what is the new total distance? _____

    _____

3. (10 points) Given the Fort Lauderdale Country Club case,

    a. What is the total distance of pipes needed? _____

    b. If there were no limitation on the number of sprinklers hooked up per line, what would happen to the total distance? Explain briefly. _____

    _____

    c. If all the water-main connections had to be used, would the total distance change? How?

    _____

    d. If you could hook up seven sprinklers per line, would the total distance change? How and why?

    _____

4. (10 points) A medical missionary visits 12 villages by foot, and each village is equipped with a radio to notify her of any medical needs. She wants to know the quickest route from the mission to each village. Given the times in hours on the map below, determine the quickest route to each village.

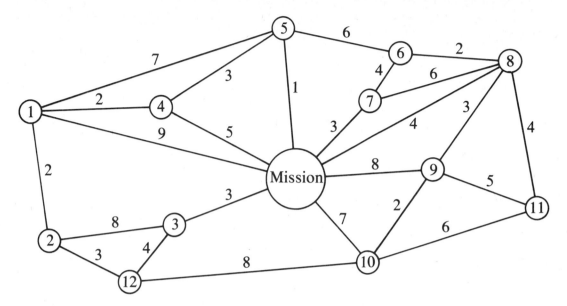

5. (10 points) Jan would like to find the overall cheapest cost to relay a telephone message between her relatives living in different cities in the state. Charges are for three minutes, enough time to give the message, and these are minimum charges. Determine the lowest cost and show your work.

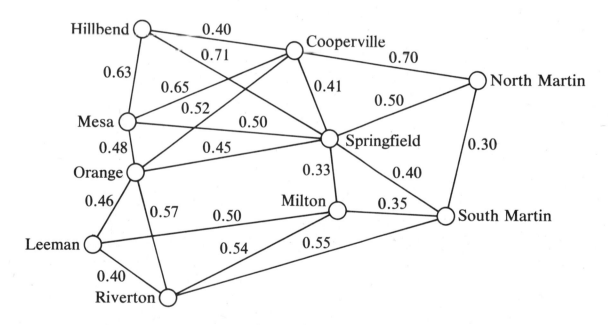

6. (10 points) For the Brookside Winery case find the shortest routes as follows:

a. From Bonita to Glendale stopping at San Pedro: _____

b. From Bonita to Guasti via San Pedro: _____

7. (10 points) Given the network below, find the maximal flow and the minimal cut from source A to sink K. List the paths and flow, the cuts and cost.

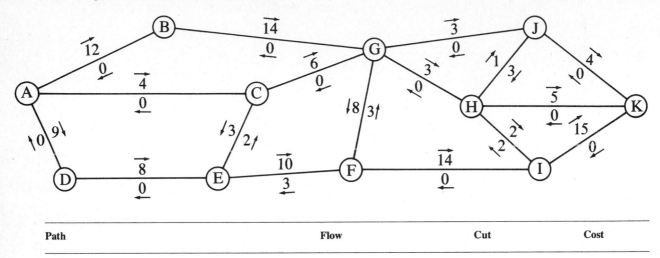

Path	Flow	Cut	Cost

8. (10 points) Consider the Reservoir System case. What is the total flow if the following changes are made? (Consider each change separately as the only change from the original problem.) Also explain what the change means in physical terms of the problem.

a. H–L capacity is 6   Total: _____   Change means: _____

b. K–L capacity is 10   Total: _____   Change means: _____

c. Source–C is 5   Total: _____   Change means: _____

9. (10 points) In order to rebuild a car engine over a weekend, the following network of activities has been laid out. Given that there are four people with a total of 80 working hours to give to the project, use a PERT method to determine if they will finish on time. Show T_E, T_L, and s for each node and identify the critical path.

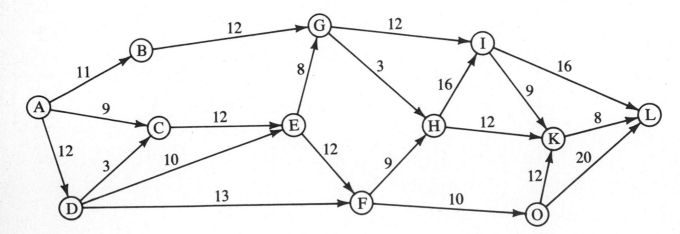

10. (10 points)

    a. What does PERT stand for? _____

    b. What does CPM stand for? _____

    c. Define what an activity is, and give one example not in the book. _____

    _____

    _____

    d. Explain why the PERT/CPM algorithms might be "dirty" instead of "clean." _____

    _____

4.9. REFERENCES

1. C. L. Liu, *Introduction to Combinatorial Mathematics* (New York: McGraw-Hill, 1968). Networks, pp. 259–261; Maximum flow/minimum cut, pp. 261–268; Minimal spanning tree, pp. 185–188.

2. R. L. Ackoff and M. W. Sasieni, *Fundamentals of Operations Research* (New York: Wiley, 1968). Shortest route, pp. 316–317; PERT, pp. 283–292; CPM, pp. 293–299.

3. M. M. Flood, "The T. S. Problem," *Operations Research*, Vol. 4, 1956, pp. 61–75.

4. S. Lin, *I.E.E.G. Spectrum*, Oct. 1966.

5. F. S. Hillier and G. J. Lieberman, *Introduction to Operations Research*, San Francisco: Holden-Day Inc., pp. 224–229.

5
assignment techniques

A host of problems can be solved using a variation of the assignment techniques. In all these problems there is the basic underlying theme of making some sort of assignment or correspondence. These techniques are essentially tabular in nature and consist of many additions and subtractions, plus a search for a maximum or a minimum, which is a table search. For problems involving more than a dozen assignments, it is usually easier to use some computerized algorithm, which is especially fast because of the fact that there are no multiplications or divisions (which take five to ten times as long as additions or subtractions). Further, all data can be scaled so that all computer operations are in fixed, not floating-point format, which takes much less time per computer instruction.

The assignment techniques in this chapter attempt to deal with problems that are combinatorial, as in Chapter 2. If there are N assignments to be made, or N cities to visit, there are $N!$ possibilities to choose from to find the optimal answer. As has been stated before, this can take quite a long time, even with the fastest computer available. Thus the techniques in this chapter attempt to take advantage of special structures present in the problems. By approaching some problems in a different manner, we will gain some more insight into their structure and solution. Thus we will again encounter the shortest route and

traveling salesman problems and solve them from a different perspective. It is important to realize that there is a difference between problems and solution techniques, and that a problem may be seen from many different angles.

The basic philosophy behind the techniques in this chapter involves a methodical way of determining trade-offs. In Chapter 3 we saw that we would be willing to trade off a decrease in average fixed costs for an increase in average available costs if the latter were less than the former. Thus we ended up balancing the two costs. In the problems in this chapter, we will be trying to minimize total costs (or time or distance) by trading off costs for several factors simultaneously. For small problems this can be done by inspection, but for larger problems this is neither simple nor intuitive.

As usual, candor forces the authors to admit that many problems presented in this chapter can be solved better as network flow problems. However, mitigation is offered in that the authors are aware of actual (by hand) solutions done on cut-and-fill operations in at least two *emerging* countries. It is instructive and educational, though, to recognize that these problems can be formulated in an assignment framework.

Finally, the authors feel compelled to suggest that it

is possible that a person might be confronted with a problem such as those presented in this chapter deep in the jungles with no computer handy. There have been rumors that not every small business in the United States has affordable access to a computer, but we assure you that this is impossible in America.

5.1 ASSIGNMENT PROBLEM

The assignment problem proper entails having n people to be assigned to n jobs that need to be done. The time estimates for how long it would take each person to do each job are given, and it is desired to determine the minimum time it would take if each person would do one job (and each job were done by only one person). Thus there may be a trade-off between having one person do a job the quickest, which might force another person to do a job that he or she is very inefficient at, versus having both of them do jobs that they are not best at, but where their combined total time would be lower.

Quick & Clean Algorithm: Assignment, Part I[1]

1. Subtract the smallest number of every row from all the numbers in that row.
2. Subtract the smallest number of every column from all the numbers in that column. If there is a zero in a column, subtract zero.
3. To make the assignment, proceed as follows:
   a. Put boxes around any *single* zeros in all the rows, and cross out any zeros that appear in the same column in which a zero is being boxed.
   b. Put boxes around any *single* zeros not yet crossed out in all the columns and cross out any zeros that appear in the same row in which a zero is being crossed out.
   c. Continue steps a. and b. until no single uncrossed zeros remain.
   d. If there are still any zeros remaining, there must be at least two in each row and column; pick *any* one, box it to break the tie, and cross out any other zeros in that row and column.
   e. When there are no more zeros to mark,
      i. there are n zeros boxed. *Stop.* Assignment is complete.
      ii. there are $m < n$ zeros boxed. Assignment is incomplete, go to part II.

Example

Step 1 simply states that each job *must* be done by

Job	Person 1	Person 2	Person 3	Person 4
A	8	26	17	11
B	13	28	4	26
C	38	19	18	15
D	19	26	24	10

someone, and that the amount of time it will take must be *at least* the smallest time for any person. Thus for job A it must take at least 8 hours to be done, regardless of who does it. We will therefore reduce the times for job A for each person by 8 and obtain the numbers representing how much extra time over the minimum will be necessary to complete the job if someone other than person 1 does it. The same is done for the other jobs, so that the table of times looks as follows:

Job	Person 1	Person 2	Person 3	Person 4	Time
A	0	18	9	3	8
B	9	24	0	22	4
C	23	4	3	0	15
D	9	16	14	0	10
					37

Thus the minimum time it could take for all the jobs to be done (if there were not the restriction that each person do one and only one job) would be 37 hours.

Step 2 looks at the columns that indicate how much more time would be needed if person 1, 2, 3, or 4 were to do any job. Looking at person 2, regardless of which job he or she did, it would still take 4 more hours at the least. Thus the column is reduced by 4. Person 1, 3, and 4 would require no more time since the minimum in those columns is 0. Thus the table of times would look as follows, and there is a zero in every row and column:

Job	Person 1	Person 2	Person 3	Person 4
A	0	14	9	3
B	9	20	0	22
C	23	0	3	0
D	9	12	14	0

Time $4 + 37 = 41$

Now the minimum time for each person doing one job, and each job being done by one person, is 41 hours.

Step 3 involves trying to make assignments with all the zeros so that no more time is added to the task.

The first row, row A, has only one zero in it, so it is boxed (and if there were other zeros in the first column, they would be crossed out). The second row, row B, contains only one zero and it is boxed, too. Row C contains two zeros, so it is bypassed for the moment. Row D contains only one zero; it is boxed, and the zero in that column is crossed out. Finally row C has just one unmarked zero (and so does column 2), and it is boxed. Now there are four boxed zeros, which is a complete assignment:

	Person			
	1	**2**	**3**	**4**
A	$\boxed{0}$	14	9	3
B	9	20	$\boxed{0}$	22
C	23	$\boxed{0}$	3	⊠
D	9	12	14	$\boxed{0}$

(Job, left label)

Thus person 1 should do job A, person 2 should do job C, person 3 should do job B, and person 4 should do job D. The time to do these would be from the original table, 8 + 19 + 4 + 10 = 41 hours. This is exactly what we determined from reducing the rows and columns. Note that job C is done by person 2, who takes more time than either person 4 or person 3. But if person 4 had done job C, then job D would have had to be done by person 2, which would have led to a total time of 53 hours. Thus we see that here it does not pay to be greedy and assign each job to the person who can do it the quickest.

Now let us take a look at what happens if part I does not yield a feasible assignment. A *feasible assignment* simply means that if we have n jobs to be assigned, then we can make those n assignments without increased cost. If, however, there are only m assignments (where obviously m is less than n), then it will cost more than the amount by which we have reduced the original table. Since there already is a zero in every row and column, we need to determine how much more the table can be reduced without passing by our optimal solution. The next part of the algorithm will determine the minimum cost trade-off that will give us another zero (or more), and then perhaps we will have a feasible assignment. If not, the algorithm will be applied until it does. The mathematics behind this algorithm are extremely complicated and will not be presented here. Thus you will simply have to see that it does work, and trust it from there.

Quick & Clean Algorithm: Assignment, Part II[1]

1. With m straight lines in the rows and/or columns, cover *all* the zeros. You should be able to cover

all the zeros (marked or unmarked) with the same number of lines as there are boxed zeros.
2. Find the smallest number that does not have a line through it.
3. Subtract this number from all the numbers without a line through them. Then add it to all the numbers that lie at the *intersection* of two lines. Leave all the other numbers alone.
4. The total is increased by the smallest number times $(n-m)$. *Go back to step 3 in part I.*

Example. Given the original table of times for a 4 × 4 assignment problem, we end up without a maximal assignment:

	Person			
	1	**2**	**3**	**4**
A	11	17	8	16
B	9	7	12	6
C	13	16	15	12
D	21	24	17	28

Original

	Person			
	1	**2**	**3**	**4**
A	3	9	0	8
B	3	1	6	0
C	1	4	3	0
D	4	7	0	11

Step 1
Total time = 43

	Person			
	1	**2**	**3**	**4**
A	2	8	$\boxed{0}$	8
B	2	$\boxed{0}$	6	⊠
C	$\boxed{0}$	3	3	⊠
D	3	6	⊠	11

Steps 2 and 3
Total time = 45

Note that only three zeros can be boxed (assigned) and that it will cost more to make a complete assignment (four jobs by four persons). Part II of the algorithm is usually called the *Hungarian method*, and although it looks complicated, it simply ensures that the rows and columns will be reduced simultaneously by the least amount to give us another zero. In this case it will take only three lines to cover all the zeros. The actual lines used do not necessarily form a unique set, and sometimes there is more than one set of lines that will suffice. You simply have to pick any set of m lines:

Step 1

	Person			
	1	2	3	4
A	2	8	[0]	8
B	2	[0]	6	✗
C	[0]	3	3	✗
D	3	6	✗	11

Job

Steps 2, 3 and 4

Total time = 45 + (4 − 3)2

= 47

	Person			
	1	2	3	4
A	0	6	0	6
B	2	0	8	0
C	0	3	5	0
D	1	4	0	9

Job

Step 3, Part I

	Person			
	1	2	3	4
A	[0]	6	✗	6
B	2	[0]	8	✗
C	✗	3	5	[0]
D	1	4	[0]	9

Job

We now have a complete (or maximal) assignment. Person 1 does job A (cost or time = 11), person 2 does job B (7), person 3 does job D (17), and person 4 does job C (12) for a total time of 47. Here we will note that there are some trade-offs. If person 3 had done job A instead of person 1, we would have saved three units of time, *but* then person 1 would have done job D and it would have taken four more units of time with an overall loss of one unit. As it turns out, if we had been greedy with the first three jobs (A–3, B–2, C–1), we would have been forced to assign job D to person 4, and the total cost would have been 56 instead of 47. Thus the trade-offs for

this problem of only four jobs and four people are complex and not necessarily intuitively evident.

It should be noted that this algorithm is a *minimizing* algorithm. However, when a problem is presented that must maximize the assignments, either the algorithm must be changed to maximize, or the problem changed to minimize. You will find that it is much easier to change the problem by simply taking the largest number in the table and subtracting every other number from it. Thus if we were maximizing in the last example, we would subtract every number from 28 in the original table. Our first row would be 17, 11, 20, and 12 and so on. The problem then would be solved by the Quick & Clean algorithm and the answer converted back to the original data, and the original problem would be maximized.

transmission line crew

The available line crews are to be assigned to the jobs required to be completed. There can be up to 150 jobs available at any period of time. One crew can only work on one job at a time. There is never a case where there are more crews than jobs available.

Which *jobs* are to be worked on is usually decided by the following:

1. crew availability,
2. weather and terrain,
3. equipment available,
4. material available,
5. required operating dates,
6. permit and license availability,
7. design information available,
8. political issues, both internal and external.

The decision is not always logical, nor is it predictable by any mathematical formula.

Assuming that the decision as to which jobs will be done is out of our hands, our problem becomes one of assigning crews to the jobs selected in the most efficient manner.

Each crew is made up of personnel who have varying degrees of skill in constructing tower foundations, erecting towers, and stringing wire. The efficiency of a crew is kept in the form of a productivity rating, which is a factor in determining the number of hours it will take the crew to complete a job.

The jobs vary in difficulty and in the mix of foundation work, tower erection, and wire stringing. Some crews are better at one operation than at another and, therefore, can do some jobs faster than others.

The number of man-hours (in thousands) it will take a crew to do each job is evaluated in the following table:

	Job			
	A	B	C	D
1	100	78	81	98
Crew 2	80	82	87	90
3	85	84	80	92
4	95	86	83	92

These numbers come from an estimated average number of man-hours for the job times the crew performance rating. For example,

Job A—significant amount of stringing work
Crew 2—productivity rating for this type of work
$= 0.8$
Average estimate of man-hours $= 100$
$100 \times 0.8 = 80$ man-hours.

Assuming that we have four crews and four jobs, what is the minimum time in which we can complete this work?

Solution

Recommendation

Assuming that the time estimates are close to correct, the jobs and crews should be assigned in the following manner for a minimum time of 330,000 man-hours for all four jobs:

crew 1–job B;
crew 2–job A;
crew 3–job C;
crew 4–job D.

Numerical Answer

Crew	Job	Man-hours
1	B	78,000
2	A	80,000
3	C	80,000
4	D	92,000
		330,000

Math Work

	Job			
	A	B	C	D
1	100	78	81	98
Crew 2	80	82	87	90
3	85	84	80	92
4	95	86	83	92

Original times

	Job				
	A	B	C	D	
1	22	0	3	20	reduced by 78
Crew 2	0	2	7	10	reduced by 80
3	5	4	0	12	reduced by 80
4	12	3	0	9	reduced by 83

Reducing each row by the minimum in each row   321

	Job			
	A	B	C	D
1	22	0	3	11
Crew 2	0	2	7	1
3	5	4	0	3
4	12	3	0	0

Reduce column D by 9
Total time $= 321 + 9 = 330$

Now there is a zero cost for making an assignment in each row and each column. The assignments are made as follows:

	Job				
	A	B	C	D	
1	22	[0]	3	11	1–B
Crew 2	[0]	2	7	1	2–A
3	5	4	[0]	3	3–C
4	12	3	✗	[0]	4–D

class scheduling

The head of the math department at MSC has to make class assignments to his faculty. All classes have been given to instructors, except one section each of Mathematics 101, 111, 112, 122, and 135. All professors have a full load, except five who need one more class each to fulfill their load requirements. The department chairman has had the students in each of the classes fill out a teacher-evaluation sheet on each professor. He then rated each of the professors on a scale of 0 to 100 (100 being the best) on the basis of the teacher-evaluation sheets. His ratings were as follows:

	101	111	Classes 112	122	135
RMN	60	95	20	40	75
ALF	20	75	30	85	50
CMW	70	80	60	95	65
RMH	50	40	90	85	35
JLC	100	90	85	95	100

How should he make the assignments? Now that this has been done, you might want to obtain data from your own department and schedule the classes according to this algorithm. What problems would you run into? What assumptions have been hidden and are now brought to light?

INCIDENT: RELAY ASSIGNMENT

The first published application of the assignment problem involved the selection of the members of a swimming relay team. The coach had to pick four people for the 4 × 100-yard medley relay team. This means that each person must swim a different stroke (butterfly, backstroke, breaststroke, and freestyle). Each person had been timed in all four strokes, and of course could only swim one of them, and all four must participate. The coach used the assignment algorithm to determine the best trade-offs so that the total time for the medley relay was minimized.

billet assignment

At a U.S. Naval Training Center each member of a graduating class of enlisted trainees is carefully interviewed and tested. The testing includes a series of tests called a *battery*. Each recruit is given four tests: general classification test (GCT), arithmetic (ARI), mechanical (MECH), and clerical (CLER). In addition, a sonar test (SON) is given to those recruits who indicate an interest in electronics. The test scores received by a recruit become part of his permanent record and are a major determining factor in his ability to obtain future schools and special programs. Beginning at boot camp, the tests are used to determine which recruits are eligible for current billets (positions) at various technical (skills) schools. A recruit who scores high on the battery and who knows exactly which one of the 60 or more ratings to strike for (position) is generally given orders to that school. However, in every class there are normally

four or five recruits who score very high and who are willing to attend any electronics school that has an opening.

From the data given, consider five recruits and their test scores, and the five positions that are available, along with the test scores used to determine which recruit should be the best candidate. The highest possible test score is 80 on each test, and each position is the combination of two test scores. Assuming that the Navy wishes to maximize the total test scores used, determine the optimal allocation and assignments.

Recruit	GCT	ARI	Test MECH	CLER	SON	Position	Tests
Henderson	59	59	57	64	58	ET-1	GCT + ARI
Welks	61	60	63	56	61	ET-2	SON + ARI
Williams	65	67	59	61	51	ST-1	SON + GCT
Theo	58	59	54	53	62	HT-1	GCT + MECH
Wiggins	70	69	67	65	58	GMT-1	GCT + CLER

INCIDENT: DIFFICULTIES IN SOLVING ASSIGNMENT PROBLEMS

The department chairperson of the management science department in a school of business decided to assign classes to the professors in her department based upon their student ratings. She felt that this would maximize the effectiveness of the department. The department held a quick meeting and decided that she should no longer be chairperson. (The chairperson had solved an unconstrained assignment problem without taking into account certain constraints such as "favorite" courses, rivalries among professors, and so on.) This serves as yet another warning against blind implementation of quantitative techniques, and it also shows that not all data is purely objective.

computer programming

At the computer center of a school of business there were seven programmers at the beginning of the fall 1971 semester. The director wanted to keep all of them busy and had seven jobs that required different levels of expertise. The computer center had an IBM 360/30 with eleven time-sharing terminals that ran BASIC FORTRAN (another version of FORTRAN, not to be confused with BASIC, which is a different language). Some new programs needed to be written for statistics classes, others needed to be translated from BASIC packages. The center also had four tape drives and was able to run batch jobs on DOS in COBOL, PL/I, FORTRAN IV, or BAL. For large jobs (the core on the model 30 was only 65 K bytes) the center could use the university computer center which had just installed an IBM 370/155 with 500 K bytes. Materials had to be handcarried over to the main center as there was no batch teleprocessing available. Some of the programmers were familiar with the operating system at the university computer center and the job control language (JCL) which could be learned and retained with great difficulty.

The jobs which the director needed done were described as follows:

1. Write a BAL program on model 30 to read COMPUSTAT tapes (stock market prices, dividends, and so on).
2. Write a FORTRAN program for the Kolmogorov–Smirnoff test on model 30 on terminal.
3. Rewrite statistics program COVAR from BASIC to FORTRAN for model 30 on terminals.
4. Catalog ARRIBA code (integer programming) and Out-of-Kilter algorithm (network flow) on model 155, develop write-up and easy instructions for student use.
5. Solve large linear programming problem using MPS/360 on model 155 and provide write-up for student use.
6. Write COBOL program to generate input data for huge integer programming problem (4550 data cards), debug on model 30, and run on model 155.
7. Develop random number generator for 360/30 system that reads internal clock as random seed for series. Write in BAL.

The programmers were then asked to estimate the time it would take them (in hours) to complete the jobs. Since some were not familiar with certain languages or procedures, some estimates were high, indicating a necessary learning period, or in some cases an infinite time was given (*M*). The director was concerned with keeping everyone busy, keeping costs down, minimizing the total time involved, and reducing the spread between the shortest job and the longest job.

Given the data at the top of the next column, determine which programmers should have done which job, how much it cost, and what were the lowest time, the largest time, and the total time. Since the director was not sure whether she wanted to minimize costs or time, solve the problem twice and determine if there is any difference. If there is, present a rationale for choosing the assignments you would recommend.

	Job Number						
Programmer	1	2	3	4	5	6	7
Erol ($3.25/hour)	40	15	20	15	12	35	20
Clark ($3.50/hour)	35	15	22	13	10	20	20
Larry ($2.25/hour)	80	25	15	11	8	40	35
Kelvin ($2.50/hour)	70	30	25	17	12	50	45
Nancy ($2.00/hour)	M	35	35	25	30	M	M
Jeff ($3.00/hour)	50	30	30	16	10	45	30
Julie ($2.75/hour)	70	25	25	18	10	55	30

Supplementary Problems

1. Given the incomplete assignment below, make a complete assignment using the Quick & Clean Assignment Algorithm, Part II.

	1	2	3	4	5	6
1	0	3	6	2	8	9
2	8	7	6	0	5	3
3	2	0	9	4	4	0
4	0	6	7	6	6	5
5	9	5	0	11	2	0
6	4	3	8	9	0	5

2. At SAM's annual Halloween party, seven people were given seven minutes to get one person each to sign his or her name as to whether the person had dyed hair, drank coffee today, was left handed, had curly hair, was an only child, an ex-smoker, or played a musical instrument. Each person could only sign for one of these attributes. Given the simple table below, determine who should sign for which attribute.

Attribute	R.H.	B.G.	L.M.	C.R.	T.B.	C.K.	P.M.	Person	Attribute
Dyed Hair		X						___	___
Drank Coffee	X		X		X		X	___	___
Left-handed	X			X				___	___
Curly Hair	X		X	X				___	___
Only Child				X			X	___	___
Ex-Smoker	X		X					___	___
Play Instrument			X			X	X	___	___

3. A construction supervisor needs one person to do each of the following tasks, and the less hours it takes to do them the better. Given the hours it takes in the table below, determine the optimal assignment.

Job

	1	2	3	4	5
A	9	13	5	9	13
B	11	6	7	8	10
Person **C**	7	9	15	12	24
D	20	3	17	14	6
E	5	16	8	21	12

Job

	1	2	3	4	5
A					
B					
Person **C**					
D					
E					

Job

	1	2	3	4	5
A					
B					
Person **C**					
D					
E					

Job

	1	2	3	4	5
A					
B					
Person **C**					
D					
E					

Job

	1	2	3	4	5
A					
B					
Person **C**					
D					
E					

Job

	1	2	3	4	5
A					
B					
Person **C**					
D					
E					

Assignment ——————————————————

Hours ——————————————————

5.2 SHORTEST ROUTE

The shortest route problem, which we encountered in Chapter 4, can also be solved using the assignment method by changing the initial matrix. First the network is changed into a table of values (*direct* distances between cities). Then the table is changed according to the Quick & Clean rules, adding zeros and M's. The M simply stands for some large number that represents such a huge cost or distance between the cities that in effect you cannot go directly between them. Also the M is so large that to add any finite number or subtract a number won't alter the fact that it is huge, so that it will still be equal to M.

Quick & Clean Algorithm: Shortest Route[2]

1. Change the original table of distances or costs for going from city i to city j as follows:
   a. Set each number of the main diagonal, from upper left to lower right, to zero, which will allow subtours of length one and cost zero, thus adding no cost to the complete assignment.
   b. Set column i to all M's (this covers up one of

the diagonal zeros), which will force the tour to leave city i.

c. Set row j to all M's (this covers up another diagonal zero).

d. Set the number in row j, column i to zero. This returns the shortest route back to city i and makes a complete tour but doesn't add any cost.

2. Solve the assignment problem. There will be an assignment from city i to some city k, from city k to some city p, . . ., and so on, and from city q to city j and from city j back to city i. Thus the shortest route will be i to k to p to . . . q to j. All other subtours will be cost zero and do not affect the solution.

Example. Shortest route from 1 to 5.

		To City			
	1	**2**	**3**	**4**	**5**
1	–	4	8	3	M
2	4	–	2	M	8
3	8	2	–	2	6
4	3	M	2	–	M
5	M	8	6	M	–

(From City)

The table gives only values of *direct* connections between the cities shown in Figure 5.1.

Figure 5.1

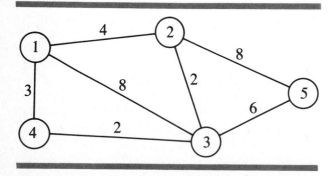

After step 1 the table for going from city 1 to city 5 will look as follows:

		To City			
	1	**2**	**3**	**4**	**5**
1	M	4	8	3	M
2	M	0	2	M	8
3	M	2	0	2	6
4	M	M	2	0	M
5	0	M	M	M	M

(From City)

The solution after step 2 looks as follows:

		To City			
	1	**2**	**3**	**4**	**5**
1	M	⊠	3	[0]	M
2	M	[0]	1	M	1
3	M	3	⊠	4	[0]
4	M	M	[0]	⊠	M
5	[0]	M	M	M	M

(From City)

The assignment is:

From City	To City	Length
1	4	3
2	2	0
3	5	6
4	3	2
5	1	0
		11

Thus we find the shortest route starting at city 1. City 1 goes to city 4, city 4 to city 3, city 3 to city 5, and city 5 returns to city 1. City 2 simply goes to city 2 at no cost. Thus the shortest route is 1–4–3–5, with a length of 11. Check this with the first method of the shortest route in Section 4.2.

Note that this method does *not* find all the shortest routes from city 1, but only the route from city 1 to city 5. However, an advantage of this method is that we can require the shortest-route tour to stop off at some city. In this case, let us require that we find the shortest route from city 1 to city 5, but have to stop at city 2. To do that, all that needs to be done to the original matrix is to set the distance from city 2 to city $2 = M$ (in other words, too high a cost for city 2 not to be included in the tour). Then solve the assignment problem. (The M could be put in the last table also and solved from that point.) If the solution contains the necessary city, it is optimal. If it does not, then there is some more work that must be done, which will be covered in the Traveling Salesman section.

The original matrix with the necessary changes for the shortest route from city 1 to city 5 stopping at city 2 is

		To City			
	1	**2**	**3**	**4**	**5**
1	M	4	8	3	M
2	M	M	2	M	8
3	M	2	0	2	6
4	M	M	2	0	M
5	0	M	M	M	M

(From City)

or continuing from the last table of the previous problem,

To City

From City		1	2	3	4	5
	1	M	0	3	0	M
	2	M	M	1	M	1
	3	M	3	0	4	0
	4	M	M	0	0	M
	5	0	M	M	M	M

The solution after step 2 is

To City

From City		1	2	3	4	5
	1	M	[0]	3	0	M
	2	M	M	[0]	M	[0]
	3	M	3	[0]	4	[0]
	4	M	M	✕	[0]	M
	5	[0]	M	M	M	M

The assignment is:

From City	To City	Length
1	2	4
2	3	2
3	5	6
4	4	0
5	1	0
		12

The tour goes 1–2–3–5 for a length of 12, which is the shortest route from city 1 to city 5 with city 2 included (it was 11 without city 2 being included). Note that an *alternate route* (dotted boxes) exists as 1–2–5.

overland rerouting

Implementing the solution to the previous Overland Moving and Storage case, the drivers have just made a stop for a customer in Des Moines. Half of the truck was emptied of household goods, furnishings, appliances, and other valuables. The other half of the truck remained with goods for another customer. The movers thought that they were going on to Cleveland, but the destination on the boxes read Cincinnati. When they checked back with the main office in Denver, it confirmed that they indeed should go on to Cincinnati and not to Cleveland, as the customer would be very upset if the goods were delivered to the wrong city. Determine the shortest route from Des Moines to Cincinnati. Table 5.1 gives the distances, where the M's are used to stand for distances that are either not direct or simply not of interest in the problem. The nice thing about using these M's is that they represent such a large number that anything added to it or subtracted from it, the number still remains equal to M. If the algorithm is to be computerized, then some large number should be used instead.

Solution

Recommendation
The movers should take the route from Des Moines to Cincinnati via Chicago and then Indianapolis for a total mileage of 647 miles.

Table 5.1

	DesM.	K.C	Chi.	St.L.	Det.	Clev.	Ind.	Lou.	Cin.
DesM.	—	205	354	360	M	M	M	M	M
K.C.	205	—	504	255	M	M	M	M	M
Chi.	354	504	—	295	294	248	185	M	M
St.L.	360	255	295	—	M	M	243	264	345
Det.	M	M	294	M	—	168	279	M	267
Clev.	M	M	248	M	168	—	315	M	255
Ind.	M	M	185	243	279	315	—	116	108
Lou.	M	M	M	264	M	M	116	—	98
Cin.	M	M	M	345	267	255	108	98	—

Numerical Answer

From	To	Miles
Des Moines	Chicago	354
Chicago	Indianapolis	185
Indianapolis	Cincinnati	108
		647 miles

Math Work. The original table of numbers is changed by the addition of zeros and *M*'s. Then the table is reduced by 205 in the first row, 98 in the last column (see Table 5.2).

Again the assignment is not complete, lacking one assignment. Since there are eight assignments, it

means that there are eight lines that can be drawn through all the zeros. The minimum element that is uncovered is 149, as shown in Table 5.3. Thus total mileage is now 488 + 149 = 637 miles.

Here again there is not a complete assignment, so that eight lines can be drawn in such a way that the smallest unlined number is 10 and the new mileage is 647 miles (see Table 5.4). Note that if the St.L. row had been lined out rather than the column, it would have taken another step.

We can now make a complete or maximal assignment at a minimum cost of 647 miles.

Table 5.2

	DesM.	K.C.	Chi.	St.L.	Det.	Clev.	Ind.	Lou.	Cin.
DesM.	*M*	[0]	149	155	*M*	*M*	*M*	*M*	*M*
K.C.	*M*	X	504	255	*M*	*M*	*M*	*M*	*M*
Chi.	*M*	504	[0]	295	294	248	(185)	*M*	*M*
St.L.	*M*	255	295	[0]	*M*	*M*	243	264	247
Det.	*M*	*M*	294	*M*	[0]	168	279	*M*	169
Clev.	*M*	*M*	248	*M*	168	[0]	315	*M*	157
Ind.	*M*	*M*	185	243	279	315	[0]	116	10
Lou.	*M*	*M*	*M*	264	*M*	*M*	116	[0]	X
Cin.	[0]	*M*	*M*	*M*	*M*	*M*	*M*	*M*	*M*

The distance is 205 + 98 = 303 miles.
This is not a complete assignment since we need nine assignments and have only eight. The smallest unlined element is 185:

	DesM.	K.C.	Chi.	St.L.	Det.	Clev.	Ind.	Lou.	Cin.
DesM.	*M*	[0]	(149)	155	*M*	*M*	*M*	*M*	*M*
K.C.	*M*	X	504	255	*M*	*M*	*M*	*M*	*M*
Chi.	*M*	504	[0]	295	109	63	X	*M*	*M*
St.L.	*M*	255	295	[0]	*M*	*M*	58	79	62
Det.	*M*	*M*	479	*M*	[0]	168	279	*M*	169
Clev.	*M*	*M*	433	*M*	168	[0]	315	*M*	157
Ind.	*M*	*M*	370	428	279	315	[0]	116	10
Lou.	*M*	*M*	*M*	449	*M*	*M*	116	[0]	X
Cin.	[0]	*M*	*M*	*M*	*M*	*M*	*M*	*M*	*M*

The distance is now 303 + 185 = 488 miles.

machine shop

A small machine shop in Fallbrook has just hired someone to make deliveries and pick up needed parts and raw materials. Many of the places that this delivery person will be going to are small towns, and the roads and routes to get there involve a lot of winding around hills and canyons. The longest trip involves going to Ajax from Fallbrook, and the owner would like to determine the shortest route. Given the distances in Table 5.5 (page 156), give the owner a recommendation for the shortest route.

INCIDENT: THE MEXICAN CONNECTION

Using the concepts of the trade-offs in the assignment algorithm, it was easy to set up a matrix of

distances for the laying out of roads between several small towns in Mexico. Rather than being "greedy" by choosing the smallest connections between towns, the planning committee arrived at an overall optimum by using the shortest-route algorithm with certain necessary stops. (Of course the matrix was in kilometers rather than miles.)

tasting rooms

The Brookside Winery acquired the Mills Brothers' Winery, which is based around the San Francisco area. Brookside has been exclusively in the southern part of California, and it can now expand its operations to the north. It sells its wine solely from its tasting rooms, which are located at strategic spots along well-traveled routes so that visitors and tourists will stop. Using the map, Figure 5.2, page 156, deter-

Table 5.3

	DesM.	K.C.	Chi.	St.L.	Det.	Clev.	Ind.	Lou.	Cin.
DesM.	M	✗	[0]	6	M	M	M	M	M
K.C.	M	[0]	355	106	M	M	M	M	M
Chi.	M	653	✗	295	109	63	✗	M	M
St.L.	M	404	295	[0]	M	M	58	79	62
Det.	M	M	479	M	[0]	168	279	M	169
Clev.	M	M	433	M	168	[0]	315	M	157
Ind.	M	M	370	428	279	315	[0]	116	(10)
Lou.	M	M	M	449	M	M	116	[0]	✗
Cin.	[0]	M	M	M	M	M	M	M	M

Table 5.4

	DesM.	K.C.	Chi.	St.L.	Det.	Clev.	Ind.	Lou.	Cin.
DesM.	M	✗	[0]	6	M	M	M	M	M
K.C.	M	[0]	355	106	M	M	M	M	M
Chi.	M	653	✗	295	99	53	[0]	M	M
St.L.	M	410	295	[0]	M	M	58	75	58
Det.	M	M	489	M	[0]	168	289	M	165
Clev.	M	M	443	M	168	[0]	325	M	153
Ind.	M	M	370	428	273	309	✗	106	[0]
Lou.	M	M	M	459	M	M	126	[0]	✗
Cin.	[0]	M	M	M	M	M	M	M	M

Table 5.5

	Fallbrook	Rainier	Riverside	Vista	Martin	Elmira	Demere	Little Valley	Ajax	Hiram
Fallbrook	M	6	17	15	21	22	36	39	52	30
Rainier	6	M	22	20	26	21	41	44	51	35
Riverside	17	22	M	7	13	17	19	22	42	13
Vista	15	20	7	M	6	10	22	25	45	16
Martin	21	26	13	6	M	4	17	20	33	11
Elmira	22	21	17	10	4	M	15	18	29	14
Demere	36	41	19	22	17	15	M	3	23	6
Little Valley	39	44	22	25	20	18	3	M	20	9
Ajax	52	51	42	45	33	29	23	20	M	29
Hiram	30	35	13	16	11	14	6	9	29	M

Figure 5.2

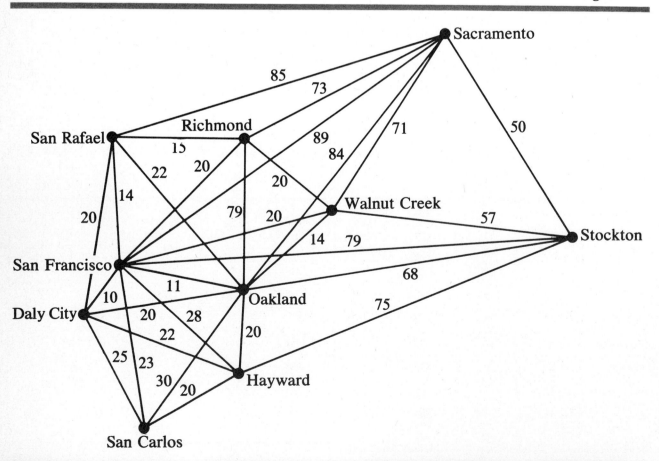

mine what would be the shortest route from Daly City to Sacramento, the state capital of California. Presently the route being used is from Daly City to Oakland, then Walnut Creek, and finally on to Sacramento. Use the assignment method to show that there is a better route.

INCIDENT: NO COMPUTER? NO PROBLEM!

In Costa Rica the laying of pipelines was facilitated by the use of the assignment algorithm where no computerized algorithm was available. Here they were interested in finding the shortest route from town to town, but with the necessity of certain junctures being hooked up. Thus in this case this algorithm is superior to the network application.

brookside winery, southern area

The Brookside Winery is interested in the shortest route from Ventura to Guasti, the company headquarters. Figure 5.3 shows a map of eleven of the wine tasting rooms that Brookside has in Southern California (there are a total of 16) and the distances between them. Ventura is the northernmost tasting room for the southern area. It is also interested in making a side trip to Torrance along the way, and needs to determine if this will make any significant

difference in the total mileage traveled. Therefore determine the shortest route from Ventura to Guasti without requiring a stop at Torrance. If Torrance is not included in the shortest route, then resolve the problem by requiring Torrance to be included and determine how many more miles that will add to the distance from Ventura to Guasti. Also determine if the route is significantly different. Assume that the problem is symmetrical, that is, the distance from point A to point B is the same as from point B to point A.

Supplementary Problems

1. A bakery truck must make a trip from city 3 to city 4 by the shortest distance. Given the table of distances below, find the shortest route and minimum mileage.

	1	2	3	4	5	6
1	—	5	8	13	9	22
2	2	—	25	6	14	13
3	3	25	—	11	20	M
4	6	6	11	—	16	10
5	8	14	20	16	—	4
6	4	7	2	5	6	

(Problem 1 continues)

Figure 5.3

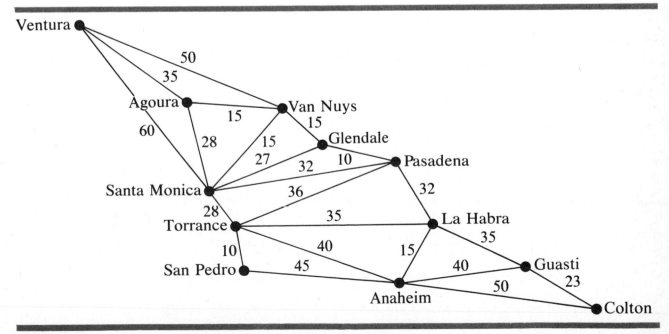

	1	2	3	4	5	6
1						
2						
3						
4						
5						
6						

	1	2	3	4	5	6
1	—	3	9	4	9	3
2	3	—	8	5	4	9
3	7	4	—	1	2	4
4	8	9	6	—	8	5
5	4	5	8	3	—	6
6	6	2	2	6	7	—

	1	2	3	4	5	6
1						
2						
3						
4						
5						
6						

	1	2	3	4	5	6
1						
2						
3						
4						
5						
6						

	1	2	3	4	5	6
1						
2						
3						
4						
5						
6						

	1	2	3	4	5	6
1						
2						
3						
4						
5						
6						

	1	2	3	4	5	6
1						
2						
3						
4						
5						
6						

Route _____

Mileage _____

2. Given the Machine Shop case:
   a. How many more miles would it take to stop at Rainier on the way to Ajax? _____
   b. What is the optimal route now? _____
   _____
   c. What would happen, looking again at the last table in your homework, if you had to stop in Demere? How many more miles would be added to the last table and why? (*Do not solve!*) _____
   _____

3. Given the table of distances at the top of the next column, find the shortest route from City 2 to City 6, stopping at City 3.

4. a. Give two good reasons for using the algorithm in Section 5.2 for the shortest route problem over the algorithm in Section 4.2 for the shortest route.

    b. Give two good reasons for preferring the algorithm in Section 4.2.

5.3 DELIVERY

The delivery problem is concerned with making deliveries or pickups at each stop or city in such a way that the total time, cost, or distance will be minimized.

There are two versions of this problem, the simpler being that the solution required will not return to a main depot, drop-off point, or pickup station. Graphically it would look as shown in Figure 5.4.

The second type is concerned with a fleet of trucks that all leave from the same spot and return there. The Post Office is concerned with such a case, where the trucks leave the office, deliver mail, and return to the same office. Also, the trucks must make pickups at the various mail boxes around the city and return to the main office; the mail is then sorted and disbursed. Graphically it would look as shown in Figure 5.5.

Figure 5.5

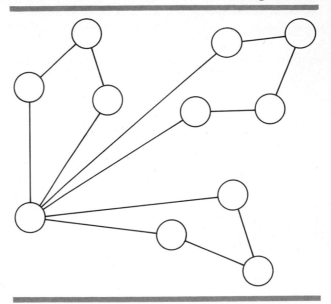

2. Solve the assignment problem. This will give the minimum length for all the vehicles to visit all the stops, and it will also give the optimum number of vehicles needed.

Example. From Figure 5.6 the following table is constructed:

		To City				
		1	2	3	4	5
	1	M	4	8	3	M
	2	4	M	2	M	8
From City	3	8	2	M	2	6
	4	3	M	2	M	M
	5	M	8	6	M	M

Original

Figure 5.4

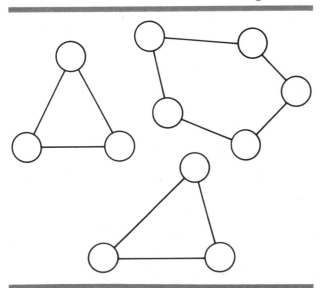

Quick & Clean Algorithm: Delivery, Case I

1. Construct the table of distances between points or cities. Put *M*'s on the diagonal from the upper left to the lower right only, thus preventing a tour of a city delivering to itself at cost zero.

Figure 5.6

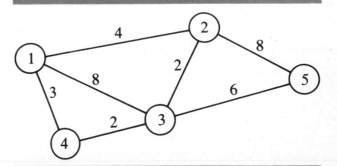

Figure 5.7

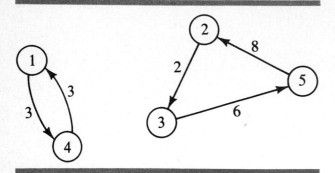

The final solution is 1–4–1 and 2–3–5–2, as shown in Figure 5.7. The length is 22 units.

To City

	1	2	3	4	5
1	M	1	7	[0]	M
2	⊠	M	[0]	M	⊠
3	6	⊠	M	⊠	[0]
4	[0]	M	1	M	M
5	M	[0]	⊠	M	M

From City (label to the left of rows 3 and 4)

Final solution: 1–4–1, 2–3–5–2

Case II is a little more difficult, and for this we shall present a Quick & Dirty algorithm for the time being. First we must determine how many vehicles or routes are needed, set up a table of distances or costs, and apply our heuristic. This will also require the establishing of one or more fictitious source cities.

Quick & Dirty Algorithm: Delivery, Case II

1. Set up the table of distances, costs, or times between cities, adding extra rows and columns for the source of the trucks or vehicles. Put M's down the main diagonal.
2. Starting with the source, pick the smallest number in that row (the shortest distance to the next city). Go to that row.
3. Continue being "greedy" (picking the smallest number in that row) with the following limitations:
   a. You cannot return to the original source node until the end.
   b. Do not return immediately to the other source nodes if possible.

This is a very "dirty" algorithm, but one that will at least provide a workable solution.

Example. In the previous example, if we were to have two trucks stationed at city 3, our graph would be that shown in Figure 5.8 and the resulting table of distances would look as follows:

	1	2	3A	3B	4	5
1	M	4	8	8	3	M
2	4	M	2	2	M	8
3A	8	2	M	M	2	6
3B	8	2	M	M	2	6
4	3	M	2	2	M	M
5	M	8	6	6	M	M

Notice that we have split city 3 into two nodes, 3A and 3B, with identical distances to the other nodes. In the table this simply means that each row and column for city 3 is identical. If we were to have three trucks, we would then have three identical rows and columns, and so on. Notice that M's are used as distances between identical nodes.

We will now start at the source node, row 3A, and pick the smallest number, which is a 2 in column 2. We now go to row 2 and see that the smallest number goes right back to column 3A or column 3B. Since our distances are symmetrical, this is of course not surprising, but heeding our step 3b, let us choose the next smallest number in row 2, which is 4 in column 1. Now we proceed to row 1 and find a 3 as the smallest number, which leads us to row 4, since the 3 was in column 4. The smallest number in row 4 is a 2, both in column 3A and column 3B. Step 3a says that we can't go back to column 3A yet, so we choose column 3B. Moving on to row 3B, we find that the smallest number in that row is a 2, but we have already visited those cities (2 and 4), so we must choose the 6 in column 5. Finally we arrive at row 5 and choose the last available number, a 6 in column 3A, and we have

Figure 5.8

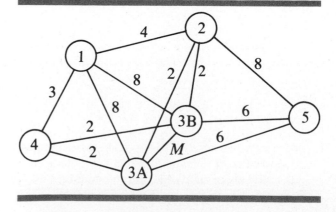

completed our algorithm. The table would look as follows:

	1	2	3A	3B	4	5
1	*M*	4	8	8	③	*M*
2	④	*M*	2	2	*M*	8
3A	8	②	*M*	*M*	2	6
3B	8	2	*M*	*M*	2	⑥
4	3	*M*	2	②	*M*	*M*
5	*M*	8	⑥	6	*M*	*M*

The possible routes are shown in Figure 5.9. In terms of the original diagram, we will have two delivery routes for a total distance of 23 units.

Figure 5.9

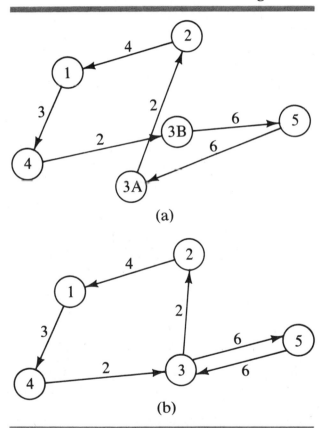

(a)

(b)

bank delivery systems

Bank Delivery Systems is a small corporation located in Jackson, in Jefferson County, which sells pneumatic tube delivery systems. It is owned and operated by one person, Mr. José Rodrigues. José is in the business of selling, producing, installing, and servicing drive-up bank teller systems. Usually there are four units at each bank. A customer drives up, deposits the papers into a carrier, and drops the carrier into the unit. The pneumatic (or vacuum) system

rushes the carrier to the teller from where it will be sent back with a traveling time of about 2 seconds. This is a very simple and efficient system with extremely low downtime when compared with similar systems from other manufacturers. There are, however, a few critical areas of the system which must be checked periodically, for example, the air seals (12 inside the bank and 4 outside), the blower unit, and the individual carriers.

In the two years that José has been in business he has sold and installed six systems. Written into the sales contract is a maintenance agreement which requires that a monthly inspection be made for a period of five years (at $500 per year). Since José wants to spend only two days each month inspecting each location, determine the two routes that will minimize the distance he must travel to do this. Remember that he must return to Jackson after each day's travel. It is possible to inspect four systems within one day, but no more. The individual distances between the cities are given below:

	Jackson	Aberdeen	Elgin	Cannon	Salem	Colton
Jackson	*M*	13	43	9	24	47
Aberdeen	13	*M*	47	21	35	50
Elgin	43	47	*M*	28	25	57
Cannon	9	21	28	*M*	14	29
Salem	24	35	32	14	*M*	36
Colton	47	52	61	32	36	*M*

Solution

Recommendation
The two routes for servicing the banks should be:

1. Jackson to Cannon to Salem back to Jackson: 47 miles,
2. Jackson to Aberdeen to Elgin to Colton back to Jackson: 164 miles.

Numerical Answer

Route 1	Distance
Jackson – Cannon	9
Cannon – Salem	14
Salem – Jackson	24
	47 miles

Route 2	Distance
Jackson – Aberdeen	13
Aberdeen – Elgin	47
Elgin – Colton	57
Colton – Jackson	47
	164 miles

Math Work. Applying the Quick & Dirty algorithm to the expanded matrix we obtain:

	Jackson A	Jackson B	Aberdeen	Elgin	Cannon	Salem	Colton
Jackson A	M	M	13	43	⑨	24	47
Jackson B	M	M	⑬	43	9	24	47
Aberdeen	13	13	M	㊼	21	35	50
Elgin	43	43	47	M	28	25	㊼
Cannon	9	9	21	28	M	⑭	29
Salem	24	㉔	35	32	14	M	36
Colton	㊼	47	52	61	23	36	M

Quick & Clean Algorithm

As an illustration of Case I and the Quick & Clean algorithm, if Bank Delivery Systems could afford any number of delivery personnel and service personnel, we would solve the assignment problem as follows.

1. Row reduction from original matrix:

	Jackson	Aberdeen	Elgin	Cannon	Salem	Colton	Distance
Jackson	M	4	34	0	15	38	9
Aberdeen	0	M	34	8	22	37	13
Elgin	18	22	M	3	0	32	25
Cannon	0	12	19	M	5	20	9
Salem	10	21	18	0	M	22	14
Colton	15	20	29	0	4	M	32

102 miles

2. Column reduction:

	Jackson	Aberdeen	Elgin	Cannon	Salem	Colton
Jackson	M	⓪	16	⤬	15	18
Aberdeen	⓪	M	16	8	22	17
Elgin	18	18	M	3	⓪	12
Cannon	⤬	8	1	M	5	⓪
Salem	10	17	⓪	⤬	M	2
Colton	15	16	11	⓪	4	M

Distance: 4 + 18 + 20 = 42 + 102 = 144 miles.

The solution gives three delivery routes and would require three persons to be stationed at one or the other of the cities. This solution is 20 miles less than having to return to Jackson but it is an impractical solution for this problem.

1. Jackson to Aberdeen back to Jackson
2. Elgin to Salem back to Elgin
3. Cannon to Colton back to Cannon.

aquatics section

Every summer the Aquatics section of the Los Angeles Department of Recreation and Parks is open to the public, and there are 52 swimming pools in the Los Angeles area and surrounding communities. The West District has seven swimming pools operated by seven crews consisting of clerks, locker attendants, pool managers, senior guards, and pool lifeguards. The pools are open six days a week for public swimming and swimming lessons. Every few days the water is chemically treated and tested so that it will pass the test by the health inspector who drops by unannounced from time to time.

At present the chlorine and other chemicals for the pool are stored at one location, but the Aquatics section would like to store them at three or four pools and then have them picked up by the neighboring pools. The state will provide these few pools with a car each so that they can deliver the chemicals to the pools near them.

Figure 5.10 shows a map of the area, and the

Figure 5.10

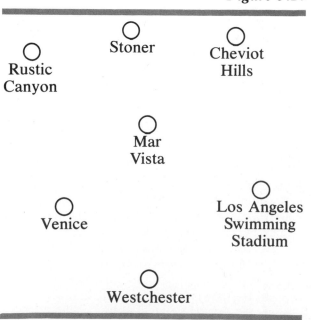

distances between pools are given in a table. Note that the distances between pools are not always symmetrical. Since the Aquatics section is willing to store chemicals at more than one location, this problem is a Case I type delivery problem. How many vehicles will be needed to minimize the total distance to deliver all the chemicals? What recommendation would you make as to where the chlorine and supplies should be delivered?

To

From	Los Angeles	Westchester	Mar Vista	Cheviot Hills	Venice	Stoner	Rustic Canyon
Los Angeles	M	7	11	10	15	12	16
Westchester	7	M	5	9	3	9	9
Mar Vista	13	5	M	4	3	3	8
Cheviot Hills	11	9	4	M	6	4	9
Venice	15	3	3	6	M	6	6
Stoner	12	9	3	4	6	M	8
Rustic Canyon	17	9	8	9	6	8	M

brookside winery, northern area

Brookside Winery has another delivery problem resulting from the acquisition of a San Francisco based winery. 2000 cases of wine are delivered monthly to the San Francisco tasting room, and during the month, 200 cases must be delivered to each tasting room by the one 5-ton truck with a 40-foot trailer that the winery has located in San Francisco. Determine the minimum number of deliveries that can be made which will reduce the total mileage involved (and thus the expense). The truck holds 1200 cases.

Obviously more than one delivery route must be used. But three routes would not be necessary, so that two deliveries would be the minimum number required. Set up the delivery problem with two locations (A and B) at San Francisco, using the mileages given in Table 5.6.

INCIDENT: CAPACITY CONSTRAINTS

A bakery must make deliveries to 110 outlets each day and has 20 bread trucks. The bakery must determine the set of routes that will minimize the time and distance so that all the bread will be delivered and that the capacity of each truck will not be

Table 5.6

	San Francisco A	San Francisco B	Daly City	San Carlos	Hayward	Oakland	San Rafael	Richmond	Sacramento	Walnut Creek	Stockton
San Francisco A	M	M	10	23	28	11	14	20	89	20	79
San Francisco B	M	M	10	23	28	11	14	20	89	20	79
Daly City	10	10	M	25	22	20	21	M	M	M	M
San Carlos	23	23	25	M	20	30	M	M	M	M	M
Hayward	28	28	22	20	M	20	M	M	M	M	75
Oakland	11	11	20	30	20	M	22	79	84	14	68
San Rafael	14	14	20	M	M	22	M	15	85	M	M
Richmond	20	20	M	M	M	79	15	M	73	20	M
Sacramento	89	89	M	M	M	84	85	73	M	71	50
Walnut Creek	20	20	M	M	M	14	M	18	71	M	57
Stockton	79	79	M	M	75	68	M	M	50	57	M

exceeded. The Quick & Dirty algorithm is used as a basis for a first solution, and then it is checked to see if there are too many stops for any one route (meaning that the truck cannot hold all that bread).

central electronic police equipment company

The Central Electronic Police Equipment Company (CEPEC) was founded in 1970 and is located in Los Angeles. It is the chief supplier of law-enforcement equipment for the police departments, cities, and counties in eleven western states. CEPEC began its operation by first delivering ammunition, its leading product, from its warehouse in Los Angeles to the Sheriff's Academy in Phoenix, Arizona.

CEPEC has now expanded its local operations and is currently providing ammunition for the following cities: Phoenix, Bakersfield, El Centro, Nogales, Tucson, and Flagstaff. The respective monthly demands for ammunition are as follows: 300,000 rounds, 100,000 rounds, 100,000 rounds, 50,000 rounds, 150,000 rounds, and 50,000 rounds.

CEPEC must deliver ammunition to these police departments once a month. The company is interested in the cheapest cost to store and deliver this ammunition and has come upon two different approaches. Warehouse costs are fixed at $250 per warehouse, regardless of how much ammunition is stored there. CEPEC already has one warehouse in Los Angeles, but is considering one or two more elsewhere. Transportation costs are figured at about $0.20 per mile for the rental of truck and driver. It is assumed that, if necessary, one truck could hold all the ammunition. The transportation can emanate from different cities, but must return to the warehouse it started from.

Thus one plan would be to have several warehouses, which would save on the mileage and transportation costs but would be more expensive in fixed costs. The other strategy would be to have just the one warehouse in Los Angeles and make one or two trips with a truck to deliver all the ammunition. In solving the delivery problem, the former plan requires using Case I and the latter using Case II. Comparing these two solutions, determine which one will give the cheapest overall costs and make your recommendation. It will be necessary to obtain the data from an atlas to develop the network and table of data.

INCIDENT: CAPACITY AND LOCATION CONSTRAINTS

To further illustrate the complexities of delivery problems, consider the case of a school district that must schedule its buses so that all the school children will be picked up within the limits of the bus capacity and minimize the total number of buses. This must also be done within a reasonable length of time so that the children are delivered to school on time without being forced to be ready at an unrealistically early time for pickup. A further complication ensues from the fact that not only do all buses start at the same node (bus terminal or yard where they are kept and serviced) but must end at school and return to the terminal.

Supplementary Problems

1. Given the distances between six cities below, solve the Delivery problem, Case I, and determine the number of cars needed and the minimum total distance.

	1	2	3	4	5	6
1	M	4	15	28	10	8
2	5	M	2	M	8	15
3	10	4	M	9	18	13
4	28	M	7	M	26	M
5	10	10	8	24	M	9
6	6	12	13	M	10	M

	1	2	3	4	5	6
1						
2						
3						
4						
5						
6						

	1	2	3	4	5	6
1						
2						
3						
4						
5						
6						

	1	2	3	4	5	6
1						
2						
3						
4						
5						
6						

	1	2	3	4	5	6
1						
2						
3						
4						
5						
6						

2. Give the two differences between the two types of Delivery Problems.

5.4 TRAVELING SALESMAN

In the previous chapter we covered the traveling salesman problem from the standpoint of a network problem. We can now formulate this same problem as a set of numbers in a table, where the numbers indicate distances, times, costs, or anything to be minimized in association with some route. There are many times when these numbers are available, but a map either is not available or would be very costly to draw to scale. Thus we are faced with the same problem as in the previous chapter, but without a way to solve it.

The first algorithm in this section is the same type of algorithm that was used for the Quick & Dirty Delivery, Case II. In this case it is necessary that the algorithm carefully avoid choosing any M's and it might be necessary that all the numbers be finite (except for the main diagonal). These numbers represent the times, costs, or distances between cities, or they might be the cost of setting up and tearing down various machines, also called changeover costs or times.

Consider the following example of seven jobs that must be done periodically. The costs involved in tearing down one job and setting up for the next are a large part of the total costs of production. This is true on large numerically controlled machines, or for large chemical vats that must be cleaned before another batch of a different chemical can be made. Thus if we have seven jobs to be done on the same machine, it might make a difference in which order they are done, for to tear down job A and then set up job B might cost much more than to tear down job B and set up job A. In one case it might be necessary to pull off the old jig and put on another, while in the second case there might simply be the addition of another part of the jig. Here we will assume that since all seven jobs must be done, they are done every month, and we will also include the cost for setting up the last job to the first again, thus making a complete "tour" or "route."

Quick & Dirty Algorithm: Traveling Salesman (Tabular)[3]

1. Set up a table of times, distances or costs from city to city or of times or cost of tearing down a job and setting up another. Put M's on the main diagonal, from the upper left corner to the lower right corner. Arbitrarily start with the first row (you *can* start with any row you want).
2. Find the smallest number in that row. Circle it. Eliminate that column. You cannot choose a number in the first column (or the column corresponding to whatever row you started with) until there is only one row left. Move to the row corresponding to the column just eliminated.
3. Continue step 2 until you have made all assignments possible.

Example. Consider the costs for setting up and tearing down (changeover) seven jobs:

		To Job						
		A	**B**	**C**	**D**	**E**	**F**	**G**
	A	M	6	12	6	4	8	1
	B	2	M	10	5	4	3	3
	C	7	4	M	11	3	11	8
From Job	**D**	6	8	4	M	5	8	6
	E	8	11	4	6	M	5	7
	F	3	3	3	5	6	M	2
	G	2	6	5	11	4	9	M

In this example you would start in row A and pick the number in column G which is the smallest (1). Eliminate column G and move down to row G. The smallest number there is a 2, but it appears in column A and thus cannot be used. The next smallest number is a 4 in column E. Eliminate that column and move to row E. The smallest number there is a 4 in column C, and so on. The final result looks as follows:

To Job

	A	B	C	D	E	F	G
A	M	6	12	6	4	8	①
B	2	M	10	5	4	③	3
C	7	④	M	11	3	11	8
D	⑥	8	4	M	5	8	6
E	8	11	④	6	M	5	7
F	3	3	3	⑤	6	M	2
G	2	6	5	11	④	9	M

From Job (row label on left)

The sequence that is derived from this algorithm is A–G–E–C–B–F–D–A and costs 27 units. Notice that the reverse order would cost 39 units. This is because the costs are not symmetrical. In the case of set-up/tear-down problems this simply means that the cost of going from job A to job B is different from that of going from job B to job A. In the case of times or distances to be traveled, going from A to B may be during rush hour, while going from B to A may be very free of traffic. With barge traffic, going the same distance from St. Louis to New Orleans versus going from New Orleans to St. Louis, it will take a lot longer going upstream than downstream. One-way streets present a contrast in distances, with an M for the distance going the wrong way.

You will note, in using this Quick & Dirty algorithm, that by being greedy in the early part of the algorithm, it is quite possible to be stuck with some very large numbers at the end. This again illustrates the difficulties involved with trade-offs. One way to apply this Quick & Dirty algorithm so that a better solution might evolve is to start with some other row and try to find a better solution. The best row to start with might be the one with the biggest difference between the highest and lowest numbers in that row. In our example, that biggest difference is found in row A, a difference of 11. If you were to start with row D, the route would be D–C–E–F–G–A–B–D for a total of 27 also. Remember that it makes no difference where you start in the traveling salesman route since you are making a complete circuit and come back to where you start. Thus the above route "started" at job D, but we could have just as easily started the route with A.

The second algorithm in this section, the Long & Clean algorithm, was developed by Shapiro[4] and uses as its base the assignment problem. The initial matrix is set up just as the delivery problem, with M's on the diagonal. The assignment problem is then solved, and if the solution is a complete tour, it is optimal. Usu-

ally, however, there are at least two subtours, as in the case of the delivery problem example (see Figure 5.7, page 160).

To City

	1	2	3	4	5
1	M	1	7	[0]	M
2	✗	M	[0]	M	✗
3	6	✗	M	✗	[0]
4	[0]	M	1	M	M
5	M	[0]	10	M	M

From City (row label on left)

Notice that we have two subroutes (1–4–1 and 2–3–5–2, see Figure 5.7), and what we want is one complete tour (or loop). The smallest subroute is chosen (for convenience more than anything), and if there are m cities in the subtour, then there will be m new problems generated. What is desired is a new solution that will not include the subtour but will not eliminate any feasible tour (that is, a loop). Thus each leg or branch of the subtour is broken. In this example we will generate two new problems, one with the cost of going from 1 to 4 being M and the other with cost of going from 4 to 1 being M. The cost for either of the two new problems will be the same as or greater than the original. Creating new problems from the shortest subtour is called *branching*. As the new problems are solved, any that produce a complete tour will be an upper bound, and those with subtours and lower costs will be lower bounds. This process is called *bounding*. When the lower bound is equal to the upper bound, the process is complete, and the lowest cost complete tour has been found. This process is called *Branch & Bound*.

Long & Clean Algorithm: Traveling Salesman[4]

1. Set up the matrix of costs, times, or distances between cities. Put M's on the diagonal.
2. Solve the assignment problem.
3. If there is one complete tour, *stop. Optimal.*
4. If there are subtours, pick the one with the least number of cities and formulate m new problems. The original problem constitutes the lower bound, and any problems that have a complete tour solution (the lowest cost) constitute an upper bound.
5. Continue to break up subtours from the problems that have been generated until there is no problem to be investigated with a lower cost than the best traveling salesman tour.

Figure 5.11

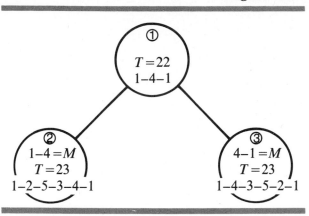

To City

		1	2	3	4	5
	1	M	0	6	M	M
	2	✗	M	✗	M	0
From City	3	6	✗	M	0	✗
	4	0	M	1	M	M
	5	M	✗	0	M	M

Tour = 23

The route is 1–2–5–3–4–1.

Problem 3 has 4–1 = M, while 1–4 remains zero. It yields the reverse tour, which is not unusual since the data is symmetrical.

To give you a better idea of the Branch & Bound algorithm, consider a hypothetical ten-city problem that generates three subtours: 1–4–7–2–1, 3–10–9–3, and 5–6–8–5. The smallest of these is broken up, and the cost for the original tour is 105. Three problems are generated (2, 3, and 4), and problem 3 yields a complete tour that costs 115. Problem 4 is still incomplete, but costs 117 already, so it will not be investigated. Problem 2 needs to be investigated, because it is possible to obtain a tour length between 108 and the upper bound of 115. The smallest sub-tour is a two-city tour, and it generates two problems (5 and 6). Problem 5 is incomplete, but its cost is above the upper bound, and so it will not be investigated further. Problem 6 yields a complete tour of length 110, which is better than the old upper bound; so it now becomes the best so far. Looking at Figure 5.12, we can see that there are no other problems that

Example. Figure 5.11 will help to explain the procedure. Problem 1 is the original problem, and problems 2 and 3 are generated from the original problem, problem 2 by setting the cost from 1 to 4 equal to M and problem 3 by setting 4–1 = M.

Problem 2: starting with problem 1, where the tour equals 22, set 1–4 = M:

To City

		1	2	3	4	5
	1	M	1	7	M	M
	2	0	M	0	M	0
From City	3	6	0	M	0	0
	4	0	M	1	M	M
	5	M	0	0	M	M

After row reduction we obtain:

Figure 5.12

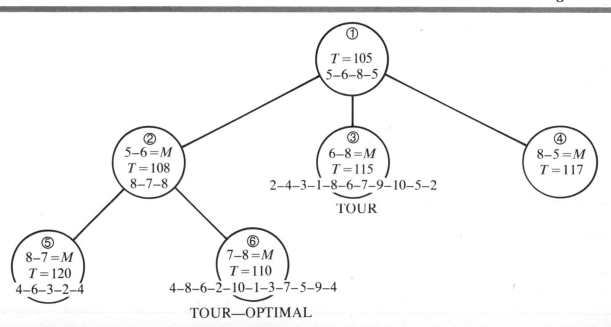

can be investigated and might yield a better tour length. Thus problem 6 is optimal.

vietnam helicopters

During the Vietnam War one of the most dangerous positions was helicopter pilot. During ground fire it was estimated that the average life of a helicopter pilot was fifteen minutes. Thus in flying missions it was necessary to minimize the amount of time that helicopters were in the air. Consider the problem of having to deliver supplies and troops starting at Saigon, visiting five other cities, and returning (Figure 5.13). The times given in the chart are not symmetrical, as the pilot has to take some evasive actions in either direction. Determine the minimum amount of time to visit all cities and return to Saigon.

	1	2	3	4	5	6
1	M	36	48	44	38	50
2	38	M	74	32	71	64
3	36	69	M	37	80	95
4	40	30	38	M	80	82
5	41	76	84	85	M	37
6	53	67	107	87	38	M

Figure 5.13

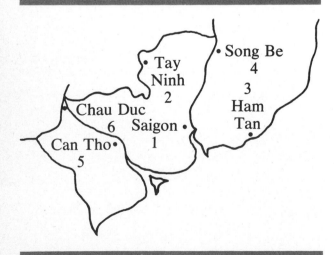

Solution

Recommendation
The pilot should fly the route from Saigon to Can Tho to Chau Duc to Tay Ninh to Song Be to Ham Tan and back to Saigon. The total time is 248 minutes, which will minimize the time spent in the air.

Numerical Answer

Quick & Dirty

Saigon – Tay Ninh	36
Tay Ninh – Song Be	32
Song Be – Ham Tan	38
Ham Tan – Can Tho	80
Can Tho – Chau Duc	37
Chau Duc – Saigon	53
	276 minutes

Long & Clean

Saigon – Can Tho	38
Can Tho – Chau Duc	37
Chau Duc – Tay Ninh	67
Tay Ninh – Song Be	32
Song Be – Ham Tan	38
Ham Tan – Saigon	36
	248 minutes

Math Work
Quick & Dirty

	1	2	3	4	5	6
1	M	㊱	48	44	38	50
2	38	M	74	㉜	71	64
3	36	69	M	37	⑧⓪	95
4	40	30	㊳	M	80	82
5	41	76	84	85	M	㊲
6	㊾	67	107	87	38	M

Starting with row 1, the smallest number is chosen, which is in column 2. Going to row 2, the smallest number is in column 4, and so on.

Long & Clean

The original table of times (with M's down the main diagonal) is solved as an assignment problem. Two subroutes result (Figure 5.14), with the smallest

Figure 5.14

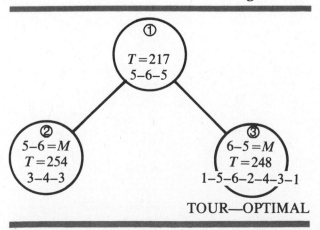

TOUR—OPTIMAL

being city 5 to city 6 back to city 5. Two problems (2 and 3) are then solved, with one yielding a tour, while the other has a higher time. Thus the tour is optimal.

Problem 1:

The rows are reduced by 36 + 32 + 36 + 30 + 37 + 38 = 209.

	1	2	3	4	5	6
1	M	0	12	8	2	14
2	6	M	42	0	39	32
3	0	33	M	1	44	59
4	10	0	8	M	50	52
5	4	39	47	48	M	0
6	15	29	69	49	0	M

The third column is reduced by 8, and the total is 209 + 8 = 217.

	1	2	3	4	5	6
1	M	[0]	4	8	2	14
2	6	M	34	[0]	39	32
3	[0]	33	M	1	44	59
4	10	X	[0]	M	50	52
5	4	39	39	48	M	[0]
6	15	29	61	49	[0]	M

The two tours are:

1. 1–2–4–3–1
2. 5–6–5.

Picking the smallest tour, we generate two more problems.

Problem 2:

Setting the cost from 5 to 6 equal to M and reducing row and column by 4 and 14, respectively, the total is 235.

	1	2	3	4	5	6
1	M	[0]	4	8	2	X
2	6	M	34	[0]	39	18
3	[0]	33	M	1	44	45
4	10	X	[0]	11	50	38
5	X	35	35	44	M	M
6	15	29	61	49	[0]	M

Total = 235+18(6–5) = 253

	1	2	3	4	5	6
1	M	[0]	4	26	20	X
2	6	M	16	[0]	39	X
3	[0]	15	M	1	44	27
4	28	X	[0]	M	68	38
5	X	17	17	44	M	M
6	15	11	43	49	[0]	M

Total = 253 + 1(6–5) = 254

	1	2	3	4	5	6
1	M	[0]	4	26	21	X
2	7	M	16	X	40	[0]
3	X	14	M	[0]	44	26
4	29	X	[0]	M	69	38
5	[0]	16	16	43	M	M
6	15	10	42	48	[0]	M

The two tours are

1. 1–2–6–5–1
2. 3–4–3.

Problem 3:

Set the cost from 6 to 5 equal to M by starting from the last table of problem 1. Reducing the row by 15 and the column by 2, the total is 217 + 15 + 2 = 234.

	1	2	3	4	5	6
1	M	[0]	4	8	X	14
2	6	M	34	[0]	37	32
3	[0]	33	M	1	42	59
4	10	X	[0]	M	48	52
5	4	39	39	48	M	[0]
6	X	14	46	34	M	M

Total = 234 + 14(6–5) = 248

	1	2	3	4	5	6
1	M	X	4	22	[0]	14
2	6	M	20	[0]	23	18
3	[0]	19	M	1	28	45
4	24	X	[0]	M	48	52
5	18	39	39	62	M	[0]
6	X	[0]	32	34	M	M

The tour is 1–5–6–2–4–3–1. This must be the optimal solution since the time is smaller than for any other problem originating from problem 2.

computer-aided design

A specific problem area of computer-aided design where the traveling salesman algorithm can be of help is as follows. The backplane of a computer serves the purpose of interconnecting integrated-circuit logic that cannot be totally connected by etching of a 6 × 8-inch printed-circuit (PC) card. In the specific application, 32 integrated-circuit chips are mounted on a PC card, and these PC cards are then inserted into the backplane. Each card contains 50 backplane connectors (pins), which allow contact to the backplane. The backplane is illustrated in Figure 5.15. Figure 5.15(a) shows the front view of a section of the backplane. (Connectors have 50 pins instead of 10 shown, and there are typically 180 cards per backplane instead of the 10 shown.) Figure 5.15(b) shows the side view.

Figure 5.15

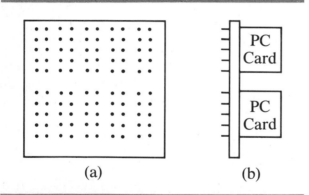

(a)   (b)

The basic problem is to connect a set of backplane terminals by the shortest possible lengths of wire. Let the distance between the two points i and j be denoted by d_{ij}. An electrical network consists of a set of points that are electrically connected to each other.

There are limitations imposed by the automatic wire-wrap machine as to the number of connections on any one pin, which is typically three for most common-size pins and most wire-wrap machines. Also, in an electrical network there can be no isolated pins, that is, no pins that are unconnected. In each network of n pins there will be $n - 1$ connections. As an example of how this is done, consider the data for an actual six-pin problem. Note that there is really no connection between pins 1 and 6, but that we will force one there at a cost of 0 (Figure 5.16). Use the Quick & Dirty method to find the smallest distance to connect all the pins.

		To Pin					
		1	2	3	4	5	6
	1	*M*	4	10	18	5	6
	2	*M*	*M*	12	8	2	6
From Pin	3	*M*	12	*M*	4	18	16
	4	*M*	8	4	*M*	14	6
	5	*M*	2	18	14	*M*	16
	6	0	*M*	*M*	*M*	*M*	*M*

Figure 5.16

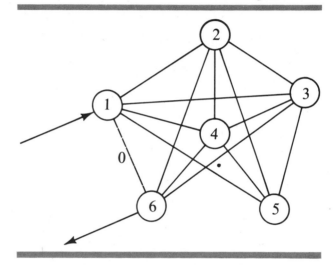

INCIDENT: CHANGEOVER SITUATION

An international chemical company headquartered in the Midwest has large vats for making batches of chemicals. Depending upon which chemical was last produced and what is being made next, there are changeover costs. The ordering of production can make quite a difference, especially if a high-grade chemical will be produced after a low-grade chemical.

This same company has a similar problem involving tank cars. It owns most cars (versus renting them), and thus must clean them from time to time. To save on the costs of cleaning, it fills the cars with "dirtier" chemicals after the "cleaner" ones. Then when the tank car is hopelessly dirty, it is brought to a special cleaning center and is out of action for a couple of days.

r. e. l. enterprises

R. E. L. Enterprises is an employment agency that handles accounting personnel. The field representative's primary function is to visit various companies in the greater Los Angeles area, familiarize them with the services offered by R.E.L., and sell the company to these prospective clients. Among the services offered by R.E.L. are bookkeepers, accountants, and certified public accountants. R.E.L. will send people with these qualifications to a client, on a temporary basis, when the client's workload goes beyond that which can be handled by the permanent employees of the firm.

A typical day involves 15 to 20 personal contacts which are brief visits with the personnel manager at each business. The field representative figures that she will spend about 15 minutes with each customer, give him some brochures and a business card, and go on to the next customer. Given the table of times between businesses (Table 5.7), determine a good route for the field representative to take so that she will finish as quickly as possible. Will it be possible to finish within an eight-hour day, before most of the personnel managers go home? Use the Quick & Dirty method to determine a good route. Since the field representative must check in at the office first thing in the morning to see if there are any important calls or contacts to make, assume that she will spend her first 15 minutes there. After the last visit of the day she must also return to file a report on each firm she visited that day.

INCIDENT: PUBLISHING DILEMMA

A large publishing company was worried about the optimization of its printing facilities. It was publishing a monthly magazine with multi-colored pages on a 16-page press and needed to know in what order the pages should be printed each month to minimize the time it took to clean the press after each run. Since the magazine is different each month, a good quick algorithm was needed to do this. The consulting company, who was approached with the problem, studied it for two weeks and then quite honestly announced that since the publisher was getting the magazine out (a feasible solution), it could guarantee

Table 5.7

	R.E.L.	Akron	Allied	Bellwood	Broadway	Bullocks	Cal Stores	Farmer John	Greyhound	Hensley	J.C. Penney	Kemper	Mart	May	Sad Sack	Sears	Sunshine	Occidental
R.E.L.	—	9	11	9	3	12	13	6	11	10	7	8	3	3	8	7	6	6
Akron	9	—	4	5	9	4	4	5	18	4	17	5	12	5	13	14	3	14
Allied	11	4	—	9	13	2	6	8	19	7	21	9	19	8	15	15	6	15
Bellwood	9	5	9	—	15	11	5	3	15	1	15	2	16	4	9	10	3	13
Broadway	3	9	13	15	—	14	14	9	11	19	14	10	2	4	10	6	6	4
Bullocks	12	4	2	11	14	—	9	12	20	10	17	9	12	9	15	14	9	5
Cal Stores	13	4	6	5	14	9	—	6	22	3	5	6	14	9	12	15	6	16
Farmer John	6	5	8	3	9	12	6	—	10	3	9	2	12	3	6	9	2	12
Greyhound	11	18	19	15	11	20	22	10	—	16	7	13	9	12	9	4	10	7
Hensley	10	4	7	1	19	10	3	3	16	—	13	4	21	5	8	15	3	11
J.C. Penney	7	17	21	15	14	17	5	9	7	13	—	6	8	5	2	4	9	6
Kemper	8	5	9	2	10	9	6	2	13	4	6	—	11	4	6	12	1	9
Mart	3	12	19	16	2	12	14	12	9	21	8	11	—	5	9	4	6	3
May	3	5	8	4	4	9	9	3	12	5	5	4	5	—	7	2	2	9
Sad Sack	8	13	15	9	10	15	12	6	9	8	2	6	9	7	—	5	8	9
Sears	7	14	15	10	6	14	15	9	4	15	4	12	4	7	5	—	9	3
Sunshine	6	3	6	3	6	9	6	2	10	3	9	1	6	2	8	9	—	10
Occidental	6	14	15	13	4	15	16	12	7	11	6	9	3	9	9	3	10	—

no better. The publishing company still has the open offer that anytime someone comes up with a good solution, it would be happy to pay for it.

california beauty and barber supply

California Beauty and Barber Supply is in the business of wholesaling beauty products. It operates five supply houses located in Phoenix, San Francisco, Stockton, Sacramento, and Rialto. Rialto is presently being used as a staging center to redistribute the supplies to the other warehouses on a need basis. From past experience it has been determined that each supply house should be visited once a week to ensure an ample supply of all products. The route now being used is from Rialto to San Francisco, to Stockton, to Sacramento, to Phoenix, and back to Rialto. The mileage between cities is:

Rialto to San Francisco	100 miles
to Stockton	80 miles
to Sacramento	110 miles
to Phoenix	140 miles
San Francisco to Stockton	35 miles
to Sacramento	50 miles
to Phoenix	220 miles
Stockton to Sacramento	40 miles
to Phoenix	195 miles
Sacramento to Phoenix	190 miles

The total cost of each trip is dependent upon the wage of the driver ($8.75 per hour), the per diem pay of the driver ($25.00 per day), the cost per mile of operating the truck ($1.67 per mile), the layover expense (motel room, meals, and so on) of the driver, and the depreciation of the equipment.

Remembering that each city should be visited once and only once during each trip, the owners of California Beauty and Barber Supply would like to know if it is possible to reduce the cost of distributing the beauty products. Use the Long & Clean algorithm.

INCIDENT: EASY RIDER

A town in a northern city in the United States has developed a public transit system called "Dial-a-Ride." There are several small buses that are used to pick up citizens who have called into the central office for rides. At the office a small minicomputer is used to quickly determine the optimal routing of these buses. The office uses a radio to contact the bus driver, who

also has a phone to contact the citizen. Thus a great deal of time and money is saved in the process.

imperial bank

Imperial Bank has its head office in the south central section of Los Angeles. It also maintains six branch banks that are located in the Wilshire district, West Los Angeles, Westchester, Torrance, Santa Ana, and Anaheim.

There is a daily distribution of a computer printout that is delivered to each branch from the main office. This output shows the running daily balance for each customer of Imperial Bank. The bank has its own delivery service, but management has become unhappy with what it feels are excessive costs involved with the distribution system as it now works.

Given the mileage between cities (Figure 5.17), what recommendation would you make to the management of Imperial Bank and why? Use the Long & Clean algorithm.

Figure 5.17

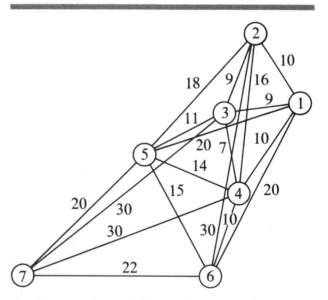

(1) Wilshire; (2) West Los Angeles; (3) Westchester; (4) Main Office; (5) Torrance; (6) Santa Ana; (7) Anaheim.

Supplementary Problems

1. Gerry is going shopping and must visit eight stores. The numbers given at the top of the first column on page 173 represent the distance between stores (because some are in the same shopping center, the distance between them will equal 0). Determine the route she should take using the Quick & Dirty algorithm, and find the total distance.

	1	2	3	4	5	6	7	8
1	M	8	7	5	4	3	2	1
2	4	M	7	0	6	2	1	5
3	8	0	M	2	1	0	3	4
4	2	5	8	M	0	2	1	7
5	1	4	7	6	M	3	0	8
6	7	3	9	4	1	M	0	2
7	6	1	2	5	3	8	M	0
8	1	1	5	1	2	4	3	M

Route __ __ __ __ __ __ __ __

Total distance _____

2. Given the Wallpaper problem and the matrix of wasted inches given below, determine the traveling salesman tour that will tell us in what order to hang the wallpaper strips to minimize waste using the Quick & Dirty algorithm.

	1	2	3	4	5	6	7	8	9
1	—	7	2	6	1	5	0	4	8
2	8	—	7	2	6	1	5	0	4
3	4	8	—	7	2	6	1	5	0
4	0	4	8	—	7	2	6	1	5
5	5	0	4	8	—	7	2	6	1
6	1	5	0	4	8	—	7	2	6
7	6	1	5	0	4	8	—	7	2
8	2	6	1	5	0	4	8	—	7
9	7	2	6	1	5	0	4	8	—

Tour __ __ __ __ __ __ __ __ __

Minimum waste _____

3. Given the distance between four stores (A, B, C, and D), determine the traveling salesman route that will minimize the total distance using the Long & Clean algorithm, filling in the appropriate parts of the circle diagram.

	A	B	C	D
A	—	5	7	3
B	6	—	8	3
C	7	9	—	5
D	8	5	6	—

	A	B	C	D
A				
B				
C				
D				

	A	B	C	D
A				
B				
C				
D				

	A	B	C	D
A				
B				
C				
D				

	A	B	C	D
A				
B				
C				
D				

Tour __ __ __ __

Length _____

4. Given the Branch & Bound diagram at the top of page 174, for the hypothetical solution of a nine-city traveling salesman problem, answer the questions below.
   a. After problem 1, what is the lower bound?

   _____

   b. After solving problems 2, 3, and 4, what is the upper bound and lower bound? _____

   c. How many problems off of Problem 4 do we need to investigate? Why? _____

   _____

   d. For problem 6, where would you put M's in the original problem 1? _____

   e. What would be a quick way to get an upper bound for problem 1 (feasible solution)?

   _____

5.5 TRANSPORTATION

This problem involves transporting products or materials from plants to warehouses at the lowest cost. It becomes complex when there are several plants and many warehouses. The number of possibilities becomes very large, and simply listing every possibility becomes very difficult. Most transportation problems of any real size are solved by computer codes using an algorithm that is based on network flow. This proves to be about ten times faster than

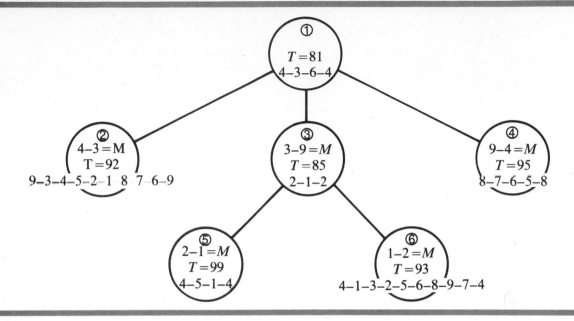

Dantzig's method (11) (dual linear programming variables), which is about ten times faster than a primal linear programming method. Most classes are taught Dantzig's method, which can be very laborious and not very practical, while the Out-of-Kilter algorithm is seldom mentioned or used. Also ignored in most classes are Quick & Dirty methods for solving the transportation problem.

The best near-optimal solution for the transportation problem comes from Russell,[5] who attempts to approximate Dantzig's dual variables and thus give an optimal solution. This has proved to be a much better approximation than a minimum-cost or Vogel's method. The following algorithm seems to work well on large problems, though it is perhaps a bit tedious.

Quick & Dirty Algorithm: Transportation[5]

1. Find the largest cost in each row and place it at the end of each row in parentheses.
2. Find the largest cost in each column and place it at the bottom of each column in parentheses.
3. For each cell, compute (largest row cost + largest column cost − cell cost) and place it in the right-hand corner of the cell. This is a measure of how much more we might have to pay for shipping if this cell is not used right away.
4. Allocate as many units as possible to the cell with the highest value in its right-hand corner. In case of ties allocate to the cell with the lowest cost. Cross off the complete row and/or column (or both).

5. Recompute steps 1 through 4 until all units are allocated.

Example. The problem can be stated as follows. Given the supply of products at each plant, the demand at each warehouse, and the cost of shipping from plant to warehouse, determine the minimum-cost allocation. First construct the table as shown in Table 5.8.

The numbers in the upper left-hand corner of each cell indicate the cost to ship one unit from a plant to a warehouse. It is assumed that these costs are proportional, that is, it would cost ten times as much to ship ten items. The numbers in the supply column indicate how much is available at each plant, and the numbers in the demand row indicate how much is needed at each warehouse.

Beginning with step 1 of the algorithm, we obtain the table shown in Table 5.9.

The largest number resulting from step 3 is 49 in the cell for plant 3, warehouse 3. Plant 3 has 20 units available and warehouse 3 needs only 15, thus 15 units will be allocated there. Column 3 will be eliminated and steps 1 through 3 repeated. In step 1 the highest cost now in row 2 (plant 2) is 22, and thus the right-hand corner numbers for step 3 will change in row 2 (Table 5.10).

The highest of the right-hand numbers is now 37, and there are two of them. However, the lowest cost belongs to plant 1, warehouse 4. Plant 1 has 30 units available and warehouse 4 needs 25, so 25 units are assigned. Column 4 is eliminated, and steps 1 through 3 are done again, the highest cost (17) again being in row 2 (Table 5.11, page 176).

Now the greatest right-hand value is 27 for plant 2, warehouse 1, and 20 units are allocated there. This

Table 5.8

	Warehouse 1	Warehouse 2	Warehouse 3	Warehouse 4	Supply
Plant 1	10	20	6	5	30
Plant 2	5	17	29	22	30
Plant 3	15	25	5	10	20
Demand	20	20	15	25	80

Table 5.9

	Warehouse 1		Warehouse 2		Warehouse 3		Warehouse 4		Supply	
Plant 1	10	25	20	25	6	43	5	37	30	(20)
Plant 2	5	39	17	37	29	29	22	29	30	(29)
Plant 3	15	25	25	25	5	49	10	37	20	(25)
Demand	20		20		15		25		80	
	(15)		(25)		(29)		(22)			

Table 5.10

	Warehouse 1		Warehouse 2		Warehouse 3		Warehouse 4		Supply	
Plant 1	10	25	20	25	6		5	37	30	(20)
Plant 2	5	32	17	30	29		22	22	30	(22)
Plant 3	15	25	25	25	5	*15*	10	37	~~20~~ 5	(25)
Demand	20		20		15		25		80	
	(15)		(25)				(22)			

Table 5.11

	Warehouse 1		Warehouse 2		Warehouse 3		Warehouse 4		Supply	
Plant 1	10	25	20	25	6		5	*25*	*5* / 30	(20)
Plant 2	5	27	17	25	29		22		30	(17)
Plant 3	15	25	25	25	5	*15*	10		*5* / 20	(25)
Demand	20		20		15		25		80	
	(15)		(25)							

Table 5.12

	Warehouse 1	Warehouse 2	Warehouse 3	Warehouse 4	Supply
Plant 1	10	20 *5*	6	5 *25*	30
Plant 2	5 *20*	17 *10*	29	22	30
Plant 3	15	25 *5*	5 *15*	10	20
Demand	20	20	15	25	80

leaves only one column left, which means that 5 units go from plant 1 to warehouse 2, 10 units from plant 2 to warehouse 2, and 5 units from plant 3 to warehouse 2 (Table 5.12).

The final allocation costs $695. This procedure does not guarantee an optimal solution, but in this case the solution is optimal.

It is important to recognize that many problems can be reformulated in different ways and thus solved by other methods. The assignment problem can be rewritten as a transportation problem, where the demand and supply are one unit each. Thus our example on page 146 can be rewritten as shown in Table 5.13.

This Quick & Dirty algorithm of the transportation problem here yields the optimal assignment solution. (However, this will not always be true.) It can be used though, and is simply another way of looking at the problem.

It is also possible to construct the transportation problem as an assignment problem (of huge dimen-

Table 5.13

	Person 1	Person 2	Person 3	Person 4	Supply
Job A	11	17	8	16	1
Job B	9	7	12	6	1
Job C	13	16	15	12	1
Job D	21	24	17	28	1
Demand	1	1	1	1	4

sions) which would be terribly inefficient, but possible. Looking at the problem in a similar manner, Stern[6] has developed an algorithm for the optimal solution of the transportation problem using a modification of the Quick & Clean Assignment algorithm.

Slower but Clean Algorithm: Transportation[6]

1. Begin with the cost table, and modify as in the assignment problem, by reducing rows and columns, thus obtaining zero in every row and column.
2. Add the supply and demand figures in the appropriate places by the cost table. For each column, find the zero(s) and add the corresponding supply figure(s) from the plant(s). Place that sum in parentheses below that column's demand. This represents how much can be shipped from plants to that particular warehouse at no extra cost. For each row, find the zero(s) and add the corresponding demand figure(s) from the warehouse(s). Place that sum in parentheses next to the supply column. This represents how much can be shipped from that particular plant to various warehouses at no extra cost.
3. Consider the numbers in parentheses:
   a. If all these numbers are greater than or equal to the number available or needed (Supply or Demand) in that row or column, an optimal solution has been determined. Go to step 5.
   b. If any number in parentheses is less than the number available or needed in the row or column, go to step 4.
4. Draw lines through columns and rows such that all zeros are covered and precedence is given to those rows or columns where the number in parentheses is strictly greater than the number available or required. As in the assignment method, find the minimum number not covered by a line. Subtract it from all unlined numbers, add it to numbers at an intersection of two lines, and leave the others alone. Go to step 2.
5. Assignments are made by first finding all rows and all columns that have only one zero and assigning the maximum amount possible to that cell.

Example. Find the reduced cost table from the original table by following step 1:

	W1	W2	W3	W4
P1	10	20	6	5
P2	5	17	29	22
P3	15	25	5	10

Original cost table

	W1	W2	W3	W4
P1	5	3	1	0
P2	0	0	24	17
P3	10	8	0	5

Reduced cost table

Now steps 2 and 3 are employed. For column 1 there is only one zero, and it is in row 2 which has a supply of 30. Thus we put 30 in parentheses below column 1. Row 2 has two zeros, one in column 1 (demand of 20) and the other in column 2 (demand of 20) so that 40 is put in parentheses at the end of row 2, and so on. It is evident that the solution is not optimal, since the numbers in parentheses are smaller than the supply in rows 1 and 3.

	W1	W2	W3	W4	Supply	
P1	5	3	1	0	30	(25)*
P2	0	0	24	17	30	(40)
P3	10	8	0	5	20	(15)*
Demand	20	20	15	25	80	
	(30)	(30)	(20)	(30)		

Now step 4 is employed. An asterisk indicates an amount not yet satisfied. Precedence is given to row 2 and all the columns.

	W1	W2	W3	W4	Supply	
P1	5	3	1	0	30	(25)*
P2	0	0	24	17	30	(40)
P3	10	8	0	5	20	(15)*
Demand	20	20	15	25	80	
	(30)	(30)	(20)	(30)		

The minimum uncovered element is now 3, which is subtracted from the unlined numbers and added to the numbers at the intersections. The final table shows that the solution is now complete.

	W.	W2	W3	W4	Supply	
P1	2	0	1	0	30	(45)
P2	0	0	27	20	30	(40)
P3	7	5	0	5	20	(15)*
Demand	20	20	15	25	80	
	(30)	(60)	(20)	(30)		

	W1	W2	W3	W4	Supply	
P1	2	0	6	0	30	(45)
P2	0	0	32	20	30	(40)
P3	2	0	0	0	20	(60)
Demand	20	20	15	25	80	
	(30)	(80)	(20)	(50)		

Table 5.14

	Warehouse 1	Warehouse 2	Warehouse 3	Warehouse 4	Supply
Plant 1	10	20 10	6	5 20	30
Plant 2	5 20	17 10	29	22	30
Plant 3	15	25	5 15	10 5	20
Demand	20	20	15	25	80

This solution is now optimal since all the numbers in parentheses are greater than the supply or demand. Now we proceed to step 5 and the assignment shown in Table 5.14 results. The cost is $695, and although the allocation is different from the first one, which we obtained with the Quick & Dirty algorithm, it is optimal also.

Finally, both the assignment problem and the transportation problem can be formulated as network problems. The network is modified with the addition of a super source and a super sink. There are two ways that the network can then be solved. The first is a modification of the Quick & Clean maximal flow/ minimum cut algorithm.

As mentioned before, the usual way to solve a transportation problem of any size is to formulate it as a network and the Out-of-Kilter algorithm[7,8] can be used (Figure 5.18). Each branch has two numbers associated with it, in parentheses. The first number is the cost of shipping along that branch and the second number is the capacity of that branch. The solution and algorithm for this problem is beyond the scope of this book; but the interested reader can investigate the texts listed in the references.

gleasen's markets

Gleasen's Markets, in an attempt to take advantage of a quantity discount offered by Paul Masson, places a weekly order for 280 cases of wine. Gleasen's has a markup policy of 42 percent on all Paul Masson

Figure 5.18

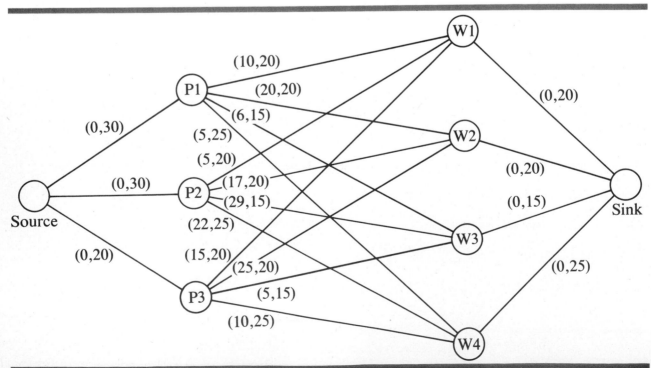

wines, and the costs range from $11.40 to $21.96 per case. A weekly order of this size does pose some problems for the company though, because it has only one store, in Emery, with a large-capacity warehouse. There Gleasen's is able to store 150 cases at room temperature with a certain amount of security (cases of wine do have a tendency to disappear).

Due to layoffs at an aerospace firm in the Brown area, the Brown store has become the only low-volume store and thus can serve as a partial warehouse also. Tabor has the capacity to store only liquor products. At the present time Gleasen's is utilizing Tabor space for 80 cases of wine and Brown for 50 cases. The weekly demand for Paul Masson at each of Gleasen's stores is as follows:

Store	Fountain	Century	Emery	Tabor	Brown
Demand	73 cases	62 cases	54 cases	60 cases	31 cases

The costs for delivering the wine from each of the warehouse facilities to the stores is given below in cents per case:

	Fountain	Century	Emery	Tabor	Brown
Emery	16	39	0	11	65
Brown	11	52	65	43	0
Tabor	26	48	11	0	43

The present schedule has Tabor fill orders for itself, Emery, and ship 20 cases to Century. Brown services itself, Fountain, and sends 42 cases to Century. The cost of this delivery schedule is $45.51 per week, and it is hoped that with a different warehouse allocation the costs should be reduced. Determine the delivery pattern and costs.

Solution

Recommendation

The new warehouse allocation is recommended with a new delivery pattern, with a saving of $8.80 per week in costs:

Emery
  to Fountain   54 cases
  to Century   42 cases
  to Emery   54 cases
Brown
  to Fountain   19 cases
  to Brown   31 cases
Tabor
  to Century   20 cases
  to Tabor   60 cases

Numerical Answer. Both the Quick & Dirty and the Slower but Clean algorithms give the same answers. The costs are as follows:

Emery
  to Fountain   54 cases ($0.16) = $ 8.64
  to Century   42 cases ($0.39) = $16.38
  to Emery   54 cases ($0.00) = $ 0.00
Brown
  to Fountain   19 cases ($0.11) = $ 2.09
  to Brown   31 cases ($0.00) = $ 0.00
Tabor
  to Century   20 cases ($0.48) = $ 9.60
  to Tabor   60 cases ($0.00) = $ 0.00
                                Total = $36.71

Old plan $45.51
New plan $36.71
Saving $ 8.80

Math Work

Quick & Dirty Algorithm

Given the initial table of costs, supply, and demand, the opportunity costs are put in the right-hand corner of each cell. There is a tie for the highest opportunity cost: 130 cents. Since both original costs are the same (zero), we will arbitrarily choose Emery to Emery which can take 54 cases. We thus eliminate that column as shown in Table 5.15. The highest opportunity cost now is 117; Brown can ship 31 cases to itself

Table 5.15

	Fountain		Century		Emery		Tabor		Brown		Supply	
Emery	16	75	39	78	0	(130) 54	11	97	65	65	96 ~~150~~	(65)
Brown	11	80	52	65	65	65	43	65	0	130	50	(65)
Tabor	26	48	48	52	11	102	0	91	43	70	80	(48)
Demand	73 (26)		62 (52)		54 (65)		60 (43)		31 (65)		280	

Table 5.16

	Fountain		Century		Tabor		Brown		Supply	
Emery	16	75	39	78	11	97	65	65	96	(65)
Brown	11	67	52	52	43	52	0	(117) 31	19 ~~50~~	(52)
Tabor	26	48	48	52	0	91	43	70	80	(48)
Demand	73 (26)		62 (52)		60 (43)		31 (65)		226	

(Table 5.16). Now the highest opportunity cost is 91, and Tabor will ship 60 units to itself. Continuing on in the same fashion, the highest row and column costs do not change. Thus 67 is the next highest opportunity cost, and 19 units are shipped from Brown to Fountain.

	Fountain		Century		Tabor		Supply	
Emery	16	49	39	52	11	71	42	(39)
~~**Brown**~~	11	(67) 19	52	52	43	52	~~19~~ (52)
Tabor	26	48	48	48	0	(91) 60	~~80~~	(48)
Demand	54 ~~73~~ (26)		62 (52)		60 (43)		195	

The remaining cells will have the following opportunity costs:

	Fountain		Century			
Emery	16	(49) 54	39	48	42 ~~96~~	(39)
Tabor	26	48	48	(48) 20	20	(48)
Demand	54 (26)		64 (48)			

Thus the cell with the greatest opportunity cost will be from Emery to Fountain and 54 cases should be allocated. This leaves only one column left which means Century needs 42 cases from Emery and 20 cases from Tabor.

Slow but Clean Algorithm

The initial cost table already has a zero in each row.

	Fountain	Century	Emery	Tabor	Brown	Supply
Emery	16	39	0	11	65	150
Brown	11	52	65	43	0	50
Tabor	26	48	11	0	43	80
Demand	73	62	54	60	31	280

The first two columns have no zeros and can be reduced by 11 and 39, respectively. Next, step 2 sums up the possible supply and demand in parentheses and we have two plants and one warehouse not yet satisfied. An asterisk indicates an amount not yet satisfied. We cover all zeros with a minimum number of lines (trying not to cover asterisks), for step 4. These are the sums of the demands (see Table 5.17).

The minimum uncovered element is a 9 and is subtracted from all uncovered costs and added to

Table 5.17

	Fountain	Century	Emery	Tabor	Brown	Supply	
Emery	~~5~~	~~0~~	~~0~~	~~11~~	~~65~~	150	(62+54 = 116)*
Brown	~~0~~	~~13~~	~~65~~	~~43~~	~~0~~	50	(73+31 = 104)
Tabor	15	9	11	0	43	80	(60)*
Demand	73 (50)*	62 (150)	54 (150)	60 (80)	31 (50)	280	

each intersection. Again, the zeros are covered with as few lines as possible whereby rows or columns with asterisks should be avoided as much as possible.

	Fountain	Century	Emery	Tabor	Brown	Supply
Emery	5	0	0	20	65	150 (116)*
Brown	0	13	65	52	0	50 (104)
Tabor	6	0	2	0	34	80 (122)
Demand	73 (50)*	62 (230)	54 (150)	60 (80)	31 (50)	280

The minimum uncovered element is a 5 which is subtracted from all uncovered elements and added to each intersection.

	Fountain	Century	Emery	Tabor	Brown	Supply
Emery	0	0	0	25	60	150 (189)
Brown	0	18	70	52	0	50 (104)
Tabor	6	0	2	0	29	80 (122)
Demand	73 (200)	62 (230)	54 (150)	60 (80)	31 (50)	280

Now assignments can be made in zero cells, starting with rows or columns that have only one zero. The last three columns each have only one zero cell and receive the units as shown.

	Fountain	Century	Emery	Tabor	Brown	
Emery			54			150 96
Brown					31	50 19
Tabor				60		80 20
Demand	73	62	54	60	31	

Next, the last two rows have only one zero cell each and receive allocations as shown.

	Fountain	Century	
Emery			96
Brown	19		19
Tabor		20	20
Demand	73	54	62 42

Finally there is only one row left and Emery must ship 54 cases to Fountain and 42 cases to Century. This allocation is the same one that was derived in the Quick & Dirty. This will not always be true.

california beauty and barber supply

Dealerships in the beauty supply business are extremely expensive and very difficult to obtain. They are allocated to wholesalers by location, and if a particular area already has a dealership, that dealership can claim territorial rights to the area—no other wholesaler can deal in that product line in that area.

California Beauty and Barber Supply (CB&BS) has just run into such a problem. Clairol products, CB&BS's most profitable line, are distributed to wholesalers in such a way that CB&BS can maintain wholesale dealerships in three locations: Phoenix, Rialto, and Sacramento. From these three locations shipments are made to the other retail outlets located in San Francisco and Stockton. In addition, CB&BS has a reciprocity agreement with another firm and supplies two stores for that company in Bishop, California, and Tucson, Arizona.

The Sacramento dealer has 1800 units of Clairol products available for shipment, while the Rialto dealer can ship 1900 units and Phoenix 1300 units. Stockton places a monthly order for 1000 units, San Francisco orders 1500, Tucson needs 1800, and Bishop requires 700 units of product each month. The costs to ship one unit of product are as follows:

From	To	Price per Unit
Sacramento	Stockton	3¢
Sacramento	San Francisco	4¢
Sacramento	Tucson	11¢
Sacramento	Bishop	8¢
Rialto	Stockton	6¢
Rialto	San Francisco	6¢
Rialto	Tucson	8¢
Rialto	Bishop	3¢
Phoenix	Stockton	12¢
Phoenix	San Francisco	12¢
Phoenix	Tucson	3¢
Phoenix	Bishop	6¢

Determine how many units each retail outlet should receive from each dealership and the cost of each shipment. Solve using both the Quick & Dirty and the Slow but Clean algorithms.

INCIDENT: SCHOOL BUS ROUTING

Jefferson County, Colorado, has many bus depots for its school buses and several schools that require the buses. Since the schools had a demand and the bus depots had a supply, it was a simple matter to solve the transportation problem, once the costs were determined.

class scheduling

The head of the math department at MSC has to make class assignments to his faculty. All classes have been given to instructors, except one Mathematics 101 class, three 111 classes, one 112 class, one 122 class, two 211 classes, one 315 class, and one 332 class. There are five faculty members without full schedules. Professors R.M.N, A.L.F, and C.M.W can each take two classes, Professor R.M.H can take only one class, and Professor J.L.C can take three classes. The head of the department has had the students in each of the classes fill out a teacher-evaluation sheet on each professor. He then rated each of the professors on a scale of 0 to 100 (100 being the best) on the basis of the teacher-evaluation sheets. How should he make the assignments? The ratings were as follows:

				Classes			
	101	111	112	122	211	315	332
RMN	60	95	20	40	55	75	25
ALF	20	75	30	85	25	95	50
CMW	70	80	60	95	50	65	90
RMH	50	40	90	85	75	65	35
JLC	100	90	85	95	35	100	40

Solve this problem using the Slow but Clean algorithm, and give the average ratings for the recommended schedule.

INCIDENT: CHANGING THE PROBLEM TO FIT THE ALGORITHM

A firm was trying to assign sales territories and sales personnel. (There were at least three salespeople to a territory.) The firm had a "profit" figure for each salesperson in each territory, that is, the amount of sales the salesperson was expected to realize. To solve this problem, it needed to be turned into a minimization problem. Thus the profit figures were all subtracted from the highest amount, and the problem was solved as a minimization.

INCIDENT: NECESSITY IS THE MOTHER OF INVENTION

During World War II, in the infancy of operations research, the United States was faced with the problem of getting a tremendous number of personnel and supplies to the European theater. This large-scale problem was tackled by a team of scientists and mathematicians and led to the Dantzig dual algorithm.

jet plastics

Jet Plastics is in the business of manufacturing molded plastic components. The market research department has found that there is a void in the area of plastic buckets and feels that if Jet Plastics were to act quickly, it could fill that void and increase the profit potential of the firm by at least 10 percent.

The lead time and changeover costs are minimal, and the management of Jet Plastics is not concerned with this aspect of the problem at the present time. What does bother Jet managers is the distribution process of getting the buckets to the marketplace.

Jet has asked various trucking firms to submit bids on the delivery job. It found that the best price that would meet its needs would amount to 80¢ per mile for each 4000 units shipped.

Jet maintains two production plants and would be able to produce $4\frac{1}{2}$ million buckets per year. The Denver plant has a maximum capability of 2 million, while the Los Angeles plant could manufacture 2.5 million buckets a year. The management of Jet Plastics is interested in how many buckets should be produced at each plant. It is estimated that it could capture 10 percent of the metal-bucket market if it could put a plastic bucket on the market within two months.

The E/S Market Potential Report provided Jet decision makers with the market demand for metal buckets broken down by states (Figure 5.19). The distances given in the table are from each plant to a staging area located in each state. The shipment is received in bulk at the staging center and broken down and further distributed by wholesalers at no cost to Jet Plastics.

Determine the optimal shipping schedule and give a breakdown of the costs involved, using the Quick & Dirty algorithm.

Distance from Los Angeles Factory (miles)	State	Distance from Denver Factory (miles)
400	Arizona	570
1450	Arkansas	800
0	California	850
850	Colorado	0
750	Idaho	450

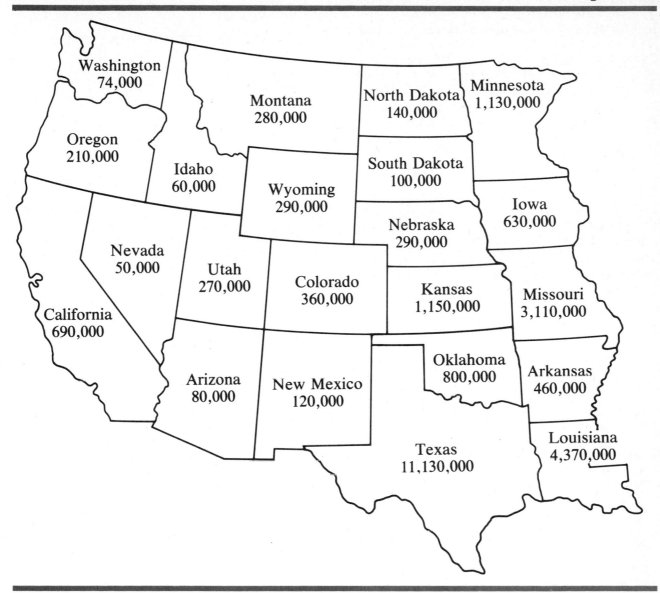

Distance from Los Angeles Factory (miles)	State	Distance from Denver Factory (miles)
1550	Iowa	800
1350	Kansas	530
1600	Louisiana	1020
1550	Minnesota	680
1400	Missouri	700
970	Montana	450
1370	Nebraska	500
280	Nevada	570
680	New Mexico	340
1200	North Dakota	470
1250	Oklahoma	550
830	Oregon	970
1320	South Dakota	520
1480	Texas	920
570	Utah	360
920	Washington	1020
900	Wyoming	220

INCIDENT: NURSING A SOLUTION

David and Ruth Stimson[9] describe a case of operations research in hospital work carried out at a large Denver hospital in December 1970. The problem was to assign night nursing personnel to floors in such a way as to maximize total patient benefit. A certain minimum number of personnel were always supposed to be available on each floor, but there were usually more people reporting for work than this minimum number. The question was where to allocate the additional people. The supervisor was asked to list all potential assignments to the various floors above and beyond the minimal required and then to rank them in order of decreasing utility in terms of patient benefit. Once these utility ratings had been determined, they were checked by several methods for internal consistency, and the differences were reconciled. The number of potential assignments made it necessary to resort to a systematic system, so the Out-of-Kilter algorithm was used.

No earth-shattering significance can be claimed for the study described, nor even any particular originality. But the outlay of time and money required was negligible, and normal staff operations were not disrupted. The problem tackled was the one the customer wanted solved (and not a broader one that the investigators might have found more interesting). The solution was found by modeling and quantifying the supervisor's own feelings about desirable and acceptable scheduling. And the result was a solution that was *used*.

All of this does not say that costly, time-consuming, and sophisticated methodologies have no place. But too often the sophisticated method will deliver the optimal answer long after the need has passed. We have learned to our pain that often an overlooked simple-minded approach will get a good answer quickly. From these premises we can at once derive two rules:

Rule I: *Until you have exhausted the set of simple-minded answers, do not proceed to sophisticated answers.*

Rule II: *The optimum solution delivered after you need it is worthless. Settle for a Quick & Dirty answer NOW.*

Supplementary Problems

1. Given the cost table below, the supply and demand, determine the allocation from plants to warehouses using the Quick & Dirty Transportation algorithm. Also find the total costs.

	W1	W2	W3	W4	W5	Supply
P1	6	9	7	8	4	60
P2	2	8	4	6	7	80
P3	4	3	9	10	3	90
Demand	10	40	20	50	40	

	W1	W2	W3	W4	W5	Supply
P1	6	9	7	8	4	
P2	2	8	4	6	7	
P3	4	3	9	10	3	
Demand						

	W1	W2	W3	W4	W5	Supply
P1	6	9	7	8	4	
P2	2	8	4	6	7	
P3	4	3	9	10	3	
Demand						

	W1	W2	W3	W4	W5	Supply
P1	6	9	7	8	4	
P2	2	8	4	6	7	
P3	4	3	9	10	3	
Demand						

Allocation _____

_____

Total costs _____

2. Given the transportation table below, use the Slow but Clean algorithm to determine the optimal allocation.

	W1	W2	W3	W4	W5	Supply
P1	10	8	4	10	8	9
P2	9	10	5	7	10	11
P3	8	4	6	8	8	10
P4	5	8	9	6	4	12
Demand	8	10	11	10	3	

	W1	W2	W3	W4	W5	Supply
P1						9
P2						11
P3						10
P4						12
Demand	8	10	11	10	3	

	W1	W2	W3	W4	W5	Supply
P1						9
P2						11
P3						10
P4						12
Demand	8	10	11	10	3	

	W1	W2	W3	W4	W5	Supply
P1						9
P2						11
P3						10
P4						12
Demand	8	10	11	10	3	

Allocation _____

_____

_____

Total costs _____

3. Consider a modified Class Scheduling case as a Transportation Problem. How could you change the Quick & Dirty Transportation algorithm without changing the ratings in the table and thus assign professors to classes to maximize the average rating? (There are several ways of doing it—pick one and explain it and use it on the simple problem below.)

	101	111	112	122	Supply
RMN	60	95	20	40	2
ALF	20	75	30	85	2
CMW	70	80	60	95	2
Demand	1	3	1	1	6

	101	111	112	122	Supply
RMN					
ALF					
CMW					
Demand					

	101	111	112	122	Supply
RMN					
ALF					
CMW					
Demand					

	101	111	112	122	Supply
RMN					
ALF					
CMW					
Demand					

4. Write the assignment problem matrix as a network flow problem:

	A	B	C
1	4	6	4
2	8	2	1
3	3	5	9

5. Referring to the Jet Plastics Case:
   a. What is the price to ship one bucket from Los Angeles to Arizona? (Show your work.)

   b. What is the total cost for the solution of the problem starting at the first city? _____

   c. Referring to the R.E.L. Enterprises case (page 170), what is the cost of the "better" answer and what is the tour? _____

   _____

   _____

   _____

5.6 BRIDGING THE GAP: THE INTERFACE

This chapter was based mostly on the assignment problem and its accompanying solution technique, the assignment algorithm. The purpose of this chapter is to show that some problems that have already been encountered (shortest route, traveling salesman, transportation) can be cast into a different form and thus be solved by different means. It is this ability to see the "familiar" in terms of another frame of reference that many times unlocks the mystery of the problem and results in a very simple solution. The purpose of this chapter was not to bore you with endless additions and subtractions (although you may have learned that doing very simple things is not all that simple), but hopefully you will have learned how complicated the trade-offs can get for even a small problem. Each table of numbers represents a trade-off that must be considered much in the same manner that we had to consider the trade-off of average fixed costs and average variable costs in Chapter 3, except that here we have n^2 trade-offs to consider rather than just two. The following notes may help bridge the gap between the mathematical theory and earlier writings and what is actually being done in practice.

1. The basis for the assignment algorithm lies with a primal/dual problem much like the maximal flow/minimal cut, which might be labeled maximal assignment/minimal cover. This is a very theoretical mathematical result involving a square table of numbers for which the minimal cover is needed. This means the minimal number of zeros to cover each row and column in a specified manner, and incidentally it is the same solution that is found when an assignment can be made for each row and column (maximal assignment). From this the practical result of the assignment algorithm was derived eons ago in a paper by Kuhn.[10] Another tie-in with earlier material is the similarity between the minimal cover and the minimal spanning tree, both accomplishing much the same objective in matrix and network terminology. A final note on the assignment problem is that the solution to part I of the assignment algorithm (which may not be feasible) is a lower-bound solution that could be used in a Branch & Bound solution to the assignment problem as was done by Hillier and Lieberman.[11]

2. In Section 5.2 it was stated that the shortest route algorithm could solve problems involving stops at "necessary" cities along the way by putting an M in the appropriate diagonal element and solving the assignment problem. If the solution that results contains subtours that have a nonzero cost, then the Branch & Bound algorithm must be employed to break up that subtour, much in the same way as it is done for the traveling salesman Long & Clean. In fact, adding an M to city 2–2 is breaking up an undesirable subtour to begin with, and to set up the traveling salesman problem, M's are put all along the major diagonal, which in essence breaks up any possible subtours of length one. It can also be seen that the shortest route algorithm is simply a special case of the traveling salesman Long & Clean and that the M's along the row and column are artificial means of making sure that the tour leaves the first city and

makes the necessary return back to it immediately after the tour reaches the destination, thus making a complete tour (traveling salesman), but with subtours of length one and cost zero. Thus the solution to the assignment problem must be the shortest route also.

3. For the delivery problem, Case II, there is a Long & Clean algorithm that is simply the application of the traveling salesman Long & Clean such that a complete tour is made with no subtours, which is the minimum cost or distance. To translate the optimal traveling salesman tour into the proper delivery solution, simply change cities 1A, 1B, 1C, and so on, back to city 1. Again, the solution using the traveling salesman algorithm will produce the optimal solution to the delivery problem, Case II.

4. Another way to use a Long & Clean Branch & Bound approach to the traveling salesman problem would be to use the minimal spanning tree as a lower bound to the solution.[12,13] In fact, the minimal spanning tree will always be less than the optimal solution because there is one less connection since it does not make a complete tour. By eliminating certain branches (branching) and forcing complete tours (upper bound) it is possible to develop an algorithm that would be more "visual" if networks were used.

5. To enlarge further on the Transportation section, the two algorithms presented were for the purpose of a quick solution (Quick & Dirty) and to show how the assignment algorithm could be changed to fit the problem (Slower but Clean). The proof for the latter algorithm lies with expanding the original problem to be an $n \times n$ assignment problem, simply using the assignment algorithm, and then allocating the shipments. However, for a problem with 100 units demanded, this would result in quite a large assignment problem. Therefore the assignment algorithm is modified a bit, rather than the problem, with the same results. Most textbooks go to laborious ends to show the MODI (Modified Distribution) method using some feasible starting solution (northwest corner, row or column maximum, matrix maximum) and then improving it until no further improvement can be made. Since the problem is linear and thus has a unimodal objective function, that solution must be optimal. Given a feasible solution to the transportation problem, we need to investigate every cell that does *not* have an assignment and ascertain whether assigning just one shipment to that cell would improve the overall cost. If there are no cells that improve the cost, we are optimal. If there is at least one cell that improves cost, allocate as many shipments as possible to it. Using

the example from Section 5.5, assume that we had the following feasible solution:

	Warehouse 1	Warehouse 2	Warehouse 3	Warehouse 4	Supply
Plant 1	10	20 (+1)	6 (−1) 5	5 25	30
Plant 2	5 20	17 10	29	22	30
Plant 3	15	25 (−1) 10	5 (+1) 10	10	20
Demand	20	20	15	25	80

The cost for this solution is $725, and as an example of testing to see if any improvement can be made, look at the cell plant 1/warehouse 2. If we add one unit there, we must subtract one from warehouse 3 or 4 in plant 1. Since doing that to the warehouse 4 cell would require adding +1 to some other empty cell in warehouse 4, we will subtract one unit from the cell plant 1/warehouse 3. Now we need to add one unit in the column for warehouse 3, and the only cell that is full (we want to work only with cells that already have allocations) is plant 3/warehouse 3. *But* adding to warehouse 3 makes an imbalance in plant 3, which means we need to subtract one unit from plant 3/warehouse 2. We have now come full circle, adding and subtracting one unit, so that all the supply and demand amounts are satisfied. There will always be one and only one such path available for an $m \times n$ problem as long as there are only $m + n - 1$ cells allocated.

Now let us see if this new allocation would help our solution. If we were to add and subtract one unit along this path, our new cost for these units (and savings) would be $20 - 6 + 5 - 25 = -6$ per unit. This means that we would save $6 per unit for every unit we could allocate to the cell plant 1/warehouse 2. To see how many we could allocate, we need to determine the minimum in each of the cells where we would be subtracting units, or minimum $(5,10) = 5$. This means that we could subtract five units from each of the cells with a -1 and add five units to each cell with a $+1$ in it. This would save us 5 units times ($6 per unit) = $30, amounting to a new cost of $695, which is our optimal cost from the Slower but Clean algorithm. There are several points to be made from this illustration.

a. This MODI method starts with a feasible solution and works down toward the minimum value, while the Slower but Clean method starts with a very cheap infeasible solution and works up toward the minimum value. Thus we see that there are two ways of solving the same problem, which again is a primal/dual approach.

b. There are easier ways of checking each cell to see if it can improve the solution, namely, by using shadow costs or marginal costs (the UV method). This method will not be detailed here, except to mention that the Quick & Dirty actually estimates these costs. This is why the Quick & Dirty is such a good approximation to the optimal solution for fair-sized problems.

c. The path that is used in the MODI method visually illustrates the trade-offs in the transportation problem; it can be quite a bit more complicated than just four cells, especially for larger problems. Thus the final solution is not always apparent by inspection.

d. The MODI method has not been presented in detail because of overriding complications involving a basis, dual variables, different possible starting solutions, and so on, which seem to do more to obfuscate the issue rather than clearing it up. Thus the Quick & Dirty and Slower but Clean algorithms were used so that we would not have to worry about fictitious warehouses or plants, incomplete bases, and an explanation of the dual variables. Since the transportation problem is in reality solved by the Out-of-Kilter algorithm (except on CPA exams), the authors felt that maybe MODI should pass by the wayside for now.

6. A final word is in order on the network approach to solving the transportation problem. There is a slight change that can be made to the maximal flow algorithm with the network setup given in Section 5.5, and a little more bookkeeping is required to solve the problem. The costs going back to the source should be M (infinite) to begin with. Then the minimum cost path may be picked from source to sink. If this path is of infinite cost, then the solution is optimal. Otherwise the cost of the path is the addition of all the costs along the path. The capacity is the minimum of all the capacities, and as with the maximal flow algorithm, subtract the minimum capacity from the path from source to sink and add it to the path from sink to source. For any capacity (in either direction) that is zero, put an infinite cost (M) on that branch. For any branch that has positive capacity, put the cost from the table (that goes for flow from sink to source). In such a manner the maximal flow algorithm can be used to solve the transportation problem; it is called the minimal cost flow algorithm.

5.7 REVIEWS

Review 1: Open book and notes; show all work and write legibly.

1. (15 points) The Internship Director in BA 404 needs one person to be at the office each day for the next week. The more hours each person can put in each day the better the office is covered. She has asked the staff to provide a list of how many hours they are available. It is required that each person be there one day and only one day and that someone be in the office each day.

   a. Given the information below, determine the schedule that gives the most coverage.

Person	Mon.	Tue.	Day Wed.	Th.	Fri.
A	2	4	8	4	6
B	3	2	7	3	2
C	6	8	6	5	4
D	7	4	3	6	8
E	4	5	3	1	4

Person	Mon.	Tue.	Day Wed.	Th.	Fri.
A					
B					
C					
D					
E					

Person	Mon.	Tue.	Day Wed.	Th.	Fri.
A					
B					
C					
D					
E					

Person	Mon.	Tue.	Day Wed.	Th.	Fri.
A					
B					
C					
D					
E					

Person	Mon.	Tue.	Day Wed.	Th.	Fri.
A					
B					
C					
D					
E					

Person	Mon.	Tue.	Day Wed.	Th.	Fri.
A					
B					
C					
D					
E					

	Mon.	Tue.	Day Wed.	Th.	Fri.
Person	____	____	____	____	____
Hours	____	____	____	____	____

   b. What if person C is unavailable for the day that he or she was assigned? How would you make a change in the last table? _____
   _____

2. (10 points) a. Explain in your own words what Part II of the assignment algorithm is attempting to do in terms of costs. _____
   _____
   _____
   _____

   b. Explain in your own words what the Quick & Dirty transportation algorithm is attempting to do in terms of costs. _____
   _____
   _____

3. (15 points) Given the network below, change it to a table of distances and determine the shortest route from city A to city D.

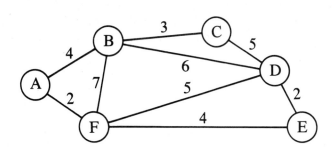

	A	B	C	D	E	F
A						
B						
C						
D						
E						
F						

	A	B	C	D	E	F
A						
B						
C						
D						
E						
F						

	A	B	C	D	E	F
A						
B						
C						
D						
E						
F						

	A	B	C	D	E	F
A						
B						
C						
D						
E						
F						

Shortest Route _____ – _____ – _____ – _____ – _____ – _____

Length _____

4. (15 points) Given the table of distances between seven locations,

	A	B	C	D	E	F	G
A	M	4	2	3	M	6	M
B	5	M	3	M	5	M	M
C	2	3	M	2	4	M	M
D	3	M	2	M	4	4	5
E	M	5	4	3	M	M	3
F	6	M	M	4	M	M	5
G	M	M	M	5	3	5	M

	A	B	C	D	E	F	G
A							
B							
C							
D							
E							
F							
G							

a. Determine the Case I solution to the delivery problem and how many trucks are needed, their routes, and the total distance.

b. Why would this total be smaller than one complete tour with one truck? _____

_____

5. (10 points) Given the following table of distances between locations, determine the shortest traveling salesman tour using the Quick & Dirty algorithm or any variation.

	A	B	C	D	E	F	G	H	I
A	M	6	4	3	6	2	6	5	6
B	5	M	1	6	4	4	4	7	3
C	3	4	M	5	2	6	3	6	1
D	3	3	3	M	2	1	3	8	3
E	2	2	5	3	M	5	1	2	2
F	6	1	6	2	5	M	8	3	2
G	5	7	2	4	7	3	M	4	5
H	7	9	1	2	2	8	7	M	4
I	9	7	1	1	3	9	2	7	M

Tour ___–___–___–___–___–___–___–___–___

Length _____

6. (10 points) Given the distances between cities, solve the Traveling Salesman problem using the Long & Clean algorithm to determine the optimal tour.

	A	B	C	D
A	M	1	4	2
B	2	M	5	1
C	4	6	M	2
D	5	2	3	M

	A	B	C	D
A				
B				
C				
D				

	A	B	C	D
A				
B				
C				
D				

	A	B	C	D
A				
B				
C				
D				

	A	B	C	D
A				
B				
C				
D				

	A	B	C	D
A				
B				
C				
D				

	A	B	C	D
A				
B				
C				
D				

	A	B	C	D
A				
B				
C				
D				

Complete the circle diagram:

Optimal Tour: ___–___–___–___

Length _____

7. (15 points) Given the cost table and demands and supply below, use the Slow but Clean algorithm to solve the transportation problem. Give the optimal allocation and cost.

	W1	W2	W3	W4	W5	Supply
P1	7	5	1	7	5	6
P2	6	7	2	6	7	8
P3	5	1	3	5	5	7
P4	2	5	6	3	1	9
Demand	5	6	8	7	4	30

	W1	W2	W3	W4	W5	Supply
P1						6
P2						8
P3						7
P4						9
Demand	5	6	8	7	4	30

	W1	W2	W3	W4	W5	Supply
P1						6
P2						8
P3						7
P4						9
Demand	5	6	8	7	4	30

	W1	W2	W3	W4	W5	Supply
P1						6
P2						8
P3						7
P4						9
Demand	5	6	8	7	4	30

	W1	W2	W3	W4	W5	Supply
P1						6
P2						8
P3						7
P4						9
Demand	5	6	8	7	4	30

Allocation _____

Cost _____

8. (10 points) Using the same data given in problem 7, determine the first two allocations using the Quick & Dirty algorithm. Show your work.

	W1	W2	W3	W4	W5	Supply
P1	7	5	1	7	5	6
P2	6	7	2	6	7	8
P3	5	1	3	5	5	7
P4	2	5	6	3	1	9
Demand	5	6	8	7	4	30

	W1	W2	W3	W4	W5	Supply
P1	7	5	1	7	5	6
P2	6	7	2	6	7	8
P3	5	1	3	5	5	7
P4	2	5	6	3	1	9
Demand	5	6	8	7	4	30

Review 2: Open book and notes; show all work and write legibly.

1. (12 points) A bootlegger wants to find the shortest route from his still in North Carolina (4) to the main dropoff point in Virginia (6). Given the graph below, *set-up only* the table to find the shortest route from 4 to 6 with required stops at 3 and 5.

	1	2	3	4	5	6
1						
2						
3						
4						
5						
6						

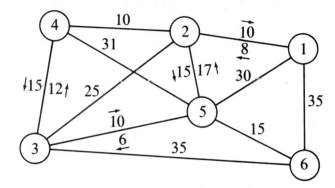

2. (13 points) A regional sales manager is responsible for six cities and would like to know the shortest route from City 1 to City 6. Given the table below, determine her shortest route (which cities) and the minimum mileage necessary.

	1	2	3	4	5	6
1	M	365	205	80	150	345
2	M	0	75	180	135	60
3	M	75	0	125	60	135
4	M	180	125	0	75	M
5	M	135	60	75	0	135
6	0	M	M	M	M	M

	1	2	3	4	5	6
1						
2						
3						
4						
5						
6						

	1	2	3	4	5	6
1						
2						
3						
4						
5						
6						

	1	2	3	4	5	6
1						
2						
3						
4						
5						
6						

Shortest Route _____ – _____ – _____ – _____ – _____ – _____

Length _____

3. (12 points) A laundry company would like to know how best to route their two trucks so as to reduce mileage and service customers quickly. Given the table of distances for the seven locations (location #1 has two trucks), complete the table, solve the problem using the Quick & Dirty for Case II. Find both routes and the total mileage.

	1A	1B	2	3	4	5	6	7
1A								
1B			8	10	15	4	20	25
2		8		30	10	15	20	5
3		10	30		20	12	5	30
4		15	10	20		15	30	5
5		4	15	12	15		10	25
6		20	20	5	30	10		15
7		25	5	30	5	25	15	

Tour 1 ___ – ___ – ___ – ___ – ___ – ___ – ___

Tour 2 ___ – ___ – ___ – ___ – ___ – ___ – ___

Total distance _____

4. (12 points) Given a hypothetical five-city traveling salesman problem, identify the optimal solution or find out what's wrong with *each* diagram (they are independent).

a. _____ c. _____

b. _____ d. _____

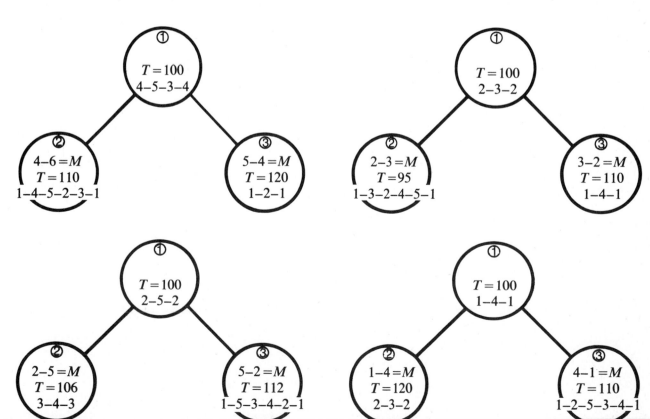

5. (15 points) Joe picks up newspapers each afternoon at the *News* office (1) and delivers to six newsstands at different locations (2–7). If Joe must have all papers delivered and be back by 3:00 at the office, and given the time in minutes between each destination below, when must he leave the office and what route should he take? Be sure to use the Long & Clean algorithm and to draw the circle diagram.

	1	2	3	4	5	6	7
1	M	11	7	10	9	13	32
2	11	M	11	9	16	20	22
3	8	11	M	14	13	22	17
4	12	11	13	M	15	13	9
5	9	9	10	11	M	7	15
6	9	8	20	15	13	M	17
7	32	25	13	16	8	18	M

	1	2	3	4	5	6	7
1							
2							
3							
4							
5							
6							
7							

	1	2	3	4	5	6	7
1							
2							
3							
4							
5							
6							
7							

	1	2	3	4	5	6	7
1							
2							
3							
4							
5							
6							
7							

Tour: _____ – _____ – _____ – _____ – _____ – _____ – _____

$T=$

6. (12 points) Given the following four-city problem,

	A	B	C	D
A	M	6	12	7
B	2	M	10	5
C	7	4	M	11
D	6	8	4	M

a. Using the Quick & Dirty traveling salesman algorithm, starting at city A, find the Quick & Dirty solution.

b. Modify the Quick & Dirty transportation algorithm and show and explain how your new method would work on the traveling salesman problem to find a good traveling salesman tour.

7. (12 points) Determine the optimal allocation which will minimize the cost by using the Slow but Clean algorithm for the following transportation problem and the total cost.

	W1	W2	W3	W4	W5	Supply
P1	10	15	5	20	30	40
P2	15	5	20	10	40	60
P3	20	10	15	50	10	20
P4	40	20	30	15	20	30
Demand	20	50	30	10	40	150

	W1	W2	W3	W4	W5	Supply
P1						40
P2						60
P3						20
P4						30
Demand	20	50	30	10	40	150

	W1	W2	W3	W4	W5	Supply
P1						40
P2						60
P3						20
P4						30
Demand	20	50	30	10	40	150

	W1	W2	W3	W4	W5	Supply
P1						40
P2						60
P3						20
P4						30
Demand	20	50	30	10	40	150

Total cost _____

8. (12 points) How would you write the Class Scheduling case (page 182) as an assignment problem? Set up only; do not solve.

5.8 REFERENCES

1. M. Sasieni, A. Yaspan, and L. Friedman, *Operations Research—Methods and Problems* (New York: Wiley, 1959), pp. 185–192.

2. R. Hesse, "Solution to the Shortest Route Problem Using the Assignment Technique," *Decision Sciences*, vol. 3, Jan. 1972.

3. J. W. Gavett, "Three Heuristic Rules for Sequencing Jobs to a Single Production Facility," *Management Science*, vol. II, June 1965, pp. 166–176.

4. D. M. Shapiro, "Algorithms for the Solution of the Optimal Cost and Bottleneck Traveling Salesman Problems," dissertation, Washington University, St. Louis, Mo., Jan. 1966.

5. E. J. Russell, "Extension of Dantzig's Algorithm to Finding an Initial Near-Optimal Basis for the Transportation Problem," *Operations Research*, vol. 17, Jan-Feb. 1969.

6. M. E. Stern, *Mathematics for Management* (Englewood Cliffs, N.J.: Prentice-Hall, 1963) pp. 396–402.

7. D. Plane and C. McMillan, *Discrete Optimization: Integer Programming and Network Analysis for Management Decisions* (Englewood Cliffs, N.J.: Prentice-Hall, 1971).

8. D. R. Fulkerson "An Out-of-Kilter Method for Minimal Cost Flow Problems," *Journal of the Society of Industrial and Applied Mathematics*, vol. 9, 1961, pp. 18–27.

9. D. Stimson and R. Stimson, *Operations Research in Hospitals: Diagnosis & Prognosis* (Chicago: Hospital Research and Educational Trust, 1972).

10. H. W. Kuhn, "The Hungarian Method for the Assignment Problem," *Naval Research Logistics Quarterly*, 1955, pp. 83–97.

11. F. S. Hillier and G. J. Lieberman, *Introduction to Operations Research* (San Francisco: Holden-Day, 1974).

12. M. Held and R. M. Karp, "The Traveling Salesman Problem and Minimum Spanning Trees," *Operations Research*, vol. 18, 1970, pp. 1138–1162.

13. M. Held and R. M. Karp, "The Traveling Salesman Problem and Minimal Spanning Trees, Part II," *Mathematical Programming*, vol. 1, 1971, pp. 6–25.

6
linear programming

Linear programming (LP) is probably the most widely known of the tools of operations research. It is a very powerful method of dealing with a large finite number of possible alternative actions in the allocation of resources while maximizing some profit or minimizing some cost. The word "programming" comes from the British, where "programme" means a methodical, step-by-step approach. It is also interesting to note that in German, linear programming is translated as "linear optimizing" or "linear optimization." The reason it is linear is that all constraints and objective functions have linear properties; that is, adding the amount A of something to the amount B of something else will result in the amount $A+B$ of the mixture. Thus all the variables are additive. If product 1 takes A minutes on a machine and product 2 takes B minutes on the same machine, the total time for that machine is $A+B$. This additive property seems intuitively obvious and realistic to most of us, and thus not a very crucial assumption, but it does *not* hold, for example, when 4 cm³ of salt is added to 6 cm³ of water (4 cm³ salt + 6 cm³ water ≠ 10 cm³ mixture). In this case we might have 9 cm³ of mixture that is fully saturated. Then adding one more cubic centimeter of salt will give one more cubic centimeter of mixture.

Ninety-nine percent of all linear programming models in the real world are solved by computerized models. The only known place where linear programming problems have been solved successfully by graphical methods is in the classroom. The only rationale for this approach might be to give a visual picture of what a simplex is, what a basis might "look" like, and what "nice" properties each linear programming problem has. This can help some to understand the process of solving linear programming problems.

We should emphasize that there is a *real* difference between each of the following aspects of operations research:

1. *Recognizing* that you have a decision problem and that linear programming might help you in making a good decision with respect to this problem. Experience is the best (and only) teacher here.
2. *Modeling* the problem (describing the effect of decisions on the problem outcome) by using linear equations and/or inequalities. The real struggle is to define the model; it is often difficult. Practice is the teacher here, and Section 6.2 will help.
3. *Solving* the model, usually with some simplex-based procedure. Frequently the friendly computer does this for you, operating as a "black

box," something that converts problems into solutions much the same way that TV converts unseen signals into pictures. Solving the model (determining the optimal value of each model variable or what decisions should be made) is usually the easiest part of operations research. Included in this chapter are many approaches to solving linear programming problems, and depending upon the depth of understanding sought, certain sections may be ignored completely. If you wish to understand the "black box" simplex operation, Sections 6.4 and 6.5 are your teachers here. Section 6.3 is a very straightforward, common-sense approach to solving and understanding linear programming solutions which you should master before becoming "sophisticated."

4. *Interpreting* the optimal solution involves checking to see that it is really feasible (possible) by verifying that it fits all the requirements, that it gives the value of the objective function printed out by the computer. Do the simple things first: never trust the "black box." Also, you would probably want to do some sensitivity analysis on the optimal solution. (How would the optimal solution change if the data changed? The data is hardly ever completely accurate.) An additional course in linear programming or someone who understands sensitivity analysis and the workings of the "black box" is the teacher here. Also included here, in Section 6.7, is a short section on this postoptimal analysis from the standpoint of the dual problem that is generated by every linear programming problem.

5. *Implementing* the optimal solution is really the test of the pudding. If you are the implementor, your only chance to solve the problem is to help the implementee understand what you are doing and why. Remember that if the implementee does not understand it, he or she may not use it. The real world, with its great variety of implementees, is the only real teacher here. However, the situations presented in this book can show you some things to avoid, and doing the simple things first is usually a good rule to follow.

Linear programming has been used to solve many types of problems. Blending of steel or aluminum alloys, paints, whiskey, coffee, feed mix, beer, ice cream, or petroleum products are problems that have been tackled by linear programming. Production problems (how much to make on each machine using different raw materials), capital budgeting (when and where to invest), and cutting stock problems (minimizing the amount of paper wasted in rolls of

paper, leather when making wallets, or aluminum in cutting out templates) are also standard linear programming problems.

The oil companies in the United States were the first to start using linear programming in the late 1940s. By this time computer technology had just gotten started, and the oil companies were the only ones with problems large enough to be unsolvable by hand. As the size of computer storage and the speed of processing increased, so did the size of the problems. Parkinson's law was validated again: The amount of work expands to meet the available space. Early models looked only at each individual refinery and were run as profit centers, trying to decide which materials to blend to make the most profit. Soon it became evident that what was profitable for one refinery was extremely unprofitable for another (the first had taken resources from the second); the total effect was robbing Peter to pay Paul, and the company as a whole was suffering. Therefore the companies started running nationwide models as profit models, which would give as solutions requirements from each individual refinery. These could be run as cost models in much greater detail, but would have the added restriction that they could not steal resources from each other.

Currently linear programming models are available on minicomputers that can solve very small and some medium-sized problems (up to 50 requirements and 200 decisions).

6.1 BANG FOR THE BUCK

The best way to explain linear programming is to illustrate it by way of a simple example. Let us assume that we have four investment opportunities and $10,000 to invest (see Table 6.1). At different times certain amounts have been invested, and a certain amount was returned. We are allowed to invest any amount and get that rate of return. We will assume that all investments were for the same period of time (1 year) and that these investment opportunities are still available. A further assumption is that we may invest any amount up to $10,000 in any or all the investments.

Table 6.1

	Savings & Loan	Apartment Houses	Shopping Center	Oil Well
Amount invested	$2000	$3000	$1000	$2000
Amount returned	$2120	$3300	$1200	$2700

Quick & Dirty Algorithm: Bang for the Buck

1. Compute the ratio of the amount returned divided by the amount invested for each investment.
2. Pick the largest ratio (Bang for the Buck) and invest all of it! *Optimal solution.*

In this case the ratios are as follows:

S & L	Apt	Shop	Oil
1.06	1.10	1.20	1.35

and the oil wells give the best return. (Another assumption is that these investments are risk free.) Thus we should put all our money into the oil wells and get a return of 10,000(1.35) = $13,500. This is the optimum.

Constraints

Life is usually a little more complicated, and there may be constraints (restrictions, requirements) to our behavior. Stated simply: *We have to do some things we don't want to do, and we can't do everything we want to do!*

Let us assume the following constraints, and see what this does to our optimal solution:

1. Being wary of all the stories about oil wells, you don't want to invest more than $2000 in oil wells.
2. Being conservative by nature, and believing in the banking system, you want to invest at least half of the $10,000 in savings & loans.
3. No more than twice as much may be invested in the shopping center as in apartments.

Constraint 1

Only $2000 at most in the oil wells limits us right away, because this gave us the greatest Bang for the Buck. If we invest $2000 in oil wells, that leaves $8000 for the other three investments. There the greatest ratio is for shopping centers, at a return of 1.20. Thus we would invest:

$2000 oil wells (return = $2700)
$8000 shopping center (return = $9600).

Our total return will then be $12,300 instead of $13,500. You will notice that the constraint has made our solution worse.

Constraint 2

Added to this is the fact that we must invest at least half in savings & loans. Considering that this is the worst alternative, we will do only as much as we are required ($5000). Our solution becomes:

$5000 savings & loans
$3000 shopping centers
$2000 oil wells.

Our return now is $11,600.

Constraint 3

Finally we must make sure that no more than twice as much is invested in shopping centers as in apartments. This means that of the $3000 now in shopping centers at least one third must be put into apartments. Since this is a lower return on our investment, we will put in only as much as we have to. Our new (and final) solution is:

$5000 savings & loans
$1000 apartments
$2000 shopping centers
$2000 oil wells.

The return is $11,500.

You will notice that by adding some requirements, or restrictions, our revenue went down. All linear programming problems are essentially trying to maximize profit or minimize costs subject to certain constraints. As the problems get larger, the number of possible solutions gets larger, and the answer becomes much more difficult to arrive at. In algebraic terms, the problem can be stated as follows:

Maximize Return =
1.06 S&L + 1.10 AH + 1.20 SC + 1.35 OW

subject to:

$$S\&L + AH + SC + OW \leq \$10,000$$
$$OW \leq \$\,2,000$$
$$S\&L \geq \$\,5,000$$
$$2AH - SC \geq 0$$

where S&L stands for the amount invested in savings and loans, AH for apartment houses, SC for shopping centers, and OW for the amount invested in oil wells.

INCIDENT: IMPLEMENTATION IS THE KEY

Regardless of how much mathematics and fancy OR techniques one learns, it still is necessary to implement the model. A midwestern chemical company acquired a southern oil company and immediately had the OR department construct a linear programming model of the refinery operation. One of the possible alternatives was to use one of the input streams from the oil company which was very low grade. This company had felt that it had to use this low-grade oil, but it made the blending process very costly. Another alternative was to buy an input stream from a competitor. The optimal solution called for the company to ignore its own crude-oil input stream and buy from the competitor; this would save approximately $100,000 per year. The bright young OR analyst rushed down South with the good news and was met with a less than enthusiastic reception. It took two years of coaxing for the oil company to try the new solution, which indeed actually saved them approximately $100,000 per year in operating costs.

Supplementary Problems

1. Given the algebraic setup for a production problem involving two types of product A and one of product B, determine the following using Quick & Dirty Inspection:

    Maximize Profit =
    $300A1+$200 A2+$400B
    subject to:
    5A1 + 4A2+10B ≤ 100 hours of labor
    2A1 + 1/2A2 + 2B ≤ 20 pounds of raw material

    a. If only the *labor* constraint were used, what would the solution be (show Bang for the Buck ratios)?

    b. If only the *raw material* constraint were used, what would the solution be (show Bang for the Buck ratios)?

c. What is the optimal solution if both constraints are used?

2. The Acme Company manufactures four products and each product uses a certain amount of raw material and a certain amount of labor. Determine the Quick & Dirty solution given the following:

    Maximize Profit =
    $1.00A + $1.50B + $2.75C + $4.00D
    subject to:
    3A+2B+2C+5D ≤ 75 units of raw material
    6A+8B+3C+4D ≤ 100 hours of labor

6.2 MODELS

Remember that in Chapter 1 we talked about changing messes into problems? Now we must also talk about changing problems into models. Once you think you know what the problem is, the following steps need to be followed in developing and solving a linear programming problem.

1. *Understand what the problem is* before you start to model it. Try to tell someone in words what decisions need to be made, and what there is about the problem that keeps you from making arbitrary decisions. If you can't *say* these things, ask more questions *before* you model. This will help you to identify the variables needed to model the problem, and to pinpoint the objective function and constraints.
2. *Determine the alternatives.* What decisions *can* be made? You must know what alternatives are feasible and could be employed. Do not try to determine which ones are best—the linear programming solution will do that.

3. Try to *relate the decisions* that need to be made in a given problem *to the variables* of the model that describes the problem. This is a simple rule that often gets overlooked, perhaps due to the awesomeness of the problem (not the model) you are trying to solve. Write the definition of each variable in longhand and include the appropriate units (tons, pounds, barrels, and so on).

4. *Determine the constraints.* What restrictions or requirements exist that must be satisfied? Determine these in English form first (doing the same as with the alternatives); then try to express them in terms of variables. Don't try and collect all your data right now; be satisfied with expressing the constraints in general form. There are four general categories that you might find useful in determining what constraints you have for the problem. You do not have to fit every constraint into one of these categories or make sure that every category has a constraint. The following constraints will be a helpful checklist for you.

   a. *Input.* These might be raw material restrictions or requirements. There may only be a certain amount of money, steel, oil, or chemicals available to be used in the making or blending of a product. It might also be that certain amounts of a particular raw material *must* be used, even though it is low grade or costly.

   b. *Capacity.* These might be restrictions or requirements on machine capacity of a mixing vat, machine times available on lathes, or workforce available during the production process. It might be the amount of storage required, plant capacity, or some facility that has a limit (or requirement).

   c. *Material balance.* These are in the form of equalities and can be chemical balances in a blending problem or, simply put, "What goes in equals what comes out." Thus in a refinery where the process is 98 percent efficient, what goes in is equal to 98 percent original plus 2 percent waste. In a production plant, production + old inventory = sales + new inventory. In a cash flow model the return is equal to the original investment times a rate of return.

   d. *Output.* These might be a limit or requirement on sales, production, or a certain rate of return. In blending models it might be the amount required to be made.

   Implicit in every model is the fact that the variables cannot be negative (we can't make a negative amount of something) and that the variables are continuous (in other words, you can make 1.26 widgets). Most of the time continuity doesn't pose much of a problem, but if it does, then the use of integer programming is recommended.

5. *Determine the objective function.* Do you want to maximize profit or revenue, or minimize cost or waste? Your constraints will be factors that keep you from making an infinite profit or producing at zero cost.

6. *Determine the data you need for the model.* The coefficients for the constraints and objective function must now be determined, and you may need to go to several sources to find these. At this point you may begin to appreciate how nice textbook problems are—the real world is a lot more difficult. You will have to quantify answers. For instance, in response to the question, "How fast does this person work?" you will probably receive the answer, "Real fast!" which of course is fairly difficult to work into a mathematical model. You will need to know if the person can produce 10 pieces per hour or 20 pieces per hour. Remember that getting data is a behavioral problem and can be very threatening to those from whom you get it.

7. *Check your model for consistency* to see that each constraint is unit consistent. The data have units, the variables have units, and it makes sense to check to see that both sides of each constraint have the same units. It does no good to have everything in ounces on one side of the constraint and in pounds on the other. This rule will help to ensure that your *model* accurately describes the decision *problem.* It can save you many headaches and embarrassments.

8. *Test the model for a simplified example.* Using some of the data, you might run a smaller model and then check the results with your employer to see if the answers relate to reality. If you have overrestrictive constraints, no solution may exist (infeasible solution). If you forgot some constraints, the answer may violate real possibilities. If you forgot some critical constraints, such as those that bound all the possibilities, the solution may be unbounded and make an infinite profit (unbounded solution). Running this small test model can help iron out a lot of the difficulties that could not be foreseen until you actually tried to solve the problem. Also this small computer solution will begin to give you an idea of the time and costs involved in running the larger model. Remember that as the size of the model increases, both time and cost usually go up proportionately as the square of the increase. So if your final model is 10 times larger (constraints and variables), it will take 100 times longer and cost 100 times more.

9. *Run the full-scale model.* For large models this does not simply mean to start from scratch and grind out the answer. It means making an educated guess (with the help from the smaller model) and starting from there, so that the running time may be significantly reduced.

10. *How valid are the answers?* Half of linear programming is setting up the model and the other half is determining how valid the answers are and for how long. What happens if certain prices change, demands change, and so on? These questions can all be answered by postoptimal analysis techniques, usually available in computer codes.

To illustrate modeling and developing linear programming models from problems, three problems are presented here. We will hold off solving them, and they are small enough not to need to be computerized.

INCIDENT: DOUBLE-CHECK YOUR MODEL

A young consultant had an interesting first experience with a large computerized model at a large chemical firm. The first computer run went so fast that it was obvious that something was wrong, and it was. The firm had made an infinite profit (something quite impossible). The consultant then started asking basic questions about the model that had been brought to her to solve. The model was to simulate making chemicals from raw materials, and the raw materials that were not used were sold off at 1¢ per barrel more than what was paid for them. One of the processes was the making of ammonia from nitrogen and hydrogen. Soon it became obvious that there was no input restriction on hydrogen and that the model simply allowed a huge pipeline to be built through the plant and to sell off an infinite amount of hydrogen at a profit of 1¢ per barrel. The consultant therefore had found the "leak," put in a constraint to restrict the amount of raw material input for hydrogen, and successfully ran the model on the computer after that. The important point here is that if the basic model is wrong, the best solution techniques in the world will not help at all.

transesco products, inc.

Transco Products, Inc., is a relatively small but very productive corporation. It was founded and designed for the manufacture of two basic product groups: antennas and switches. Most of its products are of a specialty nature, requiring a particularly high level of performance. Transco accepts orders only for those items that it feels require a high enough level of technology so that only a few firms could produce them. Productive activity includes both product modeling and production of model-substantiated items.

The organizational structure at Transco is extremely flexible. Strict regimentary scheduling of machines in relation to jobs in the production-shop area is nonexistent. Transco's philosophy in this regard is in line with the norms established throughout the industry. Most companies like Transco are run in a relatively flexible, nonuniformly scheduled manner.

The shop is run on a machine and workforce availability basis. Management feels that the 300-employee workforce can most efficiently be utilized in this type of flexible job-to-job, day-to-day approach. It also feels that due to its present capacity and level of development, a full-scale OR approach to job scheduling is prohibitive at this time. Therefore the use of OR techniques is limited to priority allocation of possible orders received, striving for profit maximization.

There are six basic machines and/or stages of production for the entire range of products manufactured at Transco. These consist of a milling machine, a lathe, a deburring machine, a painting station, an assembly stage, and the final inspection of the product.

Transco has a basic line that includes the production of three different antennas. Each of these has a selling price of $1000, and the raw materials cost the firm $475.00 for antenna I as well as for antenna II. The raw materials for antenna III cost $325.00. Additional information obtained from Transco includes the operation costs per hour and per minute and the total amount of time (in minutes) available for each stage of production. Also given in Table 6.1 is the time (in minutes) required for each antenna at each stage of production.

Transco has standing orders for 5 antenna I's, 10 antenna II's, and 5 antenna III's every month. It was determined that the market demand for antenna I is 20 units a month, the demand for antenna II is 30 units a month, and for antenna III it is 25 units a month.

Transco would like to produce for the maximum demand but doesn't have the capacity. Since all three antennas contribute different amounts to the profit structure of the firm, the management of Transco is uncertain about what quantity of each antenna to produce to create the optimal profit structure for the antenna line. Given the amount of time it takes to make one antenna on each machine (in minutes), construct a model.

Table 6.1

	Production Time (min)			Cost of Operation per Minute	Total Available Time (min)
	Antenna I	Antenna II	Antenna III		
Mill	35	38	23	$0.208	1200
Lathe	30	28	18	$0.200	1500
Deburring	12	9	6	$0.154	1600
Painting	30	35	25	$0.162	1600
Assembly	21	24	15	$0.166	1300
Inspection	35	35	25	$0.196	1100

Model

Follow the steps outlined at the beginning of this section.

1. *Understand what the problem is.* The preceding text attempts to explain the problem.
2. *Determine the alternatives.* There are three decisions that can be made: to produce a certain amount of antenna I, a certain amount of antenna II, and a certain amount of antenna III. Those amounts must be zero or greater.
3. *Relate the decisions to the variables.* We will call each decision a variable: ANT I, ANT II, and ANT III.
4. *Determine the constraints.*
   a. *Input.* There are no constraints for input for this problem.
   b. *Capacity.* There are six processes, which are capacity restrictions for making the antennas: mill, lathe, deburring, painting, assembly, and inspection:

Mill
35 ANT I + 38 ANT II + 23 ANT III ≤ 1200 min
Lathe
30 ANT I + 28 ANT II + 18 ANT III ≤ 1500 min
Deburring
12 ANT I + 9 ANT II + 6 ANT III ≤ 1600 min
Painting
30 ANT I + 35 ANT II + 25 ANT III ≤ 1600 min
Assembly
21 ANT I + 24 ANT II + 15 ANT III ≤ 1300 min
Inspection
35 ANT I + 35 ANT II + 25 ANT III ≤ 1100 min

   c. *Material balance.* There are no constraints for material balance for this problem.
   d. *Output.* There are both requirements (orders that must be filled) and restrictions (an upper limit on how much could be sold). They can be put in very simple terms:

$$5 \leq \text{ANT I} \leq 20$$
$$10 \leq \text{ANT II} \leq 30$$
$$5 \leq \text{ANT III} \leq 25$$

5. *Determine the objective function.* We want to maximize profit since we are given both cost and revenue figures. Figuring the costs for each process times the production time and the raw materials we can set up Table 6.2. The profit for each is found by subtracting the cost from the revenue of $1000 per antenna:

Maximize Profit =
$494.66 ANT I + $493.60 ANT II + $654.26 ANT III.

Steps 6–10 will not be done here, and a solution will be provided later.

We can see the consistency of the constraints by looking at the mill constraint. Each antenna I takes 35 minutes to produce, so that 35 ANT I is the total time used on the mill for antenna I. Similarly, 38 ANT II is the total time in minutes used on the mill for antenna II. Adding up the total times for all three products gives us the total minutes to be used on the mill, and this must not exceed the 1200 minutes that we have available. If we had set the left-hand side of the mill constraint less than or equal to 20, we would have minutes on the left-hand side and hours on the right-

Table 6.2

	Raw material	+ Mill	+ Lathe	+ Deburr	+ Paint	+ Assemble	+ Inspect	= Cost
ANT I	$475.00	+ $7.28	+ $6.00	+ $1.85	+ $4.86	+ $3.49	+ $6.86	= $505.34
ANT II	$475.00	+ $7.90	+ $5.60	+ $1.39	+ $5.67	+ $3.98	+ $6.86	= $506.40
ANT III	$325.00	+ $4.78	+ $3.60	+ $0.92	+ $4.05	+ $2.49	+ $4.90	= $345.74

Table 6.3

Maximize Profit = $494.66 ANT I + $493.60 ANT II + $654.26 ANT III
subject to:

35 ANT I +	38 ANT II +	23 ANT III ≤ 1200 min
30 ANT I +	28 ANT II +	18 ANT III ≤ 1500 min
12 ANT I +	9 ANT II +	6 ANT III ≤ 1600 min
30 ANT I +	35 ANT II +	25 ANT III ≤ 1600 min
21 ANT I +	24 ANT II +	15 ANT III ≤ 1300 min
35 ANT I +	35 ANT II +	25 ANT III ≤ 1100 min

5 ≤	ANT I	≤ 20 units
10 ≤	ANT II	≤ 30 units
5 ≤	ANT III ≤	25 units

hand side. Mathematically we would not even be able to make one whole antenna III.

The total model looks, mathematically, as shown in Table 6.3.

Another type of problem that linear programming techniques help to solve is blending different ingredients (usually at lowest cost) to meet some minimum requirements. The blending could be of different input streams for gasoline, different coffee beans for blends of coffee, scrap metals for metal alloys, and so on. One of the earliest applications of linear programming was by oil refineries to help determine the proper blend of inputs for different grades of gasoline (rated by octane and vapor pressure). Linear programming has also been used at steel mills to determine how to use certain alloy scraps in making new alloy blends. Previously the extra alloy scrap had to be thrown away, but now it can be used in making other alloys.

The decisions that the linear programming model makes are how much of each ingredient to put into the mix so that it meets either minimum or maximum requirements, usually at the lowest cost. Thus linear programming is used again to help determine the allocation of resources in the most effective manner. It is very easy for the number of possibilities to multiply very quickly, and thus a computerized model is usually needed to solve blending problems of any real size. Again, a Quick & Dirty solution certainly helps to gain some perspective about the blending process, and the final computerized solution should be as good or better.

whiskey blending

The D&G Whiskey Company blends three different ingredients (fermented rye, wheat, and corn) to make its two best-selling whiskies. The ingredients are blended according to a recipe found by D&G's grandmother which specifies the maximum or minimum percentage of rye, wheat, and corn mash to be added.

The cheapest of the mashes is the corn mash, and it is used to bring the cost of the blend down. Rye is the most expensive ingredient; it helps to bring the taste and quality of the blend up, while the wheat mash helps give it a good blend and cuts the taste of the corn mash. The chart below describes the ingredients, requirements, costs, revenue, and the supply of mash.

Blend/Mash	Rye	Wheat	Corn	Selling Price per Fifth
Pure Poison	At least 60%		No more than 20%	$6.80
Devilishly Deadly		At least 15%	No more than 60%	$5.70
Supply (fifths)	2000	2500	1200	
Cost per fifth	$7.00	$5.00	$4.00	

Input		Output

Rye mash ———————→ Pure Poison
Wheat mash ———————→
Corn mash ———————→ Devilishly Deadly

Determine the amount of each mash to be put into each blend that will maximize the profit subject to the input limitations and blend constraints.

Model

1. *Variables.* There are six decisions that need to be made: (3 inputs) × (2 outputs) = 6. Let us use the symbols RP, WP, and CP to stand for the amounts of rye, wheat, and corn in Pure Poison, and RD, WD, and CD for the amounts in Devilishly Deadly.
2. *Constraints.*
   a. *Input.* Each mash has a limitation put on it, so we have three constraints.

$$RP + RD \leq 2000 \text{ fifths (rye)}$$

states that the amount of rye used in both Pure Poison and Devilishly Deadly must be less than or equal to the 2000 fifths available. Similarly,

$$WP + WD \leq 2500 \text{ fifths (wheat)}$$
$$CP + CD \leq 1200 \text{ fifths (corn)}.$$

b. *Material balance blend:*

$$RP \geq 0.60(RP + WP + CP)$$

states that the amount of rye in Pure Poison must be at least 60 percent of the total mixture. This can also be written:

$$RP \geq 0.6\ RP + 0.6\ WP + 0.6\ CP$$

or

$$1.0\ RP - 0.6\ RP - 0.6\ WP - 0.6\ CP \geq 0$$

or

$$0.4\ RP - 0.6\ WP - 0.6\ CP \geq 0$$

or finally

$$2\ RP - 3\ WP - 3\ CP \geq 0.$$

In the same fashion, the other blend constraint for Pure Poison is

$$CP \leq 0.20(RP + WP + CP)$$

and would become

$$- RP - WP + 4\ CP \leq 0.$$

The blend constraints for Devilishly Deadly

$$WD \geq 0.15(RD + WD + CD)$$
$$CD \leq 0.60(RD + WD + CD)$$

become

$$- 3\ RD + 17\ WD - 3\ CD \geq 0$$
$$- 3\ RD - 3\ WD + 2\ CD \leq 0.$$

3. *Objective function.* We can see that for RP it costs $7.00 per fifth and sells for only $6.80 per fifth. Thus we will lose $0.20 per fifth, or have a profit of −$0.20. Similarly, for all the other variables:

Maximize Profit = − $0.20 RP + $1.80 WP + $2.80 CP − $1.30 RD + $0.70 WD + $1.70 CD.

The whole linear programming problem could then be written as shown in Table 6.4.

gasoline blending

One of the original uses of linear programming as an effective decision-making tool was by the oil industry for refinery operations and gasoline blending. Usually there are several input streams of crude oil into a refinery, and several decisions that need to be made during the refining process, such as how much of each stream is processed into naphthas, oils, gasoline, and so on.

In the process of blending these various inputs to make different gasolines, it is necessary to make sure that a certain octane is maintained and that at least certain amounts of regular and ethyl are produced, while not exhausting more resources than are available. Consider the simplified example shown in Table 6.5, which will serve as a model of blending. There are two input streams (isopentane and cat cracked) available from the refining process, and each has a certain octane rating. There are only two types of gasoline to be produced, regular and ethyl. They also have minimum requirements for octane rating, and a certain number of barrels can be produced (and maybe less). There is a limit to the amount of input, and cost and revenue figures are given. The problem is to determine how much of each input should go into making regular and ethyl to meet requirements and maximize profit. The abbreviation for barrels is "bbls."

Model

1. *Variables.* Here we can see that there are four decisions to be made: how much isopentane to put into regular, how much isopentane to put into ethyl, how much cat cracked to put into regular, and how much cat cracked to put into ethyl. For convenience let us use the following symbols for reference:

	Regular	Ethyl
Isopentane	IR	IE
Cat cracked	CR	CE

2. *Constraint.*
   a. *Input.* We have a limitation on the amount of isopentane and cat cracked that can be written as follows:

$$IR + IE \leq 50,000 \text{ bbls} \quad \text{isopentane}$$
$$CR + CE \leq 40,000 \text{ bbls} \quad \text{cat cracked}$$

Table 6.4

Maximize Profit	= −$0.20 RP +	$1.80 WP +	$2.80 CP −	$1.30 RD +	$0.70 WD +	$1.70 CD	
subject to:	RP		+	RD			≤ 2000 fifths
		WP	+		WD		≤ 2500 fifths
			CP	+		CD	≤ 1200 fifths
	2 RP	− 3 WP	− 3 CP				≥ 0
	− RP	− WP	+ 4 CP				≤ 0
				− 3 RD	+ 17 WD	− 3 CD	≥ 0
				− 3 RD	− 3 WD	+ 2 CD	≥ 0

Table 6.5

Inputs	Maximum Available (barrels)	Octane Rating	Cost per Barrel
Isopentane	50,000	90	$3.00
Cat cracked	40,000	110	$3.50

Input	Output

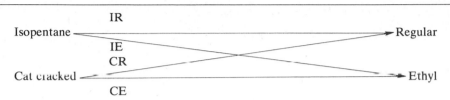

Outputs	Maximum Requirements (barrels)	Minimum Octane Rating	Revenue per Barrel
Regular	30,000	92	$4.50
Ethyl	50,000	100	$4.80

b. *Output.* We also have a requirement for only so much regular and ethyl:

IR + CR	$\leq$	30,000 bbls	regular
IE + CE	$\leq$	50,000 bbls	ethyl

c. *Material balance: Octane constraint.* There is also the minimum requirement for octane rating on regular and ethyl. Let us look at the rating requirement on ethyl first:

$$90 \text{ IE} + 110 \text{ CE} \geq 100(\text{IE} + \text{CE}).$$

This simply says that for every barrel of isopentane there is an octane of 90, and for every barrel of cat cracked an octane of 110. Thus if IE is two barrels and CE is three barrels, we would have to have at least five barrels of 100 octane. We can rewrite this inequality as

$$90 \text{ IE} + 110 \text{ CE} \geq 100 \text{ IE} + 100 \text{ CE}.$$

And further,

$$90 \text{ IE} + 110 \text{ CE} - 100 \text{ IE} - 100 \text{ CE} \geq 0$$
$$\text{or} - 10 \text{ IE} + 10 \text{ CE} \geq 0.$$

This simply means that we have to have at least as much CE as IE (or cat cracked in ethyl as isopentane in ethyl) to maintain a 100 octane rating. The constraint for the octane rating in regular is similar:

$$90 \text{ IR} + 110 \text{ CR} \geq 92(\text{IR} + \text{CR}) \text{ or}$$
$$90 \text{ IR} + 110 \text{ CR} \geq 92 \text{ IR} + 92 \text{ CR}$$

which becomes

$$90 \text{ IR} + 110 \text{ CR} - 92 \text{ IR} - 92 \text{ CR} \geq 0 \quad \text{or}$$
$$- 2 \text{ IR} + 18 \text{ CR} \geq 0.$$

This simply says that we can have up to nine times as much isopentane in regular as cat cracked, but no more. This will give us at least a 92 octane rating (and also keep the cost down and the profit up).

3. *Objective function.* Since isopentane costs $3.00 per barrel and when used in the regular blend sells for $4.50 per barrel, we will make (4.50–3.00)=$1.50 per barrel for each barrel of IR. In similar fashion, we will make (4.80–3.00)=$1.80 for each barrel of IE, $1.00 for CR and $1.30 for CE. Thus we could write our objective as:

Maximize Profit =
$1.50 IR+$1.80 IE+$1.00 CR+$1.30 CE.

The final model then looks something like that shown in Table 6.6.

Table 6.6

Maximize	Profit	=	$1.50 IR	+	$1.80 IE	+	$1.00 CR	+	$1.30 CE			
subject to:			IR	+	IE					$\leq$	50,000	bbls
							CR	+	CE	$\leq$	40,000	bbls
			IR			+	CR			$\leq$	30,000	bbls
					IE			+	CE	$\leq$	50,000	bbls
			−2 IR			+	18 CR			$\geq$	0	
					−10 IE			+	10 CE	$\geq$	0	

As a final note on modeling, it can be shown that both the transportation problem and the assignment problem can be formulated as LP problems and solved. Although the solution is not nearly as efficient as either assignment or network flow techniques, it is another way to represent these problems. An interesting point about these problems being solved as LP problems is that the optimal values will always be integer since the only divisions that ever take place in the LP algorithm are by + 1. Thus there is no round-off error (which does occur in other LP problems).

boat company

A small but highly regarded boat company located in Miami, Florida, has been producing fiberglass boats for both racing and pleasure for over 20 years. Its racing record is among the best in the world for the marathon type of racing. The products that come out of the company have to be of extremely high quality and must operate at a high level of performance to keep up with the products from other competing companies. Besides its complete boats, which are made to specific orders only, the company makes other types of specific parts, including motor mounts, U-drive mounts, and steering set-ups.

The organization as to how many of these three items will be produced is very flexible. The company has its own machine shop, so all the items are made on the premises. There are six basic machines or steps that must be followed in the production line. These consist of a bandsaw, a drill press, a lathe, a mill, a grinder, and a polisher. Most other shops that produce parts of the same design as these are run in a similar manner. No strict regimentary scheduling of machines in relation to the jobs in the production shop is necessary.

The company is run on a machine and workforce availability basis. The workforce contains seven employees and they get everything done that needs to be done. The selling price for the motor mounts,

U-drive mounts, and steering set-ups is $350.00. Raw materials for the motor mounts and U-drive mounts are $125.00, while they are $175.00 for the steering set-ups. Additional information from the company includes the operation costs per hour and per minute and the total time available for each stage of production (see Table 6.7).

The company has standing orders for three sets of motor mounts, three sets of U-drive mounts, and five sets of steering set-ups per week. It was determined that the company would like to produce more of each item up to the maximum market demand, which is substantially higher than the standing orders. However, it does not have the workforce or machines to do this, since all three parts contribute differently to the profit of the company. Management would like to know how many it can produce of each item, and what the maximum profit would be. Set up the LP problem according to the rules in this section.

INCIDENT: PAINTING THE TOWN RED

To illustrate the use of blending problems, consider that a nationwide paint company advertises that a computer system using linear programming helped formulate new paints by finding effective substitutes for scarce raw materials. It also determined the colorants in the amounts needed to color-match large paint batches during manufacture. Another paint company simply adds pigments to a white base to get any desired color. This is done right at the retail store, with a machine that has 20 different basic colors and a chart determined by a linear programming model to give the amounts of each different ingredient.

lee's bike shop

Mr. Lee wishes to start his second bike shop. He has found, through experience with his first store, that

Table 6.7

Machine Parts	Production Time (min)			Cost per Hour	Cost per Minute	Total Time Available (minutes)
	Motor Mounts	U-Drive Mounts	Steering Set-ups			
Bandsaw	42	40	28	$ 9.00	$0.15	1200
Drill press	32	35	15	$ 9.50	$0.16	1200
Lathe	—	6	10	$10.25	$0.17	1400
Mill	22	26	18	$12.00	$0.20	1400
Grinder	30	35	25	$ 8.00	$0.13	1000
Polisher	35	30	20	$11.75	$0.19	1000

Peugeot and Schwinn are the most popular of the 10-speeds. Of the Peugeots he wishes to carry two models: the A08 which sells for $105.95 and the V08 which sells for $115.95. Of the Schwinn he wishes to carry three models: the Varsity selling for $92.95, the Continental selling for $107.95, and the Super Sport selling for $139.95. For display purposes, Mr. Lee wishes to have at least three 10-speeds of each model.

Examining the sales records from his first shop, Mr. Lee found that he sold at least twice as many Peugeot V08's as Schwinn Super Sports. He also found that his total number sold of the Schwinn Varsities was at least equal to the combined total sold of the other two Schwinn models because of the Varsity's popularity among teenagers (probably due to the fact that it has a lower price). The Peugeot V08's and the Schwinn Varsities are so popular and in such demand that Mr. Lee can acquire no more than 40 V08's and 60 Varsities.

By referring again to his previous sales, Mr. Lee wishes to determine how much he must order of each model to maximize his profit. Use the sales history as a constraint for the ordering for the new store, so that Mr. Lee can maximize his profits. Since his new shop has a capacity of 200 10-speeds, he will be limited to that number of bikes. He also must stay within his budget, which allows him to spend up to $13,000 for purchasing these 10-speeds and assembling them. His cost on these bikes is 60 percent of the retail selling price, plus he must add the assembly cost, which is $3.00 per hour. Given the data below, set up the model to determine from the above requirements how many of each model Mr. Lee should order,

assuming that, if he follows the above guidelines, he would sell all that he ordered.

Make	Model	Assembly Time (min)
Peugeot	A08	30
Peugeot	V08	40
Schwinn	Varsity	20
Schwinn	Continental	30
Schwinn	Super Sport	40

disk manufacturer

A local firm manufactures rotating abrasive disks primarily for commercial usage. The disks are available in diameters of $\frac{3}{4}$, 1, $1\frac{1}{2}$, 2, 3, and 4 inches.

The raw materials used in the manufacture of the disks are abrasive, fiber, cloth, adhesive, and metal hub. The principal processes utilizing these raw materials start with the lamination of the abrasive, fiber, and cloth in two stages; next the laminated layers are punched to their final sizes. The final step is the bonding of the metal hub to the disk.

The detailed breakdown on the labor required for each processing stage is not available; however, the total labor required and the profit realized per unit (1000 disks) for each size are available and presented. In addition to the labor and profit information, other data pertaining to the resource availability and usage are shown in Table 6.8. Minimum and maximum sales requirements are also listed for each size.

Table 6.8

	Disk Size (inches)						
	$\frac{3}{4}$	1	$1\frac{1}{2}$	2	3	4	Available Resources
Total labor (hr/unit)	1.531	1.566	1.306	1.340	2.008	2.783	3040 hours
Material							
Abrasive (in²/unit)	887.7	1296	2592	4320	9600	20250	7,000,000 in²
Fiber (#/unit)							
4½ inch width	0.187	0.273	0.545			4.261	400 #
6 inch width				0.909	2.02		700 #
Cloth (in²/unit)	887.7	1296	2592	4320	9600	20250	5,184,000 in²
Adhesive (gal/unit)	0.0137	0.0200	0.0400	0.0667	0.1481	0.3125	550 gal
Metal hub (#/unit)							
1 inch diameter	2.5	2.5	2.5	2.5			2500 #
1⅜ inch diameter					3	3	2500 #
Profit ($/unit)	1.92	8.25	17.54	30.43	33.33	34.16	
Sales requirements (units)							
Minimum	25	100	150	200	200	25	
Maximum	50	150	250	300	250	50	

The primary objective of this profit analysis is to determine the production schedule (within the constraints) that would provide a maximum monthly profit. Set up the LP model for this situation.

INCIDENT: MODELING PROVIDES INSIGHT

Sometimes a great deal can be learned by just trying to construct the model. A large Southwestern oil firm was trying to decide whether to merge with a plastics manufacturer located in the South. Since their plants were near each other, the outputs from the oil refinery could become inputs to the plastics factory at a minimum cost (about the only cost would be transportation over a short distance). A large model was constructed which combined the two plants and gave a total profit figure for a 5-year period. If the rate of return was over 15 percent per year, the oil firm would merge; if under 12 percent per year, it would not. In between it would take more data and further analysis. By the time the model was constructed with all the necessary interactions, the firm had learned so much from the simple construction of the model that it decided to hold off on the merger and never needed to run the model.

ralston purina

Ralston Purina makes many types of feed mixes and runs as many as a hundred linear programming problems every day. A typical problem involves several ingredients that can be used to blend a feed mix requiring 20,000 therms to meet state requirements. For simplicity there are five possible ingredients (there can be from 30 to 40). These are alfalfa meal, barley, corn meal, dical phosphate, and fish meal. They need to be mixed in such a way as to meet requirements at minimum cost.

A ton (2000 pounds) of feed mix is needed such that alfalfa meal makes up no more than 2.75 percent of the total mix (this would mean 55 pounds). Barley has a maximum amount of 10 percent, dical phosphate a maximum limit of 7.5 percent, and fish meal is unlimited. Corn meal may be used if it comprises between 60 and 80 percent of the total mixture.

Nutrient restrictions require that no more than 8 percent and at least 3 percent fat be present (that is between 60 and 160 pounds of fat). Fiber is limited to no more than 5 percent allowed to be present in the mix. This is for digestive purposes, for if the mix contains too much fiber, problems can result. The most important ingredient, as far as nutrition goes, is the amount of protein, which must be at least 22 percent. Calcium must be between 1.0 and 1.5 percent, while phosphorous must be between 0.6 percent and 1.0 percent. A minimum of 1.1 percent of the total must be lysine. At least 0.5 percent of the mixture should be methionine, while the combination of methionine and cystine needs to be at least 1.0 percent of the total mix.

The costs for the ingredients are $610 per ton for alfalfa meal, $630 per ton for barley, $540 per ton for corn meal, $720 per ton for dical phosphate, and $1250 per ton for fish meal. As far as productive energy goes, for each pound of alfalfa meal there are 3.9 therms of energy, and for barley 8.0, while corn meal has the most energy available with 11.45 therms for every pound. Fish meal is the next highest with 9.2 therms for each pound, and dical phosphate has virtually nothing to offer in the way of productive energy.

Given the percentages of the nutrients in each ingredient listed in the table and the requirements above, determine the LP model that would find what blend of feed should be used to minimize the cost of the feed mix.

	Alfalfa Meal	Barley	Corn Meal	Dical Phosphate	Fish Meal
Fat	0.025	0.018	0.038	0.000	0.075
Fiber	0.180	0.080	0.015	0.000	0.100
Protein	0.200	0.115	0.086	0.000	0.600
Calcium	0.017	0.006	0.001	0.260	0.050
Phosphorus	0.001	0.001	0.002	0.180	0.029
Lysine	0.009	0.003	0.002	0.000	0.051
Methionine	0.003	0.002	0.002	0.000	0.018
Methionine and cystine	0.006	0.003	0.003	0.000	0.028

Supplementary Problems

1. The 31 Flavors Ice Cream Shops make their Vanilla, Pecan Crunch, Black Walnut, and Chocolate Chip flavors using cream, sugar, vanilla extract, salt, pecans, walnuts, and chocolate chips. For one gallon of ice cream, each flavor uses 8 cups of cream, a cup of sugar, and one tablespoon of salt. All of the flavors use a tablespoon of vanilla extract except vanilla, which uses three tablespoons. The Pecan Crunch needs a half pound of pecans, Black Walnut uses a half pound of walnuts, and the Chocolate Chip needs a whole pound of chips. Each gallon of ice cream sells for $2.39 regardless of flavor. The store selection of ice cream has the following constraints: at least 5 gallons of Vanilla, 4 gallons of Chocolate Chip, and no more than 25 percent of all the ice cream

made can be the flavors with nuts. Given the costs and supplies below, write a complete model (*do not solve*) to maximize the profit.

Ingredient	Cost	Supply (cups)
Cream	11¢/cup	6400 cups
Sugar	10¢/cup	100 cups
Vanilla extract	3¢/T.	100 T.
Salt	2¢/T.	300 T.
Pecans	90¢/lb.	25 lbs.
Walnuts	100¢/lb.	25 lbs.
Chocolate chips	50¢/lb.	20 lbs.

2. Develop constraints for the following situations:
   a. For the Ralston Purina case (page 208), no more than 3 percent lysine is allowed in the mixture:

   b. For the Lee's Bike Shop case (page 207), 20 percent of the stock must be Peugeot brand bikes:

   c. Again, considering Lee's Bike Shop, assume no more than 50 percent should be Schwinn brand:

d. Further considering Lee's Bike Shop, Continentals should compose 10–40 percent of the Schwinns:

3. Assume the gasoline blending problem has a new input stream, Arkansas Crude, with an octane rating of 95 and 20,000 bbls available, costing $3.30 per barrel.

   a. Write the new variable(s) to the problem:

   b. What is the new objective function?

   c. What is the octane constraint for regular gasoline?

6.3 SOLUTION BY INSPECTION

Continuing to believe that it makes sense to do the simple things first, let us now look at the models that we have developed and determine a Quick & Dirty solution. We will use the philosophy of Bang for the Buck in trying to either maximize according to restrictions or minimize according to requirements to get the most efficient use of our resources. We have seen that restrictions are written as less than or equal ($\leq$) inequalities and requirements are written as greater than or equal ($\geq$) inequalities. Requirements or restrictions may also be represented by strict equalities. The idea behind inspecting the linear programming model is to try and determine which alternatives must be employed, which might be employed, and those that would never be used. Some constraints will be "active," meaning that if they were removed, the solution would be different. Other constraints do not influence the solution at all. The former are also called "tight" constraints and the latter "loose." As we saw in the Bang for the Buck model for investing money, each constraint that was added was a tight constraint, forcing us to invest in a different pattern than if there were no constraint. If another constraint had been added that said savings & loans must be less than $8000, it would not be an active constraint since we only invested $5000 and would only do what we were forced to do. Thus it would be a loose constraint. It is also a special type of constraint in that it bounds the variable or alternative. These types of constraints are called upper and lower bounds. Obviously a variable cannot be at its upper and lower bound simultaneously. Generally, when maximizing, a variable will try to be as large as possible if it has a high Bang for the Buck ratio, and it will be at or near its lower bound if it has a low Bang for the Buck ratio.

While inspecting a model for a solution that is near optimal, we will be paying close attention to variables with lower bounds, forcing us to use an alternative. We will look for constraints that are active, either forcing us to do something that is not so profitable or keeping us from being too profitable. The upper bounds on the most profitable variables (or those with the highest Bang for the Buck) will keep us from making too much profit. Let us try to formalize the procedure for inspecting a solution.

Quick & Dirty Linear Programming Inspection

1. Set *all* variables at their lower bounds. Determine how much of each resource that uses.
2. Determine which constraints will bind the solution the most. (What keeps you from making an infinite profit *first*?)
3. Picking the tightest constraint, use the Bang for the Buck to determine which variable should increase. Make that variable as large as possible. You will either be stopped by the upper bound of that variable or use up all the resources for that constraint. If the former case applies, pick the next best Bang for the Buck variable and continue.
4. Investigate if there are other variables that may be increased and do not affect the constraint that has just been used. If so, use Bang for the Buck criteria where possible.
5. Make sure that all requirements are met. It may be that some constraints will force you to not make so much profit.

This general solution is for maximizing profit. To minimize cost we simply will do as little as is required, picking variables that have the *lowest* Bang for the Buck ratio. To illustrate this Quick & Dirty, we will solve the three models in Section 6.2 by inspection.

transco products inc.: solution

Recommendation

It is recommended that Transco produce 5 of antenna I, 10 of antenna II, and 23 of antenna III. The solution is bound by the inspection time, and less profit is made because of orders that have to be filled for antenna I and antenna II.

Numerical Answer

Variable		Profit
ANT I	5	$2,473.30
ANT II	10	$4,936.00
ANT III	23	$15,047.98
		$22,457.28

Math Work. Given the model in Section 6.2, we see that there are lower bounds on all three alternatives, that is, we *must* make 5 ANT I, 10 ANT II, and 5 ANT III. Thus our model now becomes:

$$35 \text{ ANT I} + 38 \text{ ANT II} + 23 \text{ ANT III} \le 530 \text{ min Mill}$$
$$30 \text{ ANT I} + 28 \text{ ANT II} + 18 \text{ ANT III} \le 980 \text{ min}$$
$$12 \text{ ANT I} + 9 \text{ ANT II} + 6 \text{ ANT III} \le 1420 \text{ min}$$
$$30 \text{ ANT I} + 35 \text{ ANT II} + 25 \text{ ANT III} \le 975 \text{ min}$$
$$21 \text{ ANT I} + 24 \text{ ANT II} + 15 \text{ ANT III} \le 880 \text{ min}$$
$$35 \text{ ANT I} + 35 \text{ ANT II} + 25 \text{ ANT III} \le 450 \text{ min Inspection}$$
$$\text{ANT I} \le 15$$
$$\text{ANT II} \le 20$$
$$\text{ANT III} \le 20$$

1. Notice that the right-hand sides of the first six constraints have been reduced by the amount of time that it took to produce the three types of antennas on that particular process. The last three constraints have been reduced by the number of antennas already produced (5, 10, and 5). Thus ANT I now stands for the number of antennas I that are produced above the lower limit of 5.
2. Step 2 suggests that we look now to see which constraint or constraints bind us the most. The last process (inspection) has only 450 minutes left, while the first process (mill) has 530 left. The coefficients on each variable are about the same for the two constraints, and these values are as large as or larger than the others. Thus we would run out of inspection time or mill time before anything else.
3. Looking at the Bang for the Buck ratios for these two constraints, we have:

Ratio	ANT I	ANT II	ANT III
Mill	$494.66/35	$493.60/38	$654.26/23
	= $14.13	= $12.98	= $28.44
Inspection	$494.66/35	$493.60/35	$654.26/25
	= $14.13	= $14.10	= $26.17

We see that, regardless of which constraint might be tight, the most profitable variable is antenna III. We would like to have as many as 20 more units, which would not violate the first constraint but would violate the last one. We can only have 18 more of antennas III, which will use up all the inspection time.

4. There are no other alternatives that can become positive, and all requirements are met. This is our Quick & Dirty solution (and also an optimal solution in this case):

5 ANT I,   10 ANT II,   23 ANT III.

---

whiskey blending: solution

Recommendation
Make as much Pure Poison as cheaply as possible by using the rye with as much corn as allowable. The rest will be as much wheat as possible. Use the remaining mash to make Devilishly Deadly. Therefore make 3332 fifths of Pure Poison and 2368 fifths of Devilishly Deadly.

Numerical Answer

	Pure Poison (fifths)	Profit		Devilishly Deadly (fifths)	Profit
Rye	2000	−$ 400.00	Rye	0	$ 0.00
Wheat	666	$1198.80	Wheat	1834	$1283.80
Corn	666	$1864.80	Corn	534	$ 907.80
	3332	$2630.60		2368	$2191.60

total profit = $2630.60 + $2191.60 = $4822.20.

Math Work

1. There are no lower bounds for each single variable, except of course zero. Thus our constraints are the same as for the model in Section 6.2.
2. The constraints that are binding are the input constraints for rye, wheat, and corn mash. If there were no limitations here, we could make as much of both whiskeys as we wanted (and an infinite profit also).
3. Since all coefficients in the input constraints are $+1$, we can simply use the profit figures for our Bang for the Buck ratio. The best is corn mash in Pure Poison, but to use this we must also have at least 60 percent rye, no more than 20 percent corn, and obviously the rest would be wheat mash since it has a better profit than rye. We therefore need to see how much Pure Poison we could make having 60 percent rye, 20 percent wheat, and 20 percent corn (RP, WP, and CP, respec-

tively). Thus for 100 fifths of Pure Poison, we would need 60 fifths of RP, 20 fifths of WP, and 20 fifths of CP. As we increase the amount of Pure Poison we can make, we will run out of RP first. Thus we will make our mixture with 2000 fifths of RP, 666 fifths of WP, and 666 fifths of CP. We cannot add any more wheat or corn because we would upset the necessary ratio for rye in Pure Poison.

4. This leaves us with the following reduced problem:

Maximize Profit = $0.90 WD + $1.90 CD

subject to:

$$WD \leq 1834 \text{ fifths}$$
$$CD \leq 534 \text{ fifths}$$

$$17 \, WD - 3 \, CD \geq 0$$
$$-3 \, WD + 2 \, CD \leq 0$$

Since there is no more rye at all, RD *must* be zero. If we use all the wheat and corn possible, setting WD = 1834 and CD = 534, we see that all the constraints are satisfied and nothing is violated. This is our Quick & Dirty solution (and it is also optimal).

---

gasoline blending: solution

Recommendation
Produce 50,000 barrels of ethyl by mixing 25,000 barrels of isopentane and 25,000 barrels of cat cracked, and produce 30,000 barrels of regular by mixing 25,000 barrels of isopentane with 5,000 barrels of cat cracked. A profit of $120,000 will result.

Numerical Answer

	Ethyl		Regular		Total
Isopentane	25,000 bbls	$45,000	25,000 bbls	$37,500	50,000 bbls
Cat cracked	25,000 bbls	$32,500	5,000 bbls	$ 5,000	30,000 bbls
	50,000 bbls	$77,500	30,000 bbls	$42,500	

total profit = $77,500 + $42,500 = $120,000.

Math Work.
Looking at the model in Section 6.2, we proceed as follows:

1. We see that, as in the whiskey blending problem, there are no lower bounds or requirements on the variables.
2. The constraining factors might be the raw material input (isopentane and cat cracked) or the output (regular or ethyl).
3. For all four of these constraints, the coefficient for each variable is $+1$, so that the Bang for the Buck ratio is simply the profit for each vari-

able. The highest profit is for IE, isopentane to make ethyl. From the last constraint in the mixture we can see that we *must* have at least as much cat cracked in ethyl. We are limited on the input by the 40,000 barrels of cat cracked, so that the most ethyl we could make is 80,000 barrels. But the output constraint keeps us from making more than 50,000 barrels. Therefore we will mix 25,000 barrels of IE and 25,000 barrels of CE.

4. Now our model becomes:

Maximize Profit = $\$1.50$ IR + $\$1.00$ CR

$$
\begin{aligned}
\text{subject to:} \quad \text{IR} \qquad &\leqslant 25{,}000 \text{ bbls} \\
\text{CR} &\leqslant 15{,}000 \text{ bbls} \\
\text{IR} \quad + \quad \text{CR} &\leqslant 30{,}000 \text{ bbls} \\
-2\,\text{IR} \quad + 18\,\text{CR} &\geqslant 0
\end{aligned}
$$

The biggest profit is from IR and thus we would like to use as much as possible. We are bounded on the input by 25,000 barrels of IR, which means that we would have 5000 barrels left from the output constraint for CR. Blending 5000 barrels of CR and 25,000 barrels of IR would not violate the last constraint, and would give a higher octane rating (93.3) than necessary.

INCIDENT: A COMMONSENSE SOLUTION

A consultant reported the following experience when invited to give a talk to the Amalgamated Iron and Steel Engineers.[1] He was given the regular tour of a foundry and shown the blast furnace, rolling mill, and so forth. The engineer then gave a short presentation of the company's linear programming model of the blast furnace burdening. It wanted to minimize the cost of seven ores, so that the objective function was:

Minimize Cost = $C_1 \text{Ore}_1 + C_2 \text{Ore}_2 + C_3 \text{Ore}_3 + C_4 \text{Ore}_4 + C_5 \text{Ore}_5 + C_6 \text{Ore}_6 + C_7 \text{Ore}_7$

where C_1–C_7 are the costs per ton of finished steel from a specific ore, and Ore_1–Ore_7 are the amounts of each type of ore used.

The first constraint was the capacity S of the sintering plant:

$S_1 \text{Ore}_1 + S_2 \text{Ore}_2 + S_3 \text{Ore}_3 + S_4 \text{Ore}_4 + S_5 \text{Ore}_5 + S_6 \text{Ore}_6 + S_7 \text{Ore}_7 \leqslant S$

where S_1–S_7 are tons of sinter per ton of input ore, and S is the sintering plant capacity. So far they were minimizing, subject to a less than or equal constraint.

The consultant has the optimal solution in his head (don't make anything!).

The next constraint was the net tons of hot metal (NTHM):

$H_1 \text{Ore}_1 + H_2 \text{Ore}_2 + H_3 \text{Ore}_3 + H_4 \text{Ore}_4 + H_5 \text{Ore}_5 + H_6 \text{Ore}_6 + H_7 \text{Ore}_7 = \text{NTHM}$

where H_1–H_7 are the net tons of hot metal per ton of input ore of a given type.

The engineer said that NTHM was the number of tons of hot metal they wanted and that they had to hit it *right on the button!* Thus it was an equality and right away the consultant thinks, "Six variables."

Then he was told that they received a trainload of Ore_3, the Woody Creek ore, every week, and that they *had* to use it up. Therefore Ore_3 is always a constant known beforehand. In short,

$\text{Ore}_3 = K.$

The consultant is thinking, "Five variables."

Then the engineer stated that as concerns the last three ores, management kept telling him that they were going to have all three, but that they never had more than one at a time. The one they usually had was Ore_5, the U.S. Fines Stock Material. And further, of Ore_4, the Sunrise Fine Ore, they never had any. In symbols:

$\text{Ore}_4 = 0, \qquad \text{Ore}_6 = 0, \qquad \text{Ore}_7 = 0.$

The consultant is thinking, "This has got to be some kind of a joke, there are only two variables left!"

The last constraint turned out to be the requirement that, when the first two ores were used, they always had to be in a set ratio to each other. Again, in symbols:

$R(\text{Ore}_1) = \text{Ore}_2.$

The consultant said, "Is that all?" He replied, "Yes." The consultant asked, "You've been running this as a linear programming problem, right?" "Right." "How long have you been doing this?" "Three years." "Do you do this on your own computer?" "No, no. We buy time." "You set it up every time, is that right?" "Oh, yes."

The consultant then asked the engineer to go through it again. He wanted to make sure that he was getting it right. So they went through it again, and it was revealed that the last constraint had three cases, the ratio case was case 3. Case 1 was where they got a trainload of Ore_1 and had to use it up, and case 2 was the same for the second ore.

The consultant then asked the engineer if he had any data for this model that he could see. So he was brought a listing of the last run (a case 3 situation). He looked at the data and asked for a slide rule. He then sent everybody out to get him a cup of coffee. When the coffee came, he said, "Well, the way I look at this data, you're going to have about 219 tons of Sunrise Ore, 352 tons of Comstock, 51 tons of Woody Creek (a constant), and 146 tons of U.S. Fines Stock Material." The engineer said, "You know, I've never seen anybody simplex in his head before, you must have done a lot of LP's."

The consultant then pointed out that in all three cases the model boiled down to minimizing one variable subject to that one variable being greater than or equal to a constant. In symbols:

Minimize Cost = Ore_2
subject to: Ore_2 = constant   case 1

and

Minimize Cost = Ore_1
subject to: Ore_1 = constant   case 2 or 3.

Further, whichever one of the last three ores is present can always be determined by the following formula:

$$Ore_k = constant_1 - constant_2(Ore_j)$$
where k = 5, 6, 7 and j = 1, 2.

He then pointed out that a simple chart could easily be constructed, cast in steel, and bolted to the wall of the blast furnace for the operator to use. The facts of the matter turned out to be that the company had been preparing the data for this program for some three years and running it on a time-sharing computer in another city.

The consultant usually asks his class this question when he has told them the above story. "Were these people bad engineers?" The answer is that they were very *good* engineers. Their model did what it was supposed to do, it even did it *optimally*. The only problem was that they got so wrapped up in the method that, after the initial formulation, the model was no longer necessary. They did it *right*, they just did it with more power than they needed. In short, they did it with more when they could have done it with less. There are many times when a Quick & Dirty inspection of the problem can lead to many useful results without the sophistication of an expensive computerized simplex model.

---

cases

For the cases given in Section 6.2, find the solutions using the Quick & Dirty inspection algorithm.

Supplementary Problems

1. An on-campus sorority is having a bake sale in front of the library and one of the members has decided to make three kinds of brittle—peanut brittle, cashew brittle, and pistachio brittle. The kitchen at the sorority house has enough ingredients to make sixteen pounds of brittle (not counting the weight of the nuts).

   Jeri has $10.00 to invest in the nuts which cost $1.00 per pound for peanuts, $2.00 per pound for cashews, and $4.00 per pound for pistachios. The amount of nuts needed for one pound of brittle is $\frac{1}{2}$ pound for peanut, $\frac{1}{4}$ pound for cashew, and $\frac{1}{2}$ pound for pistachio.

   After making the brittle, she will package it into $\frac{1}{8}$-pound bags and sell each bag of peanut brittle for $0.25, cashew for $0.75 and pistachio for $1.00. Since pistachio brittle is very expensive and requires a well-developed taste, Jeri will limit production of it to 2 pounds. Assuming that she will sell all she makes, develop the LP model for this situation and solve using the Quick & Dirty Inspection algorithm to maximize the revenue for the brittle being sold.

2. Given the Boat Company case, the company has just discontinued Steering Set-ups and will not be producing any more. Determine the new solution to the problem using the Quick & Dirty Inspection algorithm. *Hint*: Look at your previous answer to determine which constraints to worry about. Show your work.

6.4 GRAPHICAL SOLUTION

Now that we have looked at a very simple straightforward solution, let us turn to more complicated solutions. To do this, we need to start very simply with a problem that has only two variables so that we can "draw" the solution, and then in the next section we will introduce the simplex method. What is important in this visual section is that all the possible solutions are within an area bounded by straight lines, called the feasible region. These solutions satisfy all the constraints and are indicated by a hatched area. As you will see, there are an infinite number of possible solutions, which can make it difficult to enumerate them. The saving grace of linear programming is that because only linear equations and inequalities are used, we know that the optimal solution will occur on the boundary of the feasible region, whether we are maximizing profit or minimizing cost. In fact, the optimal solution will always occur at a corner point of the feasible region (where two constraints intersect). Since there are a finite number of these points, all that needs to be done is to find the values of the variables at these points and the resulting value of the objective function (profit or cost) and pick the best of these.

Obviously this technique falls apart when we get past three variables (and for most people, graphing in three dimensions is impossible). Thus as a solution technique it is severely limited, but it is pedagogical in that we may be able to illustrate what is happening as we systematically solve using algebra in the simplex technique. For this section we will present two problems, model them, graph them, and solve them.

bartender problem

This classic problem has been used for years by students of linear programming. It serves a good purpose to show the interactions in using up resources. A bartender is limited in his knowledge of mixing drinks; he can only make two: Tom Collins and Gin Sours. They each use varying amounts of gin, sugar, and mix (tonic), and he makes a profit of $1.00 and $2.00, respectively, on each drink (actually enough for two drinks each). The drinks are made in the proportions given below.

	Tom Collins	Gin Sours	Available
Gin	2 ounces	6 ounces	3600 ounces
Sugar	2 teaspoons	1 teaspoon	1200 teaspoons
Mix	1 bottle	1 bottle	800 bottles
Profit	$1.00	$2.00	

Model

Let us develop the model first.

1. *Variables*. Let TC be the number of Tom Collins made, GS the number of Gin Sours.
2. We are limited by three resources: gin, sugar, and mix. Algebraically,

$$2\ TC + 6\ GS \le 3600 \text{ ounces of gin}$$
$$2\ TC + 1\ GS \le 1200 \text{ teaspoons of sugar}$$
$$TC + 1\ GS \le 800 \text{ bottles of mix}$$

3. Our objective is to maximize profit:

$$\text{Maximize Profit} = \$1.00\ TC + \$2.00\ GS.$$

Solution

To graph this, we must remember that the number of TC and GS must be 0 or greater; thus we are only dealing with the first quadrant of the graph (these are actually constraints). To draw the three resource constraints, we first need to find the line that represents each inequality as an equality (=). Thus we set $2\ TC + 6\ GS = 3600$. To draw this, we need to know two points. Thus we will set $TC = 0$, which means $GS = 600$. This is one point. Now we set $GS = 0$, this means $TC = 1800$. This is another point on the graph. Now we draw a line between the two points, and this is the equality. To find out the feasible regions (what points satisfy this inequality), we test the origin. Does the point (0,0) satisfy the inequality; $2(0) + 6(0) \le 3600$. Yes it does. Therefore all the points *on* the line and toward the origin satisfy the first constraint and the nonnegativity requirements (shaded area in Figure 6.1). Adding the other two constraints, we reduce the feasible region further and get Figure 6.2 (page 216). The shaded area represents all the feasible possibilities, but as was mentioned earlier, due to the linear properties of this problem, the solution will be found at one of the corner points A through E (circled). Each point is the intersection of two constraints. We will now solve for the values of TC and GS and find the value of the profit function:

Point	Equations		Solution		Profit
A	TC = 0		TC = 0		$ 0
	GS = 0		GS = 0		
B	TC = 0		TC = 0		$1200
	2 TC + 6 GS = 3600		GS = 600		
C	TC + GS = 800		TC = 300		$1300
	2 TC + 6 GS = 3600		GS = 500		

Table continues on next page.

Figure 6.1

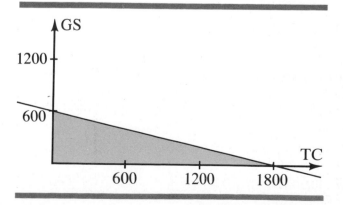

Point	Equations	Solution	Profit
D	TC + GS = 800 2 TC + GS = 1200	TC = 400 GS = 400	$1200
E	GS = 0 2 TC + GS = 1200	TC = 600 GS = 0	$ 600

The optimum solution occurs at point C at a profit of $1300. At this point all the mix and the gin are used, while point C is below the sugar inequality, meaning that there is still some sugar resource left. This represents the best use of all three resources for this problem. If the profit function were different, then another point might be optimal. Checking our solution with the original constraints, we have:

Gin   2(300) + 6(500) = 3600 all gin used
Sugar 2(300) + 1(500) = 1100 there are 100 teaspoons
                              of sugar left
Mix   1(300) + 1(500) = 800 all mix used
Profit 1(300) + 2(500) = $1300

feed mix

For our second example let us consider two food supplements that need to be added to every 100 pounds of grain. Each contains different amounts of vitamins, protein, and calcium. The first, HiPro, costs $3.00 per ounce and the second, Vita, costs $4.00 per ounce. Given the requirements below, determine the number of ounces that will meet these requirements at a minimum cost.

	Hipro	Vita	Required
Vitamin	5	25	50 units
Protein	25	10	100 units
Calcium	10	10	60 units

Thus 1 ounce of HiPro contains 5 units of vitamin, 25 units of protein, and 10 units of calcium. Let HP stand for the number of ounces of HiPro and VT for the number of ounces of Vita.

Model

The mathematical model for this is as follows:

Minimize Cost = $3.00 HP + $4.00 VT

subject to: 5 HP + 25 VT ≥ 50 Vitamins
               25 HP + 10 VT ≥100 Protein
               10 HP + 10 VT ≥ 60 Calcium

Solution

When we graph this model, we will note that the feasible area is on the line of the constraint and away

Figure 6.2

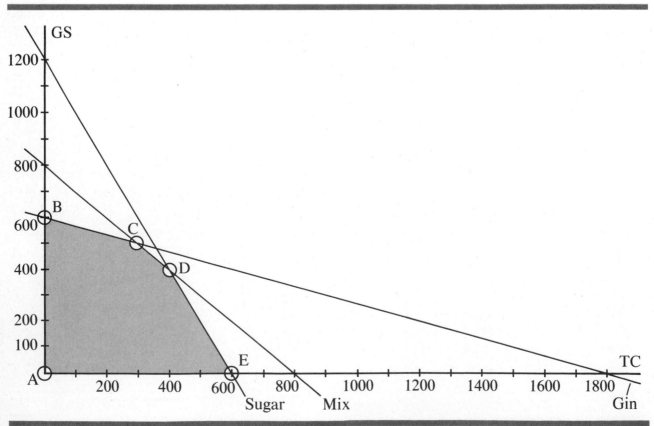

from the origin [(0,0) does not satisfy the constraint] (Figure 6.3). Again the shaded area represents all the possible feasible solutions to the problem, and the optimal solution will be found at one of the corner points.

To solve this problem we will find the values of the corner points, which are the intersections of two constraints, and choose the point that gives the minimum cost:

Point	Equations		Solution	Cost
A	HP $= 0$		HP $= 0$	$40.00
	25 HP + 10 VT = 100		VT $= 10$	
B	10 HP + 10 VT $= 60$		HP $= 2.67$	$21.33
	25 HP + 10 VT = 100		VT $= 3.33$	
C	10 HP + 10 VT $= 60$		HP $= 5$	$19.00
	5 HP + 25 VT $= 50$		VT $= 1$	
D	VT $= 0$		HP $= 10$	$30.00
	5 HP + 25 VT $= 50$		VT $= 0$	

The smallest cost occurs at point C, and thus 5 ounces of HiPro and 1 ounce of Vita should be added to every 100 pounds of grain to meet the minimum requirements at minimum cost.

It is hoped that these two examples will help in understanding that the trade-offs involved in using resources to either maximize profits or minimize costs can be very complicated, even for just two decision variables. It is therefore once again warned that solving two-variable linear programming problems by graphing is not the norm in solving linear programming problems.

INCIDENT: GRAPHICAL SOLUTIONS ARE LIMITED TO CLASSROOMS

A Midwestern aerospace company decided to diversify, and since it had a lot of computers, it decided to

Figure 6.3

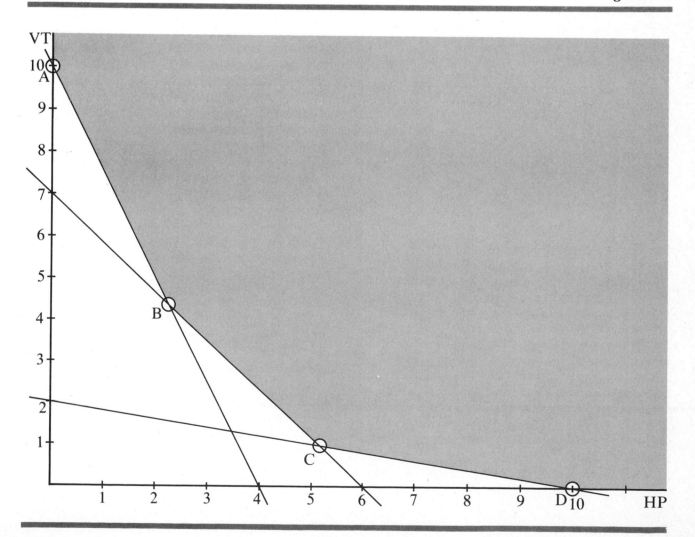

pool them together and sell computer services. Along with this, it also did OR consulting, and so it needed to hire an occasional OR analyst to keep building up its staff. During an interview with a recent graduate of one of the nation's finest schools, the manager asked if she had any linear programming experience. The young lady answered affirmatively, and the manager then asked how many models she had solved. The young lady answered that she had solved dozens of them, and the manager then wanted to know which computer codes she had used. The young lady shifted uneasily and said that she hadn't used any codes, that she had simply solved them graphically. She was politely shown the door and told not to call back, but that she would be contacted if any graphical linear programming problems arose in the real world.

the toddle house

The Toddle House Restaurant, a small chain of 24-hour short-order houses in the Midwest, serves the most fantastic hash brown potatoes that are famous for miles around. There is one restaurant located near a local university, which is the saving grace for students who are working all night on a paper or cramming for exams, and about 3:00 A.M. is the best time to get a good order of hash browns. Every order comes with a side order of hash browns, and all potato dishes are made from fresh potatoes, of which there are two kinds: Idaho, which cost about 25¢ per pound, and Russet, which cost about 20¢ per pound. The T House is able to obtain as many pounds of Russets as desired, but there is a limitation of about 900 pounds per week of Idaho potatoes. Also, for best taste, the head chef (Barrie) wants to make sure that no more than 80 percent of the potatoes used are Russets.

There are three main uses for the potatoes: french fries, hash browns, and potato pancakes. Early in the morning two workers on the graveyard shift do nothing but cut up potatoes, peeling and scrubbing, slicing and dicing, grinding and mashing. The potatoes are scientifically prepared so that the french fries come from the heart of the potato, then the hash browns, and finally the rest is used for the mashed potatoes that go into the potato pancakes. For each pound of potatoes there is a certain amount of waste, 5 percent and 20 percent for Idaho and Russet, respectively. The following table gives a breakdown of the contribution of the two types of potatoes in the different dishes and the average revenue per pound.

	Idaho	Russet	Revenue per Pound	Demand per Week
French fries	0.1	0.1	$0.25	100 lb
Hash browns	0.4	0.6	$0.27	500 lb
Potato pancakes	0.45	0.1	$0.22	125 lb

Determine the amount of potatoes of each type to buy to meet the demand and which of these demands are binding to the solution. Form the mathematical model, graph it, find the extreme points algebraically, and give the optimal solution.

golf club shafts

Frank Delaney is a senior engineer with a scientific space laboratory. His main duties revolve around working on the Mars Mariner, the Space Shuttle, and other similar projects. When he's not at work, he likes to play golf and make things he designs. The latest is making graphite golf club shafts. This project developed quite naturally when he was able to acquire arbors from a machinist and graphite from another who had a lot of scrap graphite that was too old to be used according to his occupation's regulations.

The reason graphite shafts have become so popular among golfers is that they are the lightest and stiffest type on the market. This lightness enables golfers to achieve greater velocity in the swing, and velocity is the main factor in driving distance. Mr. Delaney's unique way of using boron in the shafts also keeps the shaft from twisting sideways at contact, giving the golfer greater accuracy than most graphite shafts on the market. This combination of distance and accuracy is becoming popular around the local golf courses and has resulted in a demand he cannot meet.

This success has Mr. Delaney seriously thinking about starting a business and employing local high school students, but before he makes too big a jump into business enterprise, he has planned a trial production run. The production team will consist of himself, his daughter Kim, a UCLA graduate on the road to becoming a doctor, and his son Mike, a junior at SDSU on the long road to becoming a CPA. Each will be taking a 4-week vacation during the summer and work 40 hours a week making golf club shafts. There are two types of shafts that will be produced. B2 is made of two layers of boron and three layers of graphite, while B1 is made of one layer of boron and four layers of graphite. Each layer of boron uses 1.5 ounces of boron, and each layer of graphite uses 2 ounces of graphite. Mr. Delaney has 200 arbors for the shaping of these clubs, which requires the wrapping of each layer of boron or graphite with epoxy, reverse biases for strength, and finally applying heat sensitive tape to aid in the baking of the shafts, and then the removal of the arbor.

These shafts are made in groups of three of each type (the number that can fit into the oven Mr. Delaney purchased to cure the product). Shafts B1 take two hours to cure while B2 takes two and a half hours (the boron adding to the time). He figures that he can run the oven twelve hours per day, five days a week. For this four-week trial production run he has available twenty pounds of graphite and ten pounds of boron. He estimates the time for each group of three shafts for each of the three workers to be as follows:

	Frank	Kim	Mike
B1	6	2	2
B2	2	4	1

The cost for a single B1 club is about $12, while it sells for $35, and the cost for a single B2 club is figured around $15 with a selling price of $40 for each club. Determine the product mix that will best utilize the resources that Mr. Delaney has and maximize the profit at the same time. Also comment on which resources seem to be the most restrictive and which seem to be no problem at all.

daiquiri t.g.i.f.

On Friday afternoon everyone on campus is usually in a pretty good mood because school is out and there is a weekend ahead. Many of the beer taverns close to the university take advantage of this happy mood by offering cheap beer prices, hoping to do a large volume of business and build a reputation as a swinging place. Dave, a business student and president of his fraternity, thought he would try to take advantage of the profits that could be made by sponsoring Frozen Daiquiri T.G.I.F. (Thank God It's Friday) parties at the fraternity house. This would help the treasury and build up the reputation of the house as a real swinging bunch of guys.

There are two types of daiquiris that Dave specializes in: lime and banana. One Friday Dave went out and bought 6 half-gallons of rum (equal to about 384 ounces), 3 pounds of powdered sugar (equal to about 120 tablespoons), 25 cans of lime mix, 4 bunches of bananas (5 per bunch), and 25 bags of ice. By talking with his sorority friends and also from past experience, he had a very good idea that the minimum demand of each of the daiquiris would be about 80 lime (16 blenderfuls) and 30 bananas (5 blenderfuls).

Since he was dealing through his fraternity, Dave was able to receive a 10 percent discount on the rum which normally sells for $9.59 per half-gallon. Sugar was 42¢ per pound, lime mix 30¢ per can, a bunch of bananas sold for 30¢, and the ice cost 50¢ per bag. The daiquiris are sold for 50¢ each. The ingredients

necessary for each blenderful of daiquiri are given below.

	Rum	Sugar	Mix	Bananas	Ice	Water
Lime	5 oz	2 tbsp	$\frac{1}{2}$ can		$\frac{1}{3}$ bag	$\frac{1}{2}$ cup
Banana	4 oz	3 tbsp		1	$\frac{1}{2}$ bag	$\frac{1}{4}$ cup

Form the mathematical model that will maximize Dave's profits and the fraternity's image. Graph the model, find the extreme points algebraically, and give the optimal solution.

Supplementary Problems

1. Given the following linear programming problem and its graph, find the values of points R, S, T, U, and V algebraically.

   1. $4A + B \geq 8$
   2. $A + B \geq 6$
   3. $A + B \leq 10$
   4. $A + 2B \geq 8$

   a. The point will be
   R: $A =$ $B =$
   S: $A =$ $B =$
   T: $A =$ $B =$
   U: $A =$ $B =$
   V: $A =$ $B =$
   b. Which points are feasible?
   c. How many variables will be nonzero in the optimal solution? _____

2. Given the algebraic linear programming problem, graph the feasible area and determine the feasible extreme points algebraically and determine the optimal solution.

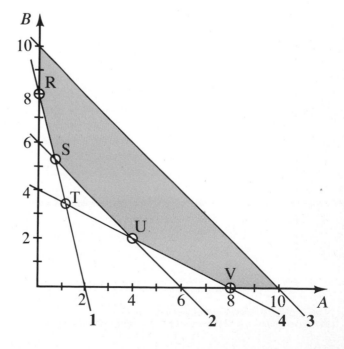

Maximize Profit = $3M + 2N$

subject to:
$$M + N \leq 10$$
$$3M + 7N \leq 42$$
$$2 \leq M \leq 8$$
$$N \geq 2$$

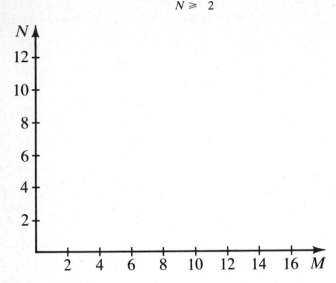

3. A small store makes two kinds of sandwiches using varying amounts of basically the same ingredients. They make a profit of $1.25 from a torpedo sandwich and $1.50 from a submarine sandwich. Given the amount of necessary ingredients below:

Ingredient	Torpedo (ounces)	Submarine (ounces)	Available (ounces)
Turkey	2	4	48
Ham	4	1	32
Salami	2	4	64

a. Write the algebraic model, graph it, and algebraically find the optimal solution:

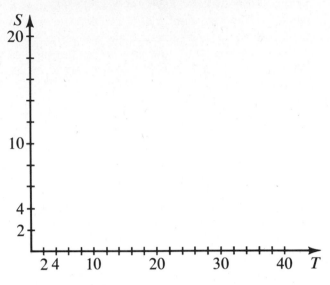

b. Which constraints are binding? _____

c. If the torpedo sandwich used 1 ounce of cheese and the submarine used 2 ounces of cheese and there were 2 pounds available, what would the constraint look like? Is it binding to the optimal solution (why or why not?). _____

4. a. Graph the Whiskey Blending problem below as it appears on page 212.

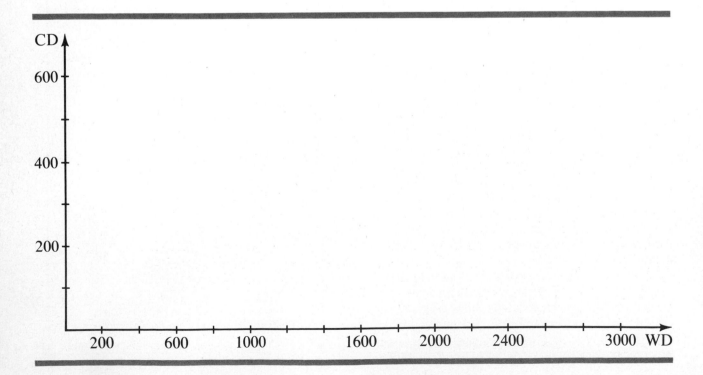

b. What are all the feasible extreme points (values of WD, CD)? _____

_____

c. What is the optimal profit (show work):

d. Which constraint(s) are never binding? ____

_____

e. Which constraints inhibit better profits? ____

_____

5. Consider the Daiquiri T.G.I.F. Case.
   a. How many feasible extreme points are there?

   _____

   b. What was the profit if we made 50 lime daiquiris and 5 banana daiquiris? _____
   c. What if the lime daiquiris only used $\frac{1}{4}$ can of mix (instead of $\frac{1}{2}$)? Which constraints are now binding to the new optimal solution? _____

   _____

   d. What is the new optimal solution? _____

   _____

6.5 SIMPLEX METHOD

The simplex method was developed in the 1940s by George Dantzig,[2,3] now a professor at Stanford University, as a systematic procedure for solving LP problems with large numbers of variables. If each linear programming problem had at most two variables, there would be no need for the simplex method, however, some problems have considerably more than two variables. Simplex does not mean "simple," but rather it comes from the mathematical jargon associated with solving LP problems. We shall avoid the mathematics (using only arithmetic and simple algebra) and esoteric jargon (using sensible words) while trying to increase the understanding of how, why, and when the simplex method works, and what it does. The advantageous thing about this method is that it can be computerized to give Quick & Clean answers to those LP problems that have an optimal solution. It does so by realizing that *solving an LP problem reduces to solving some linear equations* (even if the LP constraints are inequalities). In fact,

only particular kinds of solutions to the linear equations need to be examined in order to find the optimal solution to a given LP problem. Looking at the figures in Section 6.4 might help you to realize why this is true (but then maybe it won't help you at all).

We will now digress briefly to discuss how to solve linear equations. One thing that ought to be realized is that LP problems will have many more variables than constraints, especially after every constraint has had at least one extra variable added to it for the simplex method. To solve linear equations means to find a value for each variable so that, with these values, all the equations are true at the same time. Because of the mathematics, which we promised not to mention, some of the variables need to be set equal to zero before solving for the rest of the variables. True to our LP problem, this needs to be done when there are more variables than equations. The number of variables to be set equal to zero will be equal to the number of variables minus the number of equations. We will refer to the solution so produced as a "special solution" (basic solution to mathematicians); to the variables set equal to zero as "outs" (nonbasic variables); and to the other variables as "ins" (basic variables).

For example, to solve the single equation in two variables $2\,TC + GS = 1200$ with a special solution, let $GS = 0$ be the "out" (2 variables − 1 equation = 1 "out"), and thus $2\,TC = 1200$, or $TC = 1200/2 = 600$, is the value of the "in" variable. Note that $TC = 0$, $GS = 1200$ is another special solution with TC and GS exchanging the roles of "in" and "out." Also, while $TC = 300$ and $GS = 600$ is a solution to the equation, it is *not* a special solution. Simple? For more variables (do you remember *why* we are doing this?) and equations, it's just about as easy.

Consider $2\,TC + GS + S = 1200$ and $TC + GS + M = 800$, that is, two equations with four variables. Let GS and S be the "out" variables (equal to zero). This leaves $2\,TC = 1200$ and $TC + M = 800$, which means that $TC = 600$, $M = 200$, $GS = 0$, and $S = 0$ as a special solution to these two equations. Remember that 4 variables − 2 equations = 2 "out" variables, which must be set to zero. There are other special solutions to these two equations, and if you are clever, you can choose the "outs" so that none of the "in" variables has a negative value (as we have done above). This is called a "very special solution" (basic feasible solution). All the above special solutions we found were also very special solutions; however, sometimes they are not. Well, here we are: very special solutions to linear equations, "ins," "outs," and solving linear equations. We are almost there.

The next thing we need to explain is *why* the simplex method works (and then *how* it works). The reason simplex works is because each LP problem conforms to the following items:

1. Taken together, all solutions to the given linear programming constraints (the feasible region) form a "nice" kind of set, region, or picture. This nice set has no holes or gaps in it; the set doesn't even have dents or pockets in it; and the boundary of this feasible set is formed by straight lines (see the figures in Section 6.4).

2. The corners (extreme points) of this feasible set correspond to the very special solutions described earlier, and there are only a finite number of them (even though there are an infinite number of the plain old solutions).

3. The only difference between two very special solutions that are next to each other (are connected by a straight line) is that one "in" variable and one "out" variable have changed roles (and the remaining "ins" have adjusted their values).

4. If the objective function has an optimal value, there is some very special solution (corner point) that produces that value. This means that in the optimal solution to the LP problem only as many variables will be positive (the "ins") as there are constraints, and the remaining variables will be "out" with the value of zero.

5. If a corner point (very special solution) produces a better value of the objective function than any of its neighbors (those connected by a straight line), then that very special solution is the optimal solution, and we need look no further. Otherwise we go to the next very special solution. We will eventually find the optimal one.

Well, there you have it: "Simplexing" is just a way of enumeration or "traveling" from one very special solution to another neighboring one until the best one is identified. That's the good news. The bad news is that for even moderate-size LP problems (120 variables, 80 constraints) the number of special solutions can exceed 16 times the weight of the sun in grams, so don't try to find them by hand calculation. (At a million a second it would take approximately 1.5 million years to solve such a problem.) That's why we told you about the "black box" in the chapter introduction because LP problems cannot be solved by hand. The simplex method is very efficient and doesn't have to enumerate very many corner points or very special solutions before finding the best solution. But even at that, there is a tremendous amount of arithmetic involved that obviates hand calculations.

Now that we have tried to explain *why* the simplex method works, here is the *how*.

Quick & Clean Simplex *(if computerized)*

1. Set up the LP constraints into equations according to these rules:

   a. Put all the variables on the left, the constant on the right. Make sure that the constant is positive (if not, multiply everything by -1 and turn the inequality sign around).

   b. If the constraint is $\leq$, then add a new slack variable to the constraint. This will stand for the amount of resource not yet used up. For the gin constraint in the bartender problem $2\,TC + 6\,GS \leq 3600$ becomes $2\,TC + 6\,GS + G = 3600$, where G is the amount of gin left after the Tom Collins and Gin Sours are made. The objective function is not changed.

   c. If the constraint is $=$, then add a new artificial variable (not a real variable) and penalize that variable in the objective function. Thus if we had the equality $2\,RA + 3\,RB + 6\,RC = 10$, we would add the artificial variable A1 so that $2\,RA + 3\,RB + 6\,RC + A1 = 10$, and in the objective function we would put $+\,1000\,A1$ if we were minimizing or $-\,1000\,A1$ if we were maximizing, where the 1000 would be much larger in value than anything else in the objective function. If it isn't, simply increase the value. The idea is that we are penalizing ourselves for using that variable to get started, but it won't appear in the optimal solution (it will finally be an "out" variable).

   d. If the constraint is $\geq$, then subtract a new surplus variable and add a new artificial variable to the constraint. Again penalize the objective function for the artificial variable only. The surplus variable will stand for the amount of extra resource we are using that is not required. Thus for the feed mix problem for the protein constraint $25\,HP + 10\,VT \geq 100$ becomes $25\,HP + 10\,VT - P + A1 = 100$, where P is the surplus amount of protein and A1 is the artificial variable. The objective function for the feed mix would then have $1000\,A1$ added.

2. To begin simplexing, start by allowing the slack and artificial variables to be "in" variables and set all others to zero as "out" variables. Each equation can then be solved easily for one "in" variable, which will have the value of the right-hand side of that equation.

3. Decide if some neighboring corner point (very special solution) produces a better value of the objective function than the value produced at this corner point.

   a. If there is no better neighbor, *Stop. Optimal solution.*

   b. If there is a better neighbor, go to it: interchange the "out" variable that should become an "in" variable and allow one of the ones currently "in" to go "out." To do this, solve the proper equation for the new "in" variable and substitute it into all the other equations and the objective function. Go back to step 3.

Examples. Consider the bartender problem:

Maximize Profit = $1.00TC + $2.00 GS

subject to:
$$2TC + 6\,GS \le 3600 \text{ ounces of gin}$$
$$2TC + GS \le 1200 \text{ teaspoons of sugar}$$
$$TC + GS \le 800 \text{ bottles of mix}$$

Follow these steps:

1. Each constraint already has all the variables on the left, the right-hand side constant is non-negative.
   Convert to equations:

   Maximize Profit =
   $1.00 TC + $2.00 GS

   subject to:
   $$2\,TC + 6\,GS + G = 3600$$
   $$\qquad\qquad\qquad\qquad G \text{ is gin not used}$$
   $$2\,TC + GS + S = 1200$$
   $$\qquad\qquad\qquad\qquad S \text{ is sugar not used}$$
   $$TC + GS + M = 800$$
   $$\qquad\qquad\qquad\qquad M \text{ is mix not used}$$

2. Solve for slacks (there are no artificials) and set all other variables = 0:

   Maximize Profit = 0 + $1.00 TC + $2.00 GS
   subject to:
   $$G = 3600 - 2\,TC - 6\,GS$$
   $$S = 1200 - 2\,TC - GS$$
   $$M = 800 - TC - GS.$$

   Thus G, S, and M are "in" and GS and TC are "out" and = 0. This means G = 3600, S = 1200, and M = 800.

3. Decide if some neighbor is better. How do the "out" variables affect the profit? We see that if either "out" variable were allowed to be positive, then the profit would increase (it is now equal to 0). GS has a larger Bang for the Buck ratio than TC, so we will arbitrarily allow GS to become "in."

   This now raises the question of which "in" variable will now become "out" or zero. Let us look at what will happen to G, S, and M as we increase the value of GS from zero.

   $$G = 3600 - 2\,TC - 6\,GS.$$

   As GS gets larger (from 0 to 100, 200, and so on), G gets smaller and smaller, until GS = 600 (this

of course assumes that TC is still "out" and zero). If GS gets any bigger than 600, G will become negative, and we will no longer have a very special solution.

$$S = 1200 - 2\,TC - GS.$$

GS here can get as large as 1200 before S will be zero, but as we have already noted, if GS gets any bigger than 600, G becomes negative.

$$M = 800 - TC - GS.$$

Here GS will not get as large as in the previous constraint, but will reach 800 before M would be zero. Again, this would make G negative. So we see that GS can come "in" as long as it gets no larger than 600. It will also affect the values of the other "in" variables, and G will go "out."

a. In order to move to the next point (we are at point A in Figure 6.3, Section 6.4, and will move to point B), we must solve the equation for GS which has the "in" variable that is going "out," and then substitute that value of GS into every other equation and the objective function and repeat step 3 again.
   We now have G = 3600 − 2 TC − 6 GS, and solving for GS gives us

   $$GS = 600 = (\tfrac{1}{3})\,TC - (\tfrac{1}{6})\,G.$$

   We now substitute this into our very special solution from step 2, including the objective function. For example,

   Maximize Profit = $1.00 TC + $2.00(600 − $\tfrac{1}{3}$ TC − $\tfrac{1}{6}$ GS)
   = $1200 + $\tfrac{1}{3}$ TC − $\tfrac{1}{3}$ G.

   Since TC and G are "out" variables and = 0, profit is now $1200.
   Substituting this new value of GS into the other equations, we now get the following new very special solution:

   Maximize Profit = $1200 + $\tfrac{1}{3}$ TC − $\tfrac{1}{3}$ G
   subject to: GS = 600 − $\tfrac{1}{3}$ TC − $\tfrac{1}{6}$ G
   $$S = 600 - \tfrac{5}{3}\,TC + \tfrac{1}{6}\,G$$
   $$M = 200 - \tfrac{2}{3}\,TC + \tfrac{1}{6}\,G.$$

With TC and G "out" and = 0 we have profit = $1200, GS = 600 Gin Sours, S = 600 teaspoons of sugar, and M = 200 bottles of mix.

Step 3 asks if some "out" variable becoming positive ("in") would make more profit. Obviously if G becomes positive, it will reduce profit (in fact it would undo what we just did). But if TC is allowed to become positive, we will make one third of a dollar for each Tom Collins we could make (these coefficients are known as marginal costs or profits in economics). Thus we will allow TC to come "in," and we now investigate the variables GS, S, and M to see which would become zero first (or go "out").

An easy way to see how big TC can get before each "in" variable becomes zero is to simply divide the coefficient of TC (ignoring the minus sign) into the constant. Thus for GS, $600/\frac{1}{3} = 1800$. TC could get up to 1800 before GS would become negative. For S, $600/\frac{5}{3} = 360$, and for M, $200/\frac{2}{3} = 300$. Thus the smallest of these is TC = 300, which makes M = 0 and go "out."

Solving for TC in the equation with M in it, we get TC $= 300 + \frac{1}{4}$ G $- \frac{3}{2}$ M. Our next step is to substitute this into every other equation, including the profit function. The very special solution that results from this is:

$$\text{Maximize Profit} = \$1300 - \tfrac{1}{4}\,\text{G} - \tfrac{1}{2}\,\text{M}$$
$$\text{subject to:} \quad \text{GS} = \quad 500 - \tfrac{1}{4}\,\text{G} + \tfrac{1}{2}\,\text{M}$$
$$\text{S} = \quad 100 - \tfrac{1}{4}\,\text{G} + \tfrac{5}{2}\,\text{M}$$
$$\text{TC} = \quad 300 + \tfrac{1}{4}\,\text{G} - \tfrac{3}{2}\,\text{M}.$$

Here G and M are "out" and equal to zero, so that profit = $1300, GS = 500 Gin Sours, S = 100 teaspoons of sugar, TC = 300 Tom Collins, G = 0 ounces of gin left, and M = 0 bottles of mix left. Looking at the objective function we see that increasing either of the "out" variables will only decrease the profit. This means that we cannot find a better very special solution, and we must be optimal. This solution also corresponds to point C in Figure 6.3, which was the optimal solution, too.

Let us take the feed mix problem (page 216), simplify it by having just the one constraint for the protein requirement, and solve this by the simplex method.

$$\text{Minimize Cost} = \$3.00\ \text{HP} + \$4.00\ \text{VT}$$
$$\text{subject to:} \qquad 25\ \text{HP} + \quad 10\ \text{VT} \geqslant 100.$$

A simple graph of the problem is given in Figure 6.4. First we change the constraint to an equality: 25 HP + 10 VT − P + A1 = 100 where P is the extra protein and A1 an artificial variable so that

$$\text{Cost} = \$3\ \text{HP} + \$4\ \text{VT} + \$1000\ \text{A1}.$$

The next step is to solve for the artificial variable and substitute that value into the objective (cost) function:

$$\text{Minimize Cost} = \$100{,}000 - \$24{,}997\ \text{HP}$$
$$- \$9996\ \text{VT} + \$1000\ \text{P}$$
$$\text{subject to: A1} = 100 - 25\ \text{HP} - 10\ \text{VT} + \text{P}.$$

Figure 6.4

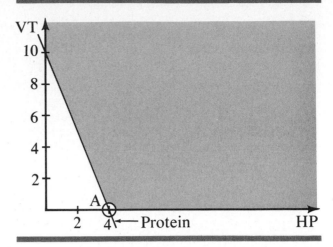

We have one "in" variable and three "out" variables. The solution is therefore to set all "outs" to zero, which gives A1 = 100 and the ghastly cost of $100,000 for the feed mix. You can now see why the variable is called "artificial," because the solution doesn't seem to be connected to reality at all. But you will also note that HP and VT = 0, and this corresponds to the origin in Figure 6.4. Although this is not a feasible solution on the graph, it is a very special solution in simplex.

Looking to the cost function, we can see that either HP or VT becoming positive would certainly decrease the cost and improve the solution, and being greedy, we will take HP because it decreases the cost faster. HP cannot get bigger than 4 (ounces of HiPro), and since there is only one equation, A1 will go "out" and HP will come "in." Solving for HP we get

$$\text{HP} = 4 - \tfrac{10}{25}\,\text{VT} + \tfrac{1}{25}\,\text{P} - \tfrac{1}{25}\,\text{A1}$$

and substituting into the cost we get:

$$\text{Minimize Cost} = \$12 + 2\tfrac{4}{5}\,\text{VT} + \tfrac{3}{25}\,\text{P} + 999\tfrac{22}{25}\,\text{A1}$$
$$\text{subject to: HP} = \quad 4 - \tfrac{10}{25}\,\text{VT} + \tfrac{1}{25}\,\text{P} - \quad \tfrac{1}{25}\,\text{A1}.$$

We can see that we have now moved to point A in Figure 6.4, another very special solution which is feasible, and also optimal, for any "out" variable that becomes positive will increase costs rather than decrease them. We should use 4 ounces of HiPro and have 0 extra units of protein, no ounces of Vita, and our artificial variable is equal to zero.

metal furniture shop

A manufacturing company makes two types of metal tables, a small table for typewriters (40 × 20 inches) and a second, larger table (60 × 30 inches) that is usually used as a second desk in an office. The parts of these tables go through several processes, including shearing, drilling, and pressing the metal, before they can be assembled. Demand for these tables has been good, and for the next month, it is expected that up to 100 of the large tables, and up to 250 of the small tables can be sold. The figures below represent the time it takes for each process for each table (in minutes) and the total time available during the next month for the machines and assembly. Given the figures below, write the algebraic representation of the problem and then solve using the simplex method.

	Large Table	Small Table	Minutes Available
Shearer	17	14	4000
Drill	14	10	5000
Press	15	8	8000
Assembly	20	26	7000
Profit per table	$275	$150	

klean karburetor company

The Klean Karburetor Company makes three basic types of carburetors: regular, four-barrel, and fuel-injected. They are molded first by a sand casting and then bored and threaded on a lathe. Each carburetor need only go through sandcasting and one lathe before it becomes a finished product. There is one large sandcasting area and then three different lathes on which the boring and threading may be done. Thus a regular carburetor may be made by sandcasting and then going to lathe 1, or by sand-casting and then going to lathe 2, and so forth. Thus, there are two *different* ways to make a regular carburetor and only one way to make the four-barrel and one for the fuel-injection (note the table has a time estimate only for the lathes that can produce each carburetor). It is assumed that as many regular carburetors can be sold as made, but that at most 100 four-barrel and 500 fuel-injected carburetors can be sold. The company wants to make sure that at least twice as many regulars are sold as the other two types combined.

Given the time in minutes for each process and the total time available for the next month, set up and solve the LP model which will maximize the profit from production.

	Regular	Four-Barrel	Fuel-Injected	Time Available (minutes)
Sandcasting	100	150	175	40,000
Lathe 1	15	27	—	10,000
Lathe 2	14	—	45	9,000
Profit	$12.50	$17.50	$22.50	

feed cooperative

A Western states cooperative makes many different kinds of feed mixes ranging from pig chow to rabbit pellets. The firm will also custom mix a feed to fit special requirements, such as feed mix for a young 4H farmer raising a competition steer, which has different nutrient needs than an animal going to market, since the latter must be consumed by human beings and the former is raised for show and breeding. The cooperative packages under the Vita-Mite label and one such mix they manufacture is Vita-Mite beef mix.

The co-op's nutritionist is the person responsible for making up the formulas for the beef mix and all other mixes. She uses the annual *Feedstuffs* magazine to find the nutrition requirements for any animal, in this case beef cattle. The magazine is a scientific journal for animal nutritionists and contains tables and charts that are used in determining feed blends. Using these tables, the nutritionist has found that the 100-pound bag must have at least 11.5 percent protein to sustain the animal and also help it put on weight. Crude fat and crude fiber are important to the animal and she doesn't want less than 2.5 percent of the mixture to be fat or the fiber to be more than 11 percent. Lastly, ash is also important to the animal, but too much can make the mixture toxic so she doesn't want more than 8 percent of the mixture to be ash.

There are seven possible ingredients for this mix (ignoring salt as a vitamin supplement that will be added at the end and not make much weight difference) and they are rolled corn, barley, milo, cottonseed crumbles, cottonseed hulls, wheat mixed feed, and cane molasses. The nutritionist wants at least 25 percent of the mix to be rolled corn. The cottonseed hulls, which help fill the fiber needs, should not be more than 7 percent of the mix; otherwise the mixture will be too hard for the animal to digest.

The costs for the ingredients per pound are 5.5¢ for rolled corn, 5.3¢ for barley, 5.0¢ for milo, 9.0¢ for cottonseed crumbles, 3.0¢ for cottonseed hulls, 6.0¢ for wheat mixed feed, and 2.5¢ for cane molasses.

Ingredient	Protein	Fat	Fiber	Ash
Rolled corn	8.9%	3.5%	2.9%	1.5%
Barley	11.5%	1.9%	5.0%	2.5%
Milo	11.0%	2.8%	2.0%	1.7%
Cottonseed crumbles	41.0%	2.1%	11.3%	6.4%
Cottonseed hulls	4.0%	4.4%	43.0%	2.5%
Wheat mixed feed	10.8%	1.7%	2.8%	2.0%
Cane molasses	2.9%	0.0%	0.0%	8.1%

These costs vary from week to week and thus the mixture that produces the lowest cost can vary each week.

Given the percentages in the table of how much protein fiber, fat, and ash are in each ingredient, use the simplex method to determine the minimum cost mix for 100 pounds.

Supplementary Problems

1. In the early 1970s, the Pentagon was faced with a decision on purchasing more planes for the Air Force and Navy in order to supply at least 300 sorties per day for a period of more than one year. The aircraft, their capabilities, and costs are as follows:

	Capability (sorties per day)	Cost per Hour
F-100	1.2	$6447
F-4	1.0	$8185
A-37	2.0	$4860

After a lot of politicking done by all concerned, it was decided that a maximum of 180 F-100s would be allowed, 160 F-4s, and 36 A-37s. Each branch of the service favored one type of plane and wanted to buy just one type exclusively. The Pentagon was looking for a "mix" of planes that would keep everyone from being too unhappy and still keep costs down. Set up the LP model and solve using the simplex method by minimizing the hourly costs of flying these planes (assume that each sortie takes the same amount of time).

2. An investor is looking for a way to diversify $10,000 and is considering four different possible investments. The first two are in slow-growth, low-risk stocks that yield about 10 and 12 percent annually. The third possiblity is in a savings & loan, that will yield 8 percent, and the fourth is a high-risk, fast-growth stock that might yield 80 percent per year. The investor wants to make sure that at least as much is put into slow-growth stocks as the other two possibilities combined, and also that at least $2000 go into the savings & loan. Write the algebraic LP model to maximize yearly revenue and solve using the simplex method.

6.6 POSTOPTIMAL ANALYSIS

Once the solution has been obtained using the simplex method on a computer, any good code will also deliver a lot of important information after (or post) the optimum. This informs the user as to what range of data the solution is good for and how sensitive the costs are and what the consequences might be if something were added or taken away. The analysis falls into different categories:

1. *Shadow prices.* These are found in the objective function of the last very special solution. Looking at the bartender problem, we see that we have $-\frac{1}{4}$ G in the profit function. This simply means that for every ounce of gin we would have left over, we would lose 25¢ in profit. It doesn't take very long to figure that the reverse is also true; that is, for every extra ounce of gin the bartender could get, he could make a 25¢ profit. For M the coefficient is $-\frac{1}{2}$, which means that for every bottle of mix left over we would lose 50¢ in profit, or for every extra bottle we could get we would make 50¢. Since sugar (S) is an "in" variable, this means that we already have some left over, in this case 100 teaspoons. Thus the cost of having 1 teaspoon of sugar left over is nonexistent.

These shadow prices give valuable information about how profitable scarce resources are. For the feed mix problem, costs would increase by $2.80 ($2\frac{4}{5}$) if one unit of Vita (VT) were required. This would be a marginal cost, since its actual cost is $4.00. For protein, for every unit required it increases the cost by $\frac{3}{25}$ or $0.12. Thus for 100 units there is a cost of $12, which is exactly what the model forces the solution to be.

These are very simple and elementary examples of the analysis done with shadow costs. They may give you an idea of the powerful data available from the answer itself.

2. *Cost ranging.* This determines the upper and lower bounds on each profit or cost coefficient in the objective function, assuming that only one coefficient is allowed to change and the others are held constant. It is done for each coefficient and will give an indication of how sensitive the data is. There may be an argument that the cost on HiPro is really $3.50 and not $3.00, and the sensitivity analysis on the costs may show that the cost could be as low as $1.00 and as high as $10.00 before the solution would change. This gives us some bounds on the degree of accuracy needed for the data.

3. *Right-hand-side ranging.* The right-hand side of the inequality is the amount of resource required

or available, and by changing the value of only one variable at a time (holding the others constant) we can determine the upper and lower bounds of these resources before our very special solution would have different "in" and "out" variables. This will also tell us what an extra unit of each resource would cost us or is worth to us.

4. *Parametrics on cost row.* Assuming that information is needed when more than one cost is changed at a time, an upper and a lower limit are given on each cost of interest. Starting at the lowest values and working upwards proportionally, the changes in the optimal solution (which variables are "in" and which are "out") are given.

5. *Parametrics on right-hand side.* Assuming that more than one right-hand-side constant is desired to be changed, an upper and a lower limit are given for each right-hand side of interest. Starting at the lowest values and working upwards proportionally, the changes in the optimal solution are given.

6. *Adding variables or constraints.* If one is interested in the effect of the addition of another variable (alternative) or constraint (restriction or requirement) there are many computer codes that will handle this. It affords the opportunity to investigate a problem in more depth or detail without starting all over again from the initial very special solution. Good codes also allow you to determine which variables you want to start out as positive ("in") rather than to assume that all decision variables are "out" to begin with. Generally speaking, half the solution time in a linear programming code is finding a feasible solution, and the other half is making it optimal.

There is a remarkable efficiency in solving LP problems: two for the price of one. In fact, each time you solve an LP problem, you actually solve two problems—the actual problem itself, called the "primal," and a slightly different but related problem, called the "dual." We have encountered duals before in our coverage of OR techniques and have noticed that the maximum of the primal is equal to the minimum of the dual. Knowledge of duality is important in LP problems for several reasons:

1. Sometimes it is considerably easier to solve one problem than it is to solve the other. It makes sense to solve whichever problem is easier for the simplex method to handle.

2. Solving either problem also produces the optimal solution to the other problem (if you know where to look for it), and you get information about

marginal profits and costs or the relative importance of the resources being used.

3. Duality helps explain a variety of human behavior.

For the bartender problem, let us construct the dual:

Primal

Maximize Profit $= \$1\ TC + \$2\ GS$

subject to:

$$
\begin{aligned}
2\ TC + 6\ GS &\leq 3600 \quad \text{gin} \\
2\ TC + GS &\leq 1200 \quad \text{sugar} \\
TC + GS &\leq 800 \quad \text{mix}
\end{aligned}
$$

Dual

Minimize Cost $= \$3600\ G + \$1200\ S + \$800\ M$

subject to:

$$
\begin{aligned}
2\ G + 2\ S + M &\geq 1 \\
6\ G + S + M &\geq 2
\end{aligned}
$$

Notice that the primal deals with the values of decisions (Tom Collins, Gin Sours) and the dual deals with the values of resources (gin, sugar, mix). Each row in the primal has become a column in the dual, and vice versa. The right-hand-side resources in the primal are now the costs in the dual, while the profits in the primal are now the right-hand-side requirements in the dual. Less than or equal constraints in the primal (all constraints in the primal must be written that way, even with negative right-hand sides, to convert to the dual) become greater than or equal constraints in the dual. The objective in the primal is to maximize profit, in the dual to minimize cost. There is a variable (the slack variable) in the dual for each constraint in the primal; this is why we called the dual variables G, S, and M.

Let us look at the optimal solution, using the simplex method, to both the primal and the dual:

Primal

$$
\begin{aligned}
\text{Maximize Profit} &= \$1300 - \tfrac{1}{4}G - \tfrac{1}{2}M \\
\text{subject to:} \quad GS &= 500 - \tfrac{1}{4}G + \tfrac{1}{2}M \\
S &= 100 - \tfrac{1}{4}G + \tfrac{3}{2}M \\
TC &= 300 - \tfrac{1}{4}G - \tfrac{3}{2}M
\end{aligned}
$$

Dual

Minimize Cost $=$

$$
\$1300 + 100\ S + 300\ TC + 500\ GS +
$$

$$
1300\ A1 + 500\ A2
$$

subject to: $M = \tfrac{1}{2} - \tfrac{3}{2}\ S + \tfrac{3}{2} \quad TC - \tfrac{1}{2}\ GS$

$$
+ \tfrac{3}{2}\ A1 + \tfrac{1}{2}\ A2
$$

$$
G = \tfrac{1}{4} + \tfrac{1}{4}\ S - \tfrac{1}{4} \quad TC + \tfrac{1}{4}\ GS
$$

$$
+ \tfrac{1}{4}\ A1 - \tfrac{1}{4}\ A2
$$

The solution of the dual is for $G = \tfrac{1}{4}$, and the shadow cost in the primal for gin is $\tfrac{1}{4}$ (ignore the minus sign in the primal). The same is true for M in the dual, which is $\tfrac{1}{2}$, and the shadow cost in the primal is $\tfrac{1}{2}$.

The same holds true for the values of the "in" variables. In the primal GS = 500, and in the dual the shadow cost is 500 for GS, and similarly for S and TC. The optimal values of the objective function are also equal ($1300). The shadow costs of the artificial variables have no interpretation.

After this staggering revelation you can see that either problem can be solved, and from the final very special solution you can find all the information needed for the other problem. With this connection between the primal and dual problems, notice that when a constraint in *either* problem is slack or loose (slack variable positive), the value of the corresponding variable in the *other* problem has a value of zero (it's "out"). Thus (slack) × (marginal value) = 0. This means that when there is a value to something you have none of it left (slack = 0) or when you have something left over it has no value (marginal value = 0). This means that the marginal value of loose constraints is zero. This principle is named "complementary slackness." The principle explains why, for example—

1. if an important paper is due on or before the last class day, you get it in on the last class day ("tight" constraint, positive shadow price),
2. if a library book has a 7-day limit, you keep it 7 days (if you like it),
3. if the law says you can't carry more than 1 ounce of some noxious weed, you carry 1 ounce (if you like it),
4. if the law says wastewater treatment plants achieve about 95 percent reductions in bacterial organisms, plants achieve about 95 percent reductions (not much more),
5. there are long lines at post offices and mailboxes at midnight on April 15 of each year (if you owe money to Uncle Sam),
6. people drive 55 mph on interstate highways (or maybe 60 mph if that's what it takes to be ticketed),
7. most workers on an 8:00 A.M. to 5:00 P.M. job don't stick around after 5:00 P.M.

We could go on, but the point is that most people *and* Mother Nature understand complementary slackness (and they must think that the world is linear). Now you too can understand and amaze your friends with this principle. And maybe you can also understand why most people won't give you any "slack."

Given the optimal solution to a linear programming problem (from either inspection, the graphical, or the simplex method), there are some Quick & Dirty ways to do postoptimal analysis.

Quick & Dirty Postoptimal Analysis

1. *Resource.* Add one unit to a resource that is binding and solve. If the constraint is a restriction, this will give the added profit for one more unit of resource. If the constraint is a requirement, the new cost will give how much it costs to be required to use one more unit of that resource.
2. *Nonsolution variable.* For a variable that is zero in the current solution, put in the requirement that the particular variable equal one unit and solve. This will give the cost of having to add a nonoptimal variable.

Examples.   As an example of the Quick & Dirty postoptimal analysis for a resource, let us consider the bartender problem in Section 6.4. The optimal solution required all the gin and the mix, while there was sugar left over. Obviously, if we allow ourselves to have one more ounce of sugar, we will make no more profit than without it. Thus the value of extra sugar is zero. But if we allow one more ounce of gin, we will have 3601 ounces available, and the optimal solution will be at the intersection of the gin and mix constraints. Algebraically,

$$TC + GS = 800$$
$$2\,TC + 6\,GS = 3601$$

Solution

$$TC = 299.75$$
$$GS = 500.25$$
$$\text{Profit} = \$1300.25.$$

We see that we would make an extra 0.25 Gin Sour but 0.25 less Tom Collins, and thus make $0.25 more in profit. Thus we can say that the marginal value of an extra ounce of gin is 25¢, and we should be willing to pay up to near that for any extra gin we might get (at least for a few ounces).

In the same way we can demonstrate from the feed mix problem the marginal cost of an extra unit of vitamin being required. The optimal solution is at the intersection of the vitamin and calcium constraints. Algebraically,

$$10\,HP + 10\,VT = 60$$
$$5\,HP + 25\,VT = 51$$

and

$$HP = 4.95$$
$$VT = 1.05$$
$$\text{Cost} = \$19.05.$$

Here we see that the change in the solution costs us 5¢ more for each extra unit of vitamin that is required in the mix.

As you can see from these simple examples, there is a lot of information in the final solution of a linear programming model, which can prove quite useful to the analyst.

Supplementary Problems

1. Given the following linear programming problem the optimal solution is $X = 2.5$ and $Y = 4.5$ with a profit of \$325. (Optimal solution is the intersection of labor and cable.)

   Maximize Profit = \$40X + \$50Y
   subject to: $3X + 5Y \le$ 30 hours of labor
   $\quad\quad\quad\quad X + Y \le$ 7 miles of cable
   $\quad\quad\quad 5X + 3Y \le$ \$30 of capital

   a. What is the marginal profit for constraint 1? _____

   b. What is the marginal profit for constraint 2? _____

   c. What is the marginal profit for constraint 3? _____

2. Given the solution to the Daiquiri T.G.I.F. case (page 219), what is the profit margin for:

   a. An extra banana? _____

   b. An extra can of lime juice? _____

   c. An extra ounce of rum? _____

   d. An extra cup of water? _____

3. Given the Toddle House case (page 218):

   a. What constraints are binding to the optimal solution? _____

   b. What constraints would *never* be binding? _____

   c. What is the optimal solution if we were maximizing instead of minimizing (give values of variables and total cost)?

6.7 COMPUTER SOLUTION

The last three sections were designed to acquaint you with what goes on in the "black box" of the computer program and the power of the simplex method. Smaller models may be constructed and solved by hand, but models of larger size are generally too complicated to solve by hand, and even to construct in the sense of putting all the data and constraints together. To determine how much it costs to make a certain product may mean determining how many machines it is made on, the production times on these various machines, machine costs, labor costs, and inventory costs. For 20 or 30 products on 10 different machines, there can be many calculations to determine costs and constraint coefficients. Thus many companies will have semiautomated management information systems (MIS). Some of these systems of necessity must be computerized, and the larger linear programming models are generated by computer programs. These are normally termed "matrix generators" or "matrix builders." Thus larger models are generated by computer programs, although the basic structure has been determined by an analyst.

When linear programming models are of meaningful size (over ten variables) it is very difficult to solve them by hand calculations. Thus there are computerized versions of simplex methods (10–100 constraints), revised simplex methods (100–200 constraints), and revised simplex methods with the product form of the inverse and bounded variables (100–10,000 constraints). The state of the art in linear programming codes has advanced rapidly in the last few years so that fast and efficient codes are available (for a price) on almost any computer.

For computer-coded solutions still another step is required. Most results of these codes are in terms intelligible only to a computer programmer, not a manager or a vice-president. Therefore another computer program is usually written to translate the answers into terminology that businesspeople will understand. These are termed "report writers" and can be coded in FORTRAN, COBOL, or some other appropriate language. Most of the operations involve moving data fields around which are alphanumeric.

The actual modeling, solution, analysis, and implementation of LP problems is beyond the scope of this book, and even graduate courses concerned only with LP, but it is hoped that an idea of the scope of linear programming has been transmitted. Included in this section are several cases that are very interesting but really need at least a small minicomputer for solution, although the modeling for these can be done and would prove instructive even without solution.

INCIDENT: PRODUCTION SCHEDULING

A large mining and manufacturing firm had a completely automated system developed by a Midwestern consulting firm. Each week the mining firm would transmit its orders for the next week (how many foils and sheets of aluminum will be needed), and this would be used as input to the total program that scheduled production. This input then generated a matrix for the problem, which was fed into the MPS (Mathematical Programming System) program, the LP problem was solved, and the solution was then fed as input into the report writer. This would finally give as output the production scheduling sheets for that week, an inventory report of how much raw material was still available, and update the management information system. The model contained about 100 constraints with 400 variables and took a total of about 10 minutes to run on an IBM 360 50/75.

crunchy granola sweet

One of the refreshing results of the health food movement has been the revival of interest in healthy breakfast cereals. Granola has been a leader in this movement, and there have been many independent brands on the market before the major cereal manufacturers took granola seriously and started making their own. One of the claims of health food freaks is that granola gives much needed protein. But what is not realized by many is that if the protein is not balanced with respect to amino acids, much of the protein is not usable. There are 8 amino acids that the body cannot produce out of the 22 present in protein. Thus each food must have a certain amount of these 8 essential amino acids (EAAs). If there is a deficiency of one acid (say by 30 percent), then there is a loss of 30 percent of usable protein.

Frank Killian, an independent computer consultant in Minneapolis, Minnesota, has taken an interest in granola and mixing the various grains and nuts in such a fashion as to maximize the available protein and minimize the cost of doing it. The ingredients are listed in Table 6.9 with the relative amounts of amino acids in each for 100 grams (0.1 kilogram), the cost of each ingredient, and the required amount of amino acids for 100 grams (0.1 kilogram) of mix.

The objective function for this problem is not to minimize cost but to minimize the total of all the surplus variables for the constraints. This will give the most usable amount of protein in 100 grams, regardless of the cost. Once the solution is determined, then the costs of the mix per 100 grams are figured out.

Thus if we had only wheat grain and filbert nut as ingredients and only two amino acid requirements (tryptophan and leucine), our model would look something like this:

Minimize Surplus = TR + LE
subject to:
$$0.9 \text{ WG} + 1.1 \text{ FN} - \text{TR} \qquad = 1.0 \text{ tryptophan}$$
$$7.7 \text{ WG} + 5.6 \text{ FN} \qquad - \text{LE} = 4.2 \text{ leucine}$$
$$\text{WG} + \quad \text{FN} \qquad = 1.0 \text{ total ingredients.}$$

Thus all constraints are now equalities, and what is being minimized is the overage or surplus for each amino acid. Using an objective function in this manner has the fancy name of "goal programming" in mathematical literature and the term "satisficing" in management literature. Rather than optimizing just one thing like cost or profit, we are trying to be satisfied at many different points and then either maximize or minimize the extra.

Given the full problem, determine what blend of ingredients and how much would give the best balance of protein usable for the granola mix.

INCIDENT: CYCLING DANGERS

Many textbooks on LP go to great lengths to show that mathematically it is impossible for a model to "cycle," that is, each iteration produces the same

Table 6.9

Amino Acid	Oats	Wheat Grain	Rye	Rice	Brazil Nut	Sunflower Seed	Filbert Nut	Need
Tryptophan	0.6	0.9	1.2	1.5	1.3	1.3	1.1	1.0
Leucine	6.5	7.7	6.0	8.0	7.2	6.2	5.6	4.2
Isoleucine	4.1	5.9	3.9	4.4	3.6	5.2	6.2	2.8
Lysine	3.6	3.0	4.0	4.4	3.2	3.8	2.8	3.2
Valine	4.1	6.2	5.0	6.3	4.8	5.2	6.2	3.6
Threonine	2.4	3.6	3.3	3.4	2.8	4.0	2.7	2.0
Methionine	1.2	1.5	1.6	1.2	4.9	3.4	0.7	1.8
Phenylalanine	4.7	5.0	4.2	4.8	3.6	5.7	3.6	3.2
Cost per 100 grams	$0.08	$0.11	$0.10	$0.05	$0.40	$0.20	$0.30	

value of the objective function, and if no one were watching, the problem would run on for eternity. The difference between the textbook world and the real world is illustrated simply by the fact that all large codes in LP have a special section dealing with this problem. It usually occurs when 75 percent or more of the right-hand sides are zero (usually from material balance equations). The codes simply add a small amount (much less than 1.000) to each right-hand side, solve the problem, then take that solution as a starting point, and reset the right-hand sides. The first time one of the authors personally encountered cycling was on a 100 by 400 problem that cycled with a complicated series of ten variables being tried as new solutions, with the objective function remaining the same and the cycle starting over again. Adding the small amount to the right-hand sides eliminated the problem, and the model was solved in 3 minutes.

space capsule design

Many problems in the field of engineering analysis have at their heart the maximization or minimization of some probability. For example, in the analysis and design of military systems it is often desired to maximize the probability of detecting a hostile aircraft, or to minimize the probability of a false alarm (usually interdependent considerations dictate a compromise). Another common problem involves the deployment of attacking units or the layout of defending units in such a manner as to maximize the effectiveness of one of our strikes, or minimize the chance of success of an enemy strike. In problems such as these, an expression for the probability of some event will appear either as a constraint or as the objective. For example, the probability of detection would most likely be constrained to be equal to or greater than a certain acceptable level, while the probability of a false alarm would be constrained to be equal to or below a certain tolerable level in search/track problems. On the other hand, in the deployment problems the probability of success would most likely appear as the objective which is to be maximized subject to appropriate constraints.

The particular problem examined here involves an objective function which again expresses a probability of concern. In this case it is the overall probability of failure of a small portable communications link that is to be minimized; or looking at it the other way, the probability of not having a failure is to be maximized. The expression for this probability of not failing is nonlinear, but it will be seen that the objective function can readily be put into a form that can be handled using the simplex technique.

In this case a relatively simple electronic com-munications link is considered, composed of three main sections: the receiver module, the transmitter module, and the electromechanical transmit/receive (T/R) switch (see Figure 6.5). It is considered that much of the hardware will be substantially standard in most designs, and it will here be treated as fixed items not under our control. Included as fixed items would be the chassis, antenna, wiring, packaging, and any coils or transformers required. The main variables under our control in this case are the transistors, resistors, capacitors, and the type of T/R switch. Finally it will be assumed that the costs of the components required are relatively constant for a given type of component, over the range of values required. Thus, for example, a glass-insulated capacitor will have a different unit cost than a dipped-mica capacitor, but all capacitors within each given type will be assumed to cost approximately the same amount over the range of values of interest. (Examining component catalogs and using an average price over the range typically encountered in similar applications shows this to be an acceptable approximation.) The types of components considered are presented in Table 6.10 (page 232), along with their important characteristics.

Given the above information, it is now desired to choose the part types to be employed in each portion of the communications link in order that we minimize the probability of failure of the communications link. (Note that, as the majority of electronics equipment failures occur with the surge at turn-on time rather than while in operation, this is considered the probability of the system not working when turned on, and is assumed to be independent of equipment age; periodically scheduled maintenance might also be assumed to justify this.) A failure in any one of the modules, or in the T/R switch, will cause a failure in the communications link. Furthermore it is pessimistically assumed here that there is no redundancy built into the design, and that each component in a module will cause that module to fail, which in turn will result in a system failure (thus, in effect, probability-wise all parts are considered in series). In light of this, the objective function of our LP model should be determined, put into a linear form, and then maximized subject to the appropriate constraints, to be discussed shortly.

Figure 6.5

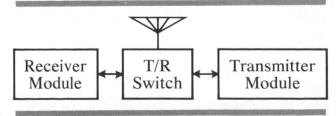

Table 6.10

Components	Cost	Probability of Failure	Weight (oz)	Volume (units the size of carbon resistors)
Transistors				
Type 1, low power, high gain	$10.80	8×10^{-5}	0.04	2.5
Type 2, high power, medium gain	$47.10	2×10^{-4}	0.98	10.0
Type 3, medium power, low gain	$4.25	8×10^{-4}	0.11	5.0
Resistors				
Etched type, miniature	$0.67	3×10^{-5}	0.01	0.1
Wirewound type, high power	$1.00	1×10^{-5}	0.17	3.0
Carbon type	$0.09	2×10^{-4}	0.08	1.0
Capacitors				
Glass-insulated, high stability	$3.60	1×10^{-4}	0.123	0.35
Dipped mica type	$0.59	3×10^{-4}	0.205	1.50
T/R Switches				
Miniaturized type	$84.37	9×10^{-4}	2.00	15.0
Regular type	$24.99	8×10^{-4}	3.50	25.0
Ruggedized type	$32.95	2×10^{-4}	4.50	33.0

Objective Function. The heart of the problem at hand is to express the objective function in a form compatible with the use of the simplex technique. This is accomplished as follows:

If P_1 is the probability of part type 1 failing, then $1 - P_1$ is the probability of part type 1 not failing. Assuming independence, the probability of X_1 of these units in module 1 having no failures is $(1 - P_1)^{X_1}$. From the above we can derive an expression for the probability of no failure in the receiver module as:

$$(1 - P_1)^{X_1} \times (1 - P_2)^{X_2} \times \ldots \times (1 - P_n)^{X_n}.$$

Similarly, the probability of no failures in the transmitter module (#2) is:

$$(1 - P_{n+1})^{X_{n+1}} \times (1 - P_{n+1})^{X_{n+2}} \times \ldots \times (1 - P_{n+m})^{X_{n+m}}$$

The probability of no failures of the transmit/receive switch is similar. Then the probability of the overall system not failing (in view of our definition of system failure) is equal to the product of the probabilities of all the modules.

This expression is obviously not linear as it stands. It is readily put into a linear form suitable for use as the linear programming objective function by taking natural logarithms of both sides, so that the new objective function is as follows:

Objective function $Z = \ln(Z) = X_1 \ln(1 - P_1) + \ldots + X_n \ln(1 - P_n) + X_{n+1} \ln(1 - P_{n+1}) + \ldots$

where $\ln(1 - P_i)$ is a constant.

Due to the fact that this will be in a spacecraft, the total weight of the components considered here must not add more than $1\frac{3}{4}$ pounds (28 ounces) to the system weight, and the volume allocated to the components considered here is limited to that occupied by 350 carbon-type resistors.

The total amount of money allocated to transistors, resistors, capacitors, and the T/R switch is $800.

The total number of high-power transistors in the system must not exceed nine due to power supply limitations.

In the receiver the gain (in decibels, which are added, not multiplied, to the overall receiver gain) required is equal to that of 28 general-purpose type transistors. The decibel gain of the type 1 high-gain transistor is twice that of the general-purpose transistor. The decibel gain of the type 2 power transistor is 1.5 times that of the general-purpose transistor.

The receiver requires a total of 63 resistors and a total of 42 capacitors.

The transmitter requires a total of 14 transistors, and at least 5 of the transistors in the transmitter must be of the high-power type 2 variety.

The transmitter requires a total of 58 resistors and capacitors. At least 12 resistors employed in the transmitter must be of the high-power-handling type 2 variety to serve in the power amplifier circuits. At least 6 capacitors employed in the transmitter must be of the glass-insulated type due to their better temperature stability characteristics.

Although just one T/R switch is required, since this is a linear programming model and not an integer programming model, it must be considered that the switches are divisible items (which of course is not true in practice), and that the total of one switch needed can be made up of fractions of the different types of switches available. Determine the optimal mix that minimizes the probability of failure.

hydraulic specialties

Hydraulic Specialties Company was founded in 1951 to produce precision hydraulic components for the aircraft industry. The business progressed from the machining of component parts to the production of precision hydraulic controls and components. Higher quality and lower cost have been made possible through the creative development of efficient processes and methods. Complete units from raw materials to final fluid testing account for 70 percent of the company's sales. The 30 percent balance of production is in components such as servo valves which are used in computers and other sophisticated components.

The more precise the production process, the higher the cost for quality machines and operators. The servo valve requires very precise machining, and tolerances must be held to within 0.00002 inch. This type of work can only be done on the newer machines by the most capable and skilled operators. The cylinder component is less precise, requiring a 0.0001-inch tolerance. The sleeve component can be produced successfully on any machine and by any operator.

Hydraulic Specialties has some extra time available on its machines and wants to make the best possible use of it. It can make as much of the three products as it has time for right now, and given the figures in the table, determine what product mix on which machines will maximize the company's profits. Note that each piece must be made on one type of each machine only. Thus the servo valve must be milled (either on mill 1 or 2 or 3, but not on all of them), then drilled (there is only one possible), put on the lathe (again just one possible), numerical control (one), deburring (two machines possible), and finally inspection (again two possibilities). Thus the number of ways the servo valve could be produced would be = (3) (1) (1) (1) (2) (2) = 12 different variables and costs for servo valves. The cylinder and sleeve are similar, except that neither of them use the numerical control machinery.

Machine costs are given in the cost column of Table 6.11, and are distributed by dividing the uncommitted time into the overhead cost given there. The operator costs must also be included, along with raw material costs. The total cost for each production combination is then subtracted from the revenue figure to give a profit for each combination.

Table 6.11

		Time Required (min)			Uncommitted Time (min)	Cost	Operator Cost per hour
		Servo Valve	Cylinder	Sleeve			
Mill	1	20	15	5	1600	$212	$3.10
	2	18	14	4	1800	$269	$3.60
	3	21	16	5	1600	$218	$3.40
Drill	1	—	—	47	1600	$201	$3.60
	2	—	35	45	1600	$218	$3.40
	3	13	32	41	1800	$266	$3.80
	4	—	36	45	1600	$227	$3.20
Lathe	1	—	90	10	1600	$324	$3.60
	2	28	82	9	1800	$369	$3.30
	3			10	1600	$216	$3.60
Numerical control		20	—	—	1200	$218	$3.40
Deburring	1	—	—	63	1600	$194	$2.20
	2	38	13	57	1600	$208	$2.90
	3	—	—	61	1600	$201	$2.55
	4	40	15	60	1600	$207	$2.85
Inspection	1	39	15	57	1800	$262	$3.40
	2	41	18	63	1600	$268	$3.50
Raw material cost		$1.10	$8.50	$0.30			
Revenue		$65.00	$75.00	$75.00			

INCIDENT: FOOD PRODUCTION PLANNING MODEL

An interesting LP model, and the largest one that one of the authors worked on, was for the United States Department of Agriculture. It involved determining where dams should be built for flood control, swamps drained, and arid regions irrigated at the cheapest cost so that projected food requirements would be met for 1980, 2000, and 2020. This was done for each river basin (there are 17) in the United States. Each model was about 4000 constraints by 50,000 variables large. A pilot study was done on the Big Sioux river basin, and then a full-fledged model of the Missouri river basin was run. The full model took 26 hours to run on an IBM 360 model 50/75. It was run in stages, with the intermediate results saved every hour, so that in case of a failure of the computer, no more than an hour of computer time would have been wasted.

6.8 BRIDGING THE GAP: THE INTERFACE

It is at this point that the gap between mathematical models as presented in most textbooks and the practice in the real world becomes a gulf and one that seems almost insurmountable. For years students have been tortured with array after array of simplex tableaus, mounds of matrices, and other irrelevant issues until the main purpose has been completely lost in the minds of both students and teachers. The best analogy that comes to mind would be to require reading *Popular Mechanics* as the textbook for driver education courses.

The problem seems to stem from the fact that most textbooks approach linear programming through quantitative methods (how to execute the simplex technique) first and then finally (if ever) through quantitative analysis. It has been our intention in this chapter to do the reverse and to leave the finer points to a further course. To continue the analogy of driver education, we have allowed the student to get behind the wheel and enjoy driving before we look under the hood. We have found that most students (and people) will never really care what is under the hood and are more than willing to go to a specialist. It is our intention to let the students know enough about the subject that they don't get taken when they do go to a mechanic (or OR analyst). With this in mind, we present a few points to ponder.

1. Most computer codes cost in the neighborhood of $10,000 to $20,000.

2. These codes do not use the simplex technique in any recognizable form that is found in textbooks. Not only is revised simplex used, but the inverse of the matrix is stored in product form, which is so complicated that it literally requires an optimization technique to determine when to reinvert the matrix to simplify it.

3. Selection techniques to determine which variable will next enter the basis are varied and usually have some optimization criteria associated with them.

4. Good codes have the ability to "crash" the basis, that is, instead of starting with all the decision variables equal to zero, they allow the user to signify which variables might be in the final solution and start from there, saving as much as 50 percent running time.

5. Unlike the mathematical world, the real world of computing linear programming problems has the real possibility of the problem cycling (or getting stuck) on the same value of the objective function and literally cycling back and forth between extreme points. This can be very costly.

6. Both the assignment problem and the transportation problem can be modeled as linear programming problems and solved by the simplex technique. This happens to be a very inefficient way to solve the problems, but it again shows that many problems can be reformulated and solved in other manners.

Assignment

Minimize $\sum_{i=1}^{n} \sum_{j=1}^{n} C_{ij} X_{ij}$

subject to: $\sum_{j=1}^{n} X_{ij} = 1, \quad i = 1, 2, \ldots, n$

$\sum_{i=1}^{n} X_{ij} = 1, \quad j = 1, 2, \ldots, n$

where X_{ij} is the ith person for the jth job.

Transportation

Minimize $\sum_{i=1}^{m} \sum_{j=1}^{n} C_{ij} X_{ij}$

subject to: $\sum_{j=1}^{n} X_{ij} \leq S_i, \quad i = 1, 2, \ldots, m,$
supply at m plants

$\sum_{i=1}^{m} X_{ij} \geq D_j, \quad j = 1, 2, \ldots, n,$
demand at n warehouses

where X_{ij} is the shipment from the ith plant to jth warehouse.

6.9 REVIEWS

Review 1: Open book and notes; show **all** *work and write legibly.*

1. (15 points) Consider the following Linear Programming problem:

Maximize Profit $= 70X + 60Y + 50Z$
subject to:
$$9X + 12Y + 4Z \leq 20 \,(1)$$
$$3X + 8Y + 6Z \leq 50 \,(2)$$
$$4X + 16Y + 4Z \leq 15 \,(3)$$

a. Solve the problem considering only constraint (1).

b. Solve considering constraints (1) and (2).

c. Solve considering the constraints (1) and (3).

2. (10 points) Determine the variables in the following problems.
   a. A nut distributor wants to use four types of nuts (peanuts, brazil, pecan, filbert) in the following mixes: less than 50 percent peanuts (*Mixed Nuts*); no peanuts (*Party Mix*), 50–70 percent peanuts (*Snack Mix*), and all peanuts (*Peanuts*). List the decision variables that you would need to model this problem.

   b. The ACME Co. can make two different products on the mill and the lathe that must use both processes. There are three possible milling machines to use and two lathes. How many decision variables are there in this problem? (Show how you got them.)

3. (10 points) Determine the new solutions for the following problems.
   a. If it were required in the Bartender problem that there be at least twice as many Tom Collins as Gin Sours, what would it do to the old optimal solution? What would the new solution be?

   b. If it were found out that the profit for Motor Mounts was $50 less in the Boat Company case, what would this do to the Quick & Dirty solution and why? What would the new solution be?

4. (15 points) Given the LP problem below for two types of products (P1 and P2), answer the following questions if the optimal solution to the problem is P1 = 5.25 and P2 = 1.50.

Maximize Profit = 3P1 + 4P2
subject to:
    5P1 + 10P2 ⩽ 60 man hours labor
    2P1 +   P2 ⩽ 12 pounds metal alloy
    3P1 +   P2 ⩽ 20 hours machine A
    4P1 + 6P2 ⩽ 30 hours machine B
    P1 +   P2 ⩽ 80 units (sales restriction)

a. What resources are completely used in the optimal solution? _____

_____

b. Will the last constraint ever be binding even if the objective function changes? _____

_____

_____

c. Write an additional constraint that forces at least 60 percent of the products to be P1. _____

_____

5. (15 points) Given the following LP problem, draw the feasible area and determine the feasible extreme points algebraically (show work) and the optimal solution.

Maximize Profit =   2A +   B
subject to: 5 ⩽ B ⩽ 10
             2A + 5B ⩽ 60
              A + B ⩽ 18

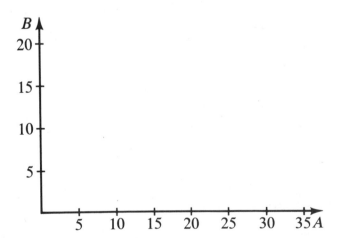

6. (15 points) Determine the postoptimal analysis for the Bartender problem.
   a. If we had ten more bottles of mix, what would the new values of the variables be at the optimal point? (Show your work.)

b. Up to how much should we be willing to pay per extra bottle? _____
_____

c. If we had 200 extra bottles of mix, should we buy all of them? Explain. _____
_____
_____

7. (20 points) Marshy Farms has two unused plots of land, one in County A (2000 acres) and the other in County B (1600 acres). They are interested in producing soybeans (maximum demand is 150,000 bushels) and sugar beets (minimum demand is 50,000 pounds). The yields and costs are given in the table below plus the revenues. It is required that at least 15 percent of each plot must be used for soybeans and that at least 20 percent of the profit come from sugar beets. Set up an algebraic model to determine the number of acres to plant for each product and maximize profit. Label all constraints and variables. *Do not solve*.

	County A Orange County	County B Riverside County	Revenue
Soybeans	30,000 bu/acre	24,000 bu/acre	$1.00/bushel
Sugar beets	4000 lbs/acre	5000 lbs/acre	$0.50/pound
Cost	$1000/acre	$1500/acre	

*Review 2: Open book and notes; show **all** work and write legibly.*

1. (10 points) Given the Boat Company problem (page 207), rewrite the objective function as one that minimizes the cost of production.

   a. Minimize Cost _____

   b. Solve the resulting new LP problem (briefly explain your solution).

2. (15 points) Bitter Water is a refreshing drink after a good run or workout and consists of water, vinegar, and honey. Since water is considered almost free and always makes up 75 percent of the solution, the only costs and constraints are for vinegar and honey. Given the following constraints and objective function, graph the feasible area, show the extreme points (feasible), solve for them algebraically and find the optimal solution. *Then* find the optimal amount of each ingredient in one gallon (128 ounces) of Bitter Water.

Minimize Cost $= \$5H + \$1V$
subject to:
$$H + V \geqslant 10$$
$$10H + 2V \geqslant 30$$
$$5H + 10V \geqslant 60$$
$$V \leqslant 12$$

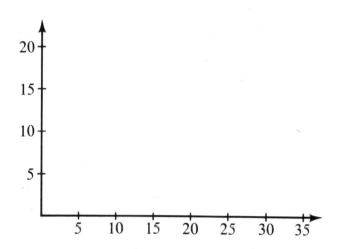

Optimal solution _____

Optimal amount of honey in one gallon _____

Optimal amount of vinegar in one gallon _____

3. (15 points) Paul's Health Food Restaurant wants to cut down on the cost of their famous salads. Their Deluxe Special is a combination of lettuce, tomatoes, broccoli, cauliflower, and mushrooms. They make a daily batch of 25 pounds of salad, of which now more than 60 percent can be greens (lettuce and broccoli). To add color, there must be at least three times as many tomatoes as mushrooms and at least four times as many crunchies (lettuce, broccoli, cauliflower) as noncrunchies (tomatoes and mushrooms). The costs per pound are: lettuce, 30¢; tomatoes, 80¢; mushrooms, $1.10; broccoli, 70¢; and cauliflower, 90¢.
    a. Set up the model by defining the variables, constraints, and objective function mathematically.

b. Solve using the Bang for the Buck principle.

4. (15 points) Considering the Feed Mix problem (page 216), answer the following questions.
   a. For the solution, how much would the cost increase if there were a requirement for one more unit of calcium?

   b. What if there were a restriction of 4 ounces of HP per mix? What is the new solution?

   c. What is the optimal solution if the amount of calcium required is 40 units? Start from the original problem, ignore the change in part b.

   d. What happens to the original optimal solution if the objective function is changed to Minimize Cost = $4HP + $2VT$? What is the new optimal solution?

5. (15 points) Considering the Whiskey Blending case (page 204), perform the following calculations.

   a. Rewrite the problem as if there were no rye available and no rye requirement for Pure Poison (but Pure Poison must still meet the other requirements).

   b. Find the optimal solution.

6. (20 points) The Mighty Mug Company is currently cashing in on the rage of moustaches for men by creating moustache cups (left- and right-handed). Their sales have been spurred by its use by a famous professor on the Johnny Carson Show. They figure unlimited demand and so want to put their production into high gear. On any given day they have 60 pounds of clay (each cup takes 20 ounces and cost $0.20) available. They also have two potting wheels with personnel to run them. Wheel 1 can turn out 15 cups per day and wheel 2 12 cups per day. It costs 50¢ per cup for wheel 1 (a newer one) and 60¢ per cup for wheel 2 (an older wheel).

   The next step is for one worker to put on the handles (left or right) and moustache guard. She can do a total of 50 cups per day at a cost of 15¢ per cup. The cups must then be baked in one of two ovens. Oven 1 is smaller, takes longer, and has a capacity of 20 cups per day, while oven 2 has a capacity of 25 cups per day. The respective costs are 45¢ and 35¢ per cup.

   Finally all these cups are put in a cooling area, which can hold up to 60 cups per day, while an overhead fan assures even cooling. The owners want to make sure that there are at least five times as many right-handed mugs as left-handed, even though they sell for less ($2.00 versus $2.50).

   a. Define the variables.

b. Write the objective function mathematically.

c. Write the constraints mathematically.

7. (10 points)

a. Relate "Complementary Slackness" with Parkinson's Law. _____
_____
_____

b. In the Bartender problem (page 215), what is the marginal profit for an extra:

ounce of gin _____ teaspoon of sugar _____ bottle of mix _____

c. How many possible extreme points are there in the Feed Mix problem? _____

How many do we investigate and why? _____
_____

d. Can a minimizing problem have an unbounded solution? Explain. _____
_____
_____

6.10   REFERENCES

1. R. E. D. Woolsey, "A Novena to St. Jude, or, Four Edifying Case Studies in Mathematical Programming," *Interfaces*, vol. 4, Nov. 1973, pp. 33–34.
2. F. S. Hillier and G. J. Lieberman, *Introduction to Operations Research* (San Francisco: Holden-Day, 1974), chaps. 5, 15.
3. H. Wagner, *Principles of Operations Research* (Englewood Cliffs, N.J.: Prentice-Hall, 1969).
4. H. S. Swanson and R. E. D. Woolsey, "Curve Fitting with Linear Programming," *SIGMAP Newsletter*, no. 19, Aug. 1975, pp. 22–27.

7
integer programming

Integer programming problems represent a class of very fascinating problems that simply require integer answers. Thus for a blending problem the answer might require 2.37 ounces of an ingredient. Integer programming problems must have solutions that are integer, not continuous.

For very large problems it might be possible to simply round off or round up linear programming answers (although it must be done *very* carefully and the solution checked to see if it satisfies all the constraints). The production problems in the linear programming chapter are treated that way.

For problems that do not have variables with large numbers, other solution techniques must be sought. Even for problems that can be rounded, the Quick & Dirty answer that results might be far from the optimum. We have already encountered several types of integer programming problems in this text. Assignment and transportation problems can be cast into integer programming formulation, requiring integer answers only (it is impossible to assign a part of a person or ship only 0.67 of a unit).

The first four sections of this chapter will be devoted to problems involved with all integer values, usually called pure integer problems; and some mixed integer problems will also be discussed. The values

that the integer variables may take on are 0, 1, 2, 3, ... A mixed integer problem simply means that some of these variables have to be integer, but not all. Some very simple heuristics will be given, which should give you a feel for the type of solution needed. Section 7.4 is included to show you some of the techniques used in trying to get optimal solutions to pure or mixed integer problems. These require some understanding of calculus, and of course are simplified for hand solution, which cannot be done on problems of any realistic size. But it is felt that it is important for you to know what lies behind these computerized algorithms.

The last three sections are devoted to problems called 0–1 integer problems. These problems involve variables that can take only the values 0 or 1. The network problems which we have already studied can also be formulated as integer problems, with the variables being whether a certain branch from A to B is being used or not. If the branch is to be a part of the solution, the variable is equal to 1; otherwise it is 0. These are sometimes referred to as "go–no go" variables, where 1 means "go" or do a project, ship a product, or buy an investment, and 0 is "no go" or don't do it. Section 7.7 is included to also show you some optimal techniques for these types of problems,

which although mathematically guaranteed to converge to an optimal solution within a finite amount of time may not do so within your lifetime.

The authors feel required to warn that integer programming is definitely within the twilight zone of operations research. The problems that *can* be formulated as integer programs far outrun the problems that *should* be formulated as such. The beginning student who seeks truth from the literature of this profession will find a vast number of papers on integer programming by veritable demigods of the profession. The conclusion might be that great progress is being made in the field and that all that needs to be done is to select the proper algorithm from the SHARE computer user's library to solve the problem at hand. *Wrong!* It turns out that integer programming problem solving is still an art, and that some do it rather well and some (with the same tools) don't do it at all. We can immediately divide these two groups into good integer programmers and bad integer programmers. Therefore what we have presented here is simply a bag of tricks, or simple heuristics, which have the failing that they do not work very well in the absence of common sense. (However, any purchaser of this volume clearly has more common sense than is *usually* found.*)

7.1 BANG FOR THE BUCK

Integer programming problems are very similar to linear programming problems, with the exception that the values of the variables must be integers rather than continuous (4.3, 7.60321). Let us consider the problem that concerns maximizing the number of people reached by an advertising campaign subject to budget restrictions. Each unit of advertising can reach a certain number of people and costs a certain amount of money. We must buy a whole number of units, which may correspond to $\frac{1}{4}$-page ads, 15-second spots on TV or radio; it is impossible to have 1.3267 $\frac{1}{4}$-page ads or 0.034 part of a 15-second TV commercial.

From the data given in Table 7.1, the integer programming problem can be written as:

Maximize People =
120,000 R + 250,000 TV + 150,000 N + 220,000 M

* *Or less money, as this book is cheaper than most.*

subject to:
$8,000 R +$10,000 TV + $3,000 N + $4,000 M
$$\leq \ \$42,000$$

If we were to use the Bang for the Buck algorithm from linear programming, the solution would be very simple. The Bang for the Buck ratios are as follows:

	Radio	TV	Newspaper	Magazine
Ratio	15	25	50	55

Thus the most effective media is magazine, and we would like to spend all the money and get the most for our resource. This would mean that we would have M = $42,000/$4,000 = 10.5. The problem here is that we do not have an integer answer. If we round the answer up to 11 we overspend the budget and thus have an infeasible solution. If we round the answer down to 10, we reach 10(220,000) = 2,200,000 people with $2,000 left over in the budget. It is possible that there may be a better solution because not all the resource has been used. The problem is that there is no other resource that uses $2000. The next best Bang for the Buck ratio is for newspaper, which needs $3000 per unit. By investing in only nine units of magazine, we would have $6,000 left over which we could put completely into two units of newspaper. This solution would yield 9(220,000) + 2(150,000) = 1,980,000 + 300,000 = 2,280,000 and uses up all the money. Thus we reach 80,000 more people for the extra $2000.

We can see from this simple example that even with one constraint, the solution to integer programming problems is not as easy as it is to linear programming problems.

Quick & Dirty Algorithm: Bang for the Buck

1. Determine the ratio of each objective function coefficient divided by the corresponding constraint coefficient and choose the highest (in case of ties choose the one that uses up the resources best).
2. Use as much of the variable with the highest Bang for the Buck ratio as possible with an integer value. If all the resources are used up, the solution is *Optimal*. Otherwise go on to step 3.

Table 7.1

	Radio	TV	Newspaper	Magazine	Budget
Number of people	120,000	250,000	150,000	220,000	
Cost per unit	$8,000	$10,000	$3,000	$4,000	$42,000

3. Reduce the variable by one and try the next highest Bang for the Buck variable, seeing if you can use up more of the resources with variables that give a lesser return. In this way a higher profit *may* result.
4. Continue to reduce the higher Bang for the Buck variables and try to use up all the resources.

Now let us add another constraint to the problem and assume that there is a limit to magazine advertising and that only three units may be purchased (any more than that would represent overkill). Now the problem will look as follows:

Maximize People =
120,000 R + 250,000 TV + 150,000 N + 220,000 M

subject to:
$8,000 R + $10,000 TV + $3,000 N + $4,000 M
                                            ≤ $42,000
                              M ≤ 3.

The first thing we would like to do is use as much magazine as possible (three units), which will leave $30,000 in the budget. The next highest Bang for the Buck ratio is newspaper, and we can put ten units of newspaper and use up all the money. In this case the solution is optimal for the new problem because we did everything we wanted with the variables with the highest Bang for the Buck ratios. We will reach 2,160,000 people.

The agency then decides that this is the best mix, but the customer feels that at least some money should be put into TV advertising, at least one unit (TV ≥ 1). The customer also feels that the printed word should be no more than a total of ten units (N + M ≤ 10). The problem now becomes:

Maximize People =
120,000 R + 250,000 TV + 150,000 N + 220,000 M

subject to:
$8,000 R + $10,000 TV + $3,000 N + $4,000 M
                                            ≤ $42,000
                              M ≤ 3
                         N + M ≤ 10
            TV   ≥ 1

The solution now becomes even more complicated, but as you can see, we still want to get the best use of our resources subject to all these requirements and restrictions. The more constraints we have, the smaller becomes the optimal number of people reached, and the more variables we have that might become positive. In this last case the first greedy solution would be TV = 1, M = 3, and N = 6 to reach 1,810,000 people with $2000 left over in the budget. By reducing M down to 2, setting N = 8, with TV still

= 1, we use up all the money and reach 1,890,000 people.

A word of caution might be appropriate at this time. The optimal solution does not necessarily have to use up all the budget. If each unit of magazine reached 280,000 people instead of 220,000, then the optimal solution for the very first problem (only the budget constraint) would be to use up ten units of magazine and have $2000 left over.

Integer programming is simply a way of trying to allocate resources in such a way as to maximize or minimize some objective function subject to several restrictions and/or requirements. Thus again we see that the problem is one of trade-offs, giving up using some resources while using others, so that sales, profits, and so on, may be maximized. The more alternatives and variables there are, the more possible solutions exist. The difficulty arises when not all the resources are used up simultaneously. Thus the Quick & Dirty becomes a necessary way to determine a quick, feasible solution that can be used.

sni incorporated

SNI Incorporated makes surfboards which are sold in all the popular surfing areas of the United States, Japan, and South America. It feels that magazine ads have been very effective in its marketing approach in the United States and has been considering radio as a means of emphasizing the local market. This would be in addition to the magazine advertising that is worldwide. Its advertising budget is set at $3000 per month, and by agreement of the two partners, at least six units of advertising must go toward *International Surfer Magazine* (ISM) at $85 per unit (¼ page). It was felt that this magazine has been the most effective agent in SNI's campaign, as an estimated 160,000 surfers are reached by a single unit of advertising.

Recently though, *Surfer Magazine* (SM) has become very effective in its advertising. It is estimated that 200,000 people are reached by each unit of advertising, which costs $170 per unit. Therefore a decision must be made as to how much should be spent in magazines and how much on local radio. In the San Diego area it was decided that KGB radio would be the best vehicle for advertising, since it has both an AM and an FM station, and the AM station is known as "Mellow Radio." This is in an effort to compete with hard rock or top-40 stations by providing a lot of music and little chatter. Each unit is estimated to reach 126,000 people, and ads cost $158 per unit for 30 seconds once a week for a month. This would occur during the peak time at 6–10 A.M. or P.M. on both the AM and the FM stations.

Since SNI is already heavily committed to magazine advertising and thoroughly established there, a limit of twice as much magazine advertising as radio is to be established in terms of capital outlay. Thus at least one third of the money spent must be put into radio each month. It is also required that at least five units should be put into *Surfer Magazine*, so that it can be determined how effective the advertising there is.

Given these requirements and restrictions, determine the allocation of resources and the advertising mix that would best benefit SNI in terms of exposure. We will neglect the fact that people may have double or even triple exposure to some ads or combination of ads.

Solution

Recommendation

It is recommended that the two partners relax the requirement that at least one third of the budget be applied to radio. By so doing they will reach 194,000 more people for $12 more and still have roughly the proportion of magazine to radio advertisement that is desired. Buy fourteen units of advertisement in *International Surfer Magazine*, five units in *Surfer Magazine*, and six units of KGB radio advertising.

Numerical Answer

Units	People	Cost
12 ISM	1,920,000	$1020
5 SM	1,000,000	$ 850
7 KGB	882,000	$1106
	3,802,000	$2976

This solution meets all the requirements.

Units	People	Cost
14 ISM	2,240,000	$1190
5 SM	1,000,000	$ 850
6 KGB	756,000	$ 948
	3,996,000	$2988

This solution should spend $996 on KGB to meet all the requirements.

Math Work. The requirements can be stated as follows:

Maximize People =
160,000 ISM + 200,000 SM + 126,000 KGB

budget constraint:
$85 ISM + $170 SM + $158 KGB ≤ $3000

minimum requirements:
ISM ≥ 6 SM ≥ 5

at least ⅓ budget for KGB:
KGB ≥ ⅓ (ISM + SM + KGB)

Meeting the minimum requirements for the magazines, six units of ISM cost $510, five units of SM cost $850, thus leaving 3000 − 510 − 850 = $1640.

Determine the Bang for the Buck ratios for each alternative:

ISM = 160,000/$85 = 1,882 people per dollar
SM = 200,000/$170 = 1,176 people per dollar
KGB = 126,000/$158 = 791 people per dollar

Thus we will try to have as much advertising in ISM as possible, realizing that we must devote one third of the budget to KGB. If six units of KGB radio are purchased, the cost is $948; seven units cost $1106.

If seven units of KGB are purchased, this leaves $534 in the budget. Since ISM has the best ratio, six more units may by purchased, leaving $24 left over.

If six units of KGB are purchased, then $692 will be left in the budget. This will buy eight units of ISM, having $12 left in the budget. Since ISM is the cheapest per unit cost of any of the alternatives, it is not possible to spend the extra money.

Thus the two solutions would be:

12	ISM	14
5	SM	5
7	KGB	6

puka shells

The rage a few years ago in men's fashions was Puka shell necklaces. They have also gone over very well for women in the form of bracelets, rings, earrings, and so on, and still find a good market on the West Coast. These shells are washed up on the Hawaiian shores and are free for the collecting. It has become a very profitable business on the islands, and there have been many students who spent their summers collecting Puka shells and either selling them or making and then selling the jewelry. The whole summer can be financed, as well as tuition, books, room, and board for the next year's schooling. A surfer and his wife living on the north shore of Oahu want to supplement their income of $115 a month in food stamps. Since Puka shells are washed up on the beach with every tide and are free, they would like to determine how much jewelry they could make and sell subject to certain constraints. They will only sell on weekends when the surf is crowded and the tourists are out. They would like to work a total of only five hours a day, five days a week at the most, and then sell all they can on the weekends. From experience they know that they need a balance of products, and they have decided on five standard pieces. The profit per piece and hours to assemble are given below. Determine the best mix of jewelry, keeping in mind that they are interested in selling (moneywise) at least as much in necklaces as in earrings, bracelets, and rings combined.

Jewelry	Profit	Assemble (hours)
Necklace — large shell	$10	2
Necklace — small shell	$20	5
Rings	$ 2	$\frac{1}{4}$
Bracelets	$ 8	1
Earrings	$ 4	$\frac{1}{3}$

INCIDENT: BIG BANG OUT OF NEWSPAPERS

The Akron stores bring in 60 to 70 percent new stock twice a week and advertise solely in newspapers. Newspaper ads proved very effective, while magazines could not keep up with the stores' change in stock. TV proved to be too expensive, and an experiment with radio met with very poor results. Akron Stores takes a full-page ad in the newspaper every Wednesday and Saturday, describing all the imported items on sale that week. By the end of three days they are usually out of the advertised stock. They will repeat the same items about every six months.

Recently they have been able to justify TV advertising for some special items that are very expensive, such as diamonds, calculators, and so on. By raising the prices of their average items being advertised (TV only), they have been able to justify such an expenditure. Here is a case where the Bang for the Buck ratio is affected by the profit margin also.

northern airmotive corporation

The Northern Airmotive Corporation has decided to design and build an airplane specifically for air taxi operators. The airplane will carry 28 passengers and have a design gross weight of 12,500 pounds, which is the maximum allowable under the Federal Aviation Agency Regulation Part 25. Engineering costs are estimated to be $600,000. The decision to go ahead on this project was based largely on the extremely good market forecasts for this type of airplane. The two airplanes currently used extensively in this type of operation were not designed specifically for this purpose.

The De Haviland Twin Otter was designed for bush-type operation and under Canadian law was required to carry its fuel in the belly of the plane; the design load factors are far too conservative for most American operations. The Twin Otter can carry 19 passengers. The other plane currently in wide use is the Cessna 402. It can carry 8 passengers and has a retractable gear.

It is thought that Northern Airmotive's airplane (PAC-1) would have a direct operating cost equal to that of the Cessna 402 while carrying 20 more passengers.

It is believed that the largest problem to be overcome is getting the engineering completed in six months. This is necessary because the marketing people have word that several other manufacturers are planning an airplane similar to Pacific Airmotive's. If the competition is allowed to beat it to the market its sales forecasts will drop off significantly.

To finish the engineering in six months would require 80 engineers, and herein lies the problem. It is felt that Northern Airmotive could hire only 30 engineers at this time. This is largely due to the general prosperity of the aerospace industry. The average wage of engineers on direct charge is $13 per hour. This would leave a shortage of at least 50 engineers.

A second source of engineers is job shoppers. The average wage of the job shopper is $10 per hour. However, because of the job shopper's nomadic nature and somewhat unreliable character, management has decreed that there shall be at least three people on direct charge for every two job shoppers. This is necessary for proper supervision and continuity of effort as the job shoppers come and go. Due to parking and facilities limitations the number of job shoppers plus direct charge personnel cannot exceed 50.

The third alternative to the workforce problem is to subcontract various parts of the airplane, such as the empennage or fuselage, to various engineering firms. Subcontractor personnel costs $13 per hour. Management has decided that there must be at least ten engineers on direct charge. The problem is to decide what mix of direct engineers, job shoppers, and subcontract personnel will get the job done for the least cost.

INCIDENT: GRAB FOR THE GUSTO!

A brewery advertises using a Bang for the Buck philosophy to sell its beer. Figuring that we all operate trying to get the most for our money, several ads urge consumers to "grab for all the gusto you can get!" This implies that its beer gives a high payoff in pleasure and satisfaction in life.

space vehicle launch scheduling

The problem is to determine the economy of operation of three, six, or nine thrust-augmented solid-motor vehicles, and which should be used. These motors are used to assist the liquid propellant booster (first stage) in a greater launching thrust.

NASA has decided to have at least 70,000 pounds of satellites launched in a year's period with the least amount of cost. NASA would like to have a forecast in order to get a congressional budget for this year to launch these satellites.

It costs $4.2, $4.6, and $5.0 million to launch three, six, and nine solid-motor vehicles.

The three, six, and nine solid-motor vehicles can launch 2500, 2850, and 3100 pounds, respectively, into a 100-mile orbit (satellites can be put in many orbits; we will assume 100 miles). Various configurations such as piggy-back satellites (a multiple satellite launch) can be made to launch satellites having various weights (usually about 500 pounds).

There are four launch sites for the Thor Delta. It takes about six weeks (or 30 days) to prepare and launch a three-solid-motor vehicle and an additional two days to add three more solid motors (making it six motors) as compared to four and one half more days to add six motors (making it nine motors in all). Douglas determined that it had the workforce and the sites to launch a maximum of 35 three-solid-motor vehicles in a year.

Determine the number of three, six, or nine thrust-augmented solid-motor vehicles that should be used, bearing in mind that there will be enough launch sites and launch days to launch the necessary payload.

7.2 INTEGER SCHEDULING

Operators at a telephone company came on and off duty in 70 different ways, and this was negotiated every three years with the union and the telephone company. Given the shifts (tricks) negotiated by the union and the number of operators needed during each hour by the telephone company, minimize the number of operators needed during each 24 hours. As an example, consider the partial problem shown below.

Time	Shift 1	Shift 2	Shift 3	Shift 4	Shift 5	Need
8–9 A.M.	×					7
9–10 A.M.	×	×	×			12
10–11 A.M.		×	×	×		15
11–12 NOON	×	×		×		18
12–1 P.M.	×	×	×	×	×	20
1–2 P.M.			×		×	17
2–3 P.M.				×	×	15
3–4 P.M.					×	8

These are the needs for extra part-time operators (four-hour shifts), with or without lunch breaks. Here, for simplicity, it will be assumed that all operators are paid the same, and since they are part-time, they can be told to work whenever the phone company desires them to. Each shift can have from 0 to 20 operators on duty.

The telephone company actually breaks down the time periods into 96 15-minute periods, and there are 70 different tricks for all the operators, part-time and full-time. Thus this becomes an incredibly large problem, with many possible solutions (and only one optimal one). What has been settled for in various parts of the country is some heuristic or Quick & Dirty to get a good estimate on the optimal solution and at least reduce the number of operators currently being used. Another objective function would be to reduce the number of total hours if the shifts are not all the same number of hours.

Supplementary Problems

1. From the Puka Shells case, using the original problem for each question answer the following:
   a. If we now made only $10 profit for the small shell necklace and $20 profit for the large shell necklace, what would be the *best mix* of jewelry now? Profit?
   b. If we had to make at least one of each kind of item (return to original problem), what would be the *best mix* of jewelry now and the profit?
   c. What was the answer to the original problem in terms of mix and profit?

Quick & Dirty Algorithm: Integer Scheduling

1. Establish lower bounds for each shift. Thus if there is only one shift that can meet requirements, at least that many operators must be put on that shift.
2. Subtract that number of people from the requirements, and repeat step 1 until finished or until several shifts remain for each requirement.
3. Try several combinations of people for the remaining shifts, keeping in mind that you are minimizing either the total number of people or the number of shift-hours.

For the preceding example, since each shift is four hours long, we will be minimizing the number of people involved.

1. Shifts 1 and 5 are the only shifts from 8 to 9 A.M. and from 3 to 4 P.M. Needed from 8 to 9 are seven people, which can only be satisfied by shift 1. Needed from 3 to 4 are eight people, which can only be satisfied by shift 5.
2. Subtracting these people for each shift from the total need, we are left with a reduced problem:

Time	Shift 2	Shift 3	Shift 4	Need
9–10 A.M.	×	×		5
10–11 A.M.	×	×	×	15
11–12 NOON	×		×	11
12–1 P.M.	×	×	×	5
1–2 P.M.		×		9
2–3 P.M.			×	7

Now we return to step 1. Only shift 4 will satisfy the requirements for 2 to 3 P.M. and shift 3 for 1 to 2 P.M. Thus we must have at least seven people on shift 4 and nine people on shift 3. Now only shift 2 remains:

Time	Shift 2	Need
9–10 A.M.	×	—
10–11 A.M.	×	—
11–NOON	×	4
12–1 P.M.	×	—

Thus only four more people are needed, which can be added as shift 2 or to shift 1 or 4.

The preceding solution gives the lower bounds on each shift but does not necessarily represent the lowest total.

Our solution is:

Shift 1	7 people
Shift 2	4 people
Shift 3	9 people
Shift 4	7 people
Shift 5	8 people

Total = 35 people.

jack-in-the-box weekdays

The Jack-in-the-Box Restaurant #41 in New York has 30 employees and 6 basic work shifts (varying an hour or two either way). Jack-in-the-Box Restaurants are part of the Foodmaker Corporation, which in turn is owned by Ralston Purina. They specialize in 24-hour drive-in fast-food service. Recently, due to the overwhelming growth of McDonald's, they have been offering indoor service at their newer locations. Their marketing is quite obviously pointed toward children and families, as is McDonald's. Staffing is done by hiring very few full-time employees, thus cutting down on fringe benefits, and hiring very many part-time employees. This of course allows them to pay minimum wages and provide job opportunities for high-school-age people who would not normally be able to get jobs. It also allows for exploitation and high employee turnover, not to mention a lot of training. Since the operations at Jack-in-the-Box are very standardized, training time can be reduced to a minimum; but even then, when a new employee is on the job, the overall team performance does slow down some.

Given the requirements for the average demand on Monday, Tuesday, and Wednesday, determine the minimum number of employees needed and the minimum number of hours.

Time	Shift 1	Shift 2	Shift 3	Shift 4	Shift 5	Shift 6	Need
8–9 A.M.	×						3
9–10 A.M.	×						3
10–11 A.M.	×						4
11–12 NOON	×	×					6
12–1 P.M.	×	×					6
1–2 P.M.	×	×					6
2–3 P.M.		×					4
3–4 P.M.		×					4
4–5 P.M.		×	×		×		4
5–6 P.M.			×		×		5
6–7 P.M.			×		×		5
7–8 P.M.			×		×		6
8–9 P.M.			×				5
9–10 P.M.			×				5
10–11 P.M.			×			×	5
11–12 P.M.			×			×	5
12–1 A.M.				×		×	3
1–2 A.M.				×		×	2
2–3 A.M.				×			2
3–4 A.M.				×			2
4–5 A.M.				×			2
5–6 A.M.				×			2
6–7 A.M.				×			2
7–8 A.M.				×			2

Solution

Recommendation
It is recommended that Jack-in-the-Box be staffed as follows:

Shift 1	4 people
Shift 2	4 people
Shift 3	5 people
Shift 4	2 people
Shift 5	1 person
Shift 6	1 person.

Numerical Answer. This will yield 112 work-hours, and 93 are required. Thus there will be an extra 19 hours. At $3.20 per hour, this comes to an extra $60.80 per day.

Math Work. Starting at step 1, we see the need to have at least four people for shift 1 to satisfy the 10–11 hour. We need at least four people for shift 2 for the hours 2–4. Shift 3 requires five people from 8 to 10 P.M., and shift 4 requires two people from 2 to 8 A.M. After this is done, the problem reduces to:

Time	Shift 3	Shift 4	Shift 5	Shift 6	Need
7–8 P.M.	×		×		1
12–1 A.M.		×		×	1

For shifts 3 and 4 this simply means extra people from what has already been allocated. Since shifts 3 and 4 are eight-hour shifts and shifts 5 and 6 are only four-hour shifts, it is better to schedule the shorter shifts. Thus both shifts 5 and 6 will have one additional person each.

The number of people-hours required is found by adding up the needs for each hour; it is 93. The actual number used is found by multiplying the number of people for each shift by the hours in each shift: 4(6) + 4(6) + 5(8) + 2(8) + 1(4) + 1(4) = 112 people-hours.

INCIDENT: A VISUAL SOLUTION[1]

A company which had 40 salespersons and 400 sales districts had the problem of scheduling sales-personnel to districts in such a way that each salesperson had about the same expected sales contacts and revenue. The problem was formulated as an integer programming problem with 1600 variables and 400 constraints. This could cost tens of thousands of dollars to run and still not guarantee an optimal solution, much less a feasible one. The consultants, before tackling the problem, asked how it was currently being solved. They were told that two little old ladies had been doing the problem manually each year, spending about a week cutting out colored pieces of paper and fitting them on a map until everything seemed to balance out. The consultants asked if the company had ever tried to systematically determine what it was that the little old ladies did. It said no. Then they asked what the difference was between the salespersons and the answer was that there was a variance of only 2 percent. The consultants then delivered their professional opinion: "Give

those little old ladies a raise!" This simply illustrates that many so-called integer programming problems have been "solved" for years by people who have a feeling for the problem. Some Quick & Dirty heuristics can get a very good answer quickly, and a usable one.

---

safeway checkers

Safeway grocery store #1470 is a small store in the Cleveland area. It was one of the first Safeway stores built, and was patterned after the small mom and pop stores of that neighborhood to build up clientele trust. This particular store has only four checkstands (most Safeway stores have ten to twelve) and has half the square footage of the average store. A new Safeway store will be opened up soon and the old one closed down, but in the meantime, management is concerned with providing maximum service with a minimum number of staff. If there is a shortage of checkers, then a clerk will check, or even the assistant manager herself will check. In the morning, to limit the number of staff during the opening hours, the manager will also check from time to time.

One company policy that complicates the scheduling problem is that all Safeway stores will now always have an express lane open (ten items or less, no checks). In fact, if a customer enters the store and there is no checker in the express lane, the customer will be given a free five pounds of coffee (and the manager will be given hell). To impress upon the customers the seriousness of this policy, this particular store will also give the customer a $15.00 gift certificate for groceries. But it has put quite a strain on the staffing requirements of the store. Given the requirements below, determine the minimum number of checkers needed for each shift. It is not necessary that there be anyone on any particular shift (that is, you may not want anyone on shift 2).

Time	Shift 1	Shift 2	Shift 3	Shift 4	Shift 5	Checkers Needed
9–10 A.M.	×					2
10–11 A.M.	×	×				2
11–12 NOON	×	×	×			3
12–1 P.M.	×	×	×		×	3
1–2 P.M.	Lunch	×	×		×	2
2–3 P.M.	×	Lunch	×		×	2
3–4 P.M.	×	×	Lunch		×	4
4–5 P.M.	×	×	×	×		4
5–6 P.M.	×	×	×	×		4
6–7 P.M.		×	×	×		3
7–8 P.M.		×	×			2

INCIDENT: LAYING OUT THE PROBLEM

A small grocery store of a national chain was facing scheduling problems with its personnel. The manager and assistant manager used to meet for two hours each week on scheduling the part-time and full-time help. It seemed that no matter how they scheduled people, there were either too many checkers during slack hours, or not enough during the rush times. By keeping some figures on the number of checkers actually needed during each hour period for two weeks, they were able to spot the slack times and the busy times, readjusted the schedule of two college students, and mollified them by promising them more hours if things got busy. Thus by laying out the data, the managers were able to identify the problem, and the Quick & Dirty algorithm was a beginning of the solution of the problem.

hayes department store

The Hayes department store at the College Grove shopping center in Pennsylvania is a fairly stable store in terms of employee turnover and customer loyalty. As with most department stores, Hayes employs a few full-time and many part-time workers, usually college students from the nearby state college. In the home furnishing department the supervisor indicated that she needed a schedule for weekdays to meet the current conditions. According to store policies there must be a minimum of 10 available employees in the home furnishing department (experience has proved that less than 10 leads to understaffing and a poor store image). One employee is the head clerk who earns $3.75 per hour, while each of the remaining 9 clerks earns $2.90 per hour. The head clerk is permitted to work a full 40-hour week, which entitles her to full company benefits such as medical insurance, disability, vacations, and so on. The head clerk also has the choice of working any schedule she feels will best serve the interest of her department. In addition, there is a minimum number of clerks (including the head clerk) that must be on duty during any 1-hour period, and there must be at least 1 clerk for each shift. These data requirements are presented in Table 7.2. Determine the minimum number of clerks necessary to meet the requirements.

INCIDENT: MONEY MAKER

A midwestern consulting firm developed several heuristics to achieve a good solution to the telephone operators' scheduling problem. The most important part of the heuristic solution is to avoid "spikes," which are occasional, very bad solutions. These could cost a company much more in losses in a bad month than total annual savings. In its most recent year, though, the company has been very successful in applying heuristics: It has billed over $3,000,000 to more than ten clients.

watch out mcdonald's!

This is a continuation of the previous Jack-in-the-Box problem, only this one concerns the scheduling for Thursday and Friday, and Saturday and Sunday. These days are significantly busier than the weekdays, and thus require a different staffing than the previous problem. The six basic shifts become seven, and the requirements differ for the various hours.

For the two different requirements (Thursday–

Table 7.2

Time	Shift 1	Shift 2	Shift 3	Shift 4	Shift 5	Shift 6	Clerks Needed
10–11 A.M.	×	×					5
11–12 NOON	×	×					5
12–1 P.M.	×		×				4
1–2 P.M.	×	×	×	×			4
2–3 P.M.		×	×	×	×		4
3–4 P.M.		×	×	×	×		4
4–5 P.M.		×		×	×		4
5–6 P.M.		×	×		×	×	5
6–7 P.M.		×	×			×	4
7–8 P.M.		×	×	×		×	4
8–9 P.M.		×	×	×		×	4

Friday and Saturday–Sunday) determine the schedule that will minimize the number of hours that people must be working:

Shift 1   10 A.M.– 3 P.M.
Shift 2   8 A.M.–5 P.M.
Shift 3   8 A.M.–1 P.M.
Shift 4   11 P.M.–7 A.M.
Shift 5   7 A.M.–2 P.M.
Shift 6   5 P.M.–Midnight
Shift 7   5 P.M.–2 A.M.

Thursday–Friday requirements (129 hours needed):

8–9 A.M.	3 people
9–10 A.M.	4 people
10–11 A.M.	5 people
11 A.M.–3 P.M.	6 people
3–5 P.M.	7 people
5–8 P.M.	8 people
8 P.M.–Midnight	6 people
Midnight–2 A.M.	7 people
2–3 A.M.	5 people
3–5 A.M.	3 people
5–8 A.M.	2 people

Saturday–Sunday requirements (141 hours needed):

8–10 A.M.	5 people
10–11 A.M.	6 people
11–3 P.M.	9 people
3–7 P.M.	8 people
7 P.M.–1 A.M.	6 people
1–2 A.M.	5 people
2–3 A.M.	4 people
3–5 A.M.	3 people
5–8 A.M.	2 people

Supplementary Problems

1. The registrar's office at a local college must make up the schedule of workers for registration week now, and must minimize the number of workers (so as to slow things up as much as possible) subject to certain constraints. Given the shifts and minimum needs for each hour (bottom of first column), apply the Quick & Dirty to determine the total number of people and total number of hours plus the number of extra hours required to staff registration week.

    Total number of people _____

    Total number of hours _____

    Extra hours required _____

2. Given the Safeway Checkers case (page 256):
    a. How many people were needed for the best solution? _____
    b. How many total hours were needed and how many extra hours were there? _____
       _____
    c. If we needed one extra checker from noon to 6 P.M., how would you change the solution?
       _____
       _____
    d. Given question (c), how many extra hours would there be? _____

7.3 CUTTING STOCK

Another integer problem that arises in many situations is the cutting stock problem. This may require the decision of how many pieces of stock to cut, and what sizes, to minimize the waste (or number of pieces cut) and yet meet certain requirements. This problem occurs in many forms in business situations. Given certain lengths of window moldings, the question may be how to cut the moldings so that a minimum number of standard lengths are cut to size for all the windows in a new house. A two-dimensional case might concern the cutting of rolls of linoleum so that a homeowner has to buy the minimum amount needed, rather than have several square feet of linoleum stored in the garage. Or standard lengths of pipe may be available, and certain sizes must be cut from each standard length. Minimizing the number of pieces may not be the same as minimizing the waste (extra lengths that cannot be used). In the former case we want to minimize surplus (which is not usable later on) and scrap, whereas in the latter case we might be able to store the surplus for use later and are only concerned with waste.

Some computerized algorithms for this problem take so long to find an answer that more is spent in computer time than is saved by solving the problem. Thus we offer a *very* Quick & Dirty algorithm so that

Time	Shift 1	Shift 2	Shift 3	Shift 4	Shift 5	Minimum Number of Workers
8–9 A.M.	×					2
9–10 A.M.	×		×			3
10–11 A.M.	×	×	×		×	3
11–12 NOON	×	×	×		×	3
12–1 P.M.		×	×		×	4
1–2 P.M.	×	×		×	×	4
2–3 P.M.	×		×	×	×	3
3–4 P.M.	×		×	×	×	3
4–5 P.M.	×		×	×		2

you can at least find a feasible solution to the problem, even though it may not be optimal. It must be recognized that this problem is confronted daily by construction supervisors, carpenters, glass cutters, and so on, and some tend to be very efficient and others very wasteful.

Quick & Dirty Algorithm: Cutting Stock

1. Determine the total need (in inches, feet, square feet, and so on) and divide by the standard length (or area). If the answer is not integer, raise to the next highest integer. This is the lowest possible number of pieces that can be used and will satisfy all requirements.
2. Start with the requirement that has the fewest cuts or layouts and choose the minimum number that will satisfy that requirement. Always favor cuts that will minimize waste or meet requirements exactly.
3. Reduce any other requirements that may have been partially or completely filled by choosing the cut in step 2. Then return to step 2.

Example. An example might be the necessity of determining the number of four-foot lengths of aluminum molding needed to satisfy the following requirements. It is assumed that partial lengths cannot be put together to satisfy the requirements due to aesthetic reasons. Let us choose as our objective function minimizing the total number of moldings.

Length (inches)	Number Needed
30	5
16	4
15	2
12	3

Here we see that there is a total requirement of 280 inches of molding. This would require five four-foot lengths and part of a sixth. Thus at least six lengths must be bought. This is our lower bound. It does not automatically mean that it can be done with six four-foot lengths. To better structure this problem it is usually helpful to determine some different ways to cut this stock. Once given these few patterns, determine how many pieces are needed (and thus how they will be cut). In this case, let us use the following cuts (others may be chosen later and yield a better solution):

cut 1   30 and 16 inches, and 2 inches scrap
cut 2   30 and 15 inches, and 3 inches scrap
cut 3   15, 15, and 16 inches, and 2 inches scrap

cut 4   12, 16, and 16 inches, and 4 inches scrap
cut 5   16, 16, and 15 inches, and 1 inch scrap
cut 6   30 and 12 inches, and 6 inches scrap.

We can lay this out in table form, which might make it easier to visualize:

Cut 1	Cut 2	Cut 3	Cut 4	Cut 5	Cut 6	Need	Length (inches)
1	1				1	5	30
1		1	2	2		4	16
	1	2		1		2	15
			1		1	3	12

We can see that the 12-inch length has only two different ways that its requirement can be met. Cut 4 has less waste than cut 6, so it is preferred. If we chose to cut three pieces this way, we would satisfy the 12-inch requirement, but would have too many 16-inch pieces. Thus let us cut two pieces using cut 4 and one piece using cut 6. This fulfills the 12-inch requirement and leaves us with a problem as follows:

Cut 1	Cut 2	Cut 3	Cut 5	Need	Length (inches)
1	1			4	30
	1	2	1	2	15

The only cut that gives both 30- and 15-inch lengths is cut 2. Cutting four sections using cut 2 will satisfy all requirements. Thus our Quick & Dirty solution is:

2 lengths cut 12, 16, and 16 inches
1 length cut 30 and 12 inches
4 lengths cut 30 and 15 inches.

This will require that we purchase seven lengths and gives an upper bound to the problem.

Another possible solution would be two of cut 2, two of cut 5, and three of cut 6, which still uses seven pieces. This treats the surplus lengths as worthless as well as the 26 inches of waste for each solution.

It might also be possible to find a solution with six lengths, either by finding a better solution to the problem given the six types of cuts, or by having better cuts.

If we were interested in only minimizing waste (and saving the surplus lengths) our objective function would be as follows (cuts in inches):

	Cut 1	Cut 2	Cut 3	Cut 4	Cut 5	Cut 6
Minimize	2	3	2	4	1	6

and we would choose cuts that had the smallest waste. Thus cut 5 would be chosen first for two cuts, then cut 1 for five (which would give us five extra 16-inch pieces) and finally cut 4 for three (giving six more

16-inch pieces). This solution yields a waste of only 24 inches, but uses ten pieces of molding. Thus we will have eleven 16-inch pieces in storage to be used later. The actual situation will dictate which objective function will be used. Notice that two obvious cuts (four 12-inch, three 16-inch) were not used. How would this change the solution?

m.c.b. lumber company

The M.C.B. Lumber Company of Florida has recently won a bid to assemble front entrance sections for several tract homes. The company must precut all necessary lumber pieces at its warehouse and then ship them out to the construction site. It has been awaiting a shipment of different-length boards for several days now, and has just received word that the shipment will be delayed. It must supply the Anderson Construction Company with the necessary materials in precut form or lose the contract. Since it only has 20-foot two by fours available, it must decide how to meet the necessary requirements with the smallest number of 20-foot boards.

Length (feet)	Length (inches)	Description	Quantity
20	240	Top and bottom plates	30
8	96	Studs	130
6.66	80	Header supports	20
4	48	Header parts	30
1.50	18	Short studs	30
1	12	Fire blocks	110

There are many ways that each 20-foot board could be cut, but M.C.B. has decided that there are seven ways the boards can be cut that will use every bit of the board. Given these, determine the minimum number of boards required, and how they will be cut.

cut 1	96, 96, and 48 inches
cut 2	96, 96, 18, 18, and 12 inches
cut 3	96, 96, 12, 12, 12, and 12 inches
cut 4	96, 48, 48, and 48 inches
cut 5	96 inches, and 12 × 12 inches
cut 6	80, 80, and 80 inches
cut 7	48, 48, 48, 48, and 48 inches.

Solution

Recommendation

To fulfill the requirements, make the following cuts:

cut 1	96, 96, and 48 inches	30 boards
cut 2	96, 96, 18, 18, and 12 inches	15 boards
cut 3	96, 96, 12, 12, 12, and 12 inches	19 boards
cut 5	96 inches and 12 × 12 inches	2 boards
cut 6	80, 80, and 80 inches	7 boards

Numerical Answers. This will yield the following:

Length	Need	Surplus
96-inch studs	130	—
80-inch header supports	20	1 × 80 inches
48-inch header parts	30	—
18-inch short studs	30	—
12-inch fire blocks	110	5 × 12 inches
		140 inches of waste

Math Work. The problem can be put into tabular form and is thus easier to see:

Length	Cut 1	Cut 2	Cut 3	Cut 4	Cut 5	Cut 6	Cut 7	Need
96 inches	2	2	2	1	1			130
80 inches						3		20
48 inches	1			3			5	30
18 inches		2						30
12 inches		1	4		12			110

Here it can be seen that only cut 6 can satisfy the requirement for the 80-inch header supports, and that at least 7 boards must be cut (giving an extra 80-inch section). After that, cut 7 could be used with 6 boards to meet the header parts requirements with no scrap at all. Then the only requirements unfulfilled would be 18-inch short studs that can only be met by cut 2 and 15 boards would be needed. The requirements would be reduced to:

Length	Need	Cut 3	Cut 5
96 inches	100	2	1
12 inches	95	4	12

Cuts 1 and 4 are ignored because they would yield board lengths not required. Cut 5 will produce too many 12-inch sections as compared to cut 3, so cut 3 is used, and 50 boards are required. This solution gives over 111 board-feet of scrap. But working from this solution, one can see that the requirement for 48-inch and 18-inch boards could be met by cuts 1 and 2, which would give more 96-inch boards. From that cut 3 can be used to meet the rest of the 96-inch requirement, but not enough 12-inch boards have been made. Thus 2 boards are given to cut 5 and one less is needed for cut 3.

The total requirements for the problem are 17,380 inches, which means that we must have 17,380/240 = 72+ or 73 boards. Our solution has met the requirements with 73 boards, and it is optimal also.

INCIDENT: PRACTICALITY IS OF PRIME IMPORTANCE

The classic problem arises in the cutting of steel reinforcing bars (re-bars) and has been tackled by the finest technicians in operations research. Computer programs have been developed for some methods in an attempt to save a lot of money by reducing excessive scrap. What is needed is a simple algorithm that can be done on the shop floor. This presents a wide-open opportunity for students to make their fame and fortune.

sprinkler system

A home owner has decided that a sprinkler system would solve the problems of maintenance of her lawn and flowers. Several underground pipes need to be installed and hooked up to the outdoor faucet. Sprinkler heads will be located at strategic spots so that the minimum number of heads and lengths of pipe will be used. Employing the minimal spanning tree algorithm, she is guaranteed that she will have to dig a minimum number of feet of ditch. Since the pipe comes in six-foot lengths, there are some sections that must be cut, and she is interested in minimizing the waste or the number of six-foot sections to be purchased. The pipe is made of a special plastic that will resist high and low temperatures, but is easily cut with a hacksaw. She has the following requirements for sections less than six feet long, and needs to determine how many six-foot sections she needs to purchase, and how they will be cut.

$4\frac{1}{2}$ feet	needs 3
4 feet	needs 2
3 feet	needs 3
2 feet	needs 4
$1\frac{1}{2}$ feet	needs 4

There are several ways a six-foot pipe can be cut, but the following six options are the only ones she will consider:

cut 1	4′		2′	
cut 2	3′		3′	
cut 3	3′		$1\frac{1}{2}′$	$1\frac{1}{2}′$
cut 4	2′	2′	2′	
cut 5	$4\frac{1}{2}′$			$1\frac{1}{2}′$
cut 6	$1\frac{1}{2}′$	$1\frac{1}{2}′$	$1\frac{1}{2}′$	$1\frac{1}{2}′$

INCIDENT: TWO-DIMENSIONAL CUTS

A two-dimensional case arises in the cutting of sheet metal for standard-size pieces from standard sheets.

Here several layouts (rather than cuts) may be designed, each with a certain amount of scrap and pieces. The problem then reduces to the same one as the one-dimensional case, the only difference being the number of layouts possible.

poway frame shop

The Poway Frame Shop is able to sell as many finished Slim-Line frames as it can obtain the necessary moldings for from its suppliers. Unfortunately the supplier has had labor and material problems and cannot always meet the frame shop's demand. The next month's demand has already been determined as 200 frames in the following sizes:

Inside Measurement (inches)	Quantity
16 × 20	100
12 × 16	40
12 × 14	60

In computing the length of a frame side, an additional 2 inches must be added to the inside measurement due to the mitering of the corners. Thus the demand is now:

Actual Measurement (inches)	Quantity
14	200
16	120
18	280
22	200

The shop has a choice of taking delivery from its dealer by either United Parcel Service (UPS) or surface freight (truck). UPS limits the package to a length of 8 feet, while the freight lines will carry the standard 20-foot lengths. UPS has been chosen because of speed and less damage in shipping. Thus the molding comes in 8-foot sections to the shop, and then is cut into frame lengths and assembled. Determine the minimum number of 8-foot lengths that will meet the demand and how they should be cut.

INCIDENT: NONUNIFORMITY CAN BE A PROBLEM

Another two-dimensional case arises from the leather goods industry, which makes wallets, key cases, and other leather accessories from cowhide. Most cowhides are not square, much less uniform, but after being tanned and processed, they do have similar shapes. Again, certain patterns of layouts are recommended and then the requirements given, and decisions are made as to how many hides to cut and in which fashion so as to minimize the waste or number of hides cut.

cabinet shop

A small cabinet shop takes orders from larger furniture manufacturers and makes small items that the larger companies do not want to bother with. The orders are done on a fixed-cost basis, so that whatever costs are saved in the making of each order are passed on to the small shop. In this case the shop has received orders for 50 end tables or night stands. The main pieces that are needed for each stand are 24 × 15 inches, 20 × 12 inches, 18 × 12 inches, and 19 × 6 inches. Two of each are needed for a table, except for the last piece of which three are needed.

The basic piece out of which all these smaller pieces must be cut is 48 × 48 inches. In laying out several possibilities, the owner came up with:

Layout	Pieces (inches)	Waste (square inches)
A	6 24 × 15	144
B	8 20 × 12, 2 19 × 6	156
C	8 18 × 12, 2 20 × 12	96
D	2 24 × 15, 2 20 × 12, 2 18 × 12, 4 19 × 6	216
E	4 24 × 15, 4 18 × 12	none
F	6 20 × 12, 6 19 × 6	180

Obviously there are several other combinations that could be used, but given the above combinations, determine the minimum waste and the number of boards that must be used to build the 50 night stands. Allowance has been made for the thickness of each cut, so that each piece should be of uniform size and not $\frac{1}{4}$ inch too short. The main problem with laying out the cuts is that although there may be plenty of square inches of waste left over to make another piece, the parts would be scattered all over the place. Cut A looks as follows (dimensions in inches):

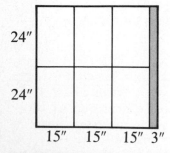

Waste = 144 square inches

INCIDENT: IMPLEMENTATION REQUIRES TRUST

A final story relates the difficulty of implementing a solution or algorithm. A professor in the Midwest has been working with a cabinet-making company for a year on the problem of determining the best cuts to minimize waste in the production of cabinets. He has developed a program that will first generate possible cuts or layouts, given the requirements for each piece of furniture. Then another program will use a heuristic to generate upper and lower bounds on the problem. Unfortunately this requires a computer, and, of course, it means that the person who has been doing the layout and carpentry must either learn to use the computer and the program or forget the whole thing. Right now, the carpenter, who has been solving this problem by hand for years, greatly distrusts the whole process. However, possible savings are evident, and the company is interested in finding a way to implement the algorithm without alienating its workers.

Supplementary Problems

1. A carpenter is doing a small home remodeling project using 6-foot lengths of boards and has decided upon the following cuts and has the stated demand. She is most interested in minimizing the waste, as she can use extra boards later on in the month. Use the Quick & Dirty to solve the problem and give the amount of waste that will be incurred as well as the number of each cut. Set up the problem in table form.

Cut	Length (inches)	Waste	Need
Cut A	60	12″	10–60″
Cut B	48, 24	0″	20–48″
Cut C	30, 30	12″	25–30″
Cut D	30, 24	18″	30–24″
Cut E	24, 24, 24	0″	

2. The following lengths of boards are needed and will be cut from 3-foot boards:

Length (inches)	Number Needed
6	20
12	10
18	5
24	12
30	8

a. Minimize the number of surplus boards given the following cuts: cut 1: 6 at 6 inches; cut 2: 1 at 12 inches, 1 at 24 inches; cut 3: 1 at 6 inches,

1 at 30 inches; cut 4: 1 at 6 inches, 1 at 12 inches, 1 at 18 inches.

   b. Give all the other possible cuts which have no

     waste. _____

     _____

     _____

3. Given the Cabinet Shop case, draw a picture of how cut B and cut E must look. Label carefully the dimensions; shade in the waste area.

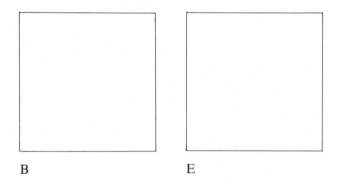

B   E

7.4 ADVANCED INTEGER PROGRAMMING TECHNIQUES

This section presents two advanced techniques that must be computerized for problems of any size above five or six variables. Both algorithms are guaranteed to lead to an optimal solution within a finite length of time (but not necessarily within our lifetime or budget constraint). You should already be familiar with the Branch & Bound concept, and you will see another application here. It is only required that there be familiarity with the graphical solution of linear programming problems and the concept that not all possible solutions need be investigated to find the optimal solution. The cutting plane technique requires knowledge of the simplex algorithm, and a simplified version is presented here to acquaint you with the process.

   The basis for both techniques is to eliminate the infeasible integer solution (the present one) without eliminating any possible feasible integer solutions. For this section there will only be an example of each technique and a few cases. You might be interested in using previous cases to test the technique or in solving each example by the other technique.

Long & Clean Algorithm: Branch & Bound Integer Programming

The technique that was used to solve the traveling salesman problem can now be employed to solve integer programming problems. We want to eliminate the linear programming answer without eliminating the integer answer. The cuts that are generated are very simple upper or lower bounds on integer variables, and several subproblems are generated (hence the branching) and upper and lower bounds are also generated again.

1. Solve the linear programming problem. If all variables that should be integer are, *Stop. Optimal.*
2. Otherwise, choose one variable that should be integer and is not ($X_i = K +$ fraction). Develop two subproblems with the constraints $X_i \leq K$ and $X_i \geq K + 1$.
3. When there are no problems with profits higher than the best integer feasible solutions, *Stop. Optimal.*

Example

Maximize Profit $= 3X_1 + 4X_2$
subject to: $3X_1 + 2X_2 \leq 8$
                $X_1 + 4X_2 \leq 10$ X_1, X_2 integer.

The resulting tree diagram and solutions are given in Figure 7.1 and Figure 7.2 (page 258).

   The first problem that is solved, problem 1, is simply the linear programming problem (ignoring the integer requirements). The optimal solution has

Figure 7.1

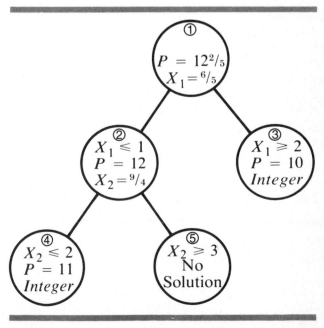

Figure 7.2

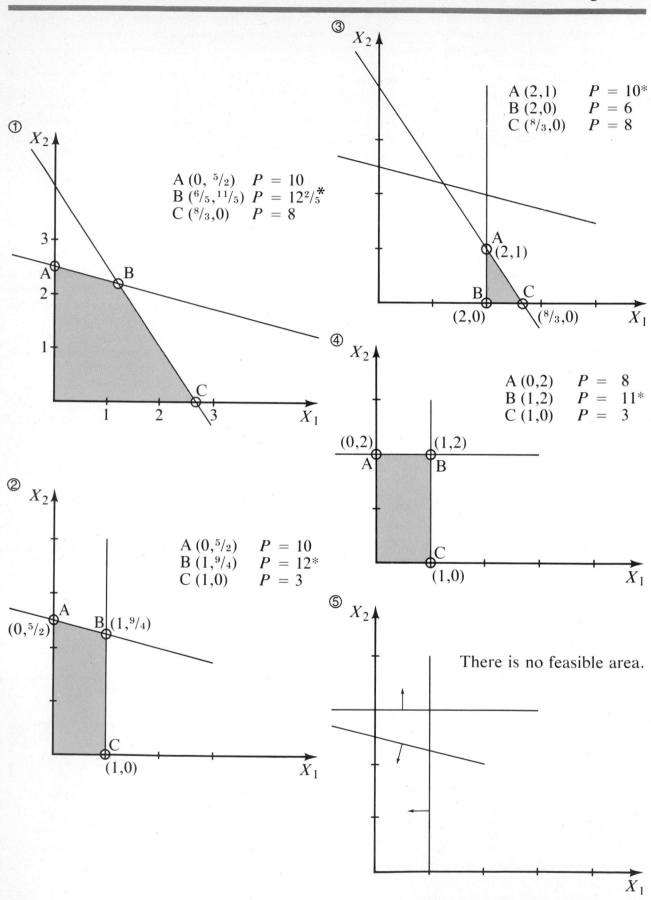

① X_2

A $(0, {}^5/_2)$ $P = 10$
B $({}^6/_5, {}^{11}/_5)$ $P = 12{}^2/_5$*
C $({}^8/_3, 0)$ $P = 8$

③ X_2

A $(2,1)$ $P = 10$*
B $(2,0)$ $P = 6$
C $({}^8/_3, 0)$ $P = 8$

④ X_2

A $(0,2)$ $P = 8$
B $(1,2)$ $P = 11$*
C $(1,0)$ $P = 3$

② X_2

A $(0, {}^5/_2)$ $P = 10$
B $(1, {}^9/_4)$ $P = 12$*
C $(1,0)$ $P = 3$

⑤ X_2

There is no feasible area.

$X_1 = \frac{6}{5}$ and $X_2 = \frac{11}{5}$ and the profit $P = 12\frac{2}{5}$. Since this answer does not satisfy the integer requirements, we must proceed to branch to two problems. Picking X_1 (we could have chosen X_2 and eventually arrived at the same answer), we make two problems: one with $X_1 \leqslant 1$ and the other with $X_1 \geqslant 2$. The solution of the first one, problem 2, yields another noninteger solution, while the second one, problem 3, yields an integer solution with a $P = 10$. This becomes the lower bound. In other words, it is the worst solution; there might be a better solution, for problem 2 has $P = 12$ and now constitutes the upper bound.

The solution to problem 2 has only one noninteger variable, $X_2 = \frac{9}{4}$. Thus we generate two more problems, problem 4: $X_2 \leqslant 2$ and problem 5: $X_2 \geqslant 3$. The solution to problem 4 is also integer and has a higher value of P than the current integer solution, so it now becomes the lower bound ($P = 11$). Problem 5 has no solution; the constraints are so restrictive that one does not exist. Thus there is no better possible solution, and the answer to problem 4 is the optimal one:

$$X_1 = 1, X_2 = 2, \text{ and } P = 11.$$

Again, this technique is not suited for hand solution, but must be computerized. The problem lies in storing all the branches and problems while working on the current problem. This can become quite a chore for a large problem. This algorithm has the advantage of working for mixed integer problems.

At the time of publication of this book, it should be noted that, in essence, most commercial mixed integer codes use considerably more sophisticated versions of the above method, usually attributed to Land & Doig.[2]

Cutting Plane

Another way to attempt to solve the integer programming problem is through taking advantage of the powerful simplex method, that is, solving the linear programming problem initially and working from that solution. The idea of the cutting plane method is to eliminate the linear programming solution (which has some variables that are not integer) but *not* eliminate any feasible integer solutions. Gomory was the pioneer in this method and gives an elaborate proof to show that the method will converge in a finite number of steps. Unfortunately, what is finite to a mathematician is infinite to a person who only lives 100 years or so. Therefore the method has been dubbed by some as the shaving plane method. Again the problem structure has to be such that it lends itself to this method. There are some small problems that will not converge to any solution in a reasonable amount of time. One of the problems with this method is that unless you reach the optimum solu-tion, you do not even have a feasible solution. Thus you may invest a couple of hours of computer time (at $900 per hour) and come up with nothing.

Long & Clean Algorithm: Cutting Plane Integer Programming

1. Solve the linear programming problem. If all variables that should be integer are, *Stop. Optimal.*
2. Otherwise, from the final simplex solution, choose the variable with the largest fractional part as the one that should be integer. Write each coefficient in that equation as an integer with a *positive* fractional part, with all the variables on the left-hand side and the constant on the right-hand side. Form a new $\geqslant$ constraint from the fractional parts only.
3. Add a surplus variable to the new constraint and solve for it, adding the new constraint to the basis.
4. Now use dual simplex to find the next linear programming solution. To do this, for the new constraint find which variable j satisfies:

$$X_j = \begin{array}{c} \text{minimum} \\ a_j > 0 \end{array} \left\{ \frac{|c_j|}{a_j} \right\}$$

5. Solve the new constraint for this variable and substitute into all other constraints and objective functions. If all variables that should be integer are, *Stop. Optimal.* Otherwise return to step 2.

The best way to illustrate this method is to first show a graph of a simple problem (Figure 7.3). Note that the dotted line is the first cut, and that it eliminates the initial linear programming solution but not any of the feasible integer points. Hereafter the

Figure 7.3

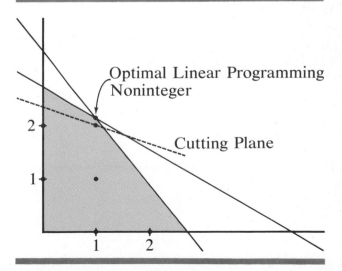

Optimal Linear Programming Noninteger

Cutting Plane

algebraic solution is given without proof. No one solves these by hand, and thus a computer code must be used.

Example

Maximize Profit $= X_1 + 5X_2$
subject to: $\qquad X_1 + 10X_2 \le 20$
$\qquad\qquad X_1 \qquad\quad \le 2$ $\qquad X_1, X_2$ integer.

The simplex solution becomes:

$$\text{Maximize Profit} = 11 - \tfrac{1}{2}X_3 - \tfrac{1}{2}X_4$$
$$\text{subject to:}\quad X_2 = \tfrac{9}{5} - \tfrac{1}{10}X_3 + \tfrac{1}{10}X_4$$
$$X_1 = 2 \qquad\quad - X_4$$

The answer is $(2,\tfrac{9}{5})$, which is not integer.

The constraint that contains the noninteger variable with the largest fractional part (in this case the X_2 constraint) is rewritten in terms of integer and positive fractional parts, and a constraint is developed from the fractional part that will eliminate the linear programming solution but no integer solutions. This will be added to the problem:

$$X_2 + \tfrac{1}{10}X_3 - \tfrac{1}{10}X_4 = \tfrac{9}{5}$$

or

$$(1 + 0)X_2 + (0 + \tfrac{1}{10})X_3 + (-1 + \tfrac{9}{10})X_4 = (1 + \tfrac{4}{5}).$$

The new constraint is:

$$0X_2 + \tfrac{1}{10}X_3 + \tfrac{9}{10}X_4 \ge \tfrac{4}{5}$$

which, by adding a surplus, becomes:

$$\tfrac{1}{10}X_3 + \tfrac{9}{10}X_4 - X_5 = \tfrac{4}{5}$$

or

$$X_5 = -\tfrac{4}{5} + \tfrac{1}{10}X_3 + \tfrac{9}{10}X_4.$$

Now dual simplex is used because one of the variables in the basis is negative. The final solution to this new problem is:

$$\text{Maximize Profit} = 10\tfrac{5}{9} - \tfrac{4}{9}X_3 - \tfrac{5}{9}X_5$$
$$\text{subject to:}\quad X_2 = \tfrac{17}{9} - \tfrac{1}{9}X_3 + \tfrac{1}{9}X_5$$
$$X_1 = \tfrac{10}{9} + \tfrac{1}{9}X_3 - \tfrac{10}{9}X_5$$
$$X_4 = \tfrac{8}{9} - \tfrac{1}{9}X_3 + \tfrac{10}{9}X_5.$$

The new constraint is taken from the X_2 constraint, which has the largest fractional part:

$$\tfrac{1}{9}X_3 + \tfrac{8}{9}X_5 \ge \tfrac{8}{9}$$

and a slack (X_6) is added.

The final solution is:

$$\text{Maximize Profit} = 10 - \tfrac{3}{8}X_3 - \tfrac{5}{8}X_6$$
$$\text{subject to:}\quad X_2 = 2 - \tfrac{1}{8}X_3 + \tfrac{1}{8}X_6$$
$$X_1 = 0 + \tfrac{1}{4}X_3 - \tfrac{5}{4}X_6$$
$$X_4 = 2 - \tfrac{1}{4}X_3 + \tfrac{5}{4}X_6$$
$$X_5 = 1 - \tfrac{1}{4}X_3 + \tfrac{9}{8}X_6.$$

The optimal solution is $(0,2)$ and $P = 10$.

You have noticed that after every cut the value of the profit got smaller. This is because the current solution was eliminated; thus the value of the profit has to be smaller. You will also notice that the size of the problem got bigger every time we added a constraint. When computerized it becomes ungainly to keep adding a new constraint and increasing the size of the problem, so that when a new constraint is added, the last one added is dropped. This can cause some problems because not all the constraints will be saved. The answer could go back to a previous one, and the problem would then cycle indefinitely.

There are many types of cuts that can be made, and the literature of mathematical programming is full of them. For specially structured problems some cuts work better than others, while for some kinds of problems nothing seems to work well. You may want to run several types of problems using these different algorithms and familiarize yourself with the idiosyncracies of each technique.

INCIDENT: PRACTICE MAKES PERFECT

A company based in the eastern United States learned the hard way when it tackled an integer problem using a computerized code for a cutting plane technique. After having spent several thousand dollars in computer time and still not obtaining a solution, it turned in desperation to an outside consultant. The consultant chastised the company for not having run small sample problems first to learn about the idiosyncracies of both the cutting plane method and the particular code. Being familiar with both, he suggested a rearrangement of variables and constraints in the problem, and a solution was found within 15 minutes. For examples, see pages 13-1–13-42 in Salkin[7] and pages 17-1–17-2 in Zionts.[8]

radio shack

The Baltimore Radio Shack outlet was granted a franchise from the Tandy Company, which has instituted a new ordering policy. This policy requires minimum orders on certain items and a limit to ordering on some others which are very popular. Since the Tandy Company has 2000 such Radio Shack outlets, it has been very concerned about balancing the ordering from its retail outlets to control inventory and production requirements. By the time the new ordering policy came through, Radio Shack had determined its ordering requirements using the old policy on everything but two receivers. These are two medium-priced production models, the ST–46 and the ST–12. The new ordering requirements on these models limit the total of these two models to 56 units and no more. This is due to the fact that Tandy can only supply a certain number per month to each of its 2000 stores.

Because the ST–12s are the slower moving of the two models, it is required that at least 6 of them be ordered. Due to local demand it would not be wise to order more than 20 of the ST–46s, and Tandy requires that at least a dozen be ordered. The budget for Radio Shack would allow $3600 to be spent for both receivers. The cost for the ST–46 is $100, and it retails for $112, while the ST–12 costs $85 and retails for $95. Being profit oriented, Radio Shack would like to determine the optimum number of receivers of each type to order to maximize profit. Since it is imperative that only whole receivers will sell, the answer must be in integers only.

INCIDENT: NOT OPTIMAL, BUT AT LEAST FEASIBLE

A midwestern computer service, having had bad luck with cutting plane codes, decided to modify an existing Branch & Bound code. Running one rather large problem, it ran out of budget before it arrived at an optimal solution. However, the saving grace of this type of code was that it had already found several feasible solutions, and the difference between the upper and lower bounds for the problem was less than 1 percent. The customer was satisfied with the solution. The biggest problem with a cutting plane algorithm, on the other hand, is that you do not have a feasible solution until you reach the optimal solution. Thus one should be very careful in the selection of the code and type of problem to be solved.

archer machine products

Archer Machine Products runs a machine shop that specializes in subcontracting with large aerospace firms. Archer receives orders from different firms, makes bids on them, and then schedules the work for bids that are accepted. When business is slow, there is no problem to allocate the work on any of the nine different machine areas, but when business is at full capacity, then scheduling must be done.

A standard production model can be used when considering the case of six products being manufactured on several machines. Included in Table 7.3 are approximate times (in hours) on each machine and a profit margin for each product. The complication arises when a linear programming code produces noninteger answers which, if rounded, can provide an infeasible solution to the problem. If the answers are required to be integer units, determine the optimal solution.

Table 7.3

Machines	Panels	O-Rings	Panel Castings	Plastic Fittings	Assembly Tracks	I Beams	Available Labor (hours)
Shearing	0.08						20
Drill press	0.34		0.50	0.46	0.72		40
Roller (large)		0.65					30
Profiler					5.90		40
Mill (hard)	0.66	5.30	0.72		1.86		40
Mill (soft)			1.60		1.12	1.13	30
Grinders	0.08					3.55	Unlimited
Lathe				0.58			40
Computer drill						10.00	20
Profit margin	$1.21	$6.55	$3.10	$1.15	$10.56	$16.15	

INCIDENT: ROUNDING SOLUTION BOMBS OUT

A systems company prepared an air-battle model for the Air Force which would determine the optimum mix of fighters and bombers to attack our Russian neighbors. The optimal solution to the linear programming model came out with 16.94 fighters and 14.03 bombers. It was rounded to an acceptable integer answer of 17 fighters and 14 bombers, which was promptly fed into the war-games model. This model had been some three years in the making, and finally there came the time to run it. Everybody was brought into the machine room to see it run, admirals and generals, and so forth. Everyone gathered around while the program ran. They loaded the program in, tapes whirled, printers printed, and out came the answer. After about 20 minutes the result was that *all* planes had been shot down and *no* bombs dropped. Immediately the Navy personnel began counting more Polaris submarines and the Air Force generals were contemplating suicide.

The linear programming code had come up with an optimal value of the objective function at 16.94 of weapon system A–2753Z (fighter) and 14.03 of weapon system A–2754K (bomber). While the answer was rounded down to the point (16, 14), they had generated the nearest integer number of weapons systems; unfortunately that point was infeasible (see Figure 7.4). In fact so were all the others around it. The only feasible point in Figure 7.4 occurred at (2,1), which called for two fighters to escort a bomber flying as low and fast as it possibly can to inflict maximum damage.

The lesson to be learned from this disaster is *not* that linear programming cannot be a good aid to solving integer programming problems, but that it only makes sense to plug the rounded values into every constraint to see if that integer solution is indeed a feasible one. Integer programming problems can be very deceiving. They sometimes do not look difficult because they look so much like linear programming problems, and yet one is lucky if one out of twenty is solved.

Supplementary Problems

1. Using the Branch & Bound method, find the optimal solution to the following integer programming problem.

    $$\text{Maximize Profit} = 3X_1 + 2X_2$$

    subject to:
    $$2X_1 + X_2 \le 5$$
    $$X_1 - X_2 \le -1$$
    $$X_2 \le 2$$

    X_1 and X_2 nonnegative and integer

2. Using Branch & Bound, show the optimal solution to the following problem.

    $$\text{Minimize Cost} = X_1 + X_2$$

    subject to:
    $$3X_1 + 4X_2 \ge 12$$
    $$2X_1 + X_2 \ge 6$$

    X_1 and X_2 nonnegative and integer

Figure 7.4

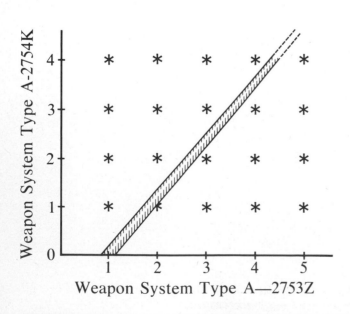

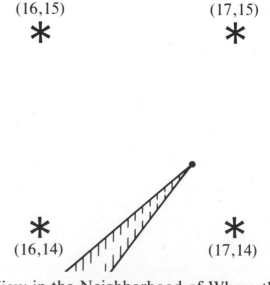

View in the Neighborhood of Where the Two Constraints Come to a Point.

3. Given the original integer programming problem in problem #2 and the optimal LP solution

$$\text{Minimize Cost} = -\tfrac{18}{5} - \tfrac{1}{5}X_3 - \tfrac{1}{5}X_4$$
$$X_2 = \tfrac{6}{5} + \tfrac{2}{5}X_3 - \tfrac{3}{5}X_4$$
$$X_1 = \tfrac{12}{5} - \tfrac{1}{5}X_3 + \tfrac{4}{5}X_4$$

where

X_3 and X_4 are surplus variables,

use the cutting plane method to eliminate the present solution to find an integer solution. Draw a graph of the original problem and the cut. By choosing the strongest cut you should arrive at an optimal integer solution.

7.5 CAPITAL BUDGETING

One of the simplest models is a capital budgeting model that is needed to allocate projects to be done (each has a payoff of some sort) subject to limitations on capital, workforce, and so on. The projects may also be portfolio selections subject to certain constraints. The value of the portfolio or project is 0 if the project is not going to be done, and 1 if it is going to be done. Thus this is a 0–1 problem. When there is only one constraint, the problem is much simpler.

This also is known as the knapsack problem (a little boy is running away from home and wants to take all his favorite things—frog, knife, marbles, and so on—to which he assigns different values. He has only so much room [volume] in his knapsack; thus he wants to maximize the value of the things he can take in his knapsack), the submarine problem (a submarine is going on a long cruise and will not be coming back to port for a long time; thus it needs to carry spare parts which take up a certain amount of weight and volume, but will increase reliability of the ship also), and the spaceship problem (which is the same as the submarine problem, except the spaceship can't come in for repairs).

Let us assume that we have six projects that can be done, but we are limited by resources. There is a payoff associated with each project, and a certain amount of capital will be required to do the project. Thus we have:

Maximize Payoff =
$$10P_1 + 7P_2 + 12P_3 + 4P_4 + 8P_5 + 5P_6$$

subject to:
$$5P_1 + 2P_2 + 4P_3 + P_4 + 3P_5 + 2P_6 \leq 8$$

where $P_i = 0$ or 1.

If the P_i's were not constrained to be integers, we could simply use the Bang for the Buck ratio and put

all our resources into one project. But since we are dealing with 0–1 variables, we must use an approximation method, the method labeled the "Slippery Algorithm."

Quick & Dirty Slippery Algorithm[4]

1. Starting with the largest Bang for the Buck ratios, set projects equal to 1 until you run out of resources.
   a. If you use up all the resources exactly, *Stop. Optimal.*
   b. Otherwise we must go to the "slippery" part of the algorithm.
2. Slip back to the last project set equal to 1 and set it to 0. Then go ahead, setting projects equal to 1 until you run out of resources again.
3. Continue "slipping back" until the first project has finally been set to 0.

The rationale behind this Quick & Dirty algorithm is that we may have been too greedy in the beginning as we decided which projects to do, and that while the Bang for the Buck ratios may be lower, we are closer to using all our resources. Thus we may get a higher total payoff for a better utilization of the resources.

The ratios for the six projects are (2.0, 3.5, 3.0, 4.0, 2.67, 2.50). The highest ratio is for project 4, so $P_4 = 1$, and that uses up 1 unit of resource; so there are 7 units remaining. Now the highest ratio left is project 2, $P_2 = 1$, which uses up 2 units of the resource, and there are 5 units remaining. Now the highest ratio is for project 3, and setting $P_3 = 1$ leaves us with only 1 unit of resource left. No other projects use only 1 unit, so that our first solution has projects 2, 3, and 4 with a payoff of 23 units. This is not guaranteed to be optimal, so we must take the last project, P_3, set it to 0 and continue on with solution 2 (see Table 7.4, page 264).

Thus the best we can do is a payoff of 24 which can take place in three ways: (P_2, P_4, P_5, P_6), (P_3, P_4, P_5), and (P_2, P_3, P_6). In 0–1 notation it can also be written as: (0, 1, 0, 1, 1, 1), (0, 0, 1, 1, 1, 0), and (0, 1, 1, 0, 0, 1).

What makes 0–1 problems so interesting is the fact that as more variables or possibilities are added, the number of possible solutions grows astronomically. If there are n decisions to make, there are 2^n possible solutions (not all would be feasible, but might have to be examined to see if they satisfied all the constraints). Further, $2^{10} = 1024$, but doubling the number of projects gives 2^{20}, which is over one million combinations. Thus even computerized solutions will tend to bog down when the number of variables increases.

Table 7.4

Bang for the Buck Ratio	Project	Solution 1			Solution 2			Solution 3			Solution 4		
		Value	Objective	Resource	Value	Objective	Resource	Value	Objective	Resource	Value	Objective	Resource
4.00	P_4	1	4	1							0	0	0
3.50	P_2	1	11	3				0	4	1	1	7	2
3.00	P_3	1	23	7	0	11	3	1	16	5	1	19	6
2.67	P_5	×			1	19	6	1	24	8	×		
2.50	P_6	×			1	24	8	×			1	24	8
2.00	P_1	×			×			×			×		

× means that the project has not been selected and will not be used (= 0).

workforce utilization

A large department store must set up several display windows for its forthcoming fall sales. The floor manager has had four different people set up windows before, and rates them on a scale from 0 to 100 in terms of effectiveness. She also knows how long it usually takes to do this work, and thus has a measure of their efficiency. She is allowed to use up to five total hours for this work, and must decide which people to use for this. The effects of working together, team spirit, synergism, and group dynamics will have to be ignored, and it will be assumed that the effectiveness ratings are additive. Store management is very concerned about its displays, as they attract a lot of customers already in the shopping mall but not originally intending to come into the store.

The following efficiency and effectiveness figures are given:

	Larry D.	Esther J.	Gerry H.	Susie C.
Effective	90	80	75	95
Efficient (hours)	1	2	1.5	2.5

From the above information, determine which workers should be used to maximize the total effectiveness, given that their work should not total more than five hours.

Solution

Recommendation

Larry D., Gerry H., and Susie C. should be assigned to set up the display windows. This will give the highest effectiveness rating.

Numerical Answer

Person	Effective	Time
Larry D.	90	1
Gerry H.	75	1.5
Susie C.	95	2.5
Total	260	5.0 hours

Math Work. The Bang for the Buck ratios are computed and the slippery algorithm is used (see Table 7.5).

Worker	Larry D.	Esther J.	Gerry H.	Susie C.
Ratio	90	40	50	38

Table 7.5

Bang for the Buck Ratio	Project	Solution 1			Solution 2			Solution 3			Solution 4		
		Value	Objective	Resource	Value	Objective	Resource	Value	Objective	Resource	Value	Objective	Resource
90	LD	1	90	1.0							0	0	0.0
50	GH	1	165	2.5				0	90	1.0	1	75	1.5
40	EJ	1	245	4.5	0	165	2.5	1	170	3.0	1	155	3.5
38	SC	×			1	260	5.0	×			×		

The highest effectiveness total is 260, with Larry D., Gerry H., and Susie C. being used.

INCIDENT: CONTINUATION INSTEAD OF CUTBACKS

An R & D supervisor discovered, at the end of the first quarter of his fiscal year, that he did not have sufficient resources to continue with all the ongoing 15 projects. He then required his manager of research and his manager of development to submit a list of what projects were to continue and what projects were to be terminated. The managers were then both asked to define the constraining factors on their actions. They both agreed that they were really only constrained by graduate engineer labor-hours and engineering associate labor-hours available. The managers were able to supply estimates of labor-hour requirements in the two groups for each project, and also the known availability of hours in each group. Five of the 15 projects required associate labor-hours, and the totals of these were 2700 labor-hours with a pool of 5600 labor-hours available. In short, this second constraint was not binding. The problem then reduced to a simple one with one constraint. A Quick & Dirty slippery algorithm was employed and the answer found. This required that some of the projects be dropped, but it didn't take too long for both managers to figure out that if they had all those extra associate labor-hours, they could fire or transfer some associates and hire some more engineers and continue *all* the projects. Thus by taking a hard look at the problem they were able to reallocate their resources and continue on instead of having to cut back. (Note, however, that this short-term solution might not be best over the long term.)

project cutbacks

A large company in the South has 12 projects that are currently in progress. The company, an industrial firm, has dictated that a 20 percent cut in the workforce budget for each department will be implemented within 2 weeks. The project director must now choose which projects will continue and which must be discontinued. She has ranked the projects on a scale from 10 to 100 in terms of several variables. These include a prospective payoff, desirability, necessity, interesting research, and degree of difficulty. With three months to go for all these projects, the workforce requirements and rankings are given in Table 7.6.

From a total of 22 people, her department must be cut down to 17. Thus for the next 3 months she will no longer have 66 worker-months available but 51 worker-months. She would definitely like to eliminate the last five projects, but wants to see if there might be some rationale for a different set of projects to be discontinued.

Determine your solution to this problem and find what areas of agreement you have. Then explain *your* reasons for your solution and why she should accept it.

INCIDENT: PROJECT MOLE

A capital budgeting procedure is useless if no one will use it. The trick is to get someone in a department interested in using the model. Then when a budget cut comes, he can quickly determine which projects to continue and which to drop. When his boss inquires how this was determined so quickly, the employee shows her the Quick & Dirty method. Of course the boss will disagree about the payoff of certain projects, and she is then invited to plug in her own numbers. Once this is done, the model is solved and both may find that they agree about most of the projects and differ on only a few. The boss, being very impressed, wishes to use the model herself. At this point one should be careful to implement it at the employee level first, for all employees who are willing. By doing this the boss has the advantage of getting the best from her resources. Those who do not cooperate cannot adapt to the change. It takes no time at all to realize that if the model can be adapted to budget cuts, it can also be adapted to budget increases. Now the wise employee comes into the boss's office and shows her what he could do with a few extra dollars or labor-hours. In no time at all the capital budgeting technique has spread throughout that level of the organization. Soon the boss's acumen comes to the attention of her department head, who wants to know how she can adapt so quickly to budget changes. The process is repeated, burrowing up from the lowest levels to the highest. One of the authors of this book has called this technique "Project Mole"[1] and considers it much more effective than the usual management technique of shoving something down everyone's throat. As always, the important

Table 7.6

Project	A	B	C	D	E	F	G	H	I	J	K	L
Ranking	100	100	90	90	80	70	60	50	40	40	20	10
Worker-Months	10	9	4	6	10	5	7	6	2	4	1	2

thing when explaining the technique to someone is to let the person use his or her own numbers. You will be surprised that not much difference will occur in the final answers, but it will be that person's answer, not yours. This is very important, as Woolsey's law of consulting points out:

A consultant never *makes the decision.*
Corollary 1: If I am right, you will never *remember.*
Corollary 2: If I am wrong, you will never *forget.*

aerospace contracts

In the aerospace industry in the 1960s it was common knowledge which companies were doing design work for government proposals. Although each company tried to keep such things secret, there was so much mobility among aerospace workers, and some industrial spying, that it was hard to keep proposal design work under wraps. From the list of candidates entering each field it was also fairly easy to guess which two or three would be finalists, and often the winner could be ascertained without too much difficulty. In response to the RFP's (request for proposals) companies would allocate a certain amount of labor-hours and budget to each possible project. If they won the award, then there would be a major allocation of people and budget to the project.

Consider the following projects under consideration by an engineering design group of a certain East Coast aerospace company. These nine projects are possible candidates for selection and are listed with a payoff (contract award). It is assumed that a contract would be awarded if the design project were completed and submitted by the company. In the case of the computer center manager, he has submitted his estimates of budget requirements for the design phase of each project. From this and his budget limitation of $70,000 for the next six months, determine which projects should be attempted in the next six months to maximize the potential payoff.

Project	Computer ($1000)	Labor-Hours	Award ($1000)
People mover	10	1,000	700
Satellite communication	12	2,000	1200
Laser gun	5	1,500	800
Nuclear waste	4	1,200	1100
Urban design	2	600	400
Infrared sensors	15	3,000	1900
Underground radar	20	4,000	2500
Tactical satellite	10	900	500
Probe III	6	1,000	800
Maximum resource	70	10,560	

Then, given the figures from the engineering design manager, determine from his constraint of labor-hours required what the optimal set of projects should be. Compare the two sets of projects and then determine what should be done if both constraints must be kept and held to.

INCIDENT: DATA COSTS CAN BE PROHIBITIVE

A fellow from a company in Canada described a capital budgeting problem as follows: It seemed that he had developed a model with 60,000 0–1 variables and 10,000 constraints. They came about in the following way. He had 1000 projects that could be done during any one of the following 60 months (5 years). Thus he had 60,000 variables and 1000 constraints. His model was maximizing the return subject to some discounted cash flow constraints. For each year he had a particular constraint on cash flow allowable. Also, he had constraints on the cash flow allowed for the first two years, the first three years, and so on. Further investigation revealed that he had gotten the last constraints by extrapolating from the first year's constraint. This meant that all those constraints were looser, or less binding, than the first. In other words, they would not really constrain the problem. When the Canadian understood that point, he reluctantly admitted that they had really gotten the 12-month cash-flow constraint from the 11th month, and so on, and that the only really tight constraint was the first month. So now the problem was down to 1 month and 1000 variables, or projects, to consider each month. For one person working 40 hours per week, 160 hours per month, 1000 projects had to be considered, or $6\frac{1}{4}$ decisions per hour. Considering that for each project it was necessary to know the initial investment, salvage value, interest rate, annual disbursements, and annual income, he was asked if he could gather the data necessary for the model before it became like a carload of old fruit (that is, rotten and useless). The Canadian was beginning to think. Then was added the "trivial" cost of gathering all this data monthly. Assuming a cost of $0.50 per item, punching it, going card to tape, and getting it ready for the model was going to make a noticeable difference in the gross national product of Canada. He had not considered this. From that a simple rule is derived: *If the cost of collecting the data for a model is greater than the amount you can save by solving it, you shouldn't do that.*

sav-on drug stores

Sav-On Drug Stores is a large chain of discount drug stores that has provided drugs, sundries, and other items such as small appliances at discount prices by having a low overhead and limited services. Checkout stands are provided, but no sales personnel are available as in a department store. One of the areas that Sav-On has been into for a while is film developing. Recently many small outlets have sprung up as competition, using a small part of a shopping center parking lot, with even lower overhead and selling exclusively to camera needs.

Thus in the summer of 1974 Sav-On Drug Stores initiated a marketing effort to keep their customers loyal. For each $25.00 or more of receipts from film purchase or development you received a free 5 × 7-inch photograph. Later on during the summer, this was changed to $15.00 or more for each free photograph. The only catch was that if you turned in $26.78 worth of receipts, you got credit only for $25.00 and you started over on the next $25. Thus it becomes important that there be some simple way to decide which receipts will be used to minimize the amount of "lost" money.

For this problem use the actual receipts of Jon and Felicia Thompson and determine solutions as follows:

1. Consider first the $25.00 problem.
2. Given your answer to the first problem, what if you find out that the $15.00 limit is in effect when you get to the store? Given the receipts that you have now, determine the optimal ordering of receipts.
3. Finally, assume that the $15.00 limit went into effect before you got to the store.

   Receipts: $4.46, $4.46, $4.29, $3.99, $2.64, $2.28, $1.49, $1.49, $1.49, $1.32, $0.76, $0.57, $0.38, $0.38, $0.19, $0.19, $0.19

This problem is a combination of a cutting stock problem and a capital budgeting problem and will require your own Quick & Dirty algorithm. Write up a one-page description of how you proceeded so that someone encountering this problem for the first time could solve it.

Supplementary Problems

1. There are six different things that Pat can do this Sunday afternoon to maximize his pleasure: Tennis (T), Sailing (S), Jogging (J), Work (W), Homework (H), Swimming (SW). Each has a certain payoff and takes a certain amount of time. Use the Slippery Algorithm to determine his maximum pleasure.

Maximize Pleasure =
$$7T + 4S + 6J + 5W + 3H + 1SW$$

subject to:
$$2T + 2S + J + 4W + 3H + 2SW \leq 6 \text{ hours}$$

2. Solve the following capital budgeting problem, in which each project is either 0 or 1 using the Quick & Dirty Slippery algorithm.

Maximize Profit =
$$3P_1 + 4P_2 + 6P_3 + 5P_4 + P_5$$

subject to:
$$4P_1 + 2P_2 + 2P_3 + 3P_4 + 2P_5 \leq 10$$

3. Consider the Sav-On Drug Case.

   a. What is the best solution you have found so far for the $25 limit (receipts & total)? _____

   _____

   b. If the limit were raised to $30, what would be the new solution in terms of receipts and the total extra spent? _____

   _____

7.6 LOCK BOX

A fascinating problem that arises with national corporations is the monthly billing procedure. Some companies bill monthly and receive payments from customers from around the United States. If bills are due (meaning postmarked) by the 10th, it may take up to three days for the money to arrive at the home office if the customer mails his check from 2000 miles away. After that it may take one day (or more) to process the paper work at the company, then two days at the bank to clear it with the Federal Reserve (because the check is written from a different bank than the billing corporation's). Thus maybe a week can be lost from the actual payment date to when the corporation can use the money. For large corporations this can run into a tremendous amount of money not being used, and if cash flow is a problem, then money must be borrowed on short-term notes at outrageous interest, which may cost the corporation a lot of money.

The solution to this is to have several lock boxes around the country. These lock boxes are simply post office boxes that are checked twice a day by a bank associated with the Federal Reserve system. This cuts down on the amount of time between the mailing of the payment and the actual use of the money. Thus several lock boxes around the country can cut the float time down to one day. The problem is that, while money is being saved, it also costs a certain amount of money to rent the lock boxes. All billing is done by the bank, which rents the post office box, sends a runner to the post office twice a day to empty out all the boxes, and handles the checks. There is usually a basic charge each month for this service (a fixed cost) regardless of the number of checks processed. This may be in the form of a flat fee, or it may require a certain balance to be maintained in the checking account, or some other arrangement. Also associated with the costs are variable costs for processing each check. Thus for each month it is possible to determine the total fixed and total variable costs for each lock box location and each customer. Given this information, the problem is simply to determine which customers will use which lock boxes, and which lock boxes will not be rented at all.

Let us assume that we have three possible lock box locations and ten customers. The following monthly variable and fixed costs are given.

Costs	Customer	Denver	Phoenix	Los Angeles
Variable	A	$25	$24	$29
	B	$20	$32	$26
	C	$16	$18	$14
	D	$16	$25	$27
	E	$40	$42	$45
	F	$18	$20	$25
	G	$19	$20	$13
	H	$16	$19	$18
	I	$24	$36	$45
	J	$32	$25	$15
Fixed		$50	$35	$70

Quick & Dirty Algorithm: Lock Box

1. Circle cheapest cost in each row and find the total of all circled numbers. This is the lower bound (cheapest possible cost usually not feasible).
2. Total each column and pick the cheapest total. This is the upper bound (most expensive possible cost).
3. The optimal solution lies somewhere between the two, and the Quick & Dirty algorithm will attempt to find it. Starting with the solution from step 2, add one lock box at a time and check how much would be saved in variable costs versus how much is added in fixed costs. If there is a savings, add the box. If not, don't. Pick the cheapest combination of two boxes.
4. If you now have two boxes, repeat the procedure for adding a third. If there are no savings, *Stop.* Otherwise continue until no more boxes will be added.

From our example above,

Costs	Customer	Denver	Phoenix	Los Angeles
Variable	A	$25	($24)	$29
	B	($20)	$32	$26
	C	$16	$18	($14)
	D	($16)	$25	$27
	E	($40)	$42	$45
	F	($18)	$20	$25
	G	$19	$20	($13)
	H	($16)	$19	$18
	I	($24)	$36	$45
	J	$32	$25	($15)
Fixed		$50	($35)	$70
Total		$276	$281	$327

Cheapest cost = $235

1. The cheapest possible cost would be $235. This is our lower bound, and is of course not possible, since we would have to use all three lock boxes rather than just one.
2. The cheapest single lock box (and the upper bound) is $276, Denver.
3. Given that we would be using the Denver box, what would be the cost savings (or increase) if Phoenix were added? We would save money for customers A ($1) and J ($7) for a total savings of $8, but we would increase the costs by $35 for the lock box. Thus we would lose money. Now we need to see if it would save money to add Los Angeles. We would save money for customers C ($2), G ($6), and J ($17) for a saving of $25, but would have an increase in the cost of the box of $70. Thus it makes no sense to add any other boxes. *Stop.*

eastern lock boxes

A company does most of its business on the East Coast, in the Southeast, and some of the Midwest (east of the Mississippi). There are ten customers that owe accounts each month, and there are four locations where this company is considering having lock boxes established. Given below are the average monthly costs for renting the lock boxes and the variable costs that would accumulate for each month. Right now the company has been receiving all its accounts in Detroit at a cost of $710 per month. What set of lock boxes would you recommend, and if there are any savings, how much would the company save each month?

Costs	Company	Atlanta	Baltimore	Chicago	Detroit
Variable	1	$40	$10	$70	$90
	2	$60	$30	$40	$80
	3	$30	$90	$50	$60
	4	$20	$80	$90	$60
	5	$70	$30	$80	$40
	6	$50	$20	$40	$70
	7	$50	$90	$30	$20
	8	$20	$50	$30	$50
	9	$60	$70	$20	$40
	10	$90	$70	$60	$30
Fixed		$150	$120	$140	$170

Solution

Recommendation

The company should not have a lock box in Detroit, but it should have lock boxes in Atlanta and Balti-more. This will save $100 per month over present costs.

Numerical Answer

Costs	Atlanta		Baltimore	
Variable	From 3 $30		From 1 $10	
	From 4 $20		From 2 $30	
	From 7 $50		From 5 $30	
	From 8 $20		From 6 $20	
	From 9 $60		From 10 $70	
Fixed	$150		$120	
Total	$330	+	$280	= $610

The savings come to $710 − $610 = $100 per month.

Math Work.   See Table 7.7.

The cheapest feasible solution to begin with is Atlanta for $640 per month. By adding Baltimore as a lock box, we would save money in variable costs at locations 1 ($30), 2 ($30), 5 ($40), 6 ($30), and 10 ($20) for a total of $150. Balanced against this is the cost of adding a lock box in Baltimore for $120; so a savings of $30 is realized. In like manner, although $120 would be saved in variable costs by having lock boxes in Atlanta and Chicago, there would be an additional fixed cost of $140 to add the Chicago lock box, so a net increase of $20 would result. Adding Detroit would also result in an increase in the total costs by $30.

Now given the solution of $610 for Atlanta and Baltimore, we want to investigate if adding another lock box will result in any savings. This means that for Chicago we must look at variable costs that are cheaper than either Atlanta or Baltimore, which only happens at locations 7, 9, and 10 for a savings of $70

Table 7.7

Costs	Company	Atlanta	Baltimore	Chicago	Detroit	Remarks
Variable	1	$40	($10)	$70	$90	
	2	60	(30)	40	80	
	3	(30)	90	50	60	
	4	(20)	80	90	60	
	5	70	(30)	80	40	
	6	50	(20)	40	70	
	7	50	90	30	(20)	
	8	(20)	50	30	50	
	9	60	70	(20)	40	
	10	90	70	60	(30)	
Fixed		$150	($120)	$140	$170	Cheapest possible cost = $350
Total		$640	$660	$650	$710	
Adding to Atlanta			−$30	+$20	+$30	Only Baltimore will reduce cost
Adding to Atlanta + Baltimore				+$70	+$80	Nothing reduces costs

in variable costs. But again, the fixed-cost increase more than wipes out any savings. The same is true for adding Detroit to the Atlanta/Baltimore solution, so that our algorithm stops at this point. We have our best solution.

west coast lock box

Consider 5 possible lock box locations for 16 customers given in Table 7.8, and determine the lock boxes to be used and which customers should use them to minimize the total cost. Remember that these boxes are actually saving money for the company, although the figures are not available.

INCIDENT: LARGE-SCALE LOCK-BOX PROBLEM

A western railroad, like all national companies, has accounts receivable coming in from all over the United States. The railroad has $600,000 coming in each month, which is quite a large amount. Considering its cash flow requirements, if it could have the money sooner, it would not have to take short-term loans at the end of each month, which has been costing $1000 per day. The solution was to use lock boxes around the country, which raised the problem of which lock boxes to use, and then which customers should use them. For this problem there were 600 customers and 200 possible lock boxes.

mine shaft location

Consider the problem of a mining company in Colorado. There are 18 possible locations for mine shafts to service a network of 50 tunnels. There are various fixed and variable costs associated with this project, the main costs being the drilling of the shaft (fixed) and the cost of transporting materials from the tunnels to the shaft (variable). The variable costs are considered over a period of 5 years (life of the tunnel).

Thus to minimize the fixed costs, the cheapest shaft should be drilled; to minimize the variable costs, all 18 shafts should be drilled. In either case the other costs would be prohibitive. The problem is to determine which mine shafts will service the network of 50 tunnels at the cheapest total costs (fixed plus variable).

Table 7.9 presents a simplified example for 12 tunnels and 5 shafts. Pertinent costs include the cost of drilling the shaft and the total variable costs for a 5-year period of transporting materials from the tunnel to that particular shaft. Decide which mine shafts should be drilled and which tunnels will use each particular mine shaft. Each tunnel must be connected to some mine shaft.

INCIDENT: WAREHOUSE LOCATION

A large midwestern chemical company wanted to add one or more warehouses to equalize the distribution load from its plant and to minimize the shipping

Table 7.8

Costs	Customer	San Diego	Los Angeles	San Francisco	Portland	Seattle
Variable	A	$15	$20	$25	$28	$32
	B	$45	$41	$36	$28	$24
	C	$18	$25	$19	$14	$16
	D	$13	$15	$20	$18	$19
	E	$25	$22	$20	$17	$18
	F	$45	$30	$42	$43	$40
	G	$27	$29	$25	$20	$16
	H	$14	$10	$18	$20	$16
	I	$26	$30	$32	$22	$20
	J	$29	$26	$24	$20	$25
	K	$28	$32	$25	$22	$26
	L	$17	$15	$21	$18	$25
	M	$38	$32	$23	$27	$20
	N	$17	$19	$24	$20	$26
	O	$20	$16	$25	$21	$24
	P	$18	$25	$32	$30	$37
Fixed		$50	$40	$35	$50	$70

Table 7.9

Shafts	Tunnels												Fixed Costs
	1	*2*	*3*	*4*	*5*	*6*	*7*	*8*	*9*	*10*	*11*	*12*	
1	40	20	40	60	80	100	20	0	20	40	60	80	$200
2	60	40	20	40	60	80	40	20	0	20	40	60	$275
3	80	60	40	20	40	60	60	40	20	0	20	40	$280
4	100	80	60	40	20	40	80	60	40	20	0	20	$150
5	120	100	80	60	40	20	100	80	60	40	20	0	$110

costs incurred by shipping materials from the plant to a distant warehouse and then shipping to the customer again. If there were several more warehouses, executives figured, then the shipping costs would be reduced. But weighed against this was the cost of building or renting new warehouse facilities. The problem then is very much like the lock box problem: determine how many warehouses to add and which customers will have shipments from them.

warehouse addition

The Jet Plastics Company has had considerable success in marketing its plastic buckets in the 22 states west of the Mississippi river. It has also decided that a continuous production for six weeks will give it a year's supply of buckets for this area and minimize the production and most inventory costs. However, it wishes to store the year's supply in different warehouses and has selected five possible sites: California, Washington, Minnesota, Colorado, and Texas. It determined the yearly cost of renting storage space (in hundreds of dollars) and the yearly cost of shipping from the warehouse to each state (see Table 7.10). This cost is a product of the mileage from the warehouse times the demand for each state times the cost per mile. Thus the problem is exactly like the lock box problem, and what is desired is to know which warehouses will minimize the total yearly costs of transportation and rental.

Table 7.10

Cost		California	Washington	Minnesota	Colorado	Texas
Variable	Arizona	$ 3	$ 9	$ 11	$ 4	$ 9
	Arkansas	$ 70	$ 90	$ 40	$ 40	$ 20
	California	$ 0	$ 63	$108	$ 60	$100
	Colorado	$ 28	$ 36	$ 26	$ 0	$ 31
	Idaho	$ 5	$ 4	$ 6	$ 3	$ 9
	Iowa	$ 91	$108	$ 15	$ 48	$ 60
	Kansas	$155	$185	$ 60	$ 65	$ 84
	Louisiana	$320	$440	$240	$200	$ 50
	Minnesota	$160	$170	$ 0	$ 75	$135
	Missouri	$210	$270	$ 75	$105	$105
	Montana	$ 25	$ 17	$ 20	$ 10	$ 37
	Nebraska	$ 40	$ 42	$ 10	$ 15	$ 30
	Nevada	$ 1	$ 5	$ 7	$ 3	$ 7
	New Mexico	$ 70	$ 15	$ 13	$ 15	$ 10
	North Dakota	$ 16	$ 14	$ 7	$ 6	$ 20
	Oklahoma	$100	$125	$ 60	$ 44	$ 40
	Oregon	$ 16	$ 30	$ 33	$ 20	$ 40
	South Dakota	$ 2	$ 2	$ 1	$ 1	$ 2
	Texas	$300	$420	$240	$200	$ 0
	Utah	$ 15	$ 20	$ 26	$ 9	$ 34
	Washington	$ 6	$ 0	$ 11	$ 7	$ 15
	Wyoming	$ 27	$ 30	$ 21	$ 7	$ 37
Fixed		$100	$150	$200	$125	$250

Supplementary Problems

1. Solve the following lock box problem.

Costs	Customer	City A	City B	City C	City D	City E
Variable	1	$29	$40	$15	$29	$36
	2	16	55	92	30	19
	3	25	24	14	65	22
	4	23	73	16	5	42
	5	21	25	26	11	76
	6	95	16	49	22	48
	7	23	22	76	25	14
	8	17	18	41	43	27
	9	15	25	14	17	35
	10	16	40	23	14	22
Fixed		$45	$65	$19	$32	$26

2. Given the Mine Shafts Case:
   a. What is the cheapest single shaft and its cost?

   _____

   _____

   b. If the fixed costs were cut in half, which is now

   the cheapest shaft and its cost? _____

   _____

   c. What is the new solution to the problem in part b (show savings of variable costs and additional fixed cost for each shaft)? Add only one shaft.
   d. Are there any prospects for adding a third shaft in part c? Why or why not?

3. a. Explain the difference between linear programming and integer programming in two

   ways: _____

   _____

   _____

   b. Explain the difference between pure integer

   problems and mixed integer problems. ____

   c. Explain the difference between integer prob-

   lems and 0–1 problems. _____

   _____

7.7 ADVANCED 0–1 TECHNIQUES

In this section you will be introduced to a basic technique for solving 0–1 problems, noting that there are certainly limitations to Quick & Dirty techniques, especially in the face of a large number of alternatives or variables. But you should also keep in mind that these simple techniques can serve as feasible answers in case none can be found from the following

algorithm, or they can serve as an upper bound to the minimum cost. Versions of these Long & Clean algorithms are computerized and usually available in many computer libraries, but you must be cautioned that several test problems should be run so that you will become familiar with how the algorithm treats each type of problem before you put large-scale problems on the machine.

The basic method to be considered in this section is called "implicit enumeration" and is due to Balas.[5] It has been modified to become a very efficient algorithm for well-structured 0–1 integer programming problems. It finds the optimal solution (or if you run out of time or money, maybe a good solution) by looking explicity at only a small subset of all the possible solutions. Since the number of possible solutions for a 0–1 problem is equal to 2^n, where n is the number of possible variables, it is necessary to determine whether each solution is feasible and then optimal.

To explain the process of implicit enumeration, we first need to contrast it with explicit enumeration. Explicit simply means that we would enumerate every single possibility and check it for feasibility. If it were feasible, we would determine the value of the objective function, and if it were the largest so far, keep that as the best answer yet. By the time we had investigated every possibility, we would have exhausted (and been exhausted by) every combination. The only problem with this approach, while it is very simple, is that for twenty 0–1 variables there are over one million possibilities. Thus this could take a very long time.

An example that might make this clear would involve a class of 40 business students. I might want to find the oldest marketing major. Thus I want to maximize age subject to the constraint of being a marketing major. If I were to do explicit enumeration, I would simply ask each and every student how old he or she was and whether he or she was a marketing major. But I would have to ask all 40 of them to find the oldest marketing major.

Implicit enumeration would involve my asking people how old they were and if they were marketing majors until I found a marketing major. Let us assume that the major is 23 years old. I would then ask all people over 23 to stand. I would then go to the people standing and ask if they were marketing majors. If they were, I would ask how old they were. Let us say the next one is 27 years old. I would then ask all people over 27 to remain standing. This would again greatly reduce the number of people standing. In this way I would find the oldest marketing major without having to explicity ask every student. But at the same time I have implicitly asked each one, and perhaps had to ask only four or five people. (Note that this probably is not the most efficient method for determining the oldest marketing major, but it serves to illustrate the difference between implicit and explicit enumeration.)

Consider an example of five projects (0–1) that can be done. Each has a certain cost that must be minimized and certain resources that must be used. Note that all the coefficients for the objective function (only) must be positive and in ascending order. The coefficients for the constraints need not be all positive, and the constraints must be greater than or equal constraints. This is the standard form for solution by implicit enumeration.

Long & Clean Algorithm: Implicit Enumeration[6]

1. Starting with the first variable, set everyone equal to 1 until one of three things happens:
   a. All constraints are satisfied. This is a feasible solution. If this solution is the best so far, it is now the upper bound.
   b. All variables are set to 0 or 1, and all constraints are not yet satisfied.
   c. All constraints are not yet satisfied, but the objective function is greater than or equal to the upper bound.
2. At this point go back to the variable just before the last one you set equal to 1.
   a. If it equals 1, set it to 0 and continue "forward" again.
   b. If it equals 0, go back to the variable before that. Then go to 2a.
3. When all variables have been set to 0, *Stop*. The best feasible solution is the *optimal solution*.

Example. Consider the following example:

Minimize Cost $= 4P_1 + 5P_2 + 7P_3 + 8P_4$

subject to:
$$P_1 + 2P_2 + 2P_3 + 3P_4 \geq 4$$
$$5P_1 + 4P_2 + 3P_3 + P_4 \geq 7$$

Starting with step 1, set variables equal to 1 starting with the first and going forward:

Variable	Cost	Feasible	Solution
$P_1 = 1$	4	No	
$P_2 = 1$	9	No	
$P_3 = 1$	16	Yes	(1,1,1,0)

We have met condition 1a and thus go on to step 2. We will go back from P_3 to P_2, set it equal to 0, and then continue forward:

Variable	Cost	Feasible
$P_2 = 0$	4	No
$P_3 = 1$	11	No
$P_4 = 1$	18	Yes, but too large

Thus we must back up again from P_4 and set $P_3 = 0$. We have not changed P_1 or P_2.

Variable	Cost	Feasible
$P_3 = 0$	4	No
$P_4 = 1$	12	No, all variables used

We must now back up to P_3, but it is already 0. Thus we back up to P_2, but it was also most recently set to 0. Finally we go all the way back to the beginning, to P_1, and set it to 0:

Variable	Cost	Feasible	Solution
$P_1 = 0$	0	No	
$P_2 = 1$	5	No	
$P_3 = 1$	12	Yes, best solution so far	(0,1,1,0)

We must now back up and set P_2 to 0:

Variable	Cost	Feasible
$P_2 = 0$	0	No
$P_3 = 1$	7	No
$P_4 = 1$	15	Too large and all variables used

Now we must set P_3 to 0 and continue:

Variable	Cost	Feasible
$P_3 = 0$	0	No
$P_4 = 1$	8	All variables used

Finally we have set all the variables to 0. The best solution is (0,1,1,0) for a minimum cost of 12 units.

You will readily agree that this is not the most exciting algorithm, yet it very methodically, explicitly, and implicitly looks at every possibility. If we had used explicit or pure enumeration of every possibility, we would have had 16 possibilities as follows:

Solution	Feasible	Cost
(0,0,0,0)	No	
(1,0,0,0)	No	
(0,1,0,0)	No	
(0,0,1,0)	No	
(0,0,0,1)	No	
(1,1,0,0)	No	
(1,0,1,0)	No	
(1,0,0,1)	No	
(0,1,1,0)	Yes	12 *(Table continues.)*

Solution	Feasible	Cost
(0,1,0,1)	No	
(0,0,1,1)	No	
(1,1,1,0)	Yes	16
(1,1,0,1)	Yes	17
(1,0,1,1)	Yes	19
(0,1,1,1)	Yes	20
(1,1,1,1)	Yes	24

So while the implicit enumeration may seem tedious and inefficient (especially for small problems), it is a vast improvement over explicit enumeration.

A final note on the standard form of the problem is in order. If a problem is in the form of maximizing subject to less than or equal constraints, it can be converted to the standard form by the following Quick & Dirty algorithm.

Quick & Dirty Conversion

1. Change the word "Maximize" to "Minimize."
2. Add the coefficients in the first constraint and subtract the right-hand value from that total. This becomes the new right-hand value.
3. Change the less than or equal sign to a greater than or equal sign.
4. Do steps 2 and 3 for all constraints.
5. Now the solution must be interpreted that 0 means *do* that project, and 1 means *don't* do it.

Example.   Given the problem:

$$\text{Maximize} \quad 3P_1 + 5P_2 + 6P_3$$

$$\text{subject to:} \quad P_1 + 4P_2 + P_3 \leq 5$$
$$2P_1 + P_2 + P_3 \leq 2$$

we have the standard form for implicit enumeration:

$$\text{Minimize} \quad 3P_1 + 5P_2 + 6P_3$$

$$\text{subject to:} \quad P_1 + 4P_2 + P_3 \geq 1$$
$$2P_1 + P_2 + P_3 \geq 2$$

The first right-hand side of 5 was changed to $(1 + 4 + 1) - 5 = 1$ and the second right-hand side became $(2 + 1 + 1) - 2 = 2$. All coefficients remain the same, but now $P_1 = 1$ means *don't* do project 1.

proposal analysis

An electronics firm in the southeastern United States has a fixed number of projects capable of producing a profit (if the proposals are successful) from available stocks of workforce in the engineering department. The question associated with this is what likely projects should be involved in proposal efforts so that there will be the maximum total payoff considering the resources available. In the manufacture of missile systems these resources would be the labor-hours available in flight mechanics, aerothermodynamics, computer simulation, and others.

Consider that this company has four possible projects within the next few months. They have available four labor-months of computer simulation time, three labor-months of aerothermodynamics, and three labor-months of flight mechanics time. We also have estimates of how much of each resource is required to complete the project and the payoff for each project. Given the information below, determine which projects should be chosen so as to maximize the total payoff.

Resource	Project			
	Tracking System	Detection Unit	Signal Device	Distorter
Computer simulation	0	1	1	3
Aerothermodynamics	0	0	2	1
Flight mechanics	4	1	0	1
Payoff	$1000	$1000	$2000	$4000

Solution

Recommendation
The projects to do are the signal device and the distorter. Do not do the other two projects. There will be two worker-months of flight mechanics time left over, while all other resources will be used fully. The total payoff for this recommendation is $6000.

Numerical Answer. $P_1 = 1$, $P_2 = 0$, $P_3 = 0$, and payoff = $1000. This translates to don't do P_1 (detection unit), do P_2 (signal device) and P_3 (distorter). The tracking system was not considered since there was not enough flight mechanics time.

Math Work.   The problem as stated can be set up as a maximization problem:

Maximize Payoff =
   $1000 TS + $1000 DU + $2000 SD + $4000 D

$$\text{subject to:} \quad DU + SD + 3D \leq 4$$
$$\text{computer simulation}$$
$$2 SD + D \leq 3$$
$$\text{aerothermodynamics}$$
$$4 TS DU + D \leq 3$$
$$\text{flight mechanics.}$$

By using the Quick & Dirty conversion we can change this to a minimization problem. We can also see from inspection that it is impossible to be able to do the tracking system project since it requires 4 worker-months of flight mechanics time and only three are available. Thus we will eliminate this from further consideration and have only three projects:

Minimize $\$1000\ DU + \$2000\ SD + \$4000\ D$

subject to:
$$DU + SD + 3D \geq 1$$
$$2SD + D \geq 0$$
$$DU + D \geq -1$$

These last two constraints will *always* be satisfied. (In the original problem all projects could be done with enough time for these.)

Thus we really have a very simple problem:

Minimize $\$1000\ P_1 + \$2000\ P_2 + \$4000\ P_3$

subject to: $P_1 + P_2 + 3P_3 \geq 1$

By setting $P_1 = 1$ we have a solution, and it must be optimal; there are no cheaper solutions.

INCIDENT: ROUNDING PREVENTS OPTIMAL SOLUTION

In the early days of operations research it was assumed that integer programs were so very similar to linear programs that one only had to solve integer problems by linear programming methods and round the answers up or down. A large washing machine manufacturer decided to buy its own bright, shiny, new OR group. Right away the group decided to tackle the problem of delivery costs, for they noticed that shipments of half-empty box cars of washers were being made by rail (the railroad is notoriously indifferent as to whether your box car is full or empty). They figured that these were 0–1 variables that could be solved by rounding to a full car or an empty car. They imagined vast savings by simply waiting until there was a box car load going to a certain city and then shipping. This meant that Sioux City had to wait until a whole box car of washers was needed before any would be shipped. People in the company began to point out that this didn't make sense, but the OR group was confident because it was the optimum plan. After all, they had just run the problem as a linear programming model and rounded the answers to integers. Well, some interesting things began to happen. The loading docks began to be cluttered

with partial pallets of washers, and soon the company had to rent extra warehouses to store them, with the added expense of transporting the washers back and forth. The accounting department soon began to see that its inventory costs were skyrocketing, and so it sent an alert to the OR department, which curtly noted that the bean counters simply didn't know anything about optimal programs. Finally the situation got so bad that the accounting department drew straws to send a representative over to talk to the head of the OR department. But he was on vacation, so the accounting representative went to the OR head's boss and presented the figures of warehouse costs (which approximated the multiplication of rabbits). When the OR head got back from vacation, he couldn't find his desk, or his department. As a matter of fact, the company has not had an OR department since. The problem was finally run as a straight integer programming problem, and the cost constraints were so tight that there was no feasible solution to the integer problem, although there had been one for the linear programming problem. In other words, it couldn't be done!

This is just to illustrate one last time that integer programming problems are very difficult to solve, and simply because one has a computerized algorithm is no excuse to throw common sense out the window.

budgeting cutbacks

In the Capital Budgeting section we considered the case of a large company in the South that has twelve on-going projects. Faced with a budget cut of approximately 20 percent, the director must make a decision as to which projects should be discontinued. This problem can be stated in the following terms as a maximization problem:

Maximize
$100A + 100B + 90C + 90D + 80E + 70F + 60G + 50H + 40I + 40J + 20K + 10L$

subject to:
$10A + 9B + 4C + 6D + 10E + 5F + 7G + 6H + 2I + 4J + 1K + 2L \leq 51.$

It can be stated as a minimization problem by applying the Quick & Dirty conversion:

Minimize
$100A + 100B + 90C + 90D + 80E + 70F + 60G + 50H + 40I + 40J + 20K + 10L$

subject to:
$10A + 9B + 4C + 6D + 10E + 5F + 7G + 6H + 2I + 4J + 1K + 2L \geq 13.$

Now we must order the projects in ascending values in the objective function, and also note that if A = 1 in this new problem, then it means to discontinue (not do) the project. For convenience, we will rename the projects $P_1, P_2, \ldots$, starting with the smallest objective coefficient:

Minimize
$$10\,P_1 + 20\,P_2 + 40\,P_3 + 40\,P_4 + 50\,P_5 + 60\,P_6 + 70\,P_7$$
$$+ 80\,P_8 + 90\,P_9 + 90\,P_{10} + 100\,P_{11} + 100\,P_{12}$$

subject to:
$$2\,P_1 + 1\,P_2 + 4\,P_3 + 2\,P_4 + 6\,P_5 + 7\,P_6 + 5\,P_7$$
$$+ 10\,P_8 + 6\,P_9 + 4\,P_{10} + 9\,P_{11} + 10\,P_{12}$$
$$\geq 13.$$

Now that the problem is set up, solve by implicit enumeration, and then recommend which projects should be discontinued and which ones continued so that the sum of the rankings (objective function) is maximized in the original problem.

---

computer contracts

The computer center director of an aerospace company is faced with considering nine projects from an engineering design group. These are the same projects that were described in the Aerospace Contracts case, and are limited by labor-hours and a budget constraint. It is assumed that a contract would be awarded if the design project were completed and submitted by the company. The payoff or contract award is listed also with the number of required man-hours and computer budget needed. With this information determine which projects should be done to maximize the total payoff. Does this answer differ from your solution to the Aerospace Contracts case, and if so, are there any major differences?

Project	Computer ($1000)	Labor-Hours	Payoff ($1000)
People mover	10	1,000	700
Satellite communication	12	2,000	1200
Laser gun	5	1,500	800
Nuclear waste	4	1,200	1100
Urban design	2	600	400
Infrared sensors	15	3,000	1900
Underground radar	20	4,000	2500
Tactical satellite	10	900	500
Probe III	6	1,000	800
Maximum resource	70	10,560	

Supplementary Problem

1. Given the following 0–1 problem,

   Maximize Profit $= 3X_1 + 2X_2 + 5X_3$

   subject to: $\quad 4X_1 + 3X_2 + 6X_3 \leq 10$
   $$X_1, X_2, \text{ and } X_3 \text{ either } 0 \text{ or } 1$$

   a. Change to the appropriate form for the implicit enumeration algorithm.
   b. Solve the problem using the implicit enumeration algorithm.

7.8 BRIDGING THE GAP: THE INTERFACE

This chapter has been different from the preceding ones in that two sections have already been devoted to the more mathematical treatment of integer programming, Sections 7.4 and 7.7. Several points need to be made or reiterated though in connection with the algorithms presented in this chapter.

1. All integer programming problems are difficult to solve.
2. The best way to try and solve integer programming problems is to take advantage of any special structure they might have. Thus the scheduling and lock box problems can be written as ordinary integer programming problems with 0–1 variables, but they are solved more quickly and easily if looked at as a table of numbers rather than as an objective function and constraints.
3. The optimal algorithms found in Sections 7.4 and 7.7 may take a very long time to solve, even for small problems on the most powerful computer available.
4. In the last chapter we noted that the assignment problem and the transportation problem could be written and solved as linear programming problems. They are technically integer programming problems, but since they are of a special structure, the answer will always come out as integers for both problems as long as the right-hand sides are integers.
5. If the integer programming problem is solved as a linear programming problem, the linear programming solution will always be greater than or equal to (if maximizing) the integer solution.
6. To illustrate the difference between the classical representation of integer programming problems

and setting them up for Quick & Dirty solutions, let us look at the lock box problem.

Assume a simple problem with two customers and two possible boxes:

Costs	Customer	Lock Box	
		1	*2*
Variable	A	2	3
	B	7	5
Fixed		20	15

Let $X_{ij} = 1$ if customer i uses lock box j
$\quad\quad = 0$ if customer i does not use box j
$\quad Y_i = 0$ if lock box i is *not* used
$\quad\quad = 1$ if lock box i is used.

The algebraic set-up would look as follows:

Minimize Cost =
$2X_{11} + 3X_{12} + 7X_{21} + 5X_{22} + 20Y_1 + 15Y_2$

subject to:
$$X_{11} + X_{12} \quad\quad\quad\quad\quad\quad = 1$$
$$X_{21} + X_{22} \quad\quad\quad = 1$$

(each customer uses only one lock box)

$$X_{11} \quad\quad + X_{21} \quad\quad - 2Y_1 \quad\quad \leq 0$$
$$X_{12} \quad\quad + X_{22} \quad\quad - 2Y_2 \leq 0$$

(insures $Y_i = 1$ if *anyone* uses a lock box)
where $Y_i = 0$ or 1.

Given M customers and N lock boxes, the problem will have $(M + 1)N$ variables. For a small problem with 500 customers and 50 possible lock boxes there will be 25,050 variables and 550 constraints. That is quite a large problem. There are 2^{25050} possible combinations of customers and lock boxes. This is simply too large to solve by conventional methods. Woolsey and Swanson[4] have come up with a code that will solve the 500 × 50 problem in 32 seconds on a PDP 10.

7. Consider the Quick & Dirty slippery algorithm for the capital budgeting problem.

What happens when we have two constraints instead of just one? A Quick & Dirty way of handling this is to make one constraint out of two. This will always produce a *weaker* constraint and will only be an approximation, but it is a lot easier than some optimal technique that may take forever or be very costly. Let us add an extra resource constraint to the example in Section 7.5. It is obvious that the optimal solution cannot be any better than 24.

Maximize Payoff =
$$10P_1 + 7P_2 + 12P_3 + 4P_4 + 8P_5 + 5P_6$$

subject to:
$$5P_1 + 2P_2 + 4P_3 + P_4 + 3P_5 + 2P_6 \leq 8$$
$$P_1 + 3P_2 + 2P_3 + 5P_4 + P_5 + 4P_6 \leq 6.$$

8. An extension of the Slippery Algorithm for Section 7.5 is to take the ordering of projects that have not completely used the resources and see if by setting the last project that was equal to 1 back to 0 and then proceeding on will yield a better result. This may increase the number of possible solutions and *may* yield a better answer. It will still be a Quick & Dirty algorithm and does not guarantee an optimal solution.

The first thing to do is to check the optimal solutions from the previous problem with just one constraint. If one of these three solutions satisfies the constraints, it is optimal.

Quick & Dirty Surrogate Constraint

1. Combine the two constraints, multiplying the first by a and the second by b, where $a + b = 1$. To begin with, arbitrarily set $a = b = \frac{1}{2}$.
2. Using the Slippery Algorithm, find the best solution. Check it against the *original* constraints. If it satisfies them, *Stop*.
3. Otherwise one of the constraints will be violated. Increase the value of the violated constraint (that is, if the first one is violated, increase the value of a, reduce b) and compute a new surrogate constraint. Go to step 2.

Surrogate means literally "substitute," and in this case we are substituting one constraint for two others.

$$\frac{1}{2}(5P_1 + 2P_2 + 4P_3 + P_4 + 3P_5 + 2P_6 \leq 8)$$
$$\frac{1}{2}(P_1 + 2P_2 + 2P_3 + 5P_4 + P_5 + 4P_6 \leq 6)$$
$$\overline{3P_1 + 2P_2 + 3P_3 + 3P_4 + 2P_5 + 3P_6 \leq 7}$$

The best solution for this is (0, 1, 1, 0, 1, 1), and the payoff = 27. Right away we know that this violates the first constraint, so instead of weighting it by 0.5, we will weight it by 0.7 and the second one by 0.3.

Our new constraint becomes:

$$3.8P_1 + 2.0P_2 + 3.4P_3 + 2.2P_4 + 2.4P_5 + 2.6P_6 \leq 7.4$$

Continuing in this fashion through steps 2 and 3 will result in the final solution of (0, 0, 1, 0, 1, 0) for a payoff of 20.

7.9 REVIEWS

Review 1: Open book and notes; show all work and write legibly.

1. (15 points) After taking an OR test, you wonder if you solved the problems in an optimal manner to get the most points in the time allotted. From experience you estimate how much time each problem takes and you know how much each problem is worth. From the data below, determine the optimal set of questions you should answer given 50 minutes for the test. Use the Slippery Algorithm and find only three solutions (you should have the optimum by then!).

   Maximize Points =
   $$20P_1 + 15P_2 + 10P_3 + 15P_1 + 20P_5 + 15P_6 + 4P_7$$

   subject to:
   $$10P_1 + 8P_2 + 6P_3 + 7P_4 + 14P_5 + 10P_6 + 5P_7 \leq 50$$

2. (15 points) The following lengths of boards are needed and will be cut from 6-foot boards.

Length (inches)	18	27	30	36	42
Number Needed	5	3	2	3	4

   a. What are all the possible cuts without any waste?

   b. What is the minimum number of boards needed (lower bound)?

c. What is the solution that gives the minimum number of boards?

3. (10 points) Given the Hayes Department Store case (page 251),
   a. What is the optimal number of hours and clerks in your answer? _____

   _____

   b. Would it make any difference in this type of problem if we minimized clerks or hours? Why? _____

   _____

4. (10 points) Given the Sav-On case (page 266), what if the free photograph was for $16.00 worth of receipts and you knew this *before* you went to the store? What receipts would you turn in for your picture

   and how much over $16.00 would you have to go? _____

   _____

   _____

5. (15 points) Solve the following lock box problem (show your work):

	Customer	A	B	City C	D	E	F
Variable	1	$15	$12	$26	$23	$83	$14
costs	2	$25	$18	$19	$15	$92	$26
	3	$30	$25	$40	$16	$14	$35
	4	$65	$29	$55	$14	$17	$19
	5	$ 5	$75	$73	$36	$23	$22
	6	$ 7	$82	$24	$29	$36	$41
	7	$23	$95	$ 4	$83	$45	$36
	8	$ 9	$ 4	$15	$16	$19	$19
	9	$16	$16	$10	$25	$23	$22
	10	$22	$17	$25	$14	$42	$49
	11	$15	$26	$16	$36	$91	$76
	12	$23	$43	$ 4	$42	$16	$41
	13	$19	$17	$16	$18	$21	$14
Fixed costs		$75	$32	$26	$17	$25	$19

6. (20 points) Solve the following integer programming problem using Branch & Bound by branching off of X_2:

Maximize Profit $= 5X_1 + 4X_2$

subject to:
$$4X_1 + 2X_2 \leq 8$$
$$3X_1 + 4X_2 \leq 12$$

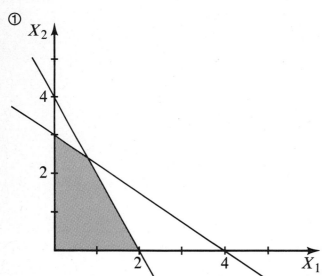

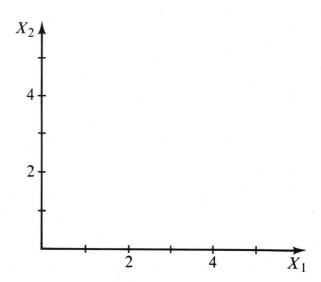

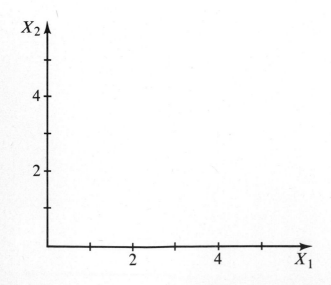

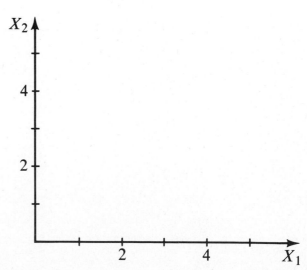

7. (15 points) Solve the following 0–1 problem by Implicit Enumeration.

Minimize Cost $= 5P_1 + 7P_2 + 8P_3 + 10P_4$

subject to:

$$5P_1 + 3P_2 + 2P_3 + 2P_4 \geqslant 6$$
$$2P_1 + 1P_2 + 3P_3 + 4P_4 \geqslant 4$$

Review 2: Open book and notes; show* all *work and write legibly.

1. (10 points) Given the Northern Airmotive Corporation case (page 247), find the new solution (cost and number of people) if the cost for jobhoppers becomes \$15 per hour. Explain your reasoning in terms of Bang for the Buck.

2. (10 points) Fruity Rudy's Smoothie Stand is doing a booming business at the college and Rudy is thinking of expanding his little stand to accommodate what he figures to be the demand on his personnel. Given the shifts, estimated need, and so on, determine how many people should be hired for each shift and minimize the number of extra hours he will have to pay personnel.

	Shift						
Time	*1*	*2*	*3*	*4*	*5*	*6*	**Need**
8–9	×	×					2
9–10	×	×					2
10–11	×					×	3
11–12	×		×		×	×	5
12–1	×		×		×		5
1–2					×	×	2
2–3			×	×		×	3
3–4			×	×			4

3. (15 points) A small contractor has agreed to build balconies for an apartment complex. She can buy the necessary lumber in 15-foot lengths for a good price and will make all cuts from these.
a. Make up as many cuts as possible without waste given the following lengths needed.

Length (feet)	Number Needed
3	180
4	180
5	60
8	90
12	30
15	30

b. Minimize the number of boards needed to fulfill the requirements.

4. (15 points) When one goes backpacking, one tries to go as light as possible, but there is always room for about 9 pounds of things that make the trip sort of special. The enjoyment of six different items has been rated and they are restricted by weight. Given the following ratings and weights, determine what should be taken to maximize enjoyment using the Slippery Algorithm. (Cheese $= C$, Tennis Shoes $= T$, Bota Bag $= B$, Novel $= N$, Toilet Paper $= TP$, Extra Butane $= X$.)

Maximize Enjoyment $= 6C + 13T + 7B + 10N + 6TP + 3X$

subject to: $2C + 4T + 2B + 3N + TP + 2X \leqslant 9$ pounds

5. (15 points) Rewrite the following problem in the correct form for Implicit Enumeration and solve the 0–1 problem.

Maximize Payoff $= 8P_1 + 6P_2 + 12P_3 + 10P_4$

subject to: $2P_1 + 3P_2 + 4P_3 + 3P_4 \leqslant 7$

6. (20 points) Solve the following Integer Programming problem by Branch & Bound, branching off of X_1.

Maximize Profit $= 5X_1 + 3X_2$
subject to: $5X_1 + 2X_2 \leq 10$
$X_1 + X_2 \leq 4$

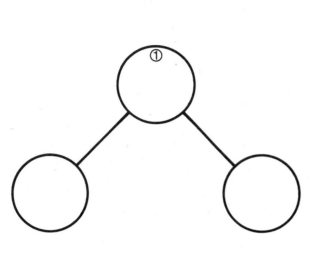

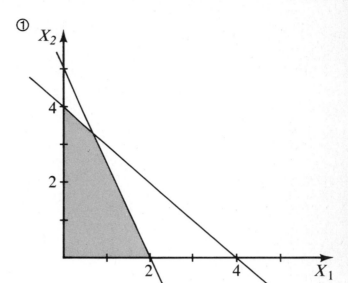

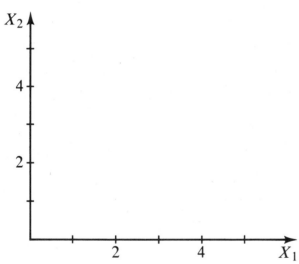

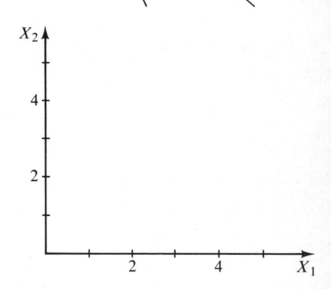

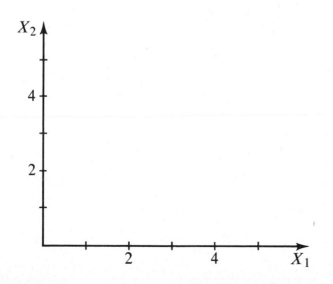

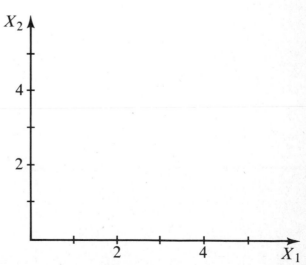

7. (15 points) Given the West Coast Lock Box case (page 270), explain what would happen to the solution if the fixed costs for San Diego and Los Angeles were switched. What would be the allocation to each box and the total costs?

7.10 REFERENCES

1. R. E. D. Woolsey, "A Candle to Saint Jude, or Four Real-World Applications of Integer Programming," *Interfaces*, vol. 2, Feb. 1972, pp. 20–27.

2. A. H. Land and A. G. Doig, "An Automatic Method of Solving Discrete Programming Problems," *Econometrica*, vol. 28, 1960, pp. 497–520.

3. R. E. D. Woolsey, "A Novena to Saint Jude, or Four Edifying Case Studies in Mathematical Programming," *Interfaces*, vol. 4, Nov. 1973, pp. 32–39.

4. R. E. D. Woolsey and H. S. Swanson, *Operations Research for Immediate Applications* (New York: Harper & Row, 1975).

5. E. Balas, "An Additive Algorithm for Solving Linear Programs with Zero-One Variables," *Operations Research*, vol. 13, 1965, pp. 517–549.

6. D. R. Plane and G. A. Kochenberger, *Operations Research for Managerial Decisions*, chap. 4: Zero–One Integer Programming (Homewood, Ill.: Irwin, 1974).

7. H. Salkin, *Integer Programming* (Reading, Mass.: Addison-Wesley, 1974).

8. S. Zionts, *Linear and Integer Programming* (Englewood Cliffs, N.J.: Prentice-Hall, 1973).

8
nonlinear programming

Nonlinear programming has been called "not linear programming" by Kenneth Boulding, economist at the University of Colorado. This is usually the classification for problems that don't fit into the nice neat categories that have preceded this chapter. Boulding also paraphrased Pascal's remark, "nothing stays put for long" by remarking that "nothing is linear for long." Essentially the reality of the dynamics of life forces us into dealing with problems that are not simple linear representations, or even combinatorial 0–1 decisions, but complicated nonlinear equations.

We experience some of these nonlinearities in our own lives: as production volume goes up, the per-unit cost goes down; the more lead we add to gasoline, the less per-unit increase we have in octane rating; we experience the "law of diminishing returns" on everything from work to investments. We quickly learn that life is not simply linear, nor static, and that we either have to make a series of simple decisions (using linear approximations to life) or one very complicated decision. In this chapter we will investigate some ways to deal with nonlinear problems, and we will again simplify the approach so that you may understand the underlying reasons for such techniques.

INCIDENT: GETTING THE LEAD OUT

Before the days of pollution control one of the easiest ways to raise the octane level in gasoline was to add lead. Unfortunately, for each ounce of lead added, the gasoline octane rating would not always go up by the same amount. Thus for the first ounce it would rise maybe 10 points, for the second 8, for the third 5, and so on. This is decidedly nonlinear, and to combat this, the objective function can be broken up into a "piecewise" linear function. By adding several extra variables, it can be incorporated into the gasoline-blending model for refineries.

INCIDENT: EXPERIENCE COUNTS

A large midwestern chemical company has the need of solving several nonlinear programming problems concerned with its distillation columns. Since the problems are always in the same form, but with different coefficients, it has discovered a search routine that seems to be very effective in its solution. Other routines did not converge or took extremely long to

converge, but after much investigation the company found an algorithm that could give good results quickly and cheaply for its specialized problem.

8.1 GEOMETRIC PROGRAMMING

Duffin, Peterson, and Zener[1] have made use of a simple theorem from mathematics that the average of n numbers is always greater than or equal to the nth root of the product of those numbers. Thus for two numbers greater than zero,

$$\frac{A + B}{2} \geq (AB)^{1/2}.$$

If A were to equal 1 and B to equal 9, we would have $(1 + 9)/2 \geq (1 \times 9)^{1/2}$ or $5 \geq 3$. Regardless of what positive weights or contributions we would have, it is generally true that

$$C_1 A + C_2 B \geq (A)^{C_1}(B)^{C_2}$$

In the above example the contributions were each $\frac{1}{2}$ or 50 percent. If $C_1 = \frac{2}{3}$ and $C_2 = \frac{1}{3}$, then

$$\tfrac{2}{3}(1) + \tfrac{1}{3}(9) \geq (1)^{\frac{2}{3}}(9)^{\frac{1}{3}}$$

or

$$3.666 \geq 2.07.$$

Obviously the contributions C_i must add up to 1.00. This can be further generalized to

$$C_1 A + C_2 B + C_3 D + \ldots + C_{10} K \geq$$
$$(A)^{C_1}(B)^{C_2}(D)^{C_3} \ldots (K)^{C_{10}}$$

Thus the minimum of the arithmetic mean (the left-hand side) will be equal to the maximum of the geometric mean (the right-hand side) when certain conditions are met. The idea then in geometric programming is to take a complicated nonlinear equation of the form of the left-hand side and convert it to an even more complicated-looking equation like the right-hand side. However, the interesting thing about this type of problem solving is that under certain conditions the second equation becomes very easy to solve. Furthermore we find the optimal minimum cost before we find the optimal values of the variables.

The only nonlinear problem that we have encountered to date is the inventory problem, which is nonlinear because the formula for the average total cost contains a term that has a variable in the denominator. This technique of geometric programming is very handy for problems that are encountered in engineering design, economics (exponential formulas), and inventory formulas.

We will also see a similarity between this technique and the maximal flow/minimal cut in that the primal and dual problems are closely associated with each other. We will be interested in solving problems having some formula that looks as follows:

$$\text{ATC} = \frac{400}{Q^2} + 6\sqrt{Q}$$

which is highly nonlinear.

The first problem, the arithmetic mean, is usually called the "primal problem" and the second problem is referred to as the "dual problem." As we have seen in previous chapters, this is not an unusual property. We will set up a dual problem from the primal, solve for the optimal profit of the dual, and use that value to find the value of the variables for the primal. The dual problem will tell us the cost contributions that each term in the primal gives to the total cost.

Quick & Clean Algorithm: Geometric Programming[2]

1. Construct the dual problem by dividing the constant in each term by its cost contribution C_i and raising that to the C_ith power. Multiply all the resulting terms together.
2. Sum up all the cost contributions to 100 percent (1.0).
3. For each variable in the primal, write another equation using the exponent of that variable in each term as the coefficient for the contribution and set = 0.
4. Solve for the value of the cost contributions C_i's.
5. Determine the maximum profit of the dual using the values of C_i.
6. From the minimum cost (which equals maximum profit) find the value(s) of each primal variable.

Example. Let us take as an example a simple inventory problem. We will assume that there is a demand of 80 units per month, a set-up cost of $4.00, and a carrying cost of the inventory of $0.10 per unit per month. Thus our average total cost (ATC) will be:

$$\text{ATC} = \frac{(4)(80)}{Q} = \frac{Q}{2}(\$0.10).$$

We wish to find the value of Q that will minimize the average total cost. This is the primal problem. We can simplify it to:

$$\text{ATC} = \frac{320}{Q} + 0.05Q$$

or

$$\text{ATC} = 320Q^{-1} + 0.05Q^1.$$

The dual problem becomes:

$$\text{Maximize Profit} = \left(\frac{320}{C_1}\right)^{C_1} \left(\frac{0.05}{C_2}\right)^{C_2}$$

where C_1 is the cost contribution for the first term of ATC and C_2 for the second term.

We know from mathematics that:

$$\text{Primal} \geq \text{Dual}$$

and

$$\text{Minimum Primal} = \text{Maximum Dual}.$$

Next we write that the sum of the cost contributions must be 100 percent:

$$C_1 + C_2 = 1.00$$

and then that the sum of the cost contributions times the exponent on Q equals zero:

$$-1C_1 + 1C_2 = 0.$$

Now we have two equations with two unknowns, which are easy to solve. In fact the last equation says that $C_1 = C_2$ or, in other words, the cost contribution of the two terms is equal. This means that the average fixed costs equal the average variable costs at the optimum, which is what we discovered in the inventory chapter. Thus,

$$C_1 = C_2 = \tfrac{1}{2} \quad \text{or} \quad 50 \text{ percent.}$$

Our next step is to determine the value of the dual:

$$\left(\frac{320}{\tfrac{1}{2}}\right)^{\tfrac{1}{2}} \left(\frac{0.05}{\tfrac{1}{2}}\right)^{\tfrac{1}{2}} = (64)^{\tfrac{1}{2}} = \$8.00.$$

Thus the maximum of the dual is equal to $8.00, and so the minimum of the primal = $8.00. Since each term of ATC equals 50 percent of the cost, $0.05Q = \tfrac{1}{2}(\$8) = \$4.00$.

Solving for Q, we find that $Q = 80$. Thus,

$$\text{ATC} = 320/80 + 0.05(80) = \$4.00 + \$4.00 = \$8.00.$$

This example is a very simple illustration of the power of geometric programming, and as was previously mentioned, under certain conditions these problems can be very quickly and easily solved. In this case the degree of difficulty of solving the problem is zero, meaning that it isn't very difficult to solve. The degree of difficulty is calculated by computing the number of terms in the original problem minus the number of variables minus 1. Thus DD = $2 - 1 - 1 = 0$ for this example. When the degree of difficulty is greater than zero, the problem solving becomes more difficult but not impossible. Much information can be gained from formulating problems as geometric programming problems, and at least bounds can be put on the solution values for the dual variables. Thus we can learn about how much each term might contribute in terms of the percentage of the overall costs. The references at the end of this chapter may be consulted for problems of more than 0 degrees of difficulty and for problems with constraints.

One last point is that you should be aware that once again we have introduced the dual of a problem and used information from it to solve our original problem.

pipeline design

An application of design engineering is the problem of designing pipelines. These lines may be used for pumping crude oil (such as the Alaskan pipeline), water, salt water, waste products, and so on. One of the factors in the design phase is to determine the diameter and length of pipe that will minimize costs. In the Minimal Spanning Tree section the problems of minimizing length were covered. Now the additional problem of determining the diameter must also be handled.

For pipes of smaller diameters the cost of pumping is less due to the fact that only so much volume can be pushed through the pipes at any one time. The larger the diameter, the larger the pumps and the amount of pressure that must be produced. The cost for pumping more water is proportional to the cube of the diameter, and in this particular case it is $100D^3$, where D is the diameter of the pipe in feet.

However, if small-diameter piping is used, the costs for laying a certain amount of pipe to handle the necessary volume go up. The larger the diameter of pipe, the lower the cost of the piping per unit of volume flow. Thus two costs need to be balanced. The cost for the piping is proportional to the square of the diameter and is $150/D^2$.

It is therefore necessary to determine the cost of the pipeline as a function of its diameter and to find out what value of the diameter will minimize this cost. Thus the balance must be made between pumping capacity and cost effectiveness:

$$\text{Cost} = 100D^3 + \frac{150}{D^2}$$

where cost is in terms of $1000. These determinations were made for a pipeline system bringing water down the Feather River system (a highly controversial and politically hot topic) in California. What value would you recommend, given the above data, and how much would it cost? Ranges of diameter values go from 6 to 30 inches, where D is in feet (thus from $\tfrac{1}{2}$ to $2\tfrac{1}{2}$ feet).

Solution

Recommendation
One-foot diameter pipe should be used to minimize the costs of the pipeline.

Numerical Answer. The minimum cost = $250,000, and the diameter = 1.0 foot. The cost contribution for the first term $(100D^3)$ = 40 percent = $100,000, and that of the second term $(150/D^2)$ = 60 percent = $150,000.

Math Work. Cost = $100D^3 + 150/D^2$.

1. Dual = $\left(\dfrac{100}{C_1}\right)^{C_1} \cdot \left(\dfrac{150}{C_2}\right)^{C_2}$.

2. The equations are:

$C_1 + C_2 = 1$ all cost contributions = 100 percent

and

3. $3C_1 - 2C_2 = 0$ all exponents on D sum to zero.

4. Solving, $2C_2 = 3C_1$ or $C_2 = \frac{3}{2}C_1$, and substituting in the first equation we get:

$$C_1 + \tfrac{3}{2}C_1 = 1 \quad \text{or} \quad \tfrac{5}{2}C_1 = 1$$

and thus,

$$C_1 = \tfrac{2}{5} \quad \text{and} \quad C_2 = \tfrac{3}{5}.$$

5. The dual is then

$$\text{Profit} = \left(\frac{100}{\frac{2}{5}}\right)^{\frac{2}{5}} \cdot \left(\frac{150}{\frac{3}{5}}\right)^{\frac{3}{5}} = (250)^{\frac{2}{5}}(250)^{\frac{3}{5}} = 250.$$

6. Now we can solve for D, knowing that the first term in the cost equation contributes $\frac{2}{5}$ or 40 percent of the cost:

$$100D^3 = \tfrac{2}{5}(250) = 100 \quad \text{or} \quad D^3 = 1$$

thus,

$$D = 1.0 \text{ foot.}$$

INCIDENT: REDUCING A COMPLEX PROBLEM TO A SIMPLE ONE

A unique application of geometric programming involves a complicated statistical equation (max-imum likelihood function) derived from data collected by the Wyoming Game and Fish Commission. The Commission had statistics on how many licenses had been sold to hunt big game (deer, elk, and antelope) for each animal. For some obscure (probably political) reason the Commission wanted to know the total hunter population. It was not practical to count all licenses held by single persons (in 1964 there were 87,993). The formula had been tediously solved each year by one method after another with varying degrees of success and at high expense. Then one year a consultant from a Midwestern university volunteered (for a fee, of course) to solve the problem using geometric programming. The only difficulty was that there were hundreds of degrees of difficulty in the problem. With, however, some clever rearranging and using some more advanced techniques, the problem was solved easily, quickly, and by an order of magnitude cheaper than before.

gray cast iron

When a cast iron melt alloy is cooled down from a temperature above 2066°F, it will produce gray or white cast iron, depending upon the cooling rate. Relatively slow cooling forms gray cast iron; very fast cooling forms white cast iron. White cast iron is brittle and not used very much. The gray cast iron has graphite flakes in the matrix, and the bigger the flakes, the less strong the cast iron will be. The big flakes have a tendency to be formed under very slow cooling and also when the melt is heated up just above 2066°F. When heated well above 2066°F, all graphite particles will be dissolved so that there is nothing in the melt to act as nucleus for graphite flakes to form around.

Thus a faster cooling rate and a high temperature of the melt hinders the production of high strength cast iron. In selling cast iron there is a higher price per pound for greater strength, but it costs more money to heat to high temperatures and to cool at fast rates (where R will be the rate of cooling at degrees Fahrenheit per minute).

The manufacturer of cast iron wants to maximize profit by balancing the cost of producing a good-grade gray cast iron and the profit for it. He gets $0.05 per pound for cast iron with a strength of 20,000 psi (pounds per square inch). For each additional 20,000 psi increase in strength he gets 4¢ extra. However, higher melt temperature costs money, and the estimated cost for this is 1¢ per 100°F above 2066°F. It also costs money to have a fast cooling rate, an estimated $(R/20)^2(2.0)$ cents per pound. But the manufacturer will also save some money if a fast cooling rate is used; that is, the casting goes faster and he saves money in labor costs. This amounts to approximately $(20/R)(0.5)$ cents per pound of cast iron. Thus he wants to minimize his cost, which is a combination of the two costs. Find the value of R that will determine this and the minimum cost.

$$\text{Cost} = \frac{R^2}{200} + \frac{10}{R}.$$

INCIDENT: GEOMETRIC PROGRAMMING PROVIDES A PRACTICAL ANSWER

Even when an exact solution cannot be found, there can be valuable information in the formulation of the problem. Such was the case for a chemical engineering problem faced by a large chemical manufacturer in the Midwest. In trying to design a certain tank for a sophisticated chemical process, the design engineers knew from practical experience that the height was always greater than the diameter when the volume was above a certain amount. Applying geometric programming, it became very evident that the cost contribution from the top and the bottom would never be greater than the contribution from the sides of the tank, and thus it should always be higher rather than wider. Thus mathematics finally proved what practical experience had known all along. (Or had practical experience proved that mathematics was correct?)

glass trees

A large gift and souvenir shop in the Northeast orders several types of glass art, including trees spun from glass which are quite elegant looking. In order to best display these, they are put on glass shelves with a special lighting that makes them very attractive. They sell for $17 each and move quite briskly, sales averaging about 2 a day or about 360 per year. The shop also handles other glass items, which are displayed in the same area as well as in another portion of the shop that sells pottery. The gift shop is located in a conveniently placed shopping mall which caters to a fairly affluent clientele. Ordering costs for these glass trees are about $15 for each order, regardless of the size of the order. The major costs for carrying inventory are the handling costs, which arise from dusting and rearranging the trees that are displayed. Since all the inventory is up front where it can be seen, this can be quite costly. But the biggest problem arises from the fact that as the inventory doubles, it seems that there is four times the work of cleaning, dusting, rearranging, and caring for the displays. Thus the cost of inventory is not linear but

nonlinear, acting as an average of the square of what is in inventory. Costs for carrying are determined to be $1.60 per tree per year, and the current ordering policy has been to treat the situation as a regular inventory problem, with the optimum amount to order being seven dozen trees each time an order is placed. Given this new model for average total costs, determine what amount should be ordered and how much the average total cost was under the old plan versus the new ordering policy that you will recommend.

$$\text{ATC} = \frac{C_0 D}{Q} + \left(\frac{Q^2}{2}\right) C_c.$$

INCIDENT: INTERNATIONAL APPLICATIONS

When the cost of materials is very expensive, it can make quite a difference whether there can be a 10 percent reduction in the surface area of a design. Such a case existed in the design of steel buildings in Europe, where geometric programming was employed to reduce costs significantly. Also in a major shipyard in Norway applications of geometric programming reduced costs by optimally designing bulkheads with proper constraints for strength and stress, as well as for the optimal size and type of a fishing fleet.

lathe speeds

In metal machine lathe operations the life expectancy of tools depends upon several factors. Cutting speed (revolutions per second) and linear feed (speed of pushing the tool into the piece) are two of the main variables that determine how long the tool will last.

The owner of a small machine shop wants to give a cost bid to the A. C. Engine Repair Company for finish-turning cast steel truck pistons. Each piston is 3.93 inches in diameter, 5.38 inches in length, and has a Brinell hardness number of 210. His shop has only one single-spindle automatic lathe, and he does not want to use cutting fluid. He buys tools at Hendrie and Bolthoff Supply for $1.48 per edge. Since shop overhead is $5.00 per hour and labor $3.70 per hour, total operating costs come to $0.145 per minute.

Feed is directly related to maximum peak-to-valley height in surface craters. For pistons the surface, before crisscross grooving, must be machined at a speed of less than 9 inches per minute. Thus he wants to determine to what speed and feed he should set his lathe so that he will minimize the cost of his tooling, but at the same time maximize his profits by producing the machined pistons as fast as possible. After due deliberation, his costs are figured as

$$\text{Cost} = \frac{10}{FS} + 50F^3S^{1/3} + \frac{4}{F}.$$

Here we have two components that will decrease the cost of our production and one that will increase the cost. The one component is related to both speed and feed and is very critical. S is measured in 100 revolutions per minute, and F is in feet per minute (and must not exceed 0.75 foot per minute). Normally a job like this is run at 500 revolutions per minute and 0.4 foot per minute. Determine the optimal speed S and feed F and the minimal cost, and compare with the current operating procedure.

Supplementary Problems

1. Solve the following geometric programming problem.

$$\text{Minimize } P = 20 \sqrt{A} + \frac{400}{A^3}$$

   a. What is the dual objective function?
   b. What are the dual constraints?
   c. Solve the dual constraints.
   d. Find the optimal value of the objective function.
   e. Find the optimal value of A.

2. Solve the geometric programming problem given on page 286. Find the minimum ATC and the optimal value of Q using geometric programming.

$$\text{Minimize ATC} = \frac{400}{Q^2} + 6 \sqrt{Q}$$

8.2 DYNAMIC PROGRAMMING

Richard Bellman[3] developed the following technique of tackling some very tough nonlinear problems by breaking down the problem into n simple problems instead of one n-dimensional nonlinear problem. Thus the problems that can be solved by this technique must be separable (that is, each term must contain only one variable). Then we are able to make one simple decision n times rather than n decisions simultaneously. These problems may be linear, integer, or nonlinear in each term, and the technique will often work for more complicated problems more

effectively than for simple problems. Each problem is broken up into a set of "stages," and at each stage a decision is made as to what value (or state) the next variable should have.

The heart of this technique is the principle of optimality, which states that for the nth step of the process to be optimal, every previous step ($n - 1$, $n - 2, \ldots$) must also be optimal. Thus most problems are solved "backwards"; that is, if we had one decision to go, what would we decide to do? After we have decided the optimal action with one decision to go, we would then back up one more variable and decide what to do if we had two variables (decisions) left. Eventually we arrive at having to decide what to do with n variables, but we are helped by the fact that we know what to do with the last $n - 1$ variables.

We have already employed this technique in the Network chapter when we solved the shortest route problem. By the time we reached the last node and found the shortest route from that node to the beginning, we had already found the solution to all the other nodes. We also only made one decision at each step, which was to find the next nearest node to the origin or beginning.

Consider the following problem: There are three investments with given returns for certain amounts invested, and there is $5000 that can be invested in these projects. Determine the amount that should be invested in each project so that no more than a total of $5000 is invested, and each project is invested in no more than once.

Invest	Investment 1	Investment 2	Investment 3
$1000	$1500	$1100	$1250
$2000	$2800	$2300	$2500
$3000	$3600	$3500	$3800
$4000	$5100	$5000	$4900
$5000	$6100	$6300	$6200

Return

It is assumed that these returns are for the same time period for all investments.

Quick & Dirty Algorithm: Dynamic Programming[3]

1. Starting at the last two stages, determine how much you would allocate for the last two variables for each possible amount of money remaining. Develop a summary table for this.
2. Add one more variable and determine how much you would allocate for it, considering the combination of the payoff in the summary table and for the current variable. Develop another summary table.

3. Continue in the same fashion until all variables have been accounted for. Then from the summary tables determine the values of all the variables that maximize the return or profit.

It is quickly noticed that the problem is not linear because the payoffs are not uniform. If they were, we would simply apply the Bang for the Buck principle and invest everything in the second investment and make $6300. If the payoffs were uniform, then for investment 1 they would increase by $1220 for each $1000 invested, by $1260 for each $1000 invested in investment 2, and finally by $1240 for each $1000 invested in investment 3.

Applying dynamic programming we will decide what we would do if we had only the third project to invest in and anywhere from 0 to $5000 to invest. This is seen from the last column of the problem. We would invest what we have left in investment 3.

Looking at our example, let us decide what we would do if we had only $1000 left to invest and only the last two investments to consider. We could invest $1000 in investment 2 and make $1100 or in investment 3 and make $1250. Obviously, if we had $1000 left, we would invest it all in investment 3.

If we had $2000 left, we could do one of three things: invest $2000 in investment 2 and make $2300, or invest $1000 in investment 2 and $1000 in investment 3 and make $1100 + $1250 = $2350, or invest it all in investment 3 and make $2500. The biggest return is to put it all into investment 3.

The total return can also be illustrated in tabular form, where the amount left to be invested is in one column, and the amount to invest is in the columns under investment 2. It will be assumed that what is not invested in investment 2 would be put into investment 3.

Amount Left	Investment 2					
	$0	$1000	$2000	$3000	$4000	$5000
$1000	$1250	$1100	—	—	—	—
$2000	$2500	$2350	$2300	—	—	—
$3000	$3800	$3600	$3550	$3500	—	—
$4000	$4900	$4900	$4800	$4750	$5000	—
$5000	$6200	$6000	$6100	$6000	$6250	$6300

The summary table that results from this tells us what we would do with a certain amount of money left over and investments 2 and 3 to consider:

Amount Left	Return	Investment 2
$1000	$1250	$0
$2000	$2500	$0
$3000	$3800	$0
$4000	$5000	$4000
$5000	$6300	$5000

Thus we see one benefit of dynamic programming already: we have the optimum solution to a problem involving only two investments right now.

Now we continue by adding the first investment. Since we have $5000 to invest, we can make up a small table as before with all the possible alternatives:

Amount Left	Investment 1					
	$0	$1000	$2000	$3000	$4000	$5000
$5000	$6300	$6500	$6600	$6100	$6350	$6100

Thus the optimal thing to do would be to invest $2000 in investment 1, which would leave $3000 to be invested in the last two projects, and from our summary table we see that with $3000 left for the last two investments, we would put $0 into investment 2 and therefore $3000 into investment 3.

Investment 1 yields $2800 for $2000 and investment 3 yields $3800 for $3000 invested, for a total of $6600.

You will notice that during this solution procedure, we were making only some very simple decisions, but a lot of them. Instead of having to decide on all three investments simultaneously, we only had to decide between one investment and what to do with the rest of the money. Thus we decided how much to invest in investment 2 and the rest would automatically go to investment 3. Then we decided how much would go into investment 1 and the rest would automatically go to the "two-investment" problem that we had solved in the summary table. If we were to add another investment, we would have to finish the above table by adding the "Amount Left" of $1000 to $4000, then summarizing and putting it into a summary table.

To give a better idea of what we are trying to do, let us return to the shortest route problem (which is really a dynamic programming algorithm) and explain what is happening. Consider the problem below, which consists of three stages and is concerned with finding the shortest route from node 1 to node 7 (Figure 8.1).

Figure 8.1

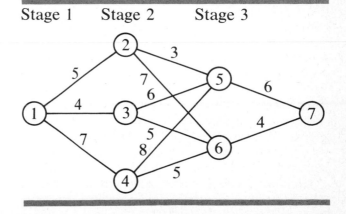

Now consider that we are at stage 3. If we are at city 5, then we will go to city 7 from there at a distance of 6 units. Alternatively, if we are at city 6 we will go to city 7 at a distance of 4 units.

Backing up one stage, we see that at stage 2, if we are at city 2 we can choose to go to city 5 or 6 at a total distance of (3+6) or (7+4) units. We will choose to go 2–5–7 for the shortest total of 9 units. The shortest route again is chosen for cities 3 and 4 with the results shown in Figure 8.2.

Now we back up to stage 1 and choose the minimum of (5+9), (4+9), and (7+9), which is 13. The shortest route is 1–3–6–7. The simplified diagram of Figure 8.2 for stage 2 is in effect the summary table for the investments. At each stage the solution is optimal from that point to the end.

Figure 8.2

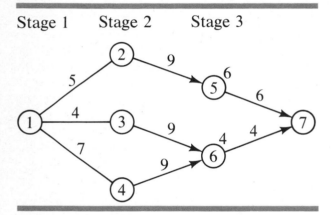

Stage 1   Stage 2   Stage 3

Another example might serve well to show the power and versatility of dynamic programming. Let us consider the proposal analysis example from Section 7.7 in which we used implicit enumeration to find an optimal solution. From inspection it can be seen that the constraints for aerothermodynamics can never be violated so they can be ignored. Also the tracking system can never be built because it requires four worker-months of flight mechanics time, and there are only three available, so we can eliminate the tracking system variable as well as the flight mechanics constraint that will never be violated by the other three variables. Thus we are left with a simple capital budgeting problem that looks as follows:

Maximize Profit =
$$\$1000 \, DU + \$2000 \, SD + \$4000 \, D$$

subject to:

$$DU + SD + 3D \leq 4$$

computer simulation budget in worker-months.

Looking at the last variable, the distorter (D), we can make up a dynamic programming table in a

slightly different fashion, realizing that these variables will have values only of 0 or 1.

Computer Simulation (worker-months left)	Distorter 0	1
1	—	—
2	—	—
3	—	$4000
4	—	$4000

The next variable to consider is the signal detector (SD), and we make up a table with the column for SD = 0 being the summary table for the previous table.

Computer Simulation (worker-months left)	Signal Detector 0	1
1	—	$2000
2	—	$2000
3	$4000	$2000
4	$4000	$6000

Finally we back up to the first variable, the detection unit (DU). In this case we know how much computer simulation time we have left, 4 worker-months.

Computer Simulation (worker-months left)	Detection Unit 0	1
4	$6000	$5000

Thus we see that the optimal strategy yields $6000, and as we look at the last table, we should not invest in the detection unit (DU = 0) and still have 4 worker-months left over. Going to the previous table shows that the optimal strategy with 4 worker-months left is to do the signal detector project, which will use up 1 worker-month and leave us 3 worker-months. Going to the first table we see that the optimal strategy there is to do the distorter project.

This example serves to show several things. First dynamic programming is a way of approaching problems by breaking down *n* simultaneous decisions into *n* single decisions, and that different problems can be cast into the same type of form for solution by dynamic programming. The second thing to note is that the capital budgeting problem can be solved by some way other than implicit enumeration or the slippery algorithm.

limited investment

Consider four investment opportunities that will allow investing either $0, $10, $20, or $30 and the fact that you have only a total of $50 to invest in any or all of these. The investments and their returns are listed at the top of the next column:

Invest	Investment 1	Investment 2	Investment 3	Investment 4
$10	$12	$14	$11	$13
$20	$25	$26	$24	$27
$30	$38	$35	$37	$34

Solution

Recommendation

Put $20 in investments 1 and 4, and $10 in investment 2 for a return of $66.

Numerical Answer

Investment	Invest	Return
1	$20	$25
2	$10	$14
3	$ 0	$ 0
4	$20	$27
		$66

Math Work. Starting with the last two investments, let us make up a table to show all the possible combinations of investments. It is assumed that what is not invested in investment 3 is put into investment 4 (up to $30).

| Amount Left | Investment 3 | | | |
	$0	*$10*	*$20*	*$30*
$10	$13	$11		
$20	$27	$24	$24	
$30	$34	$38	$37	$37
$40	$34	$45	$51	$50
$50	$34	$45	$51	$64

This leads to our summary table:

Amount Left	Return	Investment 3
$10	$13	$ 0
$20	$27	$ 0
$30	$38	$10
$40	$51	$20
$50	$64	$30

Note for the $0 column in investment 3 that it cannot rise above $34 since only $30 can be put into investment 4 and we have required that $0 go to investment 3.

The second table is now computed, adding investment 2 as an option:

| Amount Left | Investment 2 | | | |
	$0	*$10*	*$20*	*$30*
$10	$13	$14		
$20	$27	$27	$26	
$30	$38	$41	$39	$35
$40	$51	$52	$53	$48
$50	$64	$65	$64	$62

The summary table becomes:

Amount Left	Return	Investment 2
$10	$14	$10
$20	$27	$0,10
$30	$41	$10
$40	$53	$20
$50	$65	$10

Finally, we can make up our last table by adding investment 1:

| Amount Left | Investment 1 | | | |
	$0	*$10*	*$20*	*$30*
$50	$65	$65	$66	$65

Our maximum occurs with investing $20 in investment 1 and a total return of $66. This would leave us with $30, and going to the summary table for investment 2 we see that with $30 left for three investments, we would put $10 into investment 2. This now leaves us $20, and going back to the summary table for investment 3 we see that with $20 left we should invest none in investment 3 and thus all $20 in investment 4.

You may have noted that as we progressed through the tables, the second column in each new table has been the Return column for the previous summary table.

computer cutbacks

Let us consider the Computer Contracts case in Section 7.7 and that a budget cutback is being considered that will drastically affect all the scheduled projects. All that the computer department manager can ascertain is that there will at least be $8000 available in the budget for the four projects that he would deem absolutely safe to consider. These are as follows:

Project	Computer Budget	Payoff
Laser gun	$5000	$800,000
Nuclear waste	$4000	$1,100,000
Urban design	$2000	$400,000
Probe III	$6000	$800,000

The manager would like to plan upon the contingency that there may be anywhere from $8000 to $10,000 available, and because of that he is hesitant to solve this using implicit enumeration, which would have to be resolved for each specific case. Therefore dynamic programming should be employed and a final recommendation made, depending upon whether there will be $8000, $9000, or $10,000 available.

INCIDENT: APPLICATIONS STILL NEED COMMON SENSE

In a note of Rustagi and Doub[4] it was asserted that, "whether it is a fighter airplane, a ship, or a tank, the basic structure of the optimal armor-allocation decision process seems to be the same." This statement was then followed by an excellent formulation of the optimal armor-allocation problem as a dynamic program for a tank. It was strongly implied that the same formulation, or a similar one using dynamic programming, in any case could be extended to a ship or a plane. However, it should be considered that the optimal armoring of a fighter plane may introduce additional constraints to a level where dynamic programming may become computationally infeasible.

For example, the weight distribution of even a few pounds of armor must be considered in the light of relative stresses and strains on the airplane as a whole. Additional armor added to a plane will often require considerable redesign just to maintain the present performance of the aircraft, or to drop its capability as little as possible. This redesign will then alter the formulation of the dynamic program, which then may generate a different placement of armor, which then leads to redesign, which will then lead to, . . . and so on.

As an afterthought we should also note that the relationships between the design characteristics are seldom (1) linear, nor even (2) separable, thus again casting some doubt as to the efficacy of dynamic programming for this application. Finally, one just might suspect that if a plane is armored like a tank, it just might fly like a tank. Thus, quite obviously, you should not abandon common sense when applying this or any other algorithm to a problem. It is essential that the problem satisfy the assumptions for using the algorithms that are intended to find the solutions.

Consider the following five investments that are available to a certain investor. These are different projects in which she may invest $1000, $2000, $3000, $4000, or $5000 with exepcted returns. These returns are nonlinear due to certain factors of risk, and she may only invest once (or not at all) in each investment. Thus she is not allowed to invest $1000 several times in the dress shop. Given the investment possibilities in Table 8.1, determine which set of them will return the most money if a total of $10,000 is available to be invested.

The sharp investor will note that most of these investments are very nonlinear and there are incentives to either attract a lot of small investments or not have a big payoff until a lot of money is put into the investment. Thus the apartment building is a very poor investment for small amounts of money, but turns out to be much better the more money is put in. On the other hand the dress shop starts out the best and winds up as the worst for a lot of money invested.

INCIDENT: SIMPLIFYING NONLINEAR PROBLEMS

A more classic (and successful) application involves the determination of which spare parts to include for a long submarine voyage subject to limitations of size and weight. This same problem is encountered in space launches, and can be formulated as a 0–1 problem or as a dynamic programming problem. In this case the objective function is hopelessly nonlinear, since it is the product of the probability of the survival of each piece of equipment. By using logarithms, the function can be transformed to a separable function and then solved by dynamic programming. This is a much easier approach than some of the 0–1 solution techniques and has proven efficient.

Table 8.1

Invest	Apartment Building	Dress Shop	Record Store	Burger Franchise	Shopping Plaza
$1,000	$2,000	$12,000	$10,000	$6,000	$4,000
$2,000	$9,000	$15,000	$20,000	$9,000	$10,000
$3,000	$12,000	$18,000	$25,000	$15,000	$16,000
$4,000	$32,000	$21,000	$30,000	$25,000	$33,000
$5,000	$40,000	$30,000	$40,000	$48,000	$41,000

contractor capital

One of the interesting facts about small contractors is their uniform inability to collect for their jobs and keep a good cash flow in their business. In the construction industry, many times the contractor must pay for things and then collect either from the main contractor or sell the work built on speculation. More small contractors go out of business because of bad cash flow than because they could not find jobs to do. Let us consider the case of a contractor with six possible jobs to work on, each of which requires a certain amount of capital with a nice return on the investment. The problem is that this contractor would be able to obtain only $8000. Using dynamic programming, determine which projects should be undertaken to maximize the profitability of the company.

Project	Payoff	Capital
Highway section	$10,000	$5,000
Home addition	$7,000	$2,000
Bank building	$12,000	$4,000
Parking lot	$4,000	$1,000
Gas station	$8,000	$3,000
Sewer section	$5,000	$2,000

Supplementary Problems

1. Given the 0–1 problem below, solve using dynamic programming.

   maximize profit $= 3P1 + 2P2 + 4P3$

   subject to: $\qquad P1 + 3P2 + 2P3 \leq 3$

2. Given the Another Investments case:
   a. Write the *summary* table for the last four projects.
   b. Instead of having the apartment building as the first project, substitute a yogurt shop, using the payoffs given below. Determine the optimal solution to the problem using dynamic programming.

Investment	Payoff
$1000	$ 5,000
2000	15,000
3000	26,000
4000	35,000
5000	44,000

8.3 PUZZLES AND CONTESTS

When faced with a very difficult nonlinear problem, about the only thing you can do (if it is not well structured) is to simply search for a good answer, and once that is found, continue to search for a better one until you run out of time, patience or money.

There are many types of search problems, ranging from one to two, three, and more dimensions. A good example of a three-dimensional search problem is the docking of a spacecraft with an orbiting laboratory. This is a very difficult problem, and in the case of our astronauts the area of search is greatly reduced but still remains extremely difficult.

Two-dimensional problems involve helicopters looking for enemy troop movement, planes looking for submarines, or reconnaissance planes looking for missile sites.

An example of one-dimensional search is a contest that AM radio stations will play from time to time, called "Hi–Lo." There is a certain amount of money in the jackpot (between 0 and $1000). Callers guess the amount and are told whether they are high or low. As people listen, they can narrow this amount down, and eventually someone gets it. This has also been done with four-digit license plates to give away motorcycles. The idea is that the listeners become interested as the range narrows down and scoff at those who guess outside the range.

In all these problems it is necessary to develop some kind of strategy, instead of just blindly guessing. ("Battleship" is also a good two-dimensional game.) We encounter a lot of these problems in the forms of games or puzzles, without realizing that most of life is exactly like this. Most of the situations we face in life are ill-defined problems for which we never develop strategies, and so we blindly grope along, being carried about by circumstances and reacting rather than acting and anticipating. A lot of this problem solving depends upon intuitive, "gut level" feel, rather than superior rational ability. What is needed is a blend of both, an ability to "feel" a problem out and describe it to others, so that we can all act in some manner that will help us to go forward rather than grope around. These problems hopefully will be an aid toward that.

In this section several problems which have been used as contests are presented so that you may try your hand at developing some algorithm or method for finding a solution, without spending an inordinate amount of time hunting for the solution. There are many strategies to employ that we have encountered before.

1. *Greed.* This is the basic algorithm that we have learned in life and tends to give an answer, although usually it ignores trade-offs that could

yield a better answer. This is the basic Bang for the Buck type strategy.

2. *Local.* This involves hunting for the solution very carefully right where you are. Thus if hunting for submarines from reconnaissance aircraft, one hunts very carefully within that area, having a high probability of detecting the sub *if* one passes over it. This is also called "Low & Slow."

3. *Global.* This is the opposite of *Local* in that a quick search is done over the entire area. Again, if hunting for submarines, the plane would fly higher and faster, with a better probability of passing over the submarine, but a much lower probability of detecting it even if it is passed over. It is also called "High & Fast."

4. *Random.* In this case random guesses are given in the absence of any other knowledge of the problem in the hope that one will hit the right solution. This is also known as "Desperation" and is usually employed when we are running out of time, money, and especially patience.

The most discouraging thing about these puzzles and contests is that they are *not* won by mathematicians, operations researchers, or management scientists, but by grocery clerks, car salesmen, janitors, and others who have limited theoretical mathematical backgrounds. This leads us to the question of whether all this mathematical education prevents us from solving problems or if there are just some people who are born able to solve problems intuitively. In any case these problems are presented to "loosen you up" toward some intuitive problem solving along with some logic and common sense. In each case, develop a one-page algorithm explaining in simple English how to find a good solution to the problem.

baseball bingo

A sponsor of a local baseball-team radio broadcast conducts contests in the early part of the season during home stands. The winner of each contest receives $1000, and the contests are used as promotion to gain interest in attending games or in following the team. Each contestant must pick the winner of each game during a home stand. If there is a tie, then the winner is determined as the one who comes closest to guessing the total runs scored by all the teams during that home stand. Each entry must be placed on a special IBM preperforated card available at any of the sponsor's stores. The contestant must then punch out the proper holes corresponding to the teams he or she thinks will win and the total runs scored of all the teams involved. This must then be mailed in and postmarked no later than 24 hours

before the first game of the current home stand series.

During this year's season this contest was held for two home stands, one of seven games and one of nine games. Develop an algorithm or strategy to win this contest. How much money would you spend on your approach to win $1000? Would you actually do this?

amphora pipe tobacco

Amphora Pipe Tobacco offered a 14-day trip for two to the 1972 Olympic Games in Munich for the winner of this puzzle. The summary of the rules is given below. Develop a strategy for winning this game.

1. Using the letters from the words "Amphora Pipe Tobacco" make up as many words as you can, which are related to or specifically associated with *any* sport. Example: boat, hoop. "Sport" is defined as a particular activity or game (as hunting or an athletic game) engaged in for pleasure or recreation. Winners will be judged according to the highest number of eligible words made.

2. In building words you may use any letter as often as you wish. You may use a specific word only once. You may *not* use abbreviations, contractions, combining forms (such as prefixes and suffixes), words with a hyphen or apostrophe, or proper nouns. Word eligibility will be determined by independent qualified judges whose decision will be final. Only words appearing in the main body of any recent edition of Webster's New Collegiate Dictionary are eligible. "Main body" comprises words from A to Z inclusive, appearing in boldface type, but not including words referring to derivation.

3. Write your word list in alphabetical order, neatly, on a plain piece of paper. At the top you must then write your total number of words, your name, address, and zip code.

Write an algorithm that would describe how you would approach solving this puzzle.

microminiature integrated circuits

Microminiature integrated circuits are a combination of several "chips," all interconnected to perform a desired task. The number of chips that are required depends on the function of the circuit. Each chip is a circuit within itself and is connected to one or more of

Figure 8.3

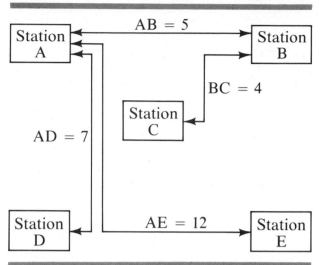

Distances	Interconnections
AB = 5	$C_1C_2 = 4$
AC = 4	$C_1C_3 = 2$
AD = 7	$C_1C_4 = 2$
AE = 12	$C_1C_5 = 0$
BC = 4	$C_2C_3 = 3$
BD = 12	$C_2C_4 = 0$
BE = 7	$C_2C_5 = 4$
CD = 4	$C_3C_4 = 4$
CE = 4	$C_3C_5 = 2$
DE = 5	$C_4C_5 = 4$

Determine a solution to this problem, and then try to design an algorithm for a more general case.

tangle towns

U.S. Tangle Towns is a syndicated puzzle run in various newspapers throughout the United States. Every few years the puzzle appears and is designed to promote sales and interest in the newspaper by offering large cash prizes and bonuses. In 1970 the top prize was $10,000 and a bonus of a new Cadillac if the winner had entered two new subscriptions. In 1975 the top prize was $12,500 and a new Lincoln Continental. There are hundreds of prizes offered, from cars to TV sets, radios, and so on. Two sets of about 30 fairly simple puzzles are solved, one each day, and then a gigantic tie breaker is offered at the end of the contest. The person with the highest total points for this tie breaker wins the contest, and it is a bear! Usually just three or four days are given for the solution, computer assistance is not allowed (and is highly impractical anyway), and the contest is consistently won by people who are not in the mathematics profession.

the other chips by etched copper strips. It is usually most desirable for economy, functionability, and reliability to minimize the lengths of copper interconnects.

In a given example it will require 5 chips to make a circuit board to perform a series of tasks within the memory circuitry of a computer. The basic layout of the board is shown in Figure 8.3.

The distance between two stations is estimated as an average. Orthogonal, rather than diagonal, distances are necessary due to etching and cross-connect restrictions.

The distance between stations and the number of interconnections between chips (Figure 8.4) are:

The game consists of a pool of available letters that can be used to spell different town names from a list of eligible names. Points are awarded for spelling these names, plus bonus points if the name contains certain letter combinations in order. If any letters are left over, points are deducted. A bonus is given if all the letters are used. The winners have always used all the letters.

This puzzle can be formulated as an integer programming problem, with the town names being 0–1 variables and the number of A's being one constraint, and so on. But the solution for such a problem would take an incredible amount of computer time on the fastest machine available. For example, three hours on an IBM 360/65 yielded an answer that was worse than just being greedy and doing it by hand.

The points and town names are given, along with a sample solution that was obtained by being greedy to show you a feasible solution. After having looked

Figure 8.4

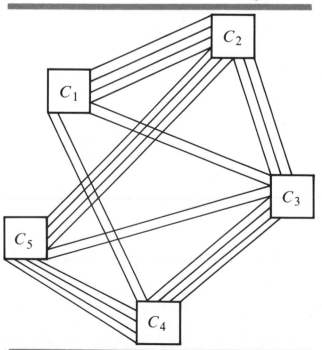

over and studied the problem, write up an algorithm to describe how you would approach solving the problem.

Score your solution on the following basis:

7 Points should be credited for each place name spelled from the puzzle letters and listed on the blank provided.

14 Points should be credited each time an "E" and an "R" appear together in a selected place name in that order, "ER."

16 Points should be credited each time an "A" and an "R" appear together in a selected place name in that order, "AR."

17 Points should be credited each time an "I" and an "N" appear together in a selected place name in that order, "IN."

21 Points should be credited each time an "A" and an "M" appear together in a selected place name in that order, "AM."

23 Points should be credited each time an "O" and an "L" appear together in a selected place name in that order, "OL."

69 Points should be credited if all puzzle letters in the Official Tie-Breaking Puzzle are used. (This credit is in addition to all credits listed.)

6 Points should be *deducted* for each letter in the Tie-Breaking Puzzle not used in the place names selected.

You have a total of 258 letters as follows:

27 A's	7 B's	12 C's	7 D's
20 E's	3 F's	7 G's	9 H's
15 I's	2 J's	7 K's	18 L's
9 M's	15 N's	18 O's	8 P's
3 Q's	15 R's	11 S's	13 T's
8 U's	4 V's	5 W's	3 X's
8 Y's	4 Z's		

The list of the 600 eligible town names with bonus points (if any) follows.

	Abbott		Allouez		Audubon		Birchleaf
	Abell		Allyn		Avoca		Birdeye
21	Abrams		Alsey		Aztec		Birney
	Absecon	14	Alverda				Birome
21	Acampo	21	Amesbury				Bivalve
	Acequia	23	Anahola		Backoo		Blairsden
14	Ackerly		Ancell		Baggs	14	Blocker
16	Acmar		Anchor		Baldwyn		Blomkest
21	Agawam	17	Angwin	21	Balsam		Bogota
	Agnos		Anselmo	16	Baraga	23	Bolivia
	Agra		Ansonia		Bashi	16	Bomarton
21	Alabama		Anvik		Belton		Bonita
21	Alamo	16	Arbyrd	14	Berwick	17	Brinklow
21	Alamosa	16	Argyle	16	Bexar		Brush
	Alkabo	21	Ashcamp	23	Bigpool		Buxton
16	Allardt	14	Aspermont		Bippus		
	Allgood		Atglen		Birchdale		

	Calais		Daisy		Gaza		
	Calcium		Dakota	14	Gerty		
	Calypso	16	Dalhart		Gilby		
17	Capulin		Dalzell	14	Girdler		
16	Caraway	17	Dauphin	14	Glazier		
16	Carrizozo	17	Daykin	21	Glenham		
	Caspian		Decatur		Glyndon		
	Catawba	21	Dedham	14	Gobler		
	Catesby		Delta	23	Goliad		
	Cayuga		Depoy		Gonvick		
	Cement		Dixmont	21	Gorham		
	Chalk		Dixon		Greig		
21	Chamois	23	Doland		Grelton		
21	Champion		Dothan		Gridley		
16	Chariton		Drasco		Grubbs		
30	Charleroi		Drewry		Grygla		
16	Charmian		Dreyfus				
	Chastang		Drift				
	Check		Driggs	21	Haddam		
	Chemult	17	Duquoin		Hagan		
	Chicota		Dutzow		Halfway		
	Chipley		Dwale		Halsey		
	Chireno			21	Hampden		
14	Chrysler			17	Hankins		
	Chula		Eagle		Hanska		
	Circle		Eakly		Happy		
	Cismont	32	Earlimart	16	Harvest		
	Clairette		Eastbank		Hatley		
	Clawson		Eastford		Hawks		
16	Clearco		Ebony		Haxtun		
	Cobalt		Ebro		Hazlet		
	Coggon		Eccles		Hebo		
	Cohoes		Eclipse		Helmuth		
	Coke		Eek		Hemlock		
23	Colburn		Ekwak		Hemple		
23	Colquitt	14	Eleroy		Hewett		
	Copake		Elijah		Higdon		
23	Corolla		Elkfork		Hiko		
17	Corwin	16	Elkhart		Hilda		
	Cowan		Excel	14	Hilger		
16	Coward			21	Hilham		
	Cowdrey				Hixton		
	Cowiche		Fabius		Hodge		
	Coyote	14	Fackler	23	Holmen		
	Cozad		Fagus	17	Hominy		
	Craig		Fairburn	17	Hopkins		
	Cremo		Fairfax	21	Hoquiam		
	Cusick		Fairgrove		Hoxie		
17	Cutshin		Fandon		Huey		
16	Cuzzart		Fanrock		Hugo		
			Felty		Hurley		
			Festus		Hytop		
			Fibre				
			Filson				
		17	Finly		Ibapah		
			Fishtrap		Idaho		
			Flatgap		Idria		
			Frakes	17	Index		
			Furlong		Iroquois		
			Furnace	17	Irvine		
			Fyffe		Island		
					Islip		
					Italy		
			Gaastra		Itasca		
			Gabbs				
			Galax				
			Galdia		Jabez		
		14	Gautier		Jamison		

14 Jasper
Jenks
Jiggs
Jodie
Joppa
Judson
14 Jupiter

Kadoka
21 Kalama
Kaliopi
Kaltag
16 Karnack
32 Kearsarge
Kechi
Kegley
Kehoe
Keith
Kenly
Kensal
Kent
Kenvir
Keokuk
Kewa
Killbuck
Kiln
17 Kinzua
Kipnuk
Kismet
Kobuk
Koch
Kokadjo
Kotzebue
Krebs
23 Kreole
Kulm

Ladd
Lake
21 Lambric
Landis
Lanexa
Langlois
Lantry
Lapel
Laquey
16 Larned
Latexo
Lawn
Leck
Lecompte
Ledoux
Lehr
Lenox
Lesage
16 Leshara
Letha
Levy
Lexsy
Limon
17 Lingle
Liscomb
Lititz
Llano

Lloyd
Lobata
Lodge
Logsden
Loma
Lopeno
Lopez
14 Louviers
Lovick
Lowry
Lugoff
17 Luling
Lutz
Lycan
Lynd
Lyons
Lytle

Macy
Madill
Madoc
Madrid
17 Magazine
Magna
16 Malabar
Manchaug
21 Mangham
Manly
17 Manquin
Mansura
Many
16 Marcum
16 Marquez
Mastic
Maud
Mayodan
Mays
Mecca
Mecosta
Medley
Melby
Meldrim
Menfro
Mexia
Micro
Middle
Milfay
Mimbres
Mims
Miracle
Miranda
Mize
Mobjack
Moffat
23 Mollusk
Mosby
Mound
Moweaqua
Moxahala
Muldrow
Mulga
Muncy
Muroc
Murphy

Nabb
Nace
Naknek
Nanuet
Napa
Nash
Nashotah
Natchez
Natick
Nauvoo
14 Naxera
Neafus
Nedrow
Nelse
Nemo
Neopit
Neshoba
Nesmith
Neva
Newdale
Newry
Ney
14 Nezperce
23 Nikolski
Niwot
Nixa
Noble
Nohly
Nucla
Nunez
14 Nursery
Nyac

Oaklyn
14 Obert
Occoquan
Odum
Ojibwa
Ojito
Okay
23 Olathe
Opelika
Oquawka
Oriskany
17 Orwin
Osage
23 Osceola
Osprey
Osyka
Otley
Ovett
17 Owings
Ozawkie

Pablo
Pachuta
Paden
Paguate
Pahrump
14 Palmer
Palmyra
Paul
Pavo
21 Pegram

21 Pelham
Penn
Penryn
Peoples
14 Peruque
23 Petrolia
Pheba
Phil
Philpot
Phlox
Piedra
14 Piercy
16 Piffard
Pima
Piqua
17 Pitkin
Pitt
Plad
14 Plover
23 Poland
Potosi
Praco
Pryse
Puxico

Quail
Quality
Quay
Quealy
Quick
17 Quinby
17 Quinque

17 Raisin
21 Ramage
Ravia
Redby
Reform
Reklaw
Remlap
Requa
21 Rhame
Riddle
14 Ritner
14 Rohwer
Romney
23 Rosholt
Rothsay
Ruby
17 Ruffin
Rusk

17 Saginaw
Salitpa
Salome
Salvia
21 Sample
Saponac
16 Sarben
16 Sarepta
Saxton
14 Schertz

Scipio
Scotia
Scotland
Scotrun
Selawik
Semmes
Seth
Shively
Shoup
14 Sibert
Silt
Sitka
16 Sparks
Stab
16 Stalwart
Staples
16 Starbuck
16 Startup
14 Steger
Stokes
Sully
14 Sumter
31 Sutherlin
Suttle
Sutton
16 Swartz
14 Switzer
Sylva

Tacna
Tallega
21 Tamaqua
16 Tarkio
Tchula
Techny
Tefft
Temvik
14 Teresita
17 Texline
23 Texola
Thida
14 Tijeras
Timken
17 Tinsman
17 Toney
Topawa
Topaz
21 Topsham
17 Trinway
23 Tripoli
Triumph
Trout
Truchas
Truro
14 Tucker
Tujunga
Tulsa
14 Tyner
Tyro

Urban
Ursa

17 Ursina
Ury
Uvalde
Uwchland
Uxbridge

Valsetz
16 Varney
Vaughn
17 Viking
17 Vindex
Viroqua
23 Volcano
Voss

21 Wadhams
Waimea
Wakita
Walburg
14 Walker
Wantagh
Waquoit
Wauna
16 Waymart
Waynoka
Webb
14 Webster
Wecota
Weems
Welaka
Welsh
Wesley
Whick
21 Whigham
Wikel
Wila
16 Wilbar
17 Windgap
14 Wister
14 Witmer
Witt
16 Wyarno
Wykoff
Wyncote

Yachats
Yeddo
14 Yerkes
Yocum
Yoncalla
Yreka
Yukon

Zahl
Zapata
Zigzag
Zumbrota
23 Zwolle

Sample Solution

	Town Name	Points
1.	ABRAMS	28
2.	ACKERLY	21
3.	ACMAR	23
4.	AGAWAM	28
5.	ALABAMA	28
6.	ALAMO	28
7.	ALAMOSA	28
8.	ALVEROA	21
9.	ARBYRD	23
10.	BEXAR	23
11.	CHARLEROI	37
12.	COGGON	7
13.	COKE	7
14.	CUTSHIN	24
15.	DUQUOIN	24
16.	EARLIMART	39
17.	EBONY	7
18.	ECCLES	7
19.	EEK	7
20.	ELKHART	23
21.	FINLY	24
22.	HOLMEN	30
23.	HOMINY	24
24.	HOPKINS	24
25.	HUGO	7
26.	HYTOP	7
27.	INDEX	24
28.	KEARSARGE	39
29.	LINGLE	24
30.	LULING	24
31.	PITKIN	24
32.	QUINBY	24
33.	SUTHERLIN	38
34.	VINDEX	24
35.	VOSS	7
36.	ZWOLLE	30
	Total	807

Unused letters: B CCCC DD FF JJ OO PPPPP Q SS TTTTTTT U V WWW Y ZZZ.
37 unused letters at 6 points a piece = 222.
Total score = 807 − 222 = 585.

8.4 BRIDGING THE GAP: THE INTERFACE

For the first time in this book the biggest gap is on the side of applications and real problems. There are many factors contributing to this. One is that because there have not been many good techniques for solving nonlinear problems, people have not cast their problems into nonlinear form, but instead they assumed linearity and used other linear techniques. Another factor has been that even though dynamic program-

ming has been around for several years, the amount of storage that is required for a fair-sized problem tends to be too large for even the largest of computers. The complexities that are introduced by non-linearities have usually prohibited any simple formulations that make the problem easily solvable. With the advent of geometric programming some problems have been extremely easy to solve, but this also may require expert mathematical skill to enable you to formulate them correctly for easy solution.

For those purists among you the following notes are of importance.

1. We have just scratched the surface in dynamic programming, and only a few problems have been formulated using dynamic programming. As you can readily see, putting the problem into the proper format is more in the line of analysis and is extremely difficult. Once a problem (like investments) has been formulated, then others like it can be solved fairly easily. But doing the first one is the challenge and one that the authors readily admit lies outside the realm of this textbook. What we wanted to convey was the principle of being able to solve n one-stage problems instead of one n-stage problem.

2. As mentioned above, the storage problems for dynamic programming can be considerable. If an investment problem such as in Section 8.2 has 100 possible values for each investment, then the last table computed must always be stored, that is $(100)^2$ numbers, and then a summary table is made up and stored. If the values of the variables are really continuous and the payoff is a non-linear function, then the question arises as to what values of the investments should be used, since dynamic programming really works from tabular values rather than from an infinite number of possible values from a formula. It is possible that although the algorithm is optimal, if we have the wrong values of the variables, the optimal solution will be missed and a pseudo-optimal one found.

3. Geometric programming is a newer technique which again requires some expert mathematical skill and probably the ability to do algebraic transformations as well as to understand engineering design and its attendant formulas. Here again the reason for including this technique is to show how to solve some problems by actually solving the dual problem first (changing the problem). We only included examples of geometric programming problems that had zero degrees of difficulty, which means that there exists a unique solution to each problem which is easily found. This is not so when the number of degrees of difficulty is greater than zero, which

can happen when there are two or more non-linear terms than variables or when there are constraints added. This complicates the situation greatly, although some unique answers can be found, as well as meaningful bounds on the variables or final cost, and useful information can be provided.

4. The section on problems and puzzles is included to humble all of us who think of ourselves as good mathematicians and analysts. The Tangle Towns puzzle is won triannually by common ordinary people who know nothing of matrix algebra, calculus, implicit enumeration, and so forth. The solution process seems to follow the infinite monkey theory: "An infinite number of monkeys working at an infinite number of typewriters in an infinite amount of time could produce the works of Shakespeare."

5. Dynamic programming can also be used to solve such inventory problems as unequal demand, versus the method of Silver and Meal.[5] It should be noted, however, that dynamic programming will *always* find the optimum answer for any data you feed it. The problem here is that the ordering policy would be generated from back (future) to front (present), which means that we are implicitly requiring that the forecasts for the last period be as accurate as the forecasts for the first period. Anyone working in the inventory control field will be quick to tell you that this assumption is fraught with difficulties. Figure 8.5 shows the accuracy of the forecast moving into the future. Old-time inventory control people call this figure the "trumpet of doom," and by the adding of a few more lines we get Figure 8.6.

Inventory people with experience know immediately that the only solid (unchangeable, deterministic) demand figure is the one already ordered (and received). If we recognize that the truth of the data is a function (nonlinear even) of time, we see at once the fatal flaw of using dynamic programming to get an optimal ordering policy. While the mathematics may be correct,

Figure 8.6

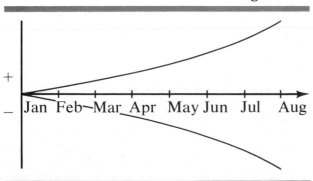

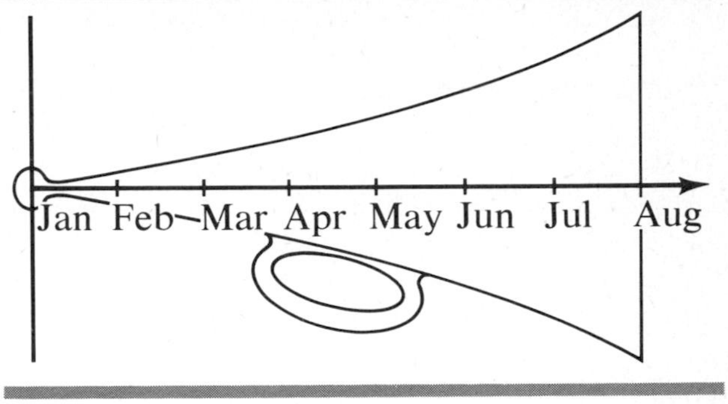

the data isn't, and our Quick & Clean becomes very dirty. Thus the Silver and Meal method tends to work best because it is a "forward" method rather than one that works backwards (and builds on the base of the most unreliable data).

6. *Mathematical notation.* For geometric programming the standard mathematical notation for primal variables has been changed from X_i to Q, R, S, or whatever the first letter of the actual variable is. Likewise the dual variables have been changed from w_i or θ_i to c_i which stands for the cost contribution of the ith term in the optimal objective function value. We also did not introduce the concept of a cost contribution for each constraint, but the mathematical formulations of the primal (consisting of "posynomials") and the dual are given below:

$$\text{Minimize} \quad y_0 = \sum_{t=1}^{T_0} \cdot \prod_{n=1}^{N} c_{0t} X_n^{a_{0tn}}$$

$$\text{subject to:} \quad y_m \leq 1, \quad m = 1, 2, \cdots, M$$
$$X_i \geq 0, \quad i = 1, 2, \cdots, N$$

becomes the dual problem:

$$\text{Maximize } D(\theta) = \prod_{m=0}^{M} \prod_{t=1}^{T_m} \left(\frac{c_{mt} \theta_{mt}}{\theta_{mt}} \right)^{\theta_{mt}}$$

subject to:

$$\sum_{t=1}^{T_0} \sum_{m=0} \theta_{0t} = 1 \qquad \text{normality condition}$$

$$\sum_{m=0}^{M} \sum_{t=1}^{T_m} a_{mtn} \theta_{mt} = 0, \qquad \text{for } n = 1, 2, \cdots, N$$

$$\text{orthogonality conditions}$$

$$\theta_{mt} \geq 0, \qquad \text{for all } m \text{ and } t.$$

Figure 8.5

As an example,[6] let us assume that a company wishes to build a steel tank to store 3141 cubic yards of oil and has only $1000.00 to spend. The tank will sit upon a concrete base, so the amount of steel needed will be for the top and sides of a cylinder. If steel costs $1.00 per square yard, will there be enough money to construct the tank, and what would be its dimensions?

Letting X_1 be the radius of the tank and X_2 its height (Figure 8.7), we will want to minimize the cost of the tank as follows:

Minimize Cost $= \pi X_1^2 + 2\pi X_1 X_2$

subject to: $X_1^2 X_2 \geq 3141$ cubic yards
(volume of the tank)

Rewriting the constraint in the proper format, we have:

$$1000 X_1^{-2} X_2^{-1} \leq 1.$$

The objective function of the dual becomes:

Maximize Profit $= \left(\dfrac{\pi}{\theta_1}\right)^{\theta_1} \left(\dfrac{2\pi}{\theta_2}\right)^{\theta_2} (1000)^{\theta_3}$

subject to:

$\theta_1 + \theta_2 = 1$ normality

$2\theta_1 + \theta_2 - 2\theta_3 = 0$ orthogonality for X_1

$\theta_2 - \theta_3 = 0$ orthogonality for X_2.

$\theta_1 = \frac{1}{3}, \theta_2 = \frac{2}{3}$, and $\theta_3 = \frac{2}{3}$ is the solution, yielding a maximum profit of $942, which is below the cost of $1000. Further the solution yields $X_1 = 10$ yards $= 30$ feet, $X_2 = 10$ yards $= 30$ feet. Thus the tank should be 30 feet high and 60 feet in diameter (30-foot radius).

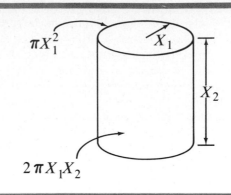

Figure 8.7

7. For dynamic programming each investment can be denoted by $P_i(s)$, where s ranges through various "states" (like 0, $10, $20, $30, $40) up to a specified upper limit (we'll denote it by $). At each stage we build a decision table, starting with the last or nth decision, such that we have:

$$f_n(s) = \underset{X_n \leq s}{\text{maximum}} \{P_n(X_n)\}$$

and thus we can start a recursive relationship:

$$f_i(s) = \underset{X_i \leq s}{\text{maximum}} \{P_i(X_i) + f_{i+1}(s - x_i)\},$$
$$1 < i < n - 1$$

and finally,

$$f_1(\$) = \underset{x_1 = \$}{\text{maximum}} \{P_1(x_1) + f_2(\$ - x_1)\}.$$

8.5 REVIEWS

*Review 1: Open book and notes; show **all** work and write legibly.*

1. (15 points) Solve the following geometric programming problem.

Minimize Cost $= \dfrac{100}{Q^2} + 100Q^2$

2. (15 points) Given the following dual problem, solve for each cost contribution (C_i) and the value of the objective function.

$$\text{Maximize Profit} = \left(\frac{9}{C_1}\right)^{C_1} \left(\frac{2}{C_2}\right)^{C_2} \left(\frac{32}{3C_3}\right)^{C_3}$$

subject to:
$$C_1 + C_2 + C_3 = 1$$
$$C_1 - C_2 + C_3 = 0$$
$$C_1 - 2C_3 = 0$$

3. (10 points) Write the primal problem from the information given in problem 2 above.

4. (15 points) Set up the dual objective function and necessary constraints for the following geometric programming problem. *DO NOT SOLVE*. How many degrees of difficulty are there?

$$\text{Minimize Cost} = 4X_1 X_2 + 3X_2^2 + \sqrt{X_1 X_2} + \frac{X_1}{2X_2}$$

5. (15 points) Consider the Limited Investment case (page 292) and determine a new solution if we add a fifth investment to the problem. Do not completely re-solve the problem, but make a summary table for the four investments and determine the optimal course of action for this new investment.

Amount	$10	$20	$30
Investment 5	$16	$28	$33

6. (20 points) Using dynamic programming, solve the capital budgeting problem below. Show your work.

Maximize Profit $= 10P_1 + 12P_2 + 8P_3 + 7P_4$

subject to: $4P_1 + 6P_2 + 3P_3 + 2P_4 \leq 9$

7. (10 points) Given the Contractor Capital case (page 295), determine the optimal strategy if there were only:
    a. $7000 available to be spent.

    b. $6000 available to be spent.

Review 2: Open book and notes; show all work and write legibly.

1. (10 points) Find the minimum ATC (don't find the value of Q) using geometric programming.

   Minimize ATC $= \dfrac{30}{Q^2} + 2Q^3$

2. (10 points) Given that the maximum dual is equal to 36.0 and $C_1 = \frac{1}{3}, C_2 = \frac{1}{2}, C_3 = \frac{1}{6}$ and the primal $= 27RS + (6/R) + (32R/S)$, find the optimal values of R and S.

3. (15 points) Solve the following equations for the cost contributions.

   a. $C_1 + \ C_2 + C_3 = 1$

   $-5C_1 + 3C_2 + C_3 = 0$

   $3C_1 - 5C_2 + C_3 = 0$

   b. If the dual function is $\left(\dfrac{12}{C_1}\right)^{C_1}\left(\dfrac{2}{C_2}\right)^{C_2}\left(\dfrac{1}{C_3}\right)^{C_3}$, determine the primal problem.

4. (15 points) With the approach of summer and an increase in surfers, a local surf shop would like to know how many surfboards to order and the minimum cost if the ATC formula were the same as the Glass Trees case (page 289). They expect demand to hold constant at 75 boards per month and the cost of ordering is known to be $25.00 while it costs $0.12 per board per month to carry the boards. Determine the optimal amount to carry and show your work.

5. (10 points) For the Dynamic Programming example (page 290), determine the optimal strategy if we only had $4000 to spend instead of $5000. Compute a table or line of values for $4000 similar to the one done for $5000.

6. (15 points) Solve the following capital budgeting problem using dynamic programming.

Maximize Profit $= 10P_1 + 12P_2 + 8P_3 + 7P_4$

subject to: $\qquad 4P_1 + 6P_2 + 3P_3 + 2P_4 \leq 10$

7. (10 points) Given the following table for Investments 2 and 3, develop the table for the optimal allocation of money for Investments 1, 2, and 3. Assume that a total of $3000 can be spent.

Invest	Investment 1	Amount Left	Investment 2 $0	$1000	$2000	$3000
$1000	$1100	$1000	$1200	$1400	—	—
$2000	$2400	$2000	$2300	$2600	$2500	—
$3000	$3900	$3000	$3500	$3700	$3700	$3600

8. (15 points) You have a total of $50 to invest, but it must be invested in $10 increments up to and including $30 in some combination of four projects. Given the values below, use dynamic programming to make up the table of optimal values *only* for Investments 3 and 4.

Invest	Investment 1	Investment 2	Investment 3	Investment 4
$10	$11	$13	$15	$12
$20	$22	$25	$23	$24
$30	$36	$38	$32	$35

8.6 REFERENCES

1. R. J. Duffin, E. L. Peterson, and C. Zener, *Geometric Programming* (New York: Wiley, 1967).
2. D. R. Plane and G. A. Kochenberger, *Operations Research for Managerial Decisions* (Homewood, Ill: Richard D. Irwin, 1974), pp. 294–304.
3. F. S. Hillier and G. J. Lieberman, *Introduction to Operations Research* (San Francisco: Holden Day, 1974), chap. 8.
4. J. S. Rustagi and T. W. Doub, "Optimum Distribution of Armor," *Operations Research*, vol. 18, 1970, pp. 559–562.
5. E. A. Silver and H. C. Meal, "In Defense of 'A Simple Modification of the EOQ for the Case of Varying Demand Rate,' " Working Paper #62, Dept. of Management Science, University of Waterloo, Waterloo, Ontario, Canada, Jan. 1972.
6. R. E. D. Woolsey and H. S. Swanson, *Operations Research for Immediate Applications* (New York: Harper & Row, 1975), pp. 84–99.

9

decision making under uncertainty

INTRODUCTION

Uncertainty and size seem to be the two biggest factors in the decision making that goes on in business and industry. We have already seen in the first eight chapters how problems can grow to large sizes, with a huge number of possible answers. As if this were not overwhelming enough, we now add the complication that everything is *not* determined. Thus we cannot count on the fact that our demand for inventory is always known. If we were attempting to find an optimal ordering policy for retailing umbrellas, it might be too low if there is a lot of rain, but way too high if it doesn't rain for six months. Thus we encounter the uncertainty of our demand, which can only be described by some possible demands and the probability for those demands. Again, we might be faced with a decision of what price to charge for a certain item. Sales may be dependent upon what our competitor does. There is a probability that he will run a special on that item, and if so, we may be stuck with a lot of them. Again, uncertainty creeps into the decision making, complicating what was already hard enough to decide. Good management tries to control size and uncertainty of the problem, while allowing for growth and flexibility at the same time. The same should be true of decision making. We need tools that

will allow us to account for some changes or uncertainty, without the decision being too restrictive or, on the other hand, too vague.

This chapter contains several types of problems that can be solved in simple, straightforward ways, taking into account the probability of certain events happening. As such, these techniques are based upon some simple suppositions of probability:

1. The probability for any single event to happen is always between 0 and 1. 0 means that it won't happen, 1 means that it will. Anything in between is not certain and is up for grabs. Thus if the probability of rain today is 60 percent (or 0.60), it may or may not rain today. For ten such days it should rain on six of the days and not rain on the other four, thus averaging out to 6/10 or 0.60.
2. The sum of the mutually exclusive probabilities of events should add up to 1.0, and such a distribution is known as the cumulative probability. Thus in the next minutes there might be three possibilities of receiving phone calls: no phone calls (0.6), one phone call (0.25), or two phone calls (0.15).

Phone Calls	0	1	2
Probability	0.60	0.25	0.15
Cumulative Probability	0.60	0.85	1.00

3. The expected value is simply the value of each event times its probability of occurring, summed up for all the possibilities. Thus for the phone calls the expected value EV (or number of calls) is

$$EV = 0(0.60) + 1(0.25) + 2(0.15) = 0.55.$$

This means that *on the average* you will receive 0.55 phone call per minute.

Armed with this knowledge of probability, we will attempt to try to solve some problems arising in operations research that require us to make decisions under uncertainty. Note that determining what these probabilities actually are is an art in itself, and may be the result of objective data gathering or subjective soul searching (for a good random number generator).

9.1 DECISION THEORY

Decision theory relates to several ways of making decisions under uncertainty from a limited amount of knowledge. There is a group of statisticians who feel that statistics took a wrong turn 100 years ago, and instead of learning sampling techniques, which require taking large numbers of data points, fitting them to distributions, and developing a theory for that, mathematicians should have been spending time working with limited amounts of information. After all, that is what happens in the real world where there are unrepeatable events that demand a decision. Do we go to war? Do we bring out a new automobile (Edsel or Mustang)? Do we expand our business (Montgomery Ward's or Sears)? Do I abdicate the throne? Real life calls for a decision based upon little or no data, and sometimes relying only on intuition, which may or may not be reliable.

Decision theory first deals with trying to write down all the possible decisions that could be made on your part (the decision maker), then a list of all the possible things that could happen but are *not* under your control. These are referred to as the states of nature. Thus you may be an artist and could spend Saturday either painting in your studio, or setting up a display in the park and hoping to sell some paintings. These are possible acts that you could decide to do. At the same time, out of your control, are the states of nature. It could be a sunny day (and thus large crowds would be in the park and there would be a high probability of selling your paintings) or it could rain (thus reducing the crowds to zero and your paintings to mush). For each possible combination of *acts* and *states*, you must determine what your *payoff* (in money, satisfaction, and so on) is. We thus generate a

table that describes all the possible important things that can happen to you, and the consequences in terms of a payoff. Next we will investigate different criteria that you could use to make the decision as to which way you should act.

A large engineering firm in Texas makes generators to produce power in remote or inaccessible places such as oil fields, deserts, the Arctic, or as standby generators when the power has failed. In the spring of 1975 a specialized team of managers studied the possibility of standardizing one of the firm's lines, which the engineering section claimed would save $550,000 per year. The sales department, though, claims that it is possible (not certain) that the firm could lose as much as $2,000,000 per year in sales. It is also conjectured that it could pick up $500,000 if its customers decided to switch over and the competition did not come out with a new model. The sales department was afraid that the standardized model would not fit anyone's need, even though the cost would be less. Another possibility was that sales would remain the same. The most controlling factor was the economy that might increase or decrease sales. After all this information was gathered, the following payoff table was constructed.

States	Acts Remain Same	Standardize
Increase Sales	$0	$1,050,000
Same Sales	$0	$550,000
Decrease Sales	$0	−$1,450,000

Here we see that we have *states*, which are called states of nature, or the possible things the future might hold for us. These are not within the company's control. Then we also have acts, which are decisions that the company can make. The table consists of payoffs or consequences of a combination of the action the company takes and the state of nature. Some are positive (in our favor) and others are negative (against us). What is desired is to act in a rational manner: we may be risk takers (optimistic) or be risk averse (pessimistic), but we must make a decision that explores alternatives and then make a decision (rather than wait until circumstances decide for us).

Another way to represent the alternative outcomes from our act and the state of nature is to draw a tree diagram with our acts first, the states of nature, and finally the payoff or consequence (see Figure 9.1, page 310).

department of public health

The Department of Public Health is charged with the health and safety of the American public and is responsible for forecasting serious epidemics and taking preventive measures. One such case involved

Figure 9.1

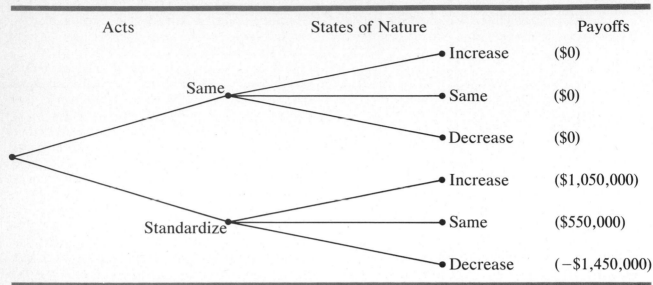

Acts	States of Nature	Payoffs
Same	Increase	($0)
	Same	($0)
	Decrease	($0)
Standardize	Increase	($1,050,000)
	Same	($550,000)
	Decrease	(−$1,450,000)

the danger of a Swine Flu epidemic and the possible need for enough vaccine to be given to every American citizen. In order to prepare for the demand for the vaccine, the D.P.H. needed to predict the response of the citizenry and this is difficult since each citizen can choose to be vaccinated or not. Some lead time was needed to develop the vaccine in laboratories, so it was necessary that the decision be made ahead of time as to how much vaccine should be prepared, with the chance that too much might be made or not enough. The public response can be seen as a state of nature in that the decision is made up of many individual decisions and produces an atmosphere that would have either not many people being vaccinated (10 million), a few (30 million), some (50 million), half (100 million), almost everyone (150 million) and virtually everyone (200 million). The department can either make up vaccine for 50 million, 100 million, 150 million, or 200 million people. It costs $200,000 per million people if the vaccine is not used, and the cost of not having enough vaccine in terms of lives lost, illness, and so on, is $100 million per million people not vaccinated.

Set up a payoff table with the states of nature and acts that the Public Health Department can take with the payoffs. Also draw a tree diagram indicating acts, states, and payoffs. Comment on the actual decision of the Public Health Department and ensuing public decision. What changed the payoff table?

pascal's bet

Blaise Pascal, the seventeenth-century French scientist, mathematician inventor, theologian, and philosopher, has a section in his *Pensées* (a collec-

tion of notes written during his lifetime) that demonstrates he was involved in a little decision theory himself. Consider the following passages:

> Let us examine this point, and say, "God is, or He is not." But to which side shall we incline? Reason can decide nothing here. A game is being played at the extremity of this infinite distance (between God and us) where heads or tails will turn up. What will you wager? According to reason, you can do neither the one thing or the other; according to reason, you can defend neither of the propositions. "The true course is not to wager at all." But you must wager; it is not optional.
> . . . Since there is an equal risk of gain or of loss, if you had only to gain two lives, instead of one, you might still wager. But if there were three lives to gain, you would have to play. But there is an eternity of life and happiness. And this being so, if there were an infinity of chances, of which one only would be for you, you would still be right in wagering one to win two, and you would act stupidly, being obliged to play, by refusing to stake one life against three at a game in which out of an infinity of chances there is one for you, if there were an infinity of an infinity of happy life to gain.[1]

From the above discourse determine a payoff table and a decision tree with the acts and states of nature and the payoff. Do this in terms of lifetimes to be gained or lost. Infinity would represent Heaven, and negative infinity Hell. A life lived on earth for your own pleasure would be +1 and a life lived for others would be −1. What does Pascal say about the decision you would have to make?

Now let us look at all the ways we could make a decision.

First, let us consider *Maximin*. This criterion assumes that the worst state of nature will occur for each act and tries to pick the best of the worst things that will happen. This can be referred to as Sad Sack, who seems to go through life picking the best of the worst possibilities.

Quick & Dirty Algorithm: Pessimist[2]

1. For each act circle the worst (lowest) payoff in the table.
2. Pick the largest of the circled payoffs and choose that act.

States	Acts Same	Standardize
Increase	(\$0)	\$1,050,000
Same	\$0	\$550,000
Decrease	\$0	(− \$1,450,000)

Thus if we keep the product line the same, there is a payoff of zero. If we standardize, we stand a chance of losing \$1,450,000 (this is the pessimist's way of looking at things). Of these two possibilities, we see that we should remain the same since \$0 is greater than − \$1,450,000. We have looked at this situation from the perspective of the worst thing happening when we make a decision or act, and we decide to keep the same product line and not to standardize.

Second, let us consider *Minimax*. In this case we are still pessimistic, but now we would like to minimize the regret we might feel by *not* choosing a certain act. Thus we need to construct a table of values that are opportunity losses (how much did we miss out on?) and minimize the maximum opportunity loss. This loss is the difference between the payoff act and the best we could have done in that same state. In the present case the *opportunity loss table* is shown below.

States	Acts Same	Standardize
Increase	\$1,050,000	\$0
Same	\$550,000	\$0
Decrease	\$0	\$1,450,000

Thus if we knew that sales were going to increase and we had chosen to keep the same product line, we would have a payoff of \$0. But if we had chosen to standardize instead, we would have made \$1,050,000. Thus our opportunity loss is \$1,050,000 − \$0 or \$1,050,000. Obviously, if we decided to standardize and sales increased, we had acted optimally and our opportunity loss would be zero.

Quick & Dirty Algorithm: Minimize Regret[2]

1. For each act circle the largest (most positive) opportunity loss.

2. Choose the act that has the smallest (minimum) circled value.

States	Acts Same	Standardize
Increase	(\$1,050,000)	\$0
Same	\$550,000	\$0
Decrease	\$0	(\$1,450,000)

The largest opportunity loss if we do not standardize (keep the same product line) is \$1,050,000 if it turns out that there is an increase in sales. If we do standardize, the largest opportunity loss is \$1,450,000, which would happen if there were a decrease in sales and in essence a sales loss of \$1,450,000. We could have lost out by simply not standardizing and breaking even (and not losing money). The smallest of these opportunity losses results from remaining the same.

Third, let us consider *Maximax*. This is the criterion for the eternal optimist. It is the strategy for the person who is a risk taker.

Quick & Dirty Algorithm: Gusto[2]

1. Find the largest number in the payoff table and circle it.
2. Choose that act.

States	Acts Same	Standardize
Increase	\$0	(\$1,050,000)
Same	\$0	\$550,000
Decrease	\$0	− \$1,450,000

Notice that our decision is now to standardize. It is an optimistic outlook to life and tries to maximize our gain rather than minimize our losses. This philosophy has been expressed earlier in history as, "Damn the torpedoes, full speed ahead!" This is certainly not a decision-making criterion for the faint of heart.

Fourth, let us consider *Expected value*. This is a balance between the optimist and the pessimist, based upon probabilities of the outcome of each state. In light of no information on these probabilities, we will use the Laplace criterion which states that nature is indifferent (or random). Otherwise we will use subjective probabilities obtained from the decision maker or those involved.

Quick & Dirty Algorithm: Expected Value[2]

1. For each act multiply the payoff for each state times its probability and sum up to get the expected value for that act.

2. Pick the largest expected value and choose the corresponding act.

First of all, using the Laplace criterion (we have *no* idea what the probabilities are of increased or decreased sales), since we have three possible outcomes of nature, each must occur with equal chance. Thus for each state there is a probability of one third (or 0.333).

If we choose to remain the same,

$$EV = \tfrac{1}{3}(0) + \tfrac{1}{3}(0) + \tfrac{1}{3}(0) = \$0.$$

If we standardize,

$$EV = \tfrac{1}{3}(\$1{,}050{,}000) + \tfrac{1}{3}(\$550{,}000) + \tfrac{1}{3}(-\$1{,}450{,}000) = \$50{,}000.$$

Choosing the largest of the expected values gives us $50,000 and means that we would choose to standardize. The philosophy behind this criterion is that if this decision were to occur several times, then on the average we would come out ahead by $50,000 each time we decided on standardizing. However, we must remember that in actuality we are only going to choose once.

Now let us assume that in a discussion with the sales force it is agreed that there is at least a 60 percent chance of a loss in sales, with a 20 percent chance for an increase and a 20 percent chance of sales remaining the same. Now our expected values are as follows. If we remain the same,

$$EV = 0.20(0) + 0.20(0) + 0.60(0) = \$0$$

and if we standardize,

$$EV = 0.20(\$1{,}050{,}000) + 0.20(\$550{,}000) + 0.60(-\$1{,}450{,}000) = -\$550{,}000.$$

Now we see that our expected value for standardizing is that we lose money on the average, whereas if we remain the same our expected value is $0. Thus the highest of these is $0, and we should remain the same.

With our subjective probabilities we can ascertain what action to take by maximizing our expected values. The questions now arise, "What is the best we could do if we knew what was going to happen for certain?" and "When is it going to happen?" Thus if we knew that 20 percent of the time sales would increase, and if we knew when that would happen, we would always choose to standardize (this is treating the problem as if we were to have this decision come up again and again). Similarly, if we knew when sales would remain the same, we would also choose to standardize. However, if we knew sales would drop, we would keep our product line the same. The

expected profit EP that would result from our ability to see into the future is then

$$EP = 0.20(\$1{,}050{,}000) + 0.20(\$550{,}000) + 0.60(\$0) = \$320{,}000.$$

This would mean that we would know exactly when sales would go up, down, or stay the same, and it also assumes that we would be encountering this problem several times. This gives us a value of the best that we could do on the average. In contrast, we would expect to make only $0 by using our subjective probabilities. The difference between these two values is called the *expected value of perfect information* (EVPI) and is the maximum price we would be willing to pay for perfect information about the states of nature. If we could hire a genius consultant, this is the most that we would be willing to pay the consultant.

Quick & Dirty Algorithm: EVPI[2]

1. Expected value of perfect information = expected profit − expected value or
2. Choosing the optimal act from the Quick & Dirty expected value, multiply each opportunity loss by the probability for that state. The sum is the expected value of perfect information.

We can see from our opportunity loss table that the optimal strategy was to remain the same, and

$$EVPI = 0.20(\$1{,}050{,}000) + 0.20(\$550{,}000) + 0.60(\$0) = \$320{,}000.$$

This is the most that we should be willing to pay the genius consultant for perfect information about the future or, more realistically, for a survey to get more data about what sales might do in the future. This might entail finding out what competitors will be doing the next few years, what the economy might be like, what the needs of the consumers of these generator sets will be, and so on.

If we believed that nature was random, then our optimal act was to standardize. Going to the opportunity loss table, we see that

$$EVPI = \tfrac{1}{3}(\$0) + \tfrac{1}{3}(\$0) + \tfrac{1}{3}(\$1{,}450{,}000) = \$483{,}333$$

or

$$EVPI = EP[\tfrac{1}{3}(\$1{,}050{,}000) + \tfrac{1}{3}(\$550{,}000) + \tfrac{1}{3}(\$0)] = -EV(\$50{,}000) = \$483{,}333.$$

In summary, four criteria have been presented by which we can decide which act to choose. Several factors may play a role when you decide which one to choose, although studies show that most of us are risk averse (life insurance, medical coverage, and so on). We might be optimistic or pessimistic, we might have some information on probabilities or none at all, we might be willing to spend money to get information or not, and so on. The reason that the algorithms in this section have been called Quick & Dirty is not that the mathematics behind them are suspect, but that the data itself is usually very "dirty." Normally it will consist of estimates of guesses based on hunches. This is not to say that these techniques should not be used, for *some* decision must be made. Theologian Harvey Cox said, "*Not* to decide *is* to decide."

Finally you must realize that most decisions are made in turbulent environments, when states of nature occur that one would never have guessed. Such things as a tornado in California, a President of the United States resigning, unemployment *and* inflation both going up have a tendency to enter new payoffs that were never dreamed of.

autospot

Autospot provides refreshments at all home football games at a small state college in the Northeast. There the weather during the fall can be quite hot (Indian summer) or cold (early frost). The team has lost 13 of its last 14 games (they won their opener two years ago), so the crowds have been quite small. Autospot must decide whether warm drinks will be needed (coffee) or cold drinks (mixed punch, nonalcoholic). In both cases the refreshment must be mixed, and if not sold, simply thrown away. Thus Autospot is quite anxious to determine how much of each should be prepared. If it is very cold, it will not sell any punch and will probably sell about 20 large containers of coffee. However, if the weather is quite warm, no one will want coffee, but it will sell about 25 large containers of punch. If the weather is moderate, it would expect to sell about 10 large containers each of punch and coffee. Given the payoff table below, determine the optimal act under each type of decision criterion and then make a recommendation as to which one you would choose.

States	Acts		
	Coffee	Both	Punch
Hot	− $50	− $20	$80
Moderate	$20	$60	$30
Cold	$75	$10	− $30

Given no information about the weather, determine what the expected value of perfect information is. In other words, what is it worth to call up the weather station? Assuming that you have determined the weather report (and believe it), you find out that since it has been cold all week, there is only a 10 percent chance of it being hot for the game, a 20 percent chance of moderate weather, but a 70 percent chance of continued cold. Determine what decision this would dictate, and also what would be the expected value of perfect information.

Solution

Recommendation

Considering that the weather has been cold lately and that forecasts give a good probability of the cold continuing, it is recommended that Autospot make all coffee (20 large containers) for the game.

Numerical Answer. The various criteria, their decision, and values are as follows:

Pessimist	Both	Minimize loss at $20
Regret	Both	Minimize regret, opportunity loss at $100
Optimist	Punch	Maximize profit at $80
Expected value (random)	Punch	EV = $26.67, EVPI = $45.00
Weather report	Coffee	EV = $51.50, EVPI = $21.00

Math Work

Maximin, Pessimist

The payoff table is:

States	Acts		
	Coffee	Both	Punch
Hot	(− $50)	(− $20)	$80
Moderate	$20	$60	$30
Cold	$75	$10	(− $30)

The minimum of each act is circled, the maximum of these is $20. Serve *both*.

Minimax, Regret

The opportunity loss table is:

States	Acts		
	Coffee	Both	Punch
Hot	($130)	($100)	$0
Moderate	$40	$0	$30
Cold	$0	$65	($105)

The maximum of each act is circled, the minimum of these is $100. Serve *both*.

Maximax, Gusto

The largest number in the payoff table above is $80. Serve *punch*.

Expected Value

If we consider that Nature is indifferent (random), then the probability of each state of nature is one third, and the expected value for each act is:

Coffee $\frac{1}{3}(-\$50) + \frac{1}{3}(\$20) + \frac{1}{3}(\$75) = \$15.00$
Both $\frac{1}{3}(-\$20) + \frac{1}{3}(\$60) + \frac{1}{3}(\$10) = \$16.67$
Punch $\frac{1}{3}(\$80) + \frac{1}{3}(\$30) + \frac{1}{3}(-\$30) = \$26.67$.

Choose *punch*, the maximum expected value.

The expected value of perfect information can be calculated as:

EP $= \frac{1}{3}(\$80) + \frac{1}{3}(\$60) + \frac{1}{3}(\$75)$ $= \$71.67$
$-$ EV $= \$26.67$ $= -\$26.67$

EVPI $= \$45.00$

or, by looking at the values in the opportunity loss table for punch,

EVPI $= \frac{1}{3}(\$0) + \frac{1}{3}(\$30) + \frac{1}{3}(\$105) = \$45.00$.

If we consider the weather report probabilities, we have the following expected values:

Coffee $0.10(-\$50) + 0.20(\$20) + 0.70(\$75) = \$51.50$.
Both $0.10(-\$20) + 0.20(\$60) + 0.70(\$10) = \$17.00$
Punch $0.10(\$80) + 0.20(\$30) + 0.70(-\$30) = -\$7.00$.

Choose *coffee*, the maximum expected value.

The expected value of perfect information can then be calculated as:

EP $0.10(\$80) + 0.20(\$60) + 0.70(\$75) = \$72.50$
$-$EV $\$51.50$ $= -\$51.50$

EVPI $= \$21.00$

or, using the values in the opportunity loss table for coffee,

EVPI $= 0.10(\$130) + 0.20(\$40) + 0.70(\$0) = \$21.00$.

INCIDENT: CONTRACT DECISION

A large international firm based in England was bidding on three contracts for underwater cable. The first two contracts only required machinery already installed and checked out at its plant in the United States. The third contract required machinery that was newer and was producing the same cable as everyone else. If the firm received this contract, it would have to buy 2 to 3 million dollars worth of machinery eventually, but the contract would help pay for this. However, there was a danger that if it waited until the notification of being awarded the contract, it would not finish the contract on time due to the long lead time for procuring the new machine. Another possibility was that the company could ship one of the new machines from its European plant to the United States for six months, while the American plant waited for its new machine. England was reluctant to spend money on new machinery, even though it was the wave of the future, as it was not too sure that the American subsidiary would continue to make money. A decision was needed as to whether to order a new machine now, wait and ship one over, or simply wait and take the chances. The states of nature were (1) getting no contracts, (2) getting only contracts involving old machines, (3) only getting contracts for the new machine, (4) getting all contracts.

glass cans

During 1964 the bottling industry introduced "glass cans" which were no-deposit, no-return bottles made from second-rate glass. These bottles proved popular with consumers. At Anheuser-Busch this presented a serious dilemma. Beer sales generally increase at about 10 percent per year, but each brand of beer can be packaged in many different ways. There are 10-, 12-, or 16-ounce cans which might be aluminum or tin and have regular tops or tab tops; different-size bottles range from 10-ounce to quarts; and so on. In all there were 32 ways to package Bud, Busch, and Michelob.

If the beer is in the wrong type of container, the public may not buy it. This was the dilemma produced by the new glass cans. They had not been out long enough for Anheuser-Busch to know whether this was just a fad that would die out completely, maintain its current level, or keep rising exponentially. It was critical that this year's orders for containers be made now before Busch was limited by the container companies themselves. The payoff table below expresses some of the alternatives. (Ordering is in 1000s of bottles, payoff in millions of dollars.) Determine the optimal act under the various criteria. Also determine the expected value of perfect information.

Demand	Order 500	1000	1500	2000
Low	3	2	-2	-5
Medium	-1	0	1	2
High	-8	-2	4	10

INCIDENT: BIDDING GAME

A favorite dynamic decision-making game is to auction off a $5 bill. Each bid must be five cents higher than the last, and the only catch is that the last *two* bids must pay. The bidding will invariably go past $5. Another variant is to have a jar of pennies to be auctioned off with the same rule. Here it is not known how much is in the jar, but again, the auctioneer generally comes out ahead.

shopping center

In the fall of 1974 the owner of a small shopping center in the Northwest found out that the tenant of the largest space building was going bankrupt and out of business. The restaurant that he had been running for the last three years just could not make a profit, and those who had backed it decided to get out with a slight loss rather than continue to lose money each year. The restaurant was a combination of fast-food (with a drive-up window) and low-budget meat and potato dinners and lunches. It was caught between the fast-food hamburger places and the fancier restaurants and could not attract enough customers. It was now time for a decision of who the new tenant should be. There are many factors that go into choosing this, including the image that it will give the shopping center, the probability of the tenant staying in business, paying bills, parking problems created, and so on. In times of economic depression the owner knows that prospective tenants are not plentiful. The problem with choosing a tenant that goes out of business is that it may take several months to lease the property again, and this can be costly. Depending upon the type of business the tenant is in, there may be a need for remodeling, and the owner usually has to contribute something to the cost of that, as well as pay a penalty for the inconvenience it may cause other tenants in the shopping center. The owner has several tenants to consider, including another small restaurant, which at least has the advantage of a minimum of remodeling, but a high risk of making it. Another possibility is a medical–dental group which would require extensive remodeling, but has a good chance of making it. Another possibility is a dress shop that has been quite successful in a smaller location two blocks away. It wants to expand and go into both men's and women's fashions. As such it is a risk, but not as great as the restaurant. Finally, there is an auto parts store that wants a large, easily accessible location and will handle mostly a retail trade from individuals versus wholesale from dealers and repair shops. The risk there is that in bad economic times people stop repairing and fixing their cars except for absolutely

necessary work. Given the following data and using the different criteria, determine what your recommendation would be and why. The subjective probability that the tenants will make it at that location is 30 percent.

	Restaurant	M–D Group	Auto Parts	Dress Shop
Make It	$5000	$4000	$4500	$3600
Bankrupt	$1000	$2000	$3000	$2500

INCIDENT: PERSONALLY RISKY DECISIONS

A very real and difficult decision-making situation is encountered on long vacations. It usually occurs when you pull into a gas station and the attendant looks at your fan belt, radiator hose, or some other object under the hood and says something like, "I don't think you'll make it too far with it in that condition!" The situation becomes even more tense when you are planning to make it across the desert, and there are not many places to stop if you run into trouble. The question now becomes what kind of decision maker you are. If you don't know much about cars, do you pay money to make sure that nothing will go wrong (being risk averse) or are you a risk taker ("I'm not going to pay money for *that*!")? Does it make a difference whether you are alone or your family is in the car? Many gas stations have been known to sell extra items that aren't really necessary in this way simply because most people are risk averse, and when our intuitive probability of something going wrong is high enough, we will buy the extra "insurance." In the early days of flying, insurance machines were selling insurance at a rapid rate, but as the public developed more confidence in flying, these insurance policies are not selling nearly as well.

Supplementary Problems

1. Lucky Lou is staring at a slot machine in Las Vegas, Nevada, flipping his last silver dollar. There are three possible payoffs if he wins: one cherry, $1.00; two cherries, $5.00; or three cherries $25.00. Anything else on the slot machine loses.
   a. Make up a Decision Table for Lucky Lou.
   b. What should Lou do if his nickname is correct?
   c. The odds for the payoffs are: one cherry, 2:3; two cherries, 1:6; and three cherries, 1:30. What is the optimum strategy for the expected value?

2. A consumer wants to buy a new car and is worried about the price of gasoline in the next three years. The table below represents the costs or savings for buying three types of cars, plus an amount for pleasure and comfort of larger cars.

| | Acts | | |
	Subcompact	Compact	Medium
Lower price	$1000	$800	$1200
Stay same	300	500	150
Up some	400	100	−200
Up a lot	100	−400	−700

   a. Which act should the consumer choose under the maximax strategy?
   b. Which act would be optimal under maximin?
   c. Which act would be optimal under minimax?
   d. What value would *you* use for the probability of each state and why? What is the expected value optimal act?

3. Lonesome Lenny has been drinking steadily at the "Passion Pit Bar" and has been eyeing Mysterious Mary for hours. He quickly sketches the payoff table below. Not knowing her well, he lists both his acts and the possible states of nature and payoffs.

| | Acts | | |
States	Make Move	Another Drink	Go Home
Woman of his dreams	+10	+5	−5
A good time	+4	+2	−1
Boring, boring	−8	+9	+10

   a. Since Lenny is really shy, he would like to minimize his regret. Determine his strategy.
   b. If he assumes each state has an equally likely probability of occurring, what is his strategy?
   c. What is the EVPI?

9.2 GAME THEORY

Game theory is developed around several people (or teams) making decisions simultaneously. In the case of two people it bears some resemblance to decision theory. Instead of one decision maker versus nature, it is now one decision maker versus another. Thus, in essence, nature is "thinking" and active. In this section we will be investigating different strategies to employ. Another distinction between decision theory and games is that games are usually played several times rather than just once, and thus we will be interested in maximizing the payoff or minimizing the losses on the average (expected value). We will only cover a few simple games to give you an idea of some of the ramifications and complications in each game.

There are two basic qualities that will describe the games:

1. The number of players. There must be at least two players to every game, and usually the more players, the more complicated the game becomes.
2. The sum of the payoffs. If the sum is zero, it is referred to as a zero-sum game. This means that at the end of every round the sum of all the winnings and losses of all the players balances out to zero. For a two-person game this means that what you win, I lose. This would be like betting another person on the outcome of some event. For more people it would be like a poker game, where some win and some lose, but the amount of money changing hands is constant. If the sum of the payoffs does not add to zero, then it is called a nonzero-sum game. In this case it could be that everyone wins, everyone loses, or again, some win and some lose, but the sum does not balance out to zero.

Thus we could classify games in another way:

1. *Win/Win*. In this type of game everyone wins. It usually requires a lot of trust and cooperation among the participants.
2. *Win/Lose*. This is the basic game. Most people see life as a game of this type. The payoff is usually a zero-sum game, where I win what you lose. Thus if you win $10, I lose $10. Games that are theoretically win/win are seen as win/lose, and thus the strategy is usually grab what you can.
3. *Lose/Lose*. In this case everyone loses. This is usually what happens when there is no trust and cooperation in the games of the first type. It probably started for us as kids when we got mad and took our toys and went home. Had there been trust and cooperation, everyone would have won and enjoyed himself. But because we tend to see games as win or lose, we play them that way, end up losing, and make sure that everyone else loses.

Let us investigate the simplest of the games, a two-person zero-sum game. The payoff table below shows us that there are two people, and player A has two strategies or acts to employ, while player B has three acts or strategies that are possible. The payoff table is always written in terms of player A, so that positive amounts are winnings and negative amounts are losses for player A. Player B simply receives the opposite.

| | Player B | | |
Player A	1	2	3
1	$6	$4	$5
2	$1	$3	$9

This game is played by both players deciding upon their strategy simultaneously. It is obvious from the table that player B is going to lose every time, but the question is, can player B minimize losses? For player A the object is to maximize winnings. This particular game is then loaded in favor of player A. Notice that if player B decides to play strategy 1 every time so that maybe only $1 will be lost, player A will simply choose strategy 1 and make $6. If player B now knows that player A will always choose strategy 1, then player B will choose strategy 2 and lose only $4 instead of $6. Player A can do no better by changing strategy, and so the two arrive at a stalemate, or *saddle point*. That is, this is the minimum of the maximum that player B can lose, and at the same time it is the maximum of the minimum that player A can win. Player A can win at least $4 from strategy 1 and $1 from strategy 2. So if strategy 1 is always played, the worst that player A can win is $4. By the same token, the most that player B can lose is $6 in choosing strategy 1, $4 with strategy 2, and $9 using strategy 3. The minimum of these three is using strategy 2 and losing only $4.

Quick & Clean Algorithm: Saddle Point[3]

1. For each strategy for player A circle the minimum amount that can be won.
2. For each strategy for player B box the maximum amount that can be lost.
3. If any payoff is both circled and boxed, it is a saddle point. This means that both players should employ that strategy. If player A fails to do so, player B may not lose so much. If player B fails to do so, player A may win more.

	Player B		
Player A	*1*	*2*	*3*
1	$6	$4	$5
2	$1		$9

Let us look at another example, this time where there are only two options for each player.

	Player B	
Player A	*1*	*2*
1	$\frac{1}{2}$	-1
2	0	$\frac{1}{2}$

Thus if player A chooses strategy 1 and player B chooses strategy 2, player A will lose $1 and player B wins $1. Applying the Quick & Clean algorithm to this payoff matrix, we get:

	Player B	
Player A	*1*	*2*
1	$\frac{1}{2}$	-1
2	0	$\frac{1}{2}$

We note that there is no saddle point. This means that there is no single strategy for either player that will either maximize minimum winnings or minimize maximum losses. Since there is no pure strategy, we must find a way of determining a mixed strategy. This means that player A will sometimes employ strategy 1 (p_1 percent of the time) and sometimes strategy 2 (p_2). Now if player B decides upon strategy 1, the expected value for player A is:

$$EV = \tfrac{1}{2}(p_1) + 0(p_2).$$

Likewise, if player B were to decide upon strategy 2, we would like to have player A's probabilities such that we would get the same expected value:

$$EV = -1(p_1) + \tfrac{1}{2}(p_2).$$

So we have three unknowns: EV (the value), p_1, and p_2. Since player A must choose either strategy 1 or 2, we know that:

$$p_1 + p_2 = 1.$$

Now we have three equations in three unknowns, which can be solved in many ways. Rearranging all variables on the left-hand side,

$$\begin{aligned} \tfrac{1}{2}p_1 \qquad\qquad - EV &= 0 \\ -p_1 + \tfrac{1}{2}p_2 - EV &= 0 \\ p_1 + \ p_2 \qquad\ &= 1. \end{aligned}$$

The values turn out to be $p_1 = \tfrac{1}{4}$, $p_2 = \tfrac{3}{4}$, and $EV = \tfrac{1}{8}$, or $0.125 per game. This says that for player A to get 12.5¢ per game, strategy 1 must be played $\tfrac{1}{4}$ of the time and strategy 2 must be played $\tfrac{3}{4}$ of the time.

Quick & Clean Algorithm: Mixed Strategy[3]

1. For each strategy for player B use the payoffs as coefficients for the probability for each strategy for player A (p_1, p_2, p_3, ...) and set equal to EV.
2. Sum up all the probabilities to equal 1.0.
3. Solve the set of simultaneous equations.
4. In like manner, for each strategy for player A use the payoffs as coefficients for the probability for each strategy for player B (q_1, q_2, q_3, ...).
5. Sum up all the probabilities to equal 1.0.
6. Solve the set of simultaneous linear equations.

This will only work for a zero-sum game that has an equal number of strategies for each player.

Applying the algorithm to the second half of the problem, we get the following equations:

$$\frac{1}{2}q_1 - 1q_2 = EV$$
$$0q_1 + \frac{1}{2}q_2 = EV$$
$$q_1 + q_2 = 1.0$$

or

$$\frac{1}{2}q_1 - q_2 - EV = 0$$
$$\frac{1}{2}q_2 - EV = 0$$
$$q_1 + q_2 = 1.$$

The solution is $q_1 = \frac{3}{4}$, $q_2 = \frac{1}{4}$, $EV = \frac{1}{8}$. The expected value is in terms of player A. This means that player B should choose strategy 1 three times out of every four, or 75 percent of the time. That does not mean to select strategy 1 three times, then strategy 2, then repeat. If that were done, then player A would always know what player B would choose and would act accordingly. By using a random number table or some other way of determining a 75 percent chance, the player should select the strategy randomly.

Short-cut Solution for a Two-Person Game. Given the payoff matrix for a two-person zero-sum game that looks as follows:

	B 1	2
A 1	a	b
2	c	d

the probabilities for player A are

$$p_1 = \frac{(d - c)}{D} \quad \text{and} \quad p_2 = \frac{(a - b)}{D}$$

$$\text{where} \quad D = a + d - b - c$$

and for player B

$$q_1 = \frac{(d - b)}{D} \quad \text{and} \quad q_2 = \frac{(a - c)}{D}$$

Finally it is possible in a two-person zero-sum game that one player has more strategies to choose from than the other. In this case it is not possible to use the above Quick & Clean algorithm, but the following Quick & Dirty algorithm is offered.

Quick & Dirty Algorithm: Mixed Strategy[3]

1. Pick a strategy for player A and write that payoff row below the table.
2. Pick the *smallest* number in that row and circle it.
3. Choose the corresponding payoff column for player B and write that column to the right of the table.
4. Pick the *largest* number in that column and circle it.

5. Choose the corresponding payoff row for player A and *add* it to the row below.
6. Circle the smallest number in the new row. Choose the corresponding payoff column for player B and *add* it to the right-hand column. Circle the largest number in that column. Go to step 5. In case of a tie, choose the least recently used row or column.
7. Continue until a pattern is established or enough times to determine the average number of times each strategy is chosen (the number of circled strategies for each player divided by the total number of rows or columns).

	Player B 1	2	3				
Player A							
1	- $1	$1	$2	①	②1②	③2③④3	
2	$3	- $1	$0	-1	-2①0	-1②1	0③
	3	-①	0				
	2	-⓪	2				
	①	-1	4				
	4	-⓪	4				
	3	-①	6				
	②	-2	8				
	5	-①	8				
	4	-②	10				
	③	-3	12				

We begin by choosing strategy 2 for player A. The smallest number is -1, which means we will now choose strategy 2 for player B. The largest number in that column is 1, which means we choose strategy 1 for player A and *add* it to the first row below the payoff table. This represents the cumulative payoff for two games, and we choose the smallest of these numbers to select player B's strategy (2). We *add* that column to the first right-hand column.

As can be seen visually, we should be playing strategy 1 two-thirds of the time for player A, and strategy 2 one-third of the time for player A. For player B we should choose strategy 1 only one-third of the time, strategy 2 two-thirds of the time, and never use strategy 3. The reason that strategy 3 is never used is that it is *dominated* by the second strategy, that is, regardless of which strategy player A would select, player B always comes out better by choosing strategy 2 instead of strategy 3. Thus we could even eliminate that strategy from consideration and be left with two strategies for each player. In that case we could also solve by simultaneous equations and find that we have indeed found the optimal answer.

Having found the probabilities that should be used, we can now get some bound on the expected value of the game. Select the smallest expected value from player A and the largest expected value from player B. The true value of the game will be bounded by these two values.

Player	Strategy 1	Strategy 2	Strategy 3
A	$-1(\frac{2}{3})+3(\frac{1}{3})=\frac{1}{3}$	$1(\frac{2}{3})-1(\frac{1}{3})=\frac{1}{3}$	$2(\frac{2}{3})=\frac{4}{3}$
B	$-1(\frac{1}{3})+1(\frac{2}{3})+2(0)$ $=\frac{1}{3}$	$3(\frac{1}{3})-1(\frac{2}{3})+0$ $=\frac{1}{3}$	

We are bounded by one-third from below and one-third from above, so the actual value of the game is one-third in favor of player A. This means that, if both players use the probabilities, on the average player A will win $0.333 each game. If either one deviates from this strategy, player A will not win as much when deviating from optimal strategy, or player B will lose more by deviating from optimal strategy.

Nonzero-sum Games

We shall now examine very quickly the area of nonzero-sum games. In these games it is possible for all the players to win or to lose. The payoff table is changed slightly; the payoffs for all players are put in parentheses, indicating how much they win or lose. Thus (3, 2, −1) indicates that for this strategy combination player A wins $3, player B wins $2, and player C loses $1. Consider the classic prisoner's dilemma:

Two petty thieves are caught with circumstantial evidence that the district attorney figures might convict them each for two years (but not as much as if they had been caught in the very act of the crime). If the district attorney could get one of them to confess, he could get the other convicted for ten years and let the confessor go after six months of serving his sentence. The district attorney figures that he needs them each in separate rooms so that he might get one of them to talk. If both squeal and turn state's evidence, the deal is off and they will each get eight years.

Prisoner A	Prisoner B Silent	Squeal
Silent	(2,2)	(10,$\frac{1}{2}$)
Squeal	($\frac{1}{2}$,10)	(8,8)

The only way that both prisoners can "win" (minimize the total number of years they serve) is for both of them to remain silent. But human nature being what it is (greedy, distrusting) and since that nature is heightened by the fact that they cannot communicate with each other, the result is inevitably the same: they both lose. They each mistrust the other or are greedy, and each ends up confessing, and they both serve eight years.

In this case a win/win game has been changed into a lose/lose game due to lack of communication and mistrust of each other. The same thing can happen in business. Consider the following same type of game.

Two grocery stores have been within a block of each other and each has been doing about $100,000 worth of business each day for years. Recently the popularity of savings stamps has risen, and although it would cost $10,000 in stamps to start a program, figures indicate that they could get $20,000 more business each day. This assumes that the other store does not have a stamp program. In terms of the payoff matrix, we have the following table:

Store A	Store B No Stamps	Stamps
No Stamps	(100,100)	(80,110)
Stamps	(110,80)	(90,90)

Of course, as soon as one store starts the stamps and the other feels the loss of business, it will also go to stamps. Thus both stores end up losing money, while the stamp company makes out like a bandit. In this case the same district attorney keeps the stores from talking to each other (it's called collusion or price fixing) so that it is hard for the outcome not to be a lose/lose one.

diving for dollars

A radio station held a contest recently called "Diving for Dollars." This contest consisted of having contestants call in and try to guess what amount a diver would bring up from the bottom of the ocean each hour. One contestant would be allowed to guess on the air, and the disc jockey would then play a tape which would have a supposed diver's voice announce the amount of money brought up. This would be anywhere from a $5 bill to a $100 bill. If the caller guessed the amount correctly, he or she won the amount. If the guess was not correct, then nothing was won (or lost). This contest went on for about ten weeks and was part of a promotional campaign to solicit more listeners.

A payoff table for this game can be constructed in terms of the caller.

Caller Guesses	Disc Jockey Plays $5	$10	$20	$50	$100
$5	$5	$0	$0	$0	$0
$10	$0	$10	$0	$0	$0
$20	$0	$0	$20	$0	$0
$50	$0	$0	$0	$50	$0
$100	$0	$0	$0	$0	$100

Obviously the caller cannot lose, while the radio station cannot win. The caller would like to maximize the chances of winning something, while the radio station does not necessarily want to give away $100 every hour. Thus it wishes to minimize its losses. To simplify the solution to this game (and thus determine the solution to this larger one), consider that there are only two alternatives for each player, $50 and $100. Then find the optimal strategy for the small game and infer the optimal strategy for both players (and expected value of the game) for the larger game.

Solution

Recommendation

Both the disc jockey and the contestant should always play the same strategies. For the small game, $50 should be guessed (or played) two-thirds of the time, and the $100 just one-third of the time. For the large game, if it is played 38 times, then $5 should be guessed or played twenty times, $10 ten times, $20 five times, $50 twice, and $100 just once.

Numerical Answer

Small Game

$$\$50 \qquad p_1 = 0.667$$
$$\$100 \qquad p_2 = 0.333$$
$$\text{EV} = \$33.33 \text{ per game.}$$

Large Game

$$\$5 \qquad p_1 = \tfrac{20}{38}$$
$$\$10 \qquad p_2 = \tfrac{10}{38}$$
$$\$20 \qquad p_3 = \tfrac{5}{38}$$
$$\$50 \qquad p_4 = \tfrac{2}{38}$$
$$\$100 \qquad p_5 = \tfrac{1}{38}$$
$$\text{EV} = \$2.63 \text{ per game.}$$

Math Work. Let us consider the small game first. We need to determine first whether there is a saddle point:

Caller	Disc Jockey $50	$100
$50	$50	$0
$100	$0	$100

As can be seen, there is no saddle point. We then apply the Quick & Clean algorithm for mixed strategy. For the caller the equations are:

$$\$50p_1 + \$0p_2 = \text{EV}$$
$$\$0p_1 + \$100p_2 = \text{EV}$$

Solving, we obtain $p_1 = \tfrac{2}{3}$, $p_2 = \tfrac{1}{3}$.

$$p_1 + p_2 = 1.0.$$

Knowing the probabilities, we can compute the expected value of the game:

$$\text{EV} = \$50(\tfrac{2}{3}) = \$33.33 \text{ per game.}$$

Finally let us show that had we used the Quick & Dirty algorithm, we would have arrived at the same set of probabilities for each strategy:

Caller	Disc Jockey $50	$100					
$50	$50	$0	$50	$100	$100	$150	$200	$200
$100	$0	$100	$0	$0	$100	$100	$100	$200

$0	$100
$50	$100
$100	$100
$100	$200
$150	$200
$200	$200

For the caller,

$$p_1 = \tfrac{4}{6} = \tfrac{2}{3} = 0.667$$
$$p_2 = \tfrac{2}{6} = \tfrac{1}{3} = 0.333.$$

For the disc jockey the probabilities are the same:

$$q_1 = \tfrac{4}{6} = \tfrac{2}{3} = 0.667$$
$$q_2 = \tfrac{2}{6} = \tfrac{1}{3} = 0.333.$$

Note that applying the Quick & Clean mixed strategy for the disc jockey also results in the same probabilities.

Now to solve the larger problem, we see that using the Quick & Clean mixed strategy results in some very simple equations (again the results will be the same for the caller and the disc jockey):

$$\$5q_1 = \text{EV} = \$10q_2 = \$20q_3 = \$50q_4 = \$100q_5$$

and

$$q_1 + q_2 + q_3 + q_4 + q_5 = 1.0.$$

Thus the higher the payoff, the lower the probability that the disc jockey will play it or that the caller should choose it. Solving all these equations gives us:

$$p_1 = \tfrac{20}{38}, \quad p_2 = \tfrac{10}{38}, \quad p_3 = \tfrac{5}{38}, \quad p_4 = \tfrac{2}{38}, \quad p_5 = \tfrac{1}{38}.$$

INCIDENT: WAR GAME

A classic example of game theory occurred during World War II. The Japanese navy had a set of tankers carrying supplies and ammunition, escorted by two destroyers and headed to reinforce the fighting in Southeast Asia. At the same time the Allied forces had their own destroyers trying to break this supply line. Stationed at opposite points around a group of islands, with weather so bad that air reconnaissance was not possible, each admiral had to decide which direction to go in. There were only two decisions for each, and the payoff table was very simple to construct. The Allied admiral simply applied the rules and found that there was a saddle point. He moved to the appropriate location and awaited the Japanese ships. As predicted, they arrived, the battle was joined, and the shipments were stopped.

food advertisements

Thursday is traditionally the day that supermarkets advertise their specials in the food section of a newspaper. This consists of some lower prices for special items plus a few coupons to give discounts. The idea behind this is to get customers from other stores to come into their stores, figuring that once they are there, other factors may come into play to build up customer loyalty.

Consider the situation in the Northwest where two stores, both independent but quite large, are near each other. By Tuesday noon each must have its layout to the newspaper and neither knows what the other store will be advertising this week or at what price certain items will be discounted. Thus it is a perfect two-person game, and if we assume that no new customers are attracted from the outside, we then can assume it is a zero-sum game.

The first store, called The Market, has three types of specials that it usually runs. It often discounts several types of fresh vegetables and fruits, while also going to great lengths to get some that are not usually available. It feels that by concentrating on one area, it has a better chance of getting people into the store. The second type of special that it could run is on meats and poultry. It feels that this is such a staple item that by giving a few cents off here and there, many customers will shop there that week. Finally, the third option entails sundry items (clothes, school supplies, and so on) that have a very high markup compared to food and thus can be marked down dramatically, and people may come for the potential savings there.

The second store, called One-Stop, has only two specials to choose from. Both involve lower prices on meats and vegetables, differing in the selection of each, with several coupons for discounts. Given the payoff table below, determine the strategy for each store and which store will come out ahead (the expected value of the game).

The Market

One-Stop	Vegetables and Fruits	Meat and Poultry	Sundries
Vegetables and Meats I	$2000	− $3000	$5000
Vegetables and Meats II	− $5000	$2000	− $4000

INCIDENT: ESCALATING SERVICES

An example of a nonzero-sum game is that of airlines giving extra frills for their passengers as an incentive to increase sales. The Civil Aeronautics Board (CAB) said in the summer of 1975 that it would look into the practice of some airlines giving free alcoholic beverages to coach passengers. The Board ordered the nation's airlines to submit data on the cost of providing free drinks to coach passengers and on the revenues they gained from selling the drinks. The order is an outgrowth of a "booze war" that started when one airline attempted to regain passengers it had lost while shut down by a strike. National began offering two free drinks to all coach passengers on certain flights. The carrier said the action was necessary because another airline was giving free champagne to coach passengers on some of its flights. The giveaway program spread to other airlines, and several carriers now give wine, champagne, or other drinks to coach passengers on some flights. The CAB said shortly after pouring free drinks began that it was worried about the effect of the programs on airline revenues. The Board added it felt that "particularly at this time of scarce resources and higher costs, it is highly questionable for the carriers to compete for such traffic by indulging in such giveaways."

rock, paper, scissors

Probably one of the earliest two-person, zero-sum games learned is the childhood game called "Rock, Paper, Scissors." This consists of two people shaking a fist three times in unison and then keeping a fist (rock), showing their hands flat (paper), or showing the first two fingers (scissors). If they both show the same thing, there is a draw and no payoff. But if they are different, the payoff is determined by the fact that "paper covers rock," "rock breaks scissors," and "scissors cut paper." This means that if player A shows scissors and player B shows paper, then player A wins. However, if player B had shown rock, player B would have won.

First make up a payoff table, using +1 for player A winning, and −1 for player A losing. A draw is zero. Then determine the optimal strategy, both by applying the Quick & Cleans and the Quick & Dirty. Next determine the expected value of the game. Given the answers that you now have, does it make sense how you usually play the game? Why or why not? Is there some factor that is not included in this analysis such as "psyching out" an opponent? Why would it be dangerous to apply the strategy in the same sequence every time?

INCIDENT: COUPON WAR

Less than 100 years ago, C. W. Post spent a good deal of time trying to figure out how to introduce his new breakfast cereal, Grape Nuts, to the American public. He decided to rouse interest by issuing certificates worth a penny each—one redeemable with each purchase of Grape Nuts. Post's idea worked and was the beginning of a major merchandising device, one that has produced repeated competitive wars in the grocery stores and supermarkets down through the years. In 1975 it was estimated that 34 billion coupons were distributed, an increase of 107 percent in 5 years. Despite the increasing barrage of coupons, only about 5 percent are redeemed annually, according to Nielsen Clearinghouse. Critics of couponing call it a gimmick—a quiet movement away from the discount pricing that supermarkets have been touting for the last several years. They say that the merchandising vehicle is unfair and costly to the vast majority of consumers who do not use coupons. They maintain that coupons cost money and that this expense helps keep food prices high. As the supermarkets and products compete with each other, they engage in a lose/lose game where the ultimate victim is the consumer.

prisoner's dilemma

A version of the prisoner's dilemma is this game that is played by three teams. There are six rounds or decisions to be made. Each team must consist of at least two people. The first, third, and fifth rounds require decisions from each team with no outside consulting at all, and each decision is given three minutes to be made. The even rounds (second, fourth, and sixth) allow for three representatives, one from each team, to meet and discuss strategy together for three minutes, then two more minutes are allowed for the representatives to consult their respective teams before the decision is made. The scoring rules are very simple, and the decision strategies are limited to two: yes and no. The rules are as follows:

All three teams mark *yes*: everyone wins one point.
Two *yes*, one *no*: *yes* teams lose one point, *no* team wins two points.
One *yes*, two *no*: *yes* team loses two points, *no* teams win one point.
All three teams mark *no*: everyone loses three points.

The object of the game is to see if trust and cooperation can be built among these teams. Even knowing the rules and the object of the game, it most often turns out that not all the teams have positive points, and sometimes that the total of all three teams is less than zero. To make the game more interesting, the number of points won in each successive round is multiplied by a larger number, thus putting a great deal of weight on the last round. An interesting way to try and secure cooperation among the teams is to have every member put in $1 at the beginning of the game, with all the money going to the team with the most points.

The instructor should collect the decisions from each team at the end of each round, determine the scores for that round, multiply them by the multiplier for that round, add the total, and hand back the score sheet to the teams for the next round. No team should *see* another team's decision, even after the game is over.

Prisoner's Dilemma, Score Sheet

	Instructions	Vote		Points	×	Multiplier	=	Total
Round 1:	Team decides strategy only. (3 minutes)	Yes	No			1		
Round 2:	Representatives, one from each team, meet for 3 minutes. Then team decides for 2 more minutes.	Yes	No			2		
Round 3:	Team decides strategy only. (3 minutes)	Yes	No			4		
Round 4:	Representatives, one from each team, meet for 3 minutes. Then team decides for 2 more minutes.	Yes	No			5		
Round 5:	Team decides strategy only. (3 minutes)	Yes	No			7		
Round 6:	Representatives, one from each team, meet for 3 minutes. Then team decides for 2 more minutes.	Yes	No			10		

Supplementary Problems

1. When planning their political campaign strategies for a remote section of their state, two candidates for governor tried to decide what it would cost them in terms of votes. Candidate A is the incumbent, married, and candidate B is the challenger, single. Candidate A expects to come out 300 votes ahead if they both campaign, and gain 1200 votes if candidate B doesn't. If candidate A doesn't campaign and candidate B does, candidate A will lose 800 votes, but gain 100 if both don't campaign. A further possibility is for candidate A to send his wife, who could cut losses down to − 200 if candidate B campaigns and pick up 400 if candidate B doesn't.

   a. Set up the payoff table in terms of candidate A, assuming a zero-sum game.
   b. Determine the solution strategy for each player.

2. For the following payoff table,

	Player B		
Player A	1	2	3
1	1	− 2	3
2	− 1	0	4

   a. Figure the strategies for player A and B using the Quick & Dirty for eight steps.
   b. Ignoring strategy 3 for player B, determine player B's strategies using the Quick & Clean formula (or solving the equations).
   c. Why would player B never choose strategy 3?

3. Given the payoff table below, determine the optimal probabilities for each strategy for each player and the expected value of the game.

	Player B		
Player A	1	2	3
1	3	5	1
2	4	6	3
3	2	1	2

4. Recalling the Rock, Paper, Scissors case (page 327), you (player A) find that your opponent is about five times larger than yourself. Considering that the loser gets punched, you decide to change the payoff for losing from −1 to −5.

   a. Write the new payoff table.
   b. Are the old probabilities for each strategy still valid? Demonstrate or explain your answer.
   c. If you use equal probabilities, in whose favor is the game? Show why.

5. Find the optimal strategy for player B and the expected value of the following game. In whose favor is this game?

	Player B	
Player A	1	2
1	−10	− 4
2	8	2

6. Given the following payoff table,

	Player B		
Player A	1	2	3
1	− 1	− 2	1
2	3	2	0

   a. Use the Quick & Dirty eight times to determine the optimal strategy for each player.
   b. Is any strategy dominated? Explain.

7. Given the following game, start with player B choosing strategy 2 and continue for 6 times for each player using the Quick & Dirty solution and determine the probabilities for each player's strategies.

	Player B		
Player A	1	2	3
1	3	2	− 1
2	0	5	− 2
3	− 1	− 4	3

9.3 MARKOV MODELS

As we have seen, the difficulty of making decisions is not limited solely to the manager or the executive, but it is also the problem of the consumer. Which laundry soap to buy, which deodorant to use, which toothpaste to purchase, which model car to drive, and so on. One of the provinces of decision making is trying to influence the decision of the consumer, not just one person, but groups of people. There are several types of products that thrive simply on the fact that the public is fickle. Half the price of laundry detergent is for the advertising to convince you that you should buy it. In a market where most brands are the same, and the price is small per item, it is easier to steal customers than to keep them. So the strategy usually is to steal more than you lose, and to hope that the total number of customers keeps growing.

Each product attempts to come up with some slogan or image that will help it take over the market from some competitor. Measured against this are very conscious attempts to create brand loyalty. This means giving the image of a product as one that its consumers are loyal to and would go to great lengths to buy.

Markov models are used to try and simulate the buying habits of a large group of consumers (rather than one individual). Surveys are taken to determine what brand you are buying now and what you bought the last time. This helps establish probabilities for either staying with the current brand or switching to another. Markov models are interested in determining how much brand switching goes on, which brands are gaining customers, and which are losing them overall. It also helps to determine how many fickle customers are "floating" around at any given time. These models assume that there is a fixed pool of customers, and that past buying habits (several periods ago) do not affect your current decision, only the last period does.

Let us take the example of two gasoline stations in the Midwest. The first is a cut-rate low-service low-priced gas station found prevalently in the Midwest. It usually finds a section or area that it feels could use another station and undercuts the competition. After it has been established for six months and has a good pool of customers, a competitor will open a gas station across the street (or as close as possible) in order to steal as many of the first station's customers as possible. The second station has found that it is tremendously successful in doing this with the particular gas station that is cut-rate. Determine the number of customers for the next five weeks if the cut-rate station starts with a customer pool of 600 customers and the probabilities shown in Figure 9.2 indicate the probability of any one customer going from one station to another, or staying there.

Quick & Dirty Algorithm: Markov Model

1. For the first product, for each arrow coming *into* that product:
   a. Multiply the probability on that arrow times the number of customers in the product from which it is coming.
   b. Add up all these numbers.

Figure 9.2

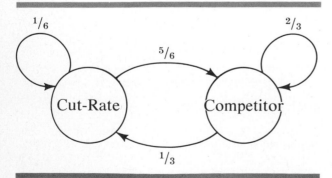

This is the new number of customers for the next time period.
2. Do the same for every product except the last.
3. For the last product add up all the new numbers of customers and subtract from the total number of customers. This will be the new number of customers for the last product.
4. Continue steps 1 to 3 until the new number of customers does not change. A steady state has now been reached.
5. The number of new customers changing to a product should now be equal to the number of old customers leaving. These are known as "floaters."

Example. For the above example, let us consider the cut-rate station first:

$$\text{cut-rate} = \tfrac{1}{6}(600) + \tfrac{1}{3}(0) = 100 \text{ customers.}$$

Here we had 600 at the cut-rate station to begin with and no customers at the competitor's. If we had a total of 600 customers, and only 100 will be at the cut-rate station this week, then the competitor must equal 500 customers ($600 - 100 = 500$). For the second week:

$$\text{cut-rate} = \tfrac{1}{6}(100) + \tfrac{1}{3}(500) = 183 \text{ (rounded).}$$

Thus,

$$\text{competitor} = 600 - 183 = 417 \text{ customers.}$$

Continuing on for the third week:

$$\text{cut-rate} = \tfrac{1}{6}(183) + \tfrac{1}{3}(417) = 170 \text{ (rounded).}$$

Also,

$$\text{competitor} = 600 - 170 = 430 \text{ customers.}$$

In table form, we get the following results:

Week	Cut-Rate	Competitor
0	600	0
1	100	500
2	183	417
3	170	430
4	172	428
5	171	429

We see that the process is very stable by the third week, with just small changes after that until the steady state is reached in the fifth week. At this point the number of customers switching from cut-rate to the competitor should be equal to the number switching the other way: $\tfrac{5}{6}(171) = \tfrac{1}{3}(429)$. These are the "floaters"; they are about 286 customers who are constantly changing brands. But this does not mean that it is always the same 286 customers. Assuming that the number of customers stays at 600, then the competitor has effectively "stolen" 429 customers from the cut-rate station.

Quick & Clean Algorithm: Markov Model

1. For each product except the last, set up an equation giving the number of that product equal to the probability of each arrow coming into that product times the amount from where it is coming (sum each of these incoming arrows).
2. Add up all products to equal the customer pool.
3. Solve the set of simultaneous linear equations that results from steps 1 and 2. These will be the steady state solutions.

Example.   For the cut-rate gasoline we can get the following equation:

$$\text{cut-rate} = \tfrac{1}{6}(\text{cut-rate}) + \tfrac{1}{3}(\text{competitor})$$

and the customer pool of 600 is equal to the sum of the two products:

$$\text{cut-rate} + \text{competitor} = 600.$$

Solving these two gives competitor = 429 (rounded) and cut-rate = 171.

deodorants

Currently on the market there are three basic types of deodorants available to the consumer. Originally most deodorants were sticks. Although very inexpensive to package, they would tend to get messy in heat. Then came the wave of spray deodorants, changing the habits of millions of Americans. Finally the "dry" spray became a fad. Thus there are basically three ways that the deodorant can be packaged. Recently the stick deodorant has become more popular because it does not use an aerosol can, which has the ecological stigma of stripping away the earth's ozone layer and thus exposing the world to deadly radiation. Given the probability that a consumer changes the type of deodorant each month, use Figure 9.3 to determine the steady state number of customers for a fixed pool of 1000 customers, and how many "floaters" there would be.

For 1000 customers there are now 500 using dry deodorant, 300 using stick, and 200 using regular spray. Market research would like to know if the stick deodorant is going to increase in popularity if these

Figure 9.3

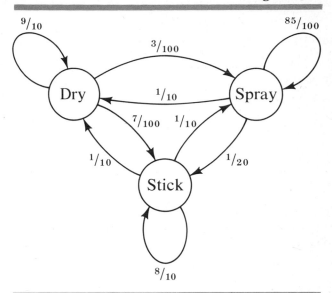

probabilities hold and if the dry spray deodorant will decrease in popularity.

Solution

Recommendation
If current probabilities are correct, the dry spray deodorant should keep 50 percent of the market that it presently has. The stick deodorant will not increase in popularity but will in fact decrease further in popularity from the present 30 percent to 24 percent of the entire market. It would not be recommended to put a lot of emphasis in advertising on the stick deodorant.

Numerical Answer.
The steady states are dry 500, stick 240, and spray 260.

The number of floaters are dry 50, stick 48, spray 39.

Math Work
Using the Quick & Dirty, for the first month,

dry $\tfrac{9}{10}(500) + \tfrac{1}{10}(200) + \tfrac{1}{10}(300) =$
                            500 customers
spray $\tfrac{85}{100}(200) + \tfrac{3}{100}(500) + \tfrac{1}{10}(300) =$
                            215 customers
stick $1000 - 500 - 215 = 285$ customers.

For the second month,

dry $\tfrac{9}{10}(500) + \tfrac{1}{10}(215) + \tfrac{1}{10}(285)$
                            $= 500$ customers
spray $\tfrac{85}{100}(215) + \tfrac{3}{100}(500) + \tfrac{1}{10}(285) = 226.25$
                            (rounded to 226 customers)
stick $1000 - 500 - 226 = 274$ customers.

We would continue this onto the steady state or use the Quick & Clean. Summarizing our results so far,

Month	Dry	Spray	Stick
0	500	200	300
1	500	215	285
2	500	226	274

Notice that for the dry deodorant a steady state has already been reached.

For the Quick & Clean,

$$\text{dry} = \tfrac{9}{10}(\text{dry}) + \tfrac{1}{10}(\text{spray}) + \tfrac{1}{10}(\text{stick})$$
$$\text{spray} = \tfrac{85}{100}(\text{spray}) + \tfrac{3}{100}(\text{dry}) + \tfrac{1}{10}(\text{stick})$$
$$\text{dry} + \text{spray} + \text{stick} = 1000.$$

Solving for each, we get:

$$\text{dry} = 500, \quad \text{spray} = 260, \quad \text{stick} = 240.$$

For floaters we have

dry	$(\tfrac{3}{100} + \tfrac{7}{100})(500)$	= 50
spray	$(\tfrac{1}{10} + \tfrac{1}{20})(260)$	= 39
stick	$(\tfrac{1}{10} + \tfrac{1}{10})(240)$	= 48.

Thus there is a total of 137 customers changing brands each month.

INCIDENT: PROMOTION MODEL

When the probability of moving or switching to another brand is interpreted as being promoted, fired, or retained, we can use the Markov model to predict how long a person might stay in an organization or how long it will take him or her to become president of the company. This of course will not work for any specific individual, but it will work for a large number of individuals in a corporation. The Air Force did a study using Markov models to track the careers of its officers throughout the world in and out of different categories. This included time spent at each rank, number promoted each year, and the number retiring (early or regular retirement). An interesting application of this Markov model occurs in civilian or military life when the probability of being retained is 1.0. This means that once entering that position, you will never leave. In Markov terms this is a trapping state, but in more popular terms this is the famous Peter principle. Thus we can describe the fact that "in a hierarchy, every employee rises to his or her level of incompetence" by a Markov model with some trapping states.

daily newspapers

The *Los Angeles Times* and the *Herald Examiner* are competitive daily newspapers serving the Los Angeles County area. The *Times* has an average circulation of about 1 million copies each day, which includes 750,000 subscribers plus newsstand sales. The *Times* is a morning newspaper, while the *Herald Examiner* is an afternoon paper. The *Examiner* has an average circulation of about 500,000 with the number of subscribers at about 350,000.

Data on brand switching was gathered by random telephone interviews of 200 people in 8 county regions (25 in each). Three regions were almost equally divided in readership. The *Times*/*Examiner* ratio was 3:2 in two of the other regions. The balance of the selected regions showed almost unanimous support of the *Times*.

The survey showed that out of 200 who were receiving either paper, 58 were getting the *Examiner* and 142 the *Times*. Further it was revealed that in the past year 11 percent of the *Times* readers had switched over to the *Examiner*, while only 6 percent of *Examiner* subscribers had changed over to the *Times*. This 2:1 ratio in favor of the *Examiner* may have been attributable in part to a recent *Examiner* strike before this data was collected. During the strike period most of its readers switched to other papers, notably the *Times*. Thus many former readers were perhaps switching back again.

Considering that these figures were for 1973, determine how many of these 200 customers will be buying each newspaper for 1974, 1975, and 1976. Then determine the steady-state solution for the 200 customers and extend that to the total circulation of both papers.

INCIDENT: PLANES STAY UP, PROFITS GO UP

Several years ago three professors did a Markov study of activity at all the airports in California and determined the least number of planes necessary to carry most of the intrastate traffic. By hiring the finest maintenance crew to make sure that all planes spent their time in the air rather than on the ground being repaired or waiting for a flight, a very profitable airline service was established.

quality assurance

The quality assurance department for a large industrial firm situated on the East Coast has been concerned about one of its assembly lines. Of the four stages of machining and assembly, three have shown considerable need for rework, which has caused a slowdown in the throughput for the company. Anything below 1 percent rework can be tolerated, but in some cases this has gone as far as 6 percent. With increased training programs the quality assurance department hopes to get throughput back up to at least 98 percent, or about 980 pieces per week, within the next 2 weeks. In very simplified terms, the assembly line can be approximated as a Markov model with a constant input into the first state of 1000 new pieces each week which need to be worked on. Each stage of production is designed to be able to handle about 1100 parts a week, but some of these areas are dangerously close to being overloaded with extra rework. The Markov model can be described in network terms as shown in Figure 9.4.

With the new training procedures the quality assurance department has figured that within 2 weeks there should be a noticeable change in the load at each stage of production. Presently there will be 1000 pieces introduced into stage I, with 30 pieces also needing rework from last week. Stage II will have 1040, stage III will have 1020, and stage IV will have 1050. Determine from this model how many will be in each stage for the next 4 weeks, and make recommendations as to whether the training program will be successful. Notice that for this problem we do not have a closed system, but that 1000 pieces will enter stage I each week. The probabilities for changing stages are weekly probabilities that are estimates by the quality assurance department.

INCIDENT: CAB STUDY

Another application of Markov models occurred in the Midwest when a consultant was hired to study the movements of cabs in a large city. Data was gathered at the airport, downtown, and in the suburbs. The results of this study showed that while a lot of traffic moved from the airport to downtown via cabs or limousines, there was not much demand for cabs from the downtown hotels back to the airport. Thus it

was advisable to drive the cab back to the airport empty rather than to wait around for a fare back.

health center

At a state-supported mental health center, fiscal-year budgeting requirements are based primarily upon the previous year's activities. This data is combined with any estimates of the next year's patient load to make a budgeting estimate. The problem could be greatly simplified if a reasonable prediction of the next year's patient load could be made. This prediction must give patient load as divided into certain specific treatment modes, each of which has a per-patient monthly cost associated with it. A by-product of this type of prediction would be an aid in determining staff requirements for the hospital.

Within the alcoholism division, patient movement from one treatment mode to another appears to approximate a Markov model. A patient can be in only one treatment mode at any one time, and as a general rule, patient movement from one mode to another is only a function of the state in which the patient presently is. Occasionally a particular family situation or background of a patient may affect movement through the program. However, this is a rare occurrence, and by taking sufficient data, this type of exception should have little influence on final predictions. Patient movement through the treatment program is dependent upon decisions made in patient–staff planning conferences. These sessions are an evaluation of the patients' past involvement in the program and their treatment objectives. The decision is made jointly by the patient and the staff subteam associated with the particular treatment mode.

For this simplified model there are four possible states: An alcoholic in the community not yet in the program, inpatient care at the mental health center, outpatient care with visits to the center, and finally the rehabilitation stage. This last stage consists of patients not in therapy, but who have been through the program and are now considered back in the community. It is estimated that there are currently 100,000 alcoholics in the community who have never been treated, 19 inpatients, 120 outpatients, and 600

Figure 9.4

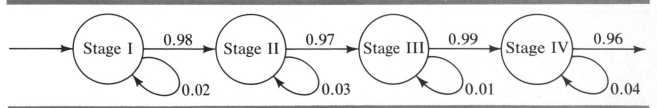

Table 9.1

This Month	Next Month			
	Community	Inpatient	Outpatient	Rehabilitation
Community	0.99988	0.00012	0.00000	0.00000
Inpatient	0.00000	0.32000	0.51000	0.17000
Outpatient	0.00000	0.00000	0.90000	0.10000
Rehabilitation	0.00000	0.00050	0.00200	0.99750

rehabilitated. Using the probabilities for changing states each month as given in Table 9.1, determine for the next 12 months what the number of inpatients and outpatients will be. Will more staff be required if the current load is about all the center can handle?

Supplementary Problems

1. The following diagram represents a Markov model for three fast food outlets, The Grease Pit, Perilous Pizza, and Chicken Clucks.

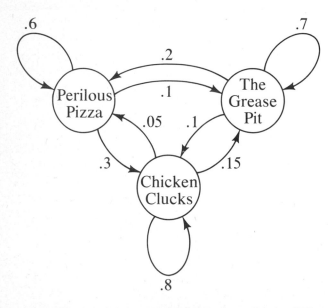

a. Determine how many customers there will be in the next two weeks if the total population is 500 customers and The Grease Pit has 200 and Perilous Pizza 200 this week.
b. Write the simultaneous equations necessary to find the steady state solution and solve.
2. Consider the Deodorants case.
a. How many customers will be buying each type of deodorant in months 3 and 4?
b. Explain why the number of customers using dry deodorant never changes from month 0.
c. Explain what is meant by "floaters" in this case.

3. At a major university in the southeastern United States a survey was taken of 1000 women to see how many were dieting each week to lose weight (dieting was defined as averaging less than 900 calories per day). In the initial survey it was determined that 782 women were dieting and 218 were not. But it was found that only 22 percent stay with their diets for a week while 60 percent say they are going on a diet next week.
a. Complete the following diagram.

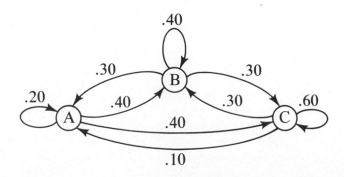

b. How many women will be in each state during weeks 1 and 2?
c. What is the steady state solution?
4. In a small Midwestern town there are two bookstores. One sells only new books and the other sells used books as well as new ones. The new bookstore can expect to receive 40 percent of the used bookstore's customers every week while they retain 30 percent of their own customers each week.
a. Draw the Markov model representing the trade between the two stores.
b. Assuming a customer population of 1000, determine the next two weeks of business if the new bookstore has 600 customers in week 0.
c. Determine the steady state number of customers for each store.
5. Consider the Markov diagram below.

a. Determine the number of customers in each state for weeks 1 and 2 if the original allocation for week 0 is as follows:

Week	A	B	C
0	600	300	100
1			
2			

b. Write the steady state equations and solve for the steady state.
c. How many floaters are there in week 2?
6. Consider the Health Center case (page 327). Write the equations for the solution of the steady state. *Do not solve*.

9.4 BRIDGING THE GAP: THE INTERFACE

The preceding three sections have barely touched upon subjects that are much more detailed and complicated than could be put into an introductory course in quantitative methods. It was the desire of the authors to give you a feeling for decision making under uncertainty problems and the kind of analysis needed to solve them. The following comments seem necessary at this point.

1. Section 9.1 is a very simplified introduction into what becomes a full semester course on its own at major universities. The whole area of prior and posterior probabilities, utility theory, and Bayesian statistics has not even been mentioned. Many books are excellent in this area, but the classic remains Schlaifer[2] and should be investigated by the serious student.
2. Section 9.2 begins to scratch the surface of competitive strategies or game theory with some simplified games and examples. Again, whole courses have been taught on the complexities of this subject and especially its predominant use in the military–aerospace complex. A linear programming model for mixed strategies is included in several books, including the one referenced in the section.[3]
3. Section 9.3 is an elementary discussion of Markov chains and their uses, but has totally ignored the important decision-making capabilities involved in the valuation determination policy of Howard.[4,5] The decision maker could choose from several options such as extra advertising, increased production, and so on, to try to change the Markov probabilities. Given a specific point in time, this can be used to aid the decision maker in finding the optimal option, thus blending in a little decision theory.

9.5 REVIEWS

Review 1: Open book and notes; show **all** *work; and write legibly.*

1. (15 points) Given the payoff table below, determine the optimal strategy for each opponent.

Player A	Player B 1	2	3
1	3	1	0
2	− 1	2	2

a. Use the Quick & Dirty algorithm starting with player A choosing strategy 1 and continuing for six times. Find the probability for each strategy.

b. Eliminate strategy 2 for player B and solve using the Quick & Clean algorithm for the strategy for player A. Also determine the expected value of the game. In whose favor is this game?

2. (10 points) Consider the following decisions to be made about a certain stock portfolio and the market conditions for the various payoffs below:

Market	Buy	Stock Keep	Sell
Up	− $600	− $400	$1000
Same	$200	0	$400
Down	$300	$200	− $800

a. Determine the Minimax strategy.

b. Determine the expected value strategy, knowing nothing about market conditions and the EVPI.

3. (15 points) After a late night you must decide whether you would go to class today or not. The question is whether the professor will give a surprise quiz. Given the payoff table below, determine what you should do according to the following strategies.

States	Acts Go to Class	Sleep
Quiz	3	− 3
No Quiz	0	5

a. Maximax.

b. Minimax.

c. Expected value.

d. EVPI.

4. (15 points) In trying to determine the effectiveness of other forms of transportation, a survey revealed that out of 10,000 people who presently ride the bus, only 50 percent return the next day to ride the bus and 10 percent go to car pools. Of the 15,000 who use car pools daily, 80 percent return with 15 percent going to drive their private cars the next day. From the 100,000 private car drivers, 2 percent will switch to the bus and 3 percent to a car pool.

a. Complete the diagram.

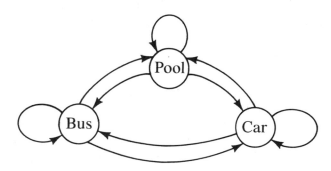

b. Write the steady state equations.

c. How many will be riding buses, car pools, or private cars the next day?

Bus: _____

Car pool: _____

Private car: _____

5. (10 points) Given the following game, start with player B choosing strategy 2 and continue six times for each player using the Quick & Dirty solution. Determine the probabilities for each player's strategies.

Player A	**Player B** 1	2	3
1	3	2	− 1
2	0	5	− 2
3	− 1	− 4	3

6. (15 points) Consider the following model of three ice cream stores servicing the area with a fixed customer pool of 2000 people in the neighborhood.

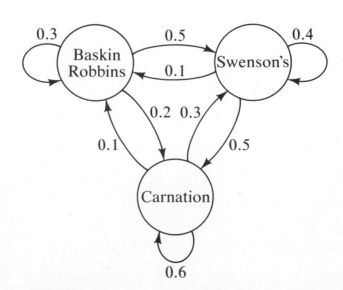

a. If there are 1000 Carnation customers and 500 Swenson's, how many will there be next week for all three stores?

b. Given the steady-state equations, find the solution:

$$\begin{aligned} BR &= 0.3\ BR + 0.1\ S + 0.1\ C \\ C &= 0.2\ BR + 0.5\ S + 0.6\ C \\ 2000 &= \quad\ BR + \quad S + \quad C \end{aligned}$$

c. Write the steady-state equation for Swenson's.

7. (10 points) In a recent amateur golf tournament Bill was facing an important approach shot to an unknown green. If the green would "hold," he could aim close to the pin and expect the ball to stop quickly, close to the hole. If the green was "hard," he must aim well short of the hole and let the ball roll up to the cup. If he chooses wrong he'll end up in the sand trap behind or in front of the green with a long difficult putt. He quickly constructed the following payoff table. The values are in terms of how many strokes he will be ahead or behind (+ is good, − is bad).

	Act	
States	*Go for Pin*	*Lay Up*
Green Holds	+ 3	− 2
Green Fast	− 3	+ 1

a. Determine the Maximin strategy. _____

b. If he were Arnold Palmer, what would he choose? (Consider that Arnie's book is entitled *Go for Broke!*)

_____

c. What is the Minimax strategy? _____

8.   (10 points) Consider the Daily Newspapers case (page 326).
a. How many of the 200 customers will be buying each newspaper in 1975, 1976, and 1977?

b. By the end of 1976, what percentage of total circulation does the *Examiner* have?

c. How does this compare with the steady-state solution?

*Review 2: Open book and notes; show **all** work; and write legibly.*

1.   (15 points) Beautiful Bob has been going out with Lovely Linda for two years now and really enjoys the arrangement. The problem is that he has just met Marvelous Martha, and she wants to go out with him. He would rate a date with her as 9 if he didn't get caught by Linda, who is extremely jealous and always checking up on him. If he does get caught on the date, he would rate it as -3, because it would take a lot of talking to convince Linda that he is not two-timing her. He knows if he doesn't go out on the date that he will really regret it (-5) if Linda wouldn't have found out, but he would be relieved ($+2$) if he didn't go out and she would have found out.

a. Set up the payoff table in terms of Bob versus Linda assuming a zero-sum game.

b. Determine the solution strategy for Bob and the expected value of the game. (In whose favor is the game?)

2. (10 points) Find the expected value of the game:

$$2p_1 \qquad - 2p_3 = EV$$
$$\qquad - 4p_2 + p_3 = EV$$
$$p_1 - 3p_2 \qquad = EV$$
$$p_1 + p_2 + p_3 = 1.0.$$

3. (15 points) From past history it is known that people in the computer software industry change jobs often. Let us assume that 30 percent of IBM's employees switch to private software houses and 20 percent to Burroughs. Burroughs, another biggie, loses 10 percent to IBM and 50 percent to private software houses. The private software houses seem to have better control. They lose about 10 percent to each of the big companies (IBM and Burroughs). These figures are for yearly changes.
a. Draw a Markov model and clearly label it (use circles, arrows, and so on).

b. Given 10,000 IBM employees, 5000 at Burroughs, and 6000 private software employees now, how many will there be in each firm a year from now, assuming a closed system?

c. Write the steady-state equations for this situation but *do not solve*.

4. (15 points) There are 1000 customers who buy drinks of some sort on campus. The only two sources of refreshment are the Commons restaurant and Fruity Rudy's. It has been determined that Fruity Rudy is able to take away 70 percent of the Commons's customers each week, while Commons gets 60 percent of Rudy's customers.

a. Draw the Markov model.

b. Assume that week zero was right before Rudy started his business on campus. Give the customer distributions for the next three weeks.

c. Determine the steady-state solution for Rudy and the Commons.

5. (15 points) Fruity Rudy has decided that he has three alternatives facing him for the fall semester. The demand for his drinks (and thus his profit) is dependent upon the weather. Given the three overall weather conditions for the fall semester, determine the expected value for each act given the payoff table below.

	Acts		
States	Increase Employees	Stay Same	Decrease Employees
Great Weather	$25,000	$15,000	$5,000
Fair Weather	$15,000	$10,000	$5,000
Poor Weather	− $5,000	− $2,000	$3,000

6. (10 points) Consider the Glass Cans case (page 314). If the probabilities of low, medium, and high demand were 0.20, 0.20, and 0.60, respectively, determine the EVPI for the optimal act.

7. (10 points) Given the Markov model below, determine the number of customers that Store A will have in the steady state solution and the number of floaters.

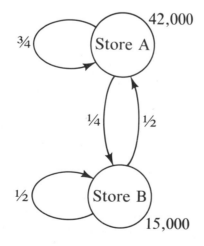

8. (10 points) Find the optimal strategy for player A and the expected value of the following game.

	Player B	
Player A	*1*	*2*
1	25	− 15
2	3	30

9.6 REFERENCES

1. B. Pascal, *Pensées*, translated by W. F. Trotter, (New York: Dutton, 1952).
2. R. Schlaifer, *Analysis of Decisions under Uncertainty* (New York: McGraw-Hill, 1969).
3. M. Sasieni, A. Yaspen, and L. Friedman, *Operations Research—Methods and Problems* (New York: Wiley, 1959).
4. R. A. Howard, *Dynamic Programming and the Markov Process* (New York: Technology Press and Wiley, 1960).
5. R. E. Bellman and S. E. Dreyfus, *Applied Dynamic Programming* (Princeton, NJ: Princeton University Press, 1962).

Additional Reference

R. E. D. Woolsey and H. S. Swanson, *Operations Research for Immediate Application* (New York: Harper & Row, 1975), Markov Processes.

10
applied probability

INTRODUCTION

This chapter is intended as an introduction to stochastic problems, or problems that involve probability, such as inventory problems where the number of items demanded is no longer constant but varies daily. This can make it very difficult to use the standard economic order quantity model developed in Chapter 3. Simple probability distributions will be used so that you will not need a thorough knowledge of statistics, although this subject should be pursued if a major in decision sciences, management sciences, or operations research is desired. The unifying theme of this chapter is that although things may occur by "chance," we can predict how often things will occur over a long period of time and thus use this knowledge to determine how much to order, when to replace, how many service facilities to open, and so on.

Two basic techniques are used to solve the problems in this chapter: analytic and simulation. You will find that simulation is a powerful tool to develop long-range patterns and results when analytic methods are either too difficult (maybe impossible) or too costly. The danger in simulation is twofold: the model may be worthless (remember our section on modeling in Chapter 1) or even if the model is valid,

simulations can be run for extensive periods of time on computers and end up costing more money than they save.

The analytic methods have an implied dangerous assumption: the probability distribution used is correct or a near-correct representation of reality. The best analysis in the world can be undermined by either the wrong assumption about the probability function or not enough data to develop an accurate probability distribution. As always, dirty data can make any Quick & Clean a Quick & Dirty.

10.1 SINGLE-PERIOD INVENTORY

There are certain items that have demand for only a single period and then lose their original value. Newspapers, bakery goods, and Christmas trees are examples of such items. Day-old newspapers do not have much value (or none), while day-old bakery goods have some value. The period for a Christmas tree is a bit longer, but there is not much sale value in a Christmas tree the day after Christmas. The problem develops because demand is not known exactly. It can be estimated with a probability distribution, but it does not follow that simply computing the mean

number demanded will give the amount that should be ordered or produced. The classic example of this problem is called the newsboy problem. A corner newsstand must decide how many papers to buy each day. They can be bought for 7 cents and sold for 10 cents, but unsold papers can only get 1 cent (for recycling). The owner feels that if he is out and someone wants a paper, he loses 25 cents in goodwill and lost sales. He has kept careful records of his business and sells anywhere from 25 to 30 papers a day. The following probabilities are given.

Customers	25	26	27	28	29	30	i
Probability	0.10	0.10	0.20	0.25	0.20	0.15	$p(i)$
Total probability	0.10	0.20	0.40	0.65	0.85	1.00	$P(i)$

Let us look at the case where the owner buys 27 newspapers. This means that 10 percent of the time only 25 customers will come in, so the revenue will be $25(10 - 7) = 75¢$ plus two unsold newspapers ($- 12¢$). Thus the expected revenue is $63¢ (0.10) = 6.3¢$. 10 percent of the time 26 customers will buy newspapers, so the revenue will be $26(10 - 7) = 78¢$ + one unsold newspaper ($- 6¢$), with an expected revenue of $72¢(0.10) = 7.2¢$. 27 customers will buy papers 20 percent of the time, and the expected revenue is $27(10 - 7) (0.20) = 16.2¢$. 25 percent of the time 28 people will want papers and only 27 will get them. Thus there will be $27(10 - 7) = 81¢$ income but a loss of 25¢ for the one customer who didn't get a paper. Thus the total revenue is 56¢ for 25 percent of the time, with the expected revenue being $56(0.25) = 14¢$. This goes on for all of the possibilities (here 29 and 30 customers). Then a total expected value is determined. This must then be compared with the case when the owner would buy 25, 26, 28, 29, or 30 papers. Needless to say, this can get monotonous.

Quick & Clean Algorithm: Single-Period Inventory[1]

Let

S = selling price per unit
R = resale (salvage) value per unit

C = cost per unit
L = lost sales cost per unit.

1. Buy, order, or make i units, where i is the smallest value for which $P(i)$ is the total probability:

$$P(i) \geq (S + L - C)/(S + L - R).$$

2. a. Set up a table as follows: Column A contains the number of items (or customers).
   b. Column B is the gross profit for selling as many as are either demanded or on hand (whichever is smaller). You can't sell what you don't have.
   c. Column C is the loss, either from selling off extra items or from not having enough and incurring the loss of customer goodwill.
   d. Column D is column B minus column C.
   e. Column E is the probability of selling that many items.
   f. Column F is column D times column E.
   g. Total column F to get the expected profit (or loss).

Example. For the newsboy example, $S = 10, C = 7, R = 1$, and $L = 25$. Find the first or smallest i such that

$$P(i) \geq (10 + 25 - 7)/(10 + 25 - 1) =$$
$$28/34 = 0.8235.$$

This occurs at $i = 29$. Any smaller value of i will not have $P(i) \geq 0.8235$. Thus to maximize the revenue, the owner ought to buy 29 newspapers each day. Some days he will make more money than others, but on the average he will make more by buying 29 newspapers each day than any other number. To determine his average daily earnings, if he buys 29 newspapers we can construct a table (Table 10.1). Thus, from Table 10.1 we can see that the newsboy will make 71.1¢ per day on the average. However there will be no day when he makes 71.1¢. Some days he will make 51¢, others 78¢, and so on, and it will average out to 71.1¢ per day.

Now let us consider that he were to buy only 28 newspapers. He can make the most profit when he buys 29 newspapers; buying any more, he will lose money because of so much scrap, with any less he will lose money through the loss of customer goodwill.

Table 10.1

Customers A	(Gross Profit B	−	Loss C)	=	Net Profit D	×	Probability E	=	Expected Net Profit F
25	75¢	−	24¢	=	51¢	×	0.10	=	5.1¢
26	78¢	−	18¢	=	60¢	×	0.10	=	6.0¢
27	81¢	−	12¢	=	69¢	×	0.20	=	13.8¢
28	84¢	−	6¢	=	78¢	×	0.25	=	19.5¢
29	87¢		0	=	87¢	×	0.20	=	17.4¢
30	87¢	−	25¢	=	52¢	×	0.15	=	9.3¢
									71.1¢

Table 10.2

Customers A	(Gross Profit B	−	Loss C)	=	Net Profit D	×	Probability E	=	Expected Net Profit F
25	75¢	−	18¢	=	57¢	×	0.10	=	5.7¢
26	78¢	−	12¢	=	66¢	×	0.10	=	6.6¢
27	81¢	−	6¢	=	75¢	×	0.20	=	15.0¢
28	84¢	−	0	=	84¢	×	0.25	=	21.0¢
29	84¢	−	25¢	=	59¢	×	0.20	=	11.8¢
30	84¢	−	50¢	=	34¢	×	0.15	=	5.1¢
									65.2¢

For 28 newspapers bought, the table would appear as shown in Table 10.2. The average daily profit when buying 28 newspapers is 65.2¢.

If 29 newspapers were ordered each day, we would expect to sell, on the average,

$$25(0.10) + 26(0.10) + 27(0.20) + 28(0.25) + 29(0.20 + 0.15) = 27.65 \text{ newspapers.}$$

The average demand is calculated the same way as the average sale, except that the last term becomes $29(0.20) + 30(0.15)$, the average daily demand being 27.80 newspapers. There will always be as much demand or more than there will be sales. Since the newsboy never has more than 29 papers, he can never sell 30.

tropical fish

The Arvada Square Aquarium is a specialty shop in Arvada, Colorado, dealing only with tropical fish and supplies. The clientele is limited to those who can afford the hobby. Prices are essentially the same as in all aquarium shops. The customers don't come to the shop to buy fish because of the price, but they come because the quality is so much better than in the large chain stores. The fish are healthier and the selection is better than at its nearest competitor's in the Lakeside Shopping Center ten miles away.

Because of the nature of the demand and the product (live fish), there is not much salvage value for dead fish. It is estimated that, due to handling and other factors, most fish will die within a month if they are not sold. Therefore the problem becomes one of determining how many fish to stock. If there are not enough, customers will stop coming to the shop. If there are too many fish, some will die and there will be losses incurred from that. The holding cost for keeping fish consists of the food consumed and some variable cost of labor.

Consider the plecostomus, a type of catfish that is in demand because of its aquarium-cleaning abilities. During the summer the following probabilities were determined from actual data for an average month:

Number of Plecostomus Sold	5	10	15	20	25	30
Probability	0.10	0.15	0.20	0.25	0.20	0.10

Each plecostomus sells for $1.98 and costs $0.65. The penalty for not having any of these in stock is put at $4.00 from the loss of sales in other fish and supplies. Determine the optimal number of plecostomus to order based on these data and the expected profit, demand, and sales.

Solution

Recommendation

It is recommended that Arvada Square Aquarium buy 25 plecostomus each month, assuming that the data given is correct. This will give an average profit of $16.40 a month.

Numerical Answer

Number of plecostomus = 25 per month
Expected demand = 18 plecostomus per month
Expected sales = 17.5 plecostomus per month
Average profit = $16.401 per month.

Math Work

$S = \$1.98$, $C = \$0.65$, $R = \$0.00$, and $L = \$4.00$.

We must determine the cumulative probabilities:

Plecostomus	5	10	15	20	25	30
Probability	0.10	0.15	0.20	0.25	0.20	0.10
Total Probability	0.10	0.25	0.45	0.70	0.90	1.00

$$P = \frac{1.98 + 4.00 - 0.65}{1.98 + 4.00 - 0.00} = 0.8913 \le 0.900.$$

The total probability for 25 plecostomus being the optimal number of fish is the first probability above, or equal to 0.891. Therefore buy 25 each month.

expected demand $5(0.10) + 10(0.15) + 15(0.20) + 20(0.25) + 25(0.20) + 30(0.10) = 18$ plecostomus

Table 10.3

Customers	(Gross Profit	–	Loss)	=	Net Profit	×	Probability	=	Expected Net Profit
5	$6.65	–	$13.00	=	– $6.35	×	0.10	=	– $0.635
10	$13.30	–	$9.75	=	$3.55	×	0.15	=	$0.533
15	$19.95	–	$6.50	=	$13.45	×	0.20	=	$2.690
20	$26.60	–	$3.25	=	$23.35	×	0.25	=	$5.838
25	$33.25	–	$0.00	=	$33.25	×	0.20	=	$6.650
30	$33.25	–	$20.00	=	$13.25	×	0.10	=	$1.325
									$16.401

expected sales $= 5(0.10) + 10(0.15) + 15(0.20) + 20(0.25) + 25(0.20 + 0.10) = 17.5$ plecostomus.

The expected net profit is shown in Table 10.3.

winchell's donut house

Winchell's is a chain of donut houses located throughout the United States. Their menu consists only of beverages and the 22 different types of donuts for which they have become quite famous. The corporate management insists that each outlet make its donuts fresh every day so as not to detract from the reputation of the chain.

A Winchell's Donut House in the south makes its donuts before opening every day, because once open, the employees do not have time to both make donuts and wait on customers. Consequently on some days Winchell's runs out before closing time, and at other times it has quantities left over that are either thrown away or given to employees. For an average day the distribution has the following probabilities:

Number Sold	600	800	1000	1200	1400	1600
Probability	0.05	0.05	0.35	0.30	0.15	0.10

The prices and costs vary for the different types of donuts, but the average figures are:

Overhead	1.7 ¢ per donut
Labor	1.2 ¢ per donut
Ingredients	0.9 ¢ per donut
Selling price	8.6 ¢ per donut

The manager says that customers actually care very little about which variety they get, for when one variety is sold out, the customer will usually select another. The manager also figures that if Winchell's runs out of donuts, it loses about 25¢ per donut from lost sales. How many donuts should be made each day in order to maximize profit? What are the expected demand, profit, and sales under this plan?

INCIDENT: DONUT ANALYSIS HAS HOLES

S.A.M., the Society for Advancement of Management at the San Diego State University School of Business, orders 15 dozen donuts every day for its coffee room, where coffee and donuts are sold 5 days a week from 8 A.M. to 8 P.M. when school is in session. On Monday through Thursday the demand for donuts is fairly constant, but Fridays have never been constant. Sometimes as many as 15 dozen donuts are sold, and other times as few as 5 dozen. Since the student members were also taking a class in operations research and studying single-period inventory models, they decided to study the problem scientifically. Lost sales were figured at $0.50 per donut, since the Accounting Society has a similar operation (offering instant coffee and no donuts), which is more accessible as most of the classrooms are on that floor. Donuts cost 9 cents each to buy and are sold for 15 cents, with the resale value of a donut being 0. After much deliberation on getting the probabilities of selling anywhere from 5 dozen to 15 dozen, it was scientifically determined to buy 7 dozen donuts on Fridays and 15 dozen the other days. The first Friday this went into effect, the company delivered 15 dozen. The next Friday they didn't deliver any. So much for science!

raymond book company

Raymond Book Company is a large book wholesaler located in New England. Its primary customers are retail book stores in the greater northeastern area.

Some books on contemporary subjects (astrology, environment, ecology, bicycling) can come into demand almost overnight by their position on the bestseller list and/or if the author is interviewed on a TV talk show. Each book must be ordered separately, and the amount ordered is dependent upon its anticipated sales by the retail outlets. Once the book is ordered, it is often five to eight weeks before additional copies can be obtained from the publishing house. Therefore the primary concern is to have enough books to satisfy immediate demand, but not so many as to clog inventory and gather dust. Books that are unsold are returned to the publishing house after a year for full credit. Carrying cost is figured as 10 percent per year of the cost of capital tied up.

A recent publication with a cost of $1.98 and selling for $2.78 had the following probability of demand:

Number of Books Ordered	100	200	300	400	500	600	700
Probability of This Number Being Sold per Month	0.05	0.05	0.20	0.30	0.20	0.10	0.10

Given that the books are returned after a year, in terms of today's value of money the wholesaler will get back $1.78. It is figured that Raymond will lose some business to the stores if it is out of stock, and so the cost of a lost sale is set at $1.50 per book. Determine how many books should be ordered, the expected demand, and the expected profit.

INCIDENT: OVERORDERING CAN HAVE BENEFITS

Another application involved a small flower stand, set up on the edge of the parking lot of a gas station. The station owner would charge rent of $25 a week, and a young couple would operate its stand from a large van. Here the probability of selling flowers depended upon several variables, such as upcoming holidays, types of flowers available, and weather conditions. Fortunately there was some resale value for the flowers, in that the couple would cut the price and sell the flowers that were not sold to another dealer at the end of the day. In the morning they would then pick up a new batch of flowers from a producer and set up shop. A bonus for running out of flowers was that they got to go home early. Nevertheless, it was important to have flowers early in the morning, at noon, and from 4 to 6 P.M. during the homeward-bound traffic. It was worth having too many of most flowers so that lost sales did not result. (The resale value helped make up some revenue lost by ordering too many.)

A final word of caution is in order. For this method to work as a Quick & Clean, the distribution of the probabilities must have a single peak. In statistical terms we would say that the distribution must be *unimodal*. If this condition is not met, the method becomes a Quick & Dirty (see Figure 10.1).

Figure 10.1

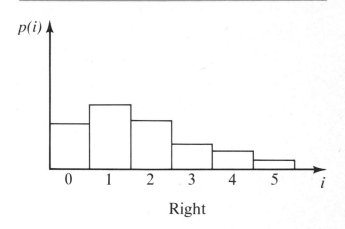

Right

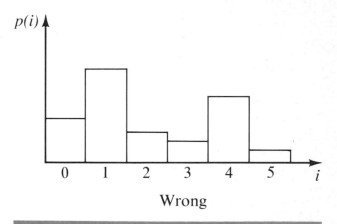

Wrong

man fook low chinese restaurant

The Man Fook Low Chinese restaurant has been in business for almost 20 years. It specializes in northern (Shanghai) Chinese food and has been a profitable concern due to its good cooking and service. One of its specialities is Chinese Tea-Cake, of which there are twelve varieties. The owner insists that the Tea-Cakes be made fresh daily so as not to detract from the restaurant's reputation. These Tea-Cakes are made before opening each day. Consequently on some days the Tea-Cakes are sold out before closing time, and at other times quantities are left over which are thrown away. For an average day the distribution is as follows:

Number Sold	3000	3200	3400	3600	3800	4000
Probability	0.05	0.05	0.35	0.15	0.20	0.20

The average prices and costs for the different types of Tea-Cakes are:

Overhead	$0.07 per cake
Labor	$0.05 per cake
Cake	$0.05 per cake.

The average selling price is $0.30. The owner says that customers are not that particular about which variety they get, but if no more Tea-Cakes are available, a lost sale is figured at $0.50 per cake. How many Chinese Tea-Cakes should be made each day to maximize the expected profit, and what would be the expected profit, demand and sales?

Supplementary Problems

1. In Hawaii a fishmonger sells fresh fish that he buys directly from the fishing fleet. He has a refrigerator so if he doesn't sell all of them the first day he can sell them to a bait shop at 5¢ each. He buys his fish for $0.50 apiece and sells them for $0.70 each. He figures he loses $0.30 per fish if he's out of fish. The probability distribution is as follows:

Number of fish	80	90	100
Probability	0.25	0.40	0.35

   a. How many fish should he buy?
   b. Assuming he buys 90 fish, what is his expected profit?
2. If the Raymond Book Company case had a price increase for its wholesale price of books from $1.98 up to $2.15,
   a. What would be the optimum number of books to order? (Show your work.)
   b. Give three examples of single period inventory items *not* given in the text.
3. The Miller Dairy has a problem with their milk going sour if they have too much production and not enough customers, and also the possibility of losing customers if there is not enough milk daily. They sell their milk for $1.30 per gallon and it costs approximately $0.75 per gallon. If it goes sour, they can get $0.05 per gallon from a pig rancher. They also lose $0.50 per gallon if they are out of milk. Given the data below, help determine what milk production should be.

Number of Gallons	500	600	700	800	900	1000
Probability	0.10	0.15	0.25	0.30	0.15	0.05

4. Consider the Winchell's Donut House case and your optimal solution. Assume that the probabilities were changed to:

Number sold	600	800	1000	1200	1400	1600
Probability	0.10	0.10	0.40	0.20	0.15	0.05

   a. What is the expected net profit if you still make

the *same* amount of donuts as your optimal answer?
   b. Should you have a new optimal amount to make? Show why or explain briefly.
5. At 14 Flavors, a town's only ice cream shop, the newest concoction is Banana Supreme. The bananas have a one day peak period (having taken two weeks to come by parcel post) and cost 25¢ a piece, but can be sold for 50¢ as an ingredient in the Banana Supreme. If not, they are sold to a neighboring restaurant for 2¢ and used in banana bread which sells for $1.95. If Banana Supreme is unavailable, the shop loses $3.00 in business. The probabilities are as follows:

Number of Customers	12	13	14	15	16	17
Probability		0.12	0.21	0.30	0.24	0.10	0.03

   a. How many bananas should be ordered daily?
   b. What are their expected sales for each day given how many they order?
   c. What is the expected demand each day?
6. Given the Man Fook Low case, would the Quick & Clean solution necessarily give the most optimal number to order? Explain.

10.2 REPLACEMENT: THINGS THAT DIE (FAIL)

The second general class of replacement problems concerns items that fail completely, such as light bulbs, electronic computer circuitry, and so on. The classic case is illustrated by a large business office or factory with a large number of incandescent light bulbs. As the bulbs burn out, they need to be replaced, which costs money in new light bulbs and labor. The two extremes in replacement are either to replace the bulbs every time they burn out and leave the others alone, or to replace all the bulbs every week, whether or not they are burned out. In the first case bulbs are only replaced when needed, but there is a high cost of replacing just one bulb. In the second case you get the economy of scale with group replacement (it is less expensive per bulb because the maintenance crew already has the large ladder out and just needs to lean over and replace another bulb), but you are replacing bulbs that are still good. The optimum solution usually lies somewhere between the two extremes: replace individual bulbs as they burn out, and after a certain period of time replace all the bulbs.

Example. Given the data for the lifetime of bulbs (in weeks), determine if they should be replaced individually (at a cost of 50¢ per bulb) or as a group (at a

Table 10.4

Bulb	\multicolumn{10}{c}{Week}
	1	*2*	*3*	*4*	*5*	*6*	*7*	*8*	*9*	*10*
1	100	100	300	400	100					
2		10	10	30	40	10				
3			11	11	33	44	11			
4				32	32	96	129	32		
5					47	47	142	190	47	
New Bulbs	100	110	321	473	252	. . .	. . .	. . .	. . .	

cost of 10¢ per bulb). Assume that there are 1000 bulbs.

Week	1	2	3	4	5	*i*
Probability	0.10	0.10	0.30	0.40	0.10	*p(i)*

This means that 10 percent of the bulbs burn out during the first week (and are replaced during that week regardless of when the group replacement will take place). Of the original 1000 bulbs, they will burn out as follows:

Week	1	2	3	4	5		
Bulbs	100	100	300	400	100	=	1000

The next week there will be 100 new bulbs, which will burn out as follows:

Week	1	2	3	4	5	6		
Bulbs	–	10	10	30	40	10	=	100

For the third week there will be 110 new bulbs (100 burned out of the original 1000 and 10 from the new bulbs for the second week):

Week	1	2	3	4	5	6	7		
Bulbs	–	–	11	11	33	44	11	=	110

We can make up a simple table (Table 10.4) to show this.

Quick & Clean Algorithm: Replacement for Things That Die (Fail)[1]

1. Set up a table as shown in Table 10.5.
   a. Column A gives simply the weeks in order.
   b. Column B is the total number of items to be replaced times the cost of group replacement.
   c. Column C is the number of items replaced that week times the cost of a single replacement.
   d. Column D is the running total of column C.
   e. Column E is column B plus column D.
   f. Column F is column E divided by column A.
2. Choose the smallest average cost in column F.
3. Determine the average life span of each part, divide into the number of parts to be replaced, and multiply by the cost of replacing a single part (or item).
4. Compare the cost in steps 2 and 3 and choose the smallest—either group replacement from step 2 or continual individual replacement from step 3.

Thus if we choose to use group replacement, we should replace individually, at a cost of 50¢ each, all the bulbs that burn out during the first two weeks. After the end of two weeks we should replace all 1000 bulbs, whether they are burned out or not.

The only thing that remains to be investigated is what it would cost if we simply replaced each bulb individually. To do that, we must determine how many weeks an average bulb lasts:

$$1(0.1) + 2(0.1) + 3(0.3) + 4(0.4) + 5(0.1) = 3.30 \text{ weeks.}$$

Table 10.5

Week A	Group Replacement B	Single Replacement C	Total Single Replacement D	Total Cost E	Average Cost F
1	1000(10¢)=$100	100(50¢)=$50.00	$50.00	$150.00	$150.00
2	$100.00	110(50¢)=$55.00	$105.00	$205.00	$102.50*
3	$100.00	321(50¢)=$160.50	$265.50	$365.50	$121.87
4	$100.00	473(50¢)=$236.50	$502.00	$602.00	$150.50
5	$100.00	252(50¢)=$126.00	$628.00	$728.00	$145.60

For 1000 bulbs this means that an average of 1000/3.30 = 303.03 bulbs burn out each week. The cost for replacing these is 303.03(0.50) = $151.52, which is considerably higher than the best average with group replacement.

los angeles memorial coliseum

The Los Angeles Memorial Coliseum seats 100,000 people and was built for the 1932 Olympic Games. Since then it has been used for numerous and varied sporting events. New seats must periodically be installed as they wear out.

As the new seats begin to wear out, the Coliseum Commission is beginning to estimate how long seats will last, and has determined that no seat lasts longer than five years. It has come up with the following distribution:

Year	1	2	3	4	5
Probability	0.10	0.15	0.20	0.25	0.30

This means that 10 percent of the seats will wear out within the first year and will have to be individually replaced within that first year. The cost involved in replacing each seat individually is $3.00 and includes installation and painting the seat brackets. When the seats are replaced as a group of 1000, the cost is $1.00 per seat. Determine what the best replacement policy would be and the average yearly cost.

Solution

Recommendation
Replace seats individually for three years, then at the end of the third year, use group replacement.

Numerical Answer. Individual replacement would cost an average of $858.00 per year. The cost of group replacement is as follows:

Year 1	$1300 per year
Year 2	$ 890 per year
Year 3	$ 833 per year
Year 4	$ 851 per year.

Math Work. Given 1000 seats per section, the number that will need to be replaced each year is shown in Table 10.6.

The average replacement cost is determined from Table 10.7. The expected number of years that a seat will last is:

$$1(0.10) + 2(0.15) + 3(0.20) + 4(0.25) + 5(0.30) = 3.50 \text{ years.}$$

Thus the average number of seats to be replaced every year is 1000/3.5 = 286. The cost of individual replacement is 286($3) = $858 per year. This is more than the group replacement at the end of three years.

football shoes

A professional football team in the western United States is faced with the problem of increasing costs as well as decreasing attendance. The team has not fared well for several years and is currently being outdrawn by the local college team. Cost effective measures are being employed everywhere, and the equipment manager is no exception. In trying to determine cost savings, he has figured out that if he

Table 10.6

Year	1	2	3	4	Year 5	6	7	8
1	100	150	200	250	300			
2		10	15	20	25	30		
3			16	24	32	40	48	
4				23.1	34.65	46.2	57.75	69.3
New Seats	100	160	231	317.1	...	...	...	...

Table 10.7

Year	Group Replacement	Single Replacement	Total Single Replacement	Total Cost	Average Cost
1	1000($1)=$1000	100($3) = $300	$300	$1300	$1300
2	$1000	160($3) = $480	$780	$1780	$890
3	$1000	231($3) = $693	$1473	$2473	$824.33*
4	$1000	317.1($3) = $951.3	$2421.3	$3421.3	$855.33

can buy 50 pairs of shoes for the team, a sporting goods outlet will give the team a discount, so that the shoes will cost only $15 per pair, rather than $25 for each single pair bought. He now must convince management that it may make sense to buy 50 pairs every few months, rather than replace the shoes individually. It is assumed that at the beginning of the season all the shoes are new. Considering a season that lasts approximately 20 weeks, he figures that shoes could be purchased at the beginning and then a lot of 50 a few times during the season. It was his hope that those who had shoes that had not been ripped, torn, or otherwise irreparable would continue wearing the old shoes (as they are broken in and comfortable), but much to his dismay he found that when there are new shoes available, the old ones do not get worn. He is now reconsidering the policy and has estimated some approximate probabilities for the shoes wearing out.

Week	1	2	3	4	5	6	7
Probability	0.05	0.10	0.15	0.30	0.20	0.10	0.10

Determine if a group replacement policy would be cheaper than individual replacement and make a recommendation.

INCIDENT: HIGH COST OF ACCIDENTS JUSTIFIES GROUP REPLACEMENT

The high reliability of atomic weapons has always been a major concern of the Defense Department. It is necessary that when these weapons are launched over enemy territory, they go off rather than fail. The only thing worse than this is a weapon that goes off *before* it is launched. Thus after a certain amount of aging the pit of an A-bomb must be replaced, or else it will go off when it is armed. These pits are replaced by group replacement of the same date group. Since there is a high cost of "failure," these pits are replaced quite often.

monkey business

The most popular animal at the zoo is the monkey, as surveys have shown again and again. There is something about its antics and similarity to us humans that lets us laugh at ourselves. Some zoos have trained monkeys and monkey shows that have proved very popular. The biggest problem with these animals, as with some other zoo animals, is that they are susceptible to colds, and the mortality rate for monkeys and

chimpanzees is not insignificant. Zoos constantly have to replace monkeys, and especially those that use them for shows find that breaking a new monkey into the act can be very difficult. The costs involved in buying, handling, shipping, and caring for monkeys can be reduced considerably if several of them are bought rather than just one at a time. If such a policy is adopted, those monkeys that are replaced are transferred to the monkey island and allowed to live out their lives performing on their own for audiences.

Consider the following data for 10 monkeys that are the basic unit for the zoo. If bought separately, they would cost approximately $400 each, while all 10 of them would cost only $1000. The yearly mortality rates are as follows:

Year	1	2	3	4
Probability	0.30	0.30	0.25	0.15

Given this data, determine if there should be a group replacement or individual replacement.

INCIDENT: PRODUCTION ROLLING ALONG

A critical part in foundry operations is the conveyor traveler for each conveyer belt that moves the ore to various parts of the foundry. If a part fails to work, the belt may come to a screeching halt, and there will be a high cost for individual replacement. Thus it is sometimes necessary to replace all the conveyer travelers between shifts, even though they have not worn out yet.

university laundromat

The University Laundromat is located near a midwestern university and is about the only place within a convenient distance of several apartments and fraternity/sorority houses for doing laundry. The laundromat is open 24 hours a day, 7 days a week, and does quite a good business. There are 20 washing machines of the top-loading variety, all bought from the same manufacturer 2 years ago. The original warranty has now run out on all the washers, and the owner does most of the repairs himself. There are also 25 dryers, which are gas dryers and require a minimum amount of servicing. Also, there are enough of them that if two or three do not work, there is no problem getting clothes dried.

The main problem, and potential source of loss of revenue, is the washing machines. If one does not work, then during the crowded hours (about eight or more hours during the whole day) no clothes can be washed, and as a consequence revenue is also lost from use of the dryers for however many machines are down. The owner will be able to repair most of the problems, but during the week two or three machines will break down in such a manner that he needs a repairman from the manufacturer to come out and service the machines. For every call made by the representative there is a cost of about $40 for a washing machine. However, if during that call each machine is checked and preventive maintenance is given, the cost goes down to about $10 for each machine.

The owner is wondering whether it would make sense to have all the washing machines periodically serviced, whether they need it or not, and if this would save money, rather than having each machine repaired when it breaks down. He has kept records for the last few months of the probability of a machine breaking down and has found that no machine can go over five weeks without some breakdown that requires the repairman.

Given this data, make a recommendation to either service the machines individually, or give a group maintenance and at what intervals.

Week	1	2	3	4	5
Probability	0.10	0.25	0.30	0.20	0.15

INCIDENT: COMPUTER MAINTENANCE

On rental equipment a large computer manufacturer has preventive maintenance once a week, and once a month he will replace certain solid logic cards, whether they need it or not. These cards have been shown to fail with a certain regularity, and tests made once a week can show if the cards are likely to fail within a certain amount of time. If there is a probability of failure of more than 20 percent, the cards are replaced. It has been found that considering the cost of downtime (having the computer break down, and the customer upset), it is much cheaper to replace parts that have not yet failed.

Supplementary Problems

1. The manager of Andy's Saloon is trying to decide whether to replace his beer mugs individually or as a group replacement. No mugs last more than two weeks at Andy's. If he buys them individually the cost is $1.75 per mug but if he buys 100 at a time the cost is $1.00 per mug. The first week, 70

percent of the mugs are broken or stolen. Assume Andy needs 100 mugs at all times.
   a. Set up a table showing how many mugs will be needed for each week for the next three weeks
   b. What is the average weekly cost for these three weeks? (Show your work.)
2. A firm services a microwave station in the mountains that has 12 separate power amplifier units that each require alignment as follows:

Quarter	1	2	3	4
Probability	0.20	0.40	0.30	0.10

If the job is done on an individual basis, it costs $300 per unit, but only $2400 for all twelve if done at the same time.
   a. How many amplifiers would you expect would need alignment in the third month?
   b. What is the expected time between alignment for each unit?
   c. How many amplifiers would need alignment during each quarter if there were no policy for repairing all of them at once?
3. An industrial plant must replace bearings on machines that provide an assembly line with parts. It is costly to shut down the line, replace one bearing ($70) when all of them can be replaced for $200 (there are 100 bearings). The frequency of breakdowns for a bearing is as follows:

Month	1	2	3	4
Probability	0.15	0.30	0.45	0.10

   a. What is the average life of a bearing?
   b. How many would be replaced on the average per month if only an individual replacement policy were used?
   c. What would be the cost of an individual replacement policy?
   d. How many bearings would be replaced in the third month if you started with 100 new bearings?
4. Consider the University Laundromat case. If the cost of group repair for machines increases from $10 to $15, how does this affect your homework recommendation? (Show your work.)

10.3 QUEUING (WAITING LINES)

The British word for line is queue, which is defined as "a file of persons or vehicles waiting in line in the order of their arrival." Thus queuing theory has to do with situations where people are waiting in line such as at a movie theater to buy tickets, at a toll booth to pay the toll, traffic on a freeway, or any place where people or things line up. The early studies of queuing were begun by Earlang, a Scandinavian scientist who studied the arrivals of telephone calls at switchboards and wanted to determine how long a person would have to wait to get through, how many incoming lines would be needed, the average time a call would take, and other measures of efficiency. Queuing has been used by traffic engineers in designing freeways, off-ramps, measuring traffic flow, and for regulating traffic. From these studies they have been able to decide where freeways need to be widened or regulated so that rush-hour traffic will travel freely and smoothly. A national chain of grocery stores uses queuing models to determine the maximum number of checkout counters needed during its busiest times so that customers will have to wait no more than 15 minutes once they reach the line. Further studies have been conducted by banks, retail stores, or almost any place where waiting will be a major part of the time spent. What queuing gives us is a model that can predict, before it happens, where the major congestion will occur, how long people or things will have to wait on the average. By changing the arrival rate in the model or the number of service areas, we can see the effect upon the average length of the line, the average waiting time, and other factors.

The models to be presented here will be very simple, with the assumption that all arrivals and services are Poisson distributed, that is, the number of arrivals per unit of time is grouped fairly close together and in graphical form would look as shown in Figure 10.2.

Figure 10.2(a) represents the distribution of arrivals that average one per minute (or hour, day, and so on). 36 percent of the time there are no arrivals during a minute, and also 36 percent of the time there is one arrival in a minute. After that, there is a lower probability of two, three, or more arrivals in a minute. Figure 10.2(b) represents arrivals that average four

per minute (or whatever time unit you are using). The exact formula for this distribution is

$$P(x) = \frac{N^x e^{-N}}{x!}$$

where N is the average number of arrivals (or services) during a span of time, and $P(x)$ is the probability of x arrivals during that span of time. The constant e often occurs in mathematics. The important thing to note is that *most* arrivals occur in this fashion, and you should be careful when applying queuing to a problem that these assumptions of a Poisson distribution are indeed met. In many cases where this is not true, the analytical formulas that we will present cannot be used, and simulation by computer is employed. This also holds true for cases that become very complicated with interactions between several lines or service areas.

Let us consider the simplest model first, where there is one line waiting for service from one station or area. We will not derive these formulas, but you may consult the references at the back of this chapter if you are interested in a derivation. The basic assumptions are that both arrival and service are Poisson distributed.

Quick & Clean Formulas for One Station Queuing[3]

1. There is a probability of x customers in line at any time; N_1 is the average number of customers arriving per unit of time and N_2 the average number of customers served per unit of time:

$$P(x) = \left(1 - \frac{N_1}{N_2}\right)\left(\frac{N_1}{N_2}\right)^x.$$

Figure 10.2

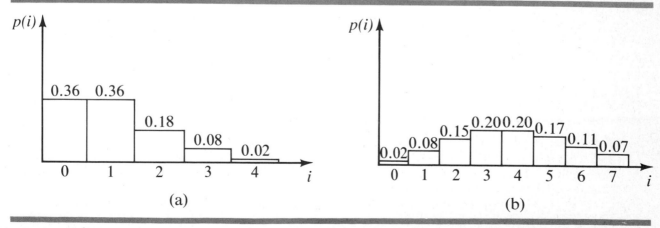

(a)

(b)

2. The average length of line Q is

$$Q = \frac{N_1^2}{N_2(N_2 - N_1)}.$$

3. The average waiting time W is

$$W = \frac{N_1}{N_2(N_2 - N_1)}.$$

4. The average number of customers N in the whole system (in line and being served) is

$$N = \frac{N_1}{(N_2 - N_1)}.$$

5. The average time a customer spends in the system (which is also the average waiting time of a customer who waits) is

$$T = \frac{1}{(N_2 - N_1)}.$$

6. The average length L of a nonempty queue (that is, *if* there is a line, what is its average length?) is

$$L = \frac{N_2}{(N_2 - N_1)}.$$

One can see from all the formulas that N_2 must be greater than N_1, or the service rate must be faster than the arrival rate. If this is not true, the line builds up indefinitely and you go out of business. Thus if we serviced less customers per hour than arrived, we would not only have trouble with the formulas, but we would have a lot of mad customers.

Example. Fotomat stores are little drive-up booths that sell film, flashbulbs, and other camera accessories. These booths are usually set up in parking lots at shopping centers, supermarkets, and so on, and are staffed by one person. Consider that during normal hours (not rush hours) arrivals take place on the average every ten minutes (that is, six arrivals per hour), and that it takes four minutes on the average to complete a transaction of buying film or getting developed pictures, ringing the sale up on the register, making change, and such. It is assumed that both arrivals and services are Poisson distributed. Given this information, let us use the Quick & Clean to find the probability of no people waiting, one person waiting, two people waiting, and so on, plus the other information gathered from the formulas.

From the problem we have $N_1 = 6$ per hour, and we can also see that N_2 (the number of services per hour) is $60/4 = 15$ possible services per hour. With $N_1 = 6$ and $N_2 = 15$, we have the following probabilities:

1. $P(0) = (1 - 6/15)(6/15)^0 =$
   $$(1 - 6/15) = 9/15 = 0.600$$
   $P(1) = (1 - 6/15)(6/15)^1 =$
   $$0.600(6/15) \qquad = 0.240$$
   $P(2) = (1 - 6/15)(6/15)^2 =$
   $$0.240(6/15) \qquad = 0.096$$
   $P(3) = (1 - 6/15)(6/15)^3 =$
   $$0.096(6/15) \qquad = 0.038$$
   $P(4) = (1 - 6/15)(6/15)^4 =$
   $$0.038(6/15) \qquad = 0.015.$$

Notice that each successive probability is simply the previous one multiplied by N_1/N_2 or 6/15. Here we see that there is a good probability of there being no one at the booth when we arrive (60 percent). There would be a very slight probability of having a line of more than two cars when we arrive.

2. The average length of line is:

$$Q = \frac{N_1^2}{N_2(N_2 - N_1)} = \frac{6^2}{15(15 - 6)} = 0.267 \text{ customer.}$$

On the average there is about one-fourth of a car or customer waiting.

3. The average waiting time is

$$W = \frac{N_1}{N_2(N_2 - N_1)} = \frac{6}{15(15 - 6)} = 0.0444 \text{ hour.}$$

In terms of minutes, this is about an average wait of 2.67 minutes for each customer.

4. The average number of customers or cars in the whole system is:

$$N = \frac{N_1}{(N_2 - N_1)} = \frac{6}{(15 - 6)} = 0.667 \text{ car or customer.}$$

5. The average time in the system is

$$T = \frac{1}{(N_2 - N_1)} = \frac{1}{(15 - 6)} = 0.111 \text{ hour or } 6.667 \text{ minutes.}$$

(This is simply taking the four-minute service average and adding it to step 3.)

6. The average length of a nonempty queue (given that there is at least one car in line) is

$$L = \frac{N_2}{(N_2 - N_1)} = \frac{15}{(15 - 6)} = 1.667 \text{ cars or customers in line.}$$

Now let us consider the situation when there is still one line, but many service areas (more than one). This is now a familiar sight and an efficient way of handling waiting. Most banks now have a single line and several tellers. When a teller is free, the next person at the head of the line goes to that window, rather than there being several lines, one behind each window. It took a few years for the customers to catch on as banks, post offices, ticket lines, and others gradually switched to this way of servicing customers. Figure 10.3 illustrates three service facilities fed by one queue.

Figure 10.3

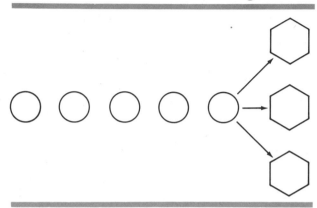

For this general model of one line and several service facilities we will again assume that all arrivals and services are Poisson distributed, and further that all service facilities have the same service rate (there is no basic difference between tellers). We will assume that we have k service facilities, and again the derivation of these formulas will not be given.

Quick & Clean Formulas for Several Station Queuing[3]

1. The probability of x customers waiting is

$$P(x) = \left(\frac{1}{x!}\right)\left(\frac{N_1}{N_2}\right)^x P(0), \quad \text{for } x = 1, 2, 3, \ldots k - 1$$

$$P(x) = \frac{1}{k! k^{x-k}} \left(\frac{N_1}{N_2}\right)^x P(0), \quad \text{for } x \geq k$$

$$P(0) = \frac{1}{\text{SUM} + \dfrac{1}{k!}\left(\dfrac{N_1}{N_2}\right)^k \dfrac{kN_2}{kN_2 - N_1}}$$

where SUM is simply the sum of

$$\frac{1}{x!}\left(\frac{N_1}{N_2}\right)^x$$

from $x = 0$ up to and including $x = k - 1$.

2. The average queue length Q is

$$Q = \frac{N_1 N_2 (N_1/N_2)^k}{(k-1)!(kN_2 - N_1)^2}\left(P(0)\right)$$

3. The average waiting time W for a customer is

$$W = \frac{Q}{N_1}.$$

4. The average number of customers N in the system is

$$N = Q + \frac{N_1}{N_2}.$$

5. The average time T a customer spends in the system is

$$T = \frac{Q}{N_1} + \frac{1}{N_2}.$$

Here we note how gruesome the first formula is, and how everything depends upon $P(0)$. As the number of service facilities increases, so does the complexity of the formulas. Again it is crucial that more customers be served per unit of time than arrive. Thus kN_2 must be greater than N_1, or the line will get infinitely long.

Example. On the West Coast there is a bridge that goes to an island which has exclusive condominiums, a nice beach, and a beautiful hotel. There are also a Navy base and a few retail stores. The toll is 60¢ per car per crossing, and there are eight booths to service the cars each way. During the day, between rush hours, usually only three of the booths are open, and if a car has to wait more than two minutes, another toll booth will be opened. The city has checked the arrival rate of cars and found that during these hours cars arrive at an average of 5 per minute and that it takes an average of 20 seconds to collect the fare. It is assumed that all arrivals and services are Poisson distributed. Determine the probability of cars waiting in line and the average length of the line, waiting time, and so on. For our purposes we will see that in essence there is one line, which splits into several as the bridge is crossed, and then chooses a toll booth to go to. $N_1 = 5$ and $N_2 = 3$ per minute, while $k = 3$ (number of toll booths).

1. SUM $= (1 + 5/3 + (1/2)(5/3)^2) = 4.056$

$$P(0) = \frac{1}{4.056 + (1/6)(5/3)^3(9/4)} = 0.1726$$

$$P(1) = \frac{1}{1!}(5/3)^1(0.1726) = 0.2876$$

$$P(2) = \frac{1}{2!}(5/3)^2(0.1726) \text{ or } (1/2)(5/3)P(1) = 0.2397$$

$$P(3) = \frac{1}{3!}(5/3)^3 P(0) = 0.1331$$

(You can use either the first or the second $P(x)$ formula here.)

$$P(4) = \frac{1}{3!3^{4-3}}(5/3)^4 P(0) \quad \text{or}$$
$$(1/3)(5/3)P(3) = 0.0739$$

$$P(5) = (1/3)(5/3)P(4) = 0.0411$$

$$P(6) = (1/3)(5/3)P(5) = 0.0228.$$

Thus there is about a 70 percent chance of finding 0, 1, or 2 cars in line (or being served) when we arrive.

2. The average queue length is

$$Q = \frac{(5)\,(3)\,(5/3)^3}{(3-1)!(9-5)^2}(0.1726) = 0.3745 \text{ car.}$$

3. The average waiting time of an arrival is

$$W = \frac{Q}{N_1} = \frac{0.3745}{5} = 0.0749 \text{ minute.}$$

which means there should hardly be any wait at all.

4. The average number of customers or cars in the system is

$$N = Q + \frac{N_1}{N_2} = 0.3745 + \frac{5}{3} = 2.0411 \text{ customers.}$$

This means that approximately two cars are in the system. Thus one toll booth should be free and there is no waiting or just a small amount of wait.

5. The average time a car must wait and spend being served is

$$S = \frac{Q}{N_1} + \frac{1}{N_2} = 0.0749 + 0.3333 = 0.4082 \text{ minute}$$
$$\text{or less than 25 seconds.}$$

Armed with these Quick & Clean formulas, you can now begin to see the effects of adding extra service facilities or taking some away, of increased service rates or faster arrivals. Again note that this is just an introduction into a field that can be very complicated, and these beginning formulas are a simplification.

drive-in dairy

A drive-in dairy takes up almost no space on a parking lot and usually consists of a large refrigerator which contains dairy products (milk, eggs, cheese, yogurt) and maybe bread and soda pop. It usually opens by 7 A.M. to catch business that most grocery stores opening at 9 A.M. would miss. If people have to be at work by 8 A.M. and need some breakfast materials, the dairy will usually meet their needs. This dairy also closes at midnight, again to get business that most stores will not give at that hour. Recently the 7/11 chain of quick-service food stores has been staying open 24 hours a day, but the owner of the drive-in dairy still thinks that its service is faster, considering that you do not have to park, get out of your car, and so on. Counting on convenience and quick service, she has not been too concerned about losing business. However, she recently spent an hour counting the number of customers that arrived and how long it took to service them. She is concerned that if on the average more than one car is waiting, customers may balk, thinking that it will take them a long time to be served. In one hour she counted 20 cars, and it took a total of 40 minutes to serve those 20 customers.

The owner's first thought on improving service was to do some remodeling and open up the other side of the dairy, but the cost would be such that it might take months to recoup the initial expense. Beside, realizing that this also meant hiring another person, it would be just as easy to have two people servicing, which might mean a little running back and forth from the dairy case to the cars, but since most of the items are small and most customers do not buy more than a few items, it would serve the same purpose as having two service facilities. Given the above data and assuming that these arrivals and services are Poisson distributed, determine the probability of a customer having to wait, the average queue length, and the wait for each type of system (one service facility or two). Is the owner's fear justified that on the average there may be more than one car waiting?

Solution

Recommendation
If the owner is concerned about more than one car waiting on the average, then she should hire another person to work at the dairy. This will reduce significantly the average number of cars waiting. It must be assumed that the number of customers not prevented from stopping at the dairy would more than pay for the extra help.

Numerical Answer

One Service Facility

probability of waiting = 0.667
average queue length = 1.333 cars
average waiting time = 4.000 minutes.

Two Service Facilities

> probability of waiting = 0.500
> average queue length = 0.083 car
> average waiting time = 0.250 minute.

Math Work

One Service Facility

$N_1 = 20$ per hour, $N_2 = 30$ per hour.
$P(0) = (1 - 20/30) = 0.333$.

Thus the probability of waiting is
$$1.000 - 0.333 = 0.667.$$

The average queue length is

$$\frac{20^2}{30(30-20)} = 1.333 \text{ cars.}$$

The average waiting time is

$$\frac{20}{30(30-20)} = 0.067 \text{ hour} = 4 \text{ minutes.}$$

Two Service Facilities, $k = 2$.

$$\text{SUM} = 1 + \left(\frac{1}{1}\right)\left(\frac{2}{3}\right) = 1.667$$

$$P(0) = \frac{1}{1.667 + \dfrac{1}{2}\left(\dfrac{2}{3}\right)^2 \dfrac{(2)(30)}{60-20}}$$

$$= \frac{1}{1.667 + 0.333} = 0.500.$$

Thus the probability of waiting is
$$1.0 - 0.500 = 0.500.$$

The average queue length is

$$\frac{(20)(30)(2/3)^2(0.500)}{(60-20)^2} = 0.083 \text{ car.}$$

The average waiting time is

$$\frac{0.083}{20} = 0.004 \text{ hour} = 0.25 \text{ minute} = 15 \text{ seconds.}$$

INCIDENT: DISNEY—MASTER OF ILLUSION

Walt Disney was the master of illusion, perfecting the art of cartooning, amusement parks, and, best of all, creating the illusion of the short line. His innovations, first at Disneyland and now at Disney World, have affected our lives; his "wrap-around queue," for example, has been copied everywhere. Rather than have you stand in a long straight line (which looks foreboding and might cause "balking," that is, not going into the line, or "reneging," that is, leaving a line once in it), his lines are designed so that they curve back and forth, creating a high density of customers but not much length. This creates the illusion of a short line, gives plenty of people around you to talk to, and, before you know it, you are at your destination. Thus rather than increase the service rate or slow down the arrival rate, Disney just engineered the illusion of faster service.

express lanes

For years, grocery stores in California fought using express checkout lanes (ten items or less, cash only). That is because of the strange social dynamics of California. In the Midwest or on the East Coast one can use express checkout lanes and everyone will observe the rules—but not in California. The dilemma arises when someone enters the express lane with a basket full of groceries. The other customers tend to ignore it, assuming that the customer must know what he is doing or that the checkout clerk will tell the person to get out of the line. But the checkout clerk is playing a lose/lose game. If she tells the person to get out of the line, a big scene ensues and the other customers feel uncomfortable and tend not to want to return to the store. Of course we won't mention the toll it takes on the clerk or on the offender. But if the clerk doesn't say anything, all the other customers feel that they have just been ripped off, and they give the clerk heat for not refusing the offender. Such has been the experience of different grocery stores that only after much pressure from a few stores, which had persisted in offering express lane service, have the other stores finally followed suit.

The advantage of the express lane is that if a customer has just a few groceries, there is a good chance of his or her getting out of the store quickly. But the main disadvantage, besides the potential disagreements and resulting arguments, is that when customers have a lot of groceries (more than ten items), they will have to wait longer because there will be one less checker available. Recently the manager of a store that advertises an express lane open at all times has kept figures to determine if the service rate needs to be improved. She has determined that it takes an average of 45 seconds to check out a customer, and that the customers arrive in the lane at the rate of about 48 per hour. From this data find the probability of there being 0, 1, 2, 3, or 4 people in line, the average length of the line, the average waiting time for each customer, and the average time a customer will spend in the whole system (waiting and being served).

INCIDENT: GUARANTEED EXPRESS LANES

To combat reneging, Von's grocery stores in California have advertised that if at any time there are more than three customers in any line, Von's will immediately open up any closed checkout counter. Emphasizing service, they are trying to keep customers who already have a basket of groceries from leaving the store rather than wait in line. The idea of the express lane, common to most grocery stores, is just increasing the service rate (since you can only have ten items or less).

law offices' switchboard

The law offices of Sullwien, McCall, Levy, and Wood have a staff of six lawyers. There are eight offices and two conference rooms plus four secretaries to help in getting all the work done. By combining resources, the lawyers have reduced costs considerably and increased their coverage and effectiveness. The main switchboard can handle five phone lines. On the average three calls come in every two minutes.

Recently there have been complaints from clients that it seems impossible to be able to get through to the office, but not much attention was paid to this—until one of the partners tried for 15 minutes to get through. At that time it was decided that perhaps this was not just chance, but that the switchboard might be overloaded. A study was instituted that showed an average call took five minutes, although some were as long as half an hour.

One suggestion to alleviate this problem was to install more phone lines, which would increase the expenses of the office. Another suggestion was to just limit the length of the calls themselves to, say, perhaps three minutes if possible. Using the last suggestion, compare it with the situation as it actually is now. Will this significantly alleviate the problem of waiting to get through to the office?

INCIDENT: CONTROLLING TRAFFIC BY CHANGING INPUT

One way to get better throughput in a system is to regulate the incoming arrivals. Such is the theory behind monitoring freeway traffic during rush hours by installing traffic signals at on-ramps and metering

the traffic. There are nearly 140 on-ramps controlled by signals on the Los Angeles region's 675 miles of freeways. The idea is to avoid slowdowns and congestion caused by too many cars getting on a freeway at the same time. Travel times during the busiest bumper-to-bumper period have improved about 35 percent, and state highway engineers believe they can be trimmed even more.

drive-through versus 7/24 banking

Middletown Trust and Savings Bank is set up so that the drive-up system has two service stations fed by a single queue. The queue is set up so that once in line, reneging is not possible until the customer reaches a service window. Additionally, the bank provided a walk-up 7/24 banking system. This is a computerized system that allows most routine transactions (checking and savings deposits and withdrawals, loan payments) to be conducted 7 days a week, 24 hours a day. The 7/24 is a single-station service facility located near the bank entrance. Customers that drive to the bank must park along the street or in the parking lot.

Data was obtained by stationing several people across from the bank to observe and time the transactions for one hour. It was assumed that

1. all transactions that were conducted at the drive-up window could also be conducted at the 7/24 station,
2. on the average it takes two minutes to park the car and walk to and from the 7/24 station.

After a careful examination of the data it was determined that it was Poisson distributed.

From the data provided in the following tables, determine N_1 and N_2 for the drive-up window and the 7/24, respectively. Next compute the average number of customers in the total system, the average waiting time for each customer, and the average time in the total system for each customer. Considering this information, which service facility (drive-up window or 7/24) would you choose to minimize your time at the bank?

Drive-Through Survey Data

Car	Arrival	Window	Begin Transaction	End Transaction
1	1201	1	1202	1205
2	1201	2	1204	1205
3	1201	2	1205	1206
4	1203	1	1205	1207
5	1204:30	2	1206	1207
6		Balk		
7	1205:15	2	1207	1208
8	1206	1	1207	1208

Car	Arrival	Window	Begin Transaction	End Transaction
9	1206:10	2	1208	1209
10	1208	2	1209	1210
11	1208:10	1	1209	1209:30
12	1210:35	2	1211	1212:15
13	1211:30	2	1212:15	1217:30
14	1212	2	1217:30	1218
15	1213:25	1	1215:15	1218:30
16	1213:30	2	1218	1224
17	1213:35	1	1219	1219:30
18	1216:05	1	1219:30	1221:45
19	1217:25	1	1222	1224:30
20	1219:55	2	1224:15	1225
21	1220:15	1	1224:30	1227:15
22	1223	2	1225:15	1228:30
23	1225:05	1	1227:15	1228:45
24	1225:15	2	1229	1230:30
25	1226	2	1230:30	1231
26	1226:15	2	1231:15	1232
27	1227:35	1	1231	1233:30
28		Renege		
29	1229	1	1233:45	1235
30	1230:45	2	1233:10	1234:15
31	1231:30	2	1234:15	1237:30
32	1231:40	1	1235:15	1243
33	1232	2	1237:45	1240:15
34	1236:30	2	1240:30	1241:30
35	1236:50	2	1242	1244
36	1237:05	2	1244:45	1249
37		Balk		
38	1238:35	1	1243:45	1245:15
39	1239	1	1245:15	1245:45
40	1239:50	1	1246	1247
41	1241:15	1	1247:15	1249:15
42	1244:45	2	1249:15	1250:45
43	1244:50	1	1249:30	1253
44	1248:45	2	1251	1253:15
45	1249	2	1253:15	1254:30
46	1249:05	1	1253:30	1254
47	1250:15	1	1254:15	1255:45
48	1251	2	1254:30	1255:15
49	1251:45	2	1255:45	1258:20
50	1253:30	1	1256	1258:45
51	1256	2	1258:30	1259
52	1256:10	2	1259	1301:45
53	1258:20	2	1301:45	1302:30
54	1259:20	2	1302:30	1303:30
55	1259:50	2	1303:30	1304:30

Sum total transaction time: _____

7/24 Survey Data

Customer	Arrival	Begin Transaction	End Transaction
1	1207:35	1207:55	1208:30
2	1207:55	1208:30	1209:35
3	1210:25	1210:25	1211:50
4	1215	1215	1217
5	1216:55	1217	1219:40
6	1229:50	1229:50	1230:55
7	1234	1234	1237:05
8	1237:10	1237:10	1238:55
9	1238:45	1238:55	1240:10
10	1240:15	1240:15	1241:45

Sum total transaction time: _____

INCIDENT: SIMULATION DOES NOT EQUAL REALITY

Flushed with success at monitoring traffic on the largest freeway system in the world, CALTRANS (California Transportation Freeway Operation Branch) decided to do something to change the habit patterns of millions of Southern California motorists. By making the inside, fastest lane of the freeway available only to cars with three or more motorists or buses, it was hoped to increase the service rate in effect by not necessarily increasing the number of cars, but the number of passengers per car. On Monday, March 15, 1976, all inside lanes had diamonds painted on them for the 15 miles of Santa Monica freeway feeding into Los Angeles. Special meters were used on the on-ramps to allow cars with three or more passengers to get on faster. Unfortunately there were at least a dozen accidents (up 100 to 200 percent rather than the 20 percent predicted) due to cars inching along and then trying to get into lanes where other cars were moving at 55 miles per hour). Long lines of cars barely able to move or even to get onto the freeway through metered signals at on-ramps had a rippling effect on street traffic and on congested freeways feeding into the jammed Santa Monica. Commuters reported that their trip to work took up to twice as long as it normally did. Tempers flared, many cars with one or two passengers decided to risk a ticket and use the diamond lane, others decided not to use the freeway ever again. Officials stuck by their position as public pressure increased. Day after day the controversy went on while traffic flowed like molasses. Hitchhikers were selling themselves for $1.00 per ride so that the driver could use the diamond lane. One woman was arrested for having an inflatable dummy in her car as a passenger. Public tolerance of this project was extremely low, and pressure continued to mount until the experiment was canceled. This simply goes to show that all the best queuing theory in the world done with the most sophisticated computer techniques of simulation will not necessarily help the implementation.

Supplementary Problems

1. During lunch time, the popcorn vender on campus has 90 customers per hour on the average. It takes 15 seconds on the average to serve each customer. Assuming a Poisson distribution of arrivals and services, determine the following:
   a. What is the average length of the line?
   b. What is the probability of three people waiting in line?
   c. What is the average waiting time in seconds?
   d. What is the length of the queue given that people are waiting?

2. At a popular hummingbird feeder, customers hover in at a rate of two every six minutes, and on the average take two minutes to eat. Assuming a Poisson distribution, determine the following:
   a. What is the probability of having no birds in line?
   b. What is the average length of the line?
   c. Another feeder will be added if the average wait is more than three minutes. Should another feeder be added? (Show why or why not.)

3. Since Space Mountain has opened at Disneyland, there have been long lines. Customers arrive at an average rate of every 2 seconds. The ride can handle 1500 customers per hour (treat as a single service facility). Determine the average length of the line.

4. Fruity Rudy's averages 20 customers per hour on a slow, rainy day, and it takes an average of two minutes to make a smoothie. The top flavors are coconut and blackberry.
   a. Assuming that it is so slow that only Rudy is on duty, what is the probability of no one in line?
   b. What is the average length of line?
   c. What is the average wait?

5. Tune-Craft advertises quick and inexpensive car tune-ups. What they fail to mention is the long wait you may have while other cars are being tuned. They have three service areas and recently observed that eight cars per hour come in and each takes an average of 20 minutes to tune. Assuming that all times are exponentially distributed:
   a. What is the probability of not waiting?
   b. What is the average queue length?

6. The local office of the Department of Motor Vehicles has three service windows for eye tests for driver's licenses. Testing takes an average of 3 minutes for each person and the applicants arrive at an average of every 1.5 minutes.
   a. What is the probability of five applicants waiting?
   b. What is the average time a customer spends in the system?

7. Consider the Express Lanes case.
   a. What is the probability of having five people in line?
   b. What is the average queue length?
   c. What is the average waiting time?
   d. What would the average queue length be if another express lane were opened to serve the same line of people and all other variables remained the same?

8. A library employs three people to check out from one to six books per student. On an average 33 students arrive per hour and the check-out process averages 4 minutes. Assuming these times are exponentially distributed, determine the following:
   a. What is the probability of a student *not* having to wait?
   b. On the average, how many students will be waiting in line?
   c. What is the average time spent in the total system?

10.4 SIMULATION

So far we have seen decision problems described (approximated) by mathematical models that are solved or optimized and the solution is then used to help make "good" decisions about the actual problem. When this approach is feasible, it should by all means be used. However, there are several instances when it is not possible to follow such a sequence of steps—

1. in cases where the data for the model is probabilistic (actually, *stochastic*), that is, there might be a whole range of possible values for what we would like to be a single known number in a model (cost of an item, for example, or availability of a resource),
2. in cases where the *model* of the problem is itself so complex that it is difficult, impossible, or too costly to solve or optimize the model,
3. in cases where we are unsure of exactly what the most appropriate model is.

   In situations of this sort, a technique called *Monte Carlo simulation* is frequently used to investigate the problem. The name is derived from the roulette wheel at Monte Carlo which has random outcomes. This wheel can be simulated by random numbers, which can be used to give probable outcomes and simulate actual results. We must understand two other points before going further:

1. simulation is a frequently used technique due to the fact that the world is uncertain and complex,
2. simulation methods do not necessarily optimize a model, but are more likely used to help answer "what if?" kinds of questions (. . . what if the price is $3.00 and the customer orders 73 units? . . . what if she orders 78 units? . . .).

Perhaps it is best to amplify upon these ideas with some examples and then cover some details. Let us first review some ideas from statistics before we go on to the examples. The probability of an event means the relative frequency, percentage, or proportion in the long run of that event occurring. Thus in flipping a fair coin (not loaded or biased), the probability that a particular flip results in a head is $\frac{1}{2}$, 50 percent, or 0.50, and, in general, this definition of probability means that no event can have a probability that is less than 0 or exceeds 1. Knowing the probability of an event does not eliminate the uncertainty associated with that event. A *probability distribution p* details all the possible outcomes of interest (it's of interest if it could possibly happen) and their associated probabilities. A *cumulative probability distribution P* just accumulates the probabilities of the probability distribution. To illustrate these two concepts from statistics, consider the experiment of rolling one fair die (single dice). The possible outcomes (there are exactly six), their probabilities, and the accumulated probabilities are shown in Table 10.8.

Monte Carlo simulation parallels a spinner in a children's game in the sense that thumping the spinner produces a move in the game corresponding to the random stopping point of the spinner on the board. Monte Carlo methods do a similar thing with the cumulative probability distribution describing the possible values of the uncertain (stochastic) data in the model of a problem.

As a specific example, consider the following problem description. You are invited to play a game of chance in which a balanced or fair coin is to be flipped and the outcomes are recorded until the fifth head in the sequence of flips is recorded, at which time the game ends. It costs $8.00 to play the game, but when the game ends you get $1.00 for each flip made to get

the total of five heads. Thus if you have to flip more than eight times to get five heads, you win something, otherwise you lose or break even. Do you want to play the game? There are probability models that will describe this game exactly, but they are *very* complicated for the average person to figure out in just a few minutes. Therefore we will see the advantage of learning to simulate the situation.

Recall that simulation results are intended to help us decide whether we want to play the game, and that we will want to play the game only if we expect a profit from it. One way to simulate this game is simply to go to another room, get a coin, and play the game by ourselves long enough to decide whether it is profitable or not. This can be done by keeping track of wins and losses over many repetitions of the game. But what if we don't have a coin to flip or it takes too long to play the game over and over? One equivalent way to simulate the results from playing the game for money can be accomplished without actually flipping a quarter. Get one white marble and one black marble (the same size as the white one), put them in a hat, shake them up, draw one out and record the results. If the marble drawn is white, record a head from the flip; if it's black, record a tail from the flip (or vice versa). Put the marble back in the hat, shake, draw, record, replace; continue until the fifth head is recorded. Play the game this way many times, then look at the results. If on the average over many games it takes 10 flips to end the game, then on the average you can expect to win $2.00 ($10.00 − $8.00).

This procedure is a valid simulation of the flipping game because the marbles are drawn with the same probability (relative frequency) that the coin would be flipped. Similarly, we could put 50 white marbles and 50 black marbles in the hat (or in a bigger hat) and simulate the game (or 100 of each, 500 of each, and so on). The important aspect here is that even though the processes are different, the uncertain part of the drawing process exactly duplicates the uncertain part of the flipping process.

To simulate the flipping game with a Monte Carlo method, we don't need either the coin or the marbles, and we won't *physically* duplicate the flipping game (as we did with the marbles). To perform a Monte

Table 10.8

Outcomes i (number of dots showing)	1	2	3	4	5	6
Probability distribution $p(i)$ (probability of exactly i dots)	$\frac{1}{6}$	$\frac{1}{6}$	$\frac{1}{6}$	$\frac{1}{6}$	$\frac{1}{6}$	$\frac{1}{6}$
Cumulative probability distribution $P(i)$ (probability of i dots or less)	$\frac{1}{6}$ (0.167)	$\frac{2}{6}$ (0.333)	$\frac{3}{6}$ (0.500)	$\frac{4}{6}$ (0.667)	$\frac{5}{6}$ (0.833)	$\frac{6}{6}$ (1.000)

Carlo simulation we enlist the help of a table of random digits (see Table A1 in the Appendix). Such tables are included in most mathematics texts and are merely lists of the digits 0, 1, 2, 3, 4, 5, 6, 7, 8, and 9, each of which occurs in the list with the same probability (relative frequency). They are statistically "mixed up" or randomized, so that their order of appearance in the list is not obviously predictable. There are a variety of ways to produce such lists so that the digits are random, but such methods are too technical to be of much interest here.

We can simulate the flipping game by letting even digits (0, 2, 4, 6, 8) represent heads and odd digits (1, 3, 5, 7, 9) represent tails, or by letting 0–4 represent heads and 5–9 represent tails, or by any assignment of digits such that there is a 50:50 chance of flipping a head. By starting at an arbitrary position in the list and proceeding from that position, the digits represent outcomes from our game, just as did drawing the marbles from a hat. For example, starting in the 4th column, 13th row of Table A1 and proceeding from left to right across with even digits being H, the outcomes are H, T, T, T, H, T, H, H, T, H, and this game is over in ten flips, thus netting $2.00 for the player. Thus with the table of random digits we can "play" (actually simulate playing) the game many times and let the outcomes of these many fictitious plays help us decide whether to actually play the game for money. Now this game needs to be played enough times to get average winnings and losses to help us decide to play the game with *real* money.

Another way to simulate the flipping of the coin is to make up a probability distribution and a cumulative probability distribution that would look as follows:

Outcome	Head	Tail
$p(i)$	0.50	0.50
$P(i)$	0.50	1.00

and use the numbers in the random number table as values between 0.0000 and 0.9999. Thus the first entry in the table would be read as 0.1758, which means a head. Going down the first column of numbers, the following outcomes would result: H, T, H, H, H, H, with the game ending in six flips and the player losing $2.00.

As a second example, let us look at the single period inventory newsboy problem in Section 10.1 and see how we can apply the Monte Carlo simulation technique. Recall that the number of customers for a day and the cumulative probabilities are:

Customers i	25	26	27	28	29	30
Total Probability $P(i)$	0.10	0.20	0.40	0.65	0.85	1.00

Quick & Dirty Algorithm: Simulation of Discrete Outcomes

1. Given a cumulative (total) probability table and the respective outcomes, find the first value of i (going from left to right) such that $P(i) >$ random number.
2. Assign the value of i as the random outcome for that number.

For the newsboy problem we will simulate ten days of sales under the policy of the newsboy buying 29 newspapers. Looking at the first column of numbers in Table A1 and going down the column, we get our first random number as 0.1758, which converts to 26 customers for the first day (0.20 > 0.1758). With 26 customers there are 3 newspapers left over for a day's profit of 60¢. (Note that if the number were 0.1000, this would mean *26* customers, not 25.) We can then develop the following table:

Day	Random Number	Number of Customers	Day's Profit (cents)
1	0.1758	26	60¢
2	0.6430	28	78¢
3	0.4893	28	78¢
4	0.1516	26	60¢
5	0.4950	28	78¢
6	0.0549	25	51¢
7	0.1018	26	60¢
8	0.2241	27	69¢
9	0.1602	26	60¢
10	0.5840	28	70¢

The average number of customers is 26.80 for these 10 days, while the statistical average should be 27.80, and the simulated average daily profit is 66.40¢ versus the expected value of 71.10¢. The difference exists because we need a large number of simulated days for the law of averages to work out, and if this were done for 100 trials, we would be much closer to the expected answers. Continuing for 10 more simulated days, the average for 20 total days is 27.0 customers with an average daily profit of 70.8¢, which is much closer than for the 10 days of simulation.

Let us now turn our attention to simulating continuous events as well as discrete ones. Assume that patrons arrive on the average every two minutes at a Xerox machine (it is also assumed that these arrival times are exponentially distributed) and then it takes *exactly* $1\frac{1}{2}$ minutes for them to Xerox their standard material. Simulate a $\frac{1}{2}$ hour of time to determine if anyone has to wait for service and how long the average wait is.

Quick & Dirty Algorithm: Simulation of Exponential Outcomes

1. Choose a random number N from Table A1 in the Appendix that is between 0.000 and 0.999.
2. Find that number in Table A2 under column N—the first two digits in the column marked N and the last digit in succeeding columns—and convert it to an x value.

    This can also be accomplished by a good calculator with an ln key. Simply enter the random number and then push the ln key, which will yield the same value as the table, except that it will be minus. For calculators that are very good there is a random number function key that will also generate a random number between 0.0000 and 0.9999.
3. Then multiply the value from Table A2 by the average time to get the simulated time t for the problem.

Thus starting in Table A1, column 10, row 11, we have the number 1024 which we convert to 0.102 (ignore the last digit). Looking at Table A2, we find 0.10 under N and then go to column 2 and find the number 2.28278. Keeping only two decimal places, we have 2.28. Now we multiply by the average time, 2.00 minutes, to get our simulated time of 5.56 for the first customer to arrive.

Table 10.9 shows the work required to simulate about $\frac{1}{2}$ hour of time for this situation. Remember that service *always* takes $1\frac{1}{2}$ minutes (in the next case we will also vary that) so that arrival time plus $1\frac{1}{2}$ minutes is the leave time for the first customer (because no one is ahead in line). Otherwise service cannot begin until the Xerox machine is free. The expected waiting time for constant service is one half the regular time from the Quick & Dirty formulas in Section 10.3. Thus $W = 2.25$ minutes.

For this simulation it becomes quickly apparent that although the average time between customers arriving is two minutes, this run of numbers is way below the average (but not outside of the laws of probability) and produces a lot of waiting. The average waiting time is 3.332 minutes, and the total time in the system is 1.5 minutes more than that (4.832 minutes). Continuation for ten more customers is shown in Table 10.10. Now the average wait is 2.564 minutes, with the longest wait being 5.78 minutes.

Table 10.9

Random Number	x	$t = 2.00x$	Arrive A	Service S	Leave L	Total Time $T = L - A$	Wait $W = T - S$
0.102	2.28	4.56	4.56	1.50	6.06	1.50	0.00
0.659	0.42	0.84	5.40	1.50	7.56	2.16	0.66
0.701	0.35	0.70	6.10	1.50	9.06	2.94	1.44
0.791	0.23	0.46	6.56	1.50	10.56	4.00	2.50
0.696	0.36	0.72	7.28	1.50	12.96	4.78	3.28
0.702	0.35	0.70	7.98	1.50	13.56	5.58	4.08
0.699	0.36	0.72	8.70	1.50	15.06	6.36	4.86
0.750	0.29	0.58	9.28	1.50	16.56	7.28	5.78
0.548	0.60	1.20	10.48	1.50	18.06	7.58	6.08
0.219	1.52	3.04	13.52	1.50	19.56	6.04	4.54

Table 10.10

Random Number	x	t	A	S	L	T	W
0.496	0.70	1.40	14.92	1.50	21.06	6.14	4.64
0.318	1.15	2.30	17.22	1.50	22.56	5.34	3.84
0.459	0.78	1.56	18.78	1.50	24.06	5.28	3.78
0.027	3.58	7.16	25.94	1.50	27.44	1.50	0.00
0.362	1.01	2.02	27.96	1.50	29.46	1.50	0.00
0.183	1.70	3.40	31.36	1.50	32.86	1.50	0.00
0.697	0.36	0.72	32.08	1.50	34.36	2.28	0.78
0.666	0.41	0.82	32.90	1.50	35.86	2.94	1.44
0.875	0.13	0.26	33.16	1.50	37.36	4.20	2.70
0.199	1.61	3.32	36.48	1.50	38.36	2.38	0.88

The number of customers out of 19 that did not have to wait is 3 (not counting the first), so the probability of not waiting is $\frac{3}{19}$ or 0.158.

From these examples it can be seen that it requires many computations over a long period of time to get meaningful averages. In the above problem it might be of interest to determine what would happen if customers arrived every $2\frac{1}{2}$ minutes on the average, and so on. Thus you would be able to simulate several situations and learn a lot about the system that you are studying. It can be said that simulation is much more art than mathematics, and more analysis than methods. Needless to say, a lot of simulation can become very tedious, and thus it is advantageous to use computers to do these same operations. There are ways to program a computer in FORTRAN or BASIC, which have subroutines to produce random numbers, and then the discrete or continuous events can be developed and the appropriate results compiled for as many repetitions of the model as desired.[2, 3] Also at present there are special computer languages available which are intended for simulation problems, such as GPSS, GASP, SIMSCRIPT, DYNAMO, and others.

single queue simulation

Consider the Drive-In Dairy case (pages 352–353) as an example of simulating a queuing problem. In this situation let us simply investigate the single service facility with the number of customers being 20 per hour and the total service time for those customers being 40 minutes. This means that the average time between customers is 3.00 minutes and the average service time per customer is 2.00 minutes. Assuming an exponential distribution of service times and time between arrivals, we can simulate these times by using Tables A1 and A2 in the Appendix. We will use the Table of Random Digits (Table A1) to generate random values of x from Table A2 and then multiply them by either 3.00 for arrival times or 2.00 for service times.

Simulate 20 customers by finding a random time of arrival and then service for each customer in the system, using Monte Carlo simulation. Start in Table A1 in the third column at the top. Use the first customer to get started and then simulate 20 more. Compare against the expected values of an average waiting time of 4.00 minutes and an average total time of 6.00 minutes in the system.

Solution

Recommendation
Several more customers should be simulated so that the average waiting time of 0.76 minute is closer to the expected value (4.00), and thus a more accurate picture of the actual flow of customers can be drawn. Considering the early results of the simulation, it would not pay for the owner to open up another service facility, but again, it is really too early to tell.

Numerical Answer. The average waiting time is 0.76 minute versus an expected 4.00 minutes.

The average total time is 2.33 minutes versus an expected 6.00 minutes.

Math Work. Let us generate the customer arrivals and their service times by multiplying each x value from Table A2 by 3.00 for arrivals and by 2.00 for service (Table 10.11). For the 20 customers the average time between arrivals is 2.83 minutes, which is lower than the expected value of 3.00 minutes, and the average for the 20 service times is 1.57 minutes, which is also lower than the expected time of 2.00 minutes per customer. Table 10.12 shows the total time and the waiting time using Monte Carlo simulation.

The average total waiting time per customer is 2.33 minutes, and the waiting time in queue is 0.76 minute, which is very low considering the expected values.

express success

Flushed with the recent success of express lanes in supermarkets, a store manager has decided upon a new policy for the rush hours. Anytime that there are five or more people waiting to be served in the express lane, or any total wait takes more than four minutes for any customer, the manager wants to open a second express lane. During the nonrush hours, customers for express lanes (ten items or less) arrive at 60 per hour, and service averages 40 seconds per customer. During the rush hours, however, the arrivals are 120 per hour with the same service time per customer as during nonrush hours.

First simulate about 20 customers, starting at the seventh column, row 16, for a single express lane and see if there would be a need to open a second lane during nonrush hours. Then using the rush-hour data, determine what the average wait and total time in line is, again simulating the same 20 random numbers and comparing with the nonrush-hour answers.

Finally, take the rush-hour data and open up two lines. Determine the average waiting time and the total time and compare with the single-line nonrush-hour answers. Is there a difference and would you expect one? As a decision rule for which line a customer should be in, choose the line with the least number of people.

Table 10.11

Customer	N	x	t_1(Arrive)	N	x	t_2(Service)
Start	0.277	1.28	3.85	0.047	3.06	6.12
1	0.171	1.77	5.30	0.732	0.31	0.62
2	0.575	0.55	1.66	0.936	0.07	0.14
3	0.756	0.28	0.84	0.972	0.03	0.06
4	0.220	1.51	4.54	0.154	1.87	3.74
5	0.748	0.29	0.87	0.894	0.11	0.22
6	0.256	1.36	4.09	0.941	0.06	0.12
7	0.646	0.44	1.31	0.310	1.17	2.34
8	0.453	0.79	2.38	0.294	1.22	2.45
9	0.831	0.19	0.56	0.193	1.65	3.29
10	0.651	0.43	1.29	0.309	1.17	2.35
11	0.123	2.10	6.29	0.719	0.33	0.66
12	0.478	0.74	2.21	0.028	3.58	7.15
13	0.367	1.00	3.00	0.482	0.73	1.46
14	0.205	1.58	4.75	0.889	0.12	0.24
15	0.913	0.09	0.27	0.572	0.56	1.12
16	0.284	1.26	3.78	0.751	0.29	0.57
17	0.300	1.20	3.60	0.395	0.93	1.86
18	0.243	1.41	4.24	0.763	0.27	0.54
19	0.231	1.47	4.40	0.802	0.22	0.44
20	0.658	0.42	1.26	0.368	1.00	2.00

Table 10.12

Customer	Arrive A	Service S	Leave L	Total Time T	Wait W = T − S
Start	3.85	6.12	9.97	6.12	0.00
1	9.15	0.62	10.59	1.44	0.82
2	10.81	0.14	10.95	0.14	0.00
3	11.65	0.06	11.71	0.06	0.00
4	16.19	3.74	19.93	3.74	0.00
5	17.06	0.22	20.15	3.09	2.87
6	21.05	0.12	21.17	0.15	0.00
7	22.36	2.34	24.70	2.34	0.00
8	24.74	2.45	27.19	2.45	0.00
9	25.30	3.29	30.48	5.18	1.89
10	26.59	2.35	32.73	6.14	3.79
11	32.88	0.66	33.54	0.66	0.00
12	35.09	7.15	42.24	7.15	0.00
13	38.09	1.46	43.70	5.61	4.15
14	42.84	0.24	43.94	1.10	0.86
15	43.11	1.12	45.06	1.95	0.83
16	46.89	0.57	47.46	0.57	0.00
17	50.49	1.86	52.35	1.86	0.00
18	54.73	0.54	55.27	0.54	0.00
19	59.13	0.44	59.57	0.44	0.00
20	60.39	2.00	62.39	2.00	0.00

INCIDENT: DATA TOO HOT TO HANDLE

A midwestern medical systems group was contracted by a city to do a simulation study of the city hospital emergency room. The analysts were to simulate the arrival, initial screening, waiting, preparation by nurses, diagnosis, and prognosis by doctors for each patient. The questions of interest in the study were how many more doctors and/or nurses need to be added to reduce the average waiting time to satisfactory levels.

After the study had been defined, the next step was to collect actual data. A day was set aside in July, time clocks were rented for the occasion so that each patient would carry a card and punch in and out at various stages, aides and nurses were trained in data gathering, and all was ready for the big day. Things went fairly smoothly for the first few hours, until it became obvious that this was not a normal day. The temperature soared to 112°F, humidity to 90 percent, and the emergency room was so full that heat prostration patients were being laid out in the halls. Needless to say, not only was the necessary data collection quickly forgotten, but even if the data had been obtained, it certainly would not have modeled normal operations at the hospital. Unfortunately the staff found it such a bad experience, that over a month passed before another attempt (this one successful) was made.

brick kiln

A factory in Tampico, Mexico, uses several brick kilns (furnaces lined with bricks) in an industrial process 24 hours a day, 7 days a week. During the process the kilns partially collapse on the inside from time to time, losing several bricks and causing necessary rebuilding and repairs. If the bricks are available, the furnace can be rebuilt almost immediately (no noticeable downtime), but if the bricks are not readily available, the furnace is allowed to cool, the rebuilding is done when the bricks finally arrive, and the furnace is heated up again. Since this causes a great loss of revenue, the management is interested in obtaining an estimate of how many bricks are needed for the factory per month and how many should be kept in supply.

The furnaces (there are ten of them) on the average break down every 22.5 days. The following distribution of bricks is needed for each breakdown:

Bricks	200	400	600	800	1000	1200
Occurrences	21	7	9	5	1	1
$p(i)$	0.477	0.159	0.205	0.115	0.022	0.022
$P(i)$	0.477	0.636	0.841	0.956	0.978	1.000

Simulate one year of operation for one of the ten furnaces, and determine the number of bricks needed each month. Make up a frequency distribution from that data (number of 1000s of bricks needed and the probability). This could then be used to solve a problem similar to the newsboy problem in Section 10.1. Actually this problem is a multiperiod stochastic dynamic programming problem, but it can be approximated by simulation to give a good approximation to an exact solution.

Assume to simplify matters that there are 30 days per month and 360 days per year.

Start at the second column, row 1, and simulate all the breakdowns (arrivals) for the year, and then simulate the number of bricks for each breakdown.

INCIDENT: FORGED SOLUTION

A young consultant was hired to simulate the running of a large forge which included several processes and over 100 workers in one area. The manager was interested in knowing what would happen if a certain number of machines were used and the resulting total time for the work flow. After several months of analyzing, model building, and computer runs, the consultant presented the first rough results, which included a layout of the individual personnel-hours required. The manager looked first at the personnel-hours and not at the costs and pronounced the solution unworkable because the daily variation between the worker who worked the least number of hours and the one who worked the most could be no more than 15 minutes. Otherwise, the manager said, the whole plant would be out on strike. The consultant began to realize that the most important constraint to the situation was to keep the workload balanced so that the shop would not go out on strike, and was careful to incorporate this constraint into further solutions.

holding bin

A production process requires work to be done consecutively on two machines. There are 40 pieces that need to be worked. Each process takes on the average 5.0 minutes per machine, with the production times exponentially distributed. The first machine cannot work on the next piece until the finished unit is moved away, either to the next machine or to a holding bin (which can hold one piece). Management is concerned about the possible bottleneck that might occur if the present practice of not using a holding bin is employed. The cost of a bin would be $30.00, and machinists are paid $7.50 per hour. Simulate the process of all 40 pieces by first assuming no holding bin available, and determine the total time for both machinists (the first one can't quit until the second is completely through) and the total costs. Then, using the same data, compare the costs with having a holding bin that will hold one piece of work only, between the two machines, thus freeing the first machine to go on to another piece. Assume that it takes no extra time to put the piece in the bin or take it from the bin. Start at the fourth column, row 11, and simulate the processing time for the first piece on the first machine. Then continue on for the second job and so on.

In effect, what we are allowing is no penalty for a queue of length 1 if there is a holding bin, and we are penalized for having any queue if there is no bin. It should be obvious that some savings should occur, but the question is how much savings and whether it is worth spending the $30.00 for the holding bin. This problem is also beyond the scope of the material presented in Section 10.3 in that we have two stations in series and not in parallel with each other. Determine if it should be recommended to purchase a $30.00 holding bin for this particular production process.

INCIDENT: SIMULATIONS SHOULD NOT BE TOO SIMPLE

A story, perhaps true, was told by an aerospace OR analyst who had been involved in a Monte Carlo simulation at an aerospace firm. The object of the simulation had been to determine the safest landing spot for the first lunar lander. This individual claimed that the Monte Carlo simulation was accomplished with the help of a large three-dimensional relief mockup of the moon's surface and a scale model of the lunar lander. A pair of dice were tossed successively to give the coordinates of a landing spot on the moon. Then the lander was dropped ten times from three feet above the surface and the number of successes were recorded. It is hoped that a more scientific approach had been used and that the individual might not have been completely accurate in the description of the process. In any event, the Apollo program was successful in all its landings and now has left billions of dollars of equipment on the moon. All of this calls to mind the statement made by one astronaut on his way to the moon when he said that he wasn't so sure he felt too good about being in the low-bid craft.

Supplementary Problems

1. A mom and pop store has just one cash register and carries mostly convenience items. Customers arrive every 30 seconds and it is assumed arrivals are Poisson distributed. The distribution of service times is as follows:

Service Time (seconds)	10	20	30	40	50	60
Probability	0.10	0.30	0.10	0.20	0.20	0.10

a. Simulate five arrivals starting at column 6, row 1 in Table A1 (keep computations in seconds).
b. Simulate five service times (in seconds) continuing at column 6, row 6 of Table A1.
c. Complete the table and determine the average time in the system and average wait.

Customer	Arrive	Service	Leave	Total	Wait
1	——	——	——	——	——
2	——	——	——	——	——
3	——	——	——	——	——
4	——	——	——	——	——
5	——	——	——	——	——

2. A car wash has determined that 90 cars arrive per hour. It takes an average of 30 seconds to vacuum the car and put it on the automatic chain that takes it through the car wash. Assume an exponential distribution of arrivals and service times.
a. Simulate five arrivals and service times given the random numbers below.

Random Number	Arrivals		Random Number	Service	
	x	t		x	t
300	——	——	410	——	——
489	——	——	270	——	——
209	——	——	539	——	——
889	——	——	106	——	——
412	——	——	336	——	——

b. Complete the table below.

	Arrive	Service	Leave	Total	Wait	Total
1	——	——	——	——	——	——
2	——	——	——	——	——	——
3	——	——	——	——	——	——
4	——	——	——	——	——	——
5	——	——	——	——	——	——

c. Compute the average waiting time and total time for the five cars.

Average waiting time _____

Average total time _____

3. Arrivals at a gas station are exponentially distributed and on the average every five minutes a customer pulls in. The service time averages two minutes per car and is *uniformly* distributed between one to three minutes (equal probability of any time between 1 to 3 minutes).

a. Simulate six customer arrivals in the system (begin at column 8, row 16, in Table A1 and go down).
b. Simulate six customer service times, continuing on in the same column of Table A1.
c. Determine the average total time per customer.
d. Determine the average waiting time per customer in the gas station.

10.5 BRIDGING THE GAP: THE INTERFACE

The area of stochastic models (probability) in operations research introduces many complications that are certainly beyond the scope of this book. The authors wanted to introduce different types of problems and algorithms so that you could get a feel for the scope and range of these and recognize some of the qualities of stochastic problems. In general there are three qualities of problems (or messes) that can make things difficult or simple: size, linearity, and certainty.

In terms of size, the larger the problem, the more difficult it becomes to solve, even with simple algorithms. Most problems that increase in size by a factor of n will increase in solution time by a factor n^2. Thus a problem that is 10 times larger may take 100 times longer to solve.

Linearity is another key factor. Linear problems are generally much easier to solve than nonlinear ones. The higher the degree of nonlinearity and complexity, the more difficult the solution becomes and the more complicated the algorithm. Usually this is an area for heuristics as the number of variables and the size increase.

Finally, certainty makes the problem deterministic and much easier to work with. The next step of complication is probability, where we know the possible outcomes and their probabilities (like knowing that it will either rain—30 percent chance—or be sunny—70 percent chance). In this case we have seen problems involving queuing theory, replacement theory, and game theory. The third level of complexity is when only the possibilities are known, but not their probabilities. Thus we might know that it will either rain or be sunny, but have no idea of the probabilities. We saw this instance happen in decision theory when we didn't know the probabilities but at least knew all the possibilities. Lastly, we enter the area known as turbulence, where we don't even know all the possibilities. Who would have guessed in 1968 that a president of the United States would resign, much less the probability of that happening. The economy is in turbulence, and thus it becomes very

difficult to predict and make logical, rational decisions.

If we think of these three factors as a three-dimensional graph which looks like the corner of a room with three axes (Figure 10.4), the farther out we go on each axis, the more difficult it is to find solutions to those problems. The dark area represents the knowledge of operations research for solving such problems, and as can be seen, if we have a large, turbulent, nonlinear problem we have no means of solving it with current OR techniques. Very large linear deterministic problems are routinely solved, but if they include a lot of uncertainty or are nonlinear, success is extremely limited.

1. The gap that exists between mathematical theory and real world problem solving is extremely wide when the problem is very stochastic or the distribution and probabilities are not even known. If past history is available, then simulation techniques can be used to approximate some reasonable strategy. This becomes risky when the historical data is very dirty or can only be a guess based on what might happen with new variables introduced into the system.

2. The same mathematical problems arise with Sections 10.1, 3.4, and 3.6 in that, if the function is not unimodal, there is no guarantee that the algorithm will find the optimal value. In Chapter 3 we were looking at replacement costs not being unimodal, and in this chapter we need to worry

Figure 10.4

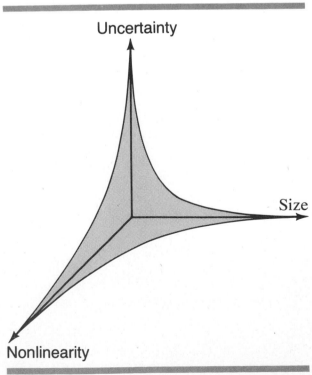

about the probability distribution not being unimodal.

3. In Section 10.2 one must be careful to realize that the average costs may not be unimodal either. They may go down, back up, and then back down again, depending upon the probability distribution for failure.

4. For Section 10.4 a note of caution should be given that most "random" numbers are really only pseudo random numbers. They are generated by mathematical formulas that make them predictable (although not apparently) and will repeat the sequence of numbers. The serious user of random number tables (in texts) or generators (on computers) should investigate using statistical techniques to test whether the numbers do indeed have a random pattern to them.

If you are interested in generating unit normal random values, a method of Box and Muller[4] used two random numbers (U_1 and U_2) to get two normal random digits with mean 0.00 and standard deviation 1.00:

$$X_1 = \cos(2\pi U_1)\ \sqrt{-2\ln(U_2)}$$

$$X_2 = \sin(2\pi U_1)\ \sqrt{-2\ln(U_2)}.$$

To change these to a mean of μ and a standard deviation σ,

$$N_1 = \mu + \sigma X_1$$

$$N_2 = \mu + \sigma X_2$$

To obtain a random exponential deviate, the following proof should suffice for the Quick & Dirty, where N is the random number between 0.000 and 0.999 and x the exponentially distributed deviate:

$$N = e^{-x}$$
$$\ln(N) = -x \quad \text{or} \quad x = -\ln(N).$$

Table A2 is simply a natural logarithm table with the minus signs removed.

10.6 REVIEWS

Review 1: Open book and notes; show all work; write legibly.

1. (10 points) The Slow Start Go-Kart race track in Spring Valley experiences blowouts on its tires as follows:

Week	1	2	3	4
Probability	0.20	0.40	0.30	0.10

It costs $3.00 per tire and $4.00 in labor to replace one tire, while it would cost $3.00 per tire and $6.00 in labor to replace all four tires. Compute the average replacement costs for a one-week and a two-week period (the first two columns of the table) and assume that we start with all new tires for 50 Go-Karts (200 tires).

2. (20 points) A drive-in hamburger stand handles ten transactions in an hour (constantly busy). Assume that arrivals are Poisson distributed.

a. What is the probability that a transaction will take less than three minutes? _____

b. What is the probability that a transaction will take more than ten minutes? _____

c. Simulate ten services, giving the transaction times and totals. Start at column 4, row 11 of Table A1.

3. (10 points) Consider the Man Fook Low Chinese Restaurant case (page 343).

    a. What is the expected demand?

    b. What are the expected sales (given the optimal quantity to make)?

    c. Would the optimum number of Tea-Cakes to make change if Mr. Low got a salvage value of 3¢ per cake? Show your work.

4. (15 points) Consider the Monkey Business case (page 347) and assume that individual monkeys cost $200 instead of $400.

   a. What is the best time for group replacement and what is the cost per year? (Show your work in a table.)

   b. What is the individual replacement cost per year? (Show your work.)

5. (20 points) A university post office has estimated that every two minutes one student will seek its services. It also estimated that it can serve three students every two minutes through its one window.

   a. What is the probability of having to wait in line? _____ _____
   _____
   _____

   b. What is the average queue length a student will encounter? _____
   _____
   _____

   c. Simulate four customers (ignoring the first one) and determine the probability of waiting in line. Start at the second column, first row of Table A1 and go down the column.

6. (10 points) Explain the following terms and give two examples of each.

   a. Renege: _____
   _____

b. Balk: _____

_____

7. (15 points) Consider the Drive-Through versus 7/24 Banking case (page 354).
   a. Determine $P(0)$ for the drive-up windows if people arrive twice as fast as in the case.

b. Determine the average queue length for the 7/24 if transaction times are twice as long as in the case.

Review 2: Open book and notes; show all work; write legibly.

1. (10 points) Boy Scout Troop 409 is selling Christmas trees and they want to determine how many trees to buy. The average selling price for a tree is $25.00, and they get trees at an average cost of $9.00 each. If they run out of trees early, they figure a loss of the profit from two sales, while there is a small salvage value of $1.00 per tree. The probability distribution for the number of trees sold each year is as follows:

Trees	50	100	150	200	250	300	350
Probability	0.05	0.15	0.20	0.30	0.10	0.10	0.10

a. Determine how many trees should be bought to maximize profit.

b. What is the expected profit if 300 trees were bought this year?

2. (15 points) Simulate ten days' demand for the Winchell's Donuts case (page 342) starting at the first row and first column of Table A1 (using 4-digit numbers) and go down the table.

Demand	600	800	1000	1200	1400	1600
Probability	0.05	0.05	0.35	0.30	0.15	0.10

3. (15 points) Arrivals at a single teller window are observed to be exponentially distributed with average intervals of 30 seconds. If each transaction is also exponentially distributed with an average of 20 seconds, simulate five people (after you have initiated the system with one person) arriving and doing business. Then give the average waiting time and total time. Start in the third column, 21st row of Table A1.

4. (15 points) Fruity Rudy's does a great business selling smoothies, especially when it is a hot, sunny day. In fact, it has been found that there is a good correlation between weather and sales. Rudy has gotten a probability breakdown of the weather and thus his future sales (in gallons of smoothies) for the month of May are estimated as follows:

			Weather			
	Rain	*Drizzle*	*Fog*	*Cloudy and Cold*	*Cloudy and Warm*	*Sunny and Hot*
Sales	200	300	400	600	1000	1600
Probability	0.02	0.04	0.12	0.15	0.18	0.49

Since Rudy must buy fresh fruit every day, he considers the cost of each gallon of smoothie and how much fruit it takes (as well as other materials such as honey, protein powder, ice, fruit juices). It costs $1.25 in raw fruit for each gallon and he can make a profit of $5.00 per gallon. He figures the cost of a lost sale as $10.00 a gallon. Since there is not much market for the sale of one-day-old fruit, he gets $0.10 for the amount of fruit needed to make a gallon of smoothies.

a. How much fruit (in gallons) should Rudy buy?

b. Give the expected sales (in gallons).

c. Give the expected demand (in gallons).

5. (15 points) Give-Us-A-Brake is a new brake specialty shop that charges $75 for a complete brake job or $30 per single brake (there are four on each car). Given the following probabilities for brakes wearing out, determine what replacement policy ought to be followed. (Do only for three years.)

Year	1	2	3
$p(i)$	0.60	0.30	0.10

6. (15 points) McDonald's feel that one service person can handle on the average four customers in ten minutes. At dinner time (their busiest) customers arrive at McDonald's every minute. Assume that there are three service persons.

a. Determine the probability of a customer having to wait.

b. Determine the average queue length.

7. (15 points) Customers arrive every ten minutes at a tobacco shop and buy either one, two, or three pouches of tobacco according to the following distribution:

Demand	1	2	3
Probability	0.50	0.30	0.20

a. Simulate one hour of customer arrivals starting in column 1, row 1 of Table A1.

b. Then simulate the number of pouches each customer buys, starting in column 2, row 11 of Table A1.

c. Determine the expected number of pouches sold per hour analytically and compare with your simulated answer.

10.7 REFERENCES

1. F. S. Hillier and G. J. Lieberman, *Introduction to Operations Research* (San Francisco: Holden-Day, 1974).

2. H. Thiel, J. C. G. Boot, and T. Kloek, *Operations Research and Quantitative Economics* (New York: McGraw-Hill, 1965).

3. M. Sasieni, A. Yaspen, and L. Friedman, *Operations Research—Methods and Problems* (New York: Wiley, 1959).

4. G. E. P. Box and M. E. Muller, "A Note on the Generation of Random Normal Deviates," *Annals of Mathematical Statistics*, vol. 29, June 1958.

11
summary

Throughout this book it has been the intention of the authors to present an introduction to OR techniques and problems such that you now have a basic grasp of the different types of problems that arise and some way to tackle them that can be actually used. As with most books that are introducing a subject, no claim is made to completeness, but it is hoped that this approach can bring you some real functional ability and perhaps encourage you to continue on in this field.

Now that you have been through the book and worked through the chapters, it might be a good idea to review where we have been and try to look at the problems and techniques in a different light.

11.1 PROBLEM TYPES

Several types of problems are presented here, grouped together by some common characteristics and not necessarily the way they appeared in the chapters in the book. In quotes will be the basic question that this type of problem is confronting to help you understand the problem better.

Sequencing and Scheduling

Job Shop and Flow Shop. "What order do jobs go in to minimize total time of throughput?" Products have to be manufactured on several different machines in a specified order, and there are a large number of ways that it can be done. The optimal sequence is usually the one that minimizes total time for all jobs through the shop (called *makespan*). Generally the more rigid and structured the problem, the easier it is to solve.

Project Scheduling. "What events are critical that, if delayed, they will delay the whole project?" Several activities and events must be scheduled so that a project may be complete, and some of these activities and events must be exactly on time or the project will be late. By determining which of these are critical, management by exception can be used, and most of the time and effort can be spent on those few activities.

Machine Changeover. "What order should jobs be done in to minimize the set-up and tear-down time or costs?" In machine shops the problem arises that as each job is done on a given machine, one set-up (the jigs to hold the piece being machined in place or the speed and depth of cut settings) must be "torn down"

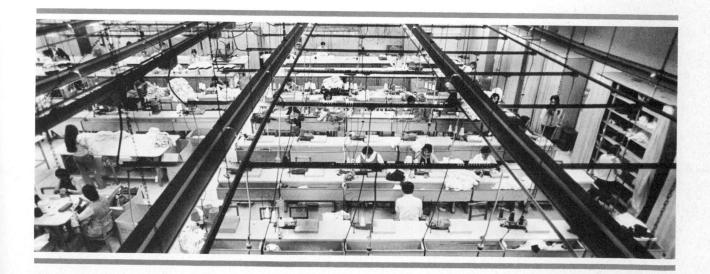

and the next one set up. In cases where it makes a difference in which order the jobs come there can be considerable savings if the best ordering is used. This problem is also known as the traveling salesman problem.

Inventory and Replacement

The basic problem here is that of equalizing average fixed costs with average variable costs. (The same is true for break-even problems.)

Inventory. The two basic questions are, "how much to order" and "when to order." The problem becomes complex when this decision has to be made for hundreds of items at several locations. Demand can be constant, unequal, or stochastic. Given when and how much someone is ordering, carrying costs or backorder costs may be imputed. Also a determination of whether or not to order low-demand items can be made. Another problem with inventory is old products or "dogs" that will not move. A quick determination can be made of how low the price can be discounted to move the products and still break even.

Replacement. The basic questions here are, "when to buy" and "when to replace." Items may be those that deteriorate over time (machinery, cars) or those that fail completely (light bulbs, stadium seats).

Location and Allocation

These problems are basically concerned with "how much (or who) goes where to minimize costs or maximize profits."

Assignment. A certain number of people are available to do an equal number of tasks with varying effectiveness. Each person must complete one and only one task at minimum cost.

Transportation. A company has several plants and many warehouses and wants to find the minimum cost of shipping the required amounts to the warehouses without exceeding the supply from the plants.

Linear Programming. Allocating resources and maximizing profits or minimizing costs is the basic problem here. Blending (gasoline, feed mix, steel alloys, paints, whiskey) at a minimum cost while not violating any requirements for the mix is another type of linear programming problem. Usually these are very large problems.

Integer Programming. Two basic types of integer programming problems are capital budgeting and fixed charge (warehouse location, lock box location). The problem is one of assigning resources that can only be integer.

Minimal Cut/Maximum Flow. Given a flow in a network of rivers, roads, pipes, and so on, what is the minimum cost to cut off all the flow (dams, road blocks, bombings, shut-off valves), and what is the maximum amount of flow possible in the system?

Routing

"What route should be used to minimize total cost, time, or distance?"

Shortest Route. What is the shortest route from point A to point B in terms of cost, time, or distance? It is assumed that no other points must be visited.

Delivery. What is the minimum number of trucks needed to deliver (or make pickups) to every point?

Minimal Spanning Tree. What is the minimum cost to make sure that every point in the network is connected by a road, sewer line, pipe line, and so on? This does not make a complete tour or circuit.

Traveling Salesman. Each point in the network must be visited once and only once, and the tour must return to the original point. The problem is to find the minimum cost tour.

Stochastic Decisions

"We decide on the course of action to take in an uncertain environment."

Decision Theory. These decisions are made against nature or an impersonal random force. They are usually one-time decisions.

Game Theory. These decisions are usually made against another person or team, each aware of the other. (There may be more than two parties involved.) These decisions are usually repeated.

Stochastic Processes

"These are dynamic, ever-changing situations in which we are trying to determine movement patterns of large groups of people or things."

Markov Chains. People who switch brands of cigarettes, laundry soaps, and so on, are examples of Markov problems. Companies are trying to steal customers from other companies without losing too many of their own. Although the switching continues, a steady state can be reached under certain conditions so that the company can tell what share of the market it will get with its new strategy.

Queuing (Waiting Lines). Any line (or a set of lines) that gives service (ticket counters, check out lanes, gas station pumps) will have people waiting eventually (or eternally). Basic properties such as average service time, waiting time, number of people in line, and so on, can be computed.

Search

This is the classic problem of finding "a needle in a hay stack."

One Dimensional. Good examples of this are trying to guess a number from 1 to 99 and being told whether you are higher or lower than the number. Radio stations will play variations of the game, guessing the amount of money in a jackpot or a six-digit license number.

Two Dimensional. A good example of this is "hot or cold" played by kids trying to guess which object in the classroom the teacher has in mind. More serious versions are a helicopter search by police for a bank robber, submarine search planes, search and destroy units, and so on.

Random. Sometimes random solutions to problems may be generated, ranked, the mean and standard deviations computed, and the process stopped when a random ordering gives a cost more than three standard deviations away from the mean.

11.2 SOLUTION TECHNIQUES

Some general comments should be made about solution techniques and ways to approach problem solving. Operations research certainly has no corner on the market of trying to solve problems, and some of the general techniques and directions can be applied to many types of problem solving. Here are five general ways that might be used in problem solving.

Reducing the Problem

There are several techniques that attempt to reduce the problem by only having to look at a few of the possible solutions.

Simplex Method. This looks at only a fraction of a percent of the number of feasible solutions and is a very efficient method for nicely structured linear problems.

Implicit Enumeration. For problems that are 0–1 in nature (either/or) this can be a very powerful method in eliminating many possible solutions and looking at only a small subset.

Branch & Bound. Not restricted to 0–1 problems or mutually exclusive subsets of the problem, it has not only been used for traveling salesman problems, but also for assignment problems, numerous job shop and flow shop problems, and integer programming.

Cutting Plane. Used in solving integer programming problems and very efficient for some classes of problems called set-covering problems, it eliminates the infeasible solution without eliminating any possible feasible solutions.

Dividing the Problem

This means trying to break down the problems into parts or stages and then solving a few simple problems rather than one big problem (in politics this is called "divide and conquer").

Dynamic Programming. This powerful technique can work on problems that can be separated into stages, but even small problems can explode into large ones.

Restructuring the Problem

Sometimes by simply redefining the problem from a different angle it can be solved very quickly and simply by another technique.

Networks. One of the nicest properties about networks is that they are very easy to see, understand, and solve. The shortest route problem can be approached as a dynamic programming problem in tabular form or as an assignment problem, but it is easily solved in network form. The same is true for the transportation problem which can be formulated as an assignment problem, as a linear programming problem, or even as an integer programming problem.

Assignment. Here the traveling salesman problem, which looks quite simple as a network problem but is very difficult to solve optimally, can be handled by being restructured.

Integer Programming. Many network problems can also be restructured as integer programming problems, and some are solved much more efficiently.

Inverting the Problem

If everything else fails, turn the problem inside out. We have seen that for many problems there lurks in the shadow the dual of the problem.

Primal. The primal problem is classically a maximizing problem. We have seen in the maximal flow problem that we can solve the dual (minimal cut) by simply solving the primal. The same is true with geometric programming and solving the inventory problem by maximizing and applying the results to minimize the average total cost (ATC).

Dual. The shadow costs or opportunity losses are used to solve the primal problem in the transportation section. In linear programming you have the choice of solving either the primal or the dual. There is always a great deal of insight to be gained by being able to see the dual of a problem.

Approaching the Problem

Some problem techniques can be described by how the optimum is approached.

Feasible. The Quick & Dirty techniques are all feasible approaches that will give some answer that is usable, although maybe far from optimal. Other algorithms will start with a feasible answer and then go step by step to the optimum. Linear programming does this with the simplex method so that if the pro-

gram were to stop at some point, there would at least be a feasible solution.

Infeasible. These techniques try to sneak in the "back door," and if they make it there is no problem. But if for some reason you have to stop before the algorithm is complete, there is no usable answer. The assignment technique is such an example. Before the last table there is no feasible answer. The same is true of the dual in linear programming. If the algorithm stops before the final solution, the answers to the dual will not be feasible or useful in the primal problem.

Combination. Several techniques use a combination of feasible and infeasible answers such as the Branch & Bound and implicit enumeration. Trying to take the best from both worlds, they will often have at least a usable answer if the algorithm is stopped short of completion.

These are just a few categorical ways of looking at problem solving which might help you to get a general idea of how to approach problems rather than getting lost in the details of each technique.

11.3 FURTHER REFERENCES

The following references will provide the reader with further information on each subject on the pages cited. This, of course, is not an exhaustive or exclusive list of references, but have been of help to the authors in the past. The notations will vary from book to book, but the concepts and principles remain the same.

1. S. K. Gupta and J. M. Cozzolino, *Fundamentals of Operations Research for Management* (San Francisco: Holden-Day, 1974).
   Sections 5.1, 5.5 Assignment and Transportation Techniques, pp. 55–94
   Section 8.2 Dynamic Programming, pp. 144–168
   Section 9.2 Game Theory, pp. 265–291
   Section 9.3 Markov Models, pp. 293–312
   Section 10.1 Single Period Inventory, pp. 217–224
   Section 10.3 Queuing, pp. 313–344
   Section 10.4 Simulation, pp. 345–371

2. I. Horowitz, *An Introduction to Quantitative Business Analysis* (New York: McGraw-Hill, 1965).
   Sections 3.1–3.6 Inventory, pp. 183–211
   Section 5.5 Transportation, pp. 157–181
   Section 7.4 Cutting Plane, pp. 139–155
   Section 9.1 Decision Theory, pp. 55–101

Section 9.2 Game Theory, pp. 235–260
Section 9.4 Utility Theory, pp. 33–54
Section 10.3 Queuing, pp. 213–234

3. T. H. Naylor, J. L. Balintfy, D. S. Burdic, and K. Chu, *Computer Simulation Techniques* (New York: Wiley, 1966).
Section 10.4 Simulation, pp. 1–300

4. T. L. Saaty, *Mathematical Models of Operations Research* (New York: McGraw-Hill, 1959).
Sections 6.1–6.5 Linear Programming, pp. 165–208
Section 9.2 Game Theory, pp. 209–227
Section 10.3 Queuing Theory, pp. 331–374

5. W. A. Spivey and R. M. Thrall, *Linear Optimization* (New York: Holt, Rinehart & Winston, 1970).
Section 5.1 Assignment Problem, pp. 213–247
Section 5.5 Transportation, pp. 248–287
Section 6.2 Models, pp. 16–60
Section 5 Simplex Method, pp. 61–138

Section 6.6 Postoptimal Analysis, pp. 158–212
Section 9.1 Decision Theory, pp. 344–350
Section 9.2 Game Theory, pp. 318–344

6. H. M. Wagner, *Principles of Operations Research* (Englewood Cliffs, N.J.: Prentice-Hall, 1969).
Sections 4.1–4.6 Networks, pp. 165–252
Section 6.2 Models, pp. 33–75
Sections 7.3–7.7 Integer Programming, pp. 445–512
Section 8.2 Dynamic Programming, pp. 253–358
Section 10.3 Queuing, pp. 837–886, A59–A75
Section 10.4 Simulation, pp. 887–924

7. D. J. Wilde and C. S. Beightler, *Foundations of Optimization* (Englewood Cliffs, N.J.: Prentice-Hall, 1967).
Sections 4.1–4.6 Networks, pp. 373–374, 383–406
Section 5.5 Transportation, pp. 187–206
Section 8.1 Geometric Programming, pp. 27–43
Section 8.2 Dynamic Programming, pp. 345–371

appendix

1758	1755	2774	1593	5693	1052	7784	1819	7365	3387
6430	9852	0478	9029	8306	0603	6703	1333	2175	1450
4893	8996	1717	0513	0560	8108	2600	2173	5278	1006
1516	6923	7326	4600	0640	1799	8260	5280	2099	2539
4950	0200	5756	4793	5957	8719	6571	8495	8102	6291
0549	3416	9360	4877	6936	0037	8649	7309	7244	8230
1018	8389	7569	5367	7577	2315	1659	8030	0123	9927
2241	3041	9729	2863	5684	9239	3332	0738	9054	4327
1602	5507	2201	8068	7339	1081	4094	5112	3293	9605
5840	9199	1549	3186	8482	3681	3214	6430	3933	7751
7422	2688	7484	1555	3008	5693	3327	9810	8463	1024
1757	4204	8940	9029	8306	8892	2291	4127	0006	6591
7469	8973	2563	0515	0560	9021	4245	6632	2582	7019
7431	2389	9418	4600	0640	9608	9977	6379	9021	7916
0431	8012	6469	4793	5597	4123	6272	6555	4503	6960
6983	0131	3106	4092	6936	4109	8700	8060	6982	7025
8478	9187	4534	5951	7557	2701	8923	2587	9653	6991
4627	0456	2946	7637	5681	5517	7309	7448	1070	7505
7903	1241	8312	3655	7339	5395	2079	0539	7035	5484
5525	1068	1933	3193	8482	6630	1820	2656	5878	0193
1032	8612	6515	9181	9371	5373	1489	9145	7311	4962
1603	7748	3097	9459	5797	3930	8803	8211	1709	3184
8102	9399	1231	9874	2373	1157	8857	2228	1303	4595
1799	8576	7193	7729	4872	2702	2733	4860	6515	0277
8719	7578	4786	4099	6721	0086	3171	2017	3237	3625
0037	6913	0280	1872	1669	2007	6776	4496	1896	1831
2315	2410	3670	9636	4933	0111	7027	2265	2521	6976
9239	7060	4821	6403	3163	6372	9965	3623	2222	6663
1081	1368	2055	4433	2774	6030	0708	9056	3116	8757
3681	7152	8899	2361	7947	1659	8381	7977	1864	1997
3068	1965	9135	4077	3007	6588	0367	6363	7511	6017
8892	0002	5728	6678	0111	4859	4175	1234	1723	1620
9021	5062	2849	6499	5207	1111	9621	0887	9700	3919
9609	0118	7513	6663	0319	6122	4584	9023	3866	9513
4123	7355	3001	9999	6105	1062	7784	1969	4114	7356
4109	1676	3954	9048	3845	2461	5412	0156	7484	5012
2701	6048	2438	5136	3654	7412	5699	2486	4666	4724
5517	5549	7632	9906	5693	7315	3791	0294	4754	0303
5395	5317	2314	4193	8182	6070	9736	5062	0707	0046
6630	2532	8026	2930	8989	7638	5537	8927	1312	0585
2219	2300	6580	6033	9813	4569	3253	6812	4702	1699
3491	1499	3686	4157	3636	7940	6744	9032	7663	1207
7448	6301	5027	1533	6572	5839	9071	3583	1811	0272
7028	6330	0319	8674	9213	2103	7104	7042	8555	0883
7448	0002	1056	3036	9047	2841	7002	7036	0211	7124
3503	1862	6865	6639	0990	1129	4995	0349	6209	0812
6524	9886	2863	7519	2539	9092	4937	5596	8821	3881
4208	5280	3012	7092	4891	8123	3849	4361	1251	3025
1807	2635	6270	9818	6241	6734	3463	2998	5506	7200
2623	6055	6789	9902	6935	6337	3011	5063	6817	8489

Table A2 Exponential Times

N	0	1	2	3	X 4	5	6	7	8	9
0.00	∞	6.90	6.21	5.80	5.52	5.29	5.11	4.96	4.82	4.71
0.01	4.60	4.50	4.42	4.34	4.26	4.19	4.13	4.07	4.01	4.96
0.02	3.91	3.86	3.81	3.77	3.72	3.68	3.64	3.61	3.57	3.54
0.03	3.50	3.47	3.44	3.41	3.38	3.35	3.32	3.29	3.27	3.24
0.04	3.21	3.19	3.17	3.14	3.12	3.10	3.07	3.05	3.03	3.01
0.05	2.99	2.97	2.95	2.93	2.91	2.90	2.88	2.86	2.84	2.83
0.06	2.81	2.79	2.78	2.76	2.74	2.73	2.71	2.70	2.68	2.67
0.07	2.65	2.64	2.63	2.61	2.60	2.59	2.57	2.56	2.55	2.53
0.08	2.52	2.51	2.50	2.48	2.47	2.46	2.45	2.44	2.43	2.41
0.09	2.40	2.39	2.38	2.37	2.36	2.35	2.34	2.33	2.32	2.31
0.10	2.30	2.29	2.28	2.27	2.26	2.25	2.24	2.23	2.22	2.21
0.11	2.20	2.19	2.18	2.18	2.17	2.16	2.15	2.14	2.13	2.12
0.12	2.12	2.11	2.10	2.09	2.08	2.07	2.07	2.06	2.05	2.04
0.13	2.04	2.03	2.02	2.01	2.00	2.00	1.99	1.98	1.98	1.97
0.14	1.96	1.95	1.95	1.94	1.93	1.93	1.92	1.91	1.91	1.90
0.15	1.89	1.89	1.88	1.87	1.87	1.86	1.85	1.85	1.84	1.83
0.16	1.83	1.82	1.82	1.81	1.80	1.80	1.79	1.78	1.78	1.77
0.17	1.77	1.76	1.76	1.75	1.74	1.74	1.73	1.73	1.72	1.72
0.18	1.71	1.70	1.70	1.69	1.69	1.68	1.68	1.67	1.67	1.66
0.19	1.66	1.65	1.65	1.64	1.63	1.63	1.62	1.62	1.61	1.61
0.20	1.60	1.60	1.59	1.59	1.58	1.58	1.57	1.57	1.57	1.56
0.21	1.56	1.55	1.55	1.54	1.54	1.53	1.53	1.52	1.52	1.51
0.22	1.51	1.50	1.50	1.50	1.49	1.49	1.48	1.48	1.47	1.47
0.23	1.46	1.46	1.46	1.45	1.45	1.44	1.44	1.43	1.43	1.43
0.24	1.42	1.42	1.41	1.41	1.41	1.40	1.40	1.39	1.39	1.39
0.25	1.38	1.38	1.37	1.37	1.37	1.36	1.36	1.35	1.35	1.35
0.26	1.34	1.34	1.33	1.33	1.33	1.32	1.32	1.32	1.31	1.31
0.27	1.30	1.30	1.30	1.29	1.29	1.29	1.28	1.28	1.28	1.27
0.28	1.27	1.26	1.26	1.26	1.25	1.25	1.25	1.24	1.24	1.24
0.29	1.23	1.23	1.23	1.22	1.22	1.22	1.21	1.21	1.21	1.20
0.30	1.20	1.20	1.19	1.19	1.19	1.18	1.18	1.18	1.17	1.17
0.31	1.17	1.16	1.16	1.16	1.15	1.15	1.15	1.14	1.14	1.14
0.32	1.13	1.13	1.13	1.13	1.12	1.12	1.12	1.11	1.11	1.11
0.33	1.10	1.10	1.10	1.09	1.09	1.09	1.09	1.08	1.08	1.08
0.34	1.07	1.07	1.07	1.07	1.06	1.06	1.06	1.05	1.05	1.05
0.35	1.04	1.04	1.04	1.04	1.03	1.03	1.03	1.03	1.02	1.02
0.36	1.02	1.01	1.01	1.01	1.01	1.00	1.00	1.00	0.99	1.99
0.37	0.99	0.99	0.98	0.98	0.98	0.98	0.97	0.97	0.97	0.97
0.38	0.96	0.96	0.96	0.95	0.95	0.95	0.95	0.94	0.94	0.94
0.39	0.94	0.93	0.93	0.93	0.93	0.92	0.92	0.92	0.92	0.91
0.40	0.91	0.91	0.91	0.90	0.90	0.90	0.90	0.89	0.89	0.89
0.41	0.89	0.88	0.88	0.88	0.88	0.87	0.87	0.87	0.87	0.86
0.42	0.86	0.86	0.86	0.86	0.85	0.85	0.85	0.85	0.84	0.84
0.43	0.84	0.84	0.83	0.83	0.83	0.83	0.83	0.82	0.82	0.82
0.44	0.82	0.81	0.81	0.81	0.81	0.80	0.80	0.80	0.80	0.80
0.45	0.79	0.79	0.79	0.79	0.78	0.78	0.78	0.78	0.78	0.77
0.46	0.77	0.77	0.77	0.77	0.76	0.76	0.76	0.76	0.75	0.75
0.47	0.75	0.75	0.75	0.74	0.74	0.74	0.74	0.74	0.73	0.73
0.48	0.73	0.73	0.72	0.72	0.72	0.72	0.72	0.71	0.71	0.71
0.49	0.71	0.71	0.70	0.70	0.70	0.70	0.70	0.69	0.69	0.69

					X					
N	**0**	**1**	**2**	**3**	**4**	**5**	**6**	**7**	**8**	**9**
0.50	0.69	0.69	0.68	0.68	0.68	0.68	0.68	0.67	0.67	0.67
0.51	0.67	0.67	0.66	0.66	0.66	0.66	0.66	0.65	0.65	0.65
0.52	0.65	0.65	0.65	0.64	0.64	0.64	0.64	0.64	0.63	0.63
0.53	0.63	0.63	0.63	0.62	0.62	0.62	0.62	0.62	0.61	0.61
0.54	0.61	0.61	0.61	0.61	0.60	0.60	0.60	0.60	0.60	0.59
0.55	0.59	0.59	0.59	0.59	0.59	0.58	0.58	0.58	0.58	0.58
0.56	0.57	0.57	0.57	0.57	0.57	0.57	0.56	0.56	0.56	0.56
0.57	0.56	0.56	0.55	0.55	0.55	0.55	0.55	0.54	0.54	0.54
0.58	0.54	0.54	0.54	0.53	0.53	0.53	0.53	0.53	0.53	0.52
0.59	0.52	0.52	0.52	0.52	0.52	0.51	0.51	0.51	0.51	0.51
0.60	0.51	0.50	0.50	0.50	0.50	0.50	0.50	0.49	0.49	0.49
0.61	0.49	0.49	0.49	0.48	0.48	0.48	0.48	0.48	0.48	0.47
0.62	0.47	0.47	0.47	0.47	0.47	0.47	0.46	0.46	0.46	0.46
0.63	0.46	0.46	0.45	0.45	0.45	0.45	0.45	0.45	0.44	0.44
0.64	0.44	0.44	0.44	0.44	0.44	0.43	0.43	0.43	0.43	0.43
0.65	0.43	0.42	0.42	0.42	0.42	0.42	0.42	0.42	0.41	0.41
0.66	0.41	0.41	0.41	0.41	0.40	0.40	0.40	0.40	0.40	0.40
0.67	0.40	0.39	0.39	0.39	0.39	0.39	0.39	0.39	0.38	0.38
0.68	0.38	0.38	0.38	0.38	0.37	0.37	0.37	0.37	0.37	0.37
0.69	0.37	0.36	0.36	0.36	0.36	0.36	0.36	0.36	0.35	0.35
0.70	0.35	0.35	0.35	0.35	0.35	0.34	0.34	0.34	0.34	0.34
0.71	0.34	0.34	0.33	0.33	0.33	0.33	0.33	0.33	0.33	0.32
0.72	0.32	0.32	0.32	0.32	0.32	0.32	0.32	0.31	0.31	0.31
0.73	0.31	0.31	0.31	0.31	0.30	0.30	0.30	0.30	0.30	0.30
0.74	0.30	0.29	0.29	0.29	0.29	0.29	0.29	0.29	0.29	0.28
0.75	0.28	0.28	0.28	0.28	0.28	0.28	0.27	0.27	0.27	0.27
0.76	0.27	0.27	0.27	0.27	0.26	0.26	0.26	0.26	0.26	0.26
0.77	0.26	0.26	0.25	0.25	0.25	0.25	0.25	0.25	0.25	0.24
0.78	0.24	0.24	0.24	0.24	0.24	0.24	0.24	0.23	0.23	0.23
0.79	0.23	0.23	0.23	0.23	0.23	0.22	0.22	0.22	0.22	0.22
0.80	0.22	0.22	0.22	0.21	0.21	0.21	0.21	0.21	0.21	0.21
0.81	0.21	0.20	0.20	0.20	0.20	0.20	0.20	0.20	0.20	0.19
0.82	0.19	0.19	0.19	0.19	0.19	0.19	0.19	0.18	0.18	0.18
0.83	0.18	0.18	0.18	0.18	0.18	0.18	0.17	0.17	0.17	0.17
0.84	0.17	0.17	0.17	0.17	0.16	0.16	0.16	0.16	0.16	0.16
0.85	0.16	0.16	0.16	0.15	0.15	0.15	0.15	0.15	0.15	0.15
0.86	0.15	0.14	0.14	0.14	0.14	0.14	0.14	0.14	0.14	0.14
0.87	0.13	0.13	0.13	0.13	0.13	0.13	0.13	0.13	0.13	0.12
0.88	0.12	0.12	0.12	0.12	0.12	0.12	0.12	0.11	0.11	0.11
0.89	0.11	0.11	0.11	0.11	0.11	0.11	0.10	0.10	0.10	0.10
0.90	0.10	0.10	0.10	0.10	0.10	0.09	0.09	0.09	0.09	0.09
0.91	0.09	0.09	0.09	0.09	0.08	0.08	0.08	0.08	0.08	0.08
0.92	0.08	0.08	0.08	0.08	0.07	0.07	0.07	0.07	0.07	0.07
0.93	0.07	0.07	0.07	0.06	0.06	0.06	0.06	0.06	0.06	0.06
0.94	0.06	0.06	0.05	0.05	0.05	0.05	0.05	0.05	0.05	0.05
0.95	0.05	0.05	0.04	0.04	0.04	0.04	0.04	0.04	0.04	0.04
0.96	0.04	0.03	0.03	0.03	0.03	0.03	0.03	0.03	0.03	0.03
0.97	0.03	0.02	0.02	0.02	0.02	0.02	0.02	0.02	0.02	0.02
0.98	0.02	0.01	0.01	0.01	0.01	0.01	0.01	0.01	0.01	0.01
0.99	0.01	0.00	0.00	0.00	0.00	0.00	0.00	0.00	0.00	0.00

index